S0-BAQ-401

KARL MARX
FREDERICK ENGELS

COLLECTED WORKS
VOLUME
15

KARL MARX
FREDERICK ENGELS

COLLECTED WORKS

INTERNATIONAL PUBLISHERS
NEW YORK

KARL MARX
FREDERICK ENGELS

Volume 15

MARX AND ENGELS: 1856-58

INTERNATIONAL PUBLISHERS
NEW YORK

This volume has been prepared jointly by Lawrence & Wishart Ltd., London, International Publishers Co. Inc., New York, and Progress Publishers, Moscow, in collaboration with the Institute of Marxism-Leninism, Moscow.

Library of Congress Cataloging in Publication Data

Marx, Karl, 1818-1883.

Karl Marx, Frederick Engels: collected works.

1. Socialism—Collected works. 2. Economics—Collected works. I. Engels, Friedrich, 1820-1895. Works. English. 1975. II. Title.
HX 39. 5. A 16 1975 335.4 73-84671
ISBN 0-7178-0515-8 (v. 15)

Printed in the Union of Soviet Socialist Republics in 1985

Contents

KARL MARX AND FREDERICK ENGELS

WORKS

May 1856-September 1858

1856

May

June

June 1856-March 1857

July

August

September

October

November

December

1857

January

February

March

September

October

November

December

1858

January

February

March

April

May

June

July

September

FROM THE PREPARATORY MATERIALS

SUPPLEMENT

NOTES AND INDEXES

ILLUSTRATIONS

Translated by

PETER and BETTY ROSS:

K. Marx, "B. Bauer's Pamphlets on the Collision with Russia"

Marx to the Editor of the *Neue Zeit*

From the Preparatory Materials

Preface

Volume 15 of the *Collected Works* of Marx and Engels contains their writings between May 1856 and September 1858. Most of them are articles and reports published in the progressive American newspaper, the *New-York Daily Tribune,* in its special issues, the *New-York Semi-Weekly Tribune* and the *New-York Weekly Tribune,* and also in the Chartist weekly, *The People's Paper,* and other newspapers.

In these years, besides his strenuous activities as a journalist, Marx was intensively engaged in the study of political economy. Between August 1857 and May 1858 he wrote the first draft of what was to become *Capital*—the Economic Manuscript of 1857-58 (see present edition, vols. 28 and 29). At that time Marx and Engels also wrote a number of articles, mainly on military and military-historical subjects for *The New American Cyclopaedia* (present edition, Vol. 18).

Their contributions to the *New-York Daily Tribune* in this period were almost the only opportunity Marx and Engels had to express their attitude on the vital international issues and on the internal politics of the European countries, to reveal the class essence of world events, and appraise them from the standpoint of the fundamental interests of the proletariat. The most notable of those events were: the economic crisis of 1857-58, the first to grip the whole capitalist world, the colonial wars, and the armed struggle of the peoples of India to liberate themselves from British rule.

Writing for the *New-York Daily Tribune* became even more important for Marx and Engels because in December 1856, in view of the changed position taken by Ernest Jones, the editor of *The People's Paper,* who had agreed to a compromise with the bourgeois radicals, they were obliged to stop contributing to that paper. This meant that in Europe there was no other press organ where they could expound their views.

A considerable portion of Marx's articles included in this volume are devoted to the economic crisis of 1857-58, and also to the specific economic problems of the major European countries.

On the basis of his analysis of European economic development since the revolutions of 1848-49 Marx had, by the autumn of 1856, already come to the conclusion that an economic crisis was approaching. He predicted that it would hit many countries and inevitably affect not only industrial production but also trade and fiscal relations. When the crisis broke in 1857, it provided vivid confirmation of the conclusion Marx had reached earlier on the cyclical nature of the development of capitalist production, and the inevitable succession of phases within each cycle. He identified the cause of the crisis in the internal contradictions inherent in the capitalist mode of production, and convincingly refuted the attempts of bourgeois economists to find an explanation for it in mere secondary causes, particularly in the wave of speculation. "The political economists who pretend to explain the regular spasms of industry and commerce by speculation," he wrote, "resemble the now extinct school of natural philosophers who considered fever as the true cause of all maladies" (see this volume, p. 401).

Marx devoted much attention to the symptoms of financial crisis, analysing their influence throughout the European economy. Step by step he traced every change on the world money market and investigated the positions of the major British and French banks. Of considerable interest in this respect are his articles on the French joint-stock company Crédit Mobilier, one of the main centres of the stock exchange speculation that exacerbated the world economic crisis. Marx described this company as "one of the most economical phenomena of our epoch" (p. 10). The activities of the Crédit Mobilier, which enjoyed the special patronage of Napoleon III, ranged far beyond the realm of credit. The company invested its capital in industrial enterprises and construction, including the building of railways.

Marx's articles on the Crédit Mobilier contain important theoretical propositions and conclusions concerning the laws of capitalist development. The enhanced role of joint-stock capital marked the appearance of trends that heralded the onset of capitalism's imperialist stage at the turn of the century. As Marx wrote, this opened "a new epoch in the economical life of modern nations" (p. 21), creating opportunities for setting up industrial enterprises that would have been beyond the means of individual capitalists. Taking the Crédit Mobilier as an example, Marx noted the appearance of "a sort of industrial kings" (p. 21), who could manipulate in their own interests capital that was far in excess of their own and which allowed them to indulge in unlimited speculation. On the other hand, Marx pointed out, this accelerated concentration of production and capital, strengthened the rule of the financial and industrial oligarchy and spelled bankruptcy for the middle and small capitalist.

In the development of large-scale bank and industrial capital Marx accurately foresaw the prospect of the capitalism of free competition becoming monopoly capitalism. As Lenin was to write later, "Imperialism is the epoch of finance capital and of monopolies, which introduce everywhere the striving for domination, not for freedom" (V. I. Lenin, *Collected Works,* Vol. 22, Moscow, 1974, p. 297). The consequent increase in the number of wage workers along with the decrease in the number of capitalists further polarised capitalist society, sharpening the endemic class struggle.

In his articles on the economic crisis of 1857 Marx gave a profound analysis of the industrial, financial and trading positions of the major European countries, studied in detail the dynamics of world exports and imports, and investigated the fluctuations of British and French bank rates and the value of securities on the European stock exchanges.

In his articles "The Economic Crisis in France", "The Trade Crisis in England", "The French Crisis", "The British Revulsion", and others, Marx accurately discerned the specific features of the crisis in each country. The worst hit country was Britain, wnere the crisis bore "the character of an industrial crisis" and struck "at the very roots of the national prosperity" (p. 390).

The articles on the crisis contain a huge amount of factual material, which Marx gleaned from British, French and German newspapers, magazines and statistical reports. His articles reflected both his own observations and researches, and information he received from Engels. The specific factual material, and his resulting generalisations and conclusions, were later used to work out his theory of economic crises.

Marx noted in particular that the crisis-ridden economies of the European countries were impoverishing the rural and urban workers and, above all, the industrial working class. "Through the whole of Europe the palsy of industrial activity and the consequent distress of the laboring classes are rapidly spreading," Marx wrote in his article "The Financial Crisis in Europe" (p. 404). Of undoubted interest in this respect are the articles "Condition of Factory Laborers" and "The English Factory System", and also "Important British Documents".

Harsh exploitation of the workers, Marx pointed out, was the other side of the thriving capitalist industry in the pre-crisis period. Circumventing the factory acts that Parliament had passed under the pressure of the proletariat's stubborn class struggle, British manufacturers lengthened the working day, reduced wages and showed a preference for employing women and children instead of adult workmen. "The infamies of the British factory system are growing with its growth," he wrote, "...the laws enacted for checking the cruel greediness of the mill-lords are a sham and a delusion, being so worded as to baffle their own ostensible end and to disarm the men entrusted with their execution" (pp. 253-54). In his article "The Economic Crisis in France" Marx observes that in that country the very first symptoms of crisis aggravated the sufferings of the workers and stimulated the growth of discontent among them (p. 133).

Regarding the period after the defeat of the 1848-49 revolutions as "a mere respite given by history to Old European Society" (p. 115) Marx and Engels believed in the inevitability of a new revolutionary upsurgence and thought that it would be triggered by the economic crisis. This was what Marx had in mind when he wrote that in 1857 material conditions were provided "for the ideal tendencies of 1848" (p. 114). This was the main reason for the great interest Marx and Engels showed in the domestic policies of the European countries, in all the facts and phenomena testifying, on the one hand, to the increasing crisis among the ruling classes themselves and, on the other to the growing revolutionary and democratic movement.

In a number of articles Marx analysed the internal situation in the European countries, particularly Britain and France, singling out political tension as a symptom of a possible revolutionary explosion. In his view Bonapartist France offered the greatest hope in this respect. The hardships caused by the economic crisis "must tend to bring the French people into that state of mind in which they are wont to embark in fresh political ventures," Marx wrote in his article "The Economic Crisis in France". "With the disappearance of material prosperity and its regular appendage of political indifference, every pretext for the prolongation of the second Empire ... disappears" (p. 463).

Marx noted the signs of mounting political crisis in the Second Empire: workers' strikes in various industries, peasant discontent, severer measures against democratic elements (pp. 135, 302). "The time of the sullen acquiescence of the nation in the rule of the Society of the perjured usurper has definitely passed away," he wrote (pp. 456-57), alluding to the Bonapartist Society of December 10, which had played an important role in the preparation of the coup d'état of December 2, 1851.

In the articles "The Attempt upon the Life of Bonaparte", "The Rule of the Pretorians", "Bonaparte's Present Position", and also in the articles on the Crédit Mobilier, Marx develops and clarifies the definition of Bonapartism which he gave in *The Eighteenth Brumaire of Louis Bonaparte* and other earlier works, for example, "The France of Bonaparte the Little" (see present edition, vols. 11 and 14). Basing himself on hard facts, he reveals such characteristic features of the Bonapartist monarchy as the undisguised dictatorship of the big bourgeoisie, relying on the force of bayonets and police terror, the wildfire spread of speculation, corruption and bribery, the embezzlement of state funds, foreign policy adventurism, the manoeuvring between various classes and sections of the population, and Napoleon III's attempts to play the role of protector of the peasantry, and in various ways "to purchase the conscience of the French working classes" (p. 478). Marx reveals the direct connections between the Bonapartist monarchy and the stock exchange speculators, a monarchy which, as Lenin put it, "is obliged to walk the tightrope in order not to fall, make advances in order to govern, bribe in order to gain affections, fraternise with the dregs of society, with plain thieves and swindlers, in order not to rely only on bayonets" (V. I. Lenin, op. cit., Vol. 15, p. 269).

One of the most important themes in Marx's journalism continued to be Britain's domestic and foreign policy, including the evolution of her parliamentary system. In his newspaper reports, "Defeat of the Palmerston Ministry", "The Coming Election in England", "The English Election", "The Defeat of Cobden, Bright and Gibson", "Political Parties in England.—Situation in Europe", and others, Marx put his finger on a characteristic phenomenon of English political life in the 1850s, the decay of the traditional political parties. Detecting in this process a manifestation of the bankruptcy of the existing oligarchic system of government, Marx notes the English bourgeoisie's "longing for compromises with the oligarchs, in order to escape concessions to the proletarians" (p. 203).

Marx emphasised that the bourgeois-oligarchic regime in England retarded the country's development. Anti-popular and counter-revolutionary in character, this regime, which was most vividly expressed in the administration of Palmerston, whom Marx ironically called a "truly British Minister", stood in the way of democratic reforms. Parliamentary legislation served the interests of the ruling clique, as was plainly demonstrated by the budgets and financial reforms of those years (see the articles "The New English Budget", "The Bank Act of 1844 and the Monetary Crisis in England", and "Mr. Disraeli's Budget"). Marx showed that, in effect, Palmerston expressed the interests of the sections of the English capitalist class that sought to expand markets, to consolidate Britain's industrial monopoly, and achieve further colonial expansion.

Analysis of the internal situation in Britain and the consequences of her colonial wars, which had diverted considerable manpower and material resources, brought Marx to the conclusion that "in case of a serious revolutionary explosion on the continent of Europe, England ... would prove unable to reassume the proud position she occupied in 1848 and 1849". Marx expressed confidence that England "will be disabled from clogging, as she did in 1848, the European Revolution that draws visibly nearer" (pp. 301-02, 567-68).

Well before the crisis broke, Marx and Engels kept a close watch for any sign of revolutionary activity among the masses in Europe, and regarded such signs as proof of the instability and impermanence of the period of political reaction that had set in during the 1850s.

In the summer of 1856 Marx's attention was once again drawn to events on the Iberian peninsula. This volume includes two articles by Marx on the revolution in Spain (pp. 97-108). Written in July-August 1856, they round off, as it were, the series of articles entitled "Revolutionary Spain", published in the *New-York Daily Tribune* in 1854, and his other articles on this subject (see present edition, Vol. 13). The articles sum up the results of the fourth Spanish bourgeois revolution, which began in June 1854 and brought the liberal Progresista party to power.

In assessing the significance and peculiarities of this revolution, Marx observes that what distinguished it from the revolutions in

Spain in the first half of the 19th century was that it had discarded its dynastic and military character. The development of industry had altered the line-up of class forces. For the first time the workers—"the product of the modern organization of labor"—were taking part in the revolution "to claim their due share of the result of victory" (this volume, p. 102). Another important new factor was the warm support given by the peasantry which, Marx points out, "would have proved a most formidable element of resistance" (p. 104). However, the bourgeois leaders of the revolution were unable and unwilling to use the peasantry's determination and energy, while the army had become a counter-revolutionary force. Both the course of the revolution itself, and its defeat, confirmed the conclusion Marx had reached on the basis of the experience of 1848-49 concerning the counter-revolutionary degeneration of the liberal bourgeoisie and its betrayal of the revolutionary cause as soon as the masses and, above all, the working class, began to put forward their own demands. "Frightened by the consequences of an alliance thus imposed on their unwilling shoulders," Marx wrote, "the middle classes shrink back again under the protecting batteries of the hated despotism." Their conduct "furnishes a new illustration of the character of most of the European struggles of 1848-49, and of those hereafter to take place in the Western portion of that continent" (p. 102).

Analysis of the revolutionary events in one of the most backward countries of Western Europe led Marx to conclude that "the next European revolution will find Spain matured for co-operation with it. The years 1854 and 1856 were phases of transition she had to pass through to arrive at that maturity" (p. 108).

Several of the works published in this volume (the never completed work consisting to a considerable extent of extracts from documents and quotations, *Revelations of the Diplomatic History of the 18th Century* and the unfinished work "B. Bauer's Pamphlets on the Collision with Russia", never published in Marx's lifetime, the article "The Right Divine of the Hohenzollerns", and a few others) reflect Marx's interest in the history of diplomacy and international relations. The special need to investigate this subject sprang from the events of those years—the growing rivalry between the European powers in the Near and the Middle East, the Crimean War, and other international conflicts. Analysis of the foreign policies of the European countries contributed a great deal to the theory of the class struggle and to the determination of the strategic and tactical objectives of the proletariat.

Marx and Engels assessed international events and international politics from the perspective of Europe's revolutionary, democratic development, an essential condition for which was the overthrow of the reactionary regimes that had established themselves after the defeat of the 1848-49 revolutions. In the 1850s, the critical study of the foreign policy of bourgeois-aristocratic England, Bonapartist France, Tsarist Russia, and the reactionary governments of Austria and Prussia became one of the main subjects of Marx's and Engels's writing for the press. To these five powers, whose governments were pursuing a reactionary political course, Marx contrasted the "sixth and greatest European power". That power was the Revolution (present edition, Vol. 12, p. 557).

The works in this volume reveal the essence and distinctive features of the diplomacy of the exploiting classes: Marx assigns diplomacy and foreign policy to the sphere of the political superstructure as something determined in the final analysis by the economic base (pp. 185-86, 188-89).

His work "B. Bauer's Pamphlets on the Collision with Russia" shows how diplomatic relations develop under capitalism, and notes the persistence of reactionary traditions in foreign policy inherited from the feudal monarchies. Marx emphasises that "the society of modern production calls for international conditions different from those of feudal society..." (p. 190). In *Revelations of the Diplomatic History of the 18th Century* he dwells on certain features of the diplomatic practice of bourgeois states. In its pursuit of profit, capital is prepared to embark on any betrayal of national interests. For the bourgeoisie, Marx wrote, its fatherland was "where the best interest for its capital was paid" (p. 64).

Dealing with some of the general principles of historical research, Marx poses the question of the relation between fact and generalisation in the analysis of this or that event, and the role and relevance of historical analogies. With biting sarcasm he criticises Bauer for drawing superficial parallels between the events that sparked off the revolution of 1789 in France and the events that took place in mid-19th century Britain, which sprang from entirely different socio-economic conditions. It would be impossible, Marx points out, "to coax into an analogy any two things of a more disparate kind" (p. 185, see also p. 186).

The *Revelations of the Diplomatic History of the 18th Century* is, in Marx's own words, only an introduction to a projected but never written work on Anglo-Russian relations. This introduction (five printers' sheets of twenty sheets for the whole work) is unfinished and breaks off with a quotation. It consists to a great extent of lengthy quotations from pamphlets and diplomatic reports. The general aim of the project was to prove that the reactionary aspirations of the English ruling oligarchy and the Tsarist autocracy had much in common, which in the mid-19th century showed itself mainly in the suppression of revolutionary and national liberation movements. Before this, Marx and Engels had exposed the counter-revolutionary nature of the foreign policy of Britain's ruling circles (see the pamphlet *Lord Palmerston* and a number of other articles, present edition, vols. 12, 13 and 14). They repeatedly stressed that these circles, unless it contradicted their own immediate interests, supported the foreign policy of Russian Tsarism, which they saw as one of the main forces of European reaction. Marx believed that the roots of this policy should be traced to the 18th century.

The *Revelations of the Diplomatic History of the 18th Century* is more a political pamphlet than a piece of historical research. Moreover, in writing it Marx deliberately concentrated attention on certain features of Anglo-Russian relations while ignoring others. In several instances this led him to make one-sided assessments and judgments, particularly in characterising British policy towards Russia, which, so he alleged, had ever since the 18th century traditionally supported the foreign-policy aims of the Tsarist autocracy.

Such one-sidedness was determined to an even greater degree by the extremely tendentious nature of the 18th-century sources Marx used, which reflected the rivalry between the two oligarchic cliques of the English ruling élite—Whigs and Tories. A large part of Marx's sources are anti-Russian pamphlets dating from the days of the Northern War (1700-21), which were often directly inspired by Sweden, Russia's main adversary in that war (see chapters II, III and V), and individual reports and letters written by diplomats and other English representatives in St. Petersburg between the mid-1730s and mid-1790s (see Chapter I). The documents relate to the period of the Russo-Turkish war of 1735-39, to the diplomatic activities of the European powers after the Seven Years' War, 1756-63, to England's war against the North American colonies, 1775-83, and to the first years of the reign of Paul I in Russia. The documents testify to the great displeasure evoked in Tory circles by the efforts of the ruling Whigs to develop a close relationship with the Imperial Russian court for the purpose of gaining its diplomatic support.

The *Revelations of the Diplomatic History of the 18th Century* also gives a brief outline of events in the history of Russia from the days of Kiev Rus to the time of Peter I (chapters IV and V). In these, to use Marx's own words, "preliminary remarks on the general history of Russian politics" (p. 74) attention is concentrated only on certain stages and some external political aspects of Russia's history, without due consideration for her internal socio-economic relations, and without analysis of the alignment of class and political forces. The whole emphasis is on external factors. The 16th and 17th centuries are totally omitted. The literature used by Marx (his basic source was a book by the French aristocrat Ph. Ségur, which had appeared in 1829) was even in those days outdated, and scarcely touched upon the socio-economic aspects of the history of ancient Russia and the state of Muscovy, the study of which had only just begun. So in this work Marx's interpretation of Russia's historical development was one-sided and far from complete. Some of his appraisals (of the activities of Ivan I Kalita and Ivan III, of the history of the founding of the centralised Russian state, the assertion that the Mongol yoke left an indelible impression on the methods of Russian diplomacy, and so on) do not correspond to the historical facts.

Following the view accepted in 19th-century historiography, Marx believed that the decisive factor in the formation of Kiev Rus was the Norman (Varangian) conquest. At that time he regarded the Norman conquests as a stage in the development of all Europe and noted that "warfare and organisation of conquest on the part of the first Ruriks differ in no point from those of the Normans in the rest of Europe" (p. 76).

The idea that for any people to acquire statehood there must be internal preconditions—the development of socio-economic relations, crisis of the communal system and formation of a class society—and that the Normans did not play a decisive role in forming the statehood of the Russian and other peoples, was clearly formulated some time later by Engels. The raids of the Normans, he wrote in his *History of Ireland*, "... came too late and emanated from nations too small for them to culminate in conquest, colonisation and the formation of states on any large scale, as had been the case with the earlier incursions of the Germanic tribes. As far as historical development is concerned, the advantages they bequeathed are quite imperceptible compared with the immense and—even for Scandinavia—fruitless disturbances they caused" (present edition, Vol. 21, 179).

Recent research, particularly the work of Soviet scholars in the 1950s-70s, the excavations in Novgorod, Kiev and other ancient Russian cities, the comparison of the archaeologists' discoveries with written sources, and anthropological, ethnographical and other data, has exploded the Norman theory of the origin of the ancient Russian state.

The *Revelations of the Diplomatic History of the 18th Century* does not reflect the struggle of the great mass of the people of Russia against the Tartar-Mongol yoke and puts no emphasis on the decisive role the Russian people played in its overthrow. In the early 1880s, however, in his "Chronological Notes" on world history Marx stressed as an important fact the victory in 1380 of Russian troops led by the Muscovite prince Dmitry Donskoi over the Tartar hordes on the "broad field of Kulikovo" (see *Marx-Engels Archives,* Russian edition, Vol. VIII, Moscow, 1946, p. 151).

Marx rightly notes the daring nature of Peter I's reforming zeal, his persistence in converting "Muscovy into Russia". But in discussing the wars waged by Peter I, and his desire to strengthen Russia's might and increase her weight in international affairs, Marx did not take into consideration the direct threat to the national interests and integrity of the Russian state from its north-western neighbours.

On the other hand in the *Revelations of the Diplomatic History of the 18th Century* Marx did make several perceptive statements. Considering Russia's past in the general context of European history, he stressed that the epoch of early feudalism, the expansion of Russian territory and feudal strife were determined in the final analysis by the same laws that characterised the early feudal states of Western Europe: "As the empire of Charlemagne precedes the foundation of modern France, Germany, and Italy, so the empire of the Ruriks precedes the foundation of Poland, Lithuania, the Baltic Settlements, Turkey and Muscovy itself" (pp. 75-76). Taking Kiev Rus as an example, Marx shows the causes and inevitability of the disintegration of the large state formations characteristic of the early Middle Ages: "The incongruous, unwieldy, and precocious Empire heaped together by the Ruriks, like the other empires of similar growth, is broken up into appanages, divided and sub-divided among the descendants of the conquerors, dilacerated by feudal wars, rent to pieces by the intervention of foreign peoples" (p. 77).

Marx showed the grave consequences of the Tartar-Mongol invasion for the Russian people. The Tartar yoke, he writes, was "a yoke not only crushing, but dishonouring and withering the very soul of the people that fell its prey" (p. 77). Referring to the "rule of systematic terror" which the Tartar-Mongols imposed in the 13th and 14th centuries, and the "wholesale slaughter" of the population, Marx compares their policy with that of the ruling classes of England at a later time, which had "depopulated the Highlands of Scotland", and also with the onslaught of the barbarians in the Campagna di Roma (p. 77-78). He draws attention to materials referring to Russia as a shield against the Tartar-Mongol invasions, "a kind of stay or stop-gap to the infidels" (p. 46).

Neither Marx, nor Engels ever attempted to have the *Revelations of the Diplomatic History of the 18th Century* republished, and as we have already noted, the one-sided approach and occasional inaccuracies that found their way into it were to a great extent overcome in their later works.

Thus, in June 1858 we find Marx already noting that Russia's internal development, the widespread peasant disturbances, point to the birth of a revolutionary movement in that country which openly opposes the official, reactionary Russia of the serf-owning landlords. Whereas in the period of European revolutions, 1848-49, Tsarist Russia had been one of the main reactionary forces blocking the advance of the revolution, now, in 1858, as Marx wrote, "combustible matter has accumulated under her own feet, which a strong blast from the West may suddenly set on fire" (p. 568). In the late 1850s and particularly after the abolition of serfdom in Russia in 1861, which accelerated the development of capitalist relations there, Marx and Engels devoted increasing attention to the study of the socio-economic processes at work there and to the Russian revolutionary movement.

In the awakening masses of Russia that were entering the struggle Marx and Engels saw a force capable of changing the situation within the country and ending the reactionary policies of Tsarist autocracy in the international field. On April 29, 1858 Marx wrote to Engels: "The movement for the emancipation of the serfs in Russia strikes me as important in so far as it indicates the beginning of an internal development that might run counter to the country's traditional foreign policy" (present edition, Vol. 40, p. 310).

Prominently represented in the volume are the articles by Marx and Engels exposing the colonial policies of the European capitalist powers, particularly Britain, and considering the national liberation struggle of the peoples of Asia against colonial oppression and enslavement.

The articles on the Anglo-Persian war of 1856-57, the second "opium" war waged by England against China in 1856-60, and particularly the popular uprising against British rule in India, 1857-59, develop ideas and propositions expressed by Marx and Engels in the first half of the 1850s (present edition, Vol. 13). These events, which they reported in detail in the *New-York Daily Tribune,* gave them enormous factual material for further generalisation, for interpreting the processes of development of the oriental states, and the colonial and dependent countries, for tracing the mutual influence of the national liberation struggle in Asia and the revolutionary movement in the European capitalist countries.

Writing of Britain's wars against Persia and China, Marx and Engels expose the methods of British colonial policy in Asia and show that Britain acquired territory either by means of direct seizure and blatant coercion or through deceit and bribery.

In several articles ("The War Against Persia", "The Prospects of the Anglo-Persian War", and others) Marx and Engels reveal such provocative methods of British diplomacy as accusing the government of this or that country of failing to observe previous treaties or agreements, of allegedly violating the rights of British citizens, and the use of other pretexts.

One example of such unceremonious action in defiance of the elementary rules of international law was the war unleashed by the British government and military against China on the pretext of protecting the lives and property of British citizens living there. Marx examines the history of the conflict and angrily condemns "this mode of invading a peaceful country, without previous declaration of war, for an alleged infringement of the fanciful code of diplomatic etiquette" (p. 163). Reminding their readers of the atrocities committed against civilians by the British aggressors during the first "opium" war (1840-42), Marx and Engels observe that this new war provoked by the British themselves was being waged by the same ruthless means (see the articles "Defeat of the Palmerston Ministry", "English Atrocities in China", "A New English Expedition to China", and others). Marx and Engels write with great sympathy of the Chinese people's resistance to the forces of the aggressor, and stress the active participation of the masses in this struggle. In his article "Persia—China" Engels cites facts showing that various sections of the population were joining in the struggle. He describes it as a people's war for the preservation of Chinese nationality and stresses that "the piratical policy of the British Government has caused this universal outbreak of all Chinese against all foreigners" (p. 281). Replying to the hypocritical comments of the British bourgeois press concerning the "horrible atrocities of the Chinese", Engels writes that the means used by a nation defending its independence cannot be measured by abstract standards, but "by the degree of civilization only attained by that insurgent nation" (p. 282).

Engels regarded the popular character of the war against the British aggressors as a symptom of the awakening of the masses, as a sign of the approaching death agony of the ancient empire.

Marx and Engels watched with particular interest the course taken by the Indian national uprising of 1857-59. Their numerous articles and reports contain a profound analysis of the causes of the uprising, its driving forces, and the circumstances that led to its defeat; the course of the military actions, the major battles and operations are considered in detail.

Countering the attempts of the authorities and the British capitalist press to belittle the significance and scale of the uprising and to portray it merely as a mutiny of the native Sepoy units in the Anglo-Indian army, Marx and Engels from the outset stressed the national character of the uprising and recognised it as a revolution of the Indian people against British rule (see articles "The Revolt in the Indian Army", "The Revolt in India" [July 17, 1857], "Indian News", and "The Relief of Lucknow"). Although the uprising did not embrace the whole territory of the country, and some groups of the population took no part in it, it was outstandingly important that "Mussulmans and Hindoos, renouncing their mutual antipathies, have combined against their common masters" (p. 298), that the insurgents included people of various castes—Brahmans, Rajputs, and others, that the uprising was supported by various sections of the population. The ramification of conspiracy in the Bengal army, the enormous scale the uprising immediately assumed, testified, as Marx noted in his article "The Indian Insurrection", to secret sympathy and support for the insurgents among the local population, while the difficulties experienced by the British in transporting and supplying their troops indicated peasant hostility towards them. "The unarmed population," Engels states in his article "The Revolt in India" [end of May 1858], "fail to afford the English either assistance or information" (p. 555).

Marx and Engels attached special importance to the fact that the native troops the British had come to rely on were the crucial force behind the uprising. In the process of conquering more and more Indian territory, the British authorities had exploited the enmity between various tribes, castes, religions, and principalities, to create a native army, which served as an instrument of their policy of conquest. When the conquest had been completed, Marx points out, this army was virtually charged with police functions. On the other hand, in the shape of this army the British without knowing it "organized the first general center of resistance which the Indian people was ever possessed of" (pp. 297-98). It was this that from the beginning endowed the uprising with unprecedented strength and extent.

The causes of the uprising lay not only in the discontent among the Sepoy troops evoked by British flouting of their religious traditions. This only triggered the indignation. The Indian peasants, the overwhelming majority of the population, were crushed by taxes, the collection of which involved the foulest methods, including violence and torture, as Marx writes in his article "Investigation of Tortures in India". He noted that of the revenues collected "no part ... is returned to the people in works of public utility, more indispensable in Asiatic countries than anywhere else" (p. 579).

Marx also placed among the causes of the uprising the British authorities' policy of annexing any as yet independent Indian principalities, as well as confiscating land, which evoked fierce opposition from the feudal landowners (see the articles "The Annexation of Oude", "Lord Canning's Proclamation and Land Tenure in India", etc.). When they defined the uprising as something national, Marx and Engels had in mind not only its territorial scale and its unifying effect on different sections and groups of the population, but also the insurgents' basic intent—to throw off the colonial oppression that had lasted almost a hundred and fifty years.

Marx and Engels write with anger and indignation about the atrocities and plunder perpetrated by the British forces in the towns and villages they captured (see the articles "The Revolt in India" [September 4, 1857], "Details of the Attack on Lucknow", etc.). Such actions as the sacking of Lucknow "will remain an everlasting disgrace to the British military service" (p. 531). Without denying the facts of brutality on the part of the insurgent Sepoys, which were exaggerated in every possible way by the British capitalist press, Marx stressed that "it is only the reflex, in a concentrated form, of England's own conduct in India, not only during the epoch of the foundation of her Eastern Empire, but even during the last ten years of a long-settled rule" (p. 353).

In many articles, particularly Engels' military reviews, the methods and means used by the insurgents are subjected to analysis. In his article "The Relief of Lucknow" Engels reaches the following conclusion: "The strength of a national insurrection does not lie in pitched battles, but in petty warfare, in the defense of towns, and in the interruption of the enemy's communications" (p. 441).

Assessing the causes of the military failures of the uprising that led to its eventual defeat, Marx and Engels in their articles "The Capture of Delhi", "The Siege and Storming of Lucknow", "The Relief of Lucknow", etc., point to the insurgents' lack of unified central command, resulting in a lack of coordinated action between their separate forces, and their lack of effective discipline. "A motley crew of mutineering soldiers who have murdered their officers, torn asunder the ties of discipline, and not succeeded in discovering a man upon whom to bestow the supreme command, are certainly the body least likely to organize a serious and protracted resistance" (p. 305).

The insurgents' military actions were much hampered by their leaders' inability to conduct large-scale military operations, and their lack of strategic or tactical experience and knowledge. "They entirely lacked," Engels writes, "the scientific element without which an army is now-a-days helpless" (p. 392).

Besides these purely military causes of the defeat, Marx and Engels note the dissension and discord among the insurgents, the renewed religious enmity between Moslems and Hindus, the ethnic diversity of the Indian population, and the treachery of the majority of the local feudal princes who found themselves at the head of the uprising.

Defining the historical importance of the Indian uprising, Marx gives priority to its internal connection with such events of the 1850s as the Chinese people's resistance to Britain's penetration of China and the Anglo-Persian war. "The revolt in the Anglo-Indian army," he writes, "has coincided with a general disaffection exhibited against English supremacy on the part of the great Asiatic nations" (p. 298). He goes on to stress that the Indian people's war of national liberation exacerbated the economic crisis in Britain and could—had there been a new revolutionary explosion in Europe—have weakened her counter-revolutionary role. "In view of the DRAIN OF MEN and BULLION which she will cost the

English, India is now our best ally," Marx wrote to Engels on January 16, 1858 (present edition, Vol. 40, p. 249).

Marx points to the fact that, although the insurrection did not bring India liberation from national oppression, it forced England to change her methods of rule and put a final end to the East India Company. The uprising revealed the deep hatred felt by the great mass of the people for the colonialists and demonstrated their ability to resist.

The ideas expressed by Marx in the articles on the national liberation struggle of the peoples of Asia were further developed by Lenin. In the new historical epoch Lenin worked out and substantiated the theory of the national-colonial problem and showed that the peoples of the colonial and dependent countries oppressed by imperialist powers are the natural allies of the proletariat in the struggle for the overthrow of capitalism, and in building the new society.

* * *

This volume contains 105 works by Marx and Engels. Only three of them were written in German and appear in English for the first time. Of the other works written in English 56 were never reprinted after their first publication.

The Supplement contains Article IX from Marx's series of articles *Revolutionary Spain,* which came to light after the appearance of Volume 13 of the present edition, where the first eight articles had been published.

In the present edition all known cases of editorial intervention in the Marx and Engels text have been indicated in the notes.

When studying the specific historical material cited in the articles, it must be remembered that Marx's and Engels' sources for their pieces on current events were newspaper reports, which were sometimes inaccurate; this too is commented on in the notes.

In the event of an article having no title, the editors have supplied a heading in square brackets.

The asterisks indicate footnotes by the author, the editors' footnotes are indicated by index letters. The spelling of proper and geographical names corresponds to that in the publications from which the texts are reproduced.

The selection of material for the volume, preparation of the text and writing of the notes was done by Valentina Smirnova (for *Revelations of the Diplomatic History of the 18th Century* and

"B. Bauer's Pamphlets on the Collision with Russia"); by Tatyana Andrushchenko (for works written between May 1856 and May 1857), Yelena Vashchenko (for works written between June and November 1857) and Natalia Martynova (for works written between November 1857 and September 1858). The Preface was prepared by Valentina Smirnova and Tatyana Andrushchenko under the editorship of Boris Tartakovsky. The editors of the volume are Tatyana Yeremeyeva and Boris Tartakovsky. Name index, index of periodicals and glossary were compiled by Yelena Vashchenko, and index of quoted and mentioned literature by Tatyana Andrushchenko, Yelena Vashchenko, and Natalia Martynova, with the participation of Felix Ryabov. Nadezhda Borodina took part in the general work of preparing the notes and indexes (CC CPSU Institute of Marxism-Leninism).

The English translations were made by Peter and Betty Ross (Lawrence & Wishart).

The volume was prepared for the press by Natalia Karmanova, Margarita Lopukhina and Yelena Vorotnikova (Progress Publishers) and Vladimir Mosolov, scientific editor (CC CPSU Institute of Marxism-Leninism).

KARL MARX
and
FREDERICK ENGELS

WORKS

May 1856-September 1858

Karl Marx

SARDINIA[1]

The history of the house of Savoy may be divided into three epochs—the first, in which it rises and aggrandises itself by taking up an equivocal position between Guelphs and Ghibellines,[2] between the Italian republics and the German empire; the second, in which it thrives upon shifting sides in the wars between France and Austria[3]; and the last, in which it endeavoured to improve the world-wide strife between revolution and counter-revolution as it had done with the antagonism of races and dynasties.[a] In the three epochs equivocation is the constant axis on which its policy revolves, and results diminutive in dimension and ambiguous in character, appear as the natural offspring of that policy. At the end of the first epoch, simultaneously with the formation of the grand monarchies in Europe, we behold the house of Savoy form a small monarchy. At the end of the second epoch the Vienna Congress condescended to surrender to it the republic of Genoa, while Austria swallowed Venice and Lombardy,[4] and the Holy Alliance[5] put its extinguisher upon all second-rate powers of whatever denomination. During the third epoch, lastly,[b] Piedmont is allowed to appear at the Conferences of Paris, drawing up a memorandum against Austria and Naples,[6] giving sage advice to the Pope,[c] clapped upon the shoulders by an Orloff, cheered on in its constitutional aspirations by the *coup d'état*,[7] and goaded in its dreams of Italian supremacy by the same Palmerston who so successfully betrayed it in 1848 and 1849.[8]

[a] The end of the sentence from the words "as it had done ..." is omitted in the *New-York Daily Tribune*.—*Ed.*

[b] This word is omitted in the *New-York Daily Tribune*.—*Ed.*

[c] Pius IX.—*Ed.*

It is a rather preposterous idea on the part of the Sardinian spokesmen that constitutionalism, the agony of which they may at this moment witness in Great Britain, and[a] with the bankruptcy of which the revolutions of 1848-49 made the European continent ring—it proving equally powerless against the bayonets of the crowns, and the barricades of the people—that this same constitutionalism is now about not only to celebrate its *restitutio in integrum*[b] on the Piedmontese stage, but even to become a conquering power. Such an idea could but originate with the great men of a little state. For any impartial observer it is an unquestionable fact that with the great monarchy in France Piedmont must remain a small one; that with an imperial despotism in France, Piedmont exists at the best but on sufferance, and that with a real republic in France, the Piedmont monarchy will disappear and melt into an Italian republic. The very conditions on which the existence of the Sardinian monarchy depends debar it from attaining its ambitious ends. It can but play the part of an Italian liberator in an epoch of revolution suspended in Europe, and of counter-revolution ruling supreme in France. Under such conditions it may imagine to take upon itself the leadership of Italy, as the only Italian state with progressive tendencies, with native rulers, and with a national army. But these very conditions place it between the pressure of imperial France on the one, and imperial Austria on the other hand. In case of serious friction between these neighbouring empires, it must become the satellite of one and the battlefield of both. In case of an *entente cordiale* between them, it must be content with an asthmatical existence, with a mere respite of life. To throw itself on the revolutionary party in Italy would be simple suicide, the events of 1848-49 having dispelled the last delusions as to its revolutionary mission. The hopes of the house of Savoy thus are bound up with the *status quo* in Europe, and the *status quo* in Europe shutting it out from extension in the Appenine Peninsula assigns it the modest part of an Italian Belgium.

In their attempt to resume at the Paris Congress the game of 1847, the Piedmontese plenipotentiaries could, therefore, exhibit but a rather lamentable spectacle. Each move they drew on the diplomatic chessboard cried *check* to themselves. While violently protesting against the Austrian occupation of central Italy, they were obliged to touch but tenderly on the occupation of Rome by

[a] Part of this sentence from the words "the agony" up to "Britain, and" is omitted in the *New-York Daily Tribune.—Ed.*

[b] Full rehabilitation.—*Ed.*

France[9]; and while grumbling against the theocracy of the Pontiff,[a] to stoop before the sanctimonious grimaces of the first-born son of the church.[b] To Clarendon, who had shown such tender mercies to Ireland in 1848,[10] they had to appeal for giving the King of Naples[c] lessons of humanity, and to the gaoler of Cayenne, Lambessa, and Belle Isle,[11] for opening the prisons of Milan, Naples, and Rome. Establishing themselves the champions of liberty in Italy, they bowed servilely to Walewski's onslaught on the liberty of the press in Belgium, and gave it as their deliberate opinion that

> "it is difficult for good relations to continue between two nations when, in one of them, journals with exaggerated doctrines, and waging war on the neighbouring governments, exist."

Bottomed on this their own foolish adhesion to Buonapartist doctrines, Austria at once turned round upon them with the imperious demand of stopping and punishing the war waged against her by the Piedmontese press.

At the same moment that they feign to oppose the international policy of the peoples to the international policy of the countries,[d] they congratulate themselves upon the treaty again, knitting together those ties of friendship which for centuries have existed between the house of Savoy and the family of Romanoff. Encouraged to display their eloquence before the Plenipotentiaries of Old Europe, they must suffer to be snubbed by Austria as a second-rate power, not with the power to discuss first-rate questions. While they enjoy the immense satisfaction of drawing up a memorandum, Austria is allowed to draw up an army the whole length of the Sardinian frontier, from the Po to the summit of the Apennines, to occupy Parma, to fortify Piacenza, notwithstanding the treaty of Vienna, and on the shore of the Adriatic to deploy her forces from Ferrara and Bologna as far as Ancona. Seven days after these complaints had been promulgated before the Congress, on the 15th of April, a special treaty was signed between France and England on the one, and Austria on the other side, proving to evidence the damage the memorandum had inflicted on Austria.

Such was the position at the Paris Congress of the worthy representatives of that Victor Emmanuel who, after his abdication, and the loss of the battle of Novara[12] went before the eyes of an

[a] Pius IX.—*Ed.*
[b] Napoleon III.—*Ed.*
[c] Ferdinand II.—*Ed.*
[d] The *New-York Daily Tribune* has "dynasties" instead of "countries".—*Ed.*

exasperated army to embrace Radetzky, Carlo Albert's spiteful foe. If Piedmont is not blind on purpose, it must now see that it is duped by the peace as it was duped by the war. Bonaparte may use it to trouble waters in Italy, with a view to fish crowns in the mud.[13] Russia may clap the shoulder of little Sardinia, with the intention of alarming Austria in the South, in order to weaken her in the North. Palmerston may, for purposes best known to himself, rehearse the comedy of 1847, without giving himself so much as the pains of playing the old song to a new tune. For all that Piedmont serves only as the catspaw of foreign powers. As to the speeches in the British Parliament Mr. Brofferio has told the Sardinian Chamber of Deputies, of which he is a member, that "they had never been Delphian oracles, but always Trophonian ones." He is only mistaken in taking echoes for oracles.[14]

The Piedmontese intermezzo considered in itself, is void of any interest but that of seeing the house of Savoy baffled again in its hereditary policy of shifts and its renewed attempts at making the Italian question the prop of its own dynastical intrigues. But there is another more important point of view, intentionally overlooked by the English and French press, but especially[a] hinted at by the Sardinian plenipotentiaries in their notorious memorandum.[b] The hostile attitude of Austria, justified by the course pursued at Paris on the part of the Sardinian plenipotentiaries, "obliges Sardinia to remain armed, and to adopt measures[c] extremely hazardous[d] to her finances, already dilapidated by the events of 1848 and 1849, and by the war in which she has taken part." But this is not all.

"The popular agitation," says the Sardinian memorandum, "has appeared to subside of late. The Italians, seeing one of their national princes allied with the great Western powers ... conceived a hope that peace would not be made before some solace had been applied to their woes. This hope rendered them calm and resigned; but when they shall learn the negative results of the Congress of Paris—when they shall know that Austria notwithstanding the good office and benevolent intervention of France and England, has opposed even discussion ... then there can be no doubt that the irritation which has been lulled for the moment will reawaken more fiercely than ever. The Italians, convinced that they have nothing more to hope from diplomacy,—will throw themselves back with Southern vehemence into the ranks of the subversive and revolutionary party,[e] and

[a] The *New-York Daily Tribune* has "anxiously".—*Ed.*

[b] Marx has in mind C. Cavour's "Note adressée au comte Walewski à lord Clarendon, le 16 avril 1856", which he quotes below.—*Ed.*

[c] The *New-York Daily Tribune* has "defensive measures".—*Ed.*

[d] The *NYDT* has "burdensome".—*Ed.*

[e] The text beginning with the words "the Italians" is italicised in the *New-York Daily Tribune.*—*Ed.*

Italy will become in turn a focus[a] of conspiracies and disorders, which may indeed be suppressed by redoubled severity, but which the most trifling European commotion will cause to break out again with the utmost violence. The awakening of revolutionary passions in all countries which surround Piedmont, by causes of a nature to excite popular sympathy, exposes the Sardinian Government to dangers of excessive gravity."

This is to the point. During the war, the wealthy middle-class of Lombardy had, so to say, expended their breath in the vain hope of winning at its conclusion by their action of diplomacy, and under the auspices of the House of Savoy, national emancipation or[b] civil liberty without a necessity of wading through the red sea of revolution, and without making to the peasantry and the proletarians those concessions which, after the experience of 1848-49, they knew to have become inseparable from any popular movement. However, their Epicurean hopes have now vanished. The only tangible results of the war, at least the only ones to be caught by an Italian eye, are material and political advantages possessed[c] by Austria—a new consolidation of that odious power secured by the co-operation of a so-called independent Italian state. The constitution also of Piedmont had again the game in their hands; they have again lost it; and stand again convicted of wanting the vocation[d] so loudly claimed of heading Italy. They will be called to account by their own army. The middle-classes are again found to throw themselves upon the bias of the people,[e] and to identify national emancipation with social regeneration. The Piedmontese nightmare is thrown off, the diplomatic spell is broken—and the volcanic heart of revolutionary Italy begins again to pant.

Written on about May 16, 1856

First published in *The People's Paper*, No. 211, May 17, 1856, signed K. M., and also in the *New-York Daily Tribune*, No. 4717, May 31, 1856, unsigned

Reproduced from *The People's Paper*

---

[a] The *New-York Daily Tribune* has "burning center".—*Ed.*

[b] The *NYDT* has "and".—*Ed.*

[c] The *NYDT* has "pocketed".—*Ed.*

[d] The *NYDT* has "as failing in the office" instead of "of wanting the vocation".—*Ed.*

[e] The *NYDT* has "mass".—*Ed.*

Karl Marx

THE FRENCH CRÉDIT MOBILIER[15]

[I]

The London *Times* of the 30th of May is much surprised at the discovery that Socialism in France had never disappeared, but had rather been forgotten for some years. Whereof it takes occasion to congratulate England for not being pestered with that plague but free from that antagonism of classes on which soil the poisonous plant is produced. A rather bold assertion this, coming from the principal journal of a country whose leading economist, Mr. Ricardo, commences his celebrated work on the principles of political economy[a] with the principle that the three fundamental classes of society, *i.e.,* of English society, viz.: the owners of the land, the capitalists, and the wages labourers, are forming a deadly and fatal antagonism; rents rising and falling in inverse ratio to the rise and fall of industrial profits, and wages rising and falling in inverse ratio to profits. If, according to English lawyers, the counterpoise of the three contesting powers is the keystone of the constitution of England, that eighth marvel of the world; according to Mr. Ricardo, who may be presumed to know something more about it than *The Times,* the deadly antagonism of the three classes representing the principal agents of production is the framework of English society.

While *The Times* contemptuously sneers at revolutionary Socialism in France, it cannot help casting a covetous glance at imperial Socialism in France, and would fain hold it up as an example for imitation to John Bull, the chief agents of that Socialism, the "Credit Mobilier", having just sent *The Times* in an advertisement of about three close columns; the Report of the Board of

---

[a] D. Ricardo, *On the Principles of Political Economy, and Taxation.—Ed.*

Administration at the ordinary general meeting of shareholders on April 23rd, 1856, Mr. Pereire in the chair.[a]

The following is the account that has enlisted the envious admiration of the *Times* shareholders, and dazzled the judgment of the *Times* editor:—

Liabilities.

On 31st December, 1855.	francs.	centimes.
Capital of the Society	60,000,000	
The balance of accounts current in December 31st, 1854, from a total of 64,924,379 to that of	103,179,308	64
Amount of bills payable of the creditors and for sundries	864,414	81
Total of reserve	1,696,083	59
Total of profits realised in 1855, after the deduction of the sum to be carried in the reserve	26,827,901	32
	192,567,708	36

Assets.

In hand.	f.	c.
1. Rents	40,069,264	40
2. Debentures	32,844,600	20
3. Railway & other shares	59,431,593	66
	132,345,458	26
From which is to be deducted for calls not made up 31st Dec. last	31,166,718	62
Balance asset	101,178,739	64
Investments for a fixed period in treasury bonds, continuations, advances on shares etc.	84,325,390	9
Value of premises and furniture	1,082,219	37
Disposable balance in hand and at the bank, and the amount of dividends to be received 31st of December last	5,981,359	26
Total assets	192,567,708	36
The total amount of rents, shares, and debentures in hand on December 31, 1854	57,460,092	94
Has been augmented by subscriptions and purchases made in 1855	265,820,907	-3
Total	323,280,999	97

[a] I. Péreire, "Rapport présenté par le conseil d'administration dans l'assemblée générale ordinaire des actionnaires du 23 avril 1856", *Le Moniteur universel*, No. 117, April 26, 1856.—*Ed.*

Amount of realisation being	217,002,431	34
To which must be added the amount of securities remaining in hand	132,345,458	26
	349,347,889	60
These results show a profit of	26,066,889	63

A profit of 26 millions on a capital of 60 millions—a profit at the rate of 43 $^{1}/_{3}$% these are indeed fascinating figures. And what has not this stirring[a] mobilier effected with its grand capital of something like two and a half millions of pounds sterling? With sixty million francs in hand they have subscribed to the French loans first 250 millions, and afterwards 375 millions more; they have acquired an interest in the principal railways of France—they have undertaken the issue of the loan contracted by the Austrian Association for the Railways of the State—they have participated in the Western and Central railways of Switzerland—they have taken an interest in a considerable operation, professing for its object the canalisation of the Ebro from Saragossa to the Mediterranean—they had their hands in the amalgamation of the omnibuses at Paris, and in the constitution of the General Maritime Company—they have brought about by their intervention the amalgamation of all the old gas companies of Paris into one enterprise—they have, as they say, made a present of 300,000 francs to the people by selling them corn below the market price—they have decided on peace and war by their loans, erected new and propped up old lines of railways—illuminated cities, given an impulse to the creations of manufacture and the speculations of commerce, and lastly extended their swindling propaganda over[b] France and scattered the fruitful seeds of their institution over the whole continent of Europe.

The "Credit Mobilier" thus presents itself as one of the most economical phenomena of our epoch wanting a thorough sifting. Without such a research it is impossible either to compute the chances of the French Empire or to understand the symptoms of the general convulsion of society manifesting themselves throughout Europe. We shall investigate first into what the board calls its theoretic principles and then test their practical execution which, possibly, as the report informs us, have been until now but partially realised, and attend as immensely greater development in the future.

---

[a] The *New-York Daily Tribune* has "wonderful".—*Ed.*

[b] The *NYDT* has "influence beyond the frontiers of France".—*Ed.*

The principles of the society are set forth in its statutes, and in the different, but principally in the first, reports made to the shareholders. According to the preamble of the statutes, and

"considering the important services which might be rendered by the establishment of a society having for its aim to favour the development of the industry of the public works, and to realise the conversion of the different titles of various enterprises through the means of consolidating them in one common fund, the founders of the 'Credit Mobilier' have resolved to carry into effect so useful a work, and consequently they have combined to lay down the basis of an anonymous society, under the denomination of the General Society of the 'Credit Mobilier'".[a]

Our readers will understand by the word "anonymous society,"[b] a joint-stock company with limited responsibility of the shareholders, and that the formation of such a society depends on a privilege arbitrarily granted by the Government.

The "Credit Mobilier" then proposes to itself firstly to "favour the development of the industry of the public works," which means to make industry of public works in general dependent on the favour of the "Credit Mobilier", and therefore on the individual favour of Bonaparte, on whose breath the existence of the society is suspended. The Board does not fail to indicate by what means it intends to bring about this its patronage, and that of its imperial patron,[c] over the whole French industry. The various industrial enterprises carried on by joint stock companies, are represented by different titles, shares, obligations, bonds, debentures, etc. Those different titles are of course rated at different prices in the money market, according to the capital they trade upon, the profits they yield, the different bearing of demand and offer upon them, and other economical conditions. Now what intends the "Credit Mobilier"?

To substitute for all these different titles carried on by different joint stock companies, one common title issued by the "Credit Mobilier" itself. But how can it effect this? By buying up with its own titles the titles of the various industrial concerns. Buying up all the bonds, shares, debentures, etc.; in one word the titles of a concern, is buying up the concern itself. Hence the "Credit Mobilier" avows the intention of making itself the proprietor, and Napoleon the Little[16] the supreme director of the whole great French industry. This is what we call Imperial Socialism.

---

[a] "Décret portant autorisation de la société anonyme formée à Paris sous la denomination de Société générale de Crédit Mobilier. 18 novembre-11 décembre 1852."—*Ed.*

[b] The *New-York Daily Tribune* has "Our readers will bear in mind that the French understand by the word..."—*Ed.*

[c] The *NYDT* has "creator".—*Ed.*

In order to realise this programme, there are needed, of course, some financial operations, and M. Isaac Péreire in tracing their operations of the "Credit Mobilier," naturally feels himself on delicate ground, is obliged to put limits to the society considered purely accidental and intended to disappear in its development, and rather throws out a feeler than to divulge at once his ultimate scheme to the world.[a]

The social fund of the society has been fixed at 60,000,000 francs divided into 120,000 shares of 500 francs each, payable to the bearer.[b]

The operations of the society, such as they are defined in the statutes, may be ranged under three heads. Firstly, operations for the support of the great industry, secondly, creation of a value issued by the society for replacing, or amalgamating the titles of different industrial enterprises, thirdly, the ordinary operations of banking, bearing upon public funds, commercial bills, etc.

The operations of the first category, intended to obtain for the society the patronage of industry, are enumerated in art. V of the statutes, which says:

"To subscribe for, or acquire public funds, shares, or obligations in the different industrial or credit enterprises, constituted as anonymous societies, and especially those of railways, canals, mines, and other public works already established, or about to be established. To undertake all loans, to transfer and realise them, as well as all enterprises of public works."[c]

We see how this article already goes beyond the pretensions of the preamble, by proposing to make the "Credit Mobilier" not only the proprietor of the great industry, but the slave of the Treasury, and the despot of commercial credit.

The operations of the second category, relating to the substitution of the titles of the "Credit Mobilier" for the titles of all other industrial enterprises, embraces the following:

"To issue in equal amounts for the sums employed for subscriptions of loans and acquisitions of industrial titles the society's own obligations."

Articles 7 and 8 indicate the limits and the nature of the obligations the society has power to issue. These obligations, or bonds

[a] The end of the sentence from the words "and rather throws..." is omitted in the *New-York Daily Tribune*.—*Ed.*

[b] The words "payable to the bearer" are omitted in the *New-York Daily Tribune*.—*Ed.*

[c] "Décret portant autorisation de la société anonyme formée à Paris..."—*Ed.*

"are allowed to reach a sum equal to ten times the amount of the capital. They must always be represented for their total amount by public funds, shares, and obligations in the society's hands. They cannot be made payable at less than 45 days notice. The total amount of the sums received in account-current and of the obligations created at less than a year's run shall not exceed twice the capital realised."

The third category, lastly, embraces the operations necessitated by the exchange of commercial values. The society "receives money at call." It is authorised "to sell or give in payment for loans all sorts of funds, papers, shares, and obligations held by it, and to exchange them for other values." It lends on "public funds, deposits of shares and obligations, and it opens account-currents on their different values." It offers to anonymous societies "all the ordinary services rendered by private bankers, such as receiving all payments on account of the societies, paying their dividends, interest, etc." It keeps a deposit of all titles of those enterprises, but in the operations relating to the trade in commercial values, bills, warrants, etc., "it is expressly understood that the society shall not make clandestine sales nor purchases for the sake of premium."

Written on about June 6, 1856

First published in *The People's Paper*, No. 214, June 7, 1856, signed K. M. and also in the *New-York Daily Tribune*, No. 4735, June 21, 1856, unsigned

Reproduced from *The People's Paper*

New-York Daily Tribune.

Vol. XVI......No. 4,737. NEW-YORK, TUESDAY, JUNE 24, 1856. PRICE TWO CENTS.

Karl Marx

THE FRENCH CRÉDIT MOBILIER

[II]

It should be recollected that Bonaparte made his *coup d'état* on two diametrically opposite pretenses: on the one hand proclaiming it was his mission to save the *bourgeoisie* and "material order" from the Red anarchy to be let loose in May, 1852[17]; and on the other hand, to save the working people from the middle-class despotism concentrated in the National Assembly. Besides, there was the personal necessity of paying his own debts and those of the respectable mob of the Society of the *Dix Décembre,*[18] and of enriching himself and them at the joint expense of bourgeoisie and workmen. The mission of the man, it must be avowed, was beset by conflicting difficulties; forced as he was to appear simultaneously as the robber and as the patriarchal benefactor of all classes. He could not give to the one class without taking from the other, and he could not satisfy his own wants and those of his followers without robbing both. In the time of the Fronde[19] the Duc de Guise was said to be the most obliging man of France. because he had transformed all his estates into obligations held by his partisans. Thus Bonaparte also proposed to become the most obliging man of France, by converting all the property and all the industry of France into a personal obligation toward Louis Bonaparte. To steal France in order to buy France—that was the great problem the man had to solve, and in this transaction of taking from France what was to be given back to France, not the least important side to him was the percentage to be skimmed off by himself and the Society of December Tenth. How were these contradictory pretenses to be reconciled? how was this nice economical problem to be solved? how this knotty point to be untwined? All the varied past experience of Bonaparte pointed to the one great resource that had carried him over the most difficult economical situations—Credit. And there happened to be in France the school of St. Simon, which in its beginning and in its decay deluded itself with the dream that all the antagonism of classes must disappear before the creation of universal wealth by some new-fangled scheme of public credit. And St. Simonism in this form had not yet died out at the epoch of the *coup d'état*. There was Michel Chevalier, the economist of the *Journal des Débats;* there was Proudhon, who tried to disguise the worst portion of the St. Simonist doctrine under the appearance of eccentric originality; and there were two Portuguese Jews, practically connected with stockjobbing and Rothschild, who had sat at the feet of the Père Enfantin, and who with their practical experience had the boldness to suspect stockjobbing behind Socialism, Law behind St. Simon. These men—Émile and Isaac Péreire—are the founders of the *Crédit Mobilier,* and the initiators of Bonapartist Socialism.

It is an old proverb, *"Habent sua fata libelli."*[a] Doctrines have also their *fate* as well as books. St. Simon to become the guardian angel of the Paris Bourse, the prophet of swindling, the Messiah of general bribery and corruption! History exhibits no example of a more cruel irony, save, perhaps, St. Just realized by the *juste milieu*[b] of Guizot, and Napoleon by Louis Bonaparte.

Events march swifter than man's consideration. While we, from an investigation of its principles and economical conditions, are pointing at the unavoidable crash foreboded by the very constitution of the *Crédit Mobilier,* history is already at work realizing our predictions. On the last of May, one of the Directors of the *Crédit Mobilier,* M. Place, failed for the sum of ten millions of francs, having only a few days before been "presented to the Emperor by M. de Morny" as one of the *dieux de la finance. Les dieux s'en vont!*[c] Almost on the same day the *Moniteur* published the new law on the *Sociétés en commandite,*[d] which, on pretense of putting a check on the speculative fever, places those societies at the mercy of the *Crédit Mobilier* by making their formation dependent on the will of the government or of the *Crédit Mobilier.* And the English

---

[a] A quotation from *De litteris, syllabis et metris* (*Carmen heroicum,* verse 258) by the Roman grammarian and poet Terentianus Maurus.—*Ed.*

[b] Golden mean.—*Ed.*

[c] Gods of finance. The Gods are passing away (cf. F. Chateaubriand, *Les Martyrs ou le Triomphe de la religion chrétienne*).—*Ed.*

[d] Joint-stock companies with limited liability; see also "Projet de loi sur les sociétés en commandite par actions", *Le Moniteur universel,* No. 153, June 1, 1856.—*Ed.*

press, ignorant of even the existence of a difference, between *Sociétés en commandite* and *Sociétés anonymes*,[a] to which latter the former are thus sacrificed, goes into ecstacies at this great "prudential act" of Bonapartist wisdom, imagining that French speculators will soon be speedily brought round to the solidity of the English Sadleirs, Spaders and Palmers. At the same time the law of drainage just passed by the famous *Corps Législatif*,[20] and which is a direct infraction of all former legislation and the Code Napoleon, sanctions the expropriation of the mortgagors of the land, in favor of the government of Bonaparte, who by this machinery proposes to seize on the land, as by the *Crédit Mobilier* he is seizing on the industry, and by the Bank of France on the commerce of France; and all this to save property from the dangers of Socialism!

Meanwhile we do not think it superfluous to continue our examination of the *Crédit Mobilier*, an institution which, we think, is destined yet to enact achievements of which the above are but small beginnings.

We have seen that the first function of the *Crédit Mobilier* consists in affording capital to such industrial concerns as are carried on by anonymous societies. We quote from the report of M. Isaac Péreire:

> "The *Crédit Mobilier* acts, with regard to the values representing industrial capital, a part analogous to the functions discharged by discount banks with regard to the values representing commercial capital. The first duty of this society is to support the development of national industry, to facilitate the formation of great enterprises which, abandoned to themselves, meet with great obstacles. Its mission in this respect will be more easily fulfilled, as it disposes of various means of information and research that escape the grasp of private individual for soundly appreciating the real value or prospects of undertakings appealing to its aid. In prosperous times our society will be a guide for capital anxious to find profitable employment; in difficult movements it is destined to offer precious resources for the maintenance of labor, and the moderation of the crises which result from a rash contraction of capitals. The pains which our society will take to invest its capital in all affairs only in such proportions and for such limited terms as will permit of a safe withdrawal, will enable it to multiply its action, to fructify in a small space of time a great number of enterprises, and to diminish the risks of its concurrence by the multiplicity of partial *commandités*" (investments in shares).[b]

Having seen in what manner Isaac develops the ideas of Bonaparte, it becomes important also to see the manner in which

---

[a] Joint-stock companies.— *Ed.*

[b] I. Péreire, "Rapport présenté par le conseil d'administration dans l'assemblée générale ordinaire et extraordinaire des actionnaires du 29 avril 1854", *Le Moniteur universel*, No. 121, May 1, 1854.— *Ed.*

Bonaparte comments upon the ideas of Isaac, a comment which may be found in the Report addressed to him by the Minister of the Interior[a] on June 21, 1854, with respect to the principles and the administration of the *Crédit Mobilier:*

"Among all the establishments of credit existing in the world, the *Banque de France* is justly considered that which boasts of the most solid constitution;"

so solid that the slight storm of February, 1848, had borne it down in a day, but for the prop afforded it by Ledru-Rollin and Co.; for not only did the Provisional Government suspend the obligation of the *Banque de France* to pay its notes in cash, and thus roll back the tide of note and bondholders blocking up its avenues, but empowered it to issue notes of 50 francs, while it had never been permitted under Louis Philippe to issue less than 500 franc notes; and not only did they thus cover the insolvent Banque by their credit, but in addition they pledged the State forests to the Banque for the privilege of obtaining credit for the State.

"The *Banque de France* is at the same time a support and a guide for our commerce, and its material and moral influence gives to our market a very precious stability."

This stability is such that the French have a regular industrial crisis each time when America and England condescend only to a little smash in their commerce.

"By the reserve and prudence which direct all its operations, this admirable institution fulfills, therefore, the part of a regulator; but the commercial genius, to generate all the wonders it carries in its womb, wants, above all things, to be stimulated; and precisely because speculation is restrained in France in the strictest limits, there existed no inconvenience, but on the contrary a great advantage, in putting alongside of the *Banque de France* an establishment conceived in quite a different order of ideas, and which should represent in the sphere of industry and commerce the spirit of initiative.

"The model for this establishment happily existed already; it is derived from a country celebrated by its severe loyalty, the prudence and solidity presiding over all its commercial operations. By placing at the disposition of all sound ideas and useful enterprises its capital, its credit, and its moral authority, the General Society of the Netherlands has multiplied in Holland canals, drainage, and a thousand other improvements which have raised the value of property a hundred fold. Why should not France likewise profit by an institution the advantages of which have been demonstrated by so dazzling an experience? This is the thought which determined the creation of the Credit Mobilier, authorized by the decree of 18th Nov., 1852.

"According to the terms of its statutes this Society can, among other operations, buy and sell public effects or industrial shares, lend and borrow on them as securities, contract for public loans, and in a word, issue its paper at long dates, to the account of the values thus acquired.

[a] F. Persigny.—*Ed.*

"It has thus the means in hand of summoning and combining at any moment, under advantageous conditions, considerable wealth. In the good use it may make of these capitals the fertility of the institution resides. Indeed, the Society may arbitrarily invest in *(commanditer)* industry, take an interest in enterprises, participate in operations of a long term, which the constitution of the Banque de France and of the Discount Office forbids these establishments to do; in one word, it is free in its movements, and may change its action just as the wants of commercial credit require it. If it knows how, among the enterprises constantly brought forth, to distinguish the fruitful; if by the timely intervention of the immense funds which it has the disposition of, it enables works to be carried out highly productive in themselves, but absorbing an unusual duration, and otherwise languishing; if its concurrence be the sure index of a useful idea or a well-conceived project, the Society of the *Crédit Mobilier* will deserve and win the public approbation; floating capital will seek its channels and direct itself in mass whithersoever the patronage of the Society indicates a guarantied employ. Thus, by the power of example, and by authority which will become attached to its support, more even than by any material aid, this Society will be the cooperator of all ideas of general utility. Thus it will powerfully encourage the efforts of industry, and stimulate everywhere the spirit of invention."[a]

We shall take an early occasion to show how all these high-flowing phrases conceal but feebly the plain scheme of dragging all the industry of France into the whirlpool of the Paris Bourse, and to make it the tennis-ball of the gentlemen of the *Crédit Mobilier,* and of their patron Bonaparte.

Written on about June 12, 1856

First published in the *New-York Daily Tribune,* No. 4737, June 24, 1856

Reproduced from the newspaper

[a] F. Persigny, "Rapport à l'Empereur", *Le Moniteur universel,* No. 172, June 21, 1854.—*Ed.*

Karl Marx

THE FRENCH CRÉDIT MOBILIER

[III]

The approaching crash in Bonapartist finance continues to announce itself in a variety of ways. On May 31 Count Montalembert, in opposing a project of law to raise the postage on all printed papers, books, and the like, sounded the note of alarm in the following strain:

"The suppression of all political life, by what has it been replaced? By the whirl of speculation. The great French nation could not resign itself to slumber, to inactivity. Political life was replaced by the fever of speculation, by the thirst for lucre, by the infatuation of gambling. On all sides, even in our small towns, even in our villages, men are carried away by the mania of making those rapid fortunes of which there are so many examples—those fortunes achieved without trouble, without labor, and often without honor. I seek for no other proof than the bill which has just been laid before you, against the *sociétés en commandite*.[a] Copies have just been distributed to us; I have not had time to examine it; I feel, however, inclined to support it, despite the somewhat Draconian regulations which I fancy I discovered there. If the remedy is so urgent and so considerable, the evil must be so likewise. The real source of that evil is the sleep of all political spirit in France.... And the evil which I point to is not the only one resulting from the same source. While the higher and middle classes—those ancient political classes—give themselves up to speculation, another labor presents itself among the lower classes of society, whence nearly all the revolutions emanated which France has suffered. At the sight of this fearful mania of gambling which has made a vast gambling booth of nearly all France, a portion of the masses, invaded by Socialists, has been more corrupted than ever, by the avidity of gain. Hence an unquestionable progress of secret societies, a greater and deeper development of those savage passions which almost calumniate Socialism by adopting its name, and which have been recently well shown up, in all their intensity, in the trials at Paris, Angers and elsewhere." [b]

[a] Joint-stock companies with limited liability. See also p. 15.—*Ed.*

[b] Count de Montalembert's speech at the sitting of the Corps Législatif on May 31, 1856, *The Times*, No. 22386, June 5, 1856.—*Ed.*

Thus speaks Montalembert—himself one of the original shareholders in the Bonapartist enterprise for saving order, religion, property and family!

We have heard, from Isaac Péreire, that one of the mysteries of the *Crédit Mobilier* was the principle of multiplying its action and diminishing its risks by embarking in the greatest possible variety of enterprises, and withdrawing from them in the shortest possible time. Now, what does this mean when divested of the flowery language of St. Simonism? Subscribing for shares to the greatest extent, in the greatest number of speculations, realizing the premiums, and getting rid of them as fast as it can be done. Stockjobbing, then, is to be the base of the industrial development, or rather all industrial enterprise is to become the mere pretext of stockjobbing. And, by the aid of what instrument is this object of the *Crédit Mobilier* to be attained? What are the means proposed to enable it thus to "multiply its action" and "diminish its risks?" The very means employed by Law. The *Crédit Mobilier* being a privileged company, backed by Government influence, and disposing of a large capital and credit, comparatively speaking, it is certain that the shares of any new enterprise started by it will, on the first emission, fetch a premium in the market. It has learned thus much from Law, to allot to its own shareholders the new shares at par, in proportion to the number of shares they hold in the mother society. The profit thus insured to them acts, in the first place, on the value of the shares of the *Crédit Mobilier* itself, while their high range, in the second place, insures a high value to the new shares to be emitted. In this manner the *Crédit Mobilier* obtains command over a large portion of the loanable capital intended for investment in industrial enterprises.

Now, apart from the fact that the premium is thus the real pivot on which the activity of the *Crédit Mobilier* turns, its object is apparently to affect capital in a manner which is the very reverse of the action of commercial banks. A commercial bank, by its discounts, loans, and emission of notes, sets free temporarily fixed capital, while the *Crédit Mobilier* fixes actually floating capital. Railway shares, for instance, may be very floating, but the capital they represent, i. e., the capital employed in the construction of the railway, is fixed. A mill-owner who would sink in buildings and machinery a part of his capital out of proportion with the part reserved for the payment of wages and the purchase of raw material, would very soon find his mill stopped. The same holds good with a nation. Almost every commercial crisis in modern times has been connected with a derangement in the due proportion between floating and fixed capital. What, then, must be the result of the working of an institution like the *Crédit Mobilier*, the direct purpose of which is to fix as much as possible of the loanable capital of the country in railways, canals, mines, docks, steamships, forges, and other industrial undertakings, without any regard to the productive capacities of the country?

According to its statutes, the *Crédit Mobilier* can patronize only such industrial concerns as are carried on by anonymous societies, or joint-stock companies with limited responsibility. Consequently there must arise a tendency to start as many such societies as possible, and, further, to bring all industrial undertakings under the form of these societies. Now, it cannot be denied that the application of joint-stock companies to industry marks a new epoch in the economical life of modern nations. On the one hand it has revealed the productive powers of association, not suspected before, and called into life industrial creations, on a scale unattainable by the efforts of individual capitalists; on the other hand, it must not be forgotten, that in joint-stock companies it is not the individuals that are associated, but the capitals. By this contrivance, proprietors have been converted into shareholders, i.e., speculators. The concentration of capital has been accelerated, and, as its natural corollary, the downfall of the small middle class. A sort of industrial kings have been created, whose power stands in inverse ratio to their responsibility—they being responsible only to the amount of their shares, while disposing of the whole capital of the society—forming a more or less permanent body, while the mass of shareholders is undergoing a constant process of decomposition and renewal, and enabled, by the very disposal of the joint influence and wealth of the society, to bribe its single rebellious members. Beneath this oligarchic Board of Directors is placed a bureaucratic body of the practical managers and agents of the society, and beneath them, without any transition, an enormous and daily swelling mass of mere wages laborers—whose dependence and helplessness increase with the dimensions of the capital that employs them, but who also become more dangerous in direct ratio to the decreasing number of its representatives. It is the immoral merit of Fourier to have predicted this form of modern industry, under the name of *Industrial Feudalism*.[a] Certainly neither Mr. Isaac, nor Mr. Émile Péreire, nor Mr. Morny, nor Mr. Bonaparte could have invented this. There existed, also, before their epoch, banks lending their credit to

[a] Cf. Ch. Fourier, *Théorie des quatre mouvements et des destinées générales*.—*Ed.*

industrial joint-stock companies. What they invented was a joint-stock bank aiming at the monopoly of the formerly divided and multiform action of the private money-lenders, and whose leading principle should be the creation of a vast number of industrial companies, not with the view of productive investments, but simply for the object of stockjobbing profits. The new idea they have started is to render the industrial feudalism tributary to stockjobbing.

According to the statutes, the capital of the *Crédit Mobilier* is fixed at 60,000,000 of francs. The same statutes allow it to receive deposits in accounts-current for twice that sum, i. e., for 120,000,000. The sum at the disposal of the society thus amounts altogether to 180,000,000 of francs. Measured by the bold scheme of obtaining the patronage of the whole industry of France, this is certainly a very small sum. But two-thirds of this sum can hardly be applied to the purchase of industrial shares, or such values as do not command the certainty of immediate realization, precisely because they are received on call. For this reason the statutes open another resource to the *Crédit Mobilier*. It is authorized to issue debentures amounting to ten times its original capital, i. e., to the amount of 600,000,000 francs; or, in other words, the institution intended for the accommodation of all the world is authorized to come into the market as a borrower for a sum ten times larger than its own capital.

"Our debentures," says M. Péreire, "will be of two kinds. The first, issued for a short period, must correspond with our various temporary investments."[a]

With this sort of debentures we have nothing to do here, as, by article VIII of the statutes, they are to be issued only to make up the supposed balance short of the 120,000,000 to be received in current account, which have been entirely received in that way. With respect to the other class of debentures,

"they are issued with remote dates of payment, reimbursable by redemption, and will correspond with the investments of like nature, which we shall have made either in public funds or in shares and debentures of manufacturing companies. According to the economy of the system which serves as the basis of our Association, these securities will not only be secured by a corresponding amount of funds purchased under the control of Government, and the united total of which will afford, by the application of the principle of mutuality, the advantages of a compensation and division of the risks, but they will have, besides, the guarantee of a capital which, for that object, we have increased to a considerable amount."

---

[a] Here and below see I. Péreire, "Rapport présenté par le conseil d'administration dans l'assemblée générale ordinaire des actionnaires du 23 avril 1856." *Le Moniteur universel*, No. 117, April 26, 1856.—*Ed.*

Now, these debentures of the *Crédit Mobilier* are simply imitations of railway bonds—obligations redeemable at certain epochs and under certain conditions, and bearing a fixed interest. But there is a difference. While railway bonds are often secured by a mortgage of the railway itself, what is the security for the *Crédit Mobilier* debentures? The *rentes*,[a] shares, debentures and the like, of industrial companies, which the *Crédit Mobilier* buys with its own debentures. Then, what is gained by their emission? The difference between the interest payable on the debentures of the *Crédit Mobilier* and the interest receivable on the shares and the like, in which it has invested its loan. To make this operation sufficiently profitable, the *Crédit Mobilier* is obliged to place the capital realized by the issue of its debentures in such investments as promise the most remunerative returns, i. e., in shares subject to great fluctuations and alterations of price. The main security for its debentures, therefore, will consist of the shares of the very industrial companies started by the Association itself.

Thus, while railway bonds are secured by a capital at least twice in amount, these *Crédit Mobilier* debentures are secured by a capital only nominally of the same amount, but which must fall below, with every downward movement of the stock-market. The holders of these debentures, accordingly, share in all the risks of the shareholders, without participating in their profits.

> "But," says the last Annual Report, "the holders of the debentures have not only the guaranty of the investments in which it [the *Crédit Mobilier*] has placed its loans, but also that of its original capital."[b]

The original capital, 60,000,000, responsible for the 120,000,000 of deposits, offers to serve as guaranty to 600,000,000 of debentures, beside the guaranties it may be required to furnish for the unlimited number of enterprises which the *Crédit Mobilier* is authorized to start. If the Association were to succeed in exchanging the shares of all industrial companies against its own debentures, it would indeed become the supreme director and proprietor of the whole industry of France, while the mass of ancient proprietors would find themselves pensioned with a fixed revenue equal to the interest on the debentures. But, on the road to this consummation, the bankruptcy which follows from the economical conditions we have above illustrated, will stop the bold adventurers. This little accident, however, has not been over-

---

[a] Here: state securities.—*Ed.*

[b] I. Péreire, "Rapport présenté par le conseil d'administration...", *Le Moniteur universel*, No. 117, April 26, 1856.—*Ed.*

looked; on the contrary, the real founders of the *Crédit Mobilier* have included it in their calculations. When that crash comes, after an immensity of French interests has been involved, the Government of Bonaparte will seem justified in interfering with the *Crédit Mobilier*, as the English Government did in 1797 with the Bank of England.[21] The Regent of France,[a] that worthy sire of Louis Philippe, tried to get rid of the public debt by converting the State obligations into obligations of Law's Bank; Louis Bonaparte, the imperial Socialist, will try to seize upon French industry by converting the debentures of the *Crédit Mobilier* into State obligations. Will he prove more solvent than the *Crédit Mobilier*? That is the question.

Written in late June 1856

First published in the *New-York Daily Tribune*, No. 4751, July 11, 1856

Reproduced from the newspaper

[a] Philip II, Duke of Orleans.— *Ed.*

KARL MARX

REVELATIONS OF THE DIPLOMATIC HISTORY OF THE 18th CENTURY[22]

Written in June 1856-March 1857

First published in full in the newspaper *The Free Press*, Vols. III-IV, Nos. 1, 2, 5, 6, 8, 13, 16, 17, 19, 26, 28, 29 and 34, August 16 and 23, September 13 and 20, October 4, November 8 and 29, December 6 and 20, 1856; February 4, 18 and 25 and April 1, 1857

Reproduced from the newspaper

Chapter I[23]

No. 1.—MR. RONDEAU TO HORACE WALPOLE[24]

Petersburg, 17th August, 1736 *

"... I heartily wish ... that the Turks could be brought to condescend to make the first step, for this Court seems resolved to hearken to nothing till that is done, to mortify the Porte, that has on all occasions spoken of the Russians with the greatest contempt, which the Czarina and her present Ministers cannot bear. Instead of being obliged to Sir Everard Fawkner and Mr. Calkoen[a] (the former the British, the latter the Dutch Ambassador at Constantinople)[b] for informing them of the good dispositions of the Turks, Count Ostermann will not be persuaded that the Porte is sincere, and seemed very much surprised that they had written to them (the Russian Cabinet) without order of the King[c] and the States-General, or without being desired by the Grand Vizier,[d] and that their letter had not been concerted with the Emperor's[e] Minister[f] at Constantinople.... I have shown Count Biron and Count Ostermann the two letters the Grand Vizier has written to the King, and at the same time told these gentlemen that as there were in them several hard reflections on this Court, I should not have communicated them, if they had not been so desirous to see them. Count Biron said that was nothing, for they were used to be treated in this manner by the Turks. I desired their Excellencies not to let the Porte know that they had seen these letters, which would sooner aggravate matters than contribute to make them up...."

---

* This letter relates to the war against Turkey, commenced by the Empress Ann, in 1735; the British diplomatist at St. Petersburg, reporting about his endeavours to induce Russia to conclude peace with the Turks.[25] The passages omitted are irrelevant.

---

[a] The newspaper has mistakenly "Mr. Thalman"; correction has been made according to the publication of this letter in *Sbornik imperatorskogo russkogo istoricheskogo obshchestva* [Records of Imperial Russian Historical Society], St. Petersburg, 1892, Vol. 80, p. 14.—*Ed.*

[b] Here and below words in parentheses are Marx's.—*Ed.*

[c] George II.—*Ed.*

[d] Esseid-Mohammed Silihdar.—*Ed.*

[e] Charles VI.—*Ed.*

[f] Thalman.—*Ed.*

No. 2.—SIR GEORGE MACARTNEY TO THE EARL OF SANDWICH

"St. Petersburgh, 1st-12th March, 1765

"*Most Secret.**

"... Yesterday, M. Panin** and the Vice-Chancellor,[a] together with M. Osten, the Danish Minister, signed a treaty of alliance between this Court and that of Copenhagen. By one of the articles, a war with Turkey is made a *casus foederis*, and whenever that event happens Denmark binds herself to pay Russia a subsidy of 500,000 rubles per annum, by quarterly payments; Denmark also, by a most secret article, promises to disengage herself from all French connections, demanding only a limited time to endeavour to obtain the arrears due to her by the Court of France. At all events, she is immediately to enter into all the views of Russia in Sweden, and to act entirely, though not openly, with her in that kingdom. Either I am deceived, or M. Gross*** has misunderstood his instructions, when he told your lordship that Russia intended to stop short, and leave all the burden of Sweden upon England; however desirous this Court may be that we should pay a large proportion of every pecuniary engagement, yet, I am assured, she will always CHOOSE to take the lead at Stockholm. Her design, her ardent wish, is to make a common cause with England and Denmark, for the total annihilation of the French interest there. This certainly cannot be done without a considerable expense, but Russia, at present, does not seem unreasonable enough to expect that WE SHOULD PAY THE WHOLE. It has been hinted to me that £1,500 per annum, on our part, would be sufficient to support our interest, and absolutely prevent the French from ever getting at Stockholm again.

"The Swedes, highly sensible of, and very much mortified at, the dependent situation they have been in for many years,[26] are extremely jealous of every power that intermeddles in their affairs, and particularly so of their neighbours the Russians. This is the reason assigned to me for this Court's desiring that we and they should act upon SEPARATE bottoms, still preserving between our respective ministers a confidence without reserve. That our first care should be, not to establish a faction under the name of a Russian or of an English faction; but, as even the wisest men are imposed upon by a mere name, to endeavour to have OUR friends distinguished as the friends of liberty and independence; at present we have a superiority, and the generality of the nation is persuaded how very ruinous their French connections have been, and, if continued, how very destructive they will be of their true interests. M. Panin does by no means desire that the smallest

---

* England was at that time negotiating a commercial treaty with Russia.

** To this time it has remained among historians a point of controverse, whether or not *Panin* was in the pay of Frederick II. of Prussia, and whether he was so behind the back of Catherine, or at her bidding. There can exist no doubt that Catherine II., in order to identify foreign courts with Russian ministers, allowed Russian ministers ostensibly to identify themselves with foreign courts. As to Panin in particular, the question is, however, decided by an authentic document which we believe has never been published. It proves that, having once become the man of Frederick II., he was forced to remain so at the risk of his honour, fortune, and life.

*** The Russian Minister at London.

---

[a] A. M. Golitsin.—*Ed.*

change should be made in the constitution of Sweden.* He wishes that the royal authority might be preserved without being augmented, and that the privileges of the people should be continued without violation. He was not, however, without his fears of the ambitious and intriguing spirit of the Queen,[a] but the great ministerial vigilances of Count Ostermann have now entirely quieted his apprehensions on that head.

"By this new alliance with Denmark and by the success in Sweden, which this Court has no doubt of, if properly seconded, M. Panin will, in some measure, have brought to bear his grand scheme of uniting the Powers of the North.** Nothing then will be wanted to render it entirely perfect, but the conclusion of a treaty alliance with Great Britain. I am persuaded this Court desires it most ardently. The Empress has expressed herself more than once, in terms that marked it strongly; her ambition is to form, by such an union, a certain counterpoise to the family compact,*** and to disappoint, as much as possible, all the views of the Courts of Vienna and Versailles, against which she is irritated with uncommon resentment. I am not, however, to conceal from your lordship that we can have no hope of any such alliance, unless we agree, by some secret article, to pay a subsidy in case of a Turkish war, for no money will be desired from us, except upon an emergency of that nature. I flatter myself I have persuaded this Court of the unreasonableness of expecting any subsidy in time of peace, and that an alliance upon an equal footing will be more safe and more honourable for both nations. I can assure your lordship that a Turkish war's being a *casus foederis*, inserted either in the body of the treaty or in a secret article, will be a *sine qua non* in every negotiation we may have to open with this Court. The obstinacy of M. Panin upon that point is owing to the accident I am going to mention. When the treaty between the Emperor[b] and the King of Prussia[c] was in agitation,[28] the Count Bestoucheff, who is a mortal enemy to the latter, proposed the Turkish clause, persuaded that the King of Prussia would never submit to it, and flattering himself with the hopes of blowing up that negotiation by his refusal. But this old politician, it seemed, was mistaken in his conjecture, for his Majesty immediately consented to the proposal on condition that Russia should make no alliance with any other power but on the same terms.**** This is the real fact, and to confirm it, a few days since, Count Solms, the Prussian Minister, came to visit me, and told me, that if this Court had any intention of concluding an alliance with ours, without such a clause, he had orders to oppose

* The oligarchic constitution set up by the Senate after the death of Charles XII.

** Thus we learn, from Sir George Macartney, that what is commonly known as Lord Chatham's "grand-conception of the Northern Alliance," was, in fact, Panin's "grand scheme of uniting the Powers of the North."[27] Chatham was *duped* into fathering the Muscovite plan.

*** The compact between the Bourbons of France and Spain, concluded at Paris on August 15th, 1761.

**** This was a subterfuge on the part of Frederick II. The manner in which Frederick was forced into the arms of the Russian Alliance, is plainly told by M. Koch, the French professor of diplomacy and teacher of Talleyrand. "Frederick II.," he says, "having been abandoned by the Cabinet of London, could not but attach himself to Russia." (See his *History of the Revolutions in Europe.*)

[a] Louisa Ulrica.—*Ed.*
[b] Peter III.—*Ed.*
[c] Frederick II.—*Ed.*

against it in the strongest manner. Hints have been given me, that if Great Britain were less inflexible in that article, Russia will be less inflexible in the article of export duties in the Treaty of Commerce, which M. Gross told your lordship this Court would never depart from. I was assured at the same time, by a person in the highest degree of confidence with M. Panin, that if we entered upon the Treaty of Alliance the Treaty of Commerce would go on with it *passibus aequis*[a]; that then the latter would be entirely taken out of the hands of the College of Trade, where so many cavils and altercations had been made, and would be settled only between the Minister and myself, and that he was sure it would be concluded to our satisfaction, provided the Turkish clause was admitted into the Treaty of Alliance. I was told also that in case the Spaniards attacked Portugal we might have 15,000 Russians in our pay to send upon that service. I must intreat your lordship on no account to mention to M. Gross the secret article of the Danish Treaty.... That gentleman, I am afraid, is no well-wisher to England."*

---

* Horace Walpole characterises his epoch by the words—"*It was the mode of the times to be paid by one favour for receiving another.*"[29] At all events, it will be seen from the text, that such was the mode of Russia in transacting business with England. The *Earl of Sandwich,* to whom *Sir George Macartney could dare* to address the above dispatch, distinguished himself, ten years later, in 1775, as First Lord of the Admiralty, in the North Administration, by the vehement opposition he made to Lord Chatham's motion for an equitable *adjustment of the American difficulties.* "He could not believe it (Chatham's motion) *the production of a British Peer:* it appeared to him rather *the work of some American.*" In 1777, we find Sandwich again blustering; "he would hazard every drop of blood, as well as the last shilling of the national treasure, rather than allow Great Britain to be defied, bullied, and dictated to, by her disobedient and rebellious subjects". Foremost as the Earl of Sandwich was in entangling England into war with her North American colonies, with France, Spain, and Holland, we behold him constantly accused in Parliament by Fox, Burke, Pitt, &c.; of keeping the naval force inadequate to the defence of the country; of intentionally opposing small English forces where he knew the enemy to have concentrated large ones; of utter mismanagement of the service in all its departments, &c. (See debates of the House of Commons of 11th March, 1778; 31st March, 1778; February, 1779, Fox's motion of censure on Lord Sandwich; 19th April, 1779, address to the King[b] for the dismissal of Lord Sandwich from his service, on account of misconduct in service; 7th February, 1782, Fox's motion that there had been gross mismanagement in the administration of naval affairs during the year 1781.) On this occasion Pitt imputed to Lord Sandwich "all our naval disasters and disgraces". The ministerial majority against the motion amounted to only 22, in a House of 388. On the 22nd February, 1782, a similar motion against Lord Sandwich was only negatived by a majority of 19 in a House of 453. Such, indeed, was the character of the Earl of Sandwich's Administration that more than thirty distinguished officers quitted the naval service, or declared they could not act under the existing system. In point of fact, during his whole tenure of office, serious apprehensions were entertained of the consequences of the dissensions then prevalent in the navy. Besides, the Earl of Sandwich was openly accused, and, as far as circumstantial evidence goes, convicted of PECULIATION. (See debates of the House of Lords, 31st March, 1778; 19th April 1779, and sqq.) When the motion for his removal from office was negatived on April 19th 1779, thirty-nine peers entered their protest.

---

[a] Literally: by equal steps; fig.—smoothly.—*Ed.*

[b] George III.—*Ed.*

No. 3.—SIR JAMES HARRIS TO LORD GRANTHAM[30]

"Petersburg, 16-27 August, 1782

"(*Private.*)

"... On my arrival here I found the Court very different from what it had been described to me. So, far from any partiality to England, its bearings were entirely French.[31] The King of Prussia[a] (then in possession of the Empress'[b] ear) was exerting his influence against us. Count Panin assisted him powerfully; Lacy and Corberon, the Bourbon Ministers, were artful and intriguing; Prince Potemkin had been wrought upon by them; and the whole tribe which surrounded the Empress—the Schuwaloffs, Stroganoffs and Chernicheffs—were what they still are, *garçons perruquiers de Paris.*[c] Events seconded their endeavours. The assistance the French affected to afford Russia in settling its disputes with the Porte, and the two Courts being immediately after united as mediators at the Peace of Teshen,[32] contributed not a little to reconcile them to each other. I was, therefore, not surprised that all my negotiations with Count Panin *from February,* 1778, *to July,* 1779, should be unsuccessful, as he meant to prevent, not to promote, an alliance. It was in vain we made concessions to obtain it. He ever started fresh difficulties; had ever fresh obstacles ready. A very serious evil resulted, in the meanwhile, from my apparent confidence in him. He availed himself of it to convey in his reports to the Empress, not the language I employed, and the sentiments I actually expressed, but the language and sentiments he wished I should employ and express. He was equally careful to conceal her opinions and feelings from me; and while he described England to her as obstinate, and overbearing, and reserved, he described the Empress to me as displeased, disgusted, and indifferent to our concerns;and he was so convinced that, by this double misrepresentation, he had shut up every avenue of success that, at the time when I presented to him the Spanish declaration,[33] he ventured to say to me, ministerially, *'That Great Britain had, by its own haughty conduct, brought down all its misfortunes on itself; that they were now at their height; that we must consent to any concession to obtain peace; and that we could expect neither assistance from our friends nor forbearance from our enemies.'* I had temper enough not to give way to my feelings on this occasion... I applied, without loss of time, to Prince Potemkin, and, by his means, the Empress *condescended* to see me alone at Peterhoff. I was so fortunate in this interview, as not only to efface all bad impressions she had against us, but by stating, in its true light, our situation, and THE INSEPARABLE INTERESTS OF GREAT BRITAIN AND RUSSIA, to raise in her mind a decided resolution to assist us. *This resolution she declared to me in express words.* When this transpired—and Count Panin was the first who knew it—he became my implacable and inveterate enemy. He not only thwarted, by falsehoods and by a most undue exertion of his influence, my public negotiations, but employed every means the lowest and most vindictive malice could suggest to depreciate and injure me personally; and, from the very infamous accusations with which he charged me, had I been prone to fear, I might have apprehended the most infamous attacks at his hands. This relentless persecution still continues; it has outlived his Ministry. *Notwithstanding the positive assurances I had received from the Empress herself,* he found means, first to stagger, and afterwards to alter her resolutions. He was, indeed, very officiously assisted by his Prussian Majesty, who, at the time, was as much bent on oversetting our interest

---

[a] Frederick II.—*Ed.*

[b] Catherine II.—*Ed.*

[c] Wigmaker's apprentices of Paris.—*Ed.*

as he now seems eager to restore it. I was not, however, disheartened by this first disappointment, and, by redoubling my efforts, *I have twice more, during the course of my mission, brought the Empress to the verge* (!) *of standing forth our professed friend,* and, each time, my *expectations were grounded on assurances from* her own *mouth.* The first was when *our enemies conjured up the armed neutrality;** the other WHEN MINORCA WAS OFFERED HER.[35] Although, on the first of these occasions, I found the same opposition from the same quarter I had experienced before, yet I am compelled to say that the principal cause of my failure was attributable to the very awkward manner in which we replied to the famous neutral declaration of February, 1780. As I well knew from what quarter the blow would come, I was prepared to parry it. *My opinion was: 'If England feels itself strong enough to do without Russia, let it reject at once these new-fangled doctrines; but if its situation is such as to want assistance, let it yield to the necessity of the hour, recognise them as far as they relate to* RUSSIA ALONE, *and by a well-timed act of complaisance insure itself a powerful friend.*** My opinion was *not* received; an ambiguous and trimming answer was given; *we seemed equally afraid to accept or dismiss them. I was instructed secretly to oppose, but avowedly to acquiesce in them,* and some unguarded expressions of one of its then confidential servants, made use of in speaking to Mr. Simolin, in direct contradiction to the temperate and cordial language that Minister had heard from Lord Stormont, *irritated* the Empress to the last degree, and completed the *dislike* and *bad opinion* she entertained of that Administration.*** Our enemies took advantage of these *circumstances....* I SUGGESTED THE IDEA OF GIVING UP MINORCA TO THE EMPRESS, *because, as it was evident to me we should at the peace be compelled to make sacrifices, it seemed to me wiser to make them to our friends than to our enemies.* THE IDEA

* Sir James Harris affects to believe that Catherine II. was not the author of, but a convert to, the armed neutrality of 1780.[34] It is one of the grand stratagems of the Court of St. Petersburg to give to its own schemes the form of proposals suggested to and pressed on itself by foreign courts. Russian diplomacy delights in those *quae pro quo.* Thus the Count of Florida Blanca was made the responsible editor of the armed neutrality, and, from a report that vainglorious Spaniard addressed to Carlos III., one may see how immensely he felt flattered at the idea of having not only hatched the armed neutrality but allured Russia into abetting it.

** This same Sir James Harris, perhaps more familiar to the reader under the name of the Earl of Malmesbury, is extolled by English historians as the man who prevented England from surrendering the right of search in the Peace Negotiations of 1782-83.[36]

*** It might be inferred from this passage and similar ones occurring in the text, that Catherine II. had caught a real Tartar in *Lord North,* whose Administration Sir James Harris is pointing at. Any such delusion will disappear before the simple statement that the first partition of Poland[37] took place under Lord North's Administration, without any protest on his part. In 1773, Catherine's war against Turkey still continuing, and her conflicts with Sweden growing serious,[38] France made preparations to send a powerful fleet into the Baltic. D'Aiguillon, the French Minister of Foreign Affairs, communicated this plan to *Lord Stormont,* the then English Ambassador at Paris. In a long conversation, D'Aiguillon dwelt largely on the ambitious designs of Russia, and the common interest that ought to blend France and England into a joint resistance against them. In answer to this confidential communication, he was informed by the English Ambassador, that, "if France sent her ships into the Baltic, they would instantly be followed by a British fleet; that the presence of two fleets would have no more effect than a neutrality; and, however, the British Court might desire to preserve the harmony now subsisting between England and France, it was impossible to foresee the

WAS ADOPTED AT HOME IN ITS WHOLE EXTENT,* *and nothing could be more perfectly calculated to the meridian of this Court than the judicious instructions I received on this occasion from Lord Stormont. Why* this project failed I am still at a loss to learn. *I never knew the Empress incline so strongly to any one measure as she did to this, before I had my full powers to treat, nor was I ever more astonished than when I found her shrink from her purpose when they arrived.* I imputed it at the same time, in my own mind, to the *rooted aversion she had for our Ministry,* and her *total want of confidence in them;* but I since am more strongly disposed to believe that she consulted the Emperor"

contingencies that might arise from accidental collision." In consequence of these representations, D'Aiguillon countermanded the squadron at Brest, but gave new orders for the equipment of an armament at Toulon. "On receiving intelligence of these renewed preparations, the British Cabinet made instant and vigorous demonstrations of resistance; Lord Stormont was ordered to declare that every argument used respecting the Baltic applied equally to the Mediterranean. A memorial also was presented to the French Minister, accompanied by a demand that it should be laid before the King[a] and Council. This produced the desired effect; the armament was countermanded, the sailors disbanded, and the chances of an extensive warfare avoided." *"Lord North,"* says the complacent writer from whom we have borrowed the last lines,[b] "*thus effectually served the cause of his ally* (Catherine II.), *and facilitated the treaty of peace* (of Kutchuk-Kainardji)[39] *between Russia and the Porte.*" Catherine II. rewarded Lord North's good services, first by withholding the aid she had promised him in case of a war between England and the North American Colonies, and in the second place, by conjuring up and leading the armed neutrality against England. Lord North DARED NOT *repay, as he was advised by Sir James Harris,* this treacherous breach of faith by giving up to Russia, and to *Russia alone,* the maritime rights of Great Britain. Hence the irritation in the nervous system of the Czarina; the hysterical fancy she caught all at once of "entertaining a bad opinion" of Lord North, of "disliking" him, of feeling a "rooted aversion" against him, of being afflicted with "a total want of confidence," etc. In order to give the Shelburne Administration a warning example, Sir James Harris draws up a minute psychological picture of the feelings of the Czarina, and the disgrace incurred by the North Administration, for having wounded these same feelings. His prescription is very simple: surrender to Russia, as our friend, everything for asking which we would consider every other power our enemy.

* It is then a fact that the English Government, not satisfied with having made Russia a Baltic power, strove hard to make her a Mediterranean power too. The offer of the surrender of Minorca appears to have been made to Catherine II. at the end of 1779, or the beginning of 1780, shortly after Lord Stormont's entrance into the North Cabinet—the same Lord Stormont we have seen thwarting the French attempts at resistance against Russia, and whom even Sir James Harris cannot deny the merit of having written "instructions perfectly calculated to the meridian of the Court of St. Petersburg." While Lord North's Cabinet, at the suggestion of Sir James Harris, offered Minorca to the *Muscovites,* the English Commoners and people were still trembling for fear lest the *Hanoverians*[40] (!) should wrest out of their hands "one of the keys of the Mediterranean." On the 26th of October, 1775, the King,[c] in his opening speech, had informed Parliament,

[a] Louis XV.—*Ed.*
[b] Th. Hughes.—*Ed.*
[c] George III.—*Ed.*

of Austria[a] "on the subject, and that he not only prevailed on her to decline the offer, but betrayed the secret to France, and that it thus became public. I cannot otherwise account for this rapid *change of sentiment in the Empress,* particularly as *Prince Potemkin* (whatever he might be in other transactions) was certainly in this *cordial and sincere* in his support, and both from what I saw at the time and from what has since come to my knowledge, *had its success at heart as much as myself.* You will observe, my lord, that *the idea of bringing the Empress forward as a friendly mediatrix went hand-in-hand with the proposed cession of Minorca.* As this idea has given rise to what has since followed, and involved us in all the dilemmas of the present mediation, it will be necessary for me to explain what my views then were, and to exculpate myself from the blame of having placed my Court in so embarrassing a situation, *my wish and intention was that she should be sole mediatrix without an adjoint;* if you have perused what passed between her and me, in December, 1780, your lordship will perceive how very potent reasons I had to suppose she would be a friendly and even a partial one.* I knew, indeed, she was unequal to the task; but I knew, too, how greatly *her vanity* would be flattered by this distinction, and was well aware that when once engaged she would persist, and be inevitably involved in our quarrel, particularly when it should appear (and appear it would),

---

amongst other things, that he had Sir James Graham's own words, when asked why they should not have kept up some blockade pending the settlement of the "plan," "*They did not take that responsibility upon themselves.*" The responsibility of executing their orders! The despatch we have quoted is the only despatch read, except one of a later date. The despatch, said to be sent on the 5th of April, in which "the Admiral is ordered to use the *largest discretionary power* in blockading the Russian ports in the Black Sea," is not read, nor any replies from Admiral Dundas.[41] The Admiralty sent *Hanoverian* troops to Gibraltar and Port Mahon (Minorca), to replace such British regiments as should be drawn from those garrisons for service in America. An amendment to the address was proposed by Lord John Cavendish, strongly condemning "the confiding *such important fortresses as Gibraltar and Port Mahon to foreigners.*"[42] After very stormy debates, in which the measure of entrusting Gibraltar and Minorca, "*the keys of the Mediterranean,*" as they were called, to *foreigners,* was furiously attacked, Lord North, acknowledging himself the adviser of the measure, felt obliged to bring in a *bill of indemnity.* However, these foreigners, these Hanoverians, were the English King's own subjects. Having virtually surrendered Minorca to Russia in 1780, Lord North was, of course, quite justified in treating, on November 27, 1781, in the House of Commons, "with utter scorn the insinuation that *Ministers were in the pay of France.*"

Let us remark, *en passant,* that Lord North, one of the most base and mischievous Ministers England can boast of, perfectly mastered the art of keeping the House in perpetual laughter. So did Lord Sunderland. So does Lord Palmerston.

* Lord North having been supplanted by the *Rockingham* Administration, on March 27th, 1782, the celebrated Fox forwarded peace proposals to Holland through the mediation of the *Russian* Minister.[b] Now what were the consequences of the *Russian mediation* so much vaunted by this Sir James Harris, the servile account-keeper of the Czarina's sentiments, humours, and feelings? While preliminary articles of peace had been convened with France, Spain, and the American States, it was found impossible to arrive at any such preliminary

---

[a] Joseph II.—*Ed.*

[b] I. M. Simolin.—*Ed.*

that we had *gratified* her with Minorca. The annexing to the mediation the other (Austrian) Imperial Court, entirely overthrew this plan. It not only afforded her a pretence for not keeping her word, but piqued and mortified her; and it was under this impression that she made over the whole business to the colleague we had given her, and ordered her Minister at Vienna[a] to subscribe implicitly to whatever the Court proposed. Hence all the evils which have since arisen, and hence those we at this moment experience. I myself could never be brought to believe that the Court of Vienne, as long as Prince Kaunitz directs its measures, can mean England any good, or France any harm. It was not with that view that I endeavoured to promote its influence here, but because *I found that of Prussia in constant opposition to me;* and because I thought that if I could by any means smite this, I should get rid of my greatest obstacle. I was mistaken, and, by a singular fatality, the Courts of Vienna and Berlin seem never to have agreed in anything but in the disposition to prejudice us here by turns.* The proposal relative to Minorca was the last attempt I made to induce the Empress to stand forth. I had exhausted my strength and resources; the freedom with which I had spoken in my last interview with her, though respectful, had *displeased;* and *from this period to the removal of the late Administration,*[44] I have been reduced to act on the defensive.... I have had more difficulty in preventing the Empress from doing harm than I ever had in attempting to engage her to do us good. It was to prevent evil, that I inclined strongly for the acceptation of *her single mediation between us and Holland, when her Imperial Majesty first offered it.* The *extreme dissatisfaction* she expressed *at our refusal* justified my opinion; and I TOOK UPON ME, when it was proposed a second time, *to urge the necessity of its being agreed to* (ALTHOUGH I KNEW IT TO BE IN CONTRADICTION OF THE SENTIMENTS OF MY PRINCIPAL), since I firmly believed, had we again declined it, the Empress would, in a *moment of anger,* have joined the Dutch against us. As it is, *all has gone on well;* our *judicious* conduct has transferred to them the *ill-humour* she originally was in with us, and she now is as partial to our cause as she was before partial to theirs. *Since the new Ministry in England, my road has been made smoother;* the great and new path struck out by *your predecessor,*** *and which you, my lord, pursue,* has operated a most advantageous change in our favour upon the Continent. Nothing, indeed, but events which come home to her,

---

agreement with Holland. Nothing but a simple cessation of hostilities was to be obtained from it. So powerful proved the *Russian mediation,* that on the 2nd September, 1783, just one day before conclusion of *definitive treaties* with America, France, and Spain,[43] Holland condescended to accede to *preliminaries of peace,* and this not in consequence of the *Russian mediation,* but through the influence of *France.*

* How much was England not prejudiced by the Courts of Vienna and Paris, thwarting the plan of the British Cabinet of ceding Minorca to Russia and by Frederick of Prussia's resistance against the great *Chatham*'s scheme of a Northern Alliance under Muscovite auspices?

** The predecessor is Fox.

Sir James Harris establishes a complete scale of British Administration, according to the degree in which they enjoyed the favour of his almighty Czarina. In spite of Lord Stormont, the Earl of Sandwich, Lord North, and Sir James Harris himself; in spite of the partition of Poland, the bullying of D'Aiguillon, the treaty of Kutchuk-Kainardji, and the intended cession of Minorca—Lord North's Administration is relegated to the bottom of the heavenly ladder; far above it has

---

[a] D. M. Golitsin.—*Ed.*

will, I believe, ever induce her Imperial Majesty to take an active part; but there is now a *strong glow of friendship* in our favour; she approves our measures; she *trusts* our Ministry,[46] and *she gives way to that predilection she certainly has for our nation.* Our enemies know and feel this; it keeps them in awe. This is a succinct, but accurate sketch of what has passed at this Court from the day of my arrival at Petersburg to the present hour. Several inferences may be deduced from it.* That the Empress is led by her passions, not by reason and argument; that her prejudices are very strong, easily acquired, and, when once fixed, irremovable; while, on the contrary, there is no sure road to her good opinion; that even when obtained, it is subject to perpetual fluctuation, and liable to be biassed by the most trifling incidents; that till she is fairly embarked in a plan, no assurances can be depended on; but that when once fairly embarked, she never retracts, and may be carried any length, that with very bright parts, an elevated mind, an uncommon sagacity, she wants *judgment, precision of idea, reflection,* and L'ESPRIT DE COMBINAISON[a] (!!) That her Ministers are either ignorant of, or indifferent to, the welfare of the State, and act from a passive submission to her will, or from motives of party and private interests." **

4.—(MANUSCRIPT)

ACCOUNT OF RUSSIA DURING THE COMMENCEMENT OF THE REIGN OF THE EMPEROR PAUL, DRAWN UP BY THE REV. L. K. PITT, CHAPLAIN TO THE FACTORY OF ST. PETERSBURG, AND A NEAR RELATIVE OF WILLIAM PITT ***

EXTRACT

"There can scarcely exist a doubt concerning the real sentiments of the late Empress of Russia on the great points which have, within the last few years, convulsed the whole system of European politics.[48] She certainly felt from the beginning the fatal tendency of the new principles, but was not, perhaps, displeased to see every European power exhausting itself in a struggle, which raised in proportion to its violence her own importance. It is more than probable

climbed the Rockingham Administration, whose soul was Fox, notorious for his subsequent intrigues with Catherine; but at the top we behold the Shelburne Administration, whose Chancellor of the Exchequer was the celebrated William Pitt. As to Lord Shelburne himself, Burke exclaimed in the House of Commons, that "if he was not a Catilina or Borgia in morals, it must not be ascribed to anything but his understanding."[45]

* Sir James Harris forgets deducing the main inference, that the Ambassador of England is the agent of Russia.

** In the eighteenth century, English diplomatists' despatches, bearing on their front the sacramental inscription, "Private," are despatches to be withheld from the King, by the Minister to whom they are addressed. That such was the case may be seen from Lord Mahon's *History of England.*[47]

*** *"To be burnt after my death."* Such are the words prefixed to the manuscript by the gentleman [William Coxe] whom it was addressed to.

[a] Ability for device.—*Ed.*

that the state of the newly acquired provinces in Poland was likewise a point which had considerable influence over the political conduct of Catherine. The fatal effects resulting from an apprehension of revolt in the late seat of conquest, seem to have been felt in a very great degree by the combined powers, who in the early period of the Revolution were so near reinstating the regular Government in France. The same dread of revolt in Poland, which divided the attention of the combined powers and hastened their retreat, deterred likewise the late Empress of Russia from entering on the great theatre of war, until a combination of circumstances rendered the progress of the French armies a more dangerous evil than any which could possibly result to the Russian Empire from active operations.... The last words which the Empress was known to utter were addressed to her Secretary when she dismissed him on the morning on which she was seized: 'Tell Prince' (Zuboff), she said, 'to come to me at twelve, and to remind me of signing the Treaty of Alliance with England.'"

Having entered into ample considerations on the Emperor Paul's acts and extravagances, the Rev. Mr. Pitt continues as follows:

"When these considerations are impressed on the mind, the nature of the late secession from the coalition,[49] and of the incalculable indignities offered to the Government of Great Britain, can alone be fairly estimated.... BUT THE TIES WHICH BIND HER (GREAT BRITAIN) TO THE RUSSIAN EMPIRE ARE FORMED BY NATURE, AND INVIOLABLE. United, these nations might almost brave the united world; divided, the strength and importance of each is FUNDAMENTALLY impaired. England has reason to regret with Russia that the imperial sceptre should be thus inconsistently wielded,[a] but it is the sovereign of Russia alone who divides the Empires."

The Reverend Gentleman concludes his account by the words:

"As far as human foresight can at this moment penetrate, the despair of an enraged individual seems a more probable means to terminate the present scene of oppression, than any more systematic combination of measures to restore the throne of Russia to its dignity and importance."

[a] The reference is to Paul I.—*Ed.*

Chapter II

The documents published in the first chapter extend from the reign of the Empress Ann to the commencement of the reign of the Emperor Paul, thus encompassing the greater part of the 18th century. At the end of that century it had become, as stated by the Rev. Mr. Pitt, the openly-professed and orthodox dogma of English diplomacy,

"that the ties which bind Great Britain to the Russian Empire are formed by nature, and inviolable."

In perusing these documents, there is something that startles us even more than their contents—viz., their form. All these letters are "confidential," "private," "secret," "most secret"; but in spite of secrecy, privacy, and confidence, the English statesmen converse among each other about Russia and her rulers in a tone of awful reserve, abject servility, and cynical submission, which would strike us even in the public despatches of Russian statesmen. To conceal intrigues against foreign nations secrecy is recurred to by Russian diplomatists. The same method is adopted by English diplomatists freely to express their devotion to a foreign court. The secret despatches of Russian diplomatists are fumigated with some equivocal perfume. It is one part the *fumée de fausseté*,[a] as the Duke of St. Simon has it, and the other part that coquet display of one's own superiority and cunning which stamps upon the reports of the French Secret Police their indelible character. Even the master despatches of Pozzo di Borgo[50] are tainted with this

[a] Veil of falsehood.—*Ed.*

common blot of the *littérature de mauvais lieu*.[a] In this point the English secret despatches prove much superior. They do not affect superiority but silliness. For instance, can there be anything more silly than Mr. Rondeau informing Horace Walpole that he has betrayed to the Russian minister the letters addressed by the Turkish Grand Vizier[b] to the King of England,[c] but that he had told

"at the same time those gentlemen that as there were several hard reflections on the Russian Court he should not have communicated them, *if they had not been so anxious to see them*," [d]

and then told their excellencies not to tell the Porte that they had seen them (those letters)! At first view the infamy of the act is drowned in the silliness of the man. Or, take Sir George Macartney. Can there be anything more silly than his happiness that Russia seemed "reasonable" enough not to expect that England "should pay the WHOLE EXPENSES" for Russia's "choosing to take the lead at Stockholm;" or his "flattering himself" that he had "persuaded the Russian Court" not to be so "unreasonable" as to ask from England, in a time of peace, subsidies for a time of war against Turkey (then the ally of England); or his warning the Earl of Sandwich "not to mention" to the Russian Ambassador[e] at London the secrets mentioned to himself by the Russian Chancellor[f] at St. Petersburg? Or can there be anything more silly than Sir James Harris confidentially whispering into the ear of Lord Grantham that Catherine II. was devoid of "judgment, precision of idea, reflection, and *l'esprit de combinaison*"?*

On the other hand, take the cool impudence with which Sir George Macartney informs his minister that because the Swedes were extremely jealous of, and mortified at, their dependence on Russia, England was directed by the Court of St. Petersburg to do its work at Stockholm, under the British colours of liberty and

* Or, to follow this affectation of silliness into more recent times, is there anything in diplomatic history that could match Lord Palmerston's proposal made to Marshal Soult (in 1839), to storm the Dardanelles, in order to afford the Sultan[g] the support of the Anglo-French fleet against Russia?

[a] Gutter literature.— *Ed.*

[b] Esseid-Mohammed Silihdar.— *Ed.*

[c] George II.— *Ed.*

[d] See this volume, p. 27.— *Ed.*

[e] H. Gross.— *Ed.*

[f] N. I. Panin.— *Ed.*

[g] Mahmud II.— *Ed.*

independence! Or Sir James Harris advising England to surrender to Russia Minorca and the right of search, and the monopoly of mediation in the affairs of the world—not in order to gain any material advantage, or even a formal engagement on the part of Russia, but only "a strong glow of friendship" from the Empress, and the transfer to France of her "ill humour."

The secret Russian despatches proceed on the very plain line that Russia knows herself to have no common interests whatever with other nations, but that every nation must be persuaded separately to have common interests with Russia to the exclusion of every other nation. The English despatches, on the contrary, never dare so much as hint that Russia has common interests with England, but only endeavour to convince England that she has Russian interests. The English diplomatists themselves tell us that this was the single argument they pleaded, when placed face to face with Russian potentates.

If the English despatches we have laid before the public were addressed to private friends, they would only brand with infamy the ambassadors who wrote them. Secretly addressed as they are to the British Government itself, they nail it for ever to the pillory of history; and, instinctively, this seems to have been felt, even by Whig writers, because none has dared to publish them.

The question naturally arises from which epoch this Russian character of English diplomacy, become traditionary in the course of the 18th century, does date its origin? To clear up this point, we must go back to the time of Peter the Great,[a] which, consequently, will form the principal subject of our researches. We propose to enter upon this task by reprinting some English pamphlets, written at the time of Peter I., and which have either escaped the attention of modern historians, or appeared to them to merit none. However, they will suffice for refuting the prejudice common to Continental and English writers, that the designs of Russia were not understood or suspected in England until at a later, and too late, epoch; that the diplomatic relations between England and Russia were but the natural offspring of the mutual material interests of the two countries; and that, therefore, in accusing the British statesmen of the 18th century of Russianism, we should commit an unpardonable hysteron proteron.[b] If we have shown by the English despatches that, at the time of the Empress Ann, England already betrayed her own allies to

---

[a] See this volume, p. 56.—*Ed.*

[b] Figure of speech in which what should come last is put first.—*Ed.*

Russia, it will be seen from the pamphlets we are now about to reprint that, even before the epoch of Ann, at the very epoch of Russian ascendency in Europe, springing up at the time of Peter I., the plans of Russia were understood, and the connivance of British statesmen at these plans was denounced by English writers.

The first pamphlet we lay before the public is called *The Northern Crisis.*[a] It was printed at London, in 1716, and relates to the intended Dano-Anglo-Russian *invasion of Scania* (Schonen).

During the year 1715 a northern alliance for the *partition,* not of Sweden proper, but of what we may call the Swedish Empire, had been concluded between Russia, Denmark, Poland, Prussia, and Hanover. That partition forms the first grand act of modern diplomacy—the logical premiss to the partition of Poland. The partition treaties relating to Spain have engrossed the interest of posterity because they were the forerunners of the War of Succession,[51] and the partition of Poland drew even a larger audience because its last act was played upon a contemporary stage.[52] However, it cannot be denied that it was the partition of the Swedish Empire which inaugurated the modern era of international policy. The partition treaty not even pretended to have a pretext, save the misfortune of its intended victim. For the first time in Europe the violation of all treaties was not only made, but proclaimed the common basis of a new treaty. Poland herself, in the drag of Russia, and personated by that commonplace of immorality, Augustus II., Elector of Saxony and King of Poland, was pushed into the foreground of the conspiracy, thus signing her own death-warrant, and not even enjoying the privilege reserved by Polyphemus to Odysseus—to be last eaten. Charles XII. predicted her fate in the manifesto flung against King Augustus and the Czar, from his voluntary exile at Bender. The manifesto is dated January 28, 1711.[53]

The participation in this partition treaty threw England within the orbit of Russia, towards whom, since the days of the "Glorious Revolution,"[54] she had more and more gravitated. George I., as King of England, was bound to a defensive alliance with Sweden by the treaty of 1700.[b] Not only as King of England, but as Elector of Hanover, he was one of the guarantees, and even of the direct parties to the treaty of Travendahl,[55] which secured to Sweden what

[a] See this volume, pp. 43-55.—*Ed.*

[b] The abridged text of the treaty is printed in Chapter III of this work for which see pp. 65-73.—*Ed.*

the partition treaty intended stripping her of. Even his German electoral dignity he partly owed to that treaty. However, as Elector of Hanover he declared war against Sweden, which he waged as King of England.

In 1715 the confederates had divested Sweden of her German provinces, and to effect that end introduced the Muscovite on the German soil. In 1716 they agreed to invade Sweden proper—to attempt an armed descent upon Schonen—the southern extremity of Sweden now constituting the districts of Malmoe and Christianstadt. Consequently, Peter of Russia brought with him from Germany a Muscovite army, which was scattered over Zealand, thence to be conveyed to Schonen, under the protection of the English and Dutch fleets sent into the Baltic, on the false pretext of protecting trade and navigation. Already in 1715, when Charles XII. was besieged in Stralsund, eight English men-of-war, lent by England to Hanover, and by Hanover to Denmark, had openly reinforced the Danish navy, and even hoisted the Danish flag. In 1716, the British navy was commanded by his Czarish Majesty in person.[56]

Everything being ready for the invasion of Schonen, there arose a difficulty from a side where it was least expected. Although the treaty stipulated only for 30,000 Muscovites, Peter, in his magnanimity, had landed 40,000 on Zealand; but now that he was to send them on the errand to Schonen, he all at once discovered that out of the 40,000 he could spare but 15,000. This declaration not only paralysed the military plan of the confederates, it seemed to threaten the security of Denmark and of Frederick IV., its king, as great part of the Muscovite army, supported by the Russian fleet, occupied Copenhagen. One of the generals of Frederick[a] proposed suddenly to fall with the Danish cavalry upon the Muscovites and to exterminate them while the English men-of-war should burn the Russian fleet. Averse to any perfidy which required some greatness of will, some force of character, and some contempt of personal danger, Frederick IV. rejected the bold proposal and limited himself to assuming an attitude of defence. He then wrote a begging letter to the Czar, intimating that he had yielded up ' is Schonen fancy, and requested the Czar to do the same and find his way home: a request the latter could not but comply with. When Peter at last left Denmark with his army, the Danish Court thought fit to communicate to the Courts of Europe a public account of the incidents and transactions which had

[a] Von Holstein.—*Ed.*

frustrated the intended descent upon Schonen—and this document forms the starting point of *The Northern Crisis.*

In a letter addressed to Baron Görtz, dated from London, January 23, 1717, by Count Gyllenborg, there occur some passages in which the latter, the then Swedish ambassador at the Court of St. James's, seems to profess himself the author of *The Northern Crisis,*[57] the title of which he does not, however, quote. Yet any idea of his having written that powerful pamphlet will disappear before the slightest perusal of the Count's authenticated writings, such as his letters to Görtz.

"THE NORTHERN CRISIS; OR, IMPARTIAL REFLECTIONS ON THE POLICIES OF THE CZAR; OCCASIONED BY MYNHEER VON STOCKEN'S REASONS FOR DELAYING THE DESCENT UPON SCHONEN. A TRUE COPY OF WHICH IS PREFIXED, VERBALLY TRANSLATED AFTER THE TENOR OF THAT IN THE GERMAN SECRETARY'S OFFICE IN COPENHAGEN, OCTOBER 10, 1716.

Parvo motu primo mox se attollit in auras.[a] *Virg.*

London, 1716.

1.—*Preface*—"... 'Tis (the present pamphlet) not fit for lawyers' clerks, but it is highly convenient to be read by those who are proper students in the laws of nations; 'twill be but lost time for any stock-jobbing, trifling dealer in Exchange-alley to look beyond the preface on't, but every merchant in England (more especially those who trade to the Baltic) will find his account in it. The Dutch (as the courants and postboys have more than once told us) are about to mend their hands, if they can, in several articles of trade with the Czar, and they have been a long time about it to little purpose. Inasmuch as they are such a frugal people, they are good examples for the imitation of our traders; but if we can outdo them for once, in the means of projecting a better and more expeditious footing to go upon, for the emolument of us both, let us, for once, be wise enough to set the example, and let them, for once, be our imitators. This little treatise will show a pretty plain way how we may do it, as to our trade in the Baltic, at this juncture. I desire no little *coffee-house politician* to meddle with it; but to give him even a disrelish for my company. I must let him know that he is not fit for mine. Those who are even proficients in state science, will find in it matter highly fit to employ all their powers of speculation, which they ever before past negligently by, and thought (too cursorily) were not worth the regarding. No outrageous party-man will find it all for his purpose; but every *honest Whig* and every *honest Tory* may each of them read it, not only without either of their disgust, but with the satisfaction of them both.... 'Tis not fit, in fine, for a mad, hectoring, Presbyterian Whig, or a raving, fretful, dissatisfied, Jacobite Tory."

[a] "Having at first little impulsion, he presently rose into the air" (Virgil, *Aeneid,* IV, 176), this epigraph is omitted in Eleanor Marx-Aveling's publication.—*Ed.*

2.—THE REASONS HANDED ABOUT BY MYNHEER VON STOCKEN FOR DELAYING THE DESCENT UPON SCHONEN.

"There being no doubt, but most courts will be surprised that the descent upon Schonen has not been put into execution, notwithstanding the great preparations made for that purpose; and that all his Czarish Majesty's troops, who were in Germany, were transported to Zealand, not without great trouble and danger, partly by his own gallies, and partly by his Danish Majesty's and other vessels; and that the said descent is deferred till another time. His Danish Majesty[a] hath therefore, in order to clear himself of all imputation and reproach, thought fit to order, that the following true account of this affair should be given to all impartial persons. Since the Swedes were entirely driven out of their *German* dominions, there was, according to all the rules of policy, and reasons of war, no other way left, than vigorously to attack the still obstinate King of Sweden,[b] in the very heart of his country; thereby, with God's assistance, to force him to a lasting, good and advantageous peace for the allies. The King of Denmark and his Czarish Majesty[c] were both of this opinion, and did, in order to put so good a design in execution, agree upon an interview, which at last (notwithstanding his Danish Majesty's presence, upon the account of Norway's being invaded, was most necessary in his own capital, and that the Muscovite Ambassador, Mr. Dolgorouki, had given quite other assurances) was held at Ham and Horn, near Hamburgh, after his Danish Majesty had stayed there six weeks for the Czar. In this conference it was, on the 3rd of June, agreed between both their Majesties, after several debates, that the descent upon Schonen should positively be undertaken this year, and everything relating to the forwarding the same was entirely consented to. Hereupon his Danish Majesty made all haste for his return to his dominions, and gave orders to work day and night to get his fleet ready to put to sea. The transport ships were also gathered from all parts of his dominions, both with inexpressible charges and great prejudice to his subjects' trade. Thus, his Majesty (as the Czar himself upon his arrival at Copenhagen owned) did his utmost to provide all necessaries, and to forward the descent, upon whose success everything depended. It happened, however, in the meanwhile, and before the descent was agreed upon in the conference at Ham and Horn, that his Danish Majesty was obliged to secure his invaded and much oppressed kingdom of Norway, by sending thither a considerable squadron out of his fleet, under the command of Vice-Admiral Gabel, which squadron could not be recalled before the enemy had left that kingdom, without endangering a great part thereof; so that out of necessity the said Vice-Admiral was forced to tarry there till the 12th of July, when his Danish Majesty sent him express orders to return with all possible speed, wind and weather permitting; but this blowing for some time contrary, he was detained.... The Swedes were all the while powerful at sea, and his Czarish Majesty himself did not think it advisable that the remainder of the Danish, in conjunction with the men-of-war then at Copenhagen, should go to convoy the Russian troops from Rostock, before the above-mentioned squadron under Vice-Admiral Gabel was arrived. This happening at last in the month of August, the confederate fleet put to sea; and the transporting of the said troops hither to Zealand was put in execution, though with a great deal of trouble and danger; but it took up so much time that the descent could not be ready till September following. Now, when all

---

[a] Frederick IV.—*Ed.*
[b] Charles XII.—*Ed.*
[c] Peter I.—*Ed.*

these preparations, as well for the descent as the embarking the armies, were entirely ready, his Danish Majesty assured himself that the descent should be made within a few days, at farthest by the 21st of September. The Russian Generals and Ministers first raised some difficulties to those of Denmark, and afterwards, on the 17th September, declared in an appointed conference, that his Czarish Majesty, considering the present situation of affairs, was of opinion that neither forage nor provision could be had in Schonen, and that consequently the descent was not advisable to be attempted this year, but ought to be put off till next spring. It may be easily imagined how much his Danish Majesty was surprised at this; especially seeing the Czar, if he had altered his opinion, as to this design so solemnly concerted, might have declared it sooner, and thereby saved his Danish Majesty several tons of gold, spent upon the necessary preparations. His Danish Majesty did, however, in a letter dated the 20th of September, amply represent to the Czar, that although the season was very much advanced, the descent might, nevertheless, easily be undertaken with such a superior force, as to get a footing in Schonen, where, being assured there had been a very plentiful harvest, he did not doubt but subsistence might be found; besides, that having an open communication with his own countries, it might easily be transported from thence. His Danish Majesty alleged also several weighty reasons why the descent was either to be made this year, or the thoughts of making it next spring entirely be laid aside. *Nor did he alone make these moving remonstrances to the Czar;* BUT HIS BRITISH MAJESTY'S[a] MINISTER[b] RESIDING HERE, AS WELL AS ADMIRAL NORRIS, *seconded the same also in a very pressing manner;* AND BY EXPRESS ORDER OF THE KING, THEIR MASTER, *endeavoured to bring the Czar into their opinion, and to persuade him to go with the descent;* but his Czarish Majesty declared by his answer, that he would adhere to the resolution he had once taken concerning this delay of making the descent; but if his Danish Majesty was resolved to venture on the descent, that he then, according to the treaty made near Stralsund,[58] would assist him only with the 15 battalions and 1,000 horse therein stipulated; that next spring he would comply with everything else, and neither could or would declare himself further in this affair. Since then, his Danish Majesty could not, without running so great a hazard, undertake so great a work alone with his own army and the said 15 battalions; he desired, in another letter of the 23rd September, his Czarish Majesty would be pleased to add 13 battalions of his troops, in which case his Danish Majesty would still this year attempt the descent; but even this could not be obtained from his Czarish Majesty, who absolutely refused it by his ambassador[c] on the 24th ditto: whereupon his Danish Majesty, in his letter of the 26th, declared to the Czar, that since things stood thus, he desired none of his troops, but that they might be all speedily transported out of his dominions; that so the transport, whose freight stood him in 40,000 Rix dollars[59] per month, might be discharged, and his subjects eased of the intolerable contributions they now underwent. This he could not do less than agree to; and accordingly, all the Russian troops are already embarked, and intend for certain to go from here with the first favourable wind. It must be left to Providence and time, to discover what may have induced the Czar to a resolution so prejudicial to the Northern Alliance, and most advantageous to the common enemy.

[a] George I.—*Ed.*
[b] Alexander Campbell.—*Ed.*
[c] V. L. Dolgoruki.—*Ed.*

3. IMPARTIAL REFLECTIONS BY WAY OF ESSAY ON THE FOREGOING INSTRUMENT.[60]

"If we would take a true survey of men, and lay them open in a proper light to the eye of our intellects, *we must* first *consider their natures* and then *their ends;* and by this method of examination, though their conduct is, seemingly, full of intricate mazes and perplexities, and winding round with infinite meanders of state-craft, we shall be able to dive into the deepest recesses, make our way through the most puzzling labyrinths, and at length come to the most abstruse means of bringing about the master-secrets of their minds, and to unriddle their utmost mysteries....

"The Czar ... is, by *nature,* of a great and enterprising spirit, and of a genius thoroughly politic; and as for his *ends,* the manner of his own Government, where he sways arbitrary lord over the estates and honours of his people, must make him, if all the policies in the world could by far-distant aims promise him accession and accumulation of empire and wealth, be everlastingly laying schemes for the achieving of both with the extremest cupidity and ambition. Whatever ends an insatiate desire of opulency, and a boundless thirst for dominion, can ever put him upon, to satisfy their craving and voracious appetites, those must, most undoubtedly, be his.

"The next questions we are to put to ourselves are these three:

"1. By what means can he gain these ends?

"2. How far from him, and in what place, can these ends be best obtained?

"3. And by what time, using all proper methods, and succeeding in them, may he obtain these ends?

"The possessions of the Czar were prodigious, vast in extent; the people all at his nod, all his downright arrant slaves, and all the wealth of the country his own at a word's command. But then the country, though large in ground, was not quite so in produce. Every vassal had his gun, and was to be a soldier upon call; but there was never a soldier among them, nor a man that understood the calling; and though he had all their wealth, they had no commerce of consequence, and little ready money; and consequently his treasury, when he had amassed all he could, very bare and empty. He was then but in an indifferent condition to satisfy those two natural appetites, when he had neither wealth to support a soldiery, nor a soldiery trained in the art of war. The first token this Prince gave of an aspiring genius, and of an ambition that is noble and necessary in a monarch, who has a mind to flourish, was to believe none of his subjects more wise than himself, or more fit to govern. He did so, and looked upon his own proper person as the most fit to travel out among the other realms of the world and study politics for the advancing of his dominions. He then seldom pretended to any warlike dispositions against those who were instructed in the science of arms; his military dealings lay mostly with the Turks and Tartars, who, as they had numbers as well as he, had them likewise composed, as well as his, of a rude, uncultivated mob, and they appeared in the field like a raw undisciplined militia. In this his Christian neighbours liked him well, insomuch as he was a kind of stay or stop-gap to the infidels. But when he came to look into the more polished parts of the Christian world, he set out towards it, from the very threshold, like a natural-born politician. He was not for learning the game by trying chances and venturing losses in the field so soon; no, he went upon the maxim, *that it was, at that time of day, expedient and necessary for him to carry, like Samson, his strength in his head and not in his arms.* He had then, he knew, but very few commodious places for commerce of his own, and those all situated in the *White Sea,* too remote, frozen up the most part of the year, and not at all fit for a fleet of men-of-war; but he knew of many more commodious ones of his neighbours in the Baltic, and within his reach, whenever he could strengthen his hands to lay hold of them. He had a longing eye towards them; but with prudence seemingly turned his head another way, and secretly entertained the pleasant thought that he should come at them all in good time. Not to give any jealousy, he endeavours for no help from his neighbours to instruct his men in arms. That was like asking a skilful person, one intended to fight a duel with, to teach him first how to fence. *He went over to Great Britain,* where he knew that potent kingdom could, as yet, have no jealousies of his growth of power, and in the eye of which his vast extent of nation lay neglected and unconsidered and overlooked, as I am afraid it is to this very day. He was present at all our exercises, looked into all our laws, inspected our military, civil, and ecclesiastical regimen of affairs; yet all this was the least he then wanted; this was the slightest part of his errand. But by degrees, when he grew familiar with our people, he visited our docks, pretending not to have any prospect of profit, but only to take a huge delight (the effect of curiosity only) to see our manner of building ships. He kept his court, as one may say, in our shipyard, so industrious was he in affording them his continual Czarish presence, and to his immortal glory for art and industry be it spoken, that the great Czar, by stooping often to the employ, could handle an axe with the best artificer of them all; and the monarch having a good mathematical head of his own, grew in some time a very expert royal shipwright. A ship or two for his diversion, made and sent him, and then two or three more, and after that two or three more, would signify just nothing at all, if they were granted to be sold to him by the *Maritime Powers,*[a] that could, at will, lord it over the sea. It would be a puny, inconsiderable matter, and not worth the regarding. Well, but then, over and above this, he had artificially insinuated himself into the good-will of many of our best workmen, and won their hearts by his good-natured familiarities and condescension among them. To turn this to his service, he offered many very large premiums and advantages to go and settle in his country, which they gladly accepted of. A little after he sends over some private ministers and officers to negotiate for more workmen, for land officers, and likewise for picked and chosen good seamen, who might be advanced and promoted to offices by going there. Nay, even to this day, any expert seaman, that is upon our traffic to the port of Archangel, if he has the least spark of ambition, and any ardent desire to be in office, he need but offer himself to the sea-service of the Czar, and he is a lieutenant immediately. Over and above this, that Prince has even found the way to take by force into his service, out of our merchant ships, as many of their ablest seamen as he pleased, giving the masters the same number of raw Muscovites in their place, whom they afterwards were forced, in their own defence, to make fit for their own use. Neither is this all; he had, during the last war,[61] many hundreds of his subjects, both noblemen and common sailors, on board *ours, the French and the Dutch fleets;* and he has all along maintained, and still maintains numbers of them in *ours and the Dutch yards.*

"But seeing he looked all along upon all these endeavours towards improving himself and his subjects as superfluous, whilst a seaport was wanting, where he might build a fleet of his own, and from whence he might himself export the products of his country, and import those of others; and finding the King of Sweden possessed of the most convenient ones, I mean *Narva* and *Revel,* which he knew that Prince[b] never could nor would amicably part with; he at last resolved to wrest them out of his hands by force. His *Swedish* Majesty's tender youth seemed

[a] England and Holland.—*Ed.*
[b] Charles XII.—*Ed.*

the fittest time for this enterprise, but even then he would not run the hazard alone. He drew in other princes to divide the spoil with him. And the *Kings of Denmark and Poland*[a] were weak enough to serve as instruments to forward the great and ambitious views of the Czar. It is true, he met with a mighty hard rub at his very first setting out; his whole army being entirely defeated by a handful of Swedes at Narva.[62] But it was his good luck that his Swedish Majesty, instead of improving so great a victory against him, turned immediately his arms against the King of Poland, against whom he was personally piqued, and that so much the more, inasmuch as he had taken that Prince for one of his best friends, and was just upon the point of concluding with him the strictest alliance, when he unexpectedly invaded the *Swedish Livonia,* and besieged *Riga.* This was, in all respects, what the Czar could most have wished for; and foreseeing that the longer the war in Poland lasted, the more time should he have both to retrieve his first loss, and to gain Narva, he took care it should be spun out to as great a length as possible; for which end, he never sent the King of Poland succour enough to make him too strong for the King of Sweden; who, on the other hand, though he gained one signal victory after the other, yet never could subdue his enemy as long as he received continual reinforcements from his hereditary country. And had not his Swedish Majesty, contrary to most people's expectations, marched directly into Saxony itself, and thereby forced the King of Poland to peace,[63] the Czar would have had leisure enough in all conscience to bring his designs to greater maturity. This peace was one of the greatest disappointments the Czar ever met with, whereby he became singly engaged in the war. He had, however, the comfort of having beforehand taken *Narva,* and laid a foundation to his favourite town *Petersburg,* and to the seaport, the docks, and the vast magazines there; all which works, to what perfection they are now brought, let them tell who, with surprise, have seen them.

"He (Peter) used all endeavours to bring matters to an accommodation. He proffered very advantageous conditions; *Petersburg* only, a trifle as he pretended, which he had set his heart upon, he would retain; and even for that he was willing some other way to give satisfaction. But the King of Sweden was too well acquainted with the importance of that place to leave it in the hands of an ambitious Prince, and thereby to give him an inlet into the Baltic. This was the only time since the defeat at Narva, that the Czar's arms had no other end than that of self-defence. They might, perhaps, even have fallen short therein, had not the King of Sweden (through whose persuasion is still a mystery), instead of marching the shortest way to Novogorod and to Moscow, turned towards Ukraine, where his army, after great losses and sufferings, was at last entirely defeated at Pultawa. As this was a fatal period to the Swedish successes, so how great a deliverance it was to the Muscovites, may be gathered from the Czar's celebrating, every year, with great solemnity, the anniversary of that day, from which his ambitious thoughts began to soar still higher. The whole of *Livonia, Estland,* and the best and greatest part of *Finland,* was now what he demanded, after which, though he might for the present condescend to give peace to the remaining part of Sweden, he knew he could easily even add that to his conquests whenever he pleased. The only obstacle he had to fear in these his projects, was from his northern neighbours; but as the *Maritime Powers,* and even the neighbouring princes in Germany, were then so intent upon their war against France, that they seemed entirely neglectful of that of the North, so there remained only Denmark and Poland to be jealous of. The former of these

---

[a] Frederick IV. and Augustus II.—*Ed.*

kingdoms had, ever since King William,[a] of glorious memory, compelled it to make peace with Holstein[64] and, consequently, with Sweden, enjoyed an uninterrupted tranquillity, during which it had time, by a free trade and considerable subsidies from the maritime powers, to enrich itself, and was in a condition, by joining itself to Sweden, as it was its interest to do, to stop the Czar's progresses, and timely to prevent its own danger from them. The other, I mean Poland, was now quietly under the Government of King Stanislaus, who, owing in a manner his crown to the King of Sweden, could not, out of gratitude, as well as real concern for the interest of his country, fail opposing the designs of a too aspiring neighbour. The Czar was too cunning not to find out a remedy for all this; he represented to the King of Denmark how low the King of Sweden was now brought, and how fair an opportunity he had, during that Prince's long absence, to clip entirely his wings, and to aggrandise himself at his expense. In King Augustus he raised the long-hid resentment for the loss of the Polish Crown, which he told him he might now recover without the least difficulty. Thus, both these Princes were immediately caught. The Danes declared war against Sweden without so much as a tolerable pretence, and made a descent upon Schonen, where they were soundly beaten for their pains. King Augustus re-entered Poland, where everything has ever since continued in the greatest disorder, and *that in a great measure owing to Muscovite intrigues.* It happened, indeed, that these new confederates, whom the Czar had only drawn in to serve his ambition, became at first more necessary to his preservation than he had thought; for the Turks, having declared a war against him, they hindered the Swedish arms from joining with them to attack him; but that storm being soon over, through the Czar's wise behaviour, and the avarice and folly of the Grand Vizier,[b] he then made the intended use both of these his friends, as well as of them he afterwards, through hopes of gain, persuaded into his alliance, which was to lay all the burthen and hazard of the war upon them, in order entirely to weaken them, together with Sweden, whilst *he was preparing to swallow the one after the other.* He has put them on one difficult attempt after the other; their armies have been considerably lessened by battles and long sieges, whilst his own were either employed in easier conquests, and more profitable to him, or kept at the vast expense of neutral princes—near enough at hand to come up to demand a share of the booty without having struck a blow in getting it. His behaviour has been as cunning at sea, where his fleet has always kept out of harm's way and at a great distance, whenever there was any likelihood of an engagement between the Danes and the Swedes. He hoped, that when these two nations had ruined one another's fleets, his might then ride master in the Baltic. All this while he had taken care to make his men improve, by the example of foreigners, and under their command, in the art of war.... His fleets will soon considerably outnumber the Swedish and the Danish ones joined together. He need not fear their being a hindrance from his giving a finishing stroke to this great and glorious undertaking. Which done, *let us look to ourselves; he will then most certainly become our rival, and as dangerous to us as he is now neglected.* We then may, perhaps, though too late, call to mind what our own ministers and merchants have told us of his designs of carrying on, alone, all the northern trade, and of getting all that from Turkey and Persia into his hands, through the rivers which he is joining and making navigable, from the Caspian, or the Black Sea, to his Petersburg. *We shall then wonder at our blindness that we did not suspect his designs* when we heard the prodigious works he has done at Petersburg and Revel; of which last place, the *Daily Courant,* dated November 23, says:

[a] William III.—*Ed.*

[b] Baltaji Mohammed.—*Ed.*

"'HAGUE, *Nov.* 17.

"'The captains of the men-of-war of the States, who have been at Revel, advise that the Czar has put that port, and the fortifications of the place, into such a condition of defence, that it may pass for one of the most considerable fortresses, not only of the Baltic, but even of Europe.'

"Leave we him now, as to his sea affairs, commerce and manufactures, and other works both of his policy and power; and let us view him in regard to his proceedings in this last campaign, especially as to that so much talked of descent, he, in conjunction with his allies, was to make upon Schonen, and we shall find, that even therein he has acted with his usual cunning.[65] There is no doubt but the King of Denmark was the first that proposed this descent. He found that nothing but a speedy end to a war he had so rashly and unjustly begun, could save his country from ruin and from the bold attempts of the King of Sweden, either against Norway, or against Zealand and Copenhagen. To treat separately with that prince was a thing he could not do, as foreseeing that he would not part with an inch of ground to so unfair an enemy; and he was afraid that a Congress for a general peace, supposing the King of Sweden would consent to it upon the terms proposed by his enemies, would draw the negotiations out beyond what the situation of his affairs could bear. He invites, therefore, all his confederates to make a home thrust at the King of Sweden, by a descent into his country, where, having defeated him, as by the superiority of the forces to be employed in that design he hoped they should, they might force him to an immediate peace on such terms as they themselves pleased. I[a] don't know how far the rest of his confederates came into that project; but neither the *Prussian* nor the *Hanoverian* Court appeared *openly* in that project, *and how far our English fleet, under Sir John Norris, was to have forwarded it, I have nothing to say, but leave others to judge out of the King of Denmark's own declaration:* but the Czar came readily into it. He got thereby a new pretence to carry the war one campaign more at other people's expense; to march his troops into the Empire again, and to have them quartered and maintained, first in Mecklenburg[66] and then in Zealand. In the meantime he had his eyes upon *Wismar,* and upon a Swedish island, called *Gothland.* If, by surprise, he could get the first out of the hands of his confederates, he then had a good seaport, whither to transport his troops when he pleased into *Germany,* without asking the King of *Prussia*'s leave for a free passage through his territories; and if, by a sudden descent, he could dislodge the *Swedes* out of the other, he then became master of the best port in the Baltic. He miscarried, however, in both these projects; for Wismar was too well guarded to be surprised; and he found his confederates would not give him a helping hand towards conquering Gothland. After this he began to look with another eye upon the descent to be made upon Schonen. He found it equally contrary to his interest, whether it succeeded or not. For if it did, and the King was thereby forced to a general peace, he knew his interests therein would be least regarded; having already notice enough of his confederates being ready to sacrifice them, provided they got their own terms. If he did not succeed, then, besides the loss of the flower of an army he had trained and disciplined with so much care, as he very well foresaw that the English fleet would hinder the King of Sweden from attempting anything against Denmark; so he justly feared the whole shock would fall upon him, and he be thereby forced to surrender all he had taken from Sweden. These considerations made him entirely resolved not to make one of the descent; but he did not care to declare it till as late as possible: first, that he might the longer have his troops maintained at the Danish

---

[a] The author of the pamphlet, Carl Gyllenborg.—*Ed.*

expense; secondly, that it might be too late for the King of Denmark to demand the necessary troops from his other confederates, and to make the descent without him; and, lastly, that by putting the Dane to a vast expense in making necessary preparations, he might still weaken him more, and, therefore, make him now the more dependent on him, and hereafter a more easy prey.

"Thus he very carefully dissembles his real thoughts, till just when the descent was to be made, and then he, all of a sudden, refuses joining it, and defers it till next spring, with this averment, *that he will then be as good as his word.* But mark him, as some of our newspapers tell us, under this restriction, *unless he can get an advantageous peace of Sweden.* This passage, together with the common report we now have of his treating a separate peace with the King of Sweden, is a new instance of his cunning and policy. He has there two strings to his bow, of which one must serve his turn. There is no doubt but the Czar knows that an accommodation between him and the King of Sweden must be very difficult to bring about. For as he, on the one side, should never consent to part with those seaports, for the getting of which he began this war, and which are absolutely necessary towards carrying on his great and vast designs; so the King of Sweden would look upon it as directly contrary to his interest to yield up these same seaports, if possibly he could hinder it. But then again: the Czar is so well acquainted with the great and heroic spirit of his Swedish Majesty, that he does not question his yielding, rather in point of interest, than nicety of honour. From hence it is, he rightly judges, that his Swedish Majesty must be less exasperated against him who, though he began an unjust war, has very often paid *dearly* for it, and carried it on all along through various successes than against some confederates; that taking an opportunity of his Swedish Majesty's misfortunes, fell upon him in an ungenerous manner, and made a partition treaty of his provinces. The Czar, still more to accommodate himself to the genius of his great enemy, unlike his confederates, who, upon all occasions, spared no reflections and even very unbecoming ones (bullying memorials and hectoring manifestoes), spoke all along with the utmost civility of his *brother* Charles, as he calls him, maintains him to be the *greatest general in Europe,* and even publicly avers, he will more trust a word from him than the greatest assurances, oaths, nay, even treaties with his confederates. These kind of civilities may, perhaps, make a deeper impression upon the noble mind of the King of Sweden, and he be persuaded rather to sacrifice a real interest to a generous enemy, than to gratify, in things of less moment, those by whom he has been ill, and even inhumanly used. But if this should not succeed, the Czar is still a gainer by having made his confederates uneasy at these his separate negotiations; and as we find by the newspapers, the more solicitous to keep him ready to their confederacy, which must cost them very large proffers and promises. In the meantime he leaves the Dane and the Swede securely bound up together in war, and weakening one another as fast as they can, and he turns towards the Empire,[67] and views the Protestant Princes there; and, under many specious pretences, not only marches and counter-marches about their several territories his troops that came back from Denmark, but makes also slowly advance towards Germany those whom he has kept this great while in Poland, under pretence to help the King[a] against his dissatisfied subjects, whose commotions all the while he was the greatest fomenter of. He considers the Emperor[b] is in war with the Turks,[68] and therefore has found, by too successful experience, how little his Imperial Majesty is able to show his authority in

[a] Augustus II.—*Ed.*
[b] Charles VI.—*Ed.*

protecting the members of the Empire. His troops remain in Mecklenburg, notwithstanding their departure is highly insisted upon. His replies to all the demands on that subject are filled with such reasons is if he would give new laws to the Empire.

"Now let us suppose that the King of Sweden should think it more honourable to make a peace with the Czar, and to carry the force of his resentment against his less generous enemies, what a stand will then the princes of the empire, even those that unadvisedly drew in 40,000 Muscovites, to secure the tranquillity of that empire against 10,000 or 12,000 Swedes, I say what stand will they be able to make against him while the Emperor is already engaged in war with the Turks; and the Poles, when they are once in peace among themselves (if after the miseries of so long a war they are in a condition to undertake anything), are by treaty obliged to join their aids against that common enemy of Christianity.

"Some will say I make great and sudden rises from very small beginnings. My answer is, that I would have such an objector look back and reflect why I show him, from such a speck of entity, at his first origin, growing, through more improbable and almost insuperable difficulties, to such a bulk as he has already attained to, and *whereby, as his advocates, the Dutch themselves own, he is grown too formidable for the repose, not only of his neighbours, but of Europe in general.*

"But then, again, they will say he has no pretence either to make a peace with the Swede separately from the Dane, or to make war upon other princes, some of whom he is bound in alliance with. Whoever thinks these objections not answered must have considered the Czar neither as to his nature nor to his ends. The Dutch own further, *that he made war against Sweden without any specious pretence.* He that made war without any specious pretence may make a peace without any specious pretence, and make a new war without any specious pretence for it too. His Imperial Majesty (of Austria), like a wise Prince, when he was obliged to make war with the Ottomans, made it, as in policy he should, powerfully. But, in the meantime, may not the Czar, who is a wise and potent Prince too, follow the example upon the neighbouring Princes round him that are Protestants? If he should, I tremble to speak it, it is not impossible but in this age of Christianity *the Protestant religion should, in a great measure, be abolished;* and that among the Christians, the *Greeks* and *Romans* may once more come to be the only pretenders for Universal Empire. The pure possibility carries with it warning enough for the *Maritime Powers,* and all the other Protestant Princes, to mediate a peace for Sweden, and strengthen her arms again, without which no preparations can put them sufficiently upon their guard; and this must be done early and betimes, *before the King of Sweden, either out of despair or revenge, throws himself into the Czar's hands.* For 'tis a certain maxim (which all Princes ought, and the Czar seems at this time to observe too much for the repose of Christendom) that the wise man must not stand for ceremony, and only *turn* with opportunities. No, he must even *run* with them. For the Czar's part, I will venture to say so much in his commendation, that he will hardly suffer himself to be overtaken that way. He seems to act just as the tide serves. There is nothing which contributes more to the making our undertakings prosperous than the taking of times and opportunities; for time carrieth with it the seasons of opportunities of business. If you let them slip, all your designs are rendered unsuccessful.

"In short, things seem now come to that *crisis* that peace should as soon as possible, be procured to the Swede, with such advantageous articles as are consistent with the nicety of his honour to accept, and with the safety of the Protestant interest, that he should have offered to him, which can be scarce less than all the possessions which he formerly had in the Empire. As in all other things, so in politics, a long-tried certainty must be preferred before an uncertainty, tho' grounded upon ever so probable suppositions. Now can there be anything more certain, than that the provinces Sweden has had in the Empire, were given to it to make it the nearer at hand and the better able to secure the Protestant interest, which, together with the liberties of the Empire it just then had saved? Can there be anything more certain than that that kingdom has, by those means, upon all occasions, secured that said interest now near four-score years? Can there be anything more certain than, as to his present Swedish Majesty, that I may use the words of a letter her late Majesty, Queen Anne, wrote to him (Charles XII.), and *in the time of a Whig Ministry too,* viz.: 'That, as a true Prince, hero and Christian, the chief end of his endeavours has been the promotion of the fear of God among men; and that without insisting on his own particular interest.'

"On the other hand, is it not very uncertain whether those princes, who, by sharing among them the Swedish provinces in the Empire, are now going to set up as protectors of the Protestant interests there, exclusive of the Swedes, will be able to do it? *Denmark* is already so low, and will in all appearance be so much lower still before the end of the war, that very little assistance can be expected from it in a great many years. In *Saxony,* the prospect is but too dismal under a popish prince,[69] so that there remain only the two illustrious houses of Hanover and Brandenburg of all the Protestant princes, powerful enough to lead the rest. Let us therefore only make a parallel between what now happens in the Duchy of Mecklenburg, and what may happen to the Protestant interest, and we shall soon find how we may be mistaken in our reckoning. That said poor Duchy has been most miserably ruined by the Muscovite troops, and it is still so; the Electors of Brandenburg[a] and Hanover[b] are obliged, both as directors of the circle of Lower Saxony, as neighbours, and Protestant Princes, to rescue a fellow state of the Empire, and a Protestant country, from so cruel an oppression of a foreign power. But pray what have they done? The Elector of Brandenburg, cautious lest the Muscovites might on one side invade his electorate, and on the other side from Livonia and Poland, his kingdom of Prussia; and the Elector of Hanover having *the same wise caution* as to his hereditary countries, have not upon this, though very pressing occasion, thought it for their interest, to use any other means than representations. But pray with what success? The Muscovites are still in Mecklenburg, and if at last they march out of it, it will be when the country is so ruined that they cannot there subsist any longer.

"It seems the King of Sweden should be restored to all that he has lost on the side of the Czar; and this appears the *joint interest of both the Maritime Powers.* This may they please to undertake: *Holland,* because it is a maxim there that the Czar grows too great, and must not be suffered to settle in the Baltic, and that Sweden must not be abandoned; *Great Britain,* because, if the Czar compasses his vast and prodigious views, he will, by the ruin and conquest of Sweden, become our nearer and more dreadful neighbour. Besides, we are bound to it by a treaty concluded in the year 1700,[c] between King William[d] and the present King of Sweden, by virtue of which King William assisted the King of Sweden, when in more powerful circumstances, with all that he desired, with great sums of money, several hundred pieces of cloth, and considerable quantities of gunpowder.

---

[a] Frederick William I., King of Prussia.—*Ed.*

[b] Georg-Ludwig, King of Great Britain from 1714 under the name of George I.—*Ed.*

[c] See this volume, pp. 65-73.—*Ed.*

[d] William III.—*Ed.*

"But *some Politicians (whom nothing can make jealous of the growing strength and abilities of the Czar, though they are even foxes and vulpones*[a] *in the art)* either *will not see,* or *pretend they cannot see* how the Czar can ever be able to make so great a progress in power as to hurt us here in our island. To them it is easy to repeat the same answer a hundred times over, if they would be so kind as to take it at last, viz., *that what has been may be again;* and that they did not see how he could reach the height of power, which he has already arrived at, after, I must confess, a very incredible manner. Let those *incredulous* people look narrowly into the *nature* and the *ends* and the *designs* of this great monarch; they will find that they are laid very deep, and that his plans carry in them a prodigious deal of prudence and foresight, and his ends are at the long run brought about by a kind of magic in policy; and will they not after that own that we ought to fear everything from him? As he desires that the designs with which he labours may not prove abortive, so he does not assign them a certain day of their birth, but leaves them to the natural productions of fit times and occasions, like those curious artists in China, who temper the mould this day, of which a vessel may be made a hundred years hence.

"There is another sort of short-sighted politicians among us, who have more of cunning court intrigue and immediate state-craft in them, than of true policy and concern for their country's interest. These gentlemen pin entirely their faith upon other people's sleeves; ask as to everything that is proposed to them, how it is liked at Court?—what the opinion of their party is concerning it?—and if the contrary party is for or against it? Hereby they rule their judgment, and it is enough for their cunning leaders to brand anything with *Whiggism* or *Jacobitism,* for to make these people, without any further inquiry into the matter, blindly espouse it or oppose it. This, it seems, is at present the case of the subject we are upon. Anything said or written in favour of Sweden and the King thereof, is immediately said to come from a *Jacobite* pen, and thus reviled and rejected, without being read or considered. Nay, I[b] have heard gentlemen go so far as to maintain publicly, and with all the vehemence in the world, that *the King of Sweden was a Roman Catholic,* and that *the Czar was a good Protestant.* This, indeed, is one of the greatest misfortunes our country labours under, and till we begin to see with our own eyes, and inquire ourselves into the truth of things, we shall be led away, God knows whither, at last. The serving of Sweden according to our treaties and real interest has nothing to do with our party causes. Instead of seeking for and taking hold of any pretence to undo Sweden, we ought openly to assist it. Could our Protestant succession have a better friend or a bolder champion?

"I shall conclude this discourse by thus shortly recapitulating what I have said. That since the Czar has not only replied to the King of Denmark entreating the contrary, but also answered our Admiral Norris, that he would persist in his resolution to delay the descent upon Schonen, and is said by other newspapers to resolve not to make it then, if he can have peace with Sweden; every Prince, and we more particularly, ought to be jealous of his having some such design as I mention in view, and consult how to prevent them, and to clip, in time, his too aspiring wings, which cannot be effectually done, first, without the Maritime Powers please to begin to keep him in some check and awe, and 'tis to be hoped a certain potent nation, that has helped him forward, can, in some measure, bring him back; and may then speak to this great enterpriser in the language of a countryman in Spain, who coming to an image enshrined, the first making whereof he could well remember, and not finding all the respectful usage he expected,—'You need not,' quoth he, 'be so proud, for we have known you from a plum-tree.'

[a] An allusion to Ben Jonson's comedy *Volpone, or the Fox.—Ed.*

[b] Carl Gyllenborg.—*Ed.*

The next only way is to restore, by a peace, to the King of Sweden what he has lost: that checks his (the Czar's) power immediately, and on that side nothing else can. I wish it may not at last be found true, that those who have been fighting against that King, have, in the main, been fighting against themselves. If the Swede ever has his dominions again, and lowers the high spirit of the Czar, still he may say by his neighbours, as an old Greek hero[a] did, whom his countrymen constantly sent into exile whenever he had done them a service, but were forced to call him back to their aid, whenever they wanted success. 'These people,' quoth he, 'are always using me like the palm-tree. They will be breaking my branches continually, and yet, if there comes a storm, they run to me, and can't find a better place for shelter.' But if he has them not, I shall only exclaim a phrase out of Terence's *Andria:*

> *"Hoccine credibile est aut memorabile*
> *"Tanta vecordia innata cuiquam ut siet,*
> *"Ut malis gaudeant?*[b]

4. POSTSCRIPT.—"I flatter myself that this little history is of that curious nature, and on matters hitherto so unobserved, that I consider it, with pride, as a valuable New Year's gift to the present world; and that posterity will accept it, as the like, for many years after, and read it over on that anniversary, and call it their *Warning Piece.* I must have my *Exegi-Monumentum*[c] as well as others."

---

[a] Themistocles.—*Ed.*

[b] "How can you believe it, can you understand it, that anyone should be born with so much stupidity in him that he would take pleasure in wickedness?" (Terence, *Andria,* Act IV, Scene 1).—*Ed.*

[c] *Exegi monumentum* (aere perennius)—"I have completed a monument more lasting than brass" (Horace, *Odes,* III, XXX).—*Ed.*

Chapter III

To understand a limited historical epoch, we must step beyond its limits and compare it with other historical epochs. To judge Governments and their acts, we must measure them by their own times and the conscience of their contemporaries. Nobody will condemn a British statesman of the 17th century for acting on a belief in witchcraft, if he find Bacon himself ranging demonology in the catalogue of science. On the other hand, if the Stanhopes, the Walpoles, the Townshends, etc., were suspected, opposed, and denounced in their own country, by their own contemporaries, as tools or accomplices of Russia, it will no longer do to shelter their policy behind the convenient screen of prejudice and ignorance common to their time. At the head of the historical evidence we have to sift, we place, therefore, long-forgotten English pamphlets printed at the very time of Peter I. These preliminary *pièces des procès*[a] we shall, however, limit to three pamphlets, which, from three different points of view, illustrate the conduct of England towards Sweden: the first, the *Northern Crisis* (given in Chapter II.), revealing the general system of Russia, and the dangers accruing to England from the Russification of Sweden; the second, called *The Defensive Treaty*,[b] judging the acts of England by the treaty of 1700; and the third, entitled *Truth is but Truth, however it is Timed*,[70] proving that the new-fangled schemes which magnified Russia into the paramount Power of the Baltic were in flagrant opposition to the traditionary policy England had pursued during the course of a whole century.

The pamphlet called *The Defensive Treaty* bears no date of publication. Yet, in one passage it states that, for reinforcing the Danish fleet, eight English men-of-war were left at Copenhagen *"the year before last,"* and in another passage alludes to the assembling of the confederate fleet for the Schonen expedition as

---

[a] Relevant documents.—*Ed.*
[b] See this volume, pp. 65-73.—*Ed.*

having occurred *"last summer."* As the former event took place in 1715, and the latter towards the end of the summer of 1716, it is evident that the pamphlet was written and published in the earlier part of the year 1717. The Defensive Treaty between England and Sweden, the single articles of which the pamphlet comments upon in the form of queries, was concluded in 1700 between William III and Charles XII, and was not to expire before 1719. Yet, during almost the whole of this period, we find England continually assisting Russia and waging war against Sweden, either by secret intrigue or open force, although the treaty was never rescinded nor war ever declared. This fact is, perhaps, even less strange than the *conspiration de silence* under which modern historians have succeeded in burying it, and among them historians by no means sparing of censure against the British Government of that time, for having, without any previous declaration of war, destroyed the Spanish fleet in the Sicilian waters.[71] But then, at least, England was not bound to Spain by a defensive treaty. How, then, are we to explain this contrary treatment of similar cases? The piracy committed against Spain was one of the weapons which the Whig Ministers, seceding from the Cabinet in 1717, caught hold of to harass their remaining colleagues. When the latter stepped forward in 1718, and urged Parliament to declare war against Spain, Sir Robert Walpole rose from his seat in the Commons, and in a most virulent speech, denounced the late ministerial acts

> "as contrary to the laws of nations, and a breach of solemn treaties." "Giving sanction to them in the manner proposed," he said, "could have no other view than to screen ministers, who were conscious of having done something amiss, and who, having begun a war against Spain, would now make it the Parliament's war." [a]

The treachery against Sweden and the connivance at the plans of Russia, never happening to afford the ostensible pretext for a family quarrel amongst the Whig rulers (they being rather unanimous on these points), never obtained the honours of historical criticism so lavishly spent upon the Spanish incident.

How apt modern historians generally are to receive their cue from the official tricksters themselves, is best shown by their reflections on the commercial interests of England with respect to Russia and Sweden. Nothing has been more exaggerated than the dimensions of the trade opened to Great Britain by the huge market of the Russia of Peter the Great, and his immediate successors. Statements bearing not the slightest touch of criticism,

---

[a] Marx is quoting from [Ph. H.] Mahon's book *History of England from the Peace of Utrecht to the Peace of Aix-la-Chapelle*, Vol. I, p. 487.—*Ed.*

have been allowed to creep from one book-shelf to another, till they became at last historical household furniture, to be inherited by every successive historian, without even the *beneficium inventarii*.[a] Some incontrovertible statistical figures[72] will suffice to blot out these hoary common-places.

British Commerce from 1697-1700.

	£
Export to Russia	58,884
Import from Russia	112,252
Total	171,136

	£
Export to Sweden	57,555
Import from Sweden	212,094
Total	269,649

During the same period the total

	£
Export of England amounted to	3,525,906
Import	3,482,586
Total	7,008,492

In 1716, after all the Swedish provinces in the Baltic, and on the Gulfs of Finland and Bothnia, had fallen into the hands of Peter I., the

	£
Export to Russia was	113,154
Import from Russia	197,270
Total	310,424
Export to Sweden	24,101
Import from Sweden	136,959
Total	161,060

At the same time, the total of English exports and imports together reached about £10,000,000. It will be seen from these figures, when compared with those of 1697-1700, that the increase in the Russian trade is balanced by the decrease in the Swedish trade, and that what was added to the one was abstracted from the other. In 1730, the

[a] Benefit of inventory—an heir's privilege of securing himself against unlimited liability for his ancestor by giving up within a year an inventory of his heritage or real estate, to the extent of which alone he was liable.—*Ed.*

	£
Export to Russia was	46,275
Import from Russia	258,802
Total	305,077

Fifteen years, then, after the consolidation in the meanwhile of the Muscovite settlement on the Baltic, the British trade with Russia had fallen off by £5,347. The general trade of England reaching in 1730 the sum of £16,329,001; the Russian trade amounted not yet to $\frac{1}{53}$rd of its total value. Again, thirty years later, in 1760, the account between Great Britain and Russia stands thus:

	£
Import from Russia (in 1760)	536,504
Export to Russia	39,761 [a]
Total	576,265

while the general trade of England amounted to £26,361,760. Comparing these figures with those of 1716, we find that the total of the Russian commerce, after nearly half a century, has increased by the trifling sum of only £265,841. That England suffered positive loss by her new commercial relations with Russia under Peter I. and Catherine I., becomes evident on comparing, on the one side, the export and import figures, and on the other, the sums expended on the frequent naval expeditions to the Baltic which England undertook during the lifetime of Charles XII., in order to break down his resistance to Russia, and, after his death, on the professed necessity of checking the maritime encroachments of Russia.

Another glance at the statistical data given for the years 1697, 1700, 1716, 1730, and 1760, will show that the British *export* trade to Russia, was continually falling off, save in 1716, when Russia engrossed the whole Swedish trade on the eastern coast of the Baltic, and the Gulf of Bothnia, and had not yet found the opportunity of subjecting it to her own regulations. From £58,884, at which the British exports to Russia stood during 1697-1700, when Russia was still precluded from the Baltic, they had sunk to £46,275 in 1730, and to £39,761 in 1760, showing a decrease of £19,123, or about $^1/_3$rd of their original amount in 1700. If, then,

[a] A. Anderson has: import—£474,680, export—£38,710 (Vol. IV, p. 42).—*Ed.*

since the absorption of the Swedish provinces by Russia, the British market proved expanding for Russian raw produce, the Russian market, on its side, proved straitening for British manufactures, a feature of that trade which could hardly recommend it at a time when the Balance of Trade doctrine[73] ruled supreme. To trace the circumstances which produced the increase of the Anglo-Russian trade under Catherine II., would lead us too far from the period we are considering.

On the whole, then, we arrive at the following conclusions: during the first sixty years of the eighteenth century the total Anglo-Russian trade formed but a very diminutive fraction of the general trade of England, say less than $^1/_{45}$th; its sudden increase during the earliest years of Peter's sway over the Baltic did not at all affect the general balance of British trade, as it was a simple transfer from its Swedish account to its Russian account. In the later times of Peter I., as well as under his immediate successors, Catherine I. and Anne, the Anglo-Russian trade was positively declining; during the whole epoch, dating from the final settlement of Russia in the Baltic provinces, the export of British manufactures to Russia was continually falling off, so that at its end it stood one-third lower than at its beginning, when that trade was still confined to the port of Archangel; neither the contemporaries of Peter I, nor the next British generation reaped any benefit from the advancement of Russia to the Baltic. In general the Baltic trade of Great Britain was at that time trifling in regard of the capital involved, but important in regard of its character. It afforded England the raw produce for its maritime stores. That from the latter point of view the Baltic was in safer keeping in the hands of Sweden than in those of Russia, was not only proved by the pamphlets we are reprinting, but fully understood by the British Ministers themselves. Stanhope writing, fo. instance, to Townshend on October 16th, 1716[a]:

"It is certain that if the Czar[b] be let alone three years, he will be absolute master in those seas." *

---

* In the year 1657, when the Courts of Denmark and Brandenburg intended engaging the Muscovites to fall upon Sweden, they instructed their Minister so to manage the affair that the Czar might by no means get any footing in the Baltic, because "they did not know what to do with so troublesome a neighbour." (See Puffendorf's *History of Brandenburg.*[74])

---

[a] Marx is quoting from [Ph. H.] Mahon's book *History of England...*, Vol. I, p. 342.— *Ed.*

[b] Alexei Mikhailovich.— *Ed.*

If, then, neither the navigation nor the general commerce of England was interested in the treacherous support given to Russia against Sweden, there existed, indeed, one small fraction of British merchants whose interests were identical with the Russian ones—the Russian Trade Company.[75] It was this gentry that raised a cry against Sweden. See, for instance: "Several grievances of the English merchants in their trade into the dominions of the King of Sweden, whereby it does appear how dangerous it may be for the English nation to depend on Sweden only for the supply of the naval stores, when they might be amply furnished with the like stores from the dominions of the Emperor of Russia." "The case of the merchants trading to Russia" (a petition to Parliament[76]), etc. It was they who in the years 1714, 1715, and 1716, regularly assembled twice a week before the opening of Parliament, to draw up in public meetings the complaints of the British merchantmen against Sweden. On this small fraction the ministers relied; they were even busy in getting up its demonstrations, as may be seen from the letters addressed by Count Gyllenborg to Baron Görtz, dated 4th of November and 4th of December, 1716,[a] wanting, as they did, but the shadow of a pretext to drive their "mercenary *Parliament*," as Gyllenborg calls it, where they liked. The influence of these British merchants trading to Russia was again exhibited in the year 1765, and our own times have witnessed the working for his interest, of a Russian merchant[b] at the head of the Board of Trade, and of a Chancellor of the Exchequer[c] in the interest of a cousin engaged in the Archangel trade.[77]

The oligarchy which, after the "glorious revolution,"[78] usurped wealth and power at the cost of the mass of the British people, was, of course, forced to look out for allies, not only abroad, but also at home. The latter they found in what the French would call *la haute bourgeoisie*,[d] as represented by the Bank of England, the money-lenders, state creditors, East India and other trading corporations, the great manufacturers, etc. How tenderly they managed the material interests of that class, may be learned from the whole of their domestic legislation—Bank Acts, Protectionist enactments, Poor Regulations, etc. As to their *foreign policy*, they wanted to give it the appearance at least of being altogether

---

[a] [C. Gyllenborg,] *Letters which passed between Count Gyllenborg, the barons Görtz, Sparre and others...*, pp. 6-8, 17.—*Ed.*

[b] Edward Cardwell.—*Ed.*

[c] William Ewart Gladstone.—*Ed.*

[d] Big bourgeoisie.—*Ed.*

regulated by the mercantile interest, an appearance the more easily to be produced, as the exclusive interest of one or the other small fraction of that class would, of course, be always easily identified with this or that ministerial measure. The interested fraction then raised the commerce and navigation cry, which the nation stupidly re-echoed.

At that time, then, there devolved on the Cabinet, at least, the *onus* of inventing *mercantile pretexts,* however futile, for their measures of foreign policy. In our own epoch, British Ministers have thrown this burden on foreign nations, leaving to the French, the Germans, etc., the irksome task of discovering the *secret* and *hidden* mercantile springs of their actions. Lord Palmerston, for instance, takes a step apparently the most damaging to the material interests of Great Britain. Up starts a State philosopher, on the other side of the Atlantic, or of the Channel, or in the heart of Germany,[79] who puts his head to the rack to dig out the mysteries of the mercantile Machiavellism of "perfide Albion," of which Palmerston is supposed the unscrupulous and unflinching executor. We will, *en passant,* show, by a few modern instances, what desperate shifts those foreigners have been driven to, who feel themselves obliged to interpret Palmerston's acts by what they imagine to be the English commercial policy. In his valuable *Histoire Politique et Sociale des Principautés Danubiennes,* M. Elias Regnault, startled by the Russian conduct, before and during the years 1848-49, of Mr. Colqhoun, the British Consul at Bucharest, suspects that England had some secret material interest in keeping down the trade of the Principalities. The late Dr. Cunibert, private physician of old Milosh, in his most interesting account of the Russian intrigues in Servia, gives a curious relation of the manner in which Lord Palmerston, through the instrumentality of Colonel Hodges, betrayed Milosh to Russia by feigning to support him against her.[a] Fully believing in the personal integrity of Hodges, and the patriotic zeal of Palmerston, Dr. Cunibert is found to go a step further than M. Elias Regnault. He suspects England of being interested in putting down Turkish commerce generally. General Mieroslawski, in his last work on Poland,[b] is not very far from intimating that mercantile Machiavellism instigated England to sacrifice her own *prestige* in Asia Minor, by the surrender of

---

[a] B. S. Cunibert, *Essai historique sur les révolutions et l'indépendance de la Servie depuis 1804 jusqu'à 1850,* t. II, pp. 303-523.—*Ed.*

[b] Presumably this refers to L. Mieroslawski's book: *De la Nationalité polonaise dans l'équilibre européen.*—*Ed.*

Kars.[80] As a last instance may serve the present lucubrations of the Paris papers, hunting after the secret springs of commercial jealousy, which induce Palmerston to oppose the cutting of the Isthmus of Suez canal.[81]

To return to our subject. The mercantile pretext hit upon by the Townshends, Stanhopes, etc., for the hostile demonstrations against Sweden, was the following. Towards the end of 1713, Peter I. had ordered all the hemp and other produce of his dominions, destined for export, to be carried to St. Petersburg instead of Archangel. Then the Swedish Regency, during the absence of Charles XII., and Charles XII. himself, after his return from Bender, declared all the Baltic ports, occupied by the Russians, to be blockaded. Consequently, English ships, breaking through the blockade, were confiscated. The English Ministry then asserted that British merchantmen had the right of trading to those ports, according to Article XVII. of the Defensive Treaty of 1700,[a] by which English commerce, with the exception of contraband of war, was allowed to go on with ports of the enemy. The absurdity and falsehood of this pretext being fully exposed in the pamphlet we are about to reprint, we will only remark that the case had been more than once decided against commercial nations, not bound, like England, by treaty to defend the integrity of the Swedish Empire. In the year 1561, when the Russians took Narva,[82] and laboured hard to establish their commerce there, the Hanse towns, chiefly Lübeck, tried to possess themselves of this traffic. Eric XIV., then King of Sweden, resisted their pretensions. The city of Lübeck represented this resistance as altogether new, as they had carried on their commerce with the Russians time out of mind, and pleaded the common right of nations to navigate in the Baltic, provided their vessels carried no contraband of war. The King replied that he did not dispute the Hanse towns the liberty of trading with Russia, but only with Narva, which was no Russian port. In the year 1579 again, the Russians having broken the suspension of arms with Sweden, the Danes likewise claimed the navigation to Narva, by virtue of their treaty, but King John was as firm, in maintaining the contrary, as was his brother Eric.

In her open demonstrations of hostility against the King of Sweden, as well as in the false pretence on which they were founded, England seemed only to follow in the track of Holland, which declaring the confiscation of its ships to be piracy, had issued two proclamations against Sweden in 1714.

---

[a] See this volume, pp. 65-73.—*Ed.*

In one respect, the case of the States-General was the same as that of England. King William had concluded the Defensive Treaty as well for Holland as for England. Besides, Article XVI., in the Treaty of Commerce, concluded between Holland and Sweden, in 1703, expressly stipulated that no navigation ought to be allowed to the ports blocked up by either of the confederates. The then common Dutch cant that "there was no hindering traders from carrying their merchandise where they will," was the more impudent as, during the war, ending with the Peace of Ryswick,[83] the Dutch Republic had declared all France to be blocked up, forbidden the neutral powers all trade with that kingdom, and caused all their ships that went there or came thence to be brought up without any regard to the nature of their cargoes.

In another respect, the situation of Holland was different from that of England. Fallen from its commercial and maritime grandeur, Holland had then already entered upon its epoch of decline. Like Genoa and Venice, when new roads of commerce had dispossessed them of their old mercantile supremacy, it was forced to lend out to other nations its capital, grown too large for the vessels of its own commerce. Its fatherland had begun to lie there where the best interest for its capital was paid. Russia, therefore, proved an immense market, less for the commerce, than for the outlay of capital and men. To this moment Holland has remained the banker of Russia. At the time of Peter, they supplied Russia with ships, officers, arms and money, so that his fleet, as a contemporary writer remarks, ought to have been called a Dutch, rather than a Muscovite one.[84] They gloried in having sent the first European merchant ship to St. Petersburg, and returned the commercial privileges they had obtained from Peter, or hoped to obtain from him, by that fawning meanness which characterises their intercourse with Japan. Here, then, was quite another solid foundation than in England for the Russianism of statesmen, whom Peter I. had entrapped during his stay at Amsterdam and the Hague in 1697, whom he afterwards directed by his ambassadors, and with whom he renewed his personal influence during his renewed stay at Amsterdam in 1716-17. Yet, if the paramount influence England exercised over Holland during the first *decennia* of the eighteenth century be considered, there can remain no doubt that the proclamations against Sweden by the States-General would never have been issued, if not with the previous consent and at the instigation of England. The intimate connection between the English and Dutch Governments served more than once the former to put up precedents in the name of Holland, which they were resolved to act upon in the name of England. On the other hand, it is no less certain that the Dutch statesmen were employed by the Czar to influence the British ones. Thus Horace Walpole, the brother of the "Father of Corruption,"[85] the brother-in-law of the Minister, Townshend, and the British Ambassador at the Hague during 1715-16, was evidently inveigled into the Russian interest by his Dutch friends. Thus, as we shall see by-and-by, Theyls, the Secretary to the Dutch Embassy at Constantinople, at the most critical period of the deadly struggle between Charles XII. and Peter I., managed affairs at the same time for the Embassies of England and Holland at the Sublime Porte. This Theyls, in a print of his[a], openly claims it as a merit with his nation to have been the devoted and rewarded agent of Russian intrigue.

"THE DEFENSIVE TREATY CONCLUDED IN THE YEAR 1700, BETWEEN HIS LATE MAJESTY, KING WILLIAM, OF EVER-GLORIOUS MEMORY, AND HIS PRESENT SWEDISH MAJESTY, KING CHARLES XII. PUBLISHED AT THE EARNEST DESIRE OF SEVERAL MEMBERS OF BOTH HOUSES OF PARLIAMENT.[86]

'Nec rumpite foedera pacis,
Nec regnis praeferte fidem.'

Silius, Lib. II[b]

London

"*Article* I. Establishes between the Kings of Sweden and England 'a sincere and constant friendship for ever, a league and good correspondence, so that they shall never mutually or separately molest one another's kingdoms, provinces, colonies, or subjects, wheresoever situated, *nor shall they suffer or agree that this should be done by others, etc.*'

"*Article* II. 'Moreover, each of the Allies, his heirs and successors, shall be obliged to take care of, and promote, as much as in him lies, the profit and honour of the other, to detect and give notice to his other ally (as soon as it shall come to his own knowledge) of all imminent dangers, conspiracies, and hostile designs formed against him, to withstand them as much as possible, and to prevent them both by advice and assistance; and therefore *it shall not be lawful for either of the Allies, either by themselves or any other whatsoever, to act, treat, or endeavour anything to the prejudice or loss of the other,* his lands or dominions whatsoever or wheresoever, whether by land or sea; that one shall in no wise favour the other's foes, either rebels or enemies, to the prejudice of his Ally,' etc.

"*Query* I. How the words marked in italics agree with our present conduct, when our fleet acts in conjuction with the enemies of Sweden, *the Czar commands*

---

[a] W. Theyls, *Mémoires pour servir à l'histoire de Charles XII, roi de Suède.—Ed.*

[b] "Neither break peace treaties, nor prefer allegiance to kingdoms" (Silius Italicus, *De secundo bello punico,* Lib. II).—*Ed.*

our fleet, our Admiral[a] *enters into Councils of War, and is not only privy to all their designs, but together with our own Minister at Copenhagen*[b] (as the King of Denmark[c] has himself owned it in a public declaration), *pushed on the Northern Confederates to an enterprise entirely destructive to our Ally Sweden, I mean the descent designed last summer upon Schonen?*

"*Query* II. In what manner we also must explain that passage in the first article by which it is stipulated that one Ally shall not either by themselves or any other whatsoever, act, treat, or endeavour anything to the loss of the other's lands and dominions; to justify in particular our leaving in the year 1715, even when the season was so far advanced as no longer to admit of our usual pretence of convoying and protecting our trade, which was then got already safe home, eight men-of-war in the Baltic, with orders to join in one line of battle with the Danes, whereby we made them so much superior in number to the Swedish fleet, that it could not come to the relief of Stralsund, and whereby *we chiefly occasioned Sweden's entirely losing its German Provinces,* and even the *extreme danger his Swedish Majesty ran, in his own person,* in crossing the sea, before the surrender of the town.

"*Article* III. By a special defensive treaty, the Kings of Sweden and England mutually oblige themselves, 'in a strict alliance, to defend one another mutually, as well as their kingdoms, territories, provinces, states, subjects, possessions, as their rights and liberties of navigation and commerce, as well in the Northern, Deucalidonian, Western, and Britannic Sea. commonly called the Channel, the Baltic, the Sound; as also of the privileges and prerogatives of each of the Allies belonging to them, by virtue of treaties and agreements, as well as by received customs, the laws of nations, hereditary right, against any aggressors or invaders and molesters in Europe by sea or land, etc.'

"*Query.* It being by the law of nations an indisputable right and prerogative of any king or people, in case of a great necessity, or threatening ruin, to use all such means they themselves shall judge most necessary for their preservation; it having moreover been a constant prerogative and practice of the Swedes, for these several hundred years, in case of a war with their most dreadful enemies the Muscovites, to hinder all trade with them in the Baltic; and since it is also stipulated in this article that amongst other things, *one Ally ought to defend the prerogatives belonging to the other, even by received customs, and the law of nations:* how come we now, the King of Sweden stands more than ever in need of using that prerogative, not only to dispute it, but also to take thereof a pretence for an open hostility against him?

"*Articles* IV., V., VI., *and* VII., fix the strength of the auxiliary forces, England and Sweden are to send each other in case the territory of either of these powers should be invaded, or its navigation 'molested or hindered' in one of the seas enumerated in Article III. The invasion of the *German* provinces of Sweden is expressly included as a *casus foederis.*

"*Article* VIII. Stipulates that that Ally who is not attacked shall first act the part of a pacific mediator; but, the mediation having proved a failure, 'the aforesaid forces shall be sent without delay; nor shall the confederates desist before the injured party shall be satisfied in all things.'

"*Article* IX. That Ally that requires the stipulated 'help, has to choose whether he will have the above-named army either all or any [part of it], either in soldiers, ships, ammunition, or money.'

---

[a] John Norris.— *Ed.*
[b] Alexander Campbell.— *Ed.*
[c] Frederick IV.— *Ed.*

"*Article* X. Ships and armies serve under 'the command of him that required them.'

"*Article* XI. 'But if it should happen that the above-mentioned forces should not be proportionable to the danger, as supposing that perhaps the aggressor should be assisted by the forces of some other confederates of his, then one of the Allies, after previous request, shall be obliged to help the other that is injured, with greater forces, such as he shall be able to raise with safety and convenience, both by sea and land....'

"*Article* XII. 'It shall be lawful for either of the Allies and their subjects to bring their men-of-war into one another's harbours, and to winter there.' Peculiar negotiations about this point shall take place at Stockholm, but 'in the meanwhile, the articles of treaty concluded at London, 1661, relating to the navigation and commerce shall remain, in their full force, as much as if they were inserted here word for word.'

"*Article* XIII. '... The subjects of either of the Allies ... shall no way, either by sea or land, serve them (the enemies of either of the Allies), either as mariners or soldiers, and therefore it shall be forbid them upon severe penalty.'

"*Article* XVI.[a] 'If it happens that either of the confederate kings ... should be engaged in a war against a common enemy, or be molested by any other neighbouring king ... in his own kingdoms or provinces ... to the hindering of which, he that requires help, may by the force of this treaty, himself be obliged to send help: then that Ally so molested, shall not be obliged to send the promised help....'

"*Query* I. Whether in our conscience we don't think the King of Sweden most unjustly attacked by all his enemies; whether consequently we are not convinced that we owe him the assistance stipulated in these Articles; whether he has not demanded the same from us, and why it has hitherto been refused him?

"*Query* II. These articles, setting forth in the most expressing terms, in what manner Great Britain and Sweden ought to assist one another, can either of these two Allies take upon him to prescribe to the other who requires his assistance, a way of lending him it, not expressed in the treaty; and if that other Ally does not think it for his interest to accept of the same, but still insists upon the performance of the treaty, can he from thence take a pretence, not only to withhold the stipulated assistance, but also to use his Ally in a hostile way, and to join with his enemies against him? If this is not justifiable, as even common sense tells us it is not, how can the reason stand good, which we allege amongst others, for using the King of Sweden as we do, *id est,* that demanding a literal performance of his alliance with us, *he would not accept the treaty of neutrality for his German provinces,* which we proposed to him some years ago, a treaty which, not to mention its partiality in favour of the enemies of Sweden, and that it was calculated only for our own interest, and for to prevent all disturbance in the empire, whilst we were engaged in a war against France,[87] the King of Sweden had so much less reason to rely upon, as he was to conclude it with those very enemies, that had every one of them broken several treaties in beginning the present war against him, and as it was to be guaranteed by those powers, who were also every one of them guarantees of the broken treaties, without having performed their guarantee?

"*Query* III. How can we make the words in the 8th Article,[b] *that in assisting our injured Ally we shall not desist before he shall be satisfied in all things,* agree with our endeavouring, to the contrary, to help the enemies of that Prince, though all unjust

[a] The newspaper has mistakenly XIV.—*Ed.*

[b] The newspaper has mistakenly 7th.—*Ed.*

aggressors, not only to take one province after the other from him, but also to remain undisturbed possessors thereof, blaming all along the King of Sweden for not tamely submitting thereunto?

"*Query* IV. The treaty concluded in the year 1661, between Great Britain and Sweden, being in the 12th[a] Article confirmed, and the said treaty forbidding expressly one of the confederates *either himself or his subjects to lend or to sell to the other's enemies, men-of-war or ships of defence;* the 13th Article of this present treaty forbidding also expressly the subjects of either of the Allies *to help any ways the enemies of the other, to the inconvenience and loss of such an Ally;* should we not have accused the Swedes of the most notorious breach of this treaty, had they, during our late war with the French, lent them their own fleet, the better to execute any design of theirs against us, or had they, notwithstanding our representations to the contrary, suffered their subjects to furnish the French with ships of 50, 60, and 70 guns! Now, if we turn the tables, and remember upon how many occasions our fleet has of late been entirely subservient to the designs of the enemies of Sweden, even in most critical times, and that *the Czar of Muscovy has actually above a dozen English-built ships* in his fleet, will it not be very difficult for us to excuse in ourselves what we should most certainly have blamed, if done by others?

"*Article* XVII. The obligation shall not be so far extended, as that all friendship and mutual commerce with the enemies of that Ally (that requires the help) shall be taken away; for supposing that one of the confederates should send his auxiliaries, and should not be engaged in the war himself, it shall then be lawful for the subjects to trade and commerce with that enemy of that Ally that is engaged in the war, also directly and safely to merchandise with such enemies, for all goods not expressly forbid and called contraband, as in a special treaty of commerce hereafter shall be appointed.

"*Query* I. This Article being the only one out of twenty-two whose performance we have now occasion to insist upon from the Swedes, the question will be whether we ourselves, in regard to Sweden, have performed all the other articles as it was our part to do, and whether in demanding of the King of Sweden the executing of this Article, we have promised that we would also do our duty as to all the rest; if not, may not the Swedes say that we complain unjustly of the breach of one single Article, when we ourselves may perhaps be found guilty of having in the most material points, either not executed, or even acted against the whole treaty?

"*Query* II. Whether the liberty of commerce one Ally is, by virtue of this Article, to enjoy with the other's enemies, ought to have no limitation at all, neither as to time nor place; in short, whether it ought even to be extended so far as to destroy the very end of this Treaty, which is the promoting the safety and security of one another's kingdoms?

"*Query* III. Whether in case the French had in the late wars made themselves masters of Ireland or Scotland, and either in new-made seaports, or the old ones, endeavoured by trade still more firmly to establish themselves in their new conquests, we, in such a case, should have thought the Swedes our true allies and friends, had they insisted upon this Article to trade with the French in the said seaports taken from us, and to furnish them there with several necessaries of war, nay, even with armed ships, whereby the French might the easier have annoyed us here in England?

"*Query* IV. Whether, if we had gone about to hinder a trade, so prejudicial to us, and in order thereunto, brought up all Swedish ships going to the said seaports, we should not highly have exclaimed against the Swedes, had they taken from

---

[a] The newspaper has mistakenly 11th.—*Ed.*

thence a pretence to join their fleet with the French, to occasion the losing of any of our dominions and even to encourage the invasion upon us, have their fleet at hand to promote the same?

"*Query* V. Whether upon an impartial examination, this would not have been a case exactly parallel to that we insist upon, as to a Free Trade to the seaports the Czar has taken from Sweden, and to our present behaviour, upon the King of Sweden's hindering the same?

"*Query* VI. Whether we have not ever since Oliver Cromwell's time, till 1710, in all our wars with France and Holland, without any urgent necessity at all, brought up and confiscated Swedish ships, though not going to any prohibited ports, and that to a far greater number and value, than all those the Swedes have now taken from us, and whether the Swedes have ever taken a pretence from thence, to join with our enemies, and to send whole squadrons of ships to their assistance?

"*Query* VII. Whether, if we inquire narrowly into the state of commerce, as it has been carried on for these many years, we shall not find that the trade of the above-mentioned places was not so very necessary to us, at least not so far as to be put into the balance with the preservation of a Protestant confederate nation, much less to give us a just reason *to make war against that nation, which, though not declared, has done it more harm than the united efforts of all its enemies?*

"*Query* VIII. Whether, if it happened two years ago, that this trade became something more necessary to us than formerly, it is not easily proved, that it was occasioned only by the Czar's forcing us out of our old channel of trade to Archangel, and bringing us to Petersburg, and our complying therewith. So that all the inconveniences we laboured under upon that account, ought to have been laid to the Czar's door, and not to the King of Sweden's?

"*Query* IX. Whether the Czar did not in the very beginning of 1715 again permit us to trade our old way to Archangel, and whether our ministers had not notice thereof a great while before our fleet was sent that year to protect our *trade to Petersburg,* which by this alteration in the Czar's resolution was become as unnecessary for us as before?

"*Query* X. Whether the King of Sweden had not declared, that if we would forbear trading to *Petersburg,* etc., which he looked upon as ruinous to his kingdom, he would in no manner disturb our trade, neither in the Baltic nor anywhere else; but that in case we would not give him this slight proof of our friendship, he should be excused if the innocent came to suffer with the guilty?

"*Query* XI. Whether, by our insisting upon the trade to the ports prohibited by the King of Sweden, which besides its being unnecessary to us, hardly makes one part in ten of that we carry on in the Baltic, we have not drawn upon us the hazards that our trade has run all this while, been ourselves the occasion of our great expenses in fitting out fleets for its protection, and by our joining with the enemies of Sweden, fully justified his Swedish Majesty's resentment; had it ever gone so far as to seize and confiscate without distinction all our ships and effects, wheresoever he found them, either within or without his kingdoms?

"*Query* XII. If we were so tender of our trade to the northern ports in general, ought we not in policy rather to have considered the hazard that trade runs by the approaching ruin of Sweden, and *by the Czar's becoming the whole and sole master of the Baltic, and all the naval stores we want from thence?* Have we not also suffered greater hardships and losses in the said trade from the Czar, than that amounting only to sixty odd thousand pounds (whereof, by the way, two parts in three may perhaps be disputable), which provoked us first to send twenty men-of-war in the Baltic with order to attack the Swedes wherever they met them? And yet, did not this very Czar, this very aspiring and dangerous prince, *last summer command the whole confederate fleet,* as it was called, *of which our men-of-war made the most considerable part? The first instance that ever was of a Foreign Potentate having the command given him of the English fleet, the bulwark of our nation;* and did not our said men-of-war afterwards convey his" (the Czar's) "transport ships and troops on board of them, in their return from Zealand, *protecting them from the Swedish fleet,* which else would have made a considerable havoc amongst them?

"*Query* XIII. Suppose now, we had on the contrary taken hold of the great and many complaints our merchants have made, of the ill-usage they meet from the Czar, to have sent our fleet to show our resentment against that prince, to prevent his great and pernicious designs even to us, *to assist Sweden pursuant to this Treaty,* and effectually to restore the peace in the North, would not that have been more for our interest, more necessary, more honourable and just, and more according to our Treaty; and would not the several 100,000 pounds these our Northern expeditions have cost the nation, have been thus better employed?

"*Query* XIV. If the preserving and securing our trade against the Swedes, had been the only and real object of all our measures, as to the Northern affairs, how came we the year before the last to leave eight men-of-war in the Baltic and at Copenhagen, when we had no more trade there to protect, and how came Admiral Norris last summer, although he and the Dutch together made up the number of twenty-six men-of-war, and consequently were too strong for the Swedes, to attempt anything against our trade under their convoy; yet to lay above two whole months of the best season in the Sound, without convoying our and the Dutch merchantmen to the several ports they were bound for, whereby they were kept in the Baltic so late that their return could not but be very hazardous, as it even proved, both to them and our men-of-war themselves? Will not the world be apt to think that the hopes of forcing the King of Sweden to an inglorious and disadvantageous peace, by which the Duchies of Bremen and Verden ought to be added to the Hanover dominions, or that some other such view, foreign, if not contrary, to the true and old interest of Great Britain, had then a greater influence upon all these our proceedings than *the pretended care of our trade?*

"Article XVIII. 'For as much as it seems convenient for the preservation of the liberty of navigation and commerce in the Baltic Sea, that a firm and exact friendship should be kept between the Kings of Sweden and Denmark and whereas the former Kings of Sweden and Denmark[a] did oblige themselves mutually, not only by the public Articles of Peace made in the camp of Copenhagen, on the 27th of May, 1660[b] and by the ratifications of the agreement interchanged on both sides, sacredly and inviolably to observe all and every one of the clauses comprehended in the said agreement, but also declared together to ... Charles II., King of Great Britain ... a little before the treaty concluded between England and Sweden in the year 1665, that they would stand sincerely ... to all ... of the Articles of the said peace ... whereupon Charles II., with the approbation and consent of both the forementioned Kings of Sweden and Denmark, took upon himself a little after the Treaty concluded between England and Sweden, lst March, 1665, to wit 9th October, 1665, guarantee of the same agreements... Whereas an instrument of peace between ... the Kings of Sweden and Denmark[c] happened to be soon after these concluded at Lunden in Schonen, in 1679, which contains an express transaction, and repetition, and confirmation of the Treaties concluded at Roskild, Copenhagen, and Westphalia[88]; therefore ... the King of Great Britain binds

[a] Charles XI and Frederick III.—*Ed.*
[b] The newspaper has mistakenly 1610.—*Ed.*
[c] Charles XI and Christian V.—*Ed.*

himself by the force of this Treaty... that if either of the Kings of Sweden and Denmark shall consent to the violation, either of all the agreements, or of one or more articles comprehended in them, and consequently if either of the Kings shall to the prejudice of the person, provinces, territories, islands, goods, dominions and rights of the other, which by the force of the agreements so often repeated, and made in the camp of Copenhagen, on the 27th of May, 1660, as also of those made in the ... peace at Lunden in Schonen, in 1679, were attributed to every one that was interested and comprehended in the words of the peace, should either by himself or by others, presume, or secretly design or attempt, or by open molestations, or by any injury, or by any violence of arms, attempt anything; that then the ... King of Great Britain ... shall first of all, by his interposition, perform all the offices of a friend and princely ally, which may serve towards the keeping inviolable all the frequently mentioned agreements, and of every article comprehended in them, and consequently towards the preservation of peace between both kings; that afterwards if the King who is the beginner of such prejudice, or any molestation or injury, contrary to all agreements, and contrary to any Article comprehended in them, shall refuse after being admonished ... then the King of Great Britain ... shall ... assist him that is injured, as by the present agreements between the Kings of Great Britain and Sweden, in such cases is determined and agreed.'

"*Query.* Does not this article expressly tell us, how to remedy the disturbances our trade in the Baltic might suffer, in case of a misunderstanding betwixt the Kings of Sweden and Denmark, by obliging both these Princes to keep all the Treaties of Peace, that have been concluded between them from 1660-79,[a] and in case either of them in an hostile manner act against the said Treaties, by assisting the other, against the aggressor? How comes it then, that we don't make use of so just a remedy against an evil we are so great sufferers by? Can anybody though ever so partial deny, but the King of Denmark,[b] though seemingly a sincere friend to the King of Sweden,[c] from the peace of Travendahl,[89] till he went out of Saxony against the Muscovites, fell very unjustly upon him immediately after, taking ungenerously advantage of the fatal battle of Pultava[90]? Is not then the King of Denmark the violator of all the above-mentioned Treaties, and consequently the true author of the disturbances our trade meets with in the Baltic? Why in God's name don't we according to this article assist Sweden against him, and why do we on the contrary declare openly against the injured King of Sweden, send hectoring and threatening memorials to him, upon the least advantage he has over his enemies, as we did last summer upon his entering Norway, and even order our fleets to act openly against him in conjunction with the Danes?

"*Article* XIX. There shall be 'stricter confederacy and union between the above-mentioned kings of Great Britain and Sweden, for the future, *for the defence and preservation of the Protestant, Evangelic, and reformed religion.*'

"*Query* I. How do we, according to this article, join with Sweden, to *assert, protect, and preserve the Protestant religion?* Don't we suffer that nation, which has always been a bulwark to the said religion, most unmercifully to be torn to pieces? ...*Don't we ourselves give a helping hand towards its destruction?* And why all this? Because our merchants have lost their ships to the value of sixty odd thousand pounds. *For this loss and nothing else was the pretended reason why in the year 1715 we sent our fleet in the Baltic, at the expense of* £200,000, and as to what our merchants

[a] The newspaper has mistakenly 1670.—*Ed.*
[b] Frederick IV.—*Ed.*
[c] Charles XII.—*Ed.*

have suffered since, suppose we attribute it to our threatening memorials as well as open hostilities against the King of Sweden, must we not even then own that that Prince's resentment has been very moderate?

"*Query* II. How can other Princes, and especially our fellow Protestants, think us sincere, in what we have made them believe as to our zeal in spending millions of lives and money for to secure the Protestant interest only in one single branch of it, *I mean the Protestant succession here*,[91] when they see that that succession has hardly taken place, before we only for sixty odd thousand pounds (for let us always remember, that this paltry sum was the first pretence for our quarrelling with Sweden), go about to undermine the very foundation of that interest in general, by helping as we do entirely to sacrifice Sweden, the old and sincere protector of the Protestants, to its neighbours, of which some are professed Papists, some worse, and some at best but lukewarm Protestants?

"*Article* XX. 'Therefore that a reciprocal faith of the Allies and their perseverance in this agreement may appear ... both the fore-mentioned kings mutually oblige themselves and declare that ... they will not depart a tittle from the genuine and common sense of all and every article of this treaty under any pretences of friendship, profit, former treaty, agreement and promise, or upon any colour whatsoever: but that they will most fully and readily either by themselves or Ministers, or subjects, put in execution whatsoever they have promised in this treaty ... without any hesitation, exception, or excuse....'

"*Query* I. In as much as this article sets forth that at the time of concluding of the treaty, we were under no engagement contrary to it, and that it were highly unjust, should we afterwards, and while this treaty is in force, which is eighteen years after the day it was signed, have entered into any such engagements, how can we justify to the world our late proceedings against the King of Sweden, which naturally seem the consequences of a treaty either of our own making with the enemies of that Prince, *or of some Court or other that at present influences our measures?*

"*Query* II. The words in this article... how in the name of honour, faith, and justice, do they agree with the *little and pitiful pretences* we now make use of, not only for not assisting Sweden, pursuant to this treaty, *but even for going about so heartily as we do to destroy it?*

"*Article* XXI. 'This defensive treaty shall last for eighteen years, before the end of which the confederate kings may ... again treat.'

"*Ratification of the abovesaid treaty.*—We having seen and considered this treaty have approved and confirmed the same in all and every particular article and clause as by the present. We do approve the same for us, our heirs, and successors; assuring and promising, on our princely word, that we shall perform and observe sincerely and in good earnest all those things that are therein contained, for the better confirmation whereof we have ordered our grand seal of England to be put to these presents, which were given at our palace at Kensington, 25th of February, in the year of our Lord 1700, and in the 11th year of our reign (Gulielmus Rex).*

"*Query.* How can anyone of us that declares himself for the late happy revolution,[92] and that is a true and grateful lover of King William's for ever-glorious memory ... yet bear with the least patience, that the said treaty should (that I may again use the words of the 20th article), be *departed from, under any*

---

* The treaty was concluded at The Hague on the 6th and 16th January, 1700, and ratified by William III, on February 5th, 1700.

pretence of profit, or upon any colour whatsoever, especially so insignificant and trifl ng a one, as that which has been made use of for two years together to employ our ships, our men, and our money, *to accomplish the ruin of Sweden,* that same Sweden whose defence and preservation this great and wise monarch of ours, has so solemnly promised, and which he always looked upon to be of the utmost necessity for to secure the *Protestant interest* in Europe?"

Chapter IV[93]

Before entering upon an analysis of the pamphlet headed, *Truth is but truth, as it is timed,*[a] with which we shall conclude the *Introduction* to the Diplomatic Revelations, some preliminary remarks on the general history of Russian politics appear opportune.

The overwhelming influence of Russia has taken Europe at different epochs by surprise, startled the peoples of the West, and been submitted to as a fatality, or resisted only by convulsions. But alongside the fascination exercised by Russia, there runs an ever-reviving scepticism, dogging her like a shadow, growing with her growth, mingling shrill notes of irony with the cries of agonising peoples, and mocking her very grandeur as a histrionic attitude taken up to dazzle and to cheat. Other empires have met with similar doubts in their infancy; Russia has become a colossus without outliving them. She affords the only instance in history of an immense empire, the very existence of whose power, even after world-wide achievements, has never ceased to be treated like a matter of faith rather than like a matter of fact. From the outset of the eighteenth century to our days, no author, whether he intended to exalt or to check Russia, thought it possible to dispense with first proving her existence.

But whether we be spiritualists or materialists with respect to Russia—whether we consider her power as a palpable fact, or as the mere vision of the guilt-stricken consciences of the European peoples—the question remains the same: "How did this power, or this phantom of a power, contrive to assume such dimensions as to

---

[a] See this volume, pp. 92-96.—*Ed.*

rouse on the one side the passionate assertion, and on the other the angry denial of its threatening the world with a rehearsal of Universal Monarchy?" At the beginning of the eighteenth century Russia was regarded as a mushroom creation extemporised by the genius of Peter the Great. Schloezer thought it a discovery to have found out that she possessed a past; and in modern times, writers, like Fallmerayer, unconsciously following in the track beaten by Russian historians, have deliberately asserted that the northern spectre which frightens the Europe of the nineteenth century already overshadowed the Europe of the ninth century. With them the policy of Russia begins with the first Ruriks, and has, with some interruptions indeed, been systematically continued to the present hour.

Ancient maps of Russia are unfolded before us, displaying even larger European dimensions than she can boast of now: her perpetual movement of aggrandisement from the ninth to the eleventh century is anxiously pointed out; we are shown Oleg launching 88,000 men against Byzantium, fixing his shield as a trophy on the gate of that capital, and dictating an ignominious treaty to the Lower Empire; Igor making it tributary[94]; Svyataslav glorying,

> "the Greeks supply me with gold, costly stuffs, rice, fruits and wine; Hungary furnishes cattle and horses; from Russia I draw honey, wax, furs, and men"[a];

Vladimir conquering the Crimea and Livonia, extorting a daughter[b] from the Greek Emperor,[c] as Napoleon did from the German Emperor,[d] blending the military sway of a northern conqueror with the theocratic despotism of the Porphyrogeniti,[95] and becoming at once the master of his subjects on earth, and their protector in heaven.

Yet, in spite of the plausible parallelism suggested by these reminiscences, the policy of the first Ruriks differs fundamentally from that of modern Russia.[96] It was nothing more nor less than the policy of the German barbarians inundating Europe—the history of the modern nations beginning only after the deluge has passed away. The Gothic period of Russia in particular forms but a chapter of the Norman conquests. As the empire of Charlemagne precedes the foundation of modern France, Germany,

[a] Ph. Segur, *History of Russia and of Peter the Great,* London, 1829, p. 37.—*Ed.*

[b] Anna.—*Ed.*

[c] Romanus II.—*Ed.*

[d] Francis II.—*Ed.*

and Italy, so the empire of the Ruriks precedes the foundation of Poland, Lithuania, the Baltic Settlements, Turkey and Muscovy itself. The rapid movement of aggrandisement was not the result of deep-laid schemes, but the natural offspring of the primitive organisation of Norman conquest—vassalship without fiefs, or fiefs consisting only in tributes—the necessity of fresh conquests being kept alive by the uninterrupted influx of new Varangian adventurers, panting for glory and plunder. The chiefs, becoming anxious for repose, were compelled by the Faithful Band to move on, and in Russian, as in French Normandy, there arrived the moment when the chiefs despatched on new predatory excursions their uncontrollable and insatiable companions-in-arms with the single view to get rid of them. Warfare and organisation of conquest on the part of the first Ruriks differ in no point from those of the Normans in the rest of Europe. If Slavonian tribes were subjected not only by the sword, but also by mutual convention, this singularity is due to the exceptional position of those tribes, placed between a northern and eastern invasion, and embracing the former as a protection from the latter. The same magic charm which attracted other northern barbarians to the Rome of the West, attracted the Varangians to the Rome of the East.[a] The very migration of the Russian capital—Rurik fixing it at Novgorod, Oleg removing it to Kiev, and Svyataslav attempting to establish it in Bulgaria—proves beyond doubt that the invader was only feeling his way, and considered Russia as a mere halting-place from which to wander on in search of an empire in the South. If modern Russia covets the possession of Constantinople to establish her dominion over the world, the Ruriks were, on the contrary, forced by the resistance of Byzantium, under Zimiskes,[b] definitively to establish their dominion in Russia.

It may be objected that victors and vanquished amalgamated more quickly in Russia than in any other conquest of the northern barbarians, that the chiefs soon commingled themselves with the Slavonians—as shown by their marriages and their names. But then, it should be recollected that the Faithful Band, which formed at once their guard and their privy council, remained exclusively composed of Varangians; that Vladimir, who marks the summit, and Yaroslav, who marks the commencing decline of Gothic Russia, were seated on her throne by the arms of the Varangians. If any Slavonian influence is to be acknowledged in

---

[a] Constantinople.—*Ed.*

[b] John I Tzimisces.—*Ed.*

this epoch, it is that of Novgorod, a Slavonian State, the traditions, policy and tendencies of which were so antagonistic to those of modern Russia that the one could found her existence only on the ruins of the other. Under Yaroslav the supremacy of the Varangians is broken, but simultaneously with it disappears the conquering tendency of the first period, and the decline of Gothic Russia begins. The history of that decline, more still than that of the conquest and formation, proves the exclusively Gothic character of the Empire of the Ruriks.

The incongruous, unwieldy, and precocious Empire heaped together by the Ruriks, like the other empires of similar growth, is broken up into appanages, divided and sub-divided among the descendants of the conquerors, dilacerated by feudal wars, rent to pieces by the intervention of foreign peoples. The paramount authority of the Grand Prince vanishes before the rival claims of seventy princes of the blood. The attempt of Andrew of Susdal[a] at recomposing some large limbs of the empire by the removal of the capital from Kiev to Vladimir proves successful only in propagating the decomposition from the South to the centre. Andrew's third successor[b] resigns even the last shadow of supremacy, the title of Grand Prince, and the merely nominal homage still offered him.[97] The appanages to the South and to the West become by turns Lithuanian, Polish, Hungarian, Livonian, Swedish. Kiev itself, the ancient capital, follows destinies of its own, after having dwindled down from a seat of the Grand Princedom to the territory of a city. Thus, the Russia of the Normans completely disappears from the stage, and the few weak reminiscences in which it still outlived itself, dissolve before the terrible apparition of Genghis Khan. The bloody mire of Mongolian slavery, not the rude glory of the Norman epoch, forms the cradle of Muscovy, and modern Russia is but a metamorphosis of Muscovy.

The Tartar yoke lasted from 1237 to 1462—more than two centuries[98]; a yoke not only crushing, but dishonouring and withering the very soul of the people that fell its prey. The Mongol Tartars established a rule of systematic terror, devastation and wholesale massacre forming its institutions. Their numbers being scanty in proportion to their enormous conquests, they wanted to magnify them by a halo of consternation, and to thin, by wholesale slaughter, the populations which might rise in their rear. In their creations of desert they were, besides, led by the

[a] Andrei Bogolubski.—*Ed.*
[b] Vsevolod Bolshoye Gnezdo (Vsevolod of the Great Nest).—*Ed.*

same economical principle which has depopulated the Highlands of Scotland and the Campagna di Roma—the conversion of men into sheep, and of fertile lands and populous abodes into pasturage.

The Tartar yoke had already lasted a hundred years before Muscovy emerged from its obscurity.[99] To entertain discord among the Russian princes, and secure their servile submission, the Mongols had restored the dignity of the Grand Princedom. The strife among the Russian princes for this dignity was, as a modern author has it,

> "an abject strife, the strife of slaves, whose chief weapon was calumny, and who were always ready to denounce each other to their cruel rulers; wrangling for a degraded throne, whence they could not move but with plundering, parricidal hands, hands filled with gold, and stained with gore; which they dared not ascend without grovelling, nor retain but on their knees, prostrate and trembling beneath the scimitar of a Tartar, always ready to roll under his feet those servile crowns, and the heads by which they were worn."[a]

It was in this infamous strife that the Moscow branch won at last the race. In 1328 the crown of the Grand Princedom,[100] wrested from the branch of Tver[101] by dint of denunciation and assassination, was picked up at the feet of Usbeck Khan by Yury, the elder brother of Ivan Kalita. Ivan I Kalita, and Ivan III surnamed the Great, personate Muscovy rising by means of the Tartar yoke, and Muscovy getting an independent power by the disappearance of the Tartar rule. The whole policy of Muscovy, from its first entrance into the historical arena, is resumed in the history of these two individuals.

The policy of Ivan Kalita was simply this: to play the abject tool of the Khan, thus to borrow his power, and then to turn it round upon his princely rivals and his own subjects. To attain this end, he had to insinuate himself with the Tartars by dint of cynical adulation, by frequent journeys to the Golden Horde, by humble prayers for the hand of Mongol princesses, by a display of unabounded zeal for the Khan's interest, by the unscrupulous execution of his orders, by atrocious calumnies against his own kinsfolk, by blending in himself the characters of the Tartar's hangman, sycophant, and slave-in-chief. He perplexed the Khan by continuous revelations of secret plots. Whenever the branch of Tver betrayed a velleity of national independence, he hurried to the Horde to denounce it. Wherever he met with resistance, he introduced the Tartar to trample it down. But it was not sufficient

---

[a] Ph. Segur, *History of Russia and of Peter the Great*, pp. 213-14.—*Ed.*

to act a character; to make it acceptable, gold was required. Perpetual bribery of the Khan and his grandees was the only sure foundation upon which to raise his fabric of deception and usurpation. But how was the slave to get the money wherewith to bribe the master? He persuaded the Khan to instal him his tax-gatherer throughout all the Russian appanages. Once invested with this function, he extorted money under false pretences. The wealth accumulated by the dread held out of the Tartar name, he used to corrupt the Tartars themselves. By a bribe he induced the primate to transfer his episcopal seat from Vladimir to Moscow,[102] thus making the latter the capital of the empire, because the religious capital, and coupling the power of the Church with that of his throne. By a bribe he allured the boyards of the rival princes into treason against their chiefs, and attracted them to himself as their centre. By the joint influence of the Mahometan Tartar, the Greek Church, and the boyards, he unites the princes holding appanages into a crusade against the most dangerous of them, the prince of Tver[a]; and then having driven his recent allies by bold attempts at usurpation into resistance against himself, into a war for the public good, he draws not the sword but hurries to the Khan. By bribes and delusion again, he seduces him into assassinating his kindred rivals under the most cruel torments. It was the traditional policy of the Tartar to check the Russian princes the one by the other, to feed their dissensions, to cause their forces to equiponderate and to allow none to consolidate himself. Ivan Kalita converts the Khan into the tool by which he rids himself of his most dangerous competitors, and weighs down every obstacle to his own usurping march. He does not conquer the appanages, but surreptitiously turns the rights of the Tartar conquest to his exclusive profit. He secures the succession of his son[b] through the same means by which he had raised the Grand Princedom of Muscovy, that strange compound of princedom and serfdom. During his whole reign he swerves not once from the line of policy he had traced to himself; clinging to it with a tenacious firmness, and executing it with methodical boldness. Thus he becomes the founder of the Muscovite power, and characteristically his people call him Kalita—that is, the purse, because it was the purse and not the sword with which he cut his way. The very period of his reign witnesses the sudden growth of the Lithuanian power which dismembers the Russian appanages

[a] Alexander Mikhailovich.—*Ed.*
[b] Semyon Ivanovich the Proud.—*Ed.*

from the West, while the Tartar squeezes them into one mass from the East. Ivan, while he dared not repulse the one disgrace, seemed anxious to exaggerate the other. He was not to be seduced from following up his ends by the allurements of glory, the pangs of conscience, or the lassitude of humiliation. His whole system may be expressed in a few words: the Machiavellism of the usurping slave. His own weakness—his slavery—he turned into the mainspring of his strength.

The policy traced by Ivan I Kalita is that of his successors; they had only to enlarge the circle of its application. They followed it up laboriously, gradually, inflexibly. From Ivan I Kalita, we may, therefore, pass at once to Ivan III, surnamed the Great.

At the commencement of his reign (1462-1505) Ivan III was still a tributary to the Tartars; his authority was still contested by the princes holding appanages; Novgorod, the head of the Russian republics, reigned over the north of Russia; Poland-Lithuania was striving for the conquest of Muscovy; lastly, the Livonian knights were not yet disarmed. At the end of his reign we behold Ivan III seated on an independent throne, at his side the daughter of the last emperor of Byzantium,[a] at his feet Kasan, and the remnant of the Golden Horde flocking to his court; Novgorod and the other Russian republics enslaved—Lithuania diminished, and its king a tool in Ivan's hands—the Livonian knights vanquished. Astonished Europe, at the commencement of Ivan's reign, hardly aware of the existence of Muscovy, hemmed in between the Tartar and the Lithuanian, was dazzled by the sudden appearance of an immense empire on its eastern confines, and Sultan Bajazet himself, before whom Europe trembled, heard for the first time the haughty language of the Muscovite.[103] How, then, did Ivan accomplish these high deeds? Was he a hero? The Russian historians themselves show him up a confessed coward.

Let us shortly survey his principal contests, in the sequence in which he undertook and concluded them—his contests with the Tartars, with Novgorod, with the princes holding appanages, and lastly with Lithuania-Poland.

Ivan rescued Muscovy from the Tartar yoke, not by one bold stroke, but by the patient labour of about twenty years. He did not break the yoke, but disengaged himself by stealth. Its overthrow, accordingly, has more the look of the work of nature than the deed of man. When the Tartar monster expired at last, Ivan appeared at its deathbed like a physician, who prognosticated and

---

[a] Sophia (Zöe) Palaeologus.—*Ed.*

speculated on death rather than like a warrior who imparted it. The character of every people enlarges with its enfranchisement from a foreign yoke; that of Muscovy in the hands of Ivan seems to diminish. Compare only Spain in its struggles against the Arabs with Muscovy in its struggles against the Tartars.

At the period of Ivan's accession to the throne, the Golden Horde had long since been weakened, internally by fierce feuds, externally by the separation from them of the Nogay Tartars,[104] the eruption of Timour Tamerlane,[105] the rise of the Cossacks,[106] and the hostility of the Crimean Tartars.[107] Muscovy, on the contrary, by steadily pursuing the policy traced by Ivan Kalita, had grown to a mighty mass, crushed, but at the same time compactly united by the Tartar chain. The Khans, as if struck by a charm, had continued to remain instruments of Muscovite aggrandisement and concentration. By calculation they had added to the power of the Greek Church, which, in the hand of the Muscovite grand princes, proved the deadliest weapon against them.

In rising against the Horde, the Muscovite had not to invent but only to imitate the Tartars themselves. But Ivan did not rise. He humbly acknowledged himself a slave of the Golden Horde. By bribing a Tartar woman he seduced the Khan[a] into commanding the withdrawal from Muscovy of the Mongol residents. By similar imperceptible and surreptitious steps he duped the Khan into successive concessions, all ruinous to his sway. He thus did not conquer, but filch strength. He does not drive, but manoeuvre his enemy out of his strongholds. Still continuing to prostrate himself before the Khan's envoys, and to proclaim himself his tributary, he eludes the payment of the tribute under false pretences,[108] employing all the stratagems of a fugitive slave who dare not front his owner, but only steal out of his reach. At last the Mongol awakes from his torpor, and the hour of battle sounds. Ivan, trembling at the mere semblance of an armed encounter, attempts to hide himself behind his own fear, and to disarm the fury of his enemy by withdrawing the object upon which to wreak his vengeance. He is only saved by the intervention of the Crimean Tartars, his allies. Against a second invasion of the Horde, he ostentatiously gathers together such disproportionate forces that the mere rumour of their number parries the attack. At the third invasion, from the midst of 200,000 men, he absconds a disgraced deserter. Reluctantly dragged back, he attempts to haggle for conditions of slavery, and at last pouring into his army his own

---

[a] Ahmad.—*Ed.*

servile fear, he involves it in a general and disorderly flight. Muscovy was then anxiously awaiting its irretrievable doom, when it suddenly hears that by an attack on their capital made by the Crimean Khan,[a] the Golden Horde has been forced to withdraw, and has, on its retreat, been destroyed by the Cossacks and Nogay Tartars.[109] Thus defeat was turned into success, and Ivan had overthrown the Golden Horde, not by fighting it himself, but by challenging it through a feigned desire of combat into offensive movements, which exhausted its remnants of vitality and exposed it to the fatal blows of the tribes of its own race whom he had managed to turn into his allies. He caught one Tartar with another Tartar. As the immense danger he had himself summoned proved unable to betray him into one single trait of manhood, so his miraculous triumph did not infatuate him even for one moment. With cautious circumspection he dared not incorporate Kasan with Muscovy, but made it over to sovereigns belonging to the family of Menghi-Ghirei, his Crimean ally, to hold it, as it were, in trust for Muscovy. With the spoils of the vanquished Tartar, he enchained the victorious Tartar. But if too prudent to assume, with the eye-witnesses of his disgrace, the airs of a conqueror, this imposter did fully understand how the downfall of the Tartar empire must dazzle at a distance—with what halo of glory it would encircle him, and how it would facilitate a magnificent entry among the European powers. Accordingly he assumed abroad the theatrical attitude of the conqueror, and, indeed, succeeded in hiding under a mask of proud susceptibility and irritable haughtiness the obtrusiveness of the Mongol serf, who still remembered kissing the stirrup of the Khan's meanest envoy. He aped in more subdued tone the voice of his old masters, which terrified his soul. Some standing phrases of modern Russian diplomacy, such as the magnanimity, the wounded dignity of the master, are borrowed from the diplomatic instructions of Ivan III.

After the surrender of Kasan, he set out on a long-planned expedition against Novgorod, the head of the Russian republics. If the overthrow of the Tartar yoke was, in his eyes, the first condition of Muscovite greatness, the overthrow of Russian freedom was the second. As the republic of Vyatka had declared itself neutral between Muscovy and the Horde,[110] and the republic of Pskov, with its twelve cities, had shown symptoms of disaffection,[111] Ivan flattered the latter and affected to forget the former,

[a] Mengli-Ghirai.— *Ed.*

meanwhile concentrating all his forces against Novgorod the Great, with the doom of which he knew the fate of the rest of the Russian republics to be sealed. By the prospect of sharing in this rich booty, he drew after him the princes holding appanages, while he inveigled the boyards by working upon their blind hatred of Novgorodian democracy. Thus he contrived to march three armies upon Novgorod and to overwhelm it by disproportionate force.[112] But then, in order not to keep his word to the princes, not to forfeit his immutable *"Vos non vobis,"*[a] at the same time apprehensive, lest Novgorod should not yet have become digestible from the want of preparatory treatment, he thought fit to exhibit a sudden moderation; to content himself with a ransom and the acknowledgement of his suzerainty; but into the act of submission of the republic he smuggled some ambiguous words which made him its supreme judge and legislator. Then he fomented the dissensions between the patricians and plebeians raging as well in Novgorod as at Florence. Of some complaints of the plebeians he took occasion to introduce himself again into the city, to have its nobles, whom he knew to be hostile to himself, sent to Moscow loaded with chains, and to break the ancient law of the republic that

"none of its citizens should ever be tried or punished out of the limits of its own territory."[b]

From that moment he became supreme arbiter.

"Never," say the annalists, "never since Rurik had such an event happened; never had the grand princes of Kiev and Vladimir seen the Novgorodians come and submit to them as their judges. Ivan alone could reduce Novgorod to that degree of humiliation."[c]

Seven years were employed by Ivan to corrupt the republic by the exercise of his judicial authority.[113] Then, when he found its strength worn out, he thought the moment ripe for declaring himself. To doff his own mask of moderation, he wanted, on the part of Novgorod, a breach of the peace. As he had simulated calm endurance, so he simulated now a sudden burst of passion. Having bribed an envoy of the republic[d] to address him during a public audience with the name of sovereign, he claimed, at once,

[a] To have the use of you not to your advantage.—*Ed.*

[b] Ph. Segur, *History of Russia and of Peter the Great,* p. 132.—*Ed.*

[c] Ibid.—*Ed.*

[d] The envoys of the Republic were Nazar and Zakhar.—*Ed.*

all the rights of a despot—the self-annihilation of the republic.[a] As he had foreseen, Novgorod answered his usurpation with an insurrection, with a massacre of the nobles, and the surrender to Lithuania. Then this Muscovite contemporary of Machiavelli complained with the accent and the gesture of moral indignation.

"It was the Novgorodians who sought him for their sovereign; and when, yielding to their wishes, he had at last assumed that title, they disavowed him, they had the impudence to give him the lie formally in the face of all Russia; they had dared to shed the blood of their compatriots who remained faithful, and to betray heaven and the holy land of the Russians by calling into its limits a foreign religion and domination."[b]

As he had, after his first attack on Novgorod, openly allied himself with the plebeians against the patricians, so he now entered into a secret conspiracy with the patricians against the plebeians. He marched the united forces of Muscovy and its feudatories against the republic. On its refusal of unconditional submission, he recurred to the Tartar reminiscence of vanquishing by consternation. During a whole month he drew straighter and straighter around Novgorod a circle of fire and devastation, holding the sword all the while in suspense, and quietly watching till the republic, torn by factions, had run through all the phases of wild despair, sullen despondency, and resigned impotence. Novgorod was enslaved.[114] So were the other Russian republics. It is curious to see how Ivan caught the very moment of victory to forge weapons against the instruments of that victory. By the union of the domains of the Novgorod clergy with the crown, he secured himself the means of buying off the boyards, henceforth to be played off against the princes, and of endowing the followers of the boyards, henceforth to be played off against the boyards. It is still worthy of notice what exquisite pains were always taken by Muscovy as well as by modern Russia to execute republics. Novgorod and its colonies lead the dance; the republic of the Cossacks[115] follows; Poland closes it. To understand the Russian mastication of Poland, one must study the execution of Novgorod, lasting from 1478 till 1528.

Ivan seemed to have snatched the chain with which the Mongols crushed Muscovy only to bind with it the Russian republics. He seemed to enslave these republics only to republicanise the Russian princes. During twenty-three years he had recognised their

---

[a] The rest of this chapter was omitted in the edition of *Revelations...* prepared for publication by Eleanor Marx-Aveling.—*Ed.*

[b] Ph. Segur, *History of Russia and of Peter the Great,* p. 134.—*Ed.*

independence, borne with their petulance, and stooped even to their outrages. Now, by the overthrow of the Golden Horde, and by the downfall of the republics, he had grown so strong, and the princes, on the other hand, had grown so weak by the influence which the Muscovite wielded over their boyards, that the mere display of force on the part of Ivan sufficed to decide the contest. Still, at the outset, he did not depart from his method of circumspection. He singled out the prince of Tver,[a] the mightiest of the Russian feudatories, to be the first object of his operations. He began by driving him to the offensive and into an alliance with Lithuania, then denounced him as a traitor, then terrified him into successive concessions destructive of the prince's means of defence, then played upon the false position in which these concessions placed him with respect to his own subjects, and then left this system to work out its consequences. It ended in the abandonment of the contest by the prince of Tver and his flight into Lithuania. Tver united with Muscovy[116]—Ivan pushed forward with terrible vigour in the execution of his long-meditated plan. The other princes underwent their degradation into simple governors almost without resistance. There remained still two brothers of Ivan. The one was persuaded to renounce his appanage; the other, enticed to the Court and put off his guard by hypocritical demonstrations of fraternal love, was assassinated.[117]

We have now arrived at Ivan's last great contest—that with Lithuania. Beginning with his accession to the throne, it ended only some years before his death. During thirty years he confined this contest to a war of diplomacy, fomenting and improving the internal dissensions between Lithuania and Poland, drawing over disaffected Russian feudatories of Lithuania, and paralysing his foe by stirring up foes against him; Maximilian of Austria,[b] Mathias Corvinus of Hungary; and above all, Stephen,[c] the hospodar of Moldavia, whom he had attached to himself by marriage; lastly, Menghi-Ghirei, who proved as powerful a tool against Lithuania as against the Golden Horde. On the death of king Casimir,[d] however, and the accession of the weak Alexander,[e] when the thrones of Lithuania and Poland became temporarily disjoined;[118] when those two countries had crippled each other's

---

[a] Mikhail Borisovich.—*Ed.*
[b] Maximilian I.—*Ed.*
[c] Stephen III the Great.—*Ed.*
[d] Casimir IV Jagiello.—*Ed.*
[e] Alexander Jagiello.—*Ed.*

forces in mutual strife; when the Polish nobility, lost in its efforts to weaken the royal power on the one hand, and to degrade the kmetons[a] and citizens on the other, deserted Lithuania, and suffered it to recede before the simultaneous incursions of Stephen of Moldavia and of Menghi-Ghirei; when thus the weakness of Lithuania had become palpable; then Ivan understood the opportunity had ripened for putting out his strength, and that conditions exuberated for a successful explosion on his part. Still he did not go beyond a theatrical demonstration of war—the assemblage of overwhelming forces. As he had completely foreseen, the feigned desire of combat did now suffice to make Lithuania capitulate. He extorted the acknowledgement by treaty of the encroachments, surreptitiously made in king Casimir's time, and plagued Alexander at the same time with his alliance and with his daughter.[119] The alliance he employed to forbid Alexander the defence against attacks instigated by the father-in-law, and the daughter to kindle a religious war between the intolerant Catholic king and his persecuted subjects of the Greek confession. Amidst this turmoil he ventured at last to draw the sword, and seized the Russian appanages under Lithuanian sway as far as Kiev and Smolensk.[120]

The Greek religion generally proved one of his most powerful means of action. But to lay claim to the inheritance of Byzantium, to hide the stigma of Mongolian serfdom under the mantle of the Porphyrogeniti, to link the upstart throne of Muscovy to the glorious empire of St. Vladimir,[b] to give in his own person a new temporal head to the Greek Church, whom of all the world should Ivan single out? The Roman Pope. At the Pope's court there dwelt the last princess of Byzantium.[c] From the Pope Ivan embezzled her by taking an oath to apostatise—an oath which he ordered his own primate[d] to release him from.[121]

A simple substitution of names and dates will prove to evidence that between the policy of Ivan III, and that of modern Russia, there exists not similarity but sameness. Ivan III, on his part, did but perfect the traditionary policy of Muscovy, bequeathed by Ivan I, Kalita. Ivan Kalita, the Mongolian slave, acquired greatness by wielding the power of his greatest foe, the Tartar, against his minor foes, the Russian princes. He could not wield the power of the Tartar but under false pretences. Forced to dissemble before

---

[a] Peasants.— *Ed.*

[b] Vladimir Svyatoslavich.— *Ed.*

[c] Sophia (Zöe) Palaeologus.— *Ed.*

[d] Philipp I.— *Ed.*

his masters the strength he really gathered, he had to dazzle his fellow-serfs with a power he did not own. To solve his problem he had to elaborate all the *ruses* of the most abject slavery into a system, and to execute that system with the patient labour of the slave. Open force itself could enter as an intrigue only into a system of intrigues, corruption and underground usurpation. He could not strike before he had poisoned. Singleness of purpose became with him duplicity of action. To encroach by the fraudulent use of a hostile power, to weaken that power by the very act of using it, and to overthrow it at last by the effects produced through its own instrumentality—this policy was inspired to Ivan Kalita by the peculiar character both of the ruling and the serving race. His policy remained still the policy of Ivan III. It is yet the policy of Peter the Great, and of modern Russia, whatever changes of name, seat, and character the hostile power used may have undergone. Peter the Great is indeed the inventor of modern Russian policy, but he became so only by divesting the old Muscovite method of encroachment of its merely local character and its accidental admixtures, by distilling it into an abstract formula, by generalising its purpose, and exalting its object from the overthrow of certain given limits of power to the aspiration of unlimited power. He metamorphosed Muscovy into modern Russia by the generalisation of its system, not by the mere addition of some provinces.

To resume. It is in the terrible and abject school of Mongolian slavery that Muscovy was nursed and grew up. It gathered strength only by becoming a *virtuoso* in the craft of serfdom. Even when emancipated, Muscovy continued to perform its traditional part of the slave as master. At length Peter the Great coupled the political craft of the Mongol slave with the proud aspiration of the Mongol master, to whom Genghis Khan had, by will, bequeathed his conquest of the earth.

Chapter V[122]

One feature characteristic of the Slavonic race must strike every observer. Almost everywhere it confined itself to an inland country, leaving the sea-borders to non-Slavonic tribes. Finno-Tartaric tribes held the shores of the Black Sea, Lithuanians and Fins those of the Baltic and White Sea. Wherever they touched the sea-board, as in the Adriatic and part of the Baltic, the Slavonians had soon to submit to foreign rule. The Russian people shared this common fate of the Slavonian race. Their home, at the time they first appear in history, was the country about the sources and upper course of the Volga and its tributaries, the Dnieper, Don and Northern Dvina. Nowhere did their territory touch the sea except at the extremity of the Gulf of Finland. Nor had they, before Peter the Great, proved able to conquer any maritime outlet beside that of the White Sea, which, during three-fourths of the year, is itself enchained and immovable. The spot where Petersburg now stands had been for a thousand years past contested ground between Fins, Swedes, and Russians. All the remaining extent of coast from Polangen, near Memel, to Tornea, the whole coast of the Black Sea, from Akerman to Redout Kaleh, has been conquered later on. And, as if to witness the anti-maritime peculiarity of the Slavonic race, of all this line of coast, no portion of the Baltic coast has really adopted Russian nationality. Nor has the Circassian and Mingrelian east coast of the Black Sea. It is only the coast of the White Sea, as far as it was worth cultivating, some portion of the northern coast of the Black Sea, and part of the coast of the Sea of Azof, that have really been peopled with Russian inhabitants, who, however, despite the new circumstances in which they are placed, still refrain from taking to the sea, and obstinately stick to the land-lopers' traditions of their ancestors.

From the very outset, Peter the Great broke through all the traditions of the Slavonic race. "It is water that Russia wants."[a] These words he addressed as a rebuke to Prince Cantemir are inscribed on the title-page of his life. The conquest of the Sea of Azof was aimed at in his first war with Turkey, the conquest of the Baltic in his war against Sweden, the conquest of the Black Sea in his second war against the Porte, and the conquest of the Caspian Sea in his fraudulent intervention in Persia.[123] For a system of local encroachment, land was sufficient, for a system of universal aggression, water had become indispensable. It was but by the conversion of Muscovy from a country wholly of land into a sea-bordering empire, that the traditional limits of the Muscovite policy could be superseded and merged into that bold synthesis which, blending the encroaching method of the Mongol slave with the world-conquering tendencies of the Mongol master, forms the life-spring of modern Russian diplomacy.

It has been said that no great nation has ever existed, or been able to exist, in such an inland position as that of the original empire of Peter the Great; that none has ever submitted thus to see its coasts and the mouths of its rivers torn away from it; that Russia could no more leave the mouth of the Neva, the natural outlet for the produce of Northern Russia, in the hands of the Swedes, than the mouths of the Don, Dnieper, and Bug, and the Straits of Kertch, in the hands of nomadic and plundering Tartars; that the Baltic provinces, from their very geographical configuration, are naturally a corollary to whichever nation holds the country behind them; that, in one word, Peter, in this quarter, at least, but took hold of what was absolutely necessary for the natural development of his country. From this point of view, Peter the Great intended, by his war against Sweden, only rearing a Russian Liverpool, and endowing it with its indispensable strip of coast.

But then, one great fact is slighted over, the *tour de force* by which he transferred the capital of the Empire from the inland centre to the maritime extremity, the characteristic boldness with which he erected the new capital on the first strip of Baltic coast he conquered, almost within gunshot of the frontier, thus deliberately giving his dominions an *eccentric centre.* To transfer the throne of the Czars from Moscow to Petersburg was to place it in

[a] Ph. Segur, *History of Russia and of Peter the Great,* p. 312.—*Ed.*

a position where it could not be safe, even from insult, until the whole coast from Libau to Tornea was subdued—a work not completed till 1809, by the conquest of Finland.

"St. Petersburg is the window from which Russia can overlook Europe," said Algarotti.[a]

It was from the first a defiance to the Europeans, an incentive to further conquest to the Russians. The fortifications in our own days of Russian Poland are only a further step in the execution of the same idea. Modlin, Warsaw, Ivangorod, are more than citadels to keep a rebellious country in check. They are the same menace to the west which Petersburg, in its immediate bearing, was a hundred years ago to the north. They are to transform Russia into Panslavonia, as the Baltic provinces were to transform Muscovy into Russia.

Petersburg, the *eccentric centre* of the empire, pointed at once at a periphery still to be drawn.

It is, then, not the mere conquest of the Baltic provinces which separates the policy of Peter the Great from that of his ancestors, but it is the transfer of the capital which reveals the true meaning of his Baltic conquests. Petersburg was not like Muscovy, the centre of a race, but the seat of a government; not the slow work of a people, but the instantaneous creation of a man; not the medium from which the peculiarities of an inland people radiate, but the maritime extremity where they are lost; not the traditionary nucleus of a national development, but the deliberately chosen abode of a cosmopolitan intrigue. By the transfer of the capital, Peter cut off the natural ligaments which bound up the encroaching system of the old Muscovite Czars with the natural abilities and aspirations of the great Russian race. By planting his capital on the margin of a sea, he put to open defiance the anti-maritime instincts of that race, and degraded it to a mere weight in his political mechanism. Since the 16th century, Muscovy had made no important acquisitions but on the side of Siberia, and to the 16th century the dubious conquests made towards the West and the South were only brought about by direct agency of the East. By the transfer of the capital, Peter proclaimed that he, on the contrary, intended working on the East and the immediately neighbouring countries through the agency of the West. If the agency through the East was narrowly circumscribed by the stationary character and the limited relations of Asiatic peoples,

[a] *Lettres du comte Algarotti sur la Russie,* London, 1769, p. 64.—*Ed.*

the agency through the West became at once illimited and universal from the movable character and the all-sided relations of Western Europe. The transfer of the capital denoted this intended change of agency, which the conquest of the Baltic provinces afforded the means of achieving, by securing at once to Russia the supremacy among the neighbouring Northern States; by putting it into immediate and constant contact with all points of Europe; by laying the basis of a material bond with the Maritime Powers, which by this conquest became dependent on Russia for their naval stores; a dependence not existing as long as Muscovy, the country that produced the great bulk of the naval stores, had got no outlets of its own, while Sweden, the power that held these outlets, had not got the country lying behind them.

If the Muscovite Czars, who worked their encroachments by the agency principally of the Tartar Khans, were obliged to *tartarise* Muscovy, Peter the Great, who resolved upon working through the agency of the West, was obliged to *civilise* Russia. In grasping upon the Baltic provinces, he seized at once the tools necessary for this process. They afforded him not only the diplomatists and the generals, the brains with which to execute his system of political and military action on the West. They yielded him, at the same time, a crop of bureaucrats, schoolmasters, and drill-sergeants, who were to drill Russians into that varnish of civilisation that adapts them to the technical appliances of the Western peoples, without imbuing them with their ideas.

Neither the Sea of Azof, nor the Black Sea, nor the Caspian Sea, could open to Peter this direct passage to Europe. Besides, during his lifetime still Taganrog, Azof, the Black Sea, with its new-formed Russian fleets, ports, and dockyards, were again abandoned or given up to the Turk. The Persian conquest, too, proved a premature enterprise. Of the four wars which fill the military life of Peter the Great, his first war, that against Turkey, the fruits of which were lost in a second Turkish war, continued in one respect the traditionary struggle with the Tartars. In another respect, it was but the prelude to the war against Sweden, of which the second Turkish war forms an episode and the Persian war an epilogue. Thus the war against Sweden lasting during 21 years, almost absorbs the military life of Peter the Great. Whether we consider its purpose, its results, or its endurance, we may justly call it *the* war of Peter the Great. His whole creation hinges upon the conquest of the Baltic coast.

Now, suppose we were altogether ignorant of the details of his operations, military and diplomatic. The mere fact that the conversion of Muscovy into Russia was brought about by its transformation from a half-Asiatic inland country into the paramount maritime power of the Baltic, would it not enforce upon us the conclusion that England, the greatest maritime power of that epoch, a maritime power lying, too, at the very gates of the Baltic, where, since the middle of the 17th century, she had maintained the attitude of supreme arbiter; that England must have had her hand in this great change, that she must have proved the main prop, or the main impediment of the plans of Peter the Great, that during the long protracted and deadly struggle between Sweden and Russia, she must have turned the balance, that if we do not find her straining every nerve in order to save the Swede, we may be sure of her having employed all the means at her disposal for furthering the Muscovite? And yet, in what is commonly called history, England does hardly appear on the plan of this grand drama, and is represented as a spectator rather than as an actor. Real history will show that the Khans of the Golden Horde were no more instrumental in realising the plans of Ivan III. and his predecessors than the rulers of England were in realising the plans of Peter I. and his successors.

The pamphlets which we have reprinted, written as they were by English contemporaries of Peter the Great, are far from concurring in the common delusions of later historians. They emphatically denounce England as the mightiest tool of Russia. The same position is taken up by the pamphlet, of which we shall now give a short analysis, and with which we shall conclude the introduction to the diplomatic revelations. It is entitled, "*Truth is but Truth as it is timed,* or our *Ministry's present measures against the Muscovite vindicated, etc., etc.* Humbly dedicated to the House of C., London, 1719."

The former pamphlets we have reprinted,[a] were written at, or shortly after, the time when, to use the words of a modern admirer of Russia,[b]

"Peter traversed the Baltic Sea as master at the head of the combined squadrons of all the northern Powers," England included, "which gloried in sailing under his orders."[c]

In 1719, however, when *Truth is but Truth* was published, the face of affairs seemed altogether changed. Charles XII was dead, and the English Government now pretended to side with Sweden,

[a] See this volume, pp. 43-55, 65-73.—*Ed.*
[b] Ph. Segur.—*Ed.*
[c] Ph. Segur, *History of Russia...,* p. 304.—*Ed.*

and to wage war against Russia. There are other circumstances connected with this anonymous pamphlet, which claim particular notice. It purports to be an extract from a relation, which, on his return from Muscovy, in August 1715, its author,[a] by order of George I., drew up and handed over to Viscount Townshend, then Secretary of State.

"It happens," says he, "to be an advantage that at present I may own to have been the first so happy to foresee, or honest to forewarn our Court here, of the absolute necessity of our then breaking with the Czar, and shutting him out again of the Baltic." "My relation discovered his aim as to other states, and even to the German empire, to which, although an inland power, he had offered to annex Livonia as an Electorate, so that he could but be admitted as an elector. It drew attention to the Czar's then contemplated assumption of the title of Autocrator.[124] Being head of the Greek Church he would be owned by the other potentates as head of the Greek Empire. I am not to say how reluctant we would be to acknowledge that title, since we have already made an ambassador[b] treat him with the title of Imperial Majesty, which the Swede has never yet condescended to."

For some time attached to the British Embassy in Muscovy, our author, as he states, was later on

"*dismissed the service, because the Czar desired it,*" having made sure that "I had given our Court such light into his affairs as is contained in this paper; for which I beg leave to appeal to the King, and to vouch the Viscount Townshend, who heard His Majesty give that vindication." And yet, notwithstanding all this, "I have been for these five years past kept soliciting for a very long arrear still due, and whereof I contracted the greatest part in executing a commission from Her late Majesty.[c]"

The anti-Muscovite attitude, suddenly assumed by the Stanhope Cabinet, our author looks to in rather a sceptic mood.

"I do not pretend to foreclose, by this paper, the Ministry of that applause due to them from the public, when they shall satisfy us as to what the motives were, which made them, till but yesterday, straiten the Swede in everything, although then our ally as much as now. Or strengthen by all the ways they could, the Czar, although under no tie, but barely that of amity with Great Britain.... At the minute I write this I learn that the gentleman, who brought the Muscovites, not yet three years ago, as a royal navy, not under our protection, on their first appearance in the Baltic, is again authorised by the persons now in power, to give the Czar a second meeting in these seas. For what reason, or to what good end?"

The gentleman hinted at is Admiral Norris, whose Baltic campaign against Peter I. seems, indeed, to be the original pattern

---

[a] G. Mackenzie.—*Ed.*
[b] M. Withworth.—*Ed.*
[c] Anne.—*Ed.*

upon which the recent naval campaigns of Admirals Napier and Dundas were cut out.[125]

The restoration to Sweden of the Baltic provinces is required by the commercial as well as the political interest of Great Britain. Such is the pith of our author's argument:

"Trade is become the very life of our State; and what food is to life naval stores are to a fleet. The whole trade we drive with all the other nations of the earth, at best, is but lucrative; this, of the north, is indispensably needful, and may not be improperly termed the *sacra embole*[a] of Great Britain, as being its chiefest foreign vent, for the support of all our trade, and our safety at home. As woollen manufactures and minerals are the staple commodities of Great Britain, so are likewise naval stores those of Muscovy, as also of all those very provinces in the Baltic, which the Czar has so lately wrested from the crown of Sweden. Since those provinces have been in the Czar's possession, Pernau is entirely waste. At Revel we have not one British merchant left, and all the trade which was formerly at Narva, is now brought to Petersburg.... The Swede could never possibly engross the trade of our subjects, because those seaports in his hands were but so many thoroughfares from whence these commodities were uttered, the places of their produce or manufacture lying behind those ports, in the dominions of the Czar. But, if left to the Czar, these Baltic ports are no more thoroughfares, but peculiar magazines from the inland countries of the Czar's own dominions. Having already Archangel in the White Sea, to leave him but any seaport in the Baltic were to put no less in his hands than the *two keys of the general magazines of all the naval stores of Europe:* it being known, that Danes, Swedes, Poles and Prussians have but single and distinct branches of those commodities in their several dominions." If the Czar should thus engross "the supply of what we cannot do without, where then is our fleet? Or, indeed, where is the security for all our trade to any part of the earth besides?"

If then, the interest of British commerce requires to exclude the Czar from the Baltic, "the interest of our State ought to be no less a spur to quicken us to that attempt. By the interest of our State I would be understood to mean neither the party measures of a Ministry, nor any foreign motives of a court, but precisely what is, and ever must be, the immediate concern, either for the safety, ease, dignity, or emolument of the Crown, as well as the common weal of Great Britain." With respect to the Baltic, it has "from the earliest period of our naval power" always been considered a fundamental interest of our State; first, to prevent the rise there of any new maritime Power; and, secondly, to maintain the balance of power between Denmark and Sweden.

"One instance of the wisdom and foresight of our *then truly British statesmen* is the peace at Stolbowa, in the year 1617.[126] James the First was the mediator of that treaty, by which the Muscovite was obliged to give up all the provinces which he then was possessed of in the Baltic, and to be barely an inland power on this side of Europe."

The same policy of preventing a new maritime power from starting in the Baltic was acted upon by Sweden and Denmark.

"Who knows not that the Emperor's[b] attempt to get a seaport in Pomerania

[a] Sacred key.—*Ed.*

[b] Ferdinand II.—*Ed.*

weighed no less with the great Gustavus,[a] than any other motive for carrying his arms even into the bowels of the house of Austria? What befell, at the times of Charles Gustavus,[b] the crown of Poland itself, who, besides it being in those days by far the mightiest of any of the Northern powers, had then a long stretch of coast on, and some ports in the Baltic? The Danes, though then in alliance with Poland, would never allow them, even for their assistance against the Swedes, to have a fleet in the Baltic, but destroyed the Polish ships wherever they could meet them."

As to the maintenance of the balance of power between the established Maritime States of the Baltic, the tradition of British policy is no less clear.

When the Swedish power gave us some uneasiness there by threatening to crush Denmark, the honour of our country was kept up by retrieving the then inequality of the balance of power.

"The Commonwealth of England sent in a squadron to the Baltic, which brought on the treaty of Roskild (1658), afterwards confirmed at Copenhagen (1660).[127] The fire of straw kindled by the Danes in the times of King William III. was as speedily quenched by George Rooke in the treaty of Travendahl."[128]

Such was the hereditary British policy.

"It never entered into the mind of the politicians of those times, in order to bring the scale again to rights, to find out the happy *expedient of raising a third naval Power* for framing a juster balance in the Baltic.... Who has taken this counsel against Tyre, the crowning city, whose merchants are princes, whose traffickers are the honourables of the earth?[c] *Ego autem neminem nomino, quare irasci mihi nemo poterit, nisi qui ante de se voluerit confiteri.*[d] Posterity will be under some difficulty to believe that this could be the *work of any of the persons now in power* ... that *we* have opened *St. Petersburg to the Czar solely at our own expense, and without any risk to him....*"

The safest line of policy would be to return to the treaty of Stolbowa, and to suffer the Muscovite no longer "to nestle in the Baltic." Yet, it may be said, that in "the present state of affairs" it would be "difficult to retrieve the advantage we have lost by not curbing, when it was more easy, the growth of the Muscovite power."

A middle course may be thought more convenient.

"If we should find it consistent with the welfare of our State, that the Muscovite have an inlet into the Baltic, as having, of all the princes of Europe, a country that can be made most beneficial to its prince, by uttering its produce to foreign markets. In this case, it were but reasonable to expect on the other hand, that in return for our complying so far with his interest, for the improvement of his country, His Czarish Majesty, on his part, should demand nothing that may tend to the disturbance of another; and, therefore, contenting himself with ships of trade, should demand none of war."

"We should thus preclude his hopes of being ever more than an inland power," but "obviate every objection of using the Czar worse than any Sovereign Prince may expect. I shall not for this give an instance of a Republic of Genoa, or another

---

[a] Gustavus II Adolphus.— *Ed.*

[b] Charles X (Gustavus).— *Ed.*

[c] Isaiah 23:8.— *Ed.*

[d] "But I name no one, so that no one will be angry with me, other than he who might refuse to express himself openly before the event." Cicero, *Pro lege Manilia,* ch. XIII.— *Ed.*

in the Baltic itself, of the Duke of Courland; but will assign Poland and Prussia, who, though both now crowned heads, have ever contented themselves with the freedom of an open traffic, without insisting on a fleet. Or the treaty of Falczin, between the Turk[a] and Muscovite, by which Peter was forced not only to restore Asof, and to part with all his men-of-war in those parts, but also to content himself with the bare freedom of traffic in the Black Sea.[129] Even an inlet in the Baltic for trade is much beyond what he could morally have promised himself not yet so long ago on the issue of his war with Sweden."

If the Czar refuse to agree to such "a healing temperament," we shall have "nothing to regret, but the time we lost to exert all the means that Heaven has made us master of, to reduce him to a peace advantageous to Great Britain."

War would become inevitable. In that case, "it ought no less to animate our Ministry to pursue their present measures, than fire with indignation the breast of every honest Briton, that a Czar of Muscovy, who owes his naval skill to our instructions, and his grandeur to our forbearance, should so soon deny to Great Britain the terms which so few years ago he was fain to take up with from the Sublime Porte."

"'Tis every way our interest to have the Swede restored to those provinces which the Muscovite has wrested from that crown in the Baltic. *Great Britain can no longer hold the balance in that sea,*" since she "*has raised the Muscovite to be a maritime Power there....* Had we performed the articles of our alliance made by King William with the crown of Sweden, that gallant nation would ever have been a bar strong enough against the Czar coming into the Baltic.... Time must confirm us, that the Muscovite's *expulsion from the Baltic* is *now* the principal end of our Ministry."

---

[a] Sultan Ahmed III.—*Ed.*

Karl Marx

[REVOLUTION IN SPAIN]

The news brought by the *Asia* yesterday, though later by three days than our previous advices, contains nothing to indicate a speedy conclusion of the civil war in Spain. O'Donnell's coup d'état, although victorious at Madrid,[130] cannot yet be said to have finally succeeded. The French *Moniteur,* which at first put down the insurrection at Barcelona as a mere riot,[a] is now obliged to confess that

"the conflict there was very keen, but that the success of the Queen's[b] troops may be considered as secured."[c]

According to the version of that official journal the combat at Barcelona lasted from 5 o'clock in the afternoon of July 18 till the same hour on the 21st—exactly three days—when the "insurgents" are said to have been dislodged from their quarters, and fled into the country, pursued by cavalry. It is, however, averred that the insurgents still hold several towns in Catalonia, including Gerona, Junquera, and some smaller places. It also appears that Murcia, Valencia and Seville have made their *pronunciamientos*[d] against the coup d'état; that a battalion of the garrison of Pampeluna, directed by the Governor of that town on Soria, had pronounced against the Government on the road, and marched to join the insurrection at Saragossa; and lastly that at Saragossa,

---

[a] *Le Moniteur universel,* No. 203, July 21, 1856, "Partie non officielle":—*Ed.*
[b] Isabella II.—*Ed.*
[c] *Le Moniteur universel,* No. 206, July 24, 1856, "Partie non officielle".—*Ed.*
[d] Mutinies.—*Ed.*

from the beginning the acknowledged center of resistance, Gen. Falcon had passed in review 16,000 soldiers of the line, reinforced by 15,000 militia and peasants from the environs.

At all events, the French Government considers the "insurrection" in Spain as not quelled, and Bonaparte, far from contenting himself with the sending of a batch of battalions to line the frontier, has ordered one brigade to advance to the Bidassoa, which brigade is being completed to a division by reinforcements from Montpellier and Toulouse. It seems, also, that a second division has been detached immediately from the army of Lyons, according to orders sent direct from Plombières on the 23d ult., and is now marching toward the Pyrenees, where, by this time, there is assembled a full *corps d'observation* of 25,000 men. Should the resistance to the O'Donnell government be able to hold its ground; should it prove formidable enough to inveigle Bonaparte into an armed invasion of the Peninsula, then the coup d'état of Madrid may have given the signal for the downfall of the coup d'état of Paris.[131]

If we consider the general plot and the *dramatis personae,* this Spanish conspiracy of 1856 appears as the simple revival of the similar attempt of 1843,[132] with some slight alterations of course. Then, as now, Isabella at Madrid and Christina at Paris; Louis Philippe, instead of Louis Bonaparte, directing the movement from the Tuileries; on the one side, Espartero and his *Ayacuchos*[133]; on the other, O'Donnell, Serrano, Concha, with Narvaez then in the proscenium, now in the background. In 1843, Louis Philippe sent two millions of gold by land and Narvaez and his friends by sea, the compact of the Spanish marriages being settled between himself and Madame Muñoz.[134] The complicity of Bonaparte in the Spanish coup d'état—who has, perhaps, settled the marriage of his cousin Prince Napoleon with a Mdlle. Muñoz, or who, at all events, must continue his mission of mimicking his uncle[a]—that complicity is not only indicated by the denunciations hurled by the *Moniteur* for the last two months at the communist conspiracies in Castile and Navarre, by the behavior before, during and after the coup d'état of M. de Turgot, the French Embassador at Madrid, the same man who was the Foreign Minister of Bonaparte during his own coup d'état; by the Duke of Alba, Bonaparte's brother-in-law, turning up as the President of the new *ayuntamiento*[b] at Madrid, immediately after the victory of

---

[a] Napoleon I.—*Ed.*
[b] Municipal Council.—*Ed.*

O'Donnell; by Ros de Olano, an old member of the French party, being the first man offered a place in O'Donnell's Ministry; and by Narvaez being dispatched to Bayonne by Bonaparte as soon as the first news of the affair reached Paris. That complicity was suggested beforehand by the forwarding of large quantities of ammunition from Bordeaux to Bayonne a fortnight in advance of the actual crisis at Madrid. Above all, it is suggested by the plan of operations followed by O'Donnell in his razzia against the people of that city. At the very outset he announced that he would not shrink from blowing up Madrid, and during the fighting he acted up to his word. Now, although a daring fellow, O'Donnell has never ventured upon a bold step without securing a safe retreat. Like his notorious uncle,[a] the hero of treason, he never burnt the bridge when he passed the Rubicon. The organ of combativeness is singularly checked in the O'Donnells by the organs of cautiousness and secretiveness. It is plain that any general who should hold forth the threat of laying the capital in ashes, and fail in his attempt, would forfeit his head. How then did O'Donnell venture upon such delicate ground? The secret is betrayed by the *Journal des Débats,* the special organ of Queen Christina.

"O'Donnell expected a great battle, and at the most a victory hotly disputed. Into his provisions there entered the possibility of defeat. If such a misfortune had happened, the Marshal would have abandoned Madrid with the rest of his army, escorting the Queen, and turning toward the northern provinces, with a view to approach the French frontier."[b]

Does not all this look as if he had laid his plan with Bonaparte? Exactly the same plan had been settled between Louis Philippe and Narvaez in 1843, which, again, was copied from the secret convention between Louis XVIII and Ferdinand VII, in 1823.[135]

This plausible parallel between the Spanish conspiracies of 1843 and 1856 once admitted, there are still sufficiently distinct features in the two movements to indicate the immense strides made by the Spanish people within so brief an epoch. These features are: the political character of the last struggle at Madrid; its military importance; and finally, the respective position of Espartero and O'Donnell in 1856 compared with those of Espartero and Narvaez in 1843. In 1843 all parties had become tired of Espartero. To get rid of him a powerful coalition was formed between the *Moderados* and *Progresistas.*[136] Revolutionary juntas springing up like mush-

[a] Enrique Jose O'Donnell.—*Ed.*

[b] *Journal des Débats,* July 22, 1856, "France".—*Ed.*

rooms in all the towns, paved the way for Narvaez and his retainers. In 1856 we have not only the court and army on the one side against the people on the other, but within the ranks of the people we have the same divisions as in the rest of Western Europe. On the 13th of July the Ministry of Espartero offered its forced resignation; in the night of the 13th and 14th the Cabinet of O'Donnell was constituted; on the morning of the 14th the rumor spread that O'Donnell, charged with the formation of a cabinet, had invited Ryos y Rosas, the ill-omened Minister of the bloody days of July, 1854,[137] to join him. At 11 a.m. the *Gaceta* confirmed the rumor. Then the Cortes assembled, 93 deputies being present. According to the rules of that body, 20 members suffice to call a meeting, and 50 to form a quorum. Besides, the Cortes had not been formally prorogued. Gen. Infante, the President, could not but comply with the universal wish to hold a regular sitting. A proposition was submitted to the effect that the new Cabinet did not enjoy the confidence of the Cortes, and that her Majesty[a] should be informed of this resolution. At the same time, the Cortes summoned the National Guard to be ready for action. Their Committee, bearing the resolution of want of confidence, went to the Queen, escorted by a detachment of National Militia. While endeavoring to enter the palace they were driven back by the troops of the line, who fired upon them and their escort. This incident gave the signal for the insurrection. The order to commence the building of barricades was given at 7 in the evening by the Cortes, whose meeting was dispersed immediately afterward by the troops of O'Donnell. The battle commenced the same night, only one battalion of the National Militia joining the Royal troops. It should be noted that as early as the morning of the 13th, Señor Escosura, the Esparterist Minister of the Interior, had telegraphed to Barcelona and Saragossa that a coup d'état was at hand, and that they must prepare to resist it. At the head of the Madrid insurgents were Señor Madoz and Gen. Valdez, the brother of Escosura. In short, there can be no doubt that the resistance to the coup d'état originated with the Esparterists, the citizens and Liberals in general. While they, with the militia, engaged the line across Madrid from east to west, the workmen under Pucheta occupied the south and part of the north side of the town.

On the morning of the 15th, O'Donnell took the initiative. Even

---

[a] Isabella II.—*Ed.*

by the partial testimony of the *Débats*,[a] O'Donnell obtained no marked advantage during the first half of the day. Suddenly, at about 1 o'clock, without any perceptible reason, the ranks of the National Militia were broken; at 2 o'clock they were still more thinned, and at 6 o'clock they had completely disappeared from the scene of action, leaving the whole brunt of the battle to be borne by the workmen, who fought it out till 4 in the afternoon of the 16th. Thus there were, in these three days of carnage, two distinct battles—the one of the Liberal Militia of the middle class, supported by the workmen against the army, and the other of the army against the workmen deserted by the militia. As Heine has it:

> "It is an old story, but is always new."[b]

Espartero deserts the Cortes; the Cortes desert the leaders of the National Guard; the leaders desert their men, and the men desert the people. On the 15th, however, the Cortes assembled again, when Espartero appeared for a moment. He was reminded by Señor Assensio and other members of his reiterated protestations to draw his grand sword of Luchana[138] on the first day when the liberty of the country should be endangered. Espartero called Heaven to witness his unswerving patriotism, and when he left, it was fully expected that he would soon be seen at the head of the insurrection. Instead of this, he went to the house of Gen. Gurrea, where he buried himself in a bomb-proof cellar, à la Palafox, and was heard of no more. The commandants of the militia, who, on the evening before, had employed every means to excite the militiamen to take up arms, now proved as eager to retire to their private houses. At 2 1/2 p.m. Gen. Valdez, who for some hours had usurped the command of the militia, convoked the soldiers under his direct command on the Plaza Mayor, and told them that the man who naturally ought to be at their head would not come forward, and that consequently everybody was at liberty to withdraw. Hereupon the National Guards rushed to their homes and hastened to get rid of their uniforms and hide their arms. Such is the substance of the account furnished by one well-informed authority. Another gives as the reason for this sudden act of submission to the conspiracy, that it was considered that the triumph of the National Guard was likely to entail the ruin of the throne and the absolute preponderance of the Republican

---

[a] *Journal des Débats*, July 22, 1856, "France".—*Ed.*

[b] H. Heine, "Lyrisches Intermezzo".—*Ed.*

Democracy. The *Presse* of Paris also gives us to understand that Marshal Espartero, seeing the turn given to things in the Congress by the Democrats, did not wish to sacrifice the throne, or launch into the hazards of anarchy and civil war, and in consequence did all he could to produce submission to O'Donnell.

It is true that the details as to the time, circumstances, and break-down of the resistance to the coup d'état, are given differently by different writers; but all agree on the one principal point, that Espartero deserted the Cortes, the Cortes the leaders, the leaders the middle class, and that class the people. This furnishes a new illustration of the character of most of the European struggles of 1848-49, and of those hereafter to take place in the Western portion of that continent. On the one hand there are modern industry and trade, the natural chiefs of which, the middle classes, are averse to the military despotism; on the other hand, when they begin the battle against this same despotism, in step the workmen themselves, the product of the modern organization of labor, to claim their due share of the result of victory. Frightened by the consequences of an alliance thus imposed on their unwilling shoulders, the middle classes shrink back again under the protecting batteries of the hated despotism. This is the secret of the standing armies of Europe, which otherwise will be incomprehensible to the future historian. The middle classes of Europe are thus made to understand that they must either surrender to a political power which they detest, and renounce the advantages of modern industry and trade, and the social relations based upon them, or forego the privileges which the modern organization of the productive powers of society, in its primary phase, has vested in an exclusive class. That this lesson should be taught even from Spain is something equally striking and unexpected.

Written on July 25, 1856

First published in the *New-York Daily Tribune*, No. 4775, August 8, 1856 as a leading article; reprinted in the *New-York Semi-Weekly Tribune*, No. 1170, August 12, 1856 and the *New-York Weekly Tribune*, No. 779, August 16, 1856 under the title "The Spanish Coup d'État"

Reproduced from the *New-York Daily Tribune*

Karl Marx

[REVOLUTION IN SPAIN]

Saragossa surrendered on August 1, at 1:30 p.m., and thus vanished the last center of resistance to the Spanish counter-revolution. There was, in a military point of view, little chance of success after the defeats at Madrid and Barcelona, the feebleness of the insurrectionary diversion in Andalusia, and the converging advance of overwhelming forces from the Basque provinces, Navarre, Catalonia, Valencia and Castile. Whatever chance there might be was paralyzed by the circumstance that it was Espartero's old aide-de-camp, General Falcon, who directed the forces of resistance; that "Espartero and Liberty" was given as the battlecry; and that the population of Saragossa had become aware of Espartero's incommensurably ridiculous fiasco at Madrid.[139] Besides, there were direct orders from Espartero's headquarters to his bottle-holders at Saragossa, that they were to put an end to all resistance, as will be seen from the following extract from the *Journal de Madrid* of July 29:

> "One of the Esparterist ex-Ministers took part in the negotiations going on between General Dulce and the authorities of Saragossa, and the Esparterist member of the Cortes, Juan Martinez Alonso, accepted the mission of informing the insurgent leaders that the Queen,[a] her Ministers and her generals, were animated by a most conciliatory spirit."[b]

The revolutionary movement was pretty generally spread over the whole of Spain. Madrid and La Mancha in Castile; Granada, Seville, Malaga, Cadiz, Jaen, etc., in Andalusia; Murcia and

[a] Isabella II.—*Ed.*

[b] Quoted from *The Leader*, No. 333, August 9, 1856.—*Ed.*

Cartagena in Murcia; Valencia, Alicante, Alzira, etc., in Valencia; Barcelona, Reus, Figueras, Gerona, in Catalonia; Saragossa, Teruel, Huesca, Jaca, etc., in Aragon; Oviedo in Asturias; and Coruña in Galicia. There were no moves in Estremadura, Leon and old Castile, where the revolutionary party had been put down two months ago, under the joint auspices of Espartero and O'Donnell—the Basque provinces and Navarre also remaining quiet. The sympathies of the latter provinces, however, were with the revolutionary cause, although they might not manifest themselves in sight of the French army of observation. This is the more remarkable if it be considered that twenty years ago these very provinces formed the stronghold of Carlism[140]—then backed by the peasantry of Aragon and Catalonia, but who, this time, were most passionately siding with the revolution; and who would have proved a most formidable element of resistance, had not the imbecility of the leaders at Barcelona and Saragossa prevented their energies from being turned to account. Even *The London Morning Herald*, the orthodox champion of Protestantism, which broke lances for the Quixote of the auto-da-fe, Don Carlos, some twenty years ago, has stumbled over that fact, which it is fair enough to acknowledge. This is one of the many symptoms of progress revealed by the last revolution in Spain, a progress the slowness of which will astonish only those not acquainted with the peculiar customs and manners of a country, where "a la mañana"[a] is the watchword of every day's life, and where everybody is ready to tell you that "our forefathers needed eight hundred years to drive out the Moors."

Notwithstanding the general spread of *pronunciamientos*,[b] the revolution in Spain was limited only to Madrid and Barcelona. In the south it was broken by the *cholera morbus*,[c] in the north by the Espartero murrain. From a military point of view, the insurrections at Madrid and Barcelona offer few interesting and scarcely any novel features. On the one side—the army—everything was prepared beforehand; on the other everything was extemporized; the offensive never for a moment changed sides. On the one hand, a well-equipped army, moving easily in the strings of its commanding generals; on the other, leaders reluctantly pushed forward by the impetus of an imperfectly-armed people. At Madrid the revolutionists from the outset committed the mistake

---

[a] Let's do it tomorrow.—*Ed.*

[b] Mutinies.—*Ed.*

[c] Epidemic of cholera.—*Ed.*

of blocking themselves up in the internal parts of the town, on the line connecting the eastern and western extremities—extremities commanded by O'Donnell and Concha, who communicated with each other and the cavalry of Dulce through the external boulevards. Thus the people were cutting off and exposing themselves to the concentric attack preconcerted by O'Donnell and his accomplices. O'Donnell and Concha had only to effect their junction and the revolutionary forces were dispersed into the north and south quarters of the town, and deprived of all further cohesion. It was a distinct feature of the Madrid insurrection that barricades were used sparingly and only at prominent street corners, while the houses were made the centers of resistance; and—what is unheard of in street warfare—bayonet attacks met the assailing columns of the army. But, if the insurgents profited by the experience of the Paris and Dresden insurrections,[141] the soldiers had learned no less by them. The walls of the houses were broken through one by one, and the insurgents were taken in the flank and rear, while the exits into the streets were swept by cannon-shot. Another distinguished feature in this battle of Madrid was that Pucheta, after the junction of Concha and O'Donnell, when he was pushed into the southern (Toledo) quarter of the town, transplanted the guerrilla warfare from the mountains of Spain into the streets of Madrid. The insurrection, dispersed, faced about under some arch of a church, in some narrow lane, on the staircase of a house, and there defended itself to the death.

At Barcelona the fighting was still more intense, there being no leadership at all. Militarily, this insurrection, like all previous risings in Barcelona, perished by the fact of the citadel, Fort Montjuick, remaining in the hands of the army. The violence of the struggle is characterized by the burning of 150 soldiers in their barracks at Gracia, a suburb which the insurgents hotly contested, after being already dislodged from Barcelona. It deserves mention that, while at Madrid, as we have shown in a previous article,[a] the proletarians were betrayed and deserted by the bourgeoisie, the weavers of Barcelona declared at the very outset that they would have nothing to do with a movement set on foot by Esparterists, and insisted on the declaration of the Republic. This being refused, they, with the exception of some who could not resist the smell of powder, remained passive spectators of the battle, which

[a] See this volume, pp. 100-02.—*Ed.*

was thus lost—all insurrections at Barcelona being decided by its 20,000 weavers.

The Spanish revolution of 1856 is distinguished from all its predecessors by the loss of all dynastic character. It is known that the movement from 1808 to 1814[a] was national and dynastic.[142] Although the Cortes in 1812[b] proclaimed an almost republican Constitution, they did it in the name of Ferdinand VII. The movement of 1820-23,[143] timidly republican, was altogether premature and had against it the masses to whose support it appealed, those masses being bound altogether to the Church and the Crown. So deeply rooted was royalty in Spain, that the struggle between old and modern society, to become serious, needed a testament of Ferdinand VII, and the incarnation of the antagonistic principles in two dynastic branches, the Carlist and Cristina ones. Even to combat for a new principle the Spaniard wanted a time-honored standard. Under these banners the struggle was fought out, from 1833[c] to 1843. Then there was an end of revolution, and the new dynasty was allowed its trial from 1843 to 1854. In the revolution of July, 1854, there was thus necessarily implied an attack on the new dynasty; but innocent Isabel was covered by the hatred concentrated on her mother,[d] and the people reveled not only in their own emancipation but also in that of Isabel from her mother and the *camarilla*.

In 1856 the cloak had fallen and Isabel herself confronted the people by the coup d'état that fomented the revolution. She proved the worthy, coolly cruel, and cowardly hypocrite daughter of Ferdinand VII, who was so much given to lying that notwithstanding his bigotry he could never convince himself, even with the aid of the Holy Inquisition, that such exalted personages as Jesus Christ and his Apostles had spoken truth. Even Murat's massacre of the *Madrileños* in 1808[144] dwindles into an insignificant riot by the side of the butcheries of the 14-16th July, smiled upon by the innocent Isabel.[e] Those days sounded the death-knell of royalty in Spain. There are only the imbecile legitimists of Europe imagining that Isabel having fallen, Don Carlos may rise. They are forever thinking that when the last manifestation of a principle dies away, it is only to give its primitive manifestation another turn.

---

[a] The *New-York Daily Tribune* has mistakenly "from 1804 to 1815".—*Ed.*

[b] The *NYDT* has mistakenly "1824".—*Ed.*

[c] The *NYDT* has mistakenly "1831".—*Ed.*

[d] Maria Cristina.—*Ed.*

[e] See this volume, pp. 97-102.—*Ed.*

In 1856, the Spanish revolution has lost not only its dynastic, but also its military character. Why the army played such a prominent part in Spanish revolutions, may be told in a very few words. The old institution of the Captain-Generalships, which made the captains the pashas of their respective provinces[145]; the war of independence against France, which not only made the army the principal instrument of national defense, but also the first revolutionary organization and the center of revolutionary action in Spain; the conspiracies of 1814-19,[a] all emanating from the army; the dynastic war of 1833-40,[b] depending on the armies of both sides[146]; the isolation of the liberal bourgeoisie forcing them to employ the bayonets of the army against clergy and peasantry in the country; the necessity for Cristina and the camarilla to employ bayonets against the Liberals, as the Liberals had employed bayonets against the peasants; the tradition growing out of all these precedents; these were the causes which impressed on revolution in Spain a military, and on the army a pretorian character. Till 1854, revolution always originated with the army, and its different manifestations up to that time offered no external sign of difference beyond the grade in the army whence they originated. Even in 1854 the first impulse still proceeded from the army, but there is the Manzanares manifesto[c] of O'Donnell[147] to attest how slender the base of the military preponderance in the Spanish revolution had become. Under what conditions was O'Donnell finally allowed to stay his scarcely equivocal promenade from Vicálvaro to the Portuguese frontiers, and to bring back the army to Madrid? Only on the promise to immediately reduce it, to replace it by the National Guard, and not to allow the fruits of the revolution to be shared by the generals. If the revolution of 1854 confined itself thus to the expression of its distrust, only two years later, it finds itself openly and directly attacked by that army—an army that has now worthily entered the lists by the side of the Croats of Radetzky, the Africans of Bonaparte, and the Pomeranians of Wrangel.[148] How far the glories of its new position are appreciated by the Spanish army, is proved by the rebellion of a regiment at Madrid, on the 29th of July, which, not being satisfied with the mere *cigarros* of Isabel, struck for the five franc pieces, and sausages of Bonaparte,[149] and got them, too.

---

[a] The *New-York Daily Tribune* has mistakenly "1815-18".—*Ed.*

[b] The *NYDT* has mistakenly "1831-41".—*Ed.*

[c] Published in the *Journal des Débats*, July 17, 1854.—*Ed.*

This time, then, the army has been all against the people, or, indeed, it has only fought against them, and the National Guards. In short, there is an end of the revolutionary mission of the Spanish army. The man in whom centered the military, the dynastic, and the bourgeois liberal character of the Spanish revolution—Espartero—has now sunk even lower than the common law of fate would have enabled his most intimate *connoisseurs* to anticipate. If, as is generally rumored, and is very probable, the Esparterists are about to rally under O'Donnell, they will have confirmed their suicide by an official act of their own. They will not save him.

The next European revolution will find Spain matured for cooperation with it. The years 1854 and 1856 were phases of transition she had to pass through to arrive at that maturity.

Written in early August 1856

First published in the *New-York Daily Tribune,* No. 4783, August 18, 1856 as a leading article; reprinted in the *New-York Weekly Tribune,* No. 780, August 23, 1856 under the title "The Spanish Revolution Closed"

Reproduced from the *New-York Daily Tribune*

Karl Marx

[THE ECONOMIC CRISIS IN EUROPE]

What distinguishes the present period of speculation in Europe is the universality of the rage. There have been gambling manias before—corn manias, railway manias, mining manias, banking manias, cotton-spinning manias—in short, manias of every possible description; but at the epochs of the great commercial crises of 1817, 1825, 1836, 1846-'47, although every branch of industrial and commercial enterprise was affected, one leading mania gave to each epoch its distinct tone and character. Every department being invaded by the spirit of speculation, every speculator still confined himself within his department. On the contrary, the ruling principle of the Crédit Mobilier, the representative of the present mania, is not to speculate in a given line, but to speculate in speculation, and to universalize swindling at the same rate that it centralizes it. There is, besides, this further difference in the origin and growth of the present mania, that it did not begin in England, but in France. The present race of French speculators stand in the same relation to the English speculators of the above-mentioned epochs as the French Deists of the Eighteenth to the English Deists of the Seventeenth Century.[150] The one furnished the materials, while the other produced the generalizing form which enabled deism to be propagated over the whole civilized world of the eighteenth century. The British are prone to congratulate themselves upon the removal of the focus of speculation from their free and sober island to the muddled and despot-ridden Continent; but then they forget the intense anxiety with which they watch the monthly statement of the Bank of France as influencing the heap of bullion in the sanctum of the Bank of England; they forget that it is English capital, to a great extent, which supplies the great arteries of the European Crédits Mobiliers with the heavenly moisture; they forget that the "sound" over-trading and over-production in England, which they are now extolling as having reached the figure of nearly £110,000,000 of exports, is the direct offspring of the "unsound" speculation they denounce on the Continent, as much as their liberal policy of 1854 and 1856 is the offspring of the coup d'état of Bonaparte. Yet it cannot be denied that they are innocent of the breeding of that curious mixture of Imperial Socialism, St. Simonistic stock-jobbing and philosophical swindling which makes up what is called the Crédit Mobilier. In strong contradistinction to this continental refinement, English speculation has gone back to its coarsest and most primitive form of fraud, plain, unvarnished and unmitigated. Fraud was the mystery of Paul, Strahan & Bates; of the Tipperary Bank of Sadleir memory; of the great City operations of Cole, Davidson & Gordon; and fraud is the sad but simple tale of the Royal British Bank of London.[151]

For a set of directors to eat up a company's capital, while cheering on its shareholders by high dividends, and inveigling depositors and fresh shareholders by fraudulent accounts, no high degree of refinement is necessary. Nothing is wanted but English law. The case of the Royal British Bank has caused a sensation, not so much on account of the capital as on account of the number of small people involved, both among the shareholders and depositors. The division of labor in this concern appears to have been very simple, indeed. There were two sets of directors, the one content to pocket their salary of $10,000 a year for knowing nothing of the affairs of the Bank and keeping their consciences clear, the other intent upon the real direction of the Bank, only to be its first customers or rather plunderers. The latter class being dependent for accommodation upon the manager, at once begin with letting the manager accommodate himself. Beside the manager they must take into the secret the auditor and solicitor of the Company, who consequently receive bribes in the shape of advances. In addition to advances made to themselves and relatives in their own names, the directors and manager proceed to set up a number of men of straw, in whose names they pocket further advances. The whole paid-up capital amounts now to £150,000, of which £121,840 were swallowed directly and indirectly by the directors. The founder of the Company, Mr. McGregor, M.P. for Glasgow, the celebrated statistical writer,[a] saddled the Company with £7,362; ano-

[a] Main works: *The Resources and Statistics of Nations* and *The Commercial and Financial Legislation of Europe and America.—Ed.*

ther director and Member of Parliament, Mr. Humphrey Brown of Tewkesbury, who used the bank to pay his electioneering expenses, incurred at one time a liability to it of £70,000, and appears to be still in its debt to the tune of £50,000. Mr. Cameron, the manager, had advances to the amount of £30,000.

Every year since the bank went in operation, it had been losing £50,000, and yet the directors came forward every year to congratulate the shareholders upon their prosperity. Dividends of six per cent. were paid quarterly, although by the declaration of the official accountant, Mr. Coleman, the shareholders ought never to have had a dividend at all. Only last Summer, fallacious accounts to the extent of over £370,000 were presented to the shareholders, the advances made to McGregor, Humphrey Brown, Cameron & Co., figuring under the abstract head of Convertible Securities. When the bank was completely insolvent, new shares were issued, amid glowing reports of its progress and a vote of confidence in the directors. This issue of new shares was by no means contemplated as a desperate means of relieving the position of the bank, but simply to furnish fresh material for directorial fraud. Although it was one of the rules of the charter that the bank was not to traffic in its own shares, it appears to have been the constant practice to saddle it, by way of security, with its own shares whenever they had become depreciated in the directors' hands. The way in which the "honest portion" of the directors pretend to have been duped, was told by one of them, Mr. Owen, at a meeting of shareholders, as follows:

"When all arrangements for starting this concern had been made, Mr. Cameron was appointed our manager, and we soon found out the evil of having a manager who had never previously been connected with any bank in London. By reason of that circumstance arose a number of difficulties. I will state what occurred two years and some months ago when I left the bank. Why, shortly before that time, I did not know that there was a single shareholder indebted to the bank to the amount of £10,000, either for discount or advances. I at one time heard a whisper of some complaints that there was a large sum due by one of them on account of discounts, and I asked one of the bookkeepers as to the matter. I was told that when I shut the parlor door I had nothing to do with the bank. Mr. Cameron said that no director must bring his own bills to be discounted before the Board. He said that such bills should go to the general manager, for if they were brought before the Board we should never get mercantile men of high character to bank with us. In this ignorance was I until one occasion, when Mr. Cameron was taken so dangerously ill that he was not expected to recover. In consequence of his illness, the Chairman and some of the other Directors made some inquiries which disclosed to us that Mr. Cameron had a book with a private key which we had never seen. When the Chairman opened that book we were all indeed astonished."[a]

It is due to Mr. Cameron to say that, without waiting for the consequences of these discoveries, he, with great prudence and promptitude, expatriated himself from England.

One of the most extraordinary and characteristic transactions of the Royal British Bank was its connection with some Welsh Iron Works. At a time when the paid-up capital of the Company amounted to but £50,000, the advances made to these Iron Works alone reached the sum of £70,000 to £80,000. When the Company first got possession of this iron establishment it was an unworkable concern. Having become workable after an investment of something like £50,000, we find the property in the hands of a Mr. Clarke, who, after having worked it "for some time," threw it back upon the bank, while "expressing his conviction that he was throwing up a large fortune," leaving the bank, however, to bear an additional debt of £20,000 upon the "property." Thus, this concern kept going out of the hands of the bank whenever profits seemed likely to come in, and kept coming back to the bank when fresh advances were required to go out. This practical joke the Directors were endeavoring to continue even at the last moment of their confession, still holding up the profitable capacities of the works, which they say might yield £16,000 per annum, forgetting that they have cost the shareholders £17,742 during every year of the Company's existence. The affairs of the Company are now to be wound up in the Court of Chancery.[152] Long before that can be done, however, the whole adventures of the Royal British Bank will have been drowned amid the deluge of the general European crisis.

Written on about September 26, 1856

First published in the *New-York Daily Tribune*, No. 4828, October 9, 1856 as a leading article

Reproduced from the newspaper

---

[a] *The Times*, No. 22479, September 22, 1856, "The Royal British Bank".—*Ed.*

Karl Marx

THE MONETARY CRISIS IN EUROPE

London, Oct. 3, 1856

The general commercial crisis which occurred in Europe about the Autumn of 1847, and lasted till the Spring of 1848, was ushered in by a panic in the London money market, beginning in the last days of April and reaching its climax on the 4th of May, 1847. During these latter days all monetary transactions were brought to a complete stand-still; but from the 4th of May the pressure subsided, and merchants and journalists congratulated one another on the merely accidental and transitory character of the panic. A few months later the commercial and industrial crisis burst forth, of which the monetary panic had been but the symptom and the forerunner.

There is now a movement in the European money markets analogous to the panic of 1847. The analogy, however, is not complete. Instead of moving from west to east—from London via Paris to Berlin and Vienna—as did the panic of 1847, the present panic is moving from east to west, with Germany for its starting point, thence spreading to Paris, and last reaching London. Then the panic assumed a local aspect from the slowness of its progress; now it appears at once in its universal character, from the rapidity of its extension. Then it lasted about a week or so; now it has lasted already three weeks. Then there were few who suspected it to be the forerunner of a general crisis; now nobody doubts it save those Englishmen who imagine themselves to make history by reading *The Times* newspaper. What the most far-sighted politicians feared then, was a repetition of the crisis of 1825 and 1836; what they now are sure of is an enlarged edition not only of the crisis of 1847 but also of the revolutions of 1848.

The anxiety of the upper classes in Europe is as intense as their disappointment. Having had it all their own way since the middle of 1849, the war,[a] as yet, was the only cloud in their view of the social horizon. Now, after the war is over, or supposed to be over, they make the same discovery everywhere as was made by the English after the battle of Waterloo, and the peace of 1815, when the *bulletins* of battles were replaced by the reports on agricultural and industrial distress. With a view to save their property they did everything in their power to put down the Revolution, and to crush the masses. They are now discovering that they were themselves the instruments of a revolution in property greater than any contemplated by the revolutionists of 1848. A general bankruptcy is staring them in the face, which they know to be coincidental with the settlement-day of the great pawning shop at Paris; and as the English found, to their surprise, after 1815, when Castlereagh, "the man of the stern path of duty," cut off his own head, that he had been a madman, so the stock-jobbing public of Europe already begin to ask themselves, even before his head is cut off, whether Bonaparte has ever been sane. They know that every market is over-imported; that every fraction of the proprietary classes, even those never before infected, has been drawn into the vortex of the speculative mania; that no European country has escaped from it; and that the demands of Governments on their tax-paying people have been stretched to the last point. In 1848 the movements which more immediately produced the Revolution were of a merely political character, such as the reform banquets in France, the war of the Sonderbund in Switzerland, the debates of the United Diet at Berlin, the Spanish marriages, the Schleswig-Holstein quarrels,[153] &c.; and when its soldiers, the workingmen of Paris, proclaimed the social character of the Revolution of 1848, its generals were as much taken by surprise as the rest of the world. Now, on the contrary, a social revolution is generally understood, even before the political revolution is proclaimed; and a social revolution brought about by no underground plots of the secret societies among the working classes, but by the public contrivances of the Crédits Mobiliers of the ruling classes. Thus the anxiety of the upper classes in Europe is embittered by the conviction that their very victories over revolution have been but instrumental in providing the material conditions in 1857 for the ideal tendencies of 1848. The whole epoch from the middle of 1849 down to the present appears,

[a] The Crimean war, 1853-56.—*Ed.*

then, as a mere respite given by history to Old European Society, in order to allow it a last condensed display of all its tendencies. In politics, adoration of the sword; in morals, general corruption and hypocritical return to exploded superstitions; in political economy, the mania of getting rich without the pains of producing—such have been the tendencies manifested by that Society during its counter-revolutionary orgies of 1849-56.

On the other hand, if we place side by side the effect of this short monetary panic and the effect of Mazzinian and other proclamations, the whole history since 1849 of the delusions of the official revolutionists is at once deprived of its mysteries. They know nothing of the economical life of peoples, they know nothing of the real conditions of historical movement, and when the new revolution shall break out they will have a better right than Pilate to wash their hands[a] and protest that they are innocent of the blood shed.

We have said that the present monetary panic in Europe made its appearance first in Germany, and this circumstance has been hit upon by the journals of Bonaparte to exculpate his régime from the suspicion of having had the least share in precipitating it.

"Government," says the Paris *Constitutionnel*, "has endeavored to moderate the spirit of enterprise even after the conclusion of peace, by adjourning several new concessions and by forbidding the introduction of new schemes on the Bourse. Unfortunately it could do no more; it could not prevent all excesses. Now, whence did they proceed? If a part was generated in the French market, it was certainly the smaller portion. Our railway companies, from a spirit of rivalry, were, perhaps, too hasty in issuing bonds, the proceeds of which were destined to extend the branch lines. But this would not have created embarrassment but for the mass of foreign enterprise suddenly sprung into life. Germany, above all, which had taken no part in the war, threw itself recklessly into schemes of all kinds. Not possessing sufficient resources itself, it appealed to ours, and as the official market was closed to it, our speculators opened to it the Coulisse. France, therefore, became the center of cosmopolitan projects which might enrich foreign countries at the expense of national interests. Capital became, in consequence, rare on our market, and our securities, meeting with fewer buyers, suffered that depreciation which, in the presence of so many elements of wealth and prosperity, astonishes the public."[b]

Having given this specimen of imperial official nonsense on the causes of the European panic, we cannot withhold an example also of the sort of opposition tolerated under Bonaparte.

---

[a] Matthew 27:24.—*Ed.*

[b] J. Buràt, "Paris, 29 septembre", *Le Constitutionnel*, No. 274, September 30, 1856.—*Ed.*

"The existence of a crisis," says the *Assemblée Nationale*, "may be denied, but we cannot help thinking that prosperity is somewhat on the wane, when we consider the recent falling off in the receipts of our railways, in the amount of Bank advances on commercial bills, and in the duties on exportation levied during the first seven months of the year, which exhibit a decline of twenty-five millions of francs."

In Germany, then, all the active part of the middle classes have ever since the counter-revolution of 1849 devoted their energies to commercial and industrial enterprise, as the thinking part of the nation have abandoned philosophy for the natural sciences. The Germans, neutral in the war, have accumulated as much more capital as their French neighbors sank in the war. Finding them in this position, with a rapidly progressing industry and an accumulation of capital, the French Crédit Mobilier condescended to notice them as being fit subjects for its operations—the passive alliance between Bonaparte and Austria having already drawn its attention to the unexplored regions of Austria, Hungary and Italy. However, having set the example and taken the initiative of speculation in Germany, the Crédit Mobilier itself was startled at the unexpected crop of stock-jobbing and credit institutions generated by its impulse. The Germans of 1855-56 received the swindle-constitutions of the French Crédits Mobiliers as dry-cut as the Germans of 1831 had received the political constitutions of France.[154] Thus, a Frenchman of the seventeenth century would behold with astonishment the Court of Louis XIV. reproduced a hundred-fold grander on the other side of the Rhine; and thus the Frenchmen of the last decennium were surprised to behold in Germany sixty-two national assemblies where they had with so much trouble produced one. Germany is not a land of decentralization after all; only centralization itself is decentralized, so that instead of one there exist a great many centers. Such a country, then, was quite fit to develop in the shortest time and in every direction the contrivances taught it by the Crédit Mobilier, just as Paris fashions are sooner circulated in Germany than in France. This is the immediate cause of the panic having made its first and most widely-spread appearance in Germany. We shall give the history of the panic itself, as well as its immediate causes, in a future article.

Written on October 3, 1856

Reproduced from the newspaper

First published in the *New-York Daily Tribune*, No. 4833, October 15, 1856

Karl Marx

[THE CAUSES OF THE MONETARY CRISIS IN EUROPE]

The monetary crisis in Germany, which began about the middle of September last, reached its climax on the 26th of that month, when it gradually subsided; like the monetary panic in England in 1847, which first manifested itself in the last [days] of April and gradually disappeared after the 4th of May, the day of its culmination. Then, the sacrifices made by several leading houses in London, for the sake of a respite during the panic, laid the immediate foundation of the complete ruin in which they were involved a few months later. Similar results will, ere long, be experienced in Germany, since at the bottom of the panic there was no scarcity of currency, but a disproportion between the disposable capital and the vastness of the industrial, commercial and speculative enterprises then in hand. The means by which the panic was temporarily subdued was the enhancement of the rate of discount by the different Government, joint-stock and private banks; some of them raising their rate to 6, some as high as 9 per cent. Consequent upon this enhancement of the rate of discount, the efflux of bullion was checked, the importation of foreign produce paralyzed, foreign capital attracted by the bait of high interest, outstanding debts were called in, the French *Crédit Mobilier,* which in the month before had paid by bills of accommodation its installments on the German railways contracted for by it, was forced to pay in cash, and France, in general, obliged to discharge in specie the balance then due on account of corn and provisions. The monetary panic in Germany thus rebounded on France, where it at once assumed a more threatening aspect. The Bank of France, following in the track of the German banks, raised its rate of discount to 6 per cent, an advance which on the 30th of September led to an application to the Bank of England for a loan of more than a million of pounds sterling. On the first of October, consequently, the Bank of England raised its rate of discount to 5 per cent, without even waiting for the usual Thursday "parlor,"[a] a step without precedent since the monetary panic of 1847. Notwithstanding this rise of interest, bullion continued to flow from the vaults of Threadneedle street[b] at the rate of £40,000 a day, while the Bank of France was obliged to part with about 6,000,000 francs in coin daily, the Mint issuing only 3,000,000, of which only about 120,000 francs was in silver. To counteract the action of the Bank of France on the bullion reserve of the Bank of England, the latter again raised its discount about a week afterward to 6 per cent for bills of 60 days, and 7 per cent for bills of longer date; and the Bank of France, in return for this civility, issued on the 6th of October a new ukase,[c] by which it refused to discount any bills of more than 60 days' date, and declared that it would not advance more than 40 per cent on funded property, and 20 per cent on railway shares, and that it would make such advances for one month only. In spite, however, of these measures, the Bank of England was quite as unable to check the efflux of bullion to France, as the Bank of France to lessen the panic at Paris, or the drain of specie to other parts of the continent. The intensity of the panic in France is attested by a fall from 1,680 francs (quotation of Sept. 29) to 1,465 francs (Oct. 6) in the shares of the Crédit Mobilier, a fall of 215 francs within eight days, from which the utmost efforts had been unable to procure a recovery of more than 15 francs up to the 9th of October. It is needless to say that the public funds fell in proportion. There is hardly anything more ludicrous than the French lamentations on the elopement of their capital into Germany, after the magniloquent assurances we had from Mr. Isaac Péreire, the great founder of the Crédit Mobilier, that French capital was gifted with a peculiar cosmopolitan character. In the midst of all this trouble, the great wizard of France, Napoleon III., prepared his panacea. He interdicted the press from talking of the financial crisis; he suggested by gendarmes to the money-dealers the expediency of withdrawing from their windows the offer of premiums on silver; and finally, he inserted in his *Moniteur,* on the 7th of October, a report

[a] Here: a meeting of the Board of Directors.— *Ed.*

[b] The Bank of England is located in this street.— *Ed.*

[c] See *Le Moniteur universel,* No. 280, October 6, 1856.— *Ed.*

addressed to himself, by his own Minister of Finance, asserting that everything was right, and that only the appreciation of things by the people was wrong.[a] Unhappily, two days later, out pops the Governor of the Bank of France with the following feature in his monthly account:

	Oct.[b]	Sept.[c]
Cash in hand	77,062,910	113,126,401
Cash in branches	89,407,036	122,676,090
Bills discounted	271,955,426	221,308,498
Bills at branch banks	239,623,602	217,829,320
Prem. on gold and silver	2,128,594	1,496,313

In other words, during one month the cash on hand had diminished by 69,332,545 francs, discounts of bills had increased by 72,441,210 francs; while the premium on the purchase of gold and silver exceeds the figures for September by 632,281 francs. Unhappily, also, it is the fact that hoarding of the precious metals is now going on to an unprecedented degree among the French; and that the rumors of a suspension of cash payments at the Bank are daily gaining ground. The intervention of Napoleon proves to be about as efficient on the money market as his intervention in the inundated districts on the waters of the Loire.[155]

The present crisis in Europe is complicated by the fact that a drain of bullion—the common harbinger of commercial disasters—is interwoven with a depreciation of gold, as compared with silver. Independently of every other commercial and industrial agency, this depreciation could not but induce those countries, where there exists a double standard of value, and where both gold and silver must be received in payment according to proportions prescribed by law, but declared to be false by economical facts, to export their silver to those markets where gold is the standard of value, and where the official price of silver does not swerve from its market price. This being the relative position of England and France, silver must naturally flow from France to England, and gold from England to France, till the silver currency of the latter is replaced by a gold currency. On the

[a] P. Magne, "Rapport à l'Empereur", *Le Moniteur universel*, No. 281, October 7, 1856.—*Ed.*

[b] "Situation de la Banque de France et de ses succursales au jeudi 9 octobre 1856", *Le Moniteur universel*, No. 284, October 10, 1856.—*Ed.*

[c] "Situation de la Banque de France et de ses succursales au jeudi 11 septembre 1856", *Le Moniteur universel*, No. 256, September 12, 1856.—*Ed.*

one hand, it is clear that such a substitution for the usual medium of exchange must be attended by temporary difficulties, but that these difficulties can be met, either by making gold the standard, and putting silver out of circulation, as has been done, or by demonetizing gold and making silver the only standard, as was done in Holland in 1851, and more recently in Belgium. On the other hand, it is evident that if there were no other agency at work except a depreciation of gold compared with silver, the general drain of silver from all Europe and America would have counteracted and paralyzed itself, because the suddenly setting free and taking out of circulation of such a mass of silver without any particular reservoir to supply it, must have lowered its price in comparison with gold, the market price of any commodity being determined temporarily by the proportion between supply and demand, and only in an average of years by the cost of production. The demonetization of gold in the Dutch and Belgian banks could exercise but a very slight influence on the value of silver, as it had been the principal means of exchange in those countries, and therefore the change was of a legal rather than an economical character. It may be admitted, however, that these changes have opened a small market for the supply of silver, and thus in a slight degree alleviated the embarrassment.

Within the last four or five months the specie in the Austrian National Bank has, it is true, increased from $20,000,000 to $43,000,000, the whole of which, Austria not having yet returned to cash payments, is hoarded in the Bank vaults. The principal part of this increase of $23,000,000 has been drawn from Paris and Germany for railways bought by the Crédit Mobilier. This is certainly one of the causes which explain the recent drain of silver, but it would be erroneous to look upon this circumstance as in any large degree accounting for the late phenomena in the money market. It must not be forgotten that from 1848 to 1855, one hundred and five millions of gold have been thrown into the money markets of the world by the production of California and Australia,[156] exclusive of the yield of Russia and the other old established sources of supply. Of these one hundred and five millions the more sanguine free-traders suppose that fifty-two millions have been required for the modern increase of commerce, whether as currency, as bank reserves, as bullion for the settling of balances and the correction of exchanges between different countries, or as articles of luxury. Of the other fifty-three millions they suppose, and we think them rather below the mark, that they have merely replaced a similar amount of silver formerly in use in

America and France—ten millions in America, and forty-three millions in France. The manner in which this displacement has worked itself out, may be seen from the Official Customs Returns of the movement of gold and silver in France during the year 1855[a]:

Gold Imported in 1855.		*Silver Imported in* 1855.	
Ingots	£11,045,268	Ingots	£1,717,459
Coin	4,306,887	Coin	3,121,250
Total	£15,352,155	Total	£4,838,709
Gold Exported in 1855.		*Silver Exported in* 1855.	
Ingots	£203,544	Ingots	£3,067,229
Coin	6,306,060	Coin	9,783,345
Total	£6,509,604	Total	£12,850,574
Balance gold imp'ed	£8,842,551	Balance silver exp'd	£8,011,865

Nobody, then, can pretend that the setting free of so large an amount of silver (fifty-three millions sterling) is accounted for either by the displacement in the currency of France and America, or by the hoarding of the Bank of Austria, or both together. It has been justly asserted that silver, not being threatened, like gold, with a diminution in value, the Italian and Levant traders were giving it a marked preference over other coin; that the Arabs have received and hoarded large quantities of it; and lastly, that the French corn-dealers, in payment for their purchases in the Black Sea and the Sea of Azof, preferred to abstract silver from France, where it maintains its antiquated relation to gold, instead of gold, which has changed its relation to silver in the south of Russia. Taking all these causes of the drain of silver together, we cannot estimate the amount abstracted by them at more than fifteen or sixteen millions sterling. The abstraction of silver by the Oriental war[b] is most absurdly alleged by the economical writers in the English Press as another special reason of this drain, though they have included it in the general estimate of the fifty-two millions of gold absorbed by the increased requirements of modern commerce. They cannot, of course, put on the shoulders of silver what they have already put on the shoulders of gold. There is, then,

[a] *The Economist*, No. 683, September 27, 1856, "Foreign Correspondence".—*Ed.*

[b] The Crimean war, 1853-56.—*Ed.*

besides all these special influences, some greater agency at work by which the drain of silver is accounted for, and this is the trade to China and India, which, curiously enough, also formed the leading feature in the great crisis of 1847. We shall return to this subject, as it is important to study the economical forerunners of the impending crisis in Europe.

This much our readers will understand, that whatever may be the temporary cause of the monetary panic, and the drain of bullion which appears as its immediate occasion, all the elements of commercial and industrial revulsion were ripe in Europe, and aggravated in France by the failure of the silk crop, by the shortcomings of the vintage, by the enormous imports of grain necessitated by the partial failure of the harvest of 1855 and the inundations of 1856, and lastly by the scarcity of dwelling houses produced in Paris by the economical contrivances of Mr. Bonaparte. For us, the mere perusal of the financial manifesto of M. Magne, which we published on Saturday,[a] seems sufficient to justify the suspicion that in spite of the second Congress of Paris[157] now assembling, and in spite of the Naples question,[158] the third Napoleon would have good reason to congratulate himself if the year 1857 came upon France with no worse auspices than, a decade earlier, attended the year 1847.

Written on about October 14, 1856

First published in the *New-York Daily Tribune*, No. 4843, October 27, 1856 as a leading article; reprinted in the *New-York Weekly Tribune*, No. 791, November 8, 1856 under the title "The Coming Crash"

Reproduced from the *New-York Daily Tribune*

---

[a] P. Magne, "Rapport à l'Empereur", *Le Moniteur universel*, No. 281, October 7, 1856. Published in the *New-York Daily Tribune*, No. 4842, October 25, 1856. This part of the sentence belongs to the *NYDT* editors.— *Ed.*

Karl Marx

[THE MONETARY CRISIS IN EUROPE. —FROM THE HISTORY OF MONEY CIRCULATION]

We have seen from the last report of the Bank of France[a] that its bullion reserve had reached the low point of about thirty millions of dollars, having diminished twenty-five per cent within the previous month alone.[b] If this drain were to go on, the Bank would be run dry by the end of the year, and cash payments would cease. To prevent this extreme danger, two measures have been employed. On the one hand, the melting of silver for export is to be hindered by the Police, and on the other, the Bank of France has determined to double, at an enormous sacrifice, its bullion reserve by contracting for a supply of six millions sterling with the Messrs. Rothschild. That is to say, that in order to make up its deficiency of gold, the Bank augments still further the disproportion between the prices at which it buys gold on the one hand, and sells it on the other. On account of this contract £50,000 in gold were taken out of the Bank of England on the 11th, and £40,000 on the 13th of October, and the *Asia,* which arrived here yesterday, brings advices of a still further draught of above half a million. Consequently, a general apprehension prevailed at London that the Bank of England would again put on the screw by raising its rate of discount in order to protect its own stock from emigrating to France. Preparatory to this the Bank has now refused to make advances on all descriptions of Government securities except Exchequer bills.

---

[a] "Situation de la Banque de France et de ses succursales au jeudi 9 octobre 1856", *Le Moniteur universel,* No. 284, October 10, 1856.—*Ed.*

[b] See this volume, p. 119.—*Ed.*

Now, all the gold the Bank of France may succeed in drawing into its coffers will escape from them quite as fast as it flows in—partly in payment of foreign debts, for settling the balance of trade—partly by being abstracted into the interior of France, to supply the place of silver disappearing from circulation, the hoarding of which naturally keeps pace with the increasing violence of the crisis; and lastly, for the supply of the enormous industrial enterprises started in the last three or four years. For instance, the great railway companies, which reckoned, for the continuation of their works and the payment of their dividends and bonuses, on the emission of new loans, which have now become impossible, are making the most desperate attempts to fill the vacuum in their exchequers. Thus the Western Railway of France is in need of sixty millions of francs; the Eastern wants twenty-four; the Northern thirty; the Mediterranean twenty; the Orleans forty, and so on. It is estimated that the total sum wanted by all the different railway companies amounts to three hundred millions. Bonaparte, who had flattered himself that he had put down politics by setting up gambling, is now eager to withdraw attention from the money-market by all sorts of political questions: Neapolitan questions, Danubian questions, Bessarabian questions, new Congress of Paris questions,[159] but all in vain. Not only France, but all Europe, is fully convinced that the fate of what is called the Bonaparte dynasty, as well as the present state of European society, is suspended on the issue of the commercial crisis of which Paris seems now to be witnessing the beginning.

As we have already stated,[a] the first occasion for the outbreak of the crisis was afforded by the sudden enhancement of the price of silver as compared with gold. This enhancement—notwithstanding the immense production of gold in California and Australia[160]—can only be accounted for by the still increasing drain of silver from the Western World to Asia, and especially to India and China. Since the beginning of the seventeenth century, Asia, and especially China and India, have never ceased to exercise an important influence on the bullion markets of Europe and America. Silver serving as the only medium of exchange in those Eastern countries, the treasure with which Spanish America inundated Europe, was partially drained through the channel of the Oriental trade, and the import of silver from America into Europe was checked by its export from Europe to Asia. Simultaneously, indeed, there took place an export of gold from

[a] See this volume, pp. 119-22.—*Ed.*

Asia to Europe; but, setting aside the supplies furnished by the Ural Mountains from 1840 to 1850, it was on too small a scale to produce sensible results.

The circulation of silver between Asia and the West had, of course, its alternate periods of ebb and flow, depending on the fluctuations of the balance of trade. On the whole, however, three broadly-marked epochs may be distinguished in the history of this world-wide movement—the first epoch beginning with the seventeenth century, and ending about 1830; the second extending from 1831 to 1848; and the last from 1849 to the present time. In the first epoch, the silver exportation to Asia was generally increasing; in the second epoch the stream was abating, till at last an opposite current set in, and, for the first time, Asia poured back into Europe part of the treasures it had absorbed for almost two centuries and a half; in the third epoch, still in its ascending phase, the screw is again turned, and the absorption of silver by Asia is proceeding on a scale hitherto without precedent.

In earlier times, after the discovery of the silver of America,[a] and even after the foundation of the Portuguese dominion in India, the export of silver from Europe to Asia was hardly perceptible. Larger masses of that metal were wanted when, in the beginning of the seventeenth century, the Dutch, and in its later period the British, extended their trade with Eastern Asia, but especially since the rapid growth of the consumption of tea in England during the eighteenth century—the English remittances for Chinese tea consisting almost exclusively of silver. In the latter part of the eighteenth century the efflux of silver from Europe to Eastern Asia had already assumed such ample proportions as to absorb an important part of the silver imported from America. There had also already begun a direct export from America to Asia, although, on the whole, limited to the amount shipped by the Mexican Acapulco fleets to the Philippine Islands. This absorption of silver by Asia became, in the first thirty years of the nineteenth century, the more sensible in Europe, as, on account of the revolutions that had broken out in the Spanish colonies,[161] the American supply decreased from upward of forty millions of dollars in 1800, to less than twenty millions in 1829. On the other hand, the silver shipped to Asia from the United States quadrupled from 1796 to 1825, while, after the year 1809, not only Mexico but also Brazil, Chili and Peru began, although on a

---

[a] The afflux of silver from Peru and Mexico began in the sixteenth century.—*Ed.*

smaller scale, to export silver directly to the east of Asia. The excess of silver imported from Europe into India and China over the gold thence exported amounted to more than thirty millions sterling from 1811 till 1822.

A great change took place during the epoch which begins with the year 1831. The East India Company had been forced not only to resign its monopoly of the trade between Europe and its Oriental empire, but also, with the exception of its Indo-Chinese monopolies, had been completely broken up as a commercial concern.[162] The East Indian trade being thus abandoned to private enterprise, the export of British manufactures to India began by far to surpass the import of Indian raw produce into Great Britain. The balance of trade thus turned more and more decidedly in favor of Europe, and consequently the export of silver to Asia rapidly fell off. Every check that British trade encountered in the other markets of the world began now to be compensated by its new expansion in Asia. If the commercial convulsion of 1825 had already led to an increase of British exports to India, a far mightier impulse was given to them by the Anglo-American crisis of 1836, while in 1847 the British crisis even derived its characteristic features from over-trading to India and other parts of Asia.

The exports to Asia, which in 1697 had hardly reached one fifty-second part of the total of British exports, amounted in 1822 to about one-fourteenth; in 1830 to about one-ninth, and in 1842 to more than one-fifth. As long as only India and the Western portion of Asia were affected by this economical change, the efflux of silver from Europe to Asia slackened, but did not cease, and still less give place to a reflux from Asia to Europe. Such a decisive turn was not imparted to the metallic circulation until English philanthropy had imposed a regular opium trade upon China, blown down by the cannon's mouth the Chinese wall, and forcibly thrown open the Celestial Empire to intercourse with the profane world. Thus drained of its silver on its Indian frontier, China was inundated on its Pacific coast by the manufactures of England and America. Hence it happened that in 1842, for the first time in the annals of modern commerce, great shipments of silver were actually effected from Asia to Europe.

This total revulsion in the circulation between Asia and the West proved, however, of short duration. A powerful and progressive reaction set in with 1849. As China had turned the tide in the first and second epoch, so China again turned it in the third. The Chinese rebellion[163] not only checked the opium trade with India, but also put a stop to the purchase of foreign manufactures, the Chinese insisting upon payment in silver, and betaking themselves to that popular contrivance of Oriental economists in times of political and social convulsion—hoarding. The excess of Chinese exports over imports has been greatly augmented by the late failure of the European silk crops. According to the reports of Mr. Robertson,[a] the British Consul at Shanghae, the export of tea from China within the last ten years has increased some sixty-three per cent, and that of silk two hundred and eighteen per cent, while the import of manufactures has decreased sixty-six per cent. He estimates the average annual balance of silver imported from all parts of the world at £5,580,000 more than it was ten years ago. The following are the precise figures of the movement of Chinese exports and imports during the period dating from 1849 to 1856, each year concluding with the 30th of June[b]:

Exports of tea.

To Gt. Br'n and Ireland.	lbs.	To the United States.	lbs.
1849	47,242,000		18,072,000
1855	86,509,000		31,515,000
1856	91,035,000		40,246,000

Silk.

To Gt. Br'n and Ireland.	lbs.	To France.	Bales.
1849	17,228		
1855	51,486		
1856	50,489	1856	6,458

Real value of exports from China to Great Britain in 1855	£8,746,000
Real value of exports from China to the United States in 1855	2,500,000
Total	£11,246,000
Deduct 20 per cent for freight and charges	2,249,200
Total due to China	£8,996,800

[a] See "Exports from China", *The Economist*, No. 683, September 27, 1856.—*Ed.*
[b] "The Trade of India and China and the Drain of Silver", *The Economist*, No. 685, October 11, 1856.—*Ed.*

Imports.

Manufactures from England in 1852	£2,503,000
Manufactures from England in 1855	1,000,000
Manufactures from England in 1856	1,277,000
Opium and Cotton from India in 1853	3,830,000
Opium and Cotton from India in 1855	3,306,000
Opium and Cotton from India in 1856	3,284,000
Total value of imports in 1855	£4,306,000
Balance due to China in 1855	4,690,000
Value of Chinese exports to India in 1855	1,000,000
Total balance due to China from all parts of the world (1855)	£5,690,000

This drain of silver from Europe to Asia on account of China is increased by the special drain to India, produced of late years by the balance of trade having turned against Europe, as will be seen from the following table:

British imports from India in 1856	£14,578,000
Deduct £3,000,000 for remittances of the East India Company	3,000,000
Total imports	£11,578,000
Indian imports from Britain	8,927,000
Balance in favor of India	£2,651,000

Now, up to the year 1825 gold was a legal tender in India, when a measure was passed for an exclusively silver standard. As some years later, gold commanded a premium over silver in the commercial markets, the East India Company declared its readiness to receive it in payments to the Government. After the discoveries of gold in Australia, however, the Company, as apprehensive of a depreciation of gold as the Dutch Government, and not at all pleased with the prospect of receiving in gold and paying in silver, suddenly returned to the exclusive silver standard of 1825. Thus the necessity of paying the balance due to India in silver was rendered paramount, and an enormous demand for that metal was created in that country. The price of silver, compared with gold, increasing henceforth more rapidly in India than in Europe, British merchants found it profitable to export silver to India as a speculation, taking in return Indian raw produce, and thus giving another stimulus to Indian exports. Altogether, silver to the amount of twenty-one millions sterling was exported from Southampton alone, from 1848 to 1855, beside a very large amount from the Mediterranean ports; and it is calculated that in the present year ten millions have been taken from Southampton to the East.

To judge from these changes in the Indian trade and the character of the Chinese revolution, it cannot be expected that the drain of silver to Asia will come to a speedy conclusion. It is, then, no rash opinion that this Chinese revolution is destined to exercise a far greater influence upon Europe than all the Russian wars, Italian manifestoes[164] and secret societies of that Continent.

Written on about October 17, 1856

First published in the *New-York Daily Tribune,* No. 4848, November 1 as a leading article; reprinted in the *New-York Weekly Tribune,* No. 793, November 22, 1856 under the title "The Crisis in Europe"

Reproduced from the *New-York Daily Tribune*

Karl Marx

[THE ECONOMIC CRISIS IN FRANCE]

There is no sign of any alleviation in the financial world of Europe. We learn by the *Niagara* that the flow of bullion from London to the Continent is more oppressive than ever, and that a proposition to raise yet higher the rate of interest had been voted down at a meeting of the Directors of the Bank of England by only one majority. It is not necessary to say that the cause of the crisis is still to be found in France, and the last number of *The Economist* which has reached us depicts the state of things in colors of unmixed gloom.

"The absence of any amelioration," says that journal, "is virtually an aggravation, and unfortunately, moreover, no permanent improvement is foreseen. The contrast between the present month and the corresponding one of last year is very painful in nearly every respect, and yet last October the country was engaged in a terrible war,[a] the close of which appeared very distant."[b]

Led by this lament, we have taken the pains to contrast the condition of the Paris Stock Market for October with that of the preceding month, and the result of our inquiries may be seen in the following table[c]:

	30th Sept.	31st Oct.	Rise.	Fall.
Three Per Cents Rente	67f. 50c.	66f. 70c.	..	80c.
Four and a Half Per Cents.	90f.	91f.	1f.	..

---

[a] The Crimean war, 1853-56.—*Ed.*

[b] *The Economist*, No. 688, November 1, 1856, "Foreign Correspondence".—*Ed.*

[c] See "Bourse du Mardi 30 septembre 1856" and "Bourse du Vendredi 31 octobre 1856", *Le Moniteur universel*, Nos. 275 and 306, October 1 and November 1, 1856.—*Ed.*

	30th Sept.	31st Oct.	Rise.	Fall.
Bank of France	4,010f.	3,850f.	..	160f.
Crédit Foncier	600f.	585f.	..	15f.
Crédit Mobilier	1,552f.	1,372f.	..	180f.
Orleans Railroad	1,267f.	1,241f.	..	26f.
Northern Railroad	950f.	941f.	..	9f.
Eastern Railroad	877f.	865f.	..	12f.
Paris-Lyons Railroad	1,265f.	1,267f.	2f.	
Mediterranean Railroad	1,750f.	1,652f.	..	98f.
Great Central Railroad	610f.	603f.	..	7f.

During the period from Sept. to Oct. 31, the shares of various companies fell as follows[a]:

Gas Paris Company	30 f.
Union des Gaz	35 f.
Lits Militaires	$27^1/_2$f.
Docks Napoléoniens	$8^1/_2$f.
Compagnie Maritime	40 f.
Palais d'Industrie	5 f.
Omnibus Company	35 f.
Messageries Impériales	50 f.

Nothing could be more ingenious than the manner in which the Bonapartist journals of Paris endeavor to account for this perpetual fall at the Bourse. Take, for instance, the paper of M. de Girardin, the *Presse*.

"Speculation," says this journal, "is still unwilling to *renounce its ideas* of fall. The continual variations of the Crédit Mobilier cause its shares to be regarded as so dangerous that many speculators dare not touch them, and confine themselves to operating on 'primes,' in order to be able to limit beforehand their chances of loss."

The stringent measures taken by the Bank of France, with a view to prevent, or at least to delay, the suspension of cash payments, have begun to tell severely on the industrial and commercial classes. Indeed, there is now raging a regular war between the *bona fide* commerce and industry, the speculative joint-stock companies already at work and the newly-hatched schemes about to be established, all of them struggling to carry off

[a] See ibid.—*Ed.*

the floating capital of the country. The inevitable result of such a struggle must be the rise of interest, the fall of profits in all departments of industry, and the depreciation of all sorts of securities, even if there existed no Bank of France, nor any drain of bullion. That, apart from all foreign influences, this pressure on the disposable capital of France must go on increasing, a glance at the development of the French railway system sufficiently demonstrates. The facts we are about to lay before our readers are given by the *Journal des Chemins de Fer,* which, like the rest of the press in that country, can publish nothing but what is admitted by the Bonapartist Government itself. On the whole, charters have been granted for an aggregate of 5,584 miles of railroad, of which only 2,884 miles are completed and in working order. Consequently there remain still 2,700 miles now being, or about to be, constructed. Nor is this all. The Government is constructing the Pyrenean lines, and has ordered the construction of new lines between Toulouse and Bayonne, Agen and Tarbès, and Mont de Marsan and Trabestans, lines amounting to more than 900 miles. France is in fact now constructing even a greater extent of railroads than she already possesses. The amount of money disbursed on her old railroad system is calculated at $300,000,000; but then its construction extended over a protracted period—a period which saw the rise and fall of three Governments—while the lines now chartered are all to be completed within six years at the farthest, and to begin their operations in the most critical phase of the commercial cycle. The embarrassed companies harass the Government for leave to raise money by new emissions of shares and bonds. The Government, comprehending that this would simply amount to giving leave to further depreciation of the old securities in the market, attended by increased disturbance at the Bourse, dares not yield. On the other hand, the money must be found; the suspension of the works would not only be bankruptcy but revolution.

While the demand for capital to start and sustain new enterprises at home is thus kept on the increase, the absorption of French capital by foreign schemes is by no means abated. It is no novelty that French capitalists have vast obligations to fulfill in Spain, Italy, Austria and Germany, and that the Crédit Mobilier is busy involving them in new ones at this very moment. Spain particularly is now adding to the embarrassments of France, as the scarcity of silver there has reached such a pitch that manufacturers at Barcelona feel the greatest difficulty in paying the wages of their workmen.

With regard to the Crédit Mobilier, we have already observed[a] that the tendency of that institution by no means corresponds with its name. Its tendency is to fix capital, not to *mobilize* it. What it mobilizes is only the titles of property. The shares of the companies started by it are, indeed, of a purely floating nature, but the capital which they represent is sunk. The whole mystery of the Crédit Mobilier is to allure capital into industrial enterprises, where it is sunk, in order to speculate on the sale of the shares created to represent that capital. As long as the managers of the Crédit Mobilier are able to realize premiums on the first emission of new shares, they can, of course, afford to look with stoical indifference on the general pressure of the money market, the ultimate fate of the shareholders, and the difficulties of the working companies. This explains the curious phenomenon that while the shares of the Crédit Mobilier are continually falling at the Bourse, its action is as continually extending over Europe.

Beside the general pressure in the money market, there are other causes affecting French manufactures. A great number of mills at Lyons are stopped in consequence of the scarcity and high price of raw silk. Similar causes are paralyzing affairs at Mulhouse and at Rouen. There the high price of cotton has forcibly enhanced the price of yarns, while fabrics are difficult of sale, and manufacturers unable to obtain their old terms. The consequences are, increased suffering and discontent among the workmen—especially at Lyons and in the south of France—where a degree of exasperation prevails, only to be compared with that which attended the crisis of 1847.

From the Bourse, railways, commerce and manufactures, let us now turn to French agriculture. The newly published Customs Returns of France reveal the fact that the failure of the last harvest was far more severe than avowed by the *Moniteur*.[b] Against 270,146 quintals of corn imported in September, 1855, 963,616 quintals were imported in September, 1856, being a difference of 693,470 quintals above the quantity imported in September, 1855, a year of notorious scarcity. It would, however, be a mistake to limit to the inundations, bad seasons, and other natural events, the causes which are evidently at work in transforming France from a corn-exporting to a corn-importing country. Agriculture, never

[a] See this volume, pp. 20-21.—*Ed.*

[b] "Direction générale des douanes et des contributions indirectes. Tableau comparatif des principales marchandises, importées pendant le mois de septembre des années 1856, 1855 et 1854", *Le Moniteur universel*, No. 302, October 28, 1856.—*Ed.*

highly developed in France, has positively retrograded under the present régime. On the one hand we see taxes constantly increasing; on the other decreasing labor—great masses of laborers being drafted from the land temporarily by war,[a] and permanently by the railway and other public works—with the progressive withdrawal of capital from agricultural to speculative pursuits. What was called Napoleon's democratization of credit, was in fact but the generalization of stockjobbing. What the Crédit Mobilier offered to the middle and higher classes, the Imperial subscription loans did for the peasantry. They brought the Bourse home to their cottages, emptied them of their private hoardings, and carried off the small capitals formerly invested in the improvement of agriculture.

The agricultural distress in France is thus as much the effect of the present political system as the offspring of natural disasters. If the small peasantry suffer less from low prices than the large farmers of England, they suffer, on the other hand, from the dearth of provisions which to the latter often proves a source of profit. Hence their disaffection illustrated by incendiary fires, which are lamentably frequent, although, by virtue of Imperial orders, they are not recorded in the French papers. If the peasants, after the Revolution of February,[b] were exasperated at the notion that the new tax of 45 centimes[165] was thrust on them to keep up the National Workshops at Paris,[166] the present peasantry are much more so by the certainty of being charged with taxes on their exhausted resources to enable the Parisians to obtain bread under cost price. If, now, it be remembered that Napoleon, after all, was but the choice of the peasantry, the present revolutionary disposition of this class throws quite a new light on the chances of the Bonapartist dynasty. To what miserable shifts it is already driven, in order to allay and stave off the threatening claims of agricultural misery, may be seen from the language of the Prefects in their circulars for the "encouragement" of charity. The Prefect of the Sarthe, for instance, addresses his Sub-Prefects as follows:

> "You will please to take up, with all zeal and confidence, the task, which is one of the finest attributes of administration, viz: to find means of support and employment for those citizens who are in want of either, whereby you will concur in maintaining public tranquillity. You need not fear that you may find the sources of charity dried up, or the private purses exhausted by the sacrifices, however enormous they may have been, of preceding years. Proprietors and farmers have realized considerable profits for some time past, and being more especially

[a] The Crimean war, 1853-56.—*Ed.*
[b] 1848.—*Ed.*

interested in the security of the country, they will understand that for them to give is an advantage as well as a duty."

If to all the preceding causes of disaffection we add the dearth of lodgings and provisions at Paris, the pressure on the retail trade of the capital, the strikes in different branches of Parisian industry, it will be understood why the suppressed freedom of the press suddenly breaks forth from the walls of buildings in insurrectionary placards. In a private letter we have received from a trustworthy correspondent at Paris, it is stated that from the 1st to the 12th of October no less than nine hundred arrests took place. Some of the causes of these arrests are worth noticing, as they offer a striking mark of the uneasiness and anxieties of the Government. In one case a man who "does business on the Bourse," as it is called, was arrested for having said that "he saw in the Crimean war nothing but many people killed and much money wasted;" another, a tradesman, for having pretended that "business was as sick as the Government;" a third, because there was found on him a song on David d'Angers and the students [167]; a fourth, a Government official, for having published a fly-sheet on the financial crisis; a tailor, for having inquired if certain of his friends had been arrested, as he was told so; lastly, a workman, for conversing with a countryman of his, a gendarme, on the high price of provisions, the gendarme interpreting the workman's remarks as hostile to the Government.

In view of all these facts, it seems hardly possible that French commerce and industry should avoid a collapse, attended by political events more or less serious, and affecting to a most disastrous extent the stability of credit and of business, not only in Europe, but in America as well. The rushing movement toward this abyss cannot but be accelerated by the gigantic speculation in Russian railroads in which the Crédit Mobilier, in conjunction with many of the leading banking firms of Europe, have now embarked.

Written on about November 7, 1856

First published in the *New-York Daily Tribune,* No. 4866, November 22, 1856 as a leading article

Reproduced from the newspaper

Karl Marx

[THE EUROPEAN CRISIS]

The indications brought from Europe by the two steamers which have arrived this week, certainly seem to postpone to a future day the final collapse of speculation and stock-jobbing, which men on both sides of the sea instinctively anticipate as with a fearful looking forward to some inevitable doom. That collapse is none the less sure from this postponement; indeed, the chronic character assumed by the existing financial crisis only forebodes for it a more violent and destructive end. The longer the crisis lasts the worse the ultimate reckoning. Europe is now like a man on the verge of bankruptcy, forced to continue at once all the enterprises which have ruined him, and all the desperate expedients by which he hopes to put off and to prevent the last dread crash. New calls are made for payments on the stock of companies most of which exist only on paper; great sums of ready money are invested in speculations from which they can never be withdrawn; while the high rate of interest—now seven per cent at the counter of the Bank of England—stands like a stern monitor of the judgment to come.

With the utmost success of the financial devices now to be attempted, it is impossible that the countless stock-jobbing speculations of the continent should be carried much further. In Rhenish Prussia alone there are seventy-two new companies for the working of mines, with a subscription capital of 79,797,333 thalers. At this very moment the Austrian Crédit Mobilier, or rather the French Crédit Mobilier in Austria, meets with the greatest difficulties in obtaining the payment of its second call, paralyzed as it is by the measures taken by the Austrian Government for the resumption of cash payments. The purchase-money to be paid into the Imperial treasury for railroads and mines has, according to contract, to be handed over in specie, causing a drain on the resources of the Crédit Mobilier of above $1,000,000 every month till February, 1858. On the other hand, the monetary pressure is so severely felt by railroad contractors in France, that the Grand Central has been compelled to dismiss five hundred employés and fifteen thousand workmen on the Mulhouse section, and the Lyons and Geneva Company has been obliged to curtail or suspend its operations. For divulging these facts, the *Indépendance belge* has been twice seized in France. With this irritability of the French Government at any disclosure of the real situation of French commerce and industry, it is curious to note the following passage, escaped from the lips of M. Petit, the substitute of the Procureur General, upon the recent reopening of the courts at Paris.

"Consult statistics and you will find some interesting information upon the present tendencies of trade. Bankruptcies increase every year. In 1851 there were 2,305; in 1852, 2,478; in 1853, 2,671; and in 1854, 3,691. The same increase is to be noted for fraudulent as for simple bankruptcies. The increase of the former has been, since 1851, at the rate of 66 per cent, and that of the latter 100 per cent. As to the frauds committed upon the nature, the quality, and the quantity of things sold, and the employment of false measures and weights, these have augmented in a frightful proportion. In 1851, 1,717 such cases were furnished; in 1852, 3,763; in 1853, 7,074; and in 1854, 7,831."

It is true that, in the face of these phenomena on the continent, we are assured by the British press that the worst of the crisis is over, but we seek in vain for conclusive evidence of such a fact. We do not find it in the raising of discount to seven per cent by the Bank of England; nor in the last report of the Bank of France, which not only exhibits internal proofs of having been cooked, but even formally shows that in spite of the severest restriction upon loans, advances, discounts, and emission of notes, the Bank has been unable to check the efflux of bullion or to dispense with the premium on gold. But however that may be, it is certain that the French Government is far from partaking in the comfortable views which it takes care to spread both at home and abroad. At Paris it is known that the Emperor[a] has not recoiled from the most stupendous monetary sacrifices to keep, during the last six weeks, the Rente above 66, it being not a mere conviction, but a settled superstition with him, that the fall below 66 will ring the death knell of the empire. It is evident that the French differs in this

[a] Napoleon III.—*Ed.*

respect from the Roman Empire—since the one feared death from the advance of the barbarians while the other fears it from the retreat of the stockjobbers.[168]

Written on about November 21, 1856

First published in the *New-York Daily Tribune,* No. 4878, December 6, 1856 as a leading article

Reproduced from the newspaper

Karl Marx

THE MARITIME COMMERCE OF AUSTRIA[169]

The maritime commerce of Austria may be said to date from the incorporation into the Empire of Venice and its dependencies on the Adriatic shores, made over first by the peace of Campo-Formio, and confirmed to Austria by the peace of Luneville.[170] Napoleon, then, is the true founder of this branch of Austrian commerce. It is true that, on becoming aware of the advantages thus bestowed on Austria, he rescinded those cessions, first by the treaty of Presburg, and again by the peace of Vienna, in 1809.[171] But Austria, having been once put on the right track, used her opportunity to recover by the treaty of 1815[172] her ascendancy over the Adriatic. Trieste is the center of this commerce, and the superiority of that place over all the other Austrian ports, even at an earlier period, may be seen by the following table:

	Ports:	Fiume. Florins.	Trieste. Flor.	Venice. Flor.	Oth. Ports. Flor.	Total. Flor.
1838	Imports.	200,000	32,200,000	9,000,000	8,000,000	49,400,000
	Exports	1,700,000	14,400,000	5,300,000	2,000,000	23,400,000
1841	Imports.	200,000	22,300,000	8,500,000	5,300,000	36,300,000
	Exports	1,600,000	11,200,000	3,100,000	1,900,000	17,800,000
1842	Imports.	200,000	24,900,000	11,500,000	5,100,000	41,700,000
	Exports	1,300,000	11,900,000	3,400,000	2,600,000	19,200,000

In 1839 the imports of Venice were to the imports of Trieste as 1 to 2.84, and their exports respectively as 1 to 3.8. In the same year the number of ships entering each harbor were in the proportion of 1 to 4. At present the preponderance of Trieste has assumed such dimensions as to eclipse all the rest of the Austrian ports, Venice included. But if Trieste has supplanted Venice in the Adriatic, the fact is to be accounted for neither by the special favor of the Austrian Government, nor by the unceasing exertions of the Austrian Lloyd.[173] An obscure creek on an iron-bound coast, inhabited only by a few fishermen at the beginning of the eighteenth century, Trieste had grown into a commercial port numbering 23,000 souls by the time the French forces evacuated Istria in 1814, with a trade amounting to three times that of Venice in 1815. In 1835, the year before the establishment of the Austrian Lloyd, its population was above 50,000, and at a time when the Lloyd cannot yet be supposed to have attained any considerable influence, Trieste occupied the second rank after England in the Turkish, and the first rank in the Egyptian trade, as will be seen from the following tables of imports and exports from Smyrna from 1835 to 1839:

	Piasters.	Piasters.
England	126,313,146	44,618,032
Trieste	93,500,456	52,477,756
United States	57,329,165	46,608,320

The following figures, giving the imports and exports of Egypt for 1837, are also instructive on this head:

	Francs.	Francs.
Trieste	13,858,000	14,532,000
Turkey	12,661,000	12,150,000
France	10,702,000	11,703,000
England and Malta	15,158,000	5,404,000

How, then, came it to pass that Trieste, and not Venice, became the cradle of revived navigation in the Adriatic? Venice was a town of reminiscences; Trieste shared the privilege of the United States of having no past at all. Formed by a motley crew of Italian, German, English, French, Greek, Armenian and Jewish merchant-adventurers, it was not fettered by traditions like the City of the Lagunes. Thus, for instance, while the Venetian grain trade still clung during the eighteenth century to its old connections, Trieste at once attached itself to the rising fortunes of Odessa, and thus succeeded, by the commencement of the nineteenth century, in driving its rival entirely from the Mediterranean corn trade. The fatal blow sustained by the old Italian trade-republics at the end of the fifteenth century, in consequence of the circumnavigation of Africa was repeated on a small scale by the Continental customs decrees of Napoleon.[174] The last remnants of Venetian commerce were then annihilated. Despairing of all chances of profitable investment in that expiring maritime commerce, Venetian capitalists naturally transferred their capital to the opposite shore of the Adriatic, where the land-trade of Trieste promised to double its activity at that very epoch. Thus Venice itself nursed the greatness of Trieste—a fate common to all maritime despots. Thus Holland laid the foundation of the greatness of England; thus England built up the power of the United States.

Once incorporated with the Austrian Empire, Trieste commanded a natural position very different from what had ever been occupied by Venice. Trieste formed the natural outlet of the vast and inexhaustible dominions lying at its back, while Venice never had been anything but an isolated, outlying port of the Adriatic, usurping the carrying-trade of the world, and resting that usurpation on the barbarism of a world unconscious of its resources. The prosperity of Trieste, therefore, has no limits but the development of the productive forces and means of communication of the enormous complex of countries now under Austrian rule. Another advantage of Trieste is its contiguity with the eastern shore of the Adriatic, furnishing at once the basis of a coast trade almost unknown to the Venetians, and the nursery of that hardy race of seamen whom Venice never succeeded in fully turning to account. As the decline of Venice kept pace with the rise of the Ottoman power, so the opportunities of Trieste grow with the ascendancy of Austria over Turkey. Even in its best times, the trade of Venice was stunted by a division of Eastern commerce altogether dependent on political causes. On the one hand, there was the Danubian road of trade, hardly ever connected with Venetian shipping; on the other hand, while Venice, under the protection of the Catholic kings, monopolized the commerce of Morea, Cyprus, Egypt, Asia Minor, etc., the Genoese, under the protection of the Greek Emperors, almost monopolized the trade of Constantinople and the Black Sea. Trieste for the first time has united these two great channels of the Levant together with the Danubian trade. At the end of the fifteenth century Venice found itself, so to say, geographically displaced. The privileges of its neighborhood to Constantinople and Alexandria, then the centers of Asiatic trade, were forfeited by the circumnavigation of the Cape of Good Hope, transferring the center of that trade first to Lisbon, then to Holland, and afterward to England. The privilege lost to Venice is likely to be recovered in our own times by Trieste, by the cutting of the Isthmus of Suez Canal. The Trieste Chamber of Commerce has not only associated itself with the French Company for the Suez Canal, but also sent agents to explore the Red Sea and coasts of the Indian Ocean, in furtherance of the commercial operations contemplated in those parts. The Isthmus once cut, Trieste will necessarily supply all Eastern Europe with Indian goods; it will be as near to the Tropic of Cancer as it is to Gibraltar, and a navigation of 5,600 miles will bring its ships to the Sunda Straits. Having thus placed the outlines and prospects of Trieste commerce, we will now add a tabular statement of the commercial movement of that port during the period of the last ten years:

Years.	Ships.	Tunnage.	Years.	Ships.	Tunnage.
1846	16,782	985,514	1851	24,101	1,408,802
1847	17,321	1,007,330	1852	27,931	1,556,652
1848	17,812	926,815	1853	29,317	1,675,886
1849	20,553	1,269,258	1854	26,556	1,730,910
1850	21,124	1,323,796	1855	21,081	1,489,197

On comparing the average of the first three years of this period with the average of the last three years (973,220 against 1,631,664), the increase within so short a space is found to be in the proportion of 68 to 100. Marseilles is far from exhibiting the same rapidity of progress. The basis of the prosperity of Trieste, besides, is all the more solid, as it is owing to the increased intercourse both with purely Austrian and foreign ports. The national trade, for instance, from 1846 to 1848 amounted to 416,709 tuns average per annum; from 1853 to 1855 it had increased to 854,753 tuns average per year, or more than double. During the years 1850 and 1855, inclusive, the Austrian tunnage entered in and out at Trieste was 6,206,316; foreign, 2,981,928 tuns. The trade with Greece, Egypt, the Levant and Black Sea, had risen from 257,741 tuns to 496,394 tuns average per year during the same period.

With all this the actual commerce and navigation of Trieste are still far from having attained that point where traffic becomes a matter of regular routine, and the mechanical effect of fully developed resources. Let one only cast a glance at the economical situation of the Austrian States, the imperfect development of internal communications, at the great part of their populations still clad in sheep-skins, and strangers to all civilized wants. In the same measure in which Austria shall put its communications on a level say only with the German States, the commerce of Trieste will make rapid and powerful strides into the heart of the Empire. The completion of the railway from Trieste to Vienna, with a branch from Cilly to Pesth, will create a revolution in Austrian commerce from which no one will derive greater advantages than Trieste. This railway is sure to begin with a traffic greater than that of Marseilles, but the dimensions it may attain one can only realize by bearing in mind that the countries whose only outlet is the Adriatic possess a population of 30,966,000 inhabitants, equal to that of France in 1821, and that the port of Trieste will drain a territory of 60,398,000 hectares, i.e. by seven millions of hectares larger than France. Trieste, therefore, is destined to become, in its immediate future, what Marseilles, Bordeaux, Nantes and Havre united are to France.

Written in late November 1856

First published in the *New-York Daily Tribune,* No. 4906, January 9, 1857

Reproduced from the newspaper

Karl Marx

THE MARITIME COMMERCE OF AUSTRIA

(Second article)

In a former article[a] we traced the natural circumstances which have brought about the resurrection of Adriatic commerce at Trieste. The development of that commerce is, in a great measure, due to the efforts of the Austrian Lloyd—a Company founded by Englishmen, but, since 1836, in the hands of Triestine capitalists. At first, the Lloyd had only one steamer running once a week between Trieste and Venice. This communication soon became a daily one. By and by the steamers of the Lloyd engrossed the commerce of Rovigno, Fiume, Pirano, Zara and Ragusa, on the Istrian and Dalmatian coast. The Romagna was the next to be enveloped in this intercourse; then came Albania, Epirus and Greece. The steamers had not left the Adriatic, before the Archipelago, Salonica, Smyrna, Beyrout, Ptolemais and Alexandria already solicited admission into the network projected by the Lloyd. Lastly, its vessels penetrated into the Black Sea, taking possession, under the very eyes of Turkey and Russia, of the lines connecting Constantinople with Sinope, Trebizond, Varna, Ibraila and Galatz. Thus a company, organized for the mere coast service of Austria in the Adriatic, gradually pushes out into the Mediterranean, and having made sure of the Black Sea, appears to wait only for the cutting of the Isthmus of Suez to push on into the Red Sea and the Indian Ocean.

The capital of the Lloyd Company, originally fixed at 1,000,000 florins, has been increased by successive emissions of new shares, and by loans, to 13,000,000 florins. Its movement and operations

---

[a] See this volume, pp. 139-43.—*Ed.*

since the year 1836 are set forth in the last report of the Directors as follows:

	1836-7.	1853-4.
Capital	1,000,000 fl.	8,000,000 fl.
Number of steamers	7	47
Horse-power	630	7,990
Tunnage	1,944	23,665
Value of ships	798,824 fl.	8,010,000 fl.
Number of trips	87	1,465
Miles traversed	43,652	776,415
Passengers	7,967	331,688
Bullion	3,934,269 fl.	59,523,125 fl.
Letters and dispatches	35,205	748,930
Parcels	5,752	565,508
Total expenses	232,267 fl.	3,611,156 fl.
In a period of seventeen years the Company had a total of expenses (including dividends) of		25,147,403 fl.
And a total of receipts of		26,032,452 fl.
Hence there is a reserve of		885,049 fl.

The Lloyd, being itself a commercial enterprise of great importance, as may be judged from the above table, has rendered immense service to the growth of industry and commerce wherever its ships have penetrated. It is calculated that, on valuing the Austrian *quintal* at 300 fl., and each passenger's parcels at 10 fl., the Lloyd has transported between 1836 and 1853:

In merchandise	1,255,219,200 florins
In baggage	84,847,930 florins
In coins and bullion	461,113,767 florins
Total	1,801,180,897 florins

"It is certain," says a French author, "that the modest but sustained action of this company of merchants on the affairs of the Levant has been for years, to say the least, quite as efficient, and much more honorable than that of Austrian diplomacy."

The revival of commerce and the development of steam navigation in the Adriatic cannot fail to call into life, in a more or less remote future, an Adriatic navy, extinct since the downfall of Venice. Napoleon, with his peculiar turn of mind,. thought to create this navy without waiting for the reestablishment of maritime commerce—an experiment he made simultaneously at Antwerp and at Venice. Having succeeded in raising armies without a people to back them, he did not doubt his power to organize navies without a marine to rely upon. But apart from the inherent impossibilities of such a scheme, Napoleon stumbled on difficulties of a local character altogether unforeseen. Having dispatched his ablest engineers to Venice, completed the fortifications of that city, repaired the floating *matériel,* restored the ancient activity of the ship-building yards, it was all at once discovered that the technical progress in maritime war and navigation had struck with the same impotence the harbor of Venice to which the new roads of commerce had condemned its commerce and shipping. It was ascertained that, however excellent for the accommodation of the ancient galleys, the harbor of Venice lacked the depth required for modern ships of the line, and that even frigates were unable to enter the port without disembarking their guns, save with a concurrence of southern winds and spring tides. Now, for modern naval ports, it is a vital condition that they admit ships to enter at all times, and that they be deep and capacious enough to harbor a whole fleet, both for attack and defense. Bonaparte found, too, that he had committed another mistake. By the treaties of Campo Formio and Luneville,[175] he had cut off Venice from the eastern shores of the Adriatic, and thus deprived it of the crews for manning its fleets. From the mouth of the Isonzo down to Ravenna, he searched in vain for a maritime population, the gondoliers of Venice and the fishermen of the Lagunes (a timid and scanty race) being wholly unable to supply any valuable maritime force. Napoleon saw now, what the Venetians had discovered already in the tenth century, that the rule of the Adriatic can belong only to the possessor of its eastern shores. He perceived that his treaties of Campo Formio and Luneville were enormous mistakes—surrendering to Austria the maritime populations of the Adriatic, and reserving for himself the name of an obsolete harbor (*magni nominis umbram*[a]). To make good his earlier blunders, he appropriated Istria and Dalmatia by the subsequent treaties of Presburg and Vienna.[176]

Strabo long ago observed[b] that while the Adriatic coast of Italy is totally deficient in creeks and harbors, the Illyrian coast on the opposite side abounds in excellent ports; and, during the civil wars of Rome,[177] we see Pompey easily forming large fleets on the coasts of Epirus and Illyria, while Caesar, on the Italian shores, was able only after unexampled efforts to collect small force of

[a] "There stands the shadow of glorious name" (Lucan, *Pharsalia,* I, 135).— *Ed.*
[b] *Strabonis rerum geographicarum libri 17, Libr. 7, cap. 5.—Ed.*

boats for the conveyance of his troops in divisions. With its deep incisions, with the wild rocks of its islands, with the sandbanks strewed about everywhere, and with its admirable harbors of refuge, the coast of Istria and Dalmatia is a first-rate nursery of good seamen—sailors with vigorous limbs and intrepid hearts, seasoned in the storms which almost daily agitate the Adriatic. The *bora*,[a] which is the great disturber of that sea, always arises without the least warning; it attacks seamen with all the violence of a tornado, and permits none but the hardiest to keep the deck. Sometimes it rages for weeks together, and the domain of its greatest fury is comprised exactly within the mouths of Cattaro and the south point of Istria. The Dalmatian, however, accustomed to brave it from childhood, hardens under its breath, and despises the vulgar gales of other seas. Thus, air, land and sea combine to breed the robust and sober mariner of this coast.

Sismondi has remarked that silk-manufacture is as natural to the peasant of Lombardy as the spinning of silk is to the silk-worm. Thus, to take to the sea is as natural to the Dalmatian as it is to the sea-fowl. Piracy is as much the theme of their popular songs as robbery by land is the theme of the old Teutonic poetry. The Dalmatian still cherishes the memory of the wild exploits of the Uskoks, who for a century and a half kept in check the regular forces of Venice and Turkey,[178] and whose career was not stopped before the treaty concluded between Turkey and Austria in 1617, till which time the Uskoks had enjoyed the convenient protection of the Emperor. The history of the Uskoks has no parallel except in the history of the Cossacks of the Dnieper[179]—the one being exiles from Turkey and the other from Poland; the one carrying terror over the Adriatic, the other over the Black Sea; the former being at first secretly supported and then extinguished by Austria, and the latter by Russia. The Dalmatian sailors in the Mediterranean squadron of Admiral Emeriau were the admiration of Napoleon. There can be no doubt, then, that the eastern shores of the Adriatic possess all the materials for manning a first-rate navy. The only thing they want is discipline. By a census taken in 1813, Napoleon ascertained the existence of 43,500 sailors on this coast.

At Trieste	12,000	At Spalato	5,000
At Fiume	6,000	At Ragusa	8,500
At Zara	9,500	At Cattaro	2,500
Total			43,500

Their number must now be at least 55,000.

[a] Strong north-easterly wind.—*Ed.*

Having found the crews, Napoleon looked out for the harbors of an Adriatic navy. The Illyrian provinces were acquired definitely by the treaty of Vienna in 1809,[180] but they had been occupied by French troops since the battle of Austerlitz,[181] and Napoleon improved the opportunity of a state of war to prepare the great works intended to be executed during peace. In 1806 M. Beautemps-Beaupré, assisted by several engineers and hydrographers of the French Navy, was sent to survey the coasts of Istria and Dalmatia, with a view of discovering the most suitable focus for the naval foundation contemplated in the Adriatic. The whole coast was explored, and the attention of the engineers finally stuck to the harbor of Pola, situated at the southern extremity of the Istrian Peninsula. The Venetians, unwilling to fix the seat of their naval power anywhere but at Venice itself, had not only neglected Pola, but had anxiously propagated the opinion that Pola was inaccessible to ships of war on account of a pretended bar. However, M. Beaupré ascertained that no such bar existed, and that Pola answered all the conditions of a modern naval port. At different times it had been the seat of the naval forces of the Adriatic. It was the center of the naval operations of the Romans during their Illyrian and Pannonian expeditions, and it became a permanent naval station under the Roman Empire. At different times it has been in the occupation of the Genoese, the Venetians, and lastly of the Uskoks. Deep and capacious in every part, the harbor of Pola is defended in front by islands, and in the rear by rocks which command the position. Its only disadvantage is the unhealthiness and the fevers which, as M. Beautemps-Beaupré affirms,[a] will yield to a system of drainage that has hitherto not been applied.

The Austrians have been very slow in familiarizing themselves with the notion of becoming a naval power. Up to a very recent period their naval administration was, in their own eyes, merely a branch of their land service. A colonel in the army had the rank of a naval captain; a lieutenant-colonel, that of a captain of a frigate; a major, that of a captain of a corvette; and the equivalence in the rank list seemed to guarantee to the Austrians an equivalence in the services. To make a midshipman, they considered to have hit on the best expedient by making him previously a cornet of hussars. The recruits of the navy were levied in the same manner as the recruits for the army—with the

---

[a] C. F. Beautemps-Beaupré, *Rapports sur les rades, ports et mouillages de la côte orientale du golfe de Venise, visités en 1806, 1808 et 1809, par ordre de l'empereur.*—*Ed.*

only difference that the provinces of Istria and Dalmatia were allotted exclusively to the sea service. The time of service was equal, viz: Eight years, either by land or sea.

The separation of the two services, like all modern progress in Austria, is the result of the revolution of 1848. In spite of the Napoleonian precedent, Venice had remained up to 1848 the only arsenal of Austria. The defects of the Venetian harbor had failed to strike the Austrians, because they had, in fact, no modern navy at all. Their naval force consisted of but 6 frigates, 5 corvettes, 7 brigs, 6 sloops, 16 steamers, and 36 armed boats—in all 850 guns. By way of punishing the Italian revolution, the Austrians transferred from Venice to Trieste the naval school, the observatory, the hydrographic office, the floating *matériel* and the artillery park. The building-yards and the stores remained behind; and thus, by a bureaucratic vengeance, the naval service was cut in two. Instead of Venice being punished, both branches were deprived of their efficiency. Slowly the Austrian Government discovered that, however excellent Trieste might be for a commercial harbor, it was unfit for a naval station. At last they had to fall back on the lesson Napoleon had set up in the Adriatic, and to make Pola the center of their naval administration. Quite in keeping with Austrian usage, the first few years after this removal of their Admiralty to Pola have been employed in building barracks instead of ship-yards. The system of defense reposes on the establishment of a cross-fire from the islands at the entrance of the harbor, with a chain of Maximilian towers[a] to prevent ships from throwing bombs into the harbor. Beside its strategical advantages, Pola answers the indispensable condition of a good port, viz: of being able to provision a good fleet. Istria has oaks equal to Naples; Carniola, Carinthia and Styria are inexhaustible in pines, which already form the staple tunnage of Trieste exportation; Styria is rich in iron; the hemp of Ancona has no more commodious outlet than Pola; coal is hitherto received from England, but the Dalmatian works at Sebenico begin to yield a better quality; and when the Trieste-Vienna Railway opens, the best quality may be had from Semmering. All Istrian produce, being grown on a chalky soil, endures long voyages. Oil is abundant, Hungarian grain at hand, and pork in immense quantities to be had from the Danubian valley. That pork goes now to Galatz and Hamburg, but the railway will bring it to Trieste and Pola.

[a] Named after Maximilian Este.—*Ed.*

To all these excellent bases for the revival of the naval power in the Adriatic, there is only one drawback—Austria itself. If, with its present organization and under its present Government, Austria were able to found a commercial and naval power in the Adriatic, it would upset all the traditions of history, which has ever coupled maritime greatness with Freedom. On the other hand, it would upset Austria to upset tradition.

Written in late November 1856

First published in the *New-York Daily Tribune,* No. 5082, August 4, 1857

Reproduced from the newspaper

Karl Marx

THE RIGHT DIVINE OF THE HOHENZOLLERNS[182]

At the present moment there is only one great question afloat in Europe—the Neuchatel question.[183] This, at least, is the tenet of the Prussian newspapers. The principality of Neuchatel, it is true, together with the county of Valengin, may be mathematically circumscribed by the somewhat diminutive figure of fourteen square miles.[a] But then, say the royalist philosophers of Berlin, it is not quantity but quality, that generally invests things with grandeur or pettiness, and stamps them as sublime or ridiculous. To them the Neuchatel question is the eternal question between revolution and right divine, an antagonism as little affected by geographical dimensions as the law of gravitation by the difference between the sun and a tennis-ball.

Let us try to get at an understanding of what the Hohenzollern dynasty call their divine right. In the case now before us, they appeal to a protocol dated London, May 24th, 1852, by which the plenipotentiaries of France, Great Britain and Russia,

> "recognised the rights which belong to the King of Prussia over the principality of Neuchatel and the county of Valengin, according to the tenor of articles twenty-three and seventy-five of the treaty of Vienna, and which have coexisted from 1815 to 1848 with those which article seventy-three of the same treaty conferred on Switzerland." [b]

By this "diplomatic intervention" the right divine of the King of Prussia over Neuchatel is only acknowledged as far as established by the treaty of Vienna. The treaty of Vienna, in its turn, refers us

[a] In the *New-York Daily Tribune* "seventeen miles square".—*Ed.*

[b] "Protocole de Londres, du 24 mai 1852".—*Ed.*

to a title which Prussia acquired in the year 1707. Now how did the case stand in 1707?

The principality of Neuchatel and the county of Valengin, appertaining in mediaeval times to the kingdom of Burgundy, became, after the defeat of Charles le Téméraire,[a] an ally of the Swiss Confederation,[184] and such it remained under the immediate protection of Berne, during all the subsequent displacements of its feudal "suzerains," till the treaty of Vienna transformed the ally into a member of the Swiss Confederation. The suzerainty over Neuchatel was first transferred to the house of Châlons-Orange—next, by the intervention of Switzerland, to the house of Longueville, and finally, after the extinction of the magnates of that house, to the sister of the prince,[b] the dowager Duchess of Nemours. When the latter acceded to these dominions, William III., King of England and Duke of Nassau-Orange, issued a protest and made over his claims on Neuchatel and Valengin to his cousin Frederick I. of Prussia, a settlement which, however, produced no effect whatever during the lifetime of William III. On the death of Mary, Duchess of Nemours, Frederick I. stepped forward with his pretensions, but fourteen other candidates appearing in the field, he wisely abandoned the decision over the rival claims to the supreme judgement of the States of Neuchatel and Valengin, having made sure before of their sentence by bribing the judges. By dint of bribery, then, the King of Prussia became Prince of Neuchatel and Count of Valengin. As such he was unmade by the French revolution, remade by the treaty of Vienna, and unmade again by the revolution of 1848. Against the revolutionary right of the people he appeals to the right divine of the Hohenzollerns, which would seem to resolve itself into the divine right of bribery.[c]

Littleness is a characteristic feature of all feudal conflicts. Yet there is a large line of distinction to be drawn. The numberless small fights, intrigues, treasons, by which the Kings of France succeeded in supplanting their feudal vassals, are sure to remain a favourite subject with the historian, because they trace the origin of a great nation. On the other hand, the story how a vassal contrived to carve out the German Empire, a more or less extensive slice of sovereignty for his private use, is a theme altogether barren and dull, unless enlivened by a concurrence of

[a] In the *NYDT* "Charles the Bold".—*Ed.*

[b] Charles Longueville; in the *NYDT* "sister of the last prince".—*Ed.*

[c] In the *NYDT* "in the last analysis to lose itself in the divine right of bribery".—*Ed.*

extraordinary circumstances, such as distinguish the history of Austria. There we observe one and the same prince as the elective head of an empire and as the hereditary vassal of a province of that empire; conspiring in the interest of his province against the empire; proving successful in that conspiracy, because his encroachments on the south appear to revive the traditionary conflicts between the German empire and Italy, and his encroachments on the east to continue the deadly struggle between the German and Sclavonic races, and the resistance of Christian Europe against the Mahometan Orient; lastly, exalting, by artful family connections,[a] his domestic power to such a pitch that at one moment it threatened not only to absorb the empire while shedding a factitious lustre upon it, but to bury the world in the tomb of a universal monarchy. Than such colossal outlines, nothing can be stranger to the annals of the margravate of Brandenburg. Where the history of its rival reads like a diabolical epic, it only reads like an immoral family tale. There exists a striking difference, even where one expects to find likeness, if not identity of interest. The two Marches of Brandenburg and of Austria,[b] both derived their original importance from forming advanced posts for the defence as well as the attack of Germany against the neighbouring Sclavonian race. But even from this point of view the history of Brandenburg lacks colour, life, and dramatic movement, lost as it is in petty strifes with obscure Sclavonic tribes scattered over a relatively small tract of land between the Elbe and the Oder, none of which tribes ever ripened into anything like an historical existence. No Sclavonic tribe of historical mark was ever conquered or Germanised by the margravate of Brandenburg, nor did it even succeed to stretch out its arms to the bordering Wendish sea.[c] Pomerania, coveted by the margraves of Brandenburg since the 12th century, was not entirely incorporated with the kingdom of Prussia in the year 1815[185]; and when the Brandenburg electors began to appropriate it piecemeal, it had long ago ceased to be a Sclavonic state. The transformation of the southern and south-eastern shores of the Baltic, partly by the commercial enterprise of German burghers, partly by the sword of the German knights, belongs to the history of Germany and Poland, not to that of Brandenburg, which only came to gather the harvest it had not sown.

---

[a] In the *NYDT* "exalting by dint of artful family combinations".—*Ed.*
[b] Previously called Ostmark.—*Ed.*
[c] Slavonic name of the Baltic Sea.—*Ed.*

Without much risk one may go so far as to say that of the innumerable readers who have contrived to get some clue to the classical names of Achilles, Cicero, Nestor, and Hector, there exists only a very indifferent per centage who ever suspected the sandy soil of Brandenburg of not only producing potatoes and sheep at our own time, but of having once[a] exuberated in no less than four electors, going respectively under the names of Albrecht Achilles, Johann Cicero, Joachim I. Nestor, and Joachim II. Hector. The same golden mediocrity that favoured the slow growth of the electorate of Brandenburg into what is by courtesy called an European power, has screened[b] its home-spun history from too indiscreet an intimacy with the public eye. Relying on this fact Prussian statesmen and writers have exerted themselves to the utmost to impregnate the world with the notion that Prussia is the military monarchy par excellence, whence it might be induced that the right divine of the Hohenzollerns must mean the right of the sword—the right of conquest. Nothing could be more off the mark. It may be affirmed, on the contrary, that, properly speaking, of all the provinces the Hohenzollerns now possess, they have conquered only one—Silesia, a fact, so unique in the annals of their house that it earned for Frederick II. the title of the Unique. Now, the Prussian monarchy stretches over 5,062 geographical square miles,[c] of which the province of Brandenburg, even in its present extent, does not occupy more than 730, and Silesia no more than 741. How, then, did they get at Prussia with 1,178, at Posen with 536, at Pomerania with 567, at Saxony with 460, at Westphalia with 366, and at Rhenish Prussia with 479 square miles? By the divine right of bribery, open purchase, petty larceny, legacy-hunting, and treacherous partition treaties.

In the beginning of the fifteenth century the margravate of Brandenburg belonged to the house of Luxemburg, whose chief, Sigismund, simultaneously swayed the Imperial sceptre of Germany. Being very short of cash, and hard pressed by his creditors, he found a facile and accommodating friend in Frederick, burgrave of Nurnberg, a prince tracing his origin to the house of Hohenzollern. In 1411, Frederick was installed as General Administrator of Brandenburg, made over to him as a sort of mortgage for the divers sums of money he had advanced to the

[a] In the *NYDT* "some centuries ago".—*Ed.*

[b] In the *NYDT* "has safely screened".—*Ed.*

[c] *Geographical mile*—a German unit of distance equal to 7.42 km.-The *New-York Daily Tribune* uses data in statute miles.—*Ed.*

Emperor. Like a prudent money-lender who finds himself once put in preliminary possession of the premises of a spendthrift, Frederick continued to involve Sigismund in fresh debts by new advances, till 1415, when the debtor and creditor accounts were settled by the investiture of Frederick with the hereditary electorate of Brandenburg. To leave no doubt as to the nature of this act, it was encumbered with two clauses, the one reserving to the house of Luxemburg the right of redeeming the electorate on payment of 400,000 gold florins, and the other binding Frederick and his heirs to give on every new election for the empire their vote to the house of Luxemburg—the former clause stamping the contract as a barter, and the latter as a bribery. To become full proprietor of the electorate, there remained for the grasping friend of Sigismund but one further operation, the dropping of the redemption clause. Accordingly, he watched the opportune moment when Sigismund, at the council of Constance,[186] had again got at loggerheads with the costs of Imperial representation[a]; and hurrying from the March to the confines of Switzerland, he emptied his purse, and the fatal clause was struck off. Such were the ways and means of the right divine on which the still reigning dynasty of Hohenzollern founds its possession of the electorate of Brandenburg. Such was the origin of the Prussian monarchy.

Frederick's next successor,[b] a very weak man, called the "Iron," because of his fancy for always appearing in public in an iron harness, bought for 100,000 gold florins the New March from the order of the Teutonic knights,[187] as his father had bought the Old March and his dignity from the Emperor. Thence the method of buying encumbered parcels of sovereignty grew into as settled a thing with the Hohenzollern electors as intervention had once been with the Roman senate. Leaving alone the tedious details of this sordid traffic, we pass on to the times of the Reformation.

It must not be imagined that because the Reformation turned out to be the main prop of the Hohenzollern dynasty, the Hohenzollern dynasty proved themselves the main prop of the Reformation. Quite the reverse. The founder of that dynasty, Frederick I., inaugurated his reign by leading the armies of Sigismund against the Hussites,[188] who thrashed him soundly for his pains. Joachim I. Nestor, 1499-1535, treated the Reformation as though it were a Taborite.[189] He persecuted it to his death.

---

[a] In the *NYDT* "was again out of money".—*Ed.*

[b] Frederick II.—*Ed.*

Joachim II. Hector, although a convert to Lutheranism, refused to draw the sword in defence of the new faith, at the very moment when it appeared to succumb under the overwhelming forces of Charles-Quint. Not only declining to share in the armed resistance of the Schmalkalden Bund,[190] he tendered his secret support to the Emperor. On the part of the Hohenzollerns, the German Reformation then met with open hostility at its rise, at the time of its earlier struggles with a false neutrality, and during its terrible concluding scene of the thirty years' war[191] with fainthearted vacillation, cowardly inaction, and base faithlessness. It is known that the elector, George Wilhelm, tried to bar the passage of the liberating armies of Gustavus Adolphus, who was forced to drive him by kicks and blows into the Protestant camp, from which he afterwards attempted to skulk out by concluding a separate peace with Austria.[192] But if the Hohenzollerns were not the knights, they certainly were the cashiers of the German Reformation. Their reluctance to fight in its cause was equalled only by their eagerness to plunder in its name. Reformation, with them, was but the religious title for secularisation, so that the best part of their acquisitions during the 16th and 17th centuries, may be traced to one large source—church robbery—a rather queer way this for the divine right to manifest itself in.

Three events stand foremost in the history of the formation of the Hohenzollern monarchy—the acquisition of the Brandenburg electorate, the adjunction to the electorate of the duchy of Prussia, and lastly the elevation of the duchy into a kingdom. We have seen how the electorate was acquired. The duchy of Prussia was got by three steps. First: secularisation; next, marriage transactions of rather an equivocal character—the elector Joachim Frederick espousing the younger,[a] and his son, Johann Sigismund, the elder daughter[b] of the mad and sonless Duke Albrecht of Prussia—and, lastly: by bribing with the right hand the Court of the Polish King,[c] and with the left hand the Diet of the Polish Republic. So complicated were these bribery transactions as to extend over a whole series of years.[193] A similar method was adopted for the transformation of the duchy of Prussia into a kingdom. To get the royal title, the elector, Frederick III., afterwards King Frederick I., wanted the consent of the German Emperor. To get this consent, against which the Catholic conscience of the Emperor

---

[a] Eleonore.—*Ed.*

[b] Anne.—*Ed.*

[c] Sigismund.—*Ed.*

revolted, he bribed the Jesuit Wolf, the confessor of Leopold I., and threw into the bargain 30,000 Brandenburghers, to be slaughtered in the Austro-Spanish succession-war.[194] The Hohenzollern elector returned to the Old German Institution of life-money, only that the ancient Germans paid with cattle and that he paid with men. Such was the foundation of the Hohenzollern royalty, by the grace of God.

With their improving fortunes, since the commencement of the eighteenth century, the Hohenzollerns improved their method of aggrandisement by adding to bribery and barter partition treaties with Russia against states which they had not felled, but surprised when fallen. Thus we find them concurring with Peter the Great in the partition of the Swedish possessions, with Catherine II. in the partition of Poland, and with Alexander I. in the partition of Germany.[195]

Those, then, who object to the Prussian claims on Neuchatel that the Hohenzollerns got it by bribery, commit a woeful mistake in forgetting that it was by bribery that they acquired Brandenburg, that they acquired Prussia, that they acquired the royal dignity. There can exist no doubt they possess Neuchatel by the same right divine as their other states, and they cannot resign the one without exposing the others.

Written on about December 2, 1856

First published in *The People's Paper,* No. 241, December 13, 1856, signed K. M., and also in the *New-York Daily Tribune,* No. 4906, January 9, 1857, unsigned

Reproduced from *The People's Paper*

Karl Marx

[THE ANGLO-CHINESE CONFLICT]

The mails of the *America* which reached us yesterday morning bring a variety of documents concerning the British quarrel with the Chinese authorities at Canton, and the warlike operations of Admiral Seymour.[196] The result which a careful study of the official correspondence between the British and Chinese authorities at Hong-Kong and Canton must, we think, produce upon every impartial mind, is that the British are in the wrong in the whole proceeding. The alleged cause of the quarrel, as stated by the latter, is that instead of appealing to the British Consul, certain Chinese officers had violently removed some Chinese criminals from a lorcha[a] lying in Canton river, and hauled down the British flag which was flying from its mast. But, as says *The London Times*,

> "there are, indeed, matters in dispute such as whether the lorcha was carrying British colors, and whether the Consul was entirely justified in the steps that he took."[b]

The doubt thus admitted is confirmed when we remember that the provision of the treaty,[c 197] which the Consul insists should be applied to this lorcha, relates to British ships alone; while the lorcha, as it abundantly appears, was not in any just sense British. But in order that our readers may have the whole case before them, we proceed to give what is important in the official correspondence. First, we have a communication dated Oct. 21,

---

[a] Coastal sailer.— *Ed.*

[b] *The Times*, No. 22567, January 2, 1857, leading article.— *Ed.*

[c] *Traité supplémentaire entre S. M. la reine du Royaume-Uni de la Grande-Bretagne et d'Irlande et l'empereur de Chine, signé à Houmon-Schai, le 8 octobre 1843.—Ed.*

from Mr. Parkes, the British Consul at Canton, to Governor-General Yeh, as follows:

"On the morning of the 8th inst. the British lorcha *Arrow,* when lying among the shipping anchored before the city, was boarded, without any previous reference being made to the British Consul, by a large force of Chinese officers and soldiers in uniform, who, in the face of the remonstrance of the master, an Englishman, seized, bound and carried away twelve Chinese out of her crew of fourteen, and hauled down her colors. I reported all the particulars of this public insult to the British flag, and grave violation of the ninth article of the Supplementary Treaty, to your Excellency the same day, and appealed to you to afford satisfaction for the insult, and cause the provision of the treaty to be in this case faithfully observed. But your Excellency, with a strange disregard both to justice and treaty engagement, has offered no reparation or apology for the injury, and, by retaining the men you have seized in your custody, signify your approval of this violation of the treaty, and leave her Majesty's Government without assurance that a similar event shall not again occur." [a]

It seems that the Chinese on board the lorcha were seized by the Chinese officers, because the latter had been informed that some of the crew had participated in a piracy committed against a Chinese merchantman. The British Consul accuses the Chinese Governor-General of seizing the crew, of hauling down the British flag, of declining to offer any apology, and of retaining the men seized in his custody. The Chinese Governor, in a letter addressed to Admiral Seymour, affirms that, having ascertained that nine of the captives were innocent, he directed, on Oct. 10, an officer to put them on board of their vessel again, but that Consul Parkes refused to receive them. As to the lorcha itself, he states that when the Chinese on board were seized, she was supposed to be a Chinese vessel, and rightly so, because she was built by a Chinese, and belonged to a Chinese, who had fraudulently obtained possession of a British ensign, by entering his vessel on the colonial British register—a method, it seems, habitual with Chinese smugglers. As to the question of the insult to the flag, the Governor remarks:

"It has been the invariable rule with lorchas of your Excellency's nation, to haul down the flag when they drop anchor, and to hoist it again when they get under way. When the lorcha was boarded, in order that the prisoners might be seized, it has been satisfactorily proved that no flag was flying. How then could a flag have been hauled down? Yet Consul Parkes, in one dispatch after another, pretends that satisfaction is required for the insult offered to the flag." [b]

---

[a] H. Parkes' letter to Yeh, Governor-General of the two Kwang Provinces, October 21, 1856, *The Times,* No. 22571, January 7, 1857.—*Ed.*

[b] Here and below see Yeh's letter to the Naval Commander-in-Chief M. Seymour, October 31, 1856, *The Times,* No. 22567, January 2, 1857.—*Ed.*

From these premises the Chinese Governor concludes that no breach of any treaty has been committed. On Oct. 12, nevertheless, the British Plenipotentiary[a] demanded not only the surrender of the whole of the arrested crew, but also an apology. The Governor thus replies:

"Early in the morning of Oct. 22, I wrote to Consul Parkes, and at the same time forwarded to him twelve men, namely, Leong Mingtai and Leong Kee-foo, convicted on the inquiry I had instituted, and the witness, Woo Ayu, together with nine previously tendered. But Consul Parkes would neither receive the twelve prisoners nor my letter."

Parkes might, therefore, have now got back the whole of his twelve men, together with what was most probably an apology, contained in a letter which he did not open. In the evening of the same day, Governor Yeh again made inquiry why the prisoners tendered by him were not received, and why he received no answer to his letter. No notice was taken of this step, but on the 24th fire was opened on the forts, and several of them were taken; and it was not until Nov. 1 that Admiral Seymour explained the apparently incomprehensible conduct of Consul Parkes in a message to the Governor. The men, he says, has been restored to the Consul, but "not *publicly* restored to their vessel, nor had the required apology been made for the violation of the Consular jurisdiction."[b] To this quibble, then, of not restoring in state a set of men numbering three convicted criminals, the whole case is reduced. To this the Governor of Canton answers, first, that the twelve men had been actually handed over to the Consul, and that there had not been "any refusal to return them to their vessel." What was still the matter with this British Consul, the Chinese Governor only learned after the city had been bombarded for six days. As to an apology, Governor Yeh insists that none could be given, as no fault had been committed. We quote his words:

"No foreign flag was seen by my executive at the time of the capture, and as, in addition to this, it was ascertained on examination of the prisoners by the officer deputed to conduct it, that the lorcha was in no respect a foreign vessel, I maintain that there was no mistake committed."[c]

---

[a] John Bowring.—*Ed.*

[b] M. Seymour's letter to Yeh, November 2, 1856, *The Times*, No. 22567, January 2, 1857.—*Ed.*

[c] Yeh's letter to M. Seymour, November 3, 1856, *The Times*, No. 22571, January 7, 1857.—*Ed.*

Indeed, the force of this Chinaman's dialectics disposes so effectually of the whole question—and there is no other apparent case—that Admiral Seymour at last has no resource left him but a declaration like the following:

"I must positively decline any further argument on the merits of the case of the lorcha *Arrow*. I am perfectly satisfied of the facts as represented to your Excellency by Mr. Consul Parkes."[a]

But after having taken the forts, breached the walls of the city, and bombarded Canton for six days, the Admiral suddenly discovers quite a new object for his measures, as we find him writing to the Chinese Governor on Oct. 30:

"It is now for your Excellency, by immediate consultation with me, to terminate a condition of things of which the present evil is not slight, but which, if not amended, can scarcely fail to be productive of the most serious calamities."[b]

The Chinese Governor answers, that according to the Convention of 1849,[198] he had no right to ask for such a consultation. He further says:

"In reference to the admission into the city, I must observe that, in April, 1849, his Excellency the Plenipotentiary Bonham issued a public notice at the factories here, to the effect that he thereby prohibited foreigners from entering the city. The notice was inserted in the newspapers of the time, and will, I presume, have been read by your Excellency. Add to this that the exclusion of foreigners from the city is by the unanimous vote of the whole population of Kwang-Tung. It may be supposed how little to their liking has been this storming of the forts and this destruction of their dwellings; and, apprehensive as I am of the evil that may hence befall the officials and citizens of your Excellency's nation, I can suggest nothing better than a continued adherence to the policy of the Plenipotentiary Bonham, as to the correct course to be pursued. As to the consultation proposed by your Excellency, I have already, some days ago, deputed Tseang, Prefect of Luy-chow-foo."[c]

Admiral Seymour now makes a clean breast of it, declaring that he does not care for the convention of Mr. Bonham:

"Your Excellency's reply refers me to the notification of the British Plenipotentiary of 1849, prohibiting foreigners from entering Canton. Now, I must

---

[a] M. Seymour's letter to Yeh, November 2, 1856, *The Times*, No. 22567, January 2, 1857.—*Ed.*

[b] M. Seymour's letter to Yeh, October 30, 1856, *The Times*, No. 22567, January 2, 1857.—*Ed.*

[c] Yeh's letter to M. Seymour, October 31, 1856, *The Times*, No. 22567, January 2, 1857.—*Ed.*

remind you that, although we have indeed serious matter of complaint against the Chinese Government for breach of the promise given in 1847 to admit foreigners into Canton at the end of two years, my demand now made is in no way connected with former negotiations on the same subject, neither am I demanding admission of any but the foreign officials, and this only for the simple and sufficient reasons above assigned. On my proposal to treat personally with your Excellency, you do me the honor to remark that you sent a Prefect some days ago. I am compelled therefore to regard your Excellency's whole letter as unsatisfactory in the extreme, and have only to add that, unless I immediately receive an explicit assurance of your assent to what I have proposed, I shall at once resume offensive operations." [a]

Governor Yeh retorts by again entering into the details of the Convention of 1849:

"In 1848 there was a long controversial correspondence on the subject between my predecessor Seu and the British Plenipotentiary, Mr. Bonham, and Mr. Bonham, being satisfied that an interview within the city was utterly out of the question, addressed a letter to Seu in the April of 1849, in which he said, 'At the present time I can have no more discussion with your Excellency on this subject.' He further issued a notice from the factories to the effect that no foreigner was to enter the city, which was inserted in the papers, and he communicated this to the British Government. There was not a Chinese or foreigner of any nation who did not know that the question was never to be discussed again." [b]

Impatient of argument, the British Admiral hereupon forces his way into the City of Canton to the residence of the Governor, at the same time destroying the Imperial fleet in the river. Thus there are two distinct acts in this diplomatic and military drama—the first introducing the bombardment of Canton on the pretext of a breach of the Treaty of 1842 [199] committed by the Chinese Governor, and the second, continuing that bombardment on an enlarged scale, on the pretext that the Governor clung stubbornly to the Convention of 1849. First Canton is bombarded for breaking a treaty, and next it is bombarded for observing a treaty. Besides, it is not even pretended that redress was not given in the first instance, but only that redress was not given in the orthodox manner.

The view of the case put forth by *The London Times* would do no discredit even to General William Walker of Nicaragua. [200]

"By this outbreak of hostilities," says that journal, "existing treaties are annulled, and we are left free to change our relations with the Chinese Empire as we please. The recent proceedings at Canton warn us that we ought to enforce that

---

[a] M. Seymour's letter to Yeh, November 2, 1856, *The Times*, No. 22567, January 2, 1857.—*Ed.*

[b] Yeh's letter to M. Seymour, November 3, 1856, *The Times*, No. 22571, January 7, 1857.—*Ed.*

right of free entrance into the country and into the ports open to us, which was stipulated for in the Treaty of 1842. We must not again be told that our representatives must be excluded from the presence of the Chinese Governor-General, because *we have waived* the performance of the article which enabled foreigners to penetrate beyond the precincts of our factories."[a]

In other words, "we" have commenced hostilities in order to break an existing treaty and to enforce a claim which "we" have waived by an express convention! We are happy to say, however, that another prominent organ of British opinion expresses itself in a more humane and becoming tone.

"It is," says *The Daily News,* "a monstrous fact, that in order to avenge the irritated pride of a British official, and punish the folly of an Asiatic governor, we prostitute our strength to the wicked work of carrying fire and sword, and desolation and death, into the peaceful homes of unoffending men, on whose shores we were originally intruders. Whatever may be the issue of this Canton bombardment, the deed itself is a bad and a base one—a reckless and wanton waste of human life at the shrine of a false etiquette and a mistaken policy."

It is, perhaps, a question whether the civilized nations of the world will approve this mode of invading a peaceful country, without previous declaration of war, for an alleged infringement of the fanciful code of diplomatic etiquette. If the first Chinese war, in spite of its infamous pretext,[201] was patiently looked upon by other powers, because it held out the prospect of opening the trade with China, is not this second war likely to obstruct that trade for an indefinite period? Its first result must be the cutting off of Canton from the tea-growing districts, as yet, for the most part, in the hands of the imperialists[202]—a circumstance which cannot profit anybody but the Russian overland tea traders.[203]

Written on January 7, 1857

First published in the *New-York Daily Tribune,* No. 4918, January 23, 1857 as a leading article and reprinted in the *New-York Weekly Tribune,* No. 803, January 31, 1857 under the title "The Chinese War"

Reproduced from the *New-York Daily Tribune*

[a] *The Times,* No. 22567, January 2, 1857, leading article.—*Ed.*

Frederick Engels

[MOUNTAIN WARFARE IN THE PAST AND PRESENT][204]

The recent possibility, not yet entirely removed, of an invasion of Switzerland, has naturally revived the public interest not only concerning the defensive resources of the mountain Republic, but with regard to mountain warfare in general. People generally incline to regard Switzerland as impregnable, and think of an invading force as of those Roman gladiators whose "*Ave Caesar, morituri te salutant*"[a] has become so famous.[b] We are reminded of Sempach and Morgarten, Murten and Granson,[205] and we are told that it may be easy enough for a foreign army to get into Switzerland, but that, as the fool of Albert of Austria said, it will be difficult to get out again. Even military men will recite the names of a dozen mountain passes and defiles, where a handful of men might easily and successfully oppose a couple of thousands of the best soldiers.[c]

This traditional impregnability of the so-called mountain-fortress of Switzerland dates from the time of the wars with

---

[a] "Hail Caesar; those who are about to die salute you." (The expression is used by Gaius Suetonius Tranquillus in Claudius' biography in *The Lives of the Twelve Caesars*).— *Ed.*

[b] In the rough manuscript the beginning of the article reads: "Whenever there is a chance of Switzerland being involved in a war, the general public look upon that country with a certain degree of awe, and are inclined to give up the invading army for quite as lost as the Roman gladiators whose '*Ave Caesar, morituri te salutant*' has become so celebrated."— *Ed.*

[c] The manuscript further reads: "And to complete your conviction they will put a map of Switzerland before you, black with mountain-ridges and slopes, and ask you how an army is to find its road and to act in concert in this labyrinth of rocks, ravines, glaciers, torrents and impassable mountain crests."— *Ed.*

Whenever there is a chance of Switzerland being involved in a war, the general public look upon that country with a certain degree of awe, and are inclined to liken the invading army (for quitting lost as [?]) with the Roman gladiators whose: Ave, Caesar, morituri te salutant has become so celebrated. We are reminded of Sempach and Morgarten, Morat and Granson, and we are told that it may be easy enough for any foreign army to get into Switzerland, but that it will be found very difficult indeed to get out again. Even military men will recite the names of a dozen mountain passes & defiles, by aspect & tradition, perfectly impregnable, where a handful of men, might easily oppose & successfully oppose a couple of thousand of the & best soldiers. And to complete your conviction, they will put a map of Switzerland before you, black with mountain-ridges & slopes, & ask you how an army is to find its road & to act in concert in this labyrinth of rocks, ravines, glaciers, torrents & impassable mountain crests.

This traditional impregnability of the so-called mountain-fortress of Switzerland dates from the time of the wars with Austria and Burgundy in the 14th & 15th centuries. In the former [illegible], the armour-clad cavalry of the knighthood was the chief arm of the invaders; strength lay in the irresistibility of the charge against armies undefended by fire arms; this charge was impossible in a country like Switzerland where cavalry, except of the lightest kind & in small numbers, is even now useless. How much more so were the knights of the 14th century, encumbered with nearly a hundredweight of iron? They had to dismount & fight on foot, thereby their last remnant of mobility was lost; they, the invaders, were reduced to an almost absolute defensive, &, caught in a defilee, were defenceless even against clubs & big sticks. During the Burgundian wars, infantry armed with pikes, had become a more important portion of an army; fire-arms had been introduced; but the infantry was still cramped by the weight of defensive armour, the cannons were heavy, & small-arms very in their infancy. The whole equipment of the troops was still so cumbersome

The first page of Engels' rough manuscript
"Mountain Warfare in the Past and Present"

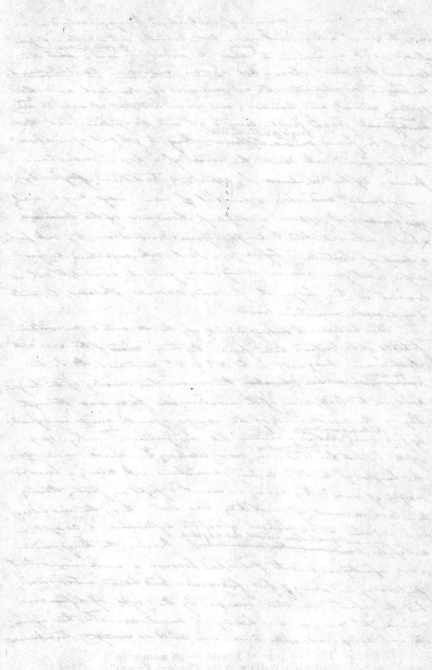

Austria and Burgundy, in the fourteenth and fifteenth centuries.[206] In the former the armor-clad cavalry of the chivalry was the chief arm of the invaders; its strength lay in the irresistible charge against armies undefended by firearms. Now, this charge was impossible in a country like Switzerland, where cavalry, except of the lightest kind, and in small numbers, is even now useless. How much more so were the knights of the fourteenth century, encumbered with nearly a hundred weight of iron. They had to dismount and fight on foot; thus, their last remnant of mobility was lost; and the invaders were reduced to the defensive, and when caught in a defile were defenseless even against clubs and sticks. During the Burgundian wars, infantry, armed with pikes, had become a more important portion of an army, and firearms had been introduced, but the infantry was still cramped by the weight of defensive armor, the cannon were heavy, and small arms clumsy and comparatively useless.[a] The whole equipment of the troops was still so cumbersome as to unfit them completely for mountain warfare, and especially at a time when roads can scarcely be said to have existed. The consequence was that, as soon as these slow-moving armies were once entangled in difficult ground, they stuck fast, while the lightly-armed Swiss peasants were enabled to act on the offensive, to out-maneuver, to surround, and finally to defeat their opponents.

For three centuries after the Burgundian wars, Switzerland was never seriously invaded. The tradition of Swiss invincibility grew venerable, until the French Revolution, an event which tore into shreds so many venerable traditions, destroyed this one too, at least for those acquainted with military history. Times had changed. The iron-clad cavalry and the heavy pikemen had passed away; tactics had been revolutionized a dozen times over; mobility was becoming the chief quality of armies; the line tactics of Marlborough, Eugene[b] and Frederick the Great were being upset by the columns and skirmishers of the revolutionary armies; and from the day that General Bonaparte passed, in 1796, the Col di Cadibone, threw himself between the scattered Austrian and Sardinian columns, defeated them in front, while at the same time intercepting their retreat in the narrow valleys of the Maritime Alps, making the most of his opponents prisoners—from that day

[a] Instead of the words "clumsy and comparatively useless" the manuscript has: "were in their infancy".—*Ed.*

[b] Of Savoy.—*Ed.*

dates the new science of mountain warfare which has put an end to the impregnability of Switzerland.

During the period of line tactics, which immediately preceded that of modern warfare, all difficult ground was studiously avoided by either adversary.[a] The more level the plain, the better it was deemed for a battle-field, if it only afforded some obstacle to support one or both wings. But with the French revolutionary armies, a different system began. An obstacle before the front, covering ground for skirmishers, as well as for the reserves, was anxiously sought for in any defensive position. Difficult ground, upon the whole, was preferred by them; their troops were far lighter in their movements; and their formations, extended order and columns, admitted not only[b] of rapid movements in all directions, but even made it advantageous to them to profit by the shelter afforded by broken ground, at the same time that their opponents were quite lost in it. In fact, the term "impracticable ground" was all but erased from the military terminology.

The Swiss were made to feel this in 1798, when four French divisions, in spite of the obstinate resistance of part of the inhabitants, and of a three times repeated insurrection of the old forest cantons, made themselves masters of the country which, for the next three years, became one of the most important theaters of the war between the French Republic and the Coalition.[207] How little the French were afraid of the inaccessible mountains and narrow gorges of Switzerland, they showed as early as March, 1798, when Masséna at once marched upon the roughest and most mountainous canton, the Grisons, then occupied by the Austrians. The latter held the upper valley of the Rhine. In concentric columns Masséna's troops marched into that valley through mountain passes hardly passable to horses, occupied all the outlets, and after a short resistance forced the Austrians to lay down their arms. The Austrians very soon profited by this lesson; under Hotze, a General who gained considerable proficiency in mountain warfare, they returned to the charge, repeated the same maneuver, and drove out the French. Then came the retreat of Masséna to the defensive position of Zurich, where he defeated Korsakoff's Russians, the invasion of Switzerland over the St. Gotthard by Souwaroff, his disastrous retreat, and finally another advance of the French through the Grisons into Tyrol, where

---

[a] Instead of the words "by either adversary" the manuscript has: "by both opposing armies in the war".—*Ed.*

[b] Here the manuscript ends.—*Ed.*

Macdonald in the depth of winter passed over three mountain ridges then scarcely thought passable in single file.[208] The great Napoleonic campaigns which then followed were fought out in the great river-basins of the Danube and the Po; the grand strategical conceptions on which they were based, all tending to cut off the hostile army from the center of its resources, to destroy that army, and then to occupy the center itself, implied a less intercepted ground and the concentration of masses for decisive battles not to be obtained in Alpine countries. But from the first Alpine campaign of Napoleon in 1796, and his march across the Julian Alps to Vienna in 1797, up to 1801, the whole history of warfare proves that Alpine ridges and valleys have completely lost their terror for modern troops; nor have the Alps ever since, up to 1815, offered any defensive positions worth speaking of to either France or the Coalition.

When you pass through one of these deep ravines which wind up the roads that lead from the northern slope of the Alps to their southern declivity, you find the most formidable defensive positions at every turn of the road. Take the well-known Via Mala, for instance. There is not an officer but will tell you he might hold that defile with a battalion against an enemy, *if* he was sure of not being turned. But that is precisely the point. There is no mountain pass, even in the highest ridge of the Alps, but can be turned. Napoleon's maxim for mountain warfare was: "Where a goat can pass, a man can pass; where a man, a battalion; where a battalion, an army." And Souwaroff had to do it, when he was closely shut up in the valley of the Reuss, and had to march his army along shepherds' tracks, where but one man could pass at a time, while Lecourbe, the best French General for mountain warfare, was at his heels.

It is this facility of turning an enemy which makes up and more for the strength of defensive positions, to attack which in front would often be perfect madness. To guard all roads by which a position can be turned would imply, in the defending party, such a dissemination of forces as must insure immediate defeat. They can, at best, be observed only, and the repulse of the turning movement must depend upon the judicious use of reserves and on the judgment and rapidity of the commanders of single detachments; and yet, if of three or four turning columns one only is successful, the defending party is placed in as bad a condition as if they had all succeeded. Thus, strategically speaking, the attack in mountain warfare is decidedly superior to the defense.

It is the same when we come to look at the subject in a purely tactical light. The defensive positions will always be narrow mountain-gorges, occupied by strong columns in the valley and protected by skirmishers on the hights. These positions may be turned either from the front, by skirmishing parties climbing up the sides of the valley and outflanking the sharp-shooters of the defense, or by parties marching along the top of the ridge where this is practicable, or by a parallel valley—the turning body profiting by a pass to fall on flank or rear of the defending post. In all these cases the turning parties have the advantage of *command;* they occupy the higher ground and overlook the valley occupied by their opponents. They may roll rocks and trees down upon them; for now-a-days no column is so foolish as to enter into a deep gorge before its sides are cleared; so that this late favorite mode of defense is now turned against the defenders. Another disadvantage of the defense is that the effect of firearms, on which it mainly rests, is very much reduced on mountainous ground. Artillery is either all but useless, or, where it is seriously used, is generally lost on a retreat. The so-called mountain artillery, consisting of light howitzers carried on the backs of mules, is of scarcely any effect, as the experience of the French in Algeria amply proves.[209] As to musketry and rifles, the cover offering itself everywhere in such ground deprives the defense of a very great advantage—that of having in front of the position open ground which the enemy must pass under fire. Tactically, then, as well as strategically, we arrive at the conclusion of the Archduke Charles of Austria, one of the best generals in mountain warfare and one of the most classical writers on that subject, that in this kind of war the attack is vastly superior to the defense.

Is it then perfectly useless to defend a mountainous country? Certainly not. It only follows that the defense must not be a merely passive one, that it must seek its strength in mobility, and act, wherever opportunity offers, on the offensive. In alpine countries battles can hardly occur; the whole war is one continuous series of small actions, of attempts, by the attacking party, to drive the thin end of the wedge in one point or the other of the enemy's position, and then to press forward. Both armies are necessarily scattered; both must expose themselves at every step to an advantageous attack; both must trust to the chapter of accidents. Now, the only advantage the defending army can take is to seek out these feeble points of the enemy and to throw itself between his divided columns. In that case the strong defensive positions on which a merely passive defense would alone rely, become so many traps for the enemy where he may be allured into taking the bull by the horns, while the main efforts of the defense are directed against the turning columns, each of which may in its turn be turned and brought into the same helpless condition into which it intended to bring the defending party. It is, however, at once evident that such an active defense presupposes active, experienced and skillful generals, highly disciplined and mobile troops, and above all very skillful and reliable leaders of brigades, battalions, and even companies; for, on the prompt, judicious action of detachments, everything depends in this case.

There is still another form of defensive mountain warfare which has become celebrated in modern times; it is that of national insurrection and the war of partisans, for which a mountainous country, at least in Europe, is absolutely required. We have four examples of it: the Tyrolese insurrection, the Spanish guerrilla war against Napoleon, the Carlist Basque insurrection,[210] and the war of the Caucasian tribes against Russia.[211] Though they have caused great trouble to the invaders, none of them, considered by itself, has proved successful. The Tyrolese insurrection was formidable only as long as it was supported, in 1809, by Austrian regular troops. The Spanish guerrillas, though they had the immense advantage of a very extensive country, owed the long continuance of their resistance chiefly to the Anglo-Portuguese army, against which the principal efforts of the French had always to be directed. The long duration of the Carlist war is explained by the degraded state to which the Spanish regular army had then been reduced, and by the constant negotiations between the Carlist and the Christina[a] generals; and it cannot be taken as a fair specimen. Finally, in the Caucasian struggle, the most glorious of all to the mountaineers, their relative success has been due to the offensive tactics predominant in the defense of their ground. Wherever the Russians—they and the British being of all troops the least fit for mountain warfare—attacked the Caucasians, the latter have generally been defeated, their villages destroyed, and their mountain-passes secured by Russian fortified posts. But their strength lay in continued sallies from their hills into the plains, in surprises of Russian stations or outposts, in rapid excursions far to the rear of the Russian advanced line, in ambushes laid for Russian columns on the march. In other words, they were lighter and more movable than the Russians, and profited by this

---

[a] Maria Cristina.—*Ed.*

advantage. In fact, in every instance, then, of even temporarily successful insurrections of mountaineers, this success has been owing to offensive operations. In this they totally differ from the Swiss insurrections of 1798 and 1799, where we find the insurgents taking up some apparently strong defensive position and there awaiting the French, who in every instance cut them to pieces.

Written between January 1 and 10, 1857

First published in the *New-York Daily Tribune,* No. 4921, January 27, 1857 as a leading article

Reproduced from the newspaper

Frederick Engels

[MOUNTAIN WARFARE IN THE PAST AND PRESENT]

(Second article)

The history of modern mountain warfare, of which we gave a short abstract in a previous article, most clearly proves that the mobility of the armies of our day is perfectly capable to overcome or to turn all the natural obstacle which an alpine country like Switzerland may oppose to their manoeuvres. Suppose, then, a war actually to break out between the king of Prussia[a] and Switzerland, the Swiss must certainly look to other defences beside their much vaunted "mountain-fortresses" for the security of their country.

In the case supposed above, the line on which Switzerland could be attacked, would extend from Constance along the Rhine to Basel: for we must consider both Austria and France as neutrals, as the active interference of either of them would secure such a crushing force to the attack that any strategical combinations against it would be useless. The northern frontier, therefore, is alone supposed to be open to invasion. It is protected in the first line by the Rhine, an obstacle of no great importance. This river runs along the attacked frontier for some 70 miles, and though deep and rapid, offers many favourable places for a passage. In the French revolutionary wars[212] its possession has never been seriously contested, and indeed, a strong attacking army may always force the passage of any river on a portion of its course 70 miles long. False alarms, feigned attacks, followed up by sudden concentration of troops on the real points of passage are sure to succeed in each case. There are, besides, several stone bridges

[a] Frederick William IV.—*Ed.*

across it which the Swiss would scarcely attempt to destroy so seriously as to make them useless for the period of a campaign; and lastly, Constance being a German town situated on the southern bank of the Rhine, offers a convenient bridge-head for the Prussians to turn the whole of the line.

But there is another obstacle at a short distance behind the Rhine, which heightens its indirect defensibility in a similar way as the Balkans, in Bulgaria, heighten the defensibility of the Danube. Three affluents of the Rhine, the Aare from the Southwest, the Reuss and Limmat from the Southeast, unite near Brugg, the two latter forming a right angle to the Aare, and then run due north towards the Rhine which they join at Coblenz (this Coblenz on the Aare and Rhine is of course not to be confounded with the fortress of that name on the Moselle and Rhine) about 10 miles from their junction. Thus the Aare from Brugg to the Rhine cuts in two the country covered by this latter stream, so that an invading army, having passed the Rhine, either above or below Coblenz, has before its front either the Limmat or the Aare, and is therefore stopped again by a defensible river. The salient angle, formed by the junction of the Aare and the Limmat (the Reuss forming but a strong second line to that of the Limmat) thus offers an important second position for defence. Its flanks are covered, to the left (west) by the lakes[a] of Zurich, Wallenstadt, Zug and of the Four Cantons; neither of which a Prussian army, under the above-supposed circumstances, *darest venture* to turn. The position of the Aare and Limmat, with the Rhine in the rear of any *army that came to attack* it, therefore forms the principal strategical defence of Switzerland against an invasion from the North. Suppose the Swiss repulsed an attack on it, and followed up the victory by a countercharge and active pursuit, the beaten army would be lost, broken up, cut off, and ruined before it could retreat over the few bridges it might have on the Rhine.

On the other hand, if the line of the lower Aare and Limmat were once forced, what would remain for the Swiss? Here again we must consult the configuration of the ground. Large armies cannot live in the high mountains, nor can they establish their chief bases of operations or magazines there. That some of the reasons why campaigns in alpine countries, if entered upon with considerable forces, have always been of very short duration. The Swiss could not, therefore, think of retreating in force into the

[a] An inaccuracy in the text. The lakes mentioned are situated on the right (east) flank of the position in question.— *Ed.*

high mountains; they must keep as long as possible to the more level territory where they find towns with all their resources and roads to facilitate transport. Now if a line is drawn from the point where the Rhône enters the lake of Geneva at Villeneuve, to the point where the Rhine enters the Lake of Constance near Rheineck, this line will cut Switzerland in two portions the northwestern of which (leaving the Jura out of consideration) will comprise the Swiss Lowlands, while the South Eastern comprises the Highlands or Alpine country. The strategy of the Swiss is thereby clearly defined. Their main body will have to retreat on the line Zurich — Berne — Lausanne — Geneva, defending the open country inch by inch, and leaving the Southeastern mountains to the protection of such portions of the army as may have been cut off, and to the irregular warfare fire of the mountaineer *Landsturm*[213] and free corps. The main body would be supported in this line of retreat by all the Southern affluents of the Aare, all of which run parallel to the Reuss and Limmat, and at Berne by the Aare itself which in its upper course also runs from the East to the Northwest. The upper Aare once forced and Berne taken, there would remain but little chance to the Swiss to bring the war to a successful issue, unless the mountaineers and the new formed bodies from the South East succeeded in again occupying part of the plain and menacing the Prussian rear so seriously that a general retreat had to follow. But that chance may well be left out of consideration altogether.

Thus the Swiss would have several good lines of defence: first, the Aare and Limmat, then the Aare and Reuss, third the Aare and Emme (not to mention the intervening smaller affluents of the Aare) and fourthly the upper Aare, the left wing behind the morass extending from the lake of Neuchâtel to that river.

The attack has its strategy equally as well prescribed by the configuration of the country as the defence. If the Prussians were to send their main body across the Rhine above Coblenz, and attack the position of the Limmat, they would take the bull by the horns; they would not only have to storm the position which Masséna in 1799 so successfully defended against the Austrians and Russians, but after taking it, find 5 miles further on the position of the Reuss, fully as strong; and then, from 2, 3, or 5 miles, another mountain-current would bar their path, until at last, after a succession of delays, combats, and losses, they would again find the Swiss posted behind the Emme, which river forms as serious an obstacle nearly as the Limmat. Unless political reasons, which we leave entirely beside, induced the Prussians to remain at a respectful distance from the French frontier, this way of attack would, therefore, be absolutely faulty. The real road into Switzerland crosses the Rhine between Basel and Coblenz; or, if part of the army should cross above Coblenz, a communication across the Aare between Brugg and Coblenz would have to be established at once so as to concentrate the main body on the left bank of the latter river. The direct attack on the line of the Aare turns the lines both of the Limmat and the Reuss, and may be made to turn the lines, too, of all the minor southern affluents of the Aare, almost as far as the Emme river. The line of the Limmat, too, is short, extending on its attackable front, from Zurich to Brugg, not more than 20 miles while the line of the Aare, from Brugg to Solothurn, offers to the attack an extent of 36 miles, and is not even absolutely secure from front attack above Solothurn. The left of the position, between Solothurn and Aarberg, is its weak point; once forced there, the line is not only lost to the Swiss, but they are cut off from Berne, Lausanne and Geneva, and have no retreat left but to the Southeastern highlands.

The defence, however, is here supported by tactical obstacles. The more you ascend the Aare towards Solothurn, the more the higher ridges of the Jura approach the river, and obstruct military operations by their peculiar longitudinal valleys running all parallel to the Aare. The intervening ridges are far from being impassable, but yet the concentration of a large corps in such ground would presuppose very complicated manoeuvres always unpleasant in the face of the enemy and not easily undertaken by a general unless he has plenty of confidence in himself and his troops. The latter quality not being very common in the old Prussian generals who scarcely can be said to have seen active service since 1815, it is not likely that they would risk such a manoeuvre, but rather stick to halfmeasures on the flanks and concentrate their chief efforts on the lower.

Written between January 1 and 10, 1857

First published in: Marx and Engels, *Works,* Second Russian Edition, Vol. 44, Moscow, 1977

Printed according to the manuscript copied by Marx

Karl Marx

THE WAR AGAINST PERSIA[214]

To understand the policy and object of the war lately undertaken by the British against Persia, and which, according to the most recent accounts, has been so energetically pushed as to lead to submission on the part of the Shah, it is necessary to take a slight retrospect of Persian affairs. The Persian dynasty, founded in 1502 by Ismael, who claimed to be descended from the ancient Persian kings, after maintaining for more than two centuries the power and dignity of a great State, received, about 1720, a severe shock in the rebellion of the Afghans inhabiting its eastern provinces. Western Persia was invaded by them, and two Afghan princes[a] succeeded in keeping themselves for a few years on the Persian throne. They were, however, speedily expelled by the famous Nadir, acting at first in the capacity of General to the Persian claimant.[b] Afterward he assumed the crown himself, and not only reduced the rebellious Afghans, but by his famous invasion of India contributed much to that disorganization of the declining Mogul empire, which opened the way for the rise of the British power in India.

Amid the anarchy that ensued in Persia after the death of Nadir Shah in 1747, there sprang up, under the rule of Ahmed Duranee, an independent Afghan kingdom comprising the Principalities of Herat, Cabul, Candahar, Pechawur, and the whole of the territories afterward owned by the Sikhs.[215] This kingdom, only superficially cemented, collapsed at the death of its founder, and was again broken up into its constituent parts, the indepen-

[a] Mahmud and Ashraf.— *Ed.*
[b] Tahmasp II.— *Ed.*

dent Afghan tribes with separate chiefs, divided by interminable feuds and only exceptionally rallied under the common pressure of a collision with Persia. This political antagonism between the Afghans and Persians, founded on diversity of race, blended with historical reminiscences, kept alive by frontier quarrels and rival claims, is also, as it were, sanctioned by religious antagonism, the Afghans being Mohammedans of the Suni sect, that is to say, of the orthodox Mahometan faith, while Persia forms the stronghold of the heretical Shiites.[216]

In spite of this intense and universal antagonism, there existed one point of contact between the Persians and Afghans—their common hostility to Russia. Russia invaded Persia for the first time under Peter the Great, but without much advantage. Alexander I, more successful, deprived Persia, by the treaty of Ghulistan,[217] of twelve provinces—the greater part of them south of the Caucasus. Nicholas, by the war of 1826-27, ending in the treaty of Turkmanchai,[218] stripped Persia of several additional districts, and interdicted her from the navigation on her own shores along the Caspian Sea. The memory of past spoliations, the endurance of present restrictions, and the fear of future encroachments, alike concurred to spur Persia into deadly opposition to Russia. The Afghans, on their part, although never involved in actual quarrels with Russia, were used to consider her as the eternal foe of their religion, and a giant which was to swallow Asia. From considering Russia as their natural foe, both races—Persians and Afghans—were induced to consider England as their natural ally. Thus, to maintain her supremacy, England had but to play the benevolent mediator between Persia and Afghanistan, and to prove the decided adversary of Russian encroachment. A show of amity on the one hand, and an earnest of resistance on the other—nothing else was required.

It cannot be said, however, that the advantages of this position have been very successfully improved. In 1834, in the matter of the selection of an heir to the Shah of Persia, the English were induced to co-operate in favour of the prince[a] proposed by Russia, and the next year to aid that prince with money and the active assistance of British military officers in maintaining his claim by arms against his rival.[b][219] The English Ambassadors dispatched to Persia were charged to warn the Persian Government against

[a] Mohammed Mirza.—*Ed.*

[b] Mohammed Mirza's rivals were the three sons of his grandfather, Fath Ali Shah.—*Ed.*

allowing itself to be pushed on to make war against the Afghans, which could only result in a waste of resources; but when these Ambassadors earnestly called for authority to prevent a threatened war of this sort, they were put in mind by the Ministry at home of an article in an old treaty of 1814, by which, in case of war between Persia and the Afghans, the English were not to interfere unless their mediation should be solicited.[220] The idea of the British envoys and of the British Indian authorities was that this war was planned by Russia, which power desired to employ the extension of Persian authority eastward as the means of opening a road by which at some time or other a Russian army might enter India. These representations seem, however, to have made little or no impression on Lord Palmerston, then at the head of the Department of Foreign Affairs, and in September, 1837, a Persian army invaded Afghanistan. Various small successes carried it to Herat, before which town it encamped and began siege operations under the personal direction of Count Simonich, the Russian Ambassador at the Persian Court. During the progress of these warlike acts, McNeill, the British Ambassador, found himself paralyzed by contradictory instructions. On the one hand, Lord Palmerston enjoined him "to refrain from making the relations of Persia" with Herat a "subject of discussion," as England had nothing to say between Persia and Herat. On the other hand, Lord Auckland, the Governor-General of India, wanted him to dissuade the Shah from pushing on his operations. At the very outset of the expedition Mr. Ellis had recalled the British officers serving in the Persian army, but Palmerston had them reinstated. So, again, the Indian Governor-General instructing McNeill to withdraw the British officers, Palmerston again reversed that decision. On March 8, 1838, McNeill proceeded to the Persian camp and offered his mediation, not in the name of England, but of India.

Toward the end of May 1838, the siege having now lasted about nine months, Palmerston sent a menacing dispatch to the Persian Court, for the first time making the affair of Herat a subject of remonstrance, and for the first time inveighing against "Persia's connection with Russia".[a] Simultaneously, a hostile expedition was ordered by the Indian Government to sail to the Persian Gulf and seize upon the Island of Karak—the same lately occupied by the

[a] See Palmerston-McNeill correspondence from May 21, 1838, especially Palmerston's letter to McNeill of July 27, 1838, *Correspondence Relating to Persia and Affghanistan*, pp. 81-89.—*Ed.*

English. At a still later epoch the English Envoy withdrew from Teheran to Erzeroum, and the Persian Ambassador[a] sent to England was refused admission. In the mean time, in spite of a very protracted blockade, Herat had held out, the Persian assaults were beaten back, and on Aug. 15, 1838, the Shah[b] was forced to raise the siege and to retreat in hurried marches from Afghanistan. Here one would have supposed the operations of the English might have ended; but so far from that, matters took a most extraordinary turn. Not content with repelling the attempts of Persia, made, it was alleged, at the instigation and in the interest of Russia, to seize a part of Afghanistan, the English undertook to occupy the whole of it for themselves. Hence the famous Afghan war,[221] the ultimate result of which was so disastrous to the English, and the real responsibility for which still remains so much a mystery.

The present war against Persia has been undertaken on grounds very similar to that which preceded the Afghan war, namely, an attack upon Herat by the Persians, resulting, on the present occasion, in the capture of that city. A striking circumstance, however, is that the English have now been acting as the allies and defenders of the same Dost Mohammed, whom, in the Afghan struggle, they so unsuccessfully undertook to dethrone. It remains to be seen whether this war is to have sequences as extraordinary and unexpected as those which attended the former one.

Written on about January 27, 1857

First published in the *New-York Daily Tribune,* No. 4937, February 14, 1857 as a leading article

Reproduced from the newspaper

[a] Husayn Khan.— *Ed.*
[b] Mohammed Shah.— *Ed.*

Karl Marx

B. BAUER'S PAMPHLETS ON THE COLLISION WITH RUSSIA[222]

a) *La Russie et l'Angleterre.* 1854

Prediction, the penetration of destiny, through the medium of a critical assessment of conditions in the states of Europe, their mutual relations and, deriving from them, contemporary history—is one of the claims made by these pamphlets. The method used in tackling this problem commends itself by a measure of cunning. Since the knowledge and foreknowledge displayed by Criticism[223] is to be tested in the light of contemporary history nothing would seem simpler than to compare the conclusions of Criticism and the facts of contemporary history, measuring the first against the second and thus convincing oneself of the justification or presumption of Criticism's claims. E.g., in the above-named pamphlet we read:

"La *pratique constitutionnelle* a gagné infiniment du terrain, et la *résistance passive* des assemblées nationales, issues de la révolution de l'année 1848, a pris de plus grandes proportions. Toute l'Europe s'est partagé, en ce moment, les différents rôles du drame constitutionnel: l'Occident s'est chargé du rôle de l'opposition honnête; la Russie représente le gouvernement, armé de la force et usant de son autorité." [a]

("Europe has apportioned itself roles in the constitutional drama; the West has assumed the role of stalwart opposition; to Russia has

---

[a] "*Constitutional practice* has gained an enormous amount of ground, and *passive resistance* on the part of the national assemblies which emerged from the revolution of the year 1848 has assumed larger dimensions. The whole of Europe has apportioned itself at this moment the various roles in the constitutional drama: the West has assumed the role of stalwart opposition; Russia plays that of government armed with might and wielding its authority" (B. Bauer, *La Russie et l'Angleterre,* p. 19).—*Ed.*

fallen the role of an *energetic* government *armed with might.*")

We shall not linger over the ill-turned phrase which, by means of an *"and"*, lumps together *"constitutional practice"* and *"the passive resistance"* of the "non-constitutional" assemblies of 1848, etc. Of all those assemblies, this might apply only to the *"assemblée législative"*.[a] But let us take the proposition as it stands. Western Europe, the *assemblée législative,* confines itself to passive resistance, and Russia, the "government armed with might", *"asserts her authority"* by means of a coup d'état, as did Bonaparte, Francis Joseph and Frederick William IV respectively.[224] Such was Criticism's assessment of the position in the month of April—an interpretation of the immediate past which at the same time purports to be a prediction of the immediate future. The weeks that immediately ensued controverted both the interpretation and prediction and demonstrated that, in its superficial precipitation, Criticism has transformed the physiognomy of a moment into a[b] permanent feature. Not only do the western powers abandon "passive resistance" and turn to aggressive acts but, before they have so done, Russia's Danubian campaigns reveal that she is *not* "armed" with might; rather, her arms are powerless and, instead of "asserting her authority", she withdraws—beats a retreat.[225] The analogy he draws with the dictatorial, coup d'état-perpetrating governments and the assemblies of 1848 falls to the ground. Was Criticism's prediction wrong, therefore? Its interpretation of the circumstances delusory? By no means. After the occurrence of the disagreeable facts which at a stroke demolished the findings of Critical pamphlet *a),* B.B., unabashed, opens brochure *b)* (*Die jetzige Stellung Russlands,* 1854) with the following diplomatic pronouncement:

"This proposition (quoted above)[226] which we advanced *as late as* (!) April, was *fully realised* by the turn things took beneath the walls of Silistria: the drama being performed by Europe is *truly* and *in every respect* a constitutional one; the government has come to resemble the opposition, it *too* has shown itself *constitutional* and has made no use of force, or, if it has, it has not been with intent to effect a decision."

The ambiguous nature of the satisfaction derived by Criticism from the "turn things took" finds expression in the peculiar "turn" of speech, "advanced *as late as* April". Does Criticism

---

[a] Crossed out in the manuscript: "and why it does not apply to the latter is something that requires no explanation here".— *Ed.*

[b] Crossed out in the manuscript: "general category".— *Ed.*

retract the proposition it advanced in April, the Russians having retreated from Silistria in March? By no means. The *as late as* should therefore read *as early as.* Our proposition, advanced "as early as" April, before the occurrence of the event, was corroborated during March. Rather, one should say, it was not corroborated. So not "as early as"—rather, "as late as", but "as late as" with a corollary which turns it into a grammatical impossibility. "The view I held *as late as* April was fulfilled in March." But Criticism does not say that its "proposition advanced as late as April" was "corroborated" as early as March. Indeed no. Rather, the new "turn things took" gave Criticism's proposition a new "turn" of which there had been no suspicion "as late as" April. That proposition was not *"corroborated"* but, it would appear, *"fully realised"* by ensuing events. VERY WELL.[a] This casts a new light on the relation of events to Criticism. Even if they do not provide proof of Criticism's assertion, they do at least help towards the further "realisation" of that assertion and reveal a content in it hitherto concealed and not suspected even by Criticism itself. Not only does Criticism stand in theoretical relation to events, but events stand in practical relation to Criticism. And what is now the position as regards the *"full realisation"* "conferred" by events in March on the proposition advanced in April?

"The drama being performed by Europe is *truly* **and** *in every respect* a constitutional one!"

Truly and in every respect! Does the "in every respect" add anything new to the "truly"? It vitiates and trivialises. That is all. But the floridity of the style, the "truly and in every respect", simply betray the same perplexed ineptitude as previously the unfortunate *"as late as"*. In the proposition advanced in April, firstly, the "passive resistance" of the national assemblies of 1848 and after was erroneously equated with "constitutional practice" and, secondly, the clash in the East was transformed into a "constitutional" drama in which, because of their "passive resistance", the western powers are compared with the national assemblies of 1848 and after and Russia with the coup d'état-perpetrating governments. This was not, in fact, a constitutional drama, since constitutionalism was confined solely to the national assemblies, whereas the governments were concerned solely with overthrowing constitutions. Now, however, when Russia has

---

[a] Here and below words in small caps are in English in the original.—*Ed.*

received a drubbing, her armed aggression having been repelled by force of arms, and has adopted a "parliamentary" tack, now the drama, formerly constitutional only in an "unreal" sense, has become "truly" and "in every respect constitutional". But the moment the government becomes "constitutional", as in England or Belgium or the France of Louis Philippe, it ceases to resemble the national assemblies of 1848 and after or the governments opposing them. Nor is that all. While Russia has begun to dally with "parliamentarianism" and hence, according to B.B., to assume the role of a "constitutional government", the western powers have, for their part, ceased to offer "passive resistance" and turned to active hostility, to an invasion. If, prior to this, the term "constitutional" was [not] applicable to Russia, it is no longer applicable to the western powers. And this Criticism describes as the "full realisation" of its proposition advanced in April! Nevertheless, there still remains the matter of the "realisation" of the term "constitutional" contained in the proposition advanced in April. Criticism's predictions, it is clear, are as ambiguous as those of the ancient oracles. If its propositions seem to have been controverted by events,[a] then it merely seems so. As soon as the opposite happens, it transpires that, in point of fact, the original critical dictum meant the "opposite" of what it said and that events have simply revealed its dialectical nature. Thanks to this sort of dialectics which proves a prognostication to have been fulfilled by the occurrence of its opposite, Criticism's prophecies are, in all circumstances, proof against attack. Urquhart adopts a different method. If his prophecies come to pass, their truth is confirmed by their having come to pass. If they do not come to pass, this is because the mere statement of what was bound to happen has prevented their fulfilment. In the first case the theoretical truth, and in the second the practical purpose, of the prediction has been fulfilled.

Criticism reproaches the daily press for its total addiction to the present instant. As for itself, it sees the instant as a moment in the context of the whole, i.e. takes a general view. What in fact transpires is that, if the daily press is, in practice, dominated by day-to-day events, Criticism experiences the same defeat in the realm of theory. The isolated event is immobilised by it and turned into the incarnation of a general proposition, which every

[a] Crossed out in the manuscript: "those propositions have been confirmed in as much as a wholly different meaning and interpretation is thereupon assigned to them".—*Ed.*

turn of events strips of even a semblance of verisimilitude. (Similarly *Proudhon.* When, in 1850 (?) the bank's bullion reserve increased more than £20 million sterling and the bank rate fell to $2^1/_2$ (?) per cent, that event instantly denoted the realisation of a new phase in the history of civil society, the time of the Banque du Peuple had come.[227] To him, in Paris, the event was a *new* one, absolutely mint-new, because his views were bounded by the southern shore of the Channel). While, therefore, the "era" of Russia was, as late as *April,* seen as the immediate expression of a new phase in world history (in pamphlet *a*), Russia's actions of as early as March prompted Criticism to ask (in pamphlet *b*) this pusillanimous question:

"Has the era of the West dawned in Russia, too? Does she already belong to the West, etc.?" (*Die jetzige Stellung Russlands,* p. 18).

In fact, since the proposition, advanced by Criticism "as late as" April concerning the constitutional drama, in which Russia assumes the role of power-wielding government and the western powers that of passive resistance, of stalwart opposition, constitutes the whole point of brochure *a),* and since events deprived it of that point as early as March, this effectively and "in every respect" brings our criticism of it to a close. However, let us consider some individual details.

In the first place, the alleged *historical illustrations.* Inter alia, a parallel is drawn between the events that paved the way for the French Revolution of 1789 and the events now supposedly paving the way for revolution in England. Turgot imagined that everything would be put right by "free corn trade" (p. 72). Likewise England at the time of the Anti-Corn Law League.[228] Would it be possible to coax into an analogy any two things of a more disparate kind? France was above all an agricultural and England an industrial country. Free trade in corn meant something altogether different in either country. In France the[a] *"fait précis* and *positif"*[b]—"financial deficit and bankruptcy" (72). In England? Well, in England there was war,[229] the government perplexed by a financial surplus and a twofold increase in imports and exports! Is that the analogy? Not so:

"in England likewise a moral and political deficit".

---

[a] Crossed out in the manuscript: "positive fact preceding the French Revolution".—*Ed.*

[b] "Precise and positive fact".—*Ed.*

What an analogy! On the one hand a "precise and positive fact", on the other the merely subjective assessment of a situation by the Criticism. The analogy lies *in* the word deficit. X died because he broke his leg. *Prophetic analogy:* Y will die because he breaks his word. The precise and positive fact of financial deficit and public bankruptcy preceded the French Revolution. In Louis XV's reign, if not before, a moral and political deficit had preceded financial deficit and public bankruptcy. In France, the reforms proposed by the government to the notables and the *Parlements* proved insignificant as compared with the presentiment of revolution. Similarly in England, no one took any interest in Russell's Reform Bill (p. 73). What an analogy! In the proposals of the French government the issue at stake was a break with the past of French monarchy, in Russell's proposals of 1831 it was a ministerial intrigue; on the one hand, a break with a centuries' old past, on the other the consequences of a measure not three decades old; on the one hand, the government's proposals were of no interest to the bourgeoisie because incommensurable with the revolution which they [the bourgeoisie] needed; on the other, *despite their own interest* in the petty manoeuvrings of the Whigs, they did not succeed in arousing the interest of the popular masses, whose disillusionment with Whig reforms was not born yesterday but goes back to the morrow of the Reform Bill.[230] And now Necker and Palmerston constitute an analogy! To please Criticism, Palmerston loses "boldness and vigour", he is "imbued with his mission" and "regards himself as his country's last saviour".[a] Not even an analogy between Robespierre and Russell could be more consummately absurd. Accordingly it need no longer surprise us when Queen Victoria turns into *reine* Antoinette[b].

In no sense do we deny that major clashes are impending in England; all we deny is that the "historical illustrations" presented show the remotest understanding of them. The most common pothouse politics is infinitely superior to this empty profundity.

In order to prove that the English are mistaken in their view of an *"influence étrangère"*[c][231] in their Cabinet, Br. B. turns his attention to *Fox* who he says, *discovered* in Russia a protector and guarantor of peace in Europe. In support he quotes a passage

---

[a] B. Bauer, *La Russie et l'Angleterre*, p. 73.— *Ed.*

[b] Queen Antoinette (Marie Antoinette).— *Ed.*

[c] Foreign influence.— *Ed.*

from Fox's speech of May 24, 1803.[a] He should have gone further, and mentioned the *"secret"* despatch of Adair by Fox in 1790[232] on the occasion of the impending 2nd partition of Poland. And what is proved by Fox's "secret" and illicit liaison with Catherine II?[233] That Palmerston is *not* in secret and illicit liaison with Nicholas.[b] Come to that, there was no discovery for Fox to make in regard to Russia. It had already been made under William III by the Marquis of Carmarthen[234] and under George I by the ruling Whigs. Diplomatic documents show that, since that time, Russian influence has been a tradition in Whig Cabinets.[235] Good reason, perhaps, to suggest that Palmerston should have broken with the Whig tradition? Why should he not rather have "realised" it in all its implications and sold himself to Russia lock, stock and barrel? No less false than this "defence" of Palmerston is the assertion that it was Fox who discovered the Anglo-French alliance. Stanhope had already done so immediately after the Peace of Utrecht.[236]

As proof of Russia's positive effect we find the allegation that, by adopting the attitude she did, she created "the *décadence de l'antagonisme anglo-français*"[c] or, alternatively, the "alliance anglo-française". In 1717 there already existed an Anglo-French alliance which, a few years later, George I endeavoured to turn into a European alliance against Russia. The Quadruple Alliance of 1834[237] was England's second alliance with France and it was directed, albeit *vainly,* also against Russia. Hence there was nothing new or unprecedented for Russia to create in this direction. But if the mere fact of an alliance between France and England is to be regarded as an enormous success on Russia's part, what was the alliance between England, Russia, Prussia and Austria against the France of Louis Philippe, the coalition of 1840[238]? Proof, according to the construction put upon it by B.B., that the France of Louis Philippe was even more dangerous than the Russia of Nicholas.

England, or so Criticism goes on to discover, having, by her war with revolutionary France, delivered the Continent into the hands of Russia—a discovery which at least has the merit of not being new—felt impelled

---

[a] B. Bauer, *La Russie et l'Angleterre,* pp. II-III.—*Ed.*

[b] Crossed out in the manuscript: "Here, where an historical analogy does exist".—*Ed.*

[c] "Decline of Anglo-French antagonism", the heading of a section in B. Bauer's *La Russie et l'Angleterre* (p. 5).—*Ed.*

"de se charger elle-même de la tâche révolutionnaire de la France. C'est *Canning* qui a rempli ce vide. Il leva en Angleterre l'étendard de la révolution, pour en faire le véritable adversaire de la Russie".[a]

By way of proof, Criticism cites the rhetorical flourish which Canning borrowed from Virgil (the *dieu Eole's "Quos ego")*[b], as though a dictum by the "CAPTAIN of Eton"[239] were any proof. It accords absolute credence and validity to the dictum concerning the "policy" of "principles"[240], which was even more false than the earlier dicta concerning the "policy of interests". For that matter, Pitt's war[241] was also blazoned abroad as a "war of principles" and "believed" to be such by a large part of the English population. And so indeed it was, in part, since the power of the oligarchy shortly before and during the outbreak of the French Revolution was threatened by movements inside the country. Canning's dictum, by the by, was not, to begin with, directed against Russia but against France. The intervention in Portugal was a riposte to France's intervention in Spain, and this "policy of principles" in its execution—recognition of the independence of what was previously Spanish America[242]—accorded singularly well with British commercial interests. Because Palmerston uses Canning's dictum as a mask for a policy determined by altogether different motives, B. B. is convinced that Canning's dictum concerning the "intervention révolutionnaire"[c] has become Britain's real policy and brought down every kind of misfortune on her head. In this connection we are told that the Reform Bill has so greatly altered the nature of the British Constitution

"que les Anglais mêmes ne reconnaissent plus en quoi se distingue leur constitution de celles du continent"[d] (p. 9).

Since George I's time, the British Constitution has altered only in so far as 1) the distribution of the ROTTEN BOROUGHS[243] has been modified in favour of the Whigs, a faction of the aristocracy, 2) the industrial bourgeoisie increased their parliamentary influ-

[a] "To assume herself France's revolutionary task. It was *Canning* who filled the gap. He raised the flag of revolution in England, to make her the true adversary of Russia" (B. Bauer, *La Russie et l'Angleterre,* p. 7).—*Ed.*

[b] Eolus the god's: Whoever I... (Virgil, *Aeneid,* I, 135). See *The Speeches of the Right Honorable George Canning with a Memoir of His Life* by R. Therry in six volumes, Vol. VI, London, 1830, p. 91.—*Ed.*

[c] B. Bauer, op. cit., p. 8.—*Ed.*

[d] "That even the English can no longer see what distinguishes their constitution from those of the Continent".—*Ed.*

ence in 1831 to the same degree as did the financial bourgeoisie by means of the "GLORIOUS REVOLUTION" of 1689.[244] Another thing B.B. discovers is that

"l'abrogation des lois des céréales, comme la proclamation du principe de la liberté du commerce renferment l'aveu que sa suprématie (of l'industrie anglaise) est perdue".[a]

What, on the contrary, they proved was 1) that the interests of the industrial bourgeoisie triumphed over those of the landed aristocracy; 2) that English industry needs no other monopoly than that of its own capital as such; it means that English industry believes it can only at present rely on its real supremacy. When war broke out, he says, England was not yet

"assez dégradée pour supporter l'idée offensante d'une alliance avec sa rivale"[b] (p. 10).

Needless to say, the England of the modern industrial bourgeoisie cannot, without degrading herself, enter into any alliances that run counter to the interests and prejudices of what was once the ruling class. England is always *"the same"* moral personage. The depths of degradation to which England has descended in this respect is demonstrated in the sentence:

"Les peuples ne sauraient oublier leur passé qu'en renonçant à l'avenir."[c]

As if the constant "unmaking" of the past were not the "making" of the future.

Thus the future of Pitt's England and the future of England are seen as identical. As soon as a "people" overcomes what was once the ruling class and thus breaks with the political past created by that class,[d] it demolishes its future.

England's nationality consists, according to B. B., in hating France and vice versa. This, England's "nationality",—the earlier feudal wars between France and England having, of course, quite a different import—was first brought into existence by the

[a] "The repeal of the Corn Laws, like the proclamation of the free trade principle, is a tacit admission that it (English industry) has lost its supremacy" (op. cit., p. 9).— *Ed.*

[b] "Debased enough to tolerate the objectionable idea of allying herself with her rival".— *Ed.*

[c] "The peoples could only forget their past at the cost of forfeiting their future" (p. 11).— *Ed.*

[d] Crossed out in the manuscript: "it must, of course, cease to exist as a people and".— *Ed.*

"Glorious Revolution" and hence "cannot be abolished". What profundity!

Russia's nationality consists in allying herself, now with France against England, now with England against France... But England and France cannot form an alliance against Russia without renouncing their "future". What Bruno is actually trying to say is this: With the exception of Russia, the national peculiarities of the European states are disappearing. France and England fight as "the West" against Russia. In this way their nationality is dissipated. But did not Russia, England, Austria, Prussia, Naples and Spain fight as Europe against France? And did this not serve to reconstruct their nationality? Criticism, needless to say, is not concerned with civil society. English and French society pass through stages of political pupation. If one of these pupae is cast off, Criticism sees this as a clear sign of decadence on the part of those societies. What, for instance, does the politically jejune chapter on the *"calculs"* and *"arrière-pensées des alliés"*[a] prove, save that those societies are still battling with political traditions which belong wholly to their preceding phases, and that they have not yet acquired the political form suited to the needs of the new phase. And this he takes as proof that the alliance, being so wretched, cannot be a means towards the attainment of that higher form? To say that the society of modern production calls for international conditions different from those of feudal society is a tautology.

What makes him think that Russia

"a formé le plan de consolider son influence sur la Turquie, sans l'aide d'un allié?"[b]

Did she not successively seek an alliance with France, England and Austria for the late war, and consistently conserve that with Prussia? And whatever the views and intentions of the French and English peoples may have been, how can he tell that Russia was not all the time certain of effecting a secret alliance with the English government? and saw therein a warranty for her insolence?

The worthy B. B. believes Russia's pretext,

---

[a] "The calculations and mental reservations of the allies", the heading of one of the chapters in B. Bauer's *La Russie et l'Angleterre* (p. 13).— *Ed.*

[b] "Has settled on the plan of consolidating her influence in Turkey without the help of an ally" (ibid., p. 12).— *Ed.*

> "the *cause des populations gréco-slaves de la Turquie*"[a] (p. 11),

to have been her true motive. So great faith is not found, no, not in Israel.[b]

A large part of the pamphlet is devoted to a portrayal of the prevarications of the British government (likewise of the French) and its concessions to Russia. It was not, in fact, the British government's fault if Russia failed to carry out her designs in Turkey. And what does this prove? That the governments of England and France, in particular the former, were constrained by the masses? No. That England is aware of "her weakness" and that the government and society, while factually divided, must in theory be identified.

Russia's demandes![c] The Russian government's real aim was to replace the autonomy of the Greco-Slav populations,[245] such as it was, with government by her consuls. In its gullibility, Criticism must needs mistake Russia's empty phrases for her true motives, only to note with chagrin in a subsequent pamphlet that the Russian government is now dropping its FALSE PRETENCES[d]. He reproaches the newspapers with ignorance of the late Turkish affair. He proves his own ignorance by overlooking the repeated attempts of the Russians—e.g. in Serbia and Greece—to undermine the autonomous administration of the communes. What Russia is seeking to conserve is the theocracy of Greek priests under Turkish suzerainty which shackles and smothers any independent civic development of the Greco-Slav communes. Criticism's erudition finds particularly brilliant expression in the

> "gages que la Russie possède dans sa participation à l'oeuvre de l'organisation en Servie"[e] and in her "règlement organique"

she has conferred through Kisseleff upon the Danubian principalities![246] *C'est par trop fort*.[f] The southern Slavs must, according to B. B., become Russians 1) en vertu *"de la nature des choses"*[g] — a most profound demonstration, the reference to this abstraction; and then, alongside the *"nature des choses"*, by virtue of *"l'histoire"*[h]

---

[a] "Cause of the Greco-Slav populations of Turkey".—*Ed.*

[b] Matthew 8:10.—*Ed.*

[c] "Les demandes de la Russie", the heading of one of the sections in B. Bauer's *La Russie et l'Angleterre* (p. 28).—*Ed.*

[d] B. Bauer, *De la Dictature occidentale,* Charlottenburg, 1854, pp. 37-38.—*Ed.*

[e] "Pledges possessed by Russia in the shape of her participation in the work of organisation in Serbia" (B. Bauer, *La Russie et l'Angleterre,* p. 33).—*Ed.*

[f] It really is the limit.—*Ed.*

[g] By virtue *"of the nature of things"* (ibid., p. 34).—*Ed.*

[h] Ibid.—*Ed.*

which, in Serbia, demonstrates precisely the reverse; finally, by virtue of the *"position géographique"*[a] whereby they are cut off from Russia by the Magyars and Romanians. And what bathos! From the *"nature des choses"* he descends to *"l'histoire"*, and from that abstraction to the particular of the *"position géographique"*.

Austria must, or so he maintains, confine herself to the role of *médiateur.* This proposition, which was correct "as late as" April, had already become "incorrect" by June, despite Criticism's absolute proof deriving from the nature of things. He maintains that Austria will not *"pourra se ranger du côté des alliés"*.[b] Additional proof of the assertion. In his lucubrations on past relations between Austria and England, he falsifies history in true Russian fashion. As regards the Treaty of Adrianople he takes very good care not to give us the real story. Namely, that the Russian army had been destroyed and would never have returned from Adrianople—not even the minute proportion of it that did so—if England had not, under false pretences, extorted the treaty from the Porte. His account of the matter of Lieven's despatch is equally false. It was not, as he says, the *"traité de paix"*[c] which was the main cause of Aberdeen's and Wellington's *perplexité,* but the blockade of Enos,[247] which was, in fact, relinquished by the Russians for fear of forcing Wellington into opposition. Incidentally Lieven remarks

"that the Duke of Wellington and Lord Aberdeen have put everything in motion to extort from us *confidences* as to the conditions of our future peace with the Turks".[d]

Lieven's answer to this was far from being the boastful remark which B. quotes from his despatch[248]; rather he went on:

"It appeared to us useful to *repeat* the assurances which on this point all the declarations of the Emperor contained, and even to add some developments to them. We shall confine ourselves to these generalities, for every circumstantial communication on a subject so delicate *would draw down real dangers,* and if once we discuss with our allies the articles of a treaty with the Porte, we shall only content them, when they would have believed that they had imposed upon us irreparable sacrifices."[e]

---

[a] Ibid.— *Ed.*

[b] "Be able to range herself alongside the allies" (ibid., p. 36).— *Ed.*

[c] "Peace treaty" (p. 39).— *Ed.*

[d] [Lieven,] Copy of a Despatch from Prince Lieven, and Count Matuszevich, addressed to Count Nesselrode, dated London, 1st (13th) June, 1829, *The Portfolio. Diplomatic Review* (New Series), London, 1843, p. 24. Here and below the despatch is quoted in English.— *Ed.*

[e] Ibid.— *Ed.*

Only then does there occur the boastful passage which, seen in the context of this nasty piece of equivocation, would have forfeited its heroism, which was not at all what Criticism intended. All Pam's knaveries are then adduced to prove his sense of "England's weakness" and the latter, too. They betray, rather, the secret of Russia's "strength" vis-à-vis England. At the same time he distorts the facts, as in the story of the *Vixen*.[249] According to him, it was enough for Russia

"à lui rappeler que ce forfait inoui avait été commis dans la mer Noire, près de la côte de la Circassie".[a]

I have shown elsewhere what complicated manoeuvres Pam and Nesselrode resorted to on that occasion.[b]

In the chapter on Austria we also learn that in 1848-49,

"toute l'Allemagne, réduite à la passivité par les illusions du principe national, aurait taxé de crime politique chaque tentative d'intervenir dans cette lutte des nationalités".[c]

"As though" the Frankfurt National Assembly had not taken a stand against Italy? Likewise against Poland! [250] It would be otiose to say anything further about this pamphlet, save that Criticism considers Omar Pasha's Danubian campaigns to be a figment on the part of the Press.

Written in January 1857

First published, in Russian, in *Letopisi marksizma,* Vol. VI, 1928

Printed according to the manuscript

Translated from the German

Published in English for the first time

---

[a] "To remind him [Palmerston] that this grave offence had been committed in the Black Sea, off the coast of Circassia" (B. Bauer, ibid., p. 42).— *Ed.*

[b] K. Marx, *Lord Palmerston* (see present edition, Vol. 12, pp. 398-406).— *Ed.*

[c] "The whole of Germany, reduced to passivity by the illusions of the nationalities principle, would have denounced as a political crime every attempt to intervene in this struggle of nationalities" (ibid., p. 43).— *Ed.*

Frederick Engels

[THE PROSPECTS OF THE ANGLO-PERSIAN WAR][251]

It is the question of the possession of Herat, an Affghan principality, but lately occupied by the Persians,[252] that has given occasion to the occupation by the English, acting in the name of the East India Company, of Bushire, the principal Persian port on the Persian Gulf. The existing political importance of Herat is derived from the fact of its being the strategical center of all the country intervening between the Persian Gulf, the Caspian Sea and the Jaxartes on the west and north, and the Indus on the east; so that in the event of a great struggle between England and Russia for supremacy in Asia—a struggle which the English invasion of Persia may tend to precipitate—Herat will form the chief object of contention, and probably the theater of the first great military operations.

That the importance ascribed to Herat is not unfounded, must be apparent to all who understand its geographical position. The interior of Persia is formed by an elevated plain, surrounded on all sides by mountain chains, allowing no egress to the waters flowing down into it. These waters are not of sufficient importance to form one or more central lakes; they either lose themselves in vast morasses, or gradually vanish in the arid sand of the great desert which fills up by far the greater portion of the Persian plateau, and forms an almost impassable barrier between Western and Northeastern Persia. The northern boundary of this desert is formed by the hills of Khorassan, stretching along from the south-eastern corner of the Caspian almost due east, the connecting link between the Elburz and the Hindoo-koosh Mountains; and it is just where these hills send a branch to the south dividing the Persian desert from the better watered regions of Affghanistan that Herat is situated, surrounded and supported by a valley of considerable extent and exuberant fertility. To the north of the Khorassan hills we find a desert similar to that at their southern foot. Here, too, mighty rivers like the Murghab are lost in the sand. But the Oxus and Jaxartes are powerful enough to traverse it, and in their lower course form valleys capable of cultivation and of large extent. Beyond the Jaxartes the desert gradually takes the character of the steppes of Southern Russia, in which it is finally lost altogether. Thus we have three distinct seats of comparative civilization intervening between the Caspian Sea and British India. First, the towns of Western Persia: Shiraz, Shuster, Teheran, Ispahan; secondly, the Affghan towns: Caboul, Ghazna, Candahar; thirdly, the towns of Turan: Khiva, Bokhara, Balkh, Samarcand. Between all these there is a considerable intercourse, and the center of all this intercourse is necessarily Herat. The roads leading from the Caspian to the Indus, from the Persian Gulf to the Oxus, all meet at that city. Between Caboul and Teheran, between Shiraz and Balkh, Herat is the half-way house. The line of oases marking the great caravan route across the Persian desert by Yezd and Shehustan, debouches in a straight line on Herat; and, on the other hand, the only road leading from Western to Eastern and Central Asia, avoiding the desert, is that through the Khorassan hills and Herat.

Thus Herat is a point which, in the hands of a strong power, can be used to command both Iran and Turan—both Persia and Transoxiana. It gives to its possessor, in the very highest degree, all the advantages of a central position, from which radiating attacks in all directions can be made with greater facility and chance of success than from any other town in either Iran or Turan. At the same time, the difficulties of intercommunication between any two of the towns of Astrabad, Khiva, Bokhara, Balkh, Caboul and Candahar are so great that a combined attack upon Herat, even from all of them, would have but little chance of success. The various columns, once marching upon Herat, would have scarcely any chance of communication with each other, and could, by an active general at Herat, be fallen upon and defeated one after the other. Still, in such a case, columns coming from Candahar, Caboul and Balkh, would certainly have a better chance than an attack concentrating from the starting points of Astrabad, Khiva and Bokhara; for the attack from the side of Affghanistan would descend from the mountains into the plain, and completely avoid the desert, while the attack from the side of the Caspian and Araxes would have only one column (that from Astrabad) avoiding the desert, while all the remainder would have to pass it, and thereby altogether lose their communications one with the others.

The three centers of civilization which have their common center in Herat, form three distinct groups of States. On the west is Persia, which the Treaty of Turkmantchai[253] has converted into a vassal of Russia. On the East are the States of Affghanistan and Beloochistan, the most important of which, Caboul and Candahar, we may class for the present with the vassal States of the Anglo-Indian Empire. On the north are the Khanats of Turan, Khiva and Bokhara, States nominally neutral, but almost sure, in the case of a conflict, to go with the conquering party. The actual dependence of Persia on Russia, and of Affghanistan on the English, is proved by the fact that the Russians have already sent troops into Persia, and the English into Caboul.

The Russians hold the whole of the western and northern shores of the Caspian. Baku, 350 miles, and Astrakhan, 750 miles from Astrabad, offer two capital points for the establishment of magazines and the concentration of reserves. With the Russian fleet on the Caspian in command of that lake, the necessary stores and re-enforcements can, with great facility, be brought down to Astrabad. The points on the eastern shore of the Caspian, whence start the roads to Lake Aral, are occupied by Russian forts. Further north and east, the line of Russian forts marking the line of the Ural Cossacks had been advanced, as far back as 1847, from the river Ural to the rivers Emba and Ulu Turgai, some 150 or 200 miles into the territory of the tributary Kirghiz hordes, and in the direction of the Lake Aral. Since then, forts have actually been established on the shores of that lake, which, as well as the river Jaxartes, is at this moment plowed by Russian steamers. There have been rumors even of an occupation of Khiva[254] by Russian troops, but they are at least premature.

The line of operations the Russians have to follow, in any serious attack on Central or Southern Asia, is pointed out by nature. A land march from the Caucasus around the south-western corner of the Caspian would find great natural obstacles in the hills of Northern Persia, and would take the invading army over 1,100 miles of ground before the chief object, Herat, was reached. A land march from Orenburg toward Herat would have to pass not only the desert in which Perowski's army, on its expedition to Khiva,[255] was lost, but two more deserts quite as inhospitable. The distance from Orenburg to Herat is 1,500 miles as the crow flies, and Orenburg is the nearest place which the Russians, advancing from that direction, could take as a base of operations. Now, both Russian Armenia and Orenburg are places all but cut off from the center of Russian power—the first by the Caucasus, the second by the steppes. To concentrate in either of them the material and men necessary for the conquest of Central Asia, is entirely out of the question. There is but one line remaining—that by the Caspian, with Astrakhan and Baku for bases, with Astrabad, on the south-eastern border of the Caspian for the point of observation, and with a march to Herat of but 500 miles. And this line combines all the advantages that Russia can wish for. Astrakhan is to the Volga what New-Orleans is to the Mississippi. Situated at the mouth of the greatest river of Russia, the upper basin of which actually forms Great Russia, the center of the Empire, Astrakhan possesses every facility for the transmission of men and stores to organize a grand expedition. In four days by steam, in eight days by sailing vessels, the opposite extremity of the Caspian at Astrabad can be reached. The Caspian itself is undisputably a Russian lake; and Astrabad, now placed by the Persian Shah at the disposal of Russia, is situated at the starting point of that only road from the west to Herat which, by passing through the Khorassan hills, totally avoids the desert.

The Russian Government acts accordingly. The main column, destined in the case of further complications to act against Herat, is concentrating at Astrabad. Then there are two flank columns, the co-operation of which with the main body is at best but problematical, and each of which has, therefore, a definite object of its own. The right column concentrating at Tabreez is destined to cover the western frontier of Persia against any hostile movements of the Turks, and eventually to march toward Hamadan and Shuster, where it covers the capital, Teheran, both against Turkey and the English troops landing in the Persian Gulf at Bushire. The left column, starting from Orenburg and very likely intended to receive reinforcements sent from Astrakhan to the western shore[a] of the Caspian, will have to secure the Aral country, to march on Khiva, Bokhara and Samarcand, to secure either the passivity or the assistance of these States, and if possible, by a march up the Oxus to Balkh, menace the flank and rear of the English at Caboul or near Herat. We know that all these columns are already on the road, and that the central and right columns are already at Astrabad and Tabreez. Of the progress of

[a] Most probably a misprint in the original. Should read "the eastern shore".— *Ed.*

the right[a] column we shall probably not hear anything for some time.

For the English, the country of the upper Indus is the base of operations; and their magazines must be fixed at Peshawur. Thence they have already moved a column on Caboul, which town is distant four hundred miles from Herat as the crow flies. But in a serious war they must occupy, beside Caboul, Ghazna and Candahar, as well as the mountain forts guarding the Affghan passes. In this they will scarcely find any more difficulty than the Russians have done in occupying Astrabad, for ostensibly they are supporting the Affghans against Persian invasion.

The march from Caboul to Herat will offer no insuperable difficulties. There will be no need of any detached flank columns, for neither of the Russian flank columns will be able to come up; and if, after a couple of campaigns, the Orenburg column should debouch from Bokhara toward Balkh, a strong reserve at Caboul would soon give a good account of it. The English have this advantage, that their line of operations is comparatively short; for, though Herat lies exactly half-way between Calcutta and Moscow, yet the English base, at the confluence of the Caboul and Indus rivers, is but 600 miles from Herat, while the Russian base at Astrakhan is 1,250 miles off. The English, at Caboul, have got the start of the Russians at Astrabad, by a hundred miles, as far as Herat is concerned; and so far as the country is known, they pass through a better cultivated and more populous district, and by better roads than the Russians would find in Khorassan. As to the two armies, that of the English is undoubtedly the better so far as standing the climate is concerned. Its European regiments would undoubtedly act with the same unflinching steadiness as their comrades at Inkermann and the sepoy infantry[256] is by no means to be lightly spoken of. Sir Charles Napier, who saw them in many a battle, had the highest opinion of them, and he was a soldier and a general, every inch of him. The regular Indian cavalry is worth very little, but the irregulars are excellent, and under their European officers decidedly preferable to the Cossacks.

It is, of course, quite useless to speculate any further on the chances of such a war. There is no possibility of guessing at the forces that may be put in motion on one side or the other. There is no way of anticipating all the accidents which may happen if such important events come to pass as now seem to be drawing nigh. One thing only is certain, from the tremendous distances

---

[a] Must be "left".— *Ed.*

either party has to traverse, that the armies which will decide the contest at Herat, the decisive point, will be comparatively small. A great deal will also depend upon diplomatic intrigues and bribery at the courts of the various potentates grouped around Herat. In these matters the Russians are almost sure to have the best of it. Their diplomacy is better and more Oriental; they know how to lavish money when it is required, and above all, they have a friend in the enemy's camp.[a] The British expedition into the Persian Gulf is but a diversion which may draw upon it an important portion of the Persian army, but which, in its direct results, can accomplish but little. Even if the 5,000 men now at Bushire be tripled, they could at the utmost march only to Shiraz, and there halt. But this expedition is not meant to do more. If it gives the Persian Government an idea of the vulnerability of the country on the seaside, it will have attained its object. To expect more, would be absurd. The line on which the fate of all Iran and Turan must really be decided, leads from Astrabad to Peshawur, and on this line the decisive point is Herat.

Written late in January-early in February 1857

First published in the *New-York Daily Tribune*, No. 4941, February 19, 1857 as a leading article

Reproduced from the newspaper

[a] An allusion to Palmerston.— *Ed.*

Karl Marx

THE NEW ENGLISH BUDGET[257]

London. Feb. 20, 1857.

Financial theatricals have suffered a severe shock at the hands of Sir George Lewis, the present Chancellor of the Exchequer. With Sir Robert Peel, the delivery of the financial statement had become a sort of religious act, to be performed with all the solemnities of State etiquette, magnified by great efforts of rhetorical plausibility, and never to be done under five hours' time. Mr. Disraeli imitated, and Mr. Gladstone almost exaggerated, Sir Robert's ceremonious behavior toward the national purse. Sir George Lewis dared not infringe upon the tradition. So he made a four hours' speech; crawling, drawling, bobbing around, till he was all at once interrupted by peals of laughter, caused by scores of honorables seizing their hats and rushing out of the House.

> "I am sorry," exclaimed the dismal actor, "to continue my speech to an audience of reduced numbers; but I must state to those who remain, what would be the effect of the proposed alterations."[a]

When still one of *The Edinburgh Review* sages, Sir George Lewis was renowned for ponderousness of argumentation rather than for solidity of argument or sprightliness of diction. His personal shortcomings account certainly, to a great extent, for his Parliamentary failure. Yet there were other circumstances, altogether beyond his control, which might have discomfited even a regular Parliamentary prize-fighter. According to Sir William Clay's indiscreet statement before his Hull constituents, Lord Palmerston

[a] G. C. Lewis's speech in the House of Commons on February 13, 1857, *The Times*, No. 22604, February 14, 1857.— *Ed.*

had originally made up his mind for a continuance of war-taxation during a time of peace, when the threatening income-tax motion which, at the meeting of the Commons, was announced by Mr. Disraeli and seconded by Mr. Gladstone, compelled him at once to beat a retreat, and to change his financial tactics all of a sudden. At shortest notice, therefore, poor Sir George Lewis had to alter all his estimates, all his figures, his whole scheme, while his speech, prepared for a war budget, had to be served up for a quasi peace budget—a *quid pro quo*[a] that might have been entertaining if it had not been drowsy. But this is not all. The budgets of Sir Robert Peel, during his administration from 1841 to 1846, derived an extraordinary interest from the fierce struggle then raging between Free Traders[258] and Protectionists,[b] profit and rent, land and town. The budget of Mr. Disraeli was looked for as a curiosity, involving as it did the revival or final abdication of Protectionism, and Mr. Gladstone's budget was unduly exaggerated as the financial settlement, for a septennial period at least, of triumphant Free Trade. The social conflicts reflected in those budgets endowed them with a positive interest, while the budget of Sir George Lewis could at the outset only claim the negative interest of forming the common point of assaults for the enemies of the Cabinet.

The Budget of Sir G. Lewis, so far as his original ways and means are concerned, may be resumed in very few words. He strikes off the nine additional pence of the income-tax imposed for the war; reducing it thus from 1s. 4d. in the pound to 7d., at which rate it is to continue till 1860. On the other hand, the whole war-tax on spirits, and part of the war-tax on sugar and tea, are to be retained. This is all.

The income-tax of the present financial year, including the additional 9d. of the war-taxation, produces a revenue of more than £16,000,000, raised from the different classes of society in about the following manner:

Schedule A—Real Property	8,000,000
Schedule B—Farmers	1,000,000
Schedule C—Public Funds	2,000,000
Schedule D—Trades and Professions	4,000,000
Schedule E—Salaries	1,000,000
Total	16,000,000

[a] A substitute.—*Ed.*

[b] The manuscript has here: "between the industrial capitalist and the landed proprietor".—*Ed.*

From this tabular statement it is evident that the income-tax weighs exclusively upon the upper and middle classes; indeed, more than two-thirds of it is made up from the incomes of the aristocracy and the higher ranks of the middle class. But, what with the other war-taxes—what with the high prices of provisions and the rising rate of discount, the lower layers of the English middle class have been severely pinched by the income-tax, and are therefore most impatient to throw it off. Nevertheless, the cries they raised would hardly have been re-echoed in the press, and certainly not in the House of Commons, if the aristocracy and upper middle class had not taken the lead of the agitation, eagerly seizing the opportunity to hide their narrow-minded selfishness under the broad mask of philanthropy, and getting rid of an impost, the burden of which they are unable to shift on the shoulders of the multitude. While in France, during the time of the *République honnête et modérée*, the establishment of an income-tax was warded off by branding it as surreptitious socialism, in England the abolition of the same tax is now attempted by pleading sympathy with popular sufferings. The game has been played very cleverly. On the return of peace,[259] the spokesmen of the petty middle class turned their attack not upon the income-tax itself, but only on its war-surplus and its unequal distribution. The upper classes feigned to embrace the popular grievance, only to sophisticate its original meaning, and to convert a cry for diminished taxation of small incomes, into a cry for the exemption from taxation of large ones. In the heat of combat, and the impatience of immediate alleviation, the lower middle class were neither aware of the shuffle played upon them, nor did they care about terms which secured the support of powerful allies. As to the working-classes, without organs in the press, and without votes in the electoral bodies, their claims were quite out of the question.

Sir Robert Peel's Free-Trade measures rested notoriously on the income-tax as their basis. It will be easily understood that direct taxation is the financial expression of Free Trade. If Free Trade means anything, it means the removal of customs, excise duties, and all imposts directly interfering with production and exchange.

Now, if taxes are not to be raised by customs and excise duties, they must be directly derived from property and income. With a certain amount of taxes, no abatement can take place in the one mode of assessment without a corresponding increase of the other. They must rise and fall in inverse ratio. If, then, the English public want to do away with the greater part of direct taxation, they must be prepared to lay heavier duties on commodities and materials of manufactures—in one word, to renounce the Free-Trade system. Thus, indeed, the present movement has been interpreted on the Continent of Europe. A Belgian paper says that

"at a meeting held at Ghent to discuss the policy of Free Trade or Protection, one of the speakers urged the new opposition in England to the income-tax as proof of a change of the national opinion in favor of protection."

Thus, in one of their recent addresses, the Financial Reformers of Liverpool utter their apprehension lest Great Britain should return to the principles of restriction.

"We can," they say, "scarcely believe in the possibility of such an exhibition of national infatuation; yet every reflecting man of ordinary intellect must see that it is to this end, and to nothing else, that the present efforts tend."[a]

As Free Trade, and consequently direct taxation, are in Great Britain offensive weapons in the hands of the industrial capitalist against the landed aristocrat, their common crusade against the income-tax bears witness of the same fact economically which was politically demonstrated by the Coalition Cabinet[260]—the lassitude of the British middle classes, and their longing for compromises with the oligarchs, in order to escape concessions to the proletarians.

Sir G. Lewis, in striking sail before the Anti-Income-Tax League, exhibited at once the reverse of the medal. No remission of the paper duty, no forsaking of the fire-insurance tax, no abatement of the wine duty; but, on the contrary, increase of the import duties on tea and sugar. According to the settlement of Mr. Gladstone,[b] the duty on tea was to be reduced[c] from 1/6 per pound, first to 1/3, and then to 1/; and the sugar duty from £1 per cwt., first to 15/, and then to 13/4.[d] This refers to refined sugar only. White sugar was to be reduced from 17/6 successively to 13/2 and 11/8; yellow sugar from 15/ to 11/8 and 10/6; brown sugar from 13/9 to 10/7 and 9/6; molasses from 5/4 to 3/9. The war arrested this settlement; but according to the law passed in 1855, it was now to be realized successively in 1857 and 1858. Sir G. Lewis, who, on the 19th April, 1855, had raised the tea duty from 1/6 to 1/9 per pound, proposes to throw its reduction over four years—diminishing it to 1/7 for 1857-58, to 1/5 for 1858-59,

[a] The Address of the President and Council of the Liverpool Financial Reform Association to the Middle, Commercial, Manufacturing and Industrial Classes of the United Kingdom, *The Times,* No. 22561, December 26, 1856.—*Ed.*

[b] The manuscript has here: "of 1855".—*Ed.*

[c] Here the manuscript reads: "in 1857".—*Ed.*

[d] The manuscript has here: "in 1858".—*Ed.*

to 1/3 for 1859-60, and finally to 1/. With the sugar duty, he proposes dealing in a similar way. It is known that the supply of sugar has fallen below its demand, and that its stocks are reduced in the markets of the world—there being in London, for instance, at present only 43,700 tuns, against 73,400 two years ago. Thus the prices of sugar are, of course, rising. As to tea, Palmerston's Chinese expedition[261] has succeeded in creating an artificial limitation of supply, and a consequent rise of prices. Now, there is no economist who will not tell you that, in a period of dearth and rising prices, any reduction of duty, to benefit not only the importer but the general consumer also, must be sudden and striking. Sir G. Lewis asserts, on the contrary, that, with rising prices, reductions of duty are the surer to accrue to the benefit of the consumer the less they are perceptible. This assertion stands on a level only with his strange doctrine that Post-Office charges are a direct tax, and that complication constitutes the redeeming feature of taxation.

Decrease in the income-tax to be counterbalanced by the increase in the duties on tea and sugar—the latter being common necessaries with the British people—means evidently diminishing the taxes on the rich by augmenting the taxes on the poor. Such a consideration, however, would not have interfered with the vote in the House of Commons. But there are the tea-dealers, who have entered into large contracts and arrangements on the express faith, as they say, in the statement made on the 19th of April, 1856, by Sir George Lewis in the House of Commons—a statement again repeated to them by the Board of Customs on the 11th November, 1856—to the effect that "the duty on tea would be reduced to 1s. 3d. on the 6th of April, 1857."[a] There they are, standing upon their bond and upon budget morality. And there is Mr. Gladstone, glad to revenge himself upon Palmerston, who quite treacherously ousted the Peelites, after having used them to overthrow, first the Derby administration, then Russell, and lastly their own patriarch, old Aberdeen.[262] Besides, as the author of the financial settlement of 1853, Mr. Gladstone must of course defend his own standard budget from Sir G. Lewis's irreverent violations. Accordingly, he gave notice[b] that he should move the following resolution:

---

[a] See: "Tea and sugar duties", *The Economist,* No. 690, November 15, 1856.—*Ed.*

[b] The manuscript has here: "on Thursday, 19 February, that on Friday, on the motion for going into Committee of ways and means, he should move...".—*Ed.*

"That this House will not agree to any addition to the rates chargeable by the Custom-duties Acts of 1855, upon the articles of tea and sugar." [a]

I have so far touched upon one side of the budget only—its ways and means. Let me now look at the other side of the balance-sheet—the proposed expenditure. If the proposed ways and means are characteristic of the present state of official English society, the intended expenditure is still more so of its actual government. Palmerston wants money, and much money, not only to plant firmly his dictatorship, but also to indulge his taste for Canton bombardments, Persian wars, Naples expeditions,[263] &c. Accordingly he proposes a peace establishment costing about £8,000,000 in excess of the highest expenditure since the peace of 1815. He wants £65,474,000, while Mr. Disraeli contented himself with £55,613,379, and Mr. Gladstone with £56,683,000. That the views of the Oriental war-glory should, in due course of time, dissolve in heavy tax-gatherers' bills, was an event of course to be anticipated by John Bull.

But the annual surplus taxation accruing from the war cannot be estimated at more than £3,600,000, viz.: £2,000,000 for Exchequer bonds falling due in May, 1857; £1,200,000 for the interest of £26,000,000 of new funded debt, and £8,000,000 of unfunded debt; lastly, about £400,000 for the new sinking fund, corresponding to the new debts. The war balances do not, then, account, in fact, for half of the surplus expenditure claimed by Lord Palmerston. But his military estimates do. The whole Army and Navy estimates from 1830 to 1840 did not average £13,000,000, but they amount in the Lewis budget to £20,699,000. If we compare them with the total military estimates of the last five years preceding the war, we find that the latter reached in 1849 to £15,823,537; in 1850, to £15,320,944; in 1851, to £15,555,171; in 1852, to £15,771,893; in 1853-54, to £17,802,000, the estimates of 1853-54 having themselves been fixed with the prospect of an imminent war.

Clinging to the orthodox Whig doctrine that the sap of the tree is destined to afford food for the vermin, Sir G. Lewis pleads the increased national wealth as shown by the export and import tables of 1856, as a reason for the increased Government expenditure. If the conclusion were true, the premise would, nevertheless, remain false. It suffices to point at the many thousands of destitute workmen now roaming through the streets

---

[a] W. Gladstone's speech in the House of Commons on February 20, 1857, *The Times*, No. 22610, February 21, 1857.—*Ed.*

of London and applying at work-houses[264] for relief; at the broad fact resulting from the official revenue returns that, during the year 1856, the British consumption of tea, sugar and coffee has considerably declined, simultaneously with a slight increase in the consumption of spirits; at the trade circulars of the past year, which, as acknowledged by Mr. Wilson himself, the present Secretary of the Treasury, plainly prove that the profits of the British trade of 1856 bear a contrary proportion to its enlargement. It would seem that the natural tactics of an opposition leader would be to direct his main batteries against this extravagant expenditure. But in so doing Mr. Disraeli would risk being stabbed in the back by his own retainers, should he directly front this aristocratic lavishness.[a] He is, therefore, driven to the over-refined maneuver[b] of resting his motion against the Palmerston Budget, not on its extravagant expenditure for 1857 and 1858, but on its prospective deficiency of revenue in 1858-'59, and in 1859-'60.

At all events, the House of Commons debates on the Budget will be highly interesting, not only that the fate of the present Administration hungs upon them, and that they will exhibit the curious spectacle of a Disraeli-Gladstone-Russell coalition against Palmerston; but the very dialectics of a financial opposition which insists upon the abolition of the income-tax, forbids the increase of the sugar and tea duties, and dares not openly strike at extravagance in expenditure, must prove quite a novelty.

Written on February 20, 1857

First published in the *New-York Daily Tribune*, No. 4956, March 9, 1857

Reproduced from the newspaper

[a] Instead of this sentence the manuscript has: "But Mr. Disraeli would risk to be attacked in the rear by his own party, should he thus seriously front the aristocratic tax-eaters." — *Ed.*

[b] Instead of the words "over-refined maneuver" the manuscript has "the most pitiful expedient".— *Ed.*

Karl Marx

PARLIAMENTARY DEBATES ON THE CHINESE HOSTILITIES[265]

London, Feb. 27, 1857

The Earl of Derby's resolution, and that of Mr. Cobden, both of them passing condemnation upon the Chinese hostilities, were moved according to notices given, the one on the 24th of February, in the House of Lords,[a] the other on the 27th of February, in the House of Commons.[b] The debates in the Lords ended on the same day when the debates in the Commons began. The former gave the Palmerston Cabinet a shock by leaving it in the comparatively weak majority of 36 votes. The latter may result in its defeat. But whatever interest may attach to the discussion in the Commons, the debates in the House of Lords have exhausted the argumentative part of the controversy—the masterly speeches of Lords Derby and Lyndhurst forestalling the eloquence of Mr. Cobden, Sir E. Bulwer, Lord John Russell, and *tutti quanti*.[c]

The only law authority on the part of the Government, the Lord Chancellor,[d] remarked that

> "unless England had a good case with regard to the *Arrow*,[266] all proceedings from the last to first were wrong."

Derby and Lyndhurst proved beyond doubt that England had no case at all with regard to that lorcha. The line of argument followed by them coincides so much with that taken up in the columns of *The Tribune*[e] on the first publication of the English

[a] E. Derby's speech in the House of Lords on February 24, 1857, *The Times*, No. 22613, February 25, 1857.—*Ed.*

[b] R. Cobden's speech in the House of Commons on February 26, 1857, *The Times*, No. 22615, February 27, 1857.—*Ed.*

[c] All the rest.—*Ed.*

[d] R. Cranworth.—*Ed.*

[e] See this volume, pp. 158-63.—*Ed.*

dispatches that I am able to condense it here into a very small compass.

What is the charge against the Chinese Government upon which the Canton massacres[267] are pretended to rest? The infringement of Art. 9 of the supplemental treaty of 1843. That article prescribes that any Chinese offenders, being in the Colony of Hong-Kong, or on board a British man-of-war, or on board a British merchant ship, are not to be seized by the Chinese authorities themselves, but should be demanded from the British Consul, and by him be handed over to the native authorities. Chinese pirates were seized in the river of Canton on board the lorcha *Arrow*, by Chinese officers, without the intervention of the British Consul. The question arises, therefore, was the *Arrow* a British vessel? It was, as Lord Derby shows,

> "a vessel Chinese built, Chinese captured, Chinese sold, Chinese bought and manned, and Chinese owned."[a]

By what means, then, was this Chinese vessel converted into a British merchantman? By purchasing at Hong-Kong a British register or sailing license. The legality of this register relies upon an ordinance of the local legislation of Hong-Kong, passed in March, 1855. That ordinance not only infringed the treaty existing between England and China,[268] but annulled the law of England herself. It was, therefore, void and null. Some semblance of English legality it could but receive from the Merchant Shipping Act, which, however, was passed only two months after the issue of the ordinance. And even with the legal provisions of that act it had never been brought into consonance. The ordinance, therefore, under which the lorcha *Arrow* received its register, was so much waste paper. But even according to this worthless paper the *Arrow* had forfeited its protection by the infringement of the provisions prescribed, and the expiration of its license. This point is conceded by Sir J. Bowring himself.[b] But then, it is said, whether or not the *Arrow* was an English vessel, it had, at all events, hoisted the English flag, and that flag was insulted. Firstly,[c]

---

[a] E. Derby's speech in the House of Lords on February 24, 1857, *The Times*, No. 22613, February 25, 1857.— *Ed.*

[b] J. Bowring's letter to Consul Parkes of October 11, 1856, *The Times*, No. 22571, January 7, 1857. The manuscript has further: "writing to Consul Parkes that the *Arrow* was not entitled to British protection".— *Ed.*

[c] The manuscript has further: "it had no right to hoist the English flag as avowed by Sir J. Bowring himself in his letter to Consul Parkes d.d. Hong-Kong, October 11".— *Ed.*

if the flag was flying, it was not legally flying. But was it flying at all? On this point there exists discrepancy between the English and Chinese declarations. The latter have, however, been corroborated by depositions, forwarded by the Consuls, of the master and crew of the Portuguese lorcha No. 83. With reference to these depositions, *The Friend of China* of Nov. 13 states that

"it is now notorious at Canton that the British flag had not been flying on board the lorcha for six days previous to its seizure." [a]

Thus falls to the ground the punctilio of honor, together with the legal case.

Lord Derby had in this speech the good taste altogether to forbear from his habitual waggishness, and thus to give his argument a strictly judicial character. No efforts, however, on his part were wanted to impregnate his speech with a deep current of irony. The Earl of Derby, the chief of the hereditary aristocracy of England, pleading against the late Doctor, now Sir John Bowring, the pet disciple of Bentham; pleading for humanity against the professional humanitarian; defending the real interests of nations against the systematic utilitarian insisting upon a punctilio of diplomatic etiquette; appealing to the "vox populi vox dei" [b] against the greatest-benefit-of-the-greatest-number man [269]; the descendant of the conquerors preaching peace where a member of the Peace Society [270] preached red-hot shell; a Derby branding the acts of the British navy as "miserable proceedings" and "inglorious operations," where a Bowring congratulates it upon cowardly outrages which met with no resistance, upon "its brilliant achievements, unparalleled bravery, and splendid union of military skill and valor"—such contrasts were the more keenly satirical the less the Earl of Derby seemed to be aware of them. He had the advantage of that great historical irony which does not flow from the wit of individuals, but from the humor of situations. The whole parliamentary history of England has, perhaps, never exhibited such an intellectual victory of the aristocrat over the parvenu.

Lord Derby declared at the outset that he

"should have to rely upon statements and documents exclusively furnished by the very parties whose conduct he was about to impugn,"

---

[a] Quoted according to E. Derby's speech in the House of Lords on February 24, 1857, *The Times*, No. 22613, February 25, 1857.—*Ed.*

[b] "The voice of the people is the voice of God" (Hesiod, *The Works and Days*).—*Ed.*

and that he was content

"to rest his case upon these documents."

Now it has been justly remarked that those documents, as laid before the public by the Government, would have allowed the latter to shift the whole responsibility upon its subordinates. So much is this the case that the attacks made by the parliamentary adversaries of the Government were exclusively directed to Bowring & Co., and could have been indorsed by the home Government itself, without at all impairing its own position. I quote from his Lordship[a]:

"I do not wish to say anything disrespectful of Dr. Bowring. He may be a man of great attainments; but it appears to me that on the subject of his admission into Canton he is possessed with a perfect *monomania* [Hear, hear, and laughter]. I believe he dreams of his entrance into Canton. I believe he thinks of it the first thing in the morning, the last thing at night, and in the middle of the night, if he happens to be awake [Laughter]. I do not believe that he would consider any sacrifice too great, any interruption of commerce to be deplored, any bloodshed to be regretted, when put in the scale with the immense advantage to be derived from the fact that Sir J. Bowring had obtained an official reception in the Yamun[b] of Canton [Laughter]."

Next came Lord Lyndhurst[c].

"Sir J. Bowring, who is a distinguished humanitarian as well as plenipotentiary [laughter], himself admits the register is void, and that the lorcha was not entitled to hoist the English flag. Now, mark what he says: 'The vessel had no protection, but the Chinese do not know this. For God's sake do not whisper it to them.' He persevered, too, for he said in effect: We know the Chinese have not been guilty of any violation of treaty, but we will not tell them so; we will insist upon reparation and a return of the men they have seized in a particular form. If the men were not returned in the form, what was to be the remedy? Why, to seize a junk—a war junk. If that was not sufficient, seize more, until we compelled them to submit, although we knew they had the right on their side and we had no justice on ours [Hear]. Was there ever conduct more abominable, more flagrant, in which—I will not say more fraudulent, but what is equal to fraud in our country—more false pretense has been put forward by a public man in the service of the British Government [Hear]? It is extraordinary that Sir J. Bowring should think he had the right of declaring war. I can understand a man in such a position having necessarily a power of carrying on defensive operations, but to carry on offensive operations upon such a ground—upon such a pretense—is one of the most extraordinary proceedings to be found in the history of the world. It is quite clear from the papers laid on the table, that from the first moment at which Sir J. Bowring was appointed to the station he now fills, his ambition was to procure

---

[a] E. Derby's speech in the House of Lords on February 24, 1857, *The Times*, No. 22613, February 25, 1857.—*Ed.*

[b] Residence of a Chinese official.—*Ed.*

[c] J. Lyndhurst's speech in the House of Lords on February 24, 1857, *The Times*, No. 22613, February 25, 1857.—*Ed.*

what his predecessors had completely failed to effect—namely, the entry within the walls of Canton. Bent only upon carrying this object of gaining admission within the walls of Canton into execution, he has, for no necessary purpose whatever, plunged the country into a war; and what is the result? Property, to the large amount of $1,500,000, belonging to British subjects, is now impounded in the City of Canton, and in addition to that our factories are burned to the ground, and all this is only owing to the mischievous policy of one of the most mischievous of men.

"———But man, proud man,
Drest in a little brief authority,
Most ignorant of what he's most assured,
His glassy essence, like an angry ape,
Plays such fantastic tricks before high heaven
As make the angels weep[a]."

And, lastly, Lord Grey[b]:

"If your Lordships will refer to the papers you will find that when Sir J. Bowring applied for an interview with Commissioner Yeh, the Commissioner was ready to meet him, but he appointed for that purpose the house of the merchant Houqua, without the city. Sir J. Bowring's dignity would not allow him to go anywhere but to the official residence of the Commissioner. I expect, if no other result, at least the good result from the adoption of the resolution—the instant recall of Sir J. Bowring."

Sir J. Bowring met with similar treatment at the hands of the Commons, and Mr. Cobden even opened his speech with a solemn repudiation of his "friend of twenty years' standing."[c]

The literal quotations from the speeches of Lords Derby, Lyndhurst and Grey prove that, to parry the attack, Lord Palmerston's Administration had only to drop Sir J. Bowring instead of identifying itself with that "distinguished humanitarian." That it owed this facility of escape neither to the indulgence nor the tactics of his adversaries, but exclusively to the papers laid before Parliament, will become evident from the slightest glance at the papers themselves as well as the debates founded upon them.

Can there remain any doubt as to Sir J. Bowring's "monomania" with respect to his entrance into Canton? Is it not proved that that individual, as *The London Times* says,

"has taken a course entirely out of his own head, without either advice from his superiors at home or any reference to their politics?"[d]

---

[a] Shakespeare, *Measure for Measure*, Act II, Scene 2.—*Ed.*

[b] G. Grey's speech in the House of Lords on February 24, 1857, *The Times*, No. 22613, February 25, 1857.—*Ed.*

[c] R. Cobden's speech in the House of Commons on February 26, 1857, *The Times*, No. 22615, February 27, 1857.—*Ed.*

[d] See *The Times*, same issue, leading article.—*Ed.*

Why, then, should Lord Palmerston, at a moment when his Government is tottering, when his way is beset with difficulties of all sorts—financial difficulties, Persian war difficulties, secret-treaty difficulties, electoral reform difficulties,[271] coalition difficulties—when he is conscious that the eyes of the House are

"upon him more earnestly but less admiringly than ever before,"

why should he single out just that moment to exhibit, for the first time in his political life, an unflinching fidelity to another man and to a subaltern, too—at the hazard of not only impairing still more his own position, but of completely breaking it up? Why should he push his new-fangled enthusiasm to such a point as to offer himself as the expiatory sacrifice for the sins of a Dr. Bowring? Of course no man in his senses thinks the noble Viscount capable of any such romantic aberrations. The line of policy he has followed up in this Chinese difficulty affords conclusive evidence of the defective character of the papers he has laid before Parliament. Apart from published papers there must exist secret papers and secret instructions which would go far to show that if Dr. Bowring was possessed of the "monomania" of entering into Canton, there stood behind him the cool-headed chief of Whitehall[a] working upon his monomania and driving it, for purposes of his own, from the state of latent warmth into that of consuming fire.

Written on February 27, 1857 — Reproduced from the newspaper

First published in the *New-York Daily Tribune*, No. 4962, March 16, 1857

[a] Palmerston.—*Ed.*

Karl Marx

DEFEAT OF THE PALMERSTON MINISTRY

London, March 6, 1857

After having raged for four nights, the Chinese debates[a] subsided at last in a vote of censure passed by the House of Commons on the Palmerston Ministry. Palmerston retorts the censure by a "penal dissolution." He punishes the Commons by sending them home.

The immense excitement prevailing on the last night of the debates, within the walls of the House as well as among the masses who had gathered in the adjoining streets, was due not only to the greatness of the interests at stake, but still more to the character of the party on trial. Palmerston's administration was not that of an ordinary Cabinet. It was a dictatorship. Since the commencement of the war with Russia,[b] Parliament had almost abdicated its constitutional functions; nor had it, after the conclusion of peace, ever dared to reassert them. By a gradual and almost imperceptible declension, it had reached the position of a Corps Législatif,[272] distinguished from the genuine, Bonapartist article by false pretenses and high-sounding pretensions only. The mere formation of the Coalition Cabinet[273] denoted the fact that the old parties, on the friction of which the movement of the Parliamentary machine depends, had become extinct. This impotence of parties, first expressed by the Coalition Cabinet, the war helped to incarnate in the omnipotence of a single individual, who, during half a century of political life, had never belonged to any party, but always used all parties. If the war with Russia had not intervened, the very exhaustion of the old official parties would

[a] See this volume, pp. 207-12.— *Ed.*

[b] The Crimean war, 1853-56.— *Ed.*

have led to transformation. New life would have been poured into the Parliamentary body by the infusion of new blood, by the admission to political rights of at least some fractions of the masses of the people who are still deprived of votes and representatives. The war cut short this natural process. Preventing the neutralization of old Parliamentary antagonisms from turning to the benefit of the masses, the war turned it to the exclusive profit of a single man. Instead of the political emancipation of the British people, we have had the dictatorship of Palmerston. War was the powerful engine by which this result was brought about, and war was the only means of insuring it. War had therefore become the vital condition of Palmerston's dictatorship. The Russian war was more popular with the British people than the Paris peace.[274] Why, then, did the British Achilles, under whose auspices the Redan disgrace and the Kars surrender[275] had occurred, not improve this opportunity? Evidently because the alternative lay beyond his control. Hence his Paris treaty, backed by his misunderstandings with the United States, his expedition to Naples, his ostensible squabbles with Bonaparte, his Persian invasion, and his Chinese massacres.[276]

In passing a vote of censure upon the latter, the House of Commons cut off the means of his usurped power. Its vote was, therefore, not a simple Parliamentary vote, but a rebellion—a forcible attempt at the resumption of the constitutional attributes of Parliament. This was the feeling which pervaded the House, and whatever may have been the peculiar motives actuating the several fractions of the heterogeneous majority—composed of Derbyites, Peelites, Manchester men,[277] Russellites, and so-called Independents—all of them were sincere in asserting that it was no vulgar anti-Ministerial conspiracy which united them in the same lobby. Such, however, was the gist of Palmerston's defense. He covered the weakness of his case by an *argumentum ad misericordiam*,[a] by presenting himself as the victim of an unprincipled conspiracy. Nothing could be more happy than Mr. Disraeli's rebuke of this plea, so common to Old Bailey[278] prisoners.

"The First Minister," he said, "is of all men the man who cannot bear a coalition. Why, he is the archtype of political coalitions without avowed principles. See how his Government is formed. It was only last year that every member of his Cabinet in this House supported a bill introduced, I think, by a late colleague. It was opposed in the other House by a member of the Government who, to excuse his apparent inconsistency, boldly declared that when he took office the First

---

[a] Appeal to mercy.—*Ed.*

Minister required no pledge from him on any subject whatever [Laughter]. Yet the noble Lord is alarmed and shocked at this unprincipled combination! The noble Lord cannot bear coalitions! The noble Lord has acted only with those among whom he was born and bred in politics [Cheers and laughter]. That infant Hercules [pointing at Lord Palmerston] was taken out of the Whig cradle and how consistent has been his political life! [Renewed laughter.] Looking back upon the last half century, during which he has professed almost every principle, and connected himself with almost every party, the noble Lord has raised a warning voice to-night against coalitions, because he fears that a majority of the House of Commons, ranking in its numbers some of the most eminent members of the House—men who have been colleagues of the noble Lord—may not approve a policy with respect to China, which has begun in outrage, and which, if pursued, will end in ruin. That, sir, is the position of the noble Lord. And what defense of that policy have we had from the noble Lord? Has he laid down a single principle on which our relations with China ought to depend? Has he enumerated a solitary political maxim which should guide us in this moment of peril and perplexity? On the contrary, he has covered a weak and shambling case by saying—what?—that he is the victim of a conspiracy. He did not enter into any manly or statesmanlike defense of his conduct. He reproduced petty observations made in the course of the debate which I thought really had become exhausted and obsolete, and then he turned round and said that the whole was a conspiracy! Accustomed to majorities which have been obtained without the assertion of a single principle, which have, indeed, been the consequence of an occasional position, and which have, in fact, originated in the noble Lord's sitting on that bench without the necessity of expressing an opinion upon any subject, foreign or domestic, that can interest the heart of the country or influence the opinion of the nation, the noble Lord will at last find that the time has come when, if he be a statesman, he must have a policy; and that it will not do, the instant that the blundering of his Cabinet is detected, and every man accustomed to influence the opinion of the House unites in condemning it, to complain to the country that he is the victim of a conspiracy."[a]

It would, however, be quite a mistake to presume that the debates were interesting because such passionate interests hinged upon them. There was one night's debate after another night's debate, and still no division. During the greater part of the battle the voices of the gladiators were drowned in the hum and hubbub of private conversation. Night after night the placemen spoke against time to win another twenty-four hours for intrigue and underground action. The first night Mr. Cobden made a clever speech. So did Bulwer and Lord John Russell[b]; but the Attorney-General was certainly right in telling them that "he could not for one moment compare their deliberations or their arguments on such a subject as this, with the arguments that had

---

[a] B. Disraeli's speech in the House of Commons on March 3, 1857, *The Times,* No. 22619, March 4, 1857.—*Ed.*

[b] Speeches of R. Cobden, E. Bulwer-Lytton and J. Russell in the House of Commons on February 26, 1857 see in *The Times,* No. 22615, February 27, 1857.—*Ed.*

been delivered in another place."[a] The second night was incumbered by the heavy special pleadings of the attorneys on both sides, the Lord-Advocate,[b] Mr. Whiteside and the Attorney-General. Sir James Graham, indeed, made an attempt to raise the debate, but he failed. When this man, the virtual murderer of the Bandiera,[279] sanctimoniously exclaimed that "he would wash his hands of the innocent blood which had been shed,"[c] a half-suppressed ironical laugh re-echoed his pathos. The third night was still duller. There was Sir F. Thesiger, the Attorney-General *in spe*,[d] answering the Attorney-General *in re*,[e] and Sergeant Shee endeavoring to answer Sir F. Thesiger. There was the agricultural eloquence of Sir John Pakington. There was General Williams of Kars, listened to with silence only for a few minutes, but after these few minutes spontaneously dropped by the House and fully understood not to be the man they had taken him for. There was, lastly, Sir Sidney Herbert. This elegant scion of Peelite statesmanship made a speech which was, indeed, terse, pointed, antithetical, but girding at the arguments of the placemen rather than producing new arguments of his own. But the last night the debate rose to a hight compatible with the natural measure of the Commons. Roebuck, Gladstone, Palmerston and Disraeli were great, each in his own way.

The difficult point was to get rid of the stalking-horse of the debate, Sir J. Bowring, and to bring home the question to Lord Palmerston himself, by making him personally responsible for the "massacre of the innocents." This was at last done. As the impending general election in England will in the main revolve upon this point, it may not be amiss to condense, in as short a compass as possible, the results of the discussion. The day after the defeat of the Ministry, and the day before the ministerial announcement of the dissolution of the House of Commons, *The London Times* ventured upon the following assertions:

"The nation will be at a loss to know the precise question to be answered. Has Lord Palmerston's Cabinet forfeited the confidence of the people on account of a series of acts committed on the other side of the world six weeks before they were even heard of here, and by public servants appointed under a former administration? It was at Christmas when Ministers heard of the matter and they were at that time as ignorant as everybody else. In fact had the scene of the

[a] R. Bethell. Here and below speeches in the House of Commons on February 27, 1857 see in *The Times*, No. 22616, February 28, 1857.—*Ed.*

[b] James Moncreiff.—*Ed.*

[c] Cf. Matthew 27 : 24.—*Ed.*

[d] In future.—*Ed.*

[e] In reality.—*Ed.*

narrative been the moon, or had it been a chapter from the *Arabian Nights*, the present Cabinet could not have less to do with it.... Is Lord Palmerston's administration to be condemned and displaced for what it never did and could not do, for what it only heard of when everybody else heard of it, for what was done by men whom it did not appoint and with whom it has not, as yet, been able to hold any communication?"[a]

To this impudent rhodomontade of a paper which has all along vindicated the Canton massacre as a supreme stroke of Palmerstonian diplomacy, we can oppose a few facts painfully elicited during a protracted debate, and not once controverted by Palmerston or his subordinates. In 1847, when at the head of the Foreign Office, Lord Palmerston's first dispatch on the admission of the British Hong-Kong authorities into Canton was couched in menacing terms. However, his ardors were damped by Earl Grey, his colleague, the then Secretary for the Colonies, who sent out a most peremptory prohibition to the officers commanding the naval forces, not only at Hong-Kong, but at Ceylon, ordering them, under no circumstances, to allow any offensive movement against the Chinese without express authority from England. On the 18th August, 1849, however, shortly before his dismissal from the Russell Cabinet, Lord Palmerston wrote the following dispatch to the British Plenipotentiary at Hong-Kong:

"Let not the great officers of Canton nor the Government of Peking deceive themselves. The forbearance which the British Government has hitherto displayed arises not from a sense of weakness, but from consciousness of superior strength. The British Government well knows that, if occasion required it, *British military force would be able to destroy the town of Canton, not leaving one single house standing,* and could thus inflict the most signal chastisement upon the people of that city."[b]

Thus the bombardment of Canton occurring in 1856, under Lord Palmerston as Premier, was foreshadowed in 1849 by the last missive sent to Hong-Kong by Lord Palmerston, as Foreign Secretary of the Russell Cabinet. All the intervening Governments have refused to allow any relaxation of the prohibition put upon the British representatives at Hong-Kong against pressing their admission into Canton. This was the case with the Earl of Granville under the Russell Ministry, the Earl of Malmesbury under the Derby Ministry, and the Duke of Newcastle under the Aberdeen Ministry. At last, in 1852, Dr. Bowring, till then Consul at Hong-Kong, was appointed Plenipotentiary. His appointment, as Mr. Gladstone states, was made by Lord Clarendon, Palmer-

[a] *The Times,* No. 22620, March 5, 1857, leading article.—*Ed.*

[b] Quoted from J. Graham's speech in the House of Commons on February 27, 1857, *The Times,* No. 22616, February 28, 1857.—*Ed.*

ston's tool, without the knowledge or consent of the Aberdeen Cabinet. When Bowring first mooted the question now at issue, Clarendon, in a dispatch dated July 5, 1854, told him that he was right, but that he should wait till there were naval forces available for his purpose. England was then at war with Russia. When the question of the *Arrow* arose,[a] Bowring had just heard that peace had been established, and in fact naval forces were being sent out to him. Then the quarrel with Yeh was picked. On the 10th of January, after having received an account of all that had passed, Clarendon informed Bowring that "Her Majesty's Government entirely approve the course which has been adopted by Sir M. Seymour and yourself." This approbation, couched in these few words, was not accompanied by any further instructions. On the contrary, Mr. Hammond, writing to the Secretary of the Admiralty,[b] was directed by Lord Clarendon to express to Admiral Seymour the Government's admiration of "the *moderation* with which he had acted, and the respect which he had shown for the lives and properties of the Chinese."

There can, then, exist no doubt that the Chinese massacre was planned by Lord Palmerston himself. Under what colors he now hopes to rally the electors of the United Kingdom is a question which I hope you will allow me to answer in another letter, as this has already exceeded the proper limits.

Written on March 6, 1857

First published in the *New-York Daily Tribune*, No. 4970, March 25, 1857

Reproduced from the newspaper

---

[a] See this volume, pp. 207-12.— *Ed.*
[b] Ralph Bernal Osborne.— *Ed.*

Karl Marx

THE COMING ELECTION IN ENGLAND[280]

London, March 13, 1857

"Stand between two churchmen, good my Lord;
For on that ground I'll make a holy descant."[a]

Palmerston does not exactly comply with the advice tendered by Buckingham to Richard III. He stands between the churchman on the one side, and the opium-smuggler on the other. While the Low Church bishops, whom the veteran impostor allowed the Earl of Shaftesbury, his kinsman, to nominate, vouch his "righteousness," the opium-smugglers, the dealers in "sweet poison for the age's tooth,"[b] vouch his faithful service to "commodity, the bias of the world."[c] Burke, the Scotchman, was proud of the London "Resurrectionists."[281] So is Palmerston of the Liverpool "poisoners." These smooth-faced gentlemen are the worthy representatives of a town, the pedigree of whose greatness may be directly traced back to the slave trade. Liverpool, otherwise not famous for poetical production, may at least claim the original merit of having enriched poetry with odes on the slave trade. While Pindar commenced his hymn on the Olympian victors with the celebrated "Water is the best thing" (Ariston men hudor),[d] a modern Liverpool Pindar might, therefore, be fairly expected to open his hymn on the Downing-street[e] prize-fighters with the more ingenious exordium, "Opium is the best thing."

Along with the holy Bishops and the unholy opium-smugglers, there go the large tea-dealers, for the greater part directly or

---

[a] Shakespeare, *King Richard III,* Act III, Scene VII.—*Ed.*
[b] Shakespeare, *King John,* Act I, Scene I.—*Ed.*
[c] Op. cit., Act II, Scene I.—*Ed.*
[d] Pindar, *The First Olympian Ode.*—*Ed.*
[e] Downing-Street—a side-turning off Whitehall, where the main government buildings in London are situated; it contains the residence of the Prime Minister (at No. 10) and the Chancellor of the Exchequer (at No. 11).—*Ed.*

indirectly engaged in the opium traffic, and, therefore, interested in oversetting the present treaties with China. They are, besides, actuated by motives of their own. Having in the past year ventured upon enormous speculations in tea, the prolongation of hostilities will at once enhance the huge stocks they hold, and enable them to postpone the large payments to their creditors at Canton. Thus, war will allow them to cheat at once their British buyers and their Chinese sellers, and consequently realize their notions of "national glory" and "commercial interests." Generally the British manufacturers disagree from the tenets of this Liverpool catechism, upon the same lofty principle which puts in opposition the Manchester man, wanting low cotton prices, to the Liverpool gentleman, wanting high ones. During the first Anglo-Chinese war, extending from 1839 to 1842, the British manufacturers had flattered themselves with false hopes of marvelously extended exports.[282] Yard by yard they had measured the cotton stuffs the Celestials were to be clothed in. Experience broke the padlock Palmerstonian politicians had put upon their mind. From 1854 to 1857 the British manufactured exports to China did not average more than £1,250,000 sterling, an amount frequently reached in years preceding the first war with China.

> "In fact," as Mr. Cobden, the spokesman of the British manufacturers, stated in the House of Commons, "since 1842 we" (the United Kingdom) "have not added to our exports to China at all, at least as far as our manufactures are concerned. We have increased our consumption of tea; that is all."[a]

Hence the broader views with which British manufacturers, in contradistinction to British Bishops, opium-smugglers, and tea-dealers, are able to take of Chinese politics. If we pass over the tax-eaters and place-hunters who hang on the skirts of every administration, and the silly coffee-house patriots who believe "the nation to pluck up a heart" under Pam's auspices, we have in fact enumerated all the *bona fide* partisans of Palmerston. Still we must not forget *The London Times* and *Punch*, the Grand Cophta[283] and the Clown of the British press, both of whom are riveted to the present administration by golden and official links, and, consequently, write up a factitious enthusiasm for the hero of the Canton massacres. But then, it ought to be considered that the vote of the House of Commons betokened a rebellion against Palmerston as much as against *The Times*. The imminent elections have, therefore, to decide not only whether Palmerston shall

---

[a] R. Cobden's speech in the House of Commons on February 26, 1857, *The Times*, No. 22615, February 27, 1857.—*Ed.*

engross all the power of the State, but also whether *The Times* shall monopolize the whole manufacture of public opinion.

Upon which principle, then, is Palmerston likely to appeal to the general election? Extension of trade with China? But he has destroyed the very port upon which that commerce depended. For a more or less protracted period he has transferred it from the sea to the land, from the five ports to Siberia, from England to Russia. In the United Kingdom he has raised the duty upon tea—the greatest bar against the extension of the Chinese trade. The safety of the British merchant-adventurers? But the Blue Book,[284] entitled "Correspondence Respecting Insults in China," laid upon the table of the Commons by the Ministry itself, proves that, since the last seven years, there occurred but six cases of insult, in two of which the English were the aggressors, while in the four others the Chinese authorities exerted themselves to the full satisfaction of the British authorities in order to punish the offenders. If, then, the fortunes and the lives of the British merchants in Hong-Kong, Singapore, &c., are at present endangered, their perils are conjured up by Palmerston himself. But the honor of the British flag! Palmerston has sold it for £50 a piece to the smugglers of Hong-Kong, and stained it by the "wholesale massacre of helpless British customers." Yet, these pleas of extension of trade, safety of British merchant-adventurers, and honor of the British flag, are the only ones put up by the Government oracles which till now have addressed their constituents. They wisely refrain from touching any point of internal policy, as the cry of "no reform," and "more taxes," would not do. One member of the Palmerstonian Cabinet, Lord Mulgrave, the Household Treasurer, tells his constituents[a] that he has "no political theories to propound." Another one, Bob Lowe, in his Kidderminster address,[b] girds at the ballot, the extension of suffrage, and similar "humbug." A third one, Mr. Labouchere, the same clever fellow who defended the Canton bombardment on the plea that, should the Commons brand it as unjust, the English people must prepare to pay a bill of about £5,000,000 to the foreign merchants whose Canton property had been destroyed—this same Labouchere, in his appeal to his Taunton constituents,[c]

[a] G. Mulgrave's speech before the Scarborough constituents in March 1857, *The Times,* No. 22627, March 13, 1857.—*Ed.*

[b] R. Lowe's speech before the Kidderminster constituents on March 10, 1857, *The Times,* same issue.—*Ed.*

[c] H. Labouchere's speech before the Taunton constituents on March 11, 1857, *The Times,* same issue.—*Ed.*

ignores politics altogether, simply resting his claims upon the high deeds of Bowring, Parkes and Seymour.

The remark, then, of a British provincial paper, that Palmerston has got, not only no "good cry for the hustings, but no cry at all," is perfectly true. Yet his case is by no means desperate. Circumstances are altogether altered since the vote of the Commons. The local outrage on Canton has led to a general war with China. There remains the question only, who is to carry on the war? The man who asserts that war to be just, is he not better enabled to push it on with vigor than his adversaries, getting in by passing sentence upon it?

During his interregnum will Palmerston not embroil matters to such a degree as to remain the indispensable man?

Then the mere fact of there taking place an electoral battle, will it not decide the question in his favor? For the greater part of the British electoral bodies, as at present constituted, an electoral battle means a battle between Whigs and Tories. Now, as he is the actual head of the Whigs, as his overthrow must bring the Tories in, will not the greater part of the so-called Liberals vote for Palmerston in order to oust Derby? Such are the true considerations upon which the Ministerialists rely. If their calculations prove correct, Palmerston's dictatorship, till now silently suffered, would be openly proclaimed. The new Parliamentary majority would owe their existence to the explicit profession of passive obedience to the minister. A coup d'état might then, in due course of time, follow Palmerston's appeal from the Parliament to the people, as it followed Bonaparte's appeal from the *Assemblée Nationale* to the nation.[285] That same people might then learn to their damage that Palmerston is the old colleague of the Castlereagh-Sidmouth Cabinet, who gagged the press, suppressed public meetings, suspended the Habeas Corpus act,[286] made it legal for the Cabinet to imprison and expulse at pleasure, and lastly butchered the people at Manchester for protesting against the Corn Laws.[287]

Written on March 13, 1857 — Reproduced from the newspaper

First published in the *New-York Daily Tribune*, No. 4975, March 31, 1857

Karl Marx

[RUSSIAN TRADE WITH CHINA]

In the matter of trade and intercourse with China, of which Lord Palmerston and Louis Napoleon have undertaken the extension by force, no little jealousy is evidently felt of the position occupied by Russia. Indeed, it is quite possible that without any expenditure of money or exertion of military force Russia may gain more in the end, as a consequence of the pending quarrel with the Chinese, than either of the belligerent nations.

The relations of Russia to the Chinese Empire are altogether peculiar. While the English and ourselves—for in the matter of the pending hostilities the French are but little more than amateurs, as they really have no trade with China—are not allowed the privilege of a direct communication even with the Viceroy of Canton, the Russians enjoy the advantage of maintaining an Embassy at Pekin. It is said, indeed, that this advantage is purchased only by submitting to allow Russia to be reckoned at the Celestial Court as one of the tributary dependencies of the Chinese Empire. Nevertheless it enables Russian diplomacy, as in Europe, to establish an influence for itself in China which is by no means limited to purely diplomatic operations.

Being excluded from the maritime trade with China, the Russians are free from any interest or involvement in past or pending disputes on that subject; and they also escape that antipathy with which from time immemorial the Chinese have regarded all foreigners approaching their country by sea, confounding them, and not entirely without reason, with the piratical adventurers by whom the Chinese coasts seem ever to have been infested. But as an indemnity for this exclusion from the maritime trade, the Russians enjoy an inland and overland trade peculiar to themselves, and in which it seems impossible for them to have any rival. This traffic, regulated by a treaty made in 1768,[288] during the reign of Catherine II, has for its principal, if not indeed its sole seat of operations, Kiakhta, situated on the frontiers of southern Siberia and of Chinese Tartary,[a] on a tributary of the Lake Baikal, and about a hundred miles south of the City of Irkootsk. This trade, conducted at a sort of annual fair, is managed by twelve factors, of whom six are Russians and six Chinese, who meet at Kiakhta, and fix the rates—since the trade is entirely by barter—at which the merchandise supplied by either party shall be exchanged. The principal articles of trade are, on the part of the Chinese, tea, and on the part of the Russians, cotton and woolen cloths. This trade, of late years, seems to have attained a considerable increase. The quantity of tea sold to the Russians at Kiakhta did not, ten or twelve years ago, exceed an average of forty thousand chests; but in 1852 it amounted to a hundred and seventy-five thousand chests, of which the larger part was of that superior quality well known to continental consumers as caravan tea, in contradistinction from the inferior article imported by sea. The other articles sold by the Chinese were some small quantities of sugar, cotton, raw silk and silk goods, but all to very limited amounts. The Russians paid about equally in cotton and woolen goods, with the addition of small quantities of Russian leather, wrought metals, furs and even opium. The whole amount of goods bought and sold—which seem in the published accounts to be stated at very moderate prices—reached the large sum of upward of fifteen millions of dollars. In 1853, owing to the internal troubles of China[289] and the occupation of the road from the tea provinces by bands of marauding rebels, the quantity of tea sent to Kiakhta fell off to fifty thousand chests, and the whole value of the trade of that year was but about six millions of dollars. In the two following years, however, this commerce revived, and the tea sent to Kiakhta for the fair of 1855 did not fall short of a hundred and twelve thousand chests.

In consequence of the increase of this trade, Kiakhta, which is situated within the Russian frontier, from a mere fort and fair-ground, has grown up into a considerable city. It has been selected as the capital of that part of the frontier region, and is to be dignified by having a military commandant and a civil governor. At the same time a direct and regular postal communi-

---

[a] Mongolia.—*Ed.*

cation for the transmission of official dispatches has lately been established between Kiakhta and Pekin, which is distant from it about nine hundred miles.

It is evident that, should the pending hostilities result in a suppression of the maritime trade, Europe might receive its entire supply of tea by this route. Indeed, it is suggested that even with the maritime trade open, Russia may, upon the completion of her system of railroads, become a powerful competitor with the maritime nations for supplying the European markets with tea. These railroads will supply a direct communication between the ports of Cronstadt and Libau and the ancient city of Nijni Novgorod in the interior of Russia, the residence of the merchants by whom the trade at Kiakhta is carried on. The supply of Europe with tea by this overland route is certainly more probable than the employment of our projected Pacific Railroad for that purpose. Silk, too, the other chief export of China, is an article of such small bulk in comparison to its cost, as to make its transportation by land by no means impossible; while this Chinese traffic opens an outlet for Russian manufactures, such as they cannot elsewhere attain.

We may observe, however, that the efforts of Russia are by no means limited to the development of this inland trade. It is several years since she took possession of the banks of the River Amour,[290] the native country of the present ruling race[a] in China. Her efforts in this direction received some check and interruption during the late war,[b] but will doubtless be revived and pushed with energy. She has possession of the Kurile Islands and the neighboring coasts of Kamtchatka. Already she maintains a fleet in those seas, and will doubtless improve any opportunity that may offer to obtain a participation in the maritime trade with China. This, however, is of little consequence to her compared with the extension of that overland trade of which she possesses the monopoly.

Written on about March 18, 1857

First published in the *New-York Daily Tribune*, No. 4981, April 7, 1857 as a leading article; reprinted in the *New-York Weekly Tribune*, No. 813, April 11, 1857 under the title "Trade with China"

Reproduced from the *New-York Daily Tribune*

---

[a] The Manchu dynasty of Ch'ing.—*Ed.*
[b] The Crimean war, 1853-56.—*Ed.*

Karl Marx

THE ENGLISH ELECTION

London, March 20, 1857

The coming historian who is to write the history of Europe from 1848 to 1858, will be struck by the similarity of the appeal made to France by Bonaparte in 1851[291] and the appeal to the United Kingdom made by Palmerston in 1857. Both pretended to appeal from Parliament to the nation, from treacherous party coalition to the unsophisticated public mind. Both set forth analogous pleas. If Bonaparte was to save France from a social, Palmerston is to save England from an international crisis. Palmerston, like Bonaparte, is to vindicate the necessity of a strong executive against the empty talk and the intermeddling importunity of the legislative power. Bonaparte addressed himself at once to the conservatives and the revolutionists; to the former as the enemy of the aristocrats, to the latter as the enemy of middle-class usurpation. Palmerston, has he not insulted every despotic Government? Can he be obnoxious to any liberal? On the other hand, has he not betrayed every revolution? Must he not be the chosen of the conservatives? He opposed every reform, and the conservatives should not stand by him! He keeps the Tories out of office, and the liberal place-hunters should desert him! Bonaparte bears a name terrible to the foreigner, and identical with French glory. And does not Palmerston do the same with respect to the United Kingdom? At least, save some slight interruptions, he has kept the Foreign Office since 1830, since the days of reformed England,[292] and, therefore, since the beginning of its modern history. Consequently, the international existence of England, however "terrible" or "glorious" it may happen to appear to foreign eyes, centers in the person of Lord Palmerston. Bonaparte by one stroke set at naught all the official great men of France, and does Palmerston not "kick into atoms" the Russells, the Grahams, the Gladstones, the Roebucks, the Cobdens, the Disraelis, and *tutti quanti*[a]? Bonaparte stood on no principle, he had no impediment, but he promised to give the country what it wanted, a man. And so does Palmerston. He is a man. His worst enemies dare not accuse him of being a principle.

The regime of the Assemblée Législative—was it not the regime of a coalition composed of Legitimists[293] and Orleanists,[294] with a sprinkling of bourgeois Republicans? Their very coalition proved the dissolution of the parties they represented, while the old party traditions did not allow them to merge in any but a negative unity. Such a negative unity is unfit for action; its acts can only be negative; it can only stop the way; hence the power of Bonaparte. Is the case not the same with Palmerston? The Parliament that has sat since 1852, was it not a coalition Parliament? and was it, therefore, from the outset, not incarnated in a coalition Cabinet? The Assemblée Nationale, when it was forcibly shut up by Bonaparte, ceased to possess a working majority. So did the House of Commons when Palmerston proclaimed its final dissolution. But here the simile ends. Bonaparte made his *coup d'état* before he appealed to the nation. Restrained by constitutional fetters, Palmerston must appeal to the nation before he attempts a *coup d'état.* In this respect it cannot be denied all the odds are on the side of Bonaparte. The massacres of Paris, the dragonnades in the provinces, the general state of siege, the proscriptions and deportations *en masse,* the bayonet placed behind and the cannon placed before the electoral urn, gave to the argumentations of the Bonapartist press (the only one not swept away by the December deluge) a sinister eloquence which its shallow sophistry, its abominable logic, and its nauseous floridness of adulation, were unable to deprive of persuasive force. Palmerston's case, on the contrary, grows the weaker the more his myrmidons inflate their lungs. Great diplomatist as he is, he has forgotten to bid his slaves be aware of the prescript of the lame who liked to lead the blind, to impress upon them Talleyrand's *"pas de zèle".*[b] And indeed,

---

[a] All the rest.—*Ed.*

[b] No zeal.—*Ed.*

they have overdone their part. Take, for instance, the following dithyrambic uttered by a metropolitan organ:

"Palmerston for ever! is a cry which we hope to hear resounded from every hustings. ... The most devoted allegiance to Lord Palmerston is the first tenet to be insisted upon in the profession of faith of every candidate... It is indispensable that liberal candidates will be compelled to admit that Lord Palmerston as Premier is a political necessity of the hour. It is requisite that he should be recognized as the man of the time, not only as the coming man, but as the man that has come; not only as the man for the crisis, but as the man and the only living man for those conjunctures which are evidently impending upon our country... He is the idol of the hour, the pet of the people, the ascending as well as the risen sun."

No wonder that John Bull should prove reluctant to stand this, and that a reaction against the Palmerstonian fever should have set in.

Palmerston's person being proclaimed a policy, no wonder that his adversaries have made it a policy to sift his person. Indeed, we find that Palmerston, as if by magic, has worked the revival from the dead of all the fallen grandeurs of Parliamentary England. In proof of this assertion, the spectacle of Lord John Russell's (the Whig's) appearance before the metropolitan electors assembled at the London Tavern[a]; the exhibition made by Sir James Graham, the Peelite, before his Carlisle constituency[b]; and lastly, the performance of Richard Cobden, the representative of the Manchester school,[295] before the crowded meeting in the Free-Trade Hall at Manchester.[c] Palmerston has not acted like Hercules. He has not killed a giant by lifting him up to the air,[d] but he has reinvigorated dwarfs by throwing them back upon the earth. If any man had sunk in public estimation, it was certainly Lord John Russell, the father of all legislative abortions, the hero of expediency, the negotiator of Vienna,[296] the man in whose hand everything fatally dwindled to nothingness. Now look at his triumphal appearance before the London electors. Whence this change? It resulted simply from the circumstances in which Palmerston had put him. I, he said, am the father of the Test and Corporation act, of the Parliamentary Reform bill, of the

[a] J. Russell's speech before the electors assembled at the London Tavern on March 19, 1857, *The Times*, No. 22633, March 20, 1857.— *Ed.*

[b] J. Graham's speech before the Carlisle constituents on March 16, 1857, *The Times*, No. 22632, March 19, 1857.— *Ed.*

[c] R. Cobden's speech before the Manchester constituents on March 18, 1857, *The Times*, No. 22633, March 20, 1857.— *Ed.*

[d] A reference to the myth about Antaeus.— *Ed.*

municipal corporation reform, of the tithes-question's settlement, of some liberal acts with respect to the Dissenters,[297] of others with respect to Ireland. In one word, I engross the substance of whatever was progressive in Whig policy. Are you to sacrifice me to a man who represents Whigism minus its popular elements, who represents Whigism not as a political party, but only as a place-hunting faction? And then he turned his very shortcomings to his advantage. I have always been an adversary of the ballot. Do you expect me now, because I am proscribed by Palmerston, to degrade myself by recanting my convictions and by pledging myself to radical reforms? No, shouted his auditory. Lord John ought at this moment not to be pledged to the ballot. It is greatness in the little man to confess himself, under present circumstances, a bit-by-bit reformer. Three cheers, and one more for John Russell without the ballot! And then he gave the last turn to the scale, by asking his audience whether they would allow a small coterie of opium dealers, at the bidding of Palmerston, to constitute themselves into an electioneering body to impose their government-hatched conclusions on the free electors of the metropolis, and to proscribe himself, Lord John Russell, their friend of 16 years' standing, at the bidding of Palmerston! No, no, shouted the auditory—down with the coterie! Long life to Lord John Russell! And he is now likely not only to be returned, but to head the poll in London.

The case of Sir James Graham was still more curious. If Lord John Russell had become ridiculous, Graham had become contemptible. But, said he to his Carlisle constituents, shall I be snuffed out like a candle that is burned down to the socket, or shall I slink away like a dog hunted off a race-course, because, once in my life, I acted conscientiously, and risked rather my political position than stoop to the dictation of a man? You have returned me as your representative in spite of all my infamies. Are you to dismiss me for one single good action I have committed? Certainly not, re-echoed the Carlisle electors.

In contradistinction to Russell and Graham, Mr. Cobden had, at Manchester, not to confront his own electors, but the electors of Bright and Gibson. He spoke not for himself, but for the Manchester School. His position waxed from this circumstance. The Palmerstonian cry at Manchester was more factitious than at any other place. The interests of the industrial capitalists differ essentially from those of the opium-smuggling merchants of London and Liverpool. The opposition raised at Manchester against Bright and Gibson was not founded upon the material interests of the community, while the cry raised for Palmerston was antagonistic to all its traditions. It proceeded from two sources—from the high-priced press, endeavoring to revenge itself for the abolition of the newspaper stamp and the reduction of the advertisement duty,[298] and from that portion of rich and snobbish manufacturers who, jealous of the political eminency of Bright, try at playing the *bourgeois gentilhommes*,[a] and think that it would be fashionable and *bon ton* to rally under the aristocratic banner of Palmerston rather than under the sober programme of Bright. This peculiar character of the Palmerstonian coterie at Manchester enabled Cobden, for the first time since the Anti-Corn-Law-League agitation,[299] to take up again the position of a plebeian leader and to summon again the laboring classes to his banners. Masterly he improved that circumstance. The high ground he took up in his attack upon Palmerston may be judged from the following extract:

"Well, now there is a great question involved in this, which I think the people of this country ought to take very much to heart. Do you want the members of the House of Commons to look after your interests, and watch the expenditure—[yes, yes]—and to guard you from getting into needless and expensive wars? [Yes.] Well, but you are not going the right way to work, if what I learn in your newspapers is going to be verified in the course of the election, for I am told that those members who joined in that vigilant care of your interests, and voted according to the evidence before us on the question of that war are all to be ostracised—sent into private life—and that you are going to send up other men—[no, no]—to do what? to look after your interests? No, to go and do the humble dirty work of the minister of the hour [Loud cheers]. In fact, that you are going to constitute Lord Palmerston the despotic ruler of this country [No, no]. Well, but if he is not checked by Parliament—if the moment Parliament does check him he dissolves Parliament, and instead of sending up men who are independent enough to assert their and your rights, you send up mere creatures of his will, what is that but investing him with the powers of a despot? Ay, and let me tell you that it is a despotism of the clumsiest, most expensive kind, and at the same time the most irresponsible on the face of the earth; because you surround the minister with the sham appearance of a representative form of government; you cannot get at him while he has got a Parliament beneath whose shield he can shelter himself; and if you don't do your duty in your elections in sending men up to the House of Commons who will vigilantly watch the minister of the day, then, I say, you are in a worse plight because governed in a more irresponsible way than if under the King of Prussia or the Emperor of the French [Loud cheers]."[b]

---

[a] An allusion to the main character in Molière's *Le bourgeois gentilhomme*.—*Ed.*

[b] R. Cobden's speech before the Manchester constituents on March 18, 1857, *The Times*, No. 22633, March 20, 1857.—*Ed.*

It will now be understood why Palmerston hurries on the elections. He can only vanquish by surprise, and time baffles surprise.

Written on March 20, 1857

First published in the *New-York Daily Tribune*, No. 4980, April 6, 1857

Reproduced from the newspaper

Karl Marx

[ENGLISH ATROCITIES IN CHINA]

A few years since, when the frightful system of torture in India was exposed in Parliament Sir James Hogg, one of the Directors of the Most Honorable East India Company, boldly asserted that the statements made were unfounded. Subsequent investigation, however, proved them to be based upon facts which should have been well known to the Directors, and Sir James had left him to admit either "willful ignorance" or "criminal knowledge" of the horrible charge laid at the Company's doors. Lord Palmerston, the present Premier of England, and the Earl of Clarendon, the Minister of Foreign Affairs, seem just now to be placed in a similar unenviable position. At the late Lord Mayor's[a] banquet, the Premier said, in his speech, while attempting to justify the atrocities committed upon the Chinese[b]:

> "If the Government had, in this case, approved of unjustifiable proceedings, they had undoubtedly followed a course which deserved to incur the censure of Parliament and of the country. We were persuaded, however, on the contrary, that these proceedings were necessary and vital. We felt that a great wrong had been inflicted on our country. We felt that our fellow-countrymen in a distant part of the globe had been exposed to a series of insults, outrages and atrocities which could not be passed over in silence [Cheers]. We felt that the treaty rights of this country had been broken, and that those locally charged with the defense of our interests in that quarter of the world were not only justified, but obliged to resent those outrages, so far as the power in their hands would enable them to do so. We felt that we should be betraying the trust which the citizens of the country had reposed in us if we had not approved of the proceedings which we thought to be right, and which we, if placed in the same circumstances, should have deemed it our duty to have pursued [Cheers]."

---

[a] Thomas Quested Finnis.— *Ed.*

[b] Palmerston's speech at the ministerial banquet at the Mansion House on March 20, 1857, *The Times*, No. 22634, March 21, 1857.— *Ed.*

Now, however much the people of England and the world at large may be deceived by such plausible statements, his Lordship himself certainly does not believe them to be true, or if he does, he has betrayed a willful ignorance almost as unjustifiable as "criminal knowledge". Ever since the first report reached us of English hostilities in China, the Government journals of England and a portion of the American Press have been heaping wholesale denunciations upon the Chinese—sweeping charges of violation of treaty obligations—insults to the English flag—degradation of foreigners residing on their soil, and the like, yet not one single distinct charge has been made or a single fact instanced in support of these denunciations, save the case of the lorcha *Arrow*, and, with respect to this case, the circumstances have been so misrepresented and glossed over by Parliamentary rhetoric as utterly to mislead those who really desire to understand the merits of the question.

The lorcha *Arrow* was a small Chinese vessel, manned by Chinese, but employed by some Englishmen. A license to carry the English flag had been temporarily granted to her, which license had expired prior to the alleged "insult". She is said to have been used to smuggle salt, and had on board of her some very bad characters—Chinese pirates and smugglers—whom, being old offenders against the laws, the authorities had long been trying to arrest. While lying at anchor in front of Canton—with sails furled, and no flag whatever displayed—the police became aware of the presence on board of these offenders, and arrested them—precisely such an act as would have taken place here, had the police along our wharves known that river-thieves and smugglers were secreted in a native or foreign vessel near by. But, as this arrest interfered with the business of the owners, the captain went to the English Consul[a] and complained. The Consul, a young man recently appointed, and, as we are informed, a person of a quick and irritable disposition, rushes on board *in propria persona*,[b] gets into an excited parley with the police, who have only discharged their simple duty, and consequently fails in obtaining satisfaction. Thence he rushes back to the Consulate, writes an imperative demand for restitution and apology to the Governor-General of the Quangtung Province, and a note to Sir John Bowring and Admiral Seymour at Hong-Kong, representing that he and his country's flag have been insulted beyond endurance, and intimat-

[a] Harry S. Parkes.—*Ed.*
[b] In person.—*Ed.*

ing in pretty broad terms that now is the time for a demonstration against Canton, such as had long been waited for.

Gov. Yeh politely and calmly responds to the arrogant demands of the excited young British Consul. He states the reason of the arrest, and regrets that there should have been any misunderstanding in the matter; at the same time he unqualifiedly denies the slightest intention of insulting the English flag, and sends back the men, whom, although lawfully arrested, he desired not to detain at the expense of so serious a misunderstanding. But this is not satisfactory to Mr. Consul Parkes—he must have an official apology, and a more formal restitution, or Gov. Yeh must abide the consequences. Next arrives Admiral Seymour with the British fleet, and then commences another correspondence, dogmatic and threatening, on the side of the Admiral; cool, unimpassioned, polite, on the side of the Chinese official. Admiral Seymour demands a personal interview within the walls of Canton. Gov. Yeh says this is contrary to all precedent, and that Sir George Bonham had agreed that it should not be required. He would readily consent to an interview, as usual, outside the walled town if necessary, or meet the Admiral's wishes in any other way not contrary to Chinese usage and hereditary etiquette. But this did not suit the bellicose representative of British power in the East.

Upon the grounds thus briefly stated—and the official accounts now before the people of England fully bear out the statement—this most unrighteous war has been waged. The unoffending citizens and peaceful tradesmen of Canton have been slaughtered, their habitations battered to the ground, and the claims of humanity violated, on the flimsy pretense that "English life and property are endangered by the aggressive acts of the Chinese!" The British Government and the British people—at least, those who have chosen to examine the question—know how false and hollow are such charges. An attempt has been made to divert investigation from the main issue, and to impress the public mind with the idea that a long series of injuries, preceding the case of the lorcha *Arrow*, form of themselves a sufficient *casus belli*. But these sweeping assertions are baseless. The Chinese have at least ninety nine injuries to complain of to one on the part of the English.

How silent is the press of England upon the outrageous violations of the treaty daily practiced by foreigners living in China under British protection! We hear nothing of the illicit opium trade, which yearly feeds the British treasury at the expense of human life and morality. We hear nothing of the constant bribery of sub-officials, by means of which the Chinese Government is defrauded of its rightful revenue on incoming and outgoing merchandise. We hear nothing of the wrongs inflicted "even unto death" upon misguided and bonded emigrants sold to worse than Slavery on the coast of Peru and into Cuban bondage. We hear nothing of the bullying spirit often exercised against the timid nature of the Chinese, or of the vice introduced by foreigners at the ports open to their trade. We hear nothing of all this and of much more, first, because the majority of people out of China care little about the social and moral condition of that country; and secondly, because it is the part of policy and prudence not to agitate topics where no pecuniary advantage would result. Thus, the English people at home, who look no farther than the grocer's where they buy their tea, are prepared to swallow all the misrepresentations which the Ministry and the Press choose to thrust down the public throat.

Meanwhile, in China, the smothered fires of hatred kindled against the English during the opium war have burst into a flame of animosity, which no tenders of peace and friendship will be very likely to quench.[300]

Written on about March 22, 1857

First published in the *New-York Daily Tribune*, No. 4984, April 10, 1857 as a leading article

Reproduced from the newspaper

Karl Marx

A TRAITOR IN CIRCASSIA

The following letter, is extracted from the *Pester Lloyd.*

"Circassian Head-quarters, Tuabs, Feb. 26.

"By means of the British steamer *Kangaroo* you will receive this letter, which will perhaps convey to Europe the first information of an event that may have very great influence on the future fate of the Circassian nations. It is known to you that Mehemed Bey (Bangya), to whose person I am attached, has acceded to the wishes of the chiefs and deputies of the Circassian tribes, and has accepted the post of commander-in-chief. On Monday the 23rd of February, we landed at Tuabs, where we have our head-quarters. Before our departure, Mehemed Bey engaged a couple of hundred excellent military instructors for the different arms, and they accompanied us hither. Mehemed Bey has already been solemnly proclaimed General-in-chief of the Circassian forces. The princes, nobles, and deputies of the people have sworn on the Koran to obey him, and a deputation of the Circassian diet has to-day sent in the flag of the prophet, which is the symbol of the highest power. The enthusiasm was very great when the new commander swore fidelity to the sacred standard. (The flag itself is green, and on it is a white sword with the crescent and the star.) The excitement is great, and the Circassians have resolved to obtain their complete independence or to perish in the struggle for it. It is expected that 150,000 (?) men will be in the field by the month of May. 'Russia,' said Mehemed Bey to me just now, 'will soon have an opportunity of convincing herself that a *new spirit* prevails.' I know the materials which are placed at my disposal (Mehemed Bey was with the Circassians during the late war), and am of opinion that a nation, which, without a military organization, could resist its enemy during thirty years, will, when properly organized, be able to *achieve* its complete independence. You may expect to receive some important news from these mountains in the coming spring. You shall have from me as early information of what happens as our means of communication will permit."

Bangya was a Hungarian chief, attached first to Kossuth, and afterwards to Szemere; was a refugee in England in 1851 and 1852, was employed by the Prussians *and* by the French Government as a spy, and of course must have an understanding with their common master; now he goes under English auspices to Circassia, where a *new spirit* is to prevail. The old spirit was anti-Russia, the new must be Russia—Circassia is to *achieve* an independence which she has never lost, and to crown the whole, a Parliament is invented which has yet to be created.

Written on about March 25, 1857

First published in *The Free Press*, No. 34, April 1, 1857

Reproduced from the newspaper

Karl Marx

THE DEFEAT OF COBDEN, BRIGHT AND GIBSON[301]

London, March 31, 1857

"The mass of candidates put forward their intention to give a general support to Lord Palmerston, as their best claim to be returned as representatives of public opinion in the new Parliament. ...Palmerston will enter the House, not as the head of a Conservative, or a Whig, or a Peelite,[302] or a Radical party, but as the leader of the English people, and as the great designer and administrator of a national party."[a]

Such are the words of *The Morning Post,* Lord Palmerston's private organ. Palmerston as dictator, the new Parliament as his *corps législatif*[303]—such is their meaning, which the electoral bulletins seem to warrant. As to the "public opinion" spoken of by *The Post,* it has been justly said that Palmerston manufactures one half of it, and laughs at the other half.

The complete rout of the Manchester School[304]—Bright and Milner Gibson being unseated at Manchester, Cobden at Huddersfield, Sir E. Armitage at Salford, Fox at Oldham and Miall at Rochdale—is the great event of the electoral battle. The issue of the Manchester election particularly took every one by surprise, even the Palmerston Government. How little stress it had laid upon the chances of victory in that quarter may be inferred from its unsettled and hesitating conduct. First, on the receipt of some Manchester addresses, Palmerston threatened to proceed himself to Cottonopolis, hurling defiance at his antagonists on "their own dunghill." On second thought, however, he shrank back. Then Bob Lowe, the Ministerial understrapper, came forward. Invited by a coterie of great mill lords to stand for Manchester, and receiving pledges that, if defeated, a sum of £2,000 should be

[a] *The Morning Post,* No. 25971, March 27, 1857, leading article.—*Ed.*

handed to him, which might enable him to buy one of the county rotten boroughs,[305] he publicly accepted the offer, and allowed an electioneering committee to set out canvassing in his name. Then came Mr. Cobden's great Manchester speech.[a] [306] Palmerston now bid Lowe retract, which he did. On further reflection still, the Manchester attempt appeared so destitute of all elements of success that *The Times* was ordered to play the part of the fox in the fable.[b] Bob Lowe had to write a leader insisting upon the re-election of Bright & Co., and warning Manchester not to disgrace itself by the repudiation of its old representatives. When, in spite of all these misgivings, the electric wire flashed to Downing street the news of Cobden's defeat, of Bright's and Gibson's rejection, and by overwhelming majorities, too, judge of the rapturous delight and the maddening cries of triumph in the Ministerial camp. As to Palmerston himself, he thought perhaps that he had been too successful for his own purposes—keenly aware, as the old trickster is, that to paralyze even a giant, you have only to get him into the House of Commons, while to hasten the breaking down of that House itself—of its basis, the privileged constituencies, and its superstructure, Ministerial usurpation—you have only to turn out its eminent members and throw them on the street, thus giving chiefs of note to the disinherited multitude outside the gates of the "British Constitution."

The defeat of the Manchester School in their own strongholds, by the bulk of their own army, bears all the appearances of a personal triumph on the part of Palmerston, not only because Cobden and Gibson moved the vote of censure, which was to drive him from the Cabinet, and which afforded the pretext for the dissolution of Parliament. A deadly antagonism of principles and situations seems to resume itself in the persons of Palmerston on the one side, of Bright, Cobden & Co., on the other. Palmerston, the trumpet of national glory, they, the organs of industrial interests; the diplomatic Viscount concentrating in his person all the usurpations of the British oligarchy, the *parvenu* demagogues representing all the vitality of the British middle classes; he deriving his strength from the decay of parties, they owing their force to the struggle of classes—the last unscrupulous incarnation of old Toryism against the chiefs of the new defunct Anti-Corn-Law League.[307] Thus the defeat of Cobden, Bright & Co. appears

---

[a] R. Cobden's speech in the Freetrade Hall, Manchester, on March 18, 1857, *The Times,* No. 22633, March 20, 1857.—*Ed.*

[b] Aesop, "The Fox and the Crow".—*Ed.*

as a personal triumph of Palmerston, the more their victorious opponents on the hustings can claim no importance of their own. Sir John Potter, for instance, the opponent of Bright, is only known as the fattest man of Manchester. He would go under the name of the Manchester Sir John Falstaff, if his small wit and his long purse did not protect him from being compared to that immortal knight. A. Turner, Milner Gibson's opponent, rested his personal claims on the fact of his being a commonplace man who would never hurt the feelings of his fellow-citizens by unpleasant pretensions to genius or brilliancy. Mr. Akroyd, finally, the opponent of Cobden, accused the latter of being an imperial man, while he (Akroyd) had never been anything, and would certainly never be anything beyond a plain Huddersfield man. All of them gloried in being not men of talent but of character, which latter gift was sure to preclude them from falling, like their predecessors, into the fault of "opposing all Governments," and of sacrificing, like Milner Gibson, lucrative offices to theoretical crotchets.

Yet, in spite of appearances, the appeal of Palmerston against Cobden and Co.[a] afforded, not the cause, but only the pretext for the explosion of combustible materials which, for a long time, were gathering round the precincts of the Manchester School. Manchester forming the nucleus of the party, and Bright being acknowledged as its true hero, it will suffice to consider his defeat to account for the simultaneous failure of his companions in arms at other manufacturing places. There were, first, the old Whigs and Tories of Manchester, eager to revenge themselves for their political nullity since the days of the Anti-Corn-Law League. The elections of 1852, when Bright carried it over them by a majority of 100 votes only, had already shown their numerical force to be by no means contemptible. Unable, as they certainly were, to vanquish under their own banners, they formed a powerful contingent for any seceding corps of the Bright army. Then, in second line, came the leaders of the high-priced press, with their inveterate rancor and lurid malignity against the parliamentary godfathers of the penny press.[308] Mr. Garnett, the editor of *The Manchester Guardian,* stirred heaven and earth against Bright, and proved indefatigable in clothing in more or less decent garbs the shabby motives of the anti-Bright coalition—an attempt facilitated by the unpopularity Bright and Cobden had incurred at the time

---

[a] A reference to Lord Palmerston's speech at the meeting in Tiverton on March 27, 1857.—*Ed.*

of the Russian war.[309] At that period they could, indeed, not venture upon fronting a public meeting at Manchester, but had to hide themselves in select tea-parties at Newall's buildings, the old abode of the Anti-Corn-Law League. Of the liberal bourgeoisie, the mill lords and the large commercial firms, an overwhelming majority voted against Bright; of the petty middle class and the shopocracy, that numerous minority only which everywhere in the United Kingdom sticks to the heels of its "natural superiors," Quakers[310] and Irishmen, stood like one man for Bright. Whence this secession of the liberal bourgeoisie? To a great extent it is explained by the impatience of the rich "men of Manchester" to become "gentlemen," like their rivals at Liverpool. If they had borne with the superiority of a man of genius like Bright so long as he was the indispensable tool of their class-interests, they now thought the opportunity ripe for indulging the envious ostracism of well-to-do mediocrities. However, they rebelled not only against his personal superiority, but still more against the superannuated pretensions of the Anti-Corn-Law League rump, which weighed upon Manchester somewhat as the Rump Parliament[311] did upon the Commonwealth of England; periodically assembling under the presidency of Mr. Wilson, that "venerable fixture" and a retired starch merchant by profession, supported on the platform by Mr. Robinson, the honorary Secretary of the League, and other men without social standing or personal eminence, whom the billows of a tempest-beaten period had thrown on the surface, who obstinately refused to subside, and could, indeed, show no cause for their protracted appearance on the political stage, but the worn-out tradition of the past, and the conventional lie of the present, of playing Manchester whenever Bright wanted to call it up. One of the leaders of the rebellion, Mr. Entwistle, declared roundly on the hustings:

"It is not the question of the Chinese war, or of the Russian war, or of any war at all. The question is, whether Manchester shall any longer submit to the dictation of the remnant of the party that assembles at Newall's buildings."

In finally burying the incubus of the Anti-Corn-Law League rump, the Manchester mill lords, while flattering themselves that they were closing the doors of their Jacobin club, were, of course, not aware that they were sweeping away the main obstruction to a new revolutionary movement.

The rationale, however, of the Manchester election was betrayed by a drunken anti-Bright man, who, during the polling, kept on crying vociferously: "We won't have home policy; we want foreign policy." In other words: Away with reform questions and class struggles! After all, the middle classes form the majority of electors, and that is all we want. The cry against the aristocracy has become tiresome, unprofitable, and is only stirring up the working men. We have got free trade, and feel marvelously at our ease, especially since the reduction of the war income tax. We dearly love a lord for all that. "We won't have home policy; we want foreign policy." Let all of us unite on that ground where we are all equals, on the national ground. Let us all be Englishmen, true John Bulls, under the leadership of the truly British Minister, Lord Palmerston.[312]

The true secret, then, of the Manchester election is, the abdication on the part of the mill lords of the revolutionary leadership they had usurped during the Anti-Corn-Law League agitation.

Written on March 31, 1857

First published in the *New-York Daily Tribune,* No. 4990, April 17, 1857

Reproduced from the newspaper

Frederick Engels

[A NEW ENGLISH EXPEDITION TO CHINA]

Should the quarrel which the English have picked with the Chinese be pushed to extremity, it may be expected to end in a new military and naval expedition similar to that undertaken in 1841-42, on the basis of the opium quarrel.[313] The easy success of the English on that occasion, in extorting an immense sum of silver from the Chinese, will be apt to recommend a new experiment of the same sort to a people who, with all their horror of *our* filibustering propensities, still retain, not less than ourselves, not a little of the old plundering buccaneering spirit which distinguished our common ancestors of the sixteenth and seventeenth centuries. Yet remarkable changes in the position of things in China, which have occurred since that former successful plundering inroad on behalf of the opium trade, make it very doubtful whether a similar expedition at the present day would be attended by anything like a similar result. The new expedition would doubtless set out, like that of 1841-42, from the island of Hong-Kong. That expedition consisted of a fleet of two seventy-fours, eight frigates, a great number of sloops and brigs-of-war, twelve steamers, and forty transports, having on board a military force, marines included, amounting to fifteen thousand men. The new expedition would hardly be attempted with any smaller force; indeed, some of the considerations we are about to state would indicate the policy of making it much larger.

The expedition of 1841-42, sailing from Hong-Kong on the 21st of August, 1841, took possession first of Amoy, and then, on the 1st of October, of the Island of Chusan, which they made the base of their future operations. The object of these operations was to penetrate into and ascend the great central river Yang-tse-Kiang as far as the City of Nankin, about two hundred miles from its mouth. The river Yang-tse-Kiang divides China into two quite distinct portions—the North and the South. About forty miles below Nankin the Imperial Canal enters and crosses the great river, affording the means of commercial intercourse between the northern and southern provinces. The theory of the campaign was that the possession of this important communication would be a fatal thing for Pekin, and would force the Emperor[a] to make peace forthwith. On the 13th of June, 1842, the English forces, under Sir Henry Pottinger, appeared off Woosung, at the entrance of the small river of that name. This river flows from the south, entering the estuary of the Yang-tse-Kiang very near its débouché into the Yellow Sea. The mouth of the Woosung River forms the harbor of Shanghae, situated a short distance up. The banks of the Woosung were covered with batteries, all of which were stormed and carried without difficulty. A column of the invading force then marched on Shanghae, which surrendered without any attempt at resistance. But, though little resistance was as yet experienced from the peaceful and timid inhabitants on the banks of the Yang-tse-Kiang, who, after a prolonged peace of nearly two hundred years, had now their first experience of war, the estuary itself, and the approach to it from the sea, were found to present great impediments. The broad estuary of the Yang-tse-Kiang enters the sea from between shores half covered with mud, and hardly discernible, as the sea for many leagues[b] off is a muddy yellow, whence comes its name. Ships intending to enter the Yang-tse-Kiang are obliged to move cautiously along the southern shore, keeping the lead constantly going, in order to avoid the bars of movable sand with which the approach is impeded. These banks extend up the estuary as high as the upper end of the great island Tsang-Ming, which lies midway in it and divides it into two channels. Above this island, which is some thirty miles long, the shores begin to show themselves above the water, but the course of the channel becomes very serpentine. The tide flows up as far as Ching-Kiang-Foo, about half way to Nankin, and where, in fact, what has hitherto been an estuary or arm of the sea, first takes on, for ascending vessels, the character of a river. Before making this point, the English fleet met with some serious difficulties. It took them fifteen days to make the distance of eighty miles from their anchorage at Chusan. Near the Island

---

[a] Tao Kuang.—*Ed.*

[b] One nautical league equals 5.56 km.—*Ed.*

of Tsang-Ming several of the larger ships ran aground, but succeeded in getting off by the help of the rising tide. Having conquered these difficulties and approached the city of Ching-Kiang, the English found abundant proof that, however deficient the Tartar-Chinese soldiers might be in military skill, they were not lacking in courage and spirit. These Tartar soldiers, who were only fifteen hundred in number, fought with the utmost desperation, and were killed to a man. Before they marched to the battle, as if anticipating the result, they strangled or drowned all their women and children, great numbers of whose dead bodies were afterward drawn from the wells into which they had been thrown. The Commander-in-Chief, seeing that the day was lost, set fire to his house and perished in the flames. The English lost a hundred and eighty-five men in the attack—a loss which they revenged by the most horrible excesses in sacking the town—the war having been conducted by the English throughout in a spirit of brutal ferocity, which was a fitting counterpart to the spirit of smuggling cupidity in which it had originated. Had the invaders met with a similar resistance everywhere they never would have reached Nankin. But such was not the case. The city of Qua-Chow, on the opposite side of the river, submitted and paid a ransom of three millions of dollars, which the English freebooters of course pocketed with immense satisfaction.

Above this point, the channel of the river had a depth of thirty fathoms,[a] and, so far as the bottom was concerned, the navigation became easy, but at some points the current ran with great swiftness, not less than six and seven miles an hour. There was nothing, however, to prevent ships-of-the-line from ascending to Nankin, under the walls of which the English at length cast anchor on the 9th of August. The effect thus produced was exactly what had been anticipated. The Emperor was frightened into signing the treaty of the 29th of August,[314] the pretended violation of which is now made the occasion of new demands which threaten a new war.

That new war, should it occur, will probably be conducted on the model of the former one. But there are several reasons why the English could not anticipate a similar easy success. The experience of that war has not been lost on the Chinese. In the recent military operations in Canton River they have exhibited such improved skill in gunnery and the art of defense as to lead to the suspicion of their having Europeans among them. In

[a] One nautical fathom equals 1.83 m.—*Ed.*

everything practical, and war is eminently practical, the Chinese far surpass all the Orientals, and there is no doubt that in military matters the English will find them apt scholars. Again, it is likely that the English may encounter artificial obstacles to the ascent of the Yang-tse-Kiang, should they again attempt it, such as do not appear to have been met with on the former occasion. But,—what is the most serious consideration of all—the reoccupation of Nankin cannot be supposed to be attended with anything like the same terror and alarm to the Imperial Court at Pekin which it caused on the former occasion. Nankin, for a considerable period past, as well as large portions of the surrounding districts, has been in possession of the rebels, one or more of whose chiefs make that city their headquarters.[315] In this state of the case its occupation by the English might be rather agreeable to the Emperor than otherwise. They might do him good service in driving the rebels from a city which, when they had got it, might prove a possession rather difficult, troublesome and dangerous to keep, and which, as recent experience has shown, may be held by a hostile power without any immediately fatal results to Pekin or the Imperial rule.

Written in early April 1857

First published in the *New-York Daily Tribune,* No. 4990, April 17, 1857 as a leading article; reprinted in the *New-York Semi-Weekly Tribune,* No. 1242, April 21, 1857 under the title "China"

Reproduced from the *New-York Daily Tribune*

Karl Marx

RESULT OF THE ELECTION

London, April 7, 1857

The electoral lists are being closed. Their clearest sum is Palmerston's triumph, a great change in the *personnel* of the House, involving about one-fourth of its members, and its unprecedented loss in intellectual character. The computations, however, of the English papers as to the numerical force of the Ministerial majority, their bickerings and squabbles about these computations, and still more, their classifications under exploded rubrics of the newly-returned members, are silly work altogether. While *The Morning Post,* for instance, glories in a Ministerial majority of 80 votes, the Disraeli *Press* estimates the loss of its own men at four in the boroughs and about 20 in the counties. According to *The London Times,* the exclusion of the Peelites and the Manchester men[316] and professional Protectionists has restored Parliament to its *status quo ante,*[a] and delivered it back to its legitimate owners, the antediluvian parties of Whigs and Tories. It would fain persuade the world that

> "the British people have gone back to what they were some thirty years ago."[b]

The Disraeli *Press* is not very far from indorsing *The Times*'s opinion. This optimist creed, with which the oligarchy may try to comfort themselves, is, however, no more absurd than that of the sham Radicals, such as *The Examiner.*

> "A Reform Parliament," says it, "answers to Lord Palmerston's appeal."

He has asked for a lot of lackeys, and the enlightened country, that is to say, a small minority of privileged electors, returns his

[a] Former state.— *Ed.*

[b] *The Times,* No. 22648, April 7, 1857, leading article.— *Ed.*

compliment by sending him a band of tribunes of the people! While roaring "Palmerston forever!" they are only playing a trick on the wily Viscount! If the new Parliament initiate a great movement, it will be certainly no fault of its own, and Great Britain, like Sinbad the Sailor, will find it more difficult to throw off the old man than to saddle him on her shoulders.[a]

In comparing the new House to its predecessors, it seems opportune to begin with the old parliamentary sections that have completely vanished during the electoral struggle—the Peelite fraction and the Manchester School.

In contradistinction to Whigs, Tories and the Manchester School, the Peelite fraction did not represent a class or fractions of a class. They were a mere Parliamentary clique, which, without the walls of both Houses, might number friends, but could never muster an army. Relics of a bygone administration; estranged from the Tories by the Corn-Law[317] treason of their late chief[b]; loth to dissolve in the Whig ranks from the memory of old feuds, and the conviction, cherished by themselves and accepted to a certain degree by the public, that the administrative talent of the country centered in them; prevented by their aristocratic connections from mixing into one mass with the Manchester School, sure of influencing Parliamentary debates from the rhetorical ability of some of their members,—this pretentious nucleus of self-styled statesmen fluctuated uncertain, impossible of classification, and representing under the form of a peculiar Parliamentary party the decomposition of all Parliamentary parties effected by Peel's free-trade legislation. This principle of dissolution to which they owed their origin, they worked out by helping to overthrow the Derby Ministry, and by giving their nominal chief[c] to the combination of parties known as the Coalition Cabinet or the Cabinet of all the talents.[318] On the visible precipitation of the Parliamentary dissolving process, on their band devolved the honor of hoisting the colors under which the mutual suicide of the old parties was to be consummated. While thus securing to themselves for a moment a supreme position, they were simultaneously destroying the only reason for their existence as a separate body. The joint stock power of the combined parties ended necessarily in their common impotence and their joint prostration before one man. The Peelites held the ladder on which Palmerston mounted.

---

[a] *Tausend und eine Nacht.* Geschichte Sinbads des Seefahrers. Fünfte Reise.—*Ed.*
[b] Robert Peel.—*Ed.*
[c] George Aberdeen.—*Ed.*

Having already, in 1852, lost half of their forces on the electoral battle-field, the elections of 1857 have swept away their whole rank and file. The two Phillimores, Lord Hervey, Sir G. Clark, Sir Stafford Northcote, Lord W. Powlett, A. Gordon, Sutton, Harcourt, Lushington, Smythe, Sir J. W. Hogg of East Indian memory, Roundell Palmer, and lastly, Mr. Cardwell, are all gone. The last-named gentleman had, on Palmerston's accession to the Premiership, had the Chancellorship of the Exchequer offered to him, which he declined, however, on the advice of Gladstone, Graham & Co. Yet, in the dying session of the now buried House of Commons, hoping to take the wind out of Gladstone's sails, he seceded from his friends and voted on the Budget division with Palmerston. Finally, during the Canton debates, being apprehensive lest the tide should turn, he again shifted sides, returned to the Peelite circle, and countersigned Mr. Cobden's motion of censure. This gentleman is thus a true pattern of the curious association, distinctive of the Peelite clique, of moral nicety with unscrupulous place-hunting. The whole Peelite rank and file being now gone to the wall, there remain only its three generals, Mr. Gladstone, Sir James Graham and Mr. Herbert, three units unable to form a trinity, opposite as they are to one another by origin and predilections; Sir James Graham having started into public life from Radicalism, Mr. Gladstone from high Toryism, and Mr. Herbert as a nondescript.

One revelation made by Mr. Herbert on the hustings to his South Wilts constituents is characteristic of the manner in which Palmerston *did* the Peelites. Nothing had made them so unpopular as the conduct of the Russian war, and especially the sparing of Odessa,[319] which was accounted for by Mr. Herbert being the nephew of Prince Woronzoff. Foremost in spreading the envenomed calumny were Palmerston's myrmidons, such as *The Morning Post, The Sun,* and *The Morning Advertiser.* Now, Mr. Herbert told his electors that he had actually signed an order to attack Odessa, and that on his secession from office Lord Palmerston issued the order to spare the place.[a] This ranks on one line with Lord John Russell's revelation on the City of London hustings.[b] He notoriously broke down in consequence of his Vienna Embassy.[320] During the election turmoil, the beery *Morning*

[a] S. Herbert's speech before the electors of the Southern division of Wiltshire on April 1, 1857, *The Times,* No. 22644, April 2, 1857.—*Ed.*

[b] J. Russell's speech before the electors of the City of London on March 27, 1857, *The Times,* No. 22640, March 28, 1857.—*Ed.*

Advertiser, the licensed victualers' own paper and Palmerston's mob-organ—he has organs of all sorts and for all tastes, from the fashionable saloon to the tap-room—almost drowned its hoary voice in the cry of Russell's great Vienna treason. Provoked by these impudent tactics, Russell found at last the courage to tell the world that Lord Clarendon had refused him the permission to publish the instructions drawn up by Palmerston himself, written in his own handwriting, and dictating that very Vienna policy for which he (Russell) had once lost his popularity. A Greek philosopher said that his compatriots, the poets, had invented worse stories about the Hellenic gods than any man would dare tell of his deadliest enemy. Modern France and England exalt as their gods Bonapartes and Palmerstons, who want no poets to blacken them.

From what has been said, it is evident that the few Peelite generals who have outlived their army will reappear in Parliament no longer in their corporate, but in their individual capacity only. As an individual, Mr. Gladstone, now cleared from the obstructions of a coterie, roused by passion, and undoubtedly the greatest orator in the new Commons, may play a more conspicuous part than ever before. During their protracted Parliamentary duel, Gladstone and Disraeli, as occurs sometimes in ardent encounters, have from time to time dropped each his own weapons to seize those of his adversary. To a certain degree Gladstone has laid hold on Disraeli's polemical pungency, while Disraeli has caught Gladstone's pompous unction—Disraeli being hardly the winner in this exchange.

In taking leave of the Peelites, we may still point out the satire of history which, dating the birth of that fraction from the decomposition by the Anti-Corn-Law League of the old Parliamentary parties, registers its death simultaneously with the Parliamentary extinction of the Manchester School.

Written on April 7, 1857

First published in the *New-York Daily Tribune,* No. 4994, April 22, 1857

Reproduced from the newspaper

Karl Marx

CONDITION OF FACTORY LABORERS

London, April 7, 1857

The reports of the Inspectors of Factories, which have been recently issued for the half year ending 31st October, 1856,[a] form a valuable contribution to the social anatomy of the United Kingdom. They will not a little help to explain the reactionary attitude taken by the mill-lords during the present general election.

During the Session of 1856, a Factory Act[b] was smuggled through Parliament by which the "radical" mill-lords first altered the law in regard to the fencing of mill-gearing and machinery, and secondly introduced the principle of arbitration in the disputes between masters and men. The one law purported to provide for the better protection of the limbs and lives of the factory laborers; the other to place that protection under cheap courts of equity.[321] In fact, the latter law intended to cheat the factory laborer out of law, and the former to cheat him out of his limbs. I quote from the joint report of the inspectors:

"Under the new statute, persons whose *ordinary occupation* brings them near to mill-gearing, and who are consequently well acquainted with the dangers to which their employment exposes them, and with the necessity of caution, are protected by the law; while protection has been *withdrawn* from those who may be obliged, in the execution of special orders, to suspend their ordinary occupation and to place themselves in positions of danger, of the existence of which they are not conscious, and from which, by reason of their ignorance, they are unable to protect

---

[a] *Reports of the Inspectors of Factories to Her Majesty's Principal Secretary of State for the Home Department, for the Half Year Ending 31st October 1856.—Ed.*

[b] "An Act for the Further Amendment of the Laws Relating to Labour in Factories".— *Ed.*

themselves, but who, on that very account, would appear to require the special protection of the Legislature."[a]

The arbitration clause, in its turn, prescribes that the arbitrators shall be chosen from persons "skilled in the construction of the kind of machinery" by which bodily harm is inflicted. In one word, engineers and machine-makers are entrusted with the monopoly of arbitration.

"It appears to us," say the Inspectors, "that engineers and machine-makers ought to be considered *as disqualified* to act as factory arbitrators, by reason of their connection in trade with the factory occupiers, who are their customers."[b]

Under such provisions, it is not to be wondered at that the number of accidents arising from machinery, such as death, amputations of hands, arms, legs or feet, fracture of limbs and bones, of head and face, lacerations, contusions, &c., amount, during the six months ending on the 31st October, 1856, to the appalling number of 1,919. Twenty cases of death, inflicted by machinery, are registered in the industrial bulletin for half a year—about ten times the number lost by the British Navy during its glorious Canton massacre.[322] Since the mill-lords, so far from endeavoring to protect the lives and limbs of their laborers, are thus only bent on escaping payment for arms and legs lost in their service, and shifting the cost of the wear and tear of their animated machines from their own shoulders, it need not surprise us that, according to the official reports,

"overworking, in violation of the factory act, is on the *increase*."

Overworking in the terms of that act means employing young persons for a longer time per day than is legally allowed. This is done in various ways: By beginning work before six in the morning, by not stopping it at six in the evening, and by abridging the terms the law has fixed for the meals of the workpeople. There are three periods of the day when the steam-engine starts, viz., when the work begins in the morning, and when it is resumed after the two meals of breakfast and dinner; and there are three periods when it stops, viz., at the beginning of each meal-time and when the work ceases in the evening. Thus there are six opportunities when five minutes may be stolen, or half an hour each day. Five minutes a day's increased work, multiplied by

[a] "Half-Yearly Joint Report of the Inspectors of Factories", *Reports of the Inspectors...*, p. 3.— *Ed.*
[b] Ibid., p. 7.— *Ed.*

weeks, is equal to two and one-half days of produce in the year; but the fraudulent overworking goes far beyond that amount. I quote Mr. Leonard Horner, the Factory Inspector for Lancashire:

> "The profit to be gained by such illegal overworking appears to be a greater temptation than the manufacturers can resist. They calculate upon the chance of not being found out; and when they see the small amount of penalty and costs which those who have been convicted have had to pay, they find that if they should be detected there will still be a considerable balance of gain." [a]

Beside the trifling fines imposed by the factory act, the mill-owners took good care to have it so framed, that the greatest facilities are afforded for passing by its enactments, and as the inspectors unanimously declare, "almost insuperable difficulties prevent them from putting an effective stop to the illegal working." They also concur in stigmatizing the willful commission of fraud by persons of large property; the mean contrivances to which they have recourse in order to elude detection; and the base intrigues they set on foot against the inspectors and sub-inspectors entrusted with the protection of the factory slave. In bringing forward a charge of overworking, the inspectors, sub-inspectors, or their constables, must be prepared to swear that the men have been employed at illegal hours. Now, suppose they appear after 6 o'clock in the evening. The manufacturing machinery is immediately stopped, and although the people could be there for no other purpose than attending upon it, the charge cannot be sustained, by reason of the wording of the act. The workmen are then sent out of the mill in great haste, often more doors than one facilitating their rapid dispersion. In some instances the gas was extinguished, when the sub-inspectors entered the room, leaving them suddenly in darkness among complicated machinery. In those places which have acquired a notoriety for overworking, there is an organized plan for giving notice at the mills of the approach of an inspector, servants at railway stations and at inns being employed for this purpose.

These vampyres, fattening on the life-blood of the young working generation of their own country, are they not the fit companions of the British opium smugglers, and the natural supporters of the "truly British Ministers[323]?"

The reports of the factory inspectors prove beyond doubt that the infamies of the British factory system are growing with its growth; that the laws enacted for checking the cruel greediness of

---

[a] [L. Horner,] "Report of Leonard Horner, Esq., Inspector of Factories, for the Half Year Ended the 31st October 1856", ibid., p. 34.—*Ed.*

the mill-lords are a sham and a delusion, being so worded as to baffle their own ostensible end and to disarm the men entrusted with their execution; that the antagonism between the mill-lords and the operatives is rapidly approaching the point of actual social war; that the number of children under 13 years, absorbed by that system, is increasing in some branches, and that of females in all; that, although the same number of hands are employed in proportion to the horse-power as at former periods, there are fewer hands employed in proportion to the machinery; that the steam-engine is enabled to drive a greater weight of machinery than ten years before by economy of force; that an increased quantity of work is now turned off by increase of speed of the machinery and other contrivances; and that the mill-lords are rapidly filling their pockets.

The interesting statistical facts illustrated in the Reports may properly claim further notice. Thus much will be understood at once, that the industrial slaveholders of Lancashire are in want of a foreign policy able to distract attention from home questions.

Written on April 7, 1857

First published in the *New-York Daily Tribune,* No. 4994, April 22, 1857

Reproduced from the newspaper

Karl Marx

THE ENGLISH FACTORY SYSTEM

London, April 10, 1857

The Reports of the Inspectors of Factories in the United Kingdom for 1856[a] contain detailed returns relating to factory statistics, such as the number of factories, the amount of horse-power employed, the quantity of machinery, and the number of persons set to work. Similar returns were ordered by the House of Commons in 1835, 1838 and 1850, the information being compiled from schedules filled up by the mill-owners. Ample materials are thus afforded for comparing different periods of the factory system, which, in its legal sense, comprises the manufactories only where steam or water-power is employed for the production of textile fabrics.

The most characteristic feature of the social history of the United Kingdom during the last six years is, undoubtedly, to be found in the rapid extension of that system.

The following are the numbers of factories at the dates of the last three returns[b]:

	1838.	1850.	1856.
Cotton Factories	1,819	1,932	2,210
Woolen Factories	1,322	1,497	1,505
Worsted Factories	416	501	525
Flax Factories	392	393	417
Silk Factories	268	277	460
Total	4,217	4,600	5,117

[a] *Reports of the Inspectors of Factories to Her Majesty's Principal Secretary of State for the Home Department, for the Half Year Ending 30th April and 31st October 1856.—Ed.*

[b] "Half-Yearly Joint Report of the Inspectors of Factories", *Reports of the Inspectors ... for the Half Year Ending 31st October 1856,* p. 11.— *Ed.*

The average increase of factories, therefore, which from 1838 to 1850 had been at the rate of 32 per annum, was almost tripled from 1850 to 1856, when it reached the rate of 86 yearly. An analysis of the aggregate increase during either epoch is given in the following summary[a]:

Aggregate Increase from 1838 to 1850.	Per Cent.	Aggregate Increase from 1850 to 1856.	Per Cent.
Cotton Factories	6	Cotton Factories	14.2
Woolen	13	Woolen	0.5
Worsted	20	Worsted	4.7
		Flax	6.1
		Silk	66.0

From this table, it will be seen that during the former period the increase was confined to the cotton, woolen and worsted manufacture, while in the latter period it also embraces the flax and silk factories. The proportions in which the various branches share in the aggregate increase differ also in the two periods. During 1838-50, the principal increase took place in the worsted and woolen trade, the latter of which appears almost stationary from 1850-56, and the former falling back to a four times lesser speed of expansion. On the other hand, cotton and silk top the movement during the latter period, the silk manufacture occupying the first rank in the proportional increase, and the cotton manufacture when the absolute increase is considered.

The localities of this expansion have varied considerably, there taking place a migration, as it were, from one part of the country to the other. Hand in hand with the general increase, there goes a local decrease, amounting in many counties and boroughs to a complete extinction of manufactories before existing. The general law ruling these changes of decay as well as of growth is the same law which pervades modern industry in all its directions—the law of concentration. Thus Lancashire, and the parts of Yorkshire adjoining it—the principal seat of the cotton manufacture—have drawn the trade from other parts of the kingdom. The number of cotton factories in Lancashire and Yorkshire having increased from 1838-56 by adding 411 to the previous number, they have decreased by 52 in the counties of Lanark (Glasgow), Renfrew

[a] Ibid., p. 12.—*Ed.*

(Paisley), and Antrim. So, too, the woolen trade is becoming concentrated in Yorkshire; while 200 woolen manufactories have been added there, we find a corresponding decrease of 82 in Cornwall, Devon, Gloucester, Monmouth, Somerset, Wilts, Wales and Clackmannan. The worsted manufacture is almost exclusively confined to Yorkshire, in which county there has been an increase of 107 factories. The flax-trade is now more vigorous in Ireland than in any other part of the United Kingdom; but the increase of 59 flax factories in Antrim, Armagh, Down and Tyrone, is accompanied by a decrease in Yorkshire of 31, in Devonshire, Dorsetshire and Gloucestershire of 9, and in Fifeshire of 18. To the increase of 76 silk factories in Cheshire, Derbyshire, Nottingham and Gloucestershire, there corresponds a decrease by 13 in Somersetshire. In some instances, the decay in one manufacturing branch is compensated by the growth of another, so that the industrial migrations would appear to be only a more definite working out of the principle of the division of employments on a large scale. Yet, on the whole, this is not the case—the progress of the system rather tending to establish a division between industrial and agricultural provinces. In England, for instance, the southern counties of Wilts, Dorset, Somerset, Gloucester, are being rapidly divested of their manufactures, while the northern counties of Lancashire, Yorkshire, Warwick, Nottingham, are strengthening their industrial monopoly. Of the aggregate increase of factories in the United Kingdom from 1838 to 1856, reaching the number of 900, Lancashire alone claims 360, Yorkshire 344, Warwick 71 and Nottingham 46—the increase in the two last-named counties having been caused by the introduction of improved machinery in two special trades—the adaptation of power to the stocking-frame at Nottingham, and the weaving of ribbons by power at Coventry.

From the increase in the number of factories must be distinguished the increase in the amount of horse-power employed, the latter not only depending on the addition of new mills, but also on the erection of more powerful engines in the old ones, the substitution of the steam-engine for water-power, the addition of steam-power to the waterwheel, and other similar contrivances. The following table contains a comparison of the nominal power of the factories in 1838, 1850 and 1856[a]:

---

[a] Ibid., p. 30.—*Ed.*

Horse-power employed in the factories in the United Kingdom.

	Steam.	Water.	Total.
1838.			
Cotton	46,826	12,977	59,803
Woolen	11,525	9,092	20,617
Worsted	5,863	1,313	7,176
Flax	7,412	3,677	11,089
Silk	2,457	927	3,384
Total	75,083	21,986	102,069
1850.			
Cotton	71,005	11,550	82,555
Woolen	13,455	8,689	22,144
Worsted	9,890	1,625	11,515
Flax	10,905	3,387	14,292
Silk	2,858	853	3,711
Total	108,113	26,104	134,217
1856.			
Cotton	88,001	9,131	97,132
Woolen	17,490	8,411	25,901
Worsted	13,473	1,431	14,904
Flax	14,387	3,935	18,322
Silk	4,360	816	5,176
Total	137,711	23,724	161,435

Great as the increase of the power apparent from the figures undoubtedly is—59,366 horse-power between 1838 and 1856—it falls, nevertheless, much below the actual additional force available and in motion for manufacturing purposes. The figures given in the return all relate to the *nominal* power only of the engines and wheels, and not to the power actually employed or capable of being employed. The modern steam-engine of 100 horse-power is capable of being driven at a much greater force than formerly, arising from improvements in its arrangements, the capacity and construction of the boilers, etc.; and thus its nominal power cannot be considered as other than an index from which its real capabilities may be calculated. Mr. Nasmyth, the civil engineer, after an explanation of the nature of recent improvements in the steam-engine, by which the same engine can be made to perform more work with a diminished consumption of fuel, sums up results as follows[a]:

"From the same weight of steam-engine machinery, we are now obtaining at least 50 per cent. more work performed, on the average, and, in many cases, the identical steam-engines which, in the days of the restricted speed of 220 feet per minute, yielded 50 horse-power, are now yielding upward of 100."

By comparing the increase of horse-power with that of factories, the concentration of the woolen industry in some few hands becomes evident. Though in 1856 there were but eight more woolen factories than in 1850, yet the power employed in them had increased 3,757 horses during the same period. The same tendency to concentration is evidently working in the cotton, worsted and flax-spinning factories. The number of spindles in the United Kingdom amounting respectively in 1850 and 1856 to 25,638,716 and to 33,503,580, the average number of spindles in each factory was as follows[b]:

	1850.	1856.
Cotton	14,000	17,000
Worsted	2,200	3,400
Flax	2,700	3,700

In the weaving factories, it is true, the tendency seems to be to an extension of the trade among many occupiers rather than to its concentration among a few, the total number of looms being 369,205 in 1856, against 301,445 in 1850, while the average number employed by each manufacturer is less in 1856 than in 1850. However, this apparent deviation from the general tendency of the British factory system is easily accounted for by the fact that in the weaving department the introduction of the factory system is of comparatively recent date, and has not yet quite superseded the hand-loom system. In 1836, steam power was employed almost exclusively for cotton looms, or for fabrics mixed with cotton; but some years later there was a rapid increase in the number of power-looms for all fabrics, for fabrics of woolen, worsted, flax and silk, and this increase continues to the present time. The following statement shows the increase of power-looms since 1836[c]:

---

[a] Ibid., p. 14, Note.— *Ed.*
[b] Ibid., p. 16.— *Ed.*
[c] Ibid.— *Ed.*

	1836.	1850.	1856.
Cotton	108,751	249,627	298,847
Woolen	2,150	9,439	14,453
Worsted	2,969	32,617	38,956
Silk	1,714	6,092	9,260
Flax	209	3,670	7,689
Total	115,793	301,445	369,205

The increase of cotton looms resulted from the extension of trade, not from the appliance of power to articles formerly woven by hand solely; but in the other fabrics power is now applied to the carpet loom, the ribbon loom, and the linen loom, where it had hitherto been little used. The application of power to wool combing, which has come extensively into operation since the introduction of the combing machine, especially of Lister's, has also had the effect to throw a large number of men out of work.

The extent of the increased power of production is clearly shown by comparing the export returns. In 1850, there being in activity 1,932 cotton factories, the average value of cotton goods and yarn exported in the three years ending January 5, 1850, was, in round numbers, £24,600,000. If the 2,210 cotton factories in activity in 1856 had produced goods or yarn in the same proportion only as the factories of 1850, the value of the exports would be £28,000,000. Yet the average value of these exports, in the three years ending December 31, 1855, amounted to about £31,000,000. The case with the woolen and worsted factories is similar. We see, then, that while the quantity of machinery kept in motion by each horse-power has considerably increased, the number of persons employed for each horse-power has remained stationary, viz.: 4 persons, on an average. This is shown by the following table[a]:

Total number of persons employed.

	1838.	1850.	1856.
Cotton	259,104	330,924	379,213
Woolen	54,808	74,443	79,091
Worsted	31,628	79,737	87,794
Flax	43,557	68,434	80,262
Silk	34,303	42,544	56,137
Total	423,400	596,082	682,497

[a] Ibid., p. 31.—*Ed.*

The aggregate working population of 682,497, appears small indeed, if it is considered that the number of handloom weavers and their families, in 1838, alone amounted to about 800,000 persons. The following table shows the centesimal proportion of the different classes of hands employed.[a]

	Children under 13.	Males bet'n 13 & 18.	Females above 13.	Males above 18.
1838	5.9	16.1	55.2	22.8
1850	6.1	11.5	55.9	26.5
1856	6.6	10.6	57.0	25.8

Between 1838 and 1850 the number of children employed had increased, but not in proportion to the general increase. The increase in the number of children between 1850 and 1856 is very considerable, amounting, as it does, to 10,761, of which 9,655 have been absorbed by the cotton trade. It may still be mentioned that the philanthropic law of 1844 permitted children to be employed in factories at 8 years of age, while prior to that it was illegal to employ them under 9 years of age.[324]

Written on April 10, 1857

First published in the *New-York Daily Tribune,* No. 4999, April 28, 1857

Reproduced from the newspaper

[a] Ibid., p. 32.—*Ed.*

Frederick Engels

[CHANGES IN THE RUSSIAN ARMY][325]

When the late war in Europe[a] broke out, a great number of military men pointed, not without a certain sense of awe, to the wonderful organization of the Russian army. While in France and England, brigades, divisions, army-corps, had to be formed from elements hitherto entirely disconnected, while commanders had to be appointed to lead bodies of troops which they had never seen before, and staffs had to be formed of officers arriving from all corners of the country—in Russia, the huge war-machine had been perfected, in all its subdivisions, years before; every regiment had its unalterable place in the organization of the whole; each body of men, from the company to the army-corps, had its standing commander, and each more important division had its regular staff. The machine was said to be, in fact, in working trim; it only awaited the word of command, the putting on of the steam, in order to move with the utmost ease; every cog, wheel, screw, pulley, strap, valve and lever in its place, doing its work and no more. That was what we were told we should see; but, unfortunately, we saw something quite different. The army-corps were scarcely ever complete, whole divisions, and still oftener brigades, being detached to distant theaters of war, while other troops were mixed up with the main bodies. The desire to keep together as much as possible the elements of each corps, division and brigade, appeared to hamper the movements of the army on the march quite as much as the strict regulations laid down for the order in which battles should be fought; and finally the nice subdivisions of command with all the generals in charge—corps,

[a] The Crimean war, 1853-56.—*Ed.*

divisions, brigades, with their respective staffs, all well known to their troops, well acquainted with each other, and well at home in their respective places and duties—all this turned out to be one vast conspiracy to swindle the Government out of its funds and the soldier out of his rations, clothing and comforts.

If these facts still required an official confirmation, the Russian Government has just given it. The new organization of the army aims first and mainly at the rooting up of those hotbeds of wholesale embezzlement, the subordinate staffs and headquarters. The staffs, both of the army-corps and of brigades, are done away with. Nay, the very name of brigade disappears from the Russian army. The whole six corps of the line are placed under the command of one man, Prince M. D. Gorchakoff I., the late commander in the Crimea. Each corps has, it is true, a commanding general; but as he has no staff—that is to say, no means of actually exercising the details of this command—he is at best but the inspector of his corps—a sort of check on the five generals of division under him. In reality, the generals of the thirty divisions (eighteen of infantry, six of cavalry and six of artillery), forming what is called the "first army," depend directly upon the commander-in-chief; and in each division again, the colonels of the four regiments, infantry or cavalry, and the chiefs of batteries, are directly dependent upon the general of the division. The generals of brigade, being entirely superseded by this new arrangement, are attached to the staff of the divisional general, as his lieutenants and seconds in command. The reason of all this is plain enough.

Upon Prince Gorchakoff the Emperor can rely; and Gorchakoff, again, can to some extent rely upon the officers of his personal staff. With the bureaucratic nicety and hierarchic gradations of the former system, the direct influence of the commander-in-chief ended with the chiefs of corps; they and their staffs had to transmit the orders to the divisions, whose staffs again handed them to the brigades, from whose staffs they reached the colonels of regiments, who saw to their actual execution. This was nothing but a well-organized scheme of fraud, embezzlement and larceny; and the better the service itself was organized, the better organized and the more successful was the plundering of the treasury. This was shown in the march of the first, second and third army-corps from Poland to the South during the war; and it is simply with a view of removing the evil that the Russian Government has done away with all but the names of the commanders of corps, and entirely with the commanders of brigades. There are now but two intermediate grades between the commander-in-chief and the company officers, namely, the general of division and the colonel; and there is but one staff, that of the division, which can be used for purposes of embezzlement. If the Government should succeed in eradicating the habit of plunder from the divisional staffs, it may reasonably expect to banish it, by and by, from the regiments also.

Thus the whole organization of the army is upset, by taking out of the chain two links, the necessity of which, in time of war, is sure to show itself. Indeed, the Russian Government acknowledges that neither chiefs of corps nor generals of brigade can be entirely left out of its military hierarchy. The chief of the corps is left there, but as a mere dummy, while the general of brigade is completely relieved from his command, and made a simple appendix to the general of division. This means nothing but that the command of these officers is suspended during peace, while they are kept in readiness for use as soon as a war breaks out. In the only army, indeed, which still faces the enemy—that of the Caucasus—the brigades have been retained. Is any other proof wanted that the abolition of brigades in the remainder of the army is only an attempt to render brigadiers and their staffs innoxious while peace lasts?

Another important change is the dissolution of the great dragoon corps, consisting of ten regiments of eight squadrons each, drilled for infantry as well as for cavalry service. This corps was intended to play a brilliant part in all great battles. When the decisive moment approached, it was to fall with the rapidity of cavalry upon some important post on the flank or rear of the enemy, to dismount, to form into sixteen battalions of infantry and defend the post, supported by its heavy horse-artillery. During the whole of the late war, this corps was nowhere; and the total unfitness of these hybrid troops for active warfare appears to have been recognized on all hands. The consequence is, the change of these amphibious mounted foot-soldiers into regular cavalry, and their distribution, in twelve regiments of eight squadrons each, with the six army-corps of the "first army." Thus the two great creations by which the Emperor Nicholas expected to establish his place among the greatest military organizers of his time, have both disappeared within a few years of his death.

Among other changes, we may mention the establishment of a second battalion of rifles for every army-corps, and the formation of two new infantry regiments in the Caucasian army. By the former innovation, the great scarcity of light cavalry is to some extent remedied. The latter shows that Russia is resolved to finish the Caucasian struggle as soon as possible. For the same reason, the reserve brigades of the Caucasian corps are still held together. It is, therefore, likely that by this time a campaign of importance has been opened in that country.

Written on about April 16, 1857

First published in the *New-York Daily Tribune,* No. 5006, May 6, 1857 as a leading article

Reproduced from the newspaper

Karl Marx

THE BRITISH WILD-CATS

London, May 1, 1857

The inquiry of the Court of Bankruptcy into the mysteries of the Royal British Bank is well nigh drawing to a close, and a more complete exposure of the recklessness, the hypocrisy, the shams and the infamies that lie hidden under the gilded outside of respectable society, has perhaps not been made since the days of Hudson the railway king's downfall. One of the gentlemen last summoned to the pillory of public opinion is Mr. Humphrey Brown, late M. P. for Tewkesbury, described in *Dodd's Parliamentary Companion* for 1855 "as a merchant," an "active promoter of railways," a "known railway statist and traffic taker," a "supporter of free-trade principles in the *fullest* sense," and a "Liberal to boot." Immediately after the burst of the Royal British Bank bubble, it became known that this influential personage had used his position as a Director of the Bank for swindling the latter out of some £70,000 sterling—which revelation, however, was not allowed to interfere any way with his customary State functions. Humphrey Brown quietly continued to make his appearance in the House of Commons, as well as on the benches of the "Great Unpaid." [326] He even gave public vent to his high sense of social responsibility by inflicting, in his quality as a county magistrate, the most severe punishment allowed by law on a poor carrier, who had happened to embezzle a small quantity of potatoes, and by administering to the culprit an unctuous sermon about the atrociousness of a breach of trust. A Tewkesbury paper thought itself warranted to improve the opportunity for finding fault with that peculiarity of the British institutions which makes great thieves the judges of small ones. Mr. Brown then threatened not only to bring the unhappy journalist to trial, but forever to turn his back on the good town of Tewkesbury, should its inhabitants fail in expiating the crime of insulted innocence by some solemn act of contrition. Accordingly there was a triumphal procession offered to the "victim of an unscrupulous conspiracy," a testimonial which, to judge by the descriptions printed at the time in the public papers, made up for its artistic shortcomings by metallic heaviness. Mr. Brown harangued the multitude from his balcony, pocketed the testimonial, declared, but for the oath binding him to secrecy in respect to the affairs of the British Bank, his innocence would appear clear as the sun at noon-day, and wound up his oration by calling himself a man more sinned against than sinning. During the last general election he stepped forward anew, as a parliamentary candidate for his snug borough, but the Cabinet, of which he had always proved a staunch partisan, was ungrateful enough to drop him.

On the 29th of April this pompous gentleman felt rescued at last from the thraldom of the oath which till now had sealed his lips, and condemned him to endure the obloquy of disgraceful slander; the Commissioner of the Court of Bankruptcy acting as his confessor. It is a general rule with joint-stock companies that their directors should possess a certain number of their shares. Mr. Brown, inverting the common order of things, became first a director and then a stockholder; but, if he held the shares, he dispensed with paying for them. He got at their possession by the following very simple method: Mr. Cameron, the fugitive manager of the British Bank, handed over to him twenty shares, of the amount of £1,000, while he (Brown) handed over to Mr. Cameron a promissory note for the amount of £1,000, on account of which he took great care never to pay one single shilling. Having become a director in the month of February, 1853, he began his banking operations in the month of March. He deposited in the Bank the handy sum of £18 14s., and on the very same day borrowed from it on a note of hand the sum of £2,000, thus proving himself at once to be no new hand in the directorial management of joint-stock companies. In fact, before and after his connection with the Royal British Bank, he honored with his directorial management the chartered Australian Importing and Refining Company, the Patent Waterproof Brick and Tile and Common Brick and Tile Company, the Wandle Water-Works Company, a Land Company, a Dock Company—in one word, companies for all the four elements. On the question of Linklater, the solicitor for the assignees, as to what had become of all these companies, Brown pertinently answered, "They are defunct, so far as this." His account with the British Bank, which began with £18 14s. paid in to his credit, ended in £77,000 standing to his debit. All these advances were made through Mr. Cameron, without the consent of the "other Directors being asked for."

"The executive officer of the Company," says Mr. Brown, "is the person through whom all the business is done. Such was the practice of this Bank, and," as he adds doctorally, "a very wholesome one it is."[a]

The truth seems to be, that the whole concern, governors, directors, managers, solicitors and accountants, were, after a preconcerted plan, playing into each other's hands, and that every one affected to ignore the share of the booty accruing to each partner. Ay, Mr. Brown is not very far from intimating that, as a Director of the Bank, he was hardly aware of his own doings as its customer. As to the customers not belonging to the managing staff, Mr. Brown seems, during his examination, still to labor under the painful impression that some of them dared encroach upon the directorial immunities. Thus he declares in respect to a Mr. Oliver:

"I have no hesitation in saying Oliver swindled the Bank out of £20,000. It is a very strong term to use, but I have no doubt about its correctness. He was a swindler."

On Mr. Linklater's asking "What were you?" he composedly replies, "Unfortunately a director much in the dark." All his answers go this same calm way. The ridiculous disproportion, for instance, between his deposits and his discounts, gives occasion for the following curious dialogue between himself and Mr. Linklater:

Mr. Linklater—Was it not one of the regular terms of the business of the Bank, that no person should have a discount account who had not also a drawing account; and on the drawing account there should always be kept a balance of one fourth of the bills current upon your discount?

Mr. Brown—It was so, and that was the Scotch system, as they told me.

Mr. Linklater—It was a system that you did not adopt?

Mr. Brown—I did not, because it was unsound.

Whenever Mr. Brown condescended to tender securities to the Bank, they consisted of notes of hand, or of ships which he took good care at the same time to have mortgaged to other people, as he generally quite freely disposed of the securities, by what the Commissioner had the hardihood to call most "fraudulent transactions." On the first of March, 1856, Mr. Brown had

[a] Here and below Marx quotes from the report on the inquiry into the causes of bankruptcy of the Royal British Bank published in *The Times*, No. 22668, April 30, 1857.—*Ed.*

virtually closed his account with the Bank; that is to say, the Board of Directors had decided upon no longer allowing him to run up his debts. Yet, on the 7th of June, we find him again getting £1,020 out of it. To Mr. Linklater's question, "by what hocus-pocus he had managed that affair?" he coolly replies, "There was no difficulty."

From the following letter, addressed by him to his bosom friend Mr. Cameron, may be inferred his general opinion about the storm of indignation the Royal British Bank disclosures roused in the public press:

"LITTLE SMITH STREET, WESTMINSTER. Oct. 5. 1855.

"DEAR MR. CAMERON: Not knowing your whereabouts at the time, I take the chance of sending this through some member of your family. As sorry news travels fast, I conclude you are no stranger to the vituperation heaped upon us in all the papers, both great and small, myself and you having the lion's share. I have some reason for believing that the very violent articles in *The Times* have been instigated by one or two of our associates, through the accountant. I am quite in ignorance of what is going on, except through the public reports, the reading of which makes me almost conclude that no one ever owed a bank any money before, and that all former intimations were made in error, and that the whole wrath of *The Times* was reserved for our individual injury.... I have not seen any other directors since the Bank stopped, which was a bungling piece of work.

"Yours truly,

"Humphrey Brown."

As if "no one ever owed a bank any money before!" Mr. Brown apparently considers all the moral indignation washed on him and his associates as mere conventional cant. "Each thing's a thief!" So says Timon,[a] and so Mr. Brown, and seems persuaded, in the depth of his soul, that every member of what is called respectable society says so. The only important thing is to be no petty thief.

Written on May 1, 1857

First published in the *New-York Daily Tribune*, No. 5015, May 16, 1857; reprinted in the *New-York Semi-Weekly Tribune*, No. 1250, May 19, 1857

Reproduced from the *New-York Daily Tribune*

[a] Shakespeare, *Timon of Athens*, Act IV, Scene 3.—*Ed.*

Karl Marx

CRÉDIT MOBILIER[327]

I

For the bulletins of the Grand Army[a] the present French Empire makes up by the reports of the Crédit Mobilier. At the last general meeting of the shareholders, on the 28th of April, Mr. Isaac Péreire, in the name of the Board of Directors, presented a report,[b] purporting to comprise the summary history for the year 1856 of this remarkable Bonapartist institution. From this grandiloquent document, mingling, in a manner peculiar to its author, financial statements with theoretical propositions, figures with sentiments, and stock-jobbing speculation with speculative philosophy, a cautious research may elicit evidence of decay, which the apologetical varnish covering the whole exposes rather than conceals.

The profits of the Crédit Mobilier continue, indeed, to dazzle the public eye. Its shares being originally fixed at 500 francs, there was paid on them, for the year 1856, 25 francs by way of interest and 90 francs by way of dividend, making together 115 francs, a sum which exactly represents 23 per cent on the funds of the Company. Yet, to arrive at safe conclusions, one must compare the Crédit Mobilier, not with ordinary commercial enterprises, but with itself, and then we shall find that, during one single year, its profits have decreased nearly one half. There are two elements to be distinguished in the net revenue of the Company—the one fixed, the other variable—the one settled by statute, the other

[a] Of Napoleon.—*Ed.*

[b] I. Péreire, "Rapport présenté par le conseil d'administration [de la Société générale du Crédit mobilier] dans l'assemblée générale ordinaire des actionnaires du 28 avril 1857", *Le Moniteur universel,* No. 120, April 30, 1857.—*Ed.*

dependent on its commercial movement—the one figuring under the head of interest, and the other under the head of dividends. The interest of 25 francs, or 5 per cent per share, forms, therefore, a standing item in the accounts of the Company, while the dividend declared is the real test of its progress. Now, we find that from 178 francs 70 centimes, to which the dividend amounted in 1855, it has dwindled down to 90 francs in 1856, a movement which cannot very well be called an ascending one. If it be considered that the smaller fry of the shareholders have, on an average, bought their shares at 1,500 francs, the real dividend they received in 1856 will hardly exceed 7 per cent.

Mr. Isaac Péreire thinks that "it would be superfluous to endeavor to point out the causes of the difference which exists between the dividend of 1856 and that of 1855." Still he condescends to intimate that the profits of 1855 bore "an exceptional character." True enough; but then it is only by keeping up the exceptional character of its profits that the Crédit Mobilier can lay claim to any character whatever. The exceptional character of its profits results from the enormous disproportion between its capital and its operations. That disproportion, so far from being merely transient, forms, in fact, the organic law of its existence. The Crédit Mobilier pretends to be neither a banking nor an industrial company, but rather the representative, on a national scale if possible, of other banking and industrial companies. The originality of its conception is founded on this representative office. Its operations purport, therefore, to be circumscribed, not by its own capital and the usual credit derived from it, but solely by the vastness of the interests it actually represents or attempts to represent. If the disproportion between its capital and its operations and consequently its "exceptional" profits were to disappear, the Crédit Mobilier would not dwindle to a common banking-house, but would miserably break down. In pursuing the enormous operations in which, by the very nature of its organization, it finds itself involved, it must rely on the progressive execution of new plans on a still more enlarged scale. With such an institution, any stagnation, and still more any regress, is a symptom of fatal decay. Take even the report of 1856. There we find on the one side the modest capital of 60,000,000 of francs, and on the other, operations involving the enormous sum of more than 6,000,000,000 of francs. Mr. Péreire himself gives the following sketch of these operations[a]:

[a] Ibid.—*Ed.*

"Our subscription to the last loan was not only preserved intact, but it increased to the amount of 40,000,000 f. by purchases intended to facilitate the installments of the subscribers.

The movement in our cash amounted to the sum of	3,085,195,176 f. 39 c.
That of our account current with the Bank was	1,216,686,271 f. 33 c.
That of our accounts current attained the amount of	2,739,111,029 f. 98 c.
Our Company has received installments on 1,455,264 shares and bonds, which have produced together the sum of	160,976,590 f. 98 c.
It has paid both on its own account and for that of the Companies to which it has acted as bankers 3,754,921 coupons, amounting to	64,259,723 f. 68 c.
The movement of our caisse of securities has been on 4,986,304 shares or bonds."	

Mr. Péreire does not deny that the part performed by the Crédit Mobilier in 1856 was of a somewhat different kind from that it had performed before. During the first three years of its existence, it had to "inaugurate important undertakings in France," to "systematize the creations of great affairs," and, consequently, to prove inexhaustible in piling fresh securities upon the stock market. But, in 1856, a sudden change occurred. As "peace had opened a new era of social activity," speculation threatened to overshoot the mark. Under these altered circumstances the conscientious gentlemen of the Crédit Mobilier, the Péreires, the Foulds, the Mornys, exclusively bent on fostering public prosperity, felt it "an imperious duty" to bridle where before they had spurred, to moderate where they had urged on, and to maintain an attitude of "reserve" where "boldness" had before been "an intelligent prudence." As all France was becoming mobile, the Crédit Mobilier, for conscience' sake, resolved upon becoming stationary. It is, however, true that this virtuous resolution was to some extent forestalled by a note inserted in the *Moniteur* of the 9th of March, 1856, which "indicated the bounds the Government wished to trace out to the issue of fresh securities." Even "if" the propensities of the Crédit Mobilier had all been the other way, "this publication," says Mr. Péreire, "would have been an order, particularly for us; it was a forced halt, which must interrupt the creation of new undertakings." This forced halt seems sufficiently to account for the self-imposed duty of moderation.

At the very moment when the Crédit Mobilier found itself thus curbed in its career by a Government halter, it unfortunately happened that unprincipled competition was busily engaged in circumscribing its sphere of action and impairing its resources. While the *Moniteur*'s note of March 9, 1856, was directly aimed at the so-called Anonymous Societies[a] whose formation and operation in France are, by law, subject to Government approbation and control, and to the starting of which the Crédit Mobilier is restricted by its statutes, French speculation now found a larger outlet under the form of Sociétés en Commandite,[b] which are exempt from Government approbation, and almost from all control. Speculation thus merely changed its channels; the stunted growth of Anonymous Societies being more than compensated by the luxuriant crop of Sociétés en Commandite. Instead of obstructing speculation, Napoleon III., with all his "exalted wisdom," as Mr. Péreire calls it, had only withdrawn a great part of it from the control of his pet concern. During the first nine months of 1856, when all France was intoxicated with speculation, and when the cream of it should have been skimmed by the Crédit Mobilier, that devoted company was thus, by a mere misunderstanding on the part of the "exalted wisdom," condemned to act upon "a restricted scale," and to humbly "wait for the official signal for the resumption of activity." It was still waiting for the official signal and "a transition to better times," when an event occurred quite beyond the control even of the "exalted wisdom" of Napoleon himself.

— The consideration of that event we will postpone to another day.

II

The financial crisis which, in September, 1856, broke out simultaneously on the Continent of Europe and in England, found the Crédit Mobilier, as Mr. Péreire says, in the attitude of "the intelligent sentinels of finance and credit," taking in "a more extended horizon" than other people "on different steps of the ladder," "capable of avoiding alarm as well as overexcitement," turning its undivided solicitude to the lofty end of "maintaining national labor and credit," indifferent "to interested or jealous

[a] See this volume, p. 11.— *Ed.*

[b] Joint-stock companies with limited liability.— *Ed.*

criticism," smiling at "violent or calculated attacks," and towering high above vulgar "misrepresentations." At that critical epoch, the Bank of France, it seems, proved rather restive against the demands which the Crédit Mobilier, prompted by its exclusive zeal for public prosperity, found itself induced to press upon it. We are, therefore, given to understand that "the crisis owed its violence and its rapidity to the measures which the Bank of France adopted under the empire of the constitution which governs it," and that "that institution is still highly imperfect from the absence of any bond, and of all harmonic combinations." While the Bank of France on one hand declined helping the Crédit Mobilier, it refused on the other to be helped by it. With characteristic boldness of conception, the Crédit Mobilier considered a financial crisis the true season for great financial strokes. At the moment of general confusion, you may take a fortress by storm which, for years, you have failed to take by regular maneuvers. Accordingly, the Crédit Mobilier offered to purchase, with the cooperation of several foreign houses, the *rentes* or public debt held by the Bank of France, so as to enable the latter establishment "effectually to increase its metallic reserve, and continue its advances on *rentes* and railway shares." When the Crédit Mobilier made this disinterested and philanthropic proposal, its treasury was encumbered with *rentes* to the amount of about 5,475,000 francs, and with railway shares to the amount of 115,000,000 francs, the Bank of France holding simultaneously *rentes* to about 50,000,000 francs. In other words, the Crédit Mobilier held more than twice the amount in railway shares which the Bank of France held in *rentes.* By throwing its *rentes* on the market, in order to strengthen its metallic reserve, the Bank of France would not only depress the *rentes,* but still more all other securities, and particularly railway shares. The proposal amounted, therefore, in fact, to an invitation to the Bank to keep the *rentes* held by itself off the market, in order to make place for the railway shares held by the Crédit Mobilier. Besides, the Bank, as Mr. Péreire says, would then have had an excuse for discontinuing its advances on railway shares. Thus it would have secretly come to the rescue of the Crédit Mobilier, while publicly owing vassalage to that magnanimous institution, and appearing to be saved by its aid. However, the Bank smelled a rat and turned a cold shoulder to the "intelligent sentinels."

As firmly resolved to save France from the financial crisis as its protector[a] had been to save her from Socialism, the Crédit

[a] Napoleon III.—*Ed.*

Mobilier made a second proposal, addressed not to the Bank of France but to the private bankers of Paris. It generously offered

"to provide for the wants of all French Railway Companies by subscribing to the amount of 300,000,000 francs to the loans which they had to issue for 1857; declaring that it was ready to engage itself in those loans to the amount of 200,000,000 francs, if the sum of 100,000,000 were subscribed by the other banking houses."[a]

Such a subscription was sure to effect a sudden rise in the price of railway shares and bonds, the very commodity of which the Crédit Mobilier was the principal holder. Moreover, the latter, by one bold stroke, would have installed itself as a great proprietor in all French railways, and drawn all the great Paris bankers into some sort of forced partnership with itself. Yet the scheme failed. Compelled "to renounce the idea of any united measure," the Crédit Mobilier had to shift for itself. The lofty conviction that "the sole fact of its having made such propositions doubtlessly contributed not a little to allay uneasiness," consoled it not a little for the tendency the crisis had "to reduce in a material manner the profits on which the Company thought it might calculate."

Quite apart from all these untoward events, the Crédit Mobilier complains of having till now been precluded from playing its trump card, namely, the emission of 600,000,000 francs in bonds—a paper money of its own invention; payable at very long dates; based, not on the capital of the company, but on the securities for which it would be exchanged.

"The resources," says Mr. Péreire, "which we should have derived from the issue of our bonds would have allowed us to absorb such securities as had not yet found their definitive investment, and to give an immense extension to the benefits rendered to industry."

In 1855, the Crédit Mobilier was just about emitting 240,000,000 of francs in such obligations, an issue authorized by its statutes, when "the exalted wisdom" of the Tuileries cut short the operation. Such an issue of fiduciary money the Crédit Mobilier calls augmenting its capital; common people are more likely to call it augmenting its debts. The forced halt, then, imposed on the Crédit Mobilier by the Government in March, 1856, the competition of the Sociétés en Commandite, the financial crisis, and the non-issue of its own paper money, all these circumstances will sufficiently account for the fall of its dividends.

In all former reports of this great swindling concern, the substitution of industrial joint-stock companies for private industry

[a] I. Péreire, op. cit.— *Ed.*

has been trumpeted as the specialty, and novelty of the institution. In this last report, the faintest allusion to this subject will be sought for in vain. Of the 60,000,000 francs which form the capital of the Company, 40,000,000 were once, during the year 1856, invested in State funds; and of the sums which credit placed in its hands, by far the greater part was employed in "continuations" in *rentes* and railway shares on the settling days of the Stock Exchange; such operations having been effected, in 1856, in French *rentes* to the amount of 421,500,000 francs, and in railway and other shares to the amount of 281,000,000 francs. Now these continuations mean nothing but advances of money to stock-jobbers in order to enable them to continue their operations, and give a bloated aspect to the fancy stocks of the Bourse. Upon this operation of turning a great part of the national capital from productive industry to unproductive gambling, the Crédit Mobilier rests its main claim to the gratitude of the nation. Louis Napoleon, indeed, derives an immense support from Messrs. Péreire & Co. Not only do they impart fictitious value to the Imperial funds, but they are constantly fostering, drilling, propping, propagating that spirit of gambling which forms the vital principle of the present empire. On the most cursory view of the operations so complacently detailed by Mr. Péreire, it must become evident that the gambling maneuvers of the Crédit Mobilier are necessarily blended with fraudulent transactions. On the one hand, in its public function as the protector of the Bourse, the Company borrows money from the public and lends it to stock-jobbing companies and individuals, in order to keep up prices of the national shares and funds. On the other hand, as a private concern, it is constantly speculating for its own account on the fluctuations of the very same securities, on their fall as well as their rise. To apparently harmonize these cross-purposes, fraud and imposture must be recurred to.

Like all professional gamblers, Louis Napoleon is as bold in the conception of his *coups* as slow and cautious in their execution. Thus he has twice checked the Crédit Mobilier in its unscrupulous career—first in 1855, when he forbade the issue of its bonds, and again in 1856, when his warning in the *Moniteur* brought it to a forced halt. But while he obstructs, the Company is pressing on. In point of fact, if full swing be given to it, it will break its neck. If Bonaparte continue to bother it with moderation, it will lose its soul. From Mr. Péreire's report, however, it appears that the "exalted wisdom" and the "intelligent prudence" have at last come to a compromise. Should the already discredited Crédit

Mobilier not be intrusted with the dangerous power of issuing its own paper money, the means it can no longer live without are to be tendered to it under the more respectable cloak of the Bank of France. Such is one of the secret ends of the new Bank law now laid before the "learned dogs and monkeys" of the *Corps Législatif*.[328] "We do not fear," says Mr. Péreire, "to proclaim it, but it would be in vain to seek elsewhere than at the Bank of France for the means of giving effectual assistance, by advances to public credit, to great undertakings, to commerce and to industry"—in other words, to the Crédit Mobilier.

Written on May 12 and 15, 1857

First published in the *New-York Daily Tribune*, Nos. 5027 and 5028, May 30 and June 1, 1857 as leading articles; reprinted in the *New-York Semi-Weekly Tribune*, No. 1254, June 2, 1857 under the title "Crédit Mobilier"

Reproduced from the *New-York Daily Tribune*

Frederick Engels

PERSIA—CHINA[329]

London, May 22, 1857

The English have just concluded an Asiatic war, and are entering upon another.[330] The resistance offered by the Persians, and that which the Chinese have so far opposed to British invasion, form a contrast worth our attention. In Persia, the European system of military organization has been engrafted upon Asiatic barbarity; in China, the rotting semi-civilization of the oldest State in the world meets the Europeans with its own resources. Persia has been signally defeated, while distracted, half-dissolved China has hit upon a system of resistance which, if followed up, will render impossible a repetition of the triumphal marches of the first Anglo-Chinese war.[331]

Persia was in a state similar to that of Turkey during the war of 1828-9 against Russia.[332] English, French, Russian officers had in turns tried their hands at the organization of the Persian army. One system had succeeded another, and each in its turn had been thwarted by the jealousy, the intrigues, the ignorance, the cupidity and corruption of the Orientals whom it was to form into European officers and soldiers. The new regular army had never had an opportunity of trying its organization and strength in the field. Its only exploits had been confined to a few campaigns against Kurds, Turcomans and Affghans, where it served as a sort of nucleus or reserve to the numerous irregular cavalry of Persia. The latter did most of the actual fighting; the regulars had generally but to impose upon the enemy by the demonstrative effect of their seemingly formidable arrays. At last, the war with England broke out.

The English attacked Bushire, and met with a gallant though ineffective resistance. But the men who fought at Bushire were not regulars; they were composed of the irregular levies of the Persian and Arab inhabitants of the coast. The regulars were only concentrating, some sixty miles off, in the hills. At last they advanced. The Anglo-Indian army met them half way; and, though the Persians used their artillery with credit to themselves, and formed their squares on the most approved principles, a single charge of one single Indian cavalry regiment swept the whole Persian army, guards and line, from the field. And to know what these Indian regular cavalry are considered to be worth in their own service, we have only to refer to Capt. Nolan's book on the subject.[a] They are, among Anglo-Indian officers, considered worse than useless, and far inferior to the irregular Anglo-Indian cavalry. Not a single action can Capt. Nolan find where they were creditably engaged. And yet, these were the men, six hundred of whom drove ten thousand Persians before them! Such was the terror spread among the Persian regulars that never since have they made a stand anywhere—the artillery alone excepted. At Mohammerah, they kept out of harm's way, leaving the artillery to defend the batteries, and retired as soon as these were silenced; and when, on a reconnaissance, the British landed three hundred riflemen and fifty irregular horse, the whole of the Persian host marched off, leaving baggage, stores and guns in the possession of the—victors you cannot call them—the invaders.

All this, however, neither brands the Persians as a nation of cowards, nor condemns the introduction of European tactics among Orientals. The Russo-Turkish wars of 1806-12 and 1828-9[333] offer plenty such examples. The principal resistance offered to the Russians was made by the irregular levies both from the fortified towns and from the mountain provinces. The regulars, wherever they showed themselves in the open field, were at once upset by the Russians, and very often ran away at the first shot; while a single company of Arnaut[b] irregulars, in a ravine at Varna, successfully opposed the Russian siege operations for weeks together. Yet, during the late war, the Turkish regular army have defeated the Russians in every single engagement from Oltenitza and Citate to Kars and to Ingur.[334]

The fact is that the introduction of European military organization with barbaric nations is far from being completed when the new army has been subdivided, equipped and drilled after the European fashion. That is merely the first step toward it. Nor will

[a] L. E. Nolan, *Cavalry, Its History and Tactics*.—*Ed.*

[b] Turkish name for the Albanians.—*Ed.*

the enactment of some European military code suffice; it will no more insure European discipline than a European set of drill-regulations will produce, by itself, European tactics and strategy. The main point, and at the same time the main difficulty, is the creation of a body of officers and sergeants, educated on the modern European system, totally freed from the old national prejudices and reminiscences in military matters, and fit to inspire life into the new formation. This requires a long time, and is sure to meet with the most obstinate opposition from Oriental ignorance, impatience, prejudice, and the vicissitudes of fortune and favor inherent to Eastern courts. A Sultan or Shah is but too apt to consider his army equal to anything as soon as the men can defile in parade, wheel, deploy and form column without getting into hopeless disorder. And as to military schools, their fruits are so slow in ripening that under the instabilities of Eastern Governments they can scarcely ever be expected to show any. Even in Turkey, the supply of educated officers is but scanty, and the Turkish army could not have done [anything] at all, during the late war, without the great number of renegades[335] and the European officers in its ranks.

The only arm which everywhere forms an exception is the artillery. Here the Orientals are so much at fault and so helpless that they have to leave the whole management to their European instructors. The consequence is that as in Turkey, so in Persia, the artillery was far ahead of the infantry and cavalry.

That under these circumstances the Anglo-Indian army, the oldest of all Eastern armies organized on the European system, the only one that is subject not to an Eastern, but an exclusively European government, and officered almost entirely by Europeans—that this army, supported by a strong reserve of British troops and a powerful navy, should easily disperse the Persian regulars, is but a matter of course. The reverse will do the Persians the more good the more signal it was. They will now see, as the Turks have seen before, that European dress and parade-drill is no talisman in itself, and may be, twenty years hence, the Persians will turn out as respectable as the Turks did in their late victories.

The troops which conquered Bushire and Mohammerah will, it is understood, be at once sent to China. There they will find a different enemy. No attempts at European evolutions, but the irregular array of Asiatic masses, will oppose them there. Of these they no doubt will easily dispose; but what if the Chinese wage against them a national war, and if barbarism be unscrupulous enough to use the only weapons which it knows how to wield?

There is evidently a different spirit among the Chinese now to what they showed in the war of 1840 to '42. Then, the people were quiet; they left the Emperor's soldiers to fight the invaders, and submitted after a defeat with Eastern fatalism to the power of the enemy. But now, at least in the southern provinces, to which the contest has so far been confined, the mass of the people take an active, nay, a fanatical part in the struggle against the foreigners. They poison the bread of the European community at Hong-Kong by wholesale, and with the coolest premeditation. (A few loaves have been sent to Liebig for examination. He found large quantities of arsenic pervading all parts of them, showing that it had already been worked into the dough. The dose, however, was so strong that it must have acted as an emetic, and thereby counteracted the effects of the poison.) They go with hidden arms on board trading steamers, and, when on the journey, massacre the crew and European passengers and seize the boat. They kidnap and kill every foreigner within their reach. The very coolies emigrating to foreign countries rise in mutiny, and as if by concert, on board every emigrant ship, and fight for its possession, and, rather than surrender, go down to the bottom with it, or perish in its flames. Even out of China, the Chinese colonists, the most submissive and meek of subjects hitherto, conspire and suddenly rise in nightly insurrection, as at Sarawak; or, as at Singapore, are held down by main force and vigilance only. The piratical policy of the British Government has caused this universal outbreak of all Chinese against all foreigners, and marked it as a war of extermination.

What is an army to do against a people resorting to such means of warfare? Where, how far, is it to penetrate into the enemy's country, how to maintain itself there? Civilization-mongers who throw hot shell on a defenseless city and add rape to murder, may call the system cowardly, barbarous, atrocious; but what matters it to the Chinese if it be only successful? Since the British treat them as barbarians, they cannot deny to them the full benefit of their barbarism. If their kidnappings, surprises, midnight massacres are what we call cowardly, the civilization-mongers should not forget that according to their own showing they could not stand against European means of destruction with their ordinary means of warfare.

In short, instead of moralizing on the horrible atrocities of the Chinese, as the chivalrous English press does, we had better recognize that this is a war *pro aris et focis*,[a] a popular war for the maintenance of Chinese nationality, with all its overbearing prejudice, stupidity, learned ignorance and pedantic barbarism if you like; but yet a popular war. And in a popular war the means used by the insurgent nation cannot be measured by the commonly recognized rules of regular warfare, nor by any other abstract standard, but by the degree of civilization only attained by that insurgent nation.

The English are this time placed in a difficult position. Thus far, the national Chinese fanaticism seems to extend no further than over those southern provinces which have not adhered to the great rebellion.[336] Is the war to be confined to these? Then it would certainly lead to no result, no vital point of the empire being menaced. At the same time, it would be a very dangerous war for the English if the fanaticism extends to the people of the interior. Canton may be totally destroyed and the coasts nibbled at in all possible points, but all the forces the British could bring together would not suffice to conquer and hold the two provinces of Kwang-tung and Kwang-si. What, then, can they do further? The country north of Canton, as far as Shanghae and Nankin, is in the hands of the Chinese insurgents, whom it would be bad policy to offend; and north of Nankin the only point an attack on which might lead to a decisive result is Pekin. But where is the army to form a fortified and garrisoned base of operations on the shore, to overcome every obstacle on the road, to leave detachments to secure the communications with the shore, and to appear in anything like formidable strength before the walls of a town, the size of London, a hundred miles from its landing place? On the other side, a successful demonstration against the capital would shake to its ground-works the very existence of the Chinese Empire—accelerate the upsetting of the Ch'ing dynasty and pave the way, not for British, but for Russian progress.

The new Anglo-Chinese war presents so many complications that it is utterly impossible to guess the turn it may take. For some months the want of troops, and for a still longer time the want of decision, will keep the British pretty inactive except, perhaps, on some unimportant point, to which under actual circumstances Canton too may be said to belong.

One thing is certain, that the death-hour of Old China is rapidly drawing nigh. Civil war has already divided the South from the

---

[a] *Pro aris et focis certamen* (battle for our altars and our hearths), Cicero, *De Natura Deorum*, III, 40.—*Ed.*

North of the Empire, and the Rebel King[a] seems to be as secure from the Imperialists (if not from the intrigues of his own followers)[337] at Nankin, as the Heavenly Emperor[b] from the rebels at Pekin. Canton carries on, so far, a sort of independent war with the English, and all foreigners in general; and while British and French fleets and troops flock to Hong-Kong, slowly but steadily the Siberian-line Cossacks advance their stanitzas from the Daoorian mountains to the banks of the Amour, and the Russian marines close in by fortifications the splendid harbors of Mantchooria. The very fanaticism of the southern Chinese in their struggle against foreigners seems to mark a consciousness of the supreme danger in which Old China is placed; and before many years pass away, we shall have to witness the death-struggle of the oldest empire in the world, and the opening day of a new era for all Asia.

Written on about May 20, 1857

First published in the *New-York Daily Tribune,* No. 5032, June 5, 1857; reprinted in the *New-York Semi-Weekly Tribune,* No. 1256, June 9, 1857

Reproduced from the *New-York Daily Tribune*

[a] Hung Hsiu-ch'üan.—*Ed.*
[b] Hsien Fung.—*Ed.*

Karl Marx

INTERESTING REVELATIONS[338]

London, May 26, 1857

O'Donnell's speech in the Spanish Senate on the 18th of May contains most curious revelations of the secret history of cotemporaneous Spain. His betrayal of Espartero and his *coup d'état* having paved the way for Narváez, the Polacos,[339] in their turn, are now trying to rid themselves of the latter. To this purpose Gen. Calonge, himself a Christina rebel of 1843,[340] and the Captain-General of Pampeluna at the time of the outbreak of the revolution in 1854,[341] was induced on the 18th of May, during the Senate's debates on the address to the Queen,[a] to move a series of amendments to the paragraph recommending a general amnesty. In a virulent attack on military insurrections in general, and on the military insurrection of 1854 in particular, he demanded "that the policy of conciliation should not go the length to encourage, by granting absolute impunity, *incorrigible perturbers.*" This stroke, premeditated by the friends of Sartorius, was aimed at O'Donnell as well as at the Duke of Valencia (Narváez). The Polacos had, in fact, ascertained that O'Donnell would seize upon the first occasion to denounce Narváez as his secret accomplice in the insurrection of the camp of the Guards. Such an opportunity was, accordingly, offered to O'Donnell by General Calonge. To prevent the threatened explosion, Narváez ventured upon a desperate maneuver. He, the man of order, justified the revolution of 1854, which, he said, was "inspired by the loftiest patriotism, and provoked by the excesses of the preceding cabinets." Thus, at the very moment that Mr. de Nocedal, the Minister of the Interior, was proposing to the Cortes a Draconian press-law, Narváez, the

[a] Isabella II.— *Ed.*

chief of the ministry, acted in the Senate as the *advocatus diaboli*[a]—the vindicator of revolution and military insurrection. But in vain. During the subsequent sitting of the Senate, on the 18th of May, while forced by the Polacos to recant his censure of "former Cabinets," Narváez had, at the same time, to writhe under O'Donnell's indiscreet revelations, the truth of which he himself admitted, by complaining that "O'Donnell had revealed private and confidential conversations," and by asking "what confidence could now be placed in friendship!" In the eyes of the Court, Narváez is now a convicted rebel, and before long will have to give way to Bravo Murillo and Sartorius, the sure forerunners of a new revolution.

The following is a literal translation of O'Donnell's speech:

"*O'Donnell*—I cannot remain silent in this eminently political discussion, after the important events that have occurred since the last meeting of the Senate. The part I have played in these events obliges me to speak. The chief of the rising of the camp of the Guards: the author of the programme of Manzanares[342]; the War Minister in the Cabinet of the Duke of Vittoria[b]; summoned, two years later, by the crown, under solemn circumstances, to save the crown and endangered society; fortunate enough to obtain that result without being forced, after the combat, to shed one drop of blood or to pronounce a single sentence of banishment—I should have felt obliged to take part in the pending discussion. But it would be a crime to keep silence after the accusations directed by General Calonge against myself and the worthy generals who, during two years, were connected with me, and, in the days of the crisis, assisted in saving society and the crown. General Calonge has described as a rebellion the rising of the camp of the Guards. Wherefore? Has he so soon forgotten all the events that preceded it, and, in due course, would have precipitated the country into a revolution not to be subdued? I thank the President of the Council for the energy with which he has repelled the accusation of General Calonge. It is true that, in thus acting, he displayed the energy of one that defends his own cause [Profound sensation]. Being obliged to enter into details indispensable for the vindication of this fact, wishing above all to dismiss from these debates whatever might bear a personal appearance, I should feel grateful if the President of the Cabinet deigned to answer the following questions: Is it true that the Duke of Valencia[c] was, since 1852, united by close ties to the Generals of Vicalvaro? Is it true that he was informed of all their undertakings since the closing of the Senate after the vote of the 105? Is it true that he was disposed to join them in the accomplishment of their projects? Is it true that, although prevented from doing so by motives which I respect, he, nevertheless, sent later on one of his aides-de-camp to congratulate us upon our triumph?"

"*Narváez*—After the words the Count of Lucena has addressed to me, I must declare that in all he planned and afterward executed, in the form in which he planned and executed it, I did not participate at all, whatever may have been our former relations."

---

[a] Devil's advocate.—*Ed.*

[b] Espartero.—*Ed.*

[c] Narváez.—*Ed.*

"*O'Donnell*—The President of the Cabinet has answered in the manner he thought the most opportune. I should have liked not to be obliged to give further explications, but, as I am driven to it, I shall give them. Everybody knows that, in the year 1852, there reigned in politics the most profound calm. Unfortunately for the Government and the country, then, for the first time, began to be whispered the words, 'Constitutional Reform.' The gentlemen of the Senate will recollect the agitation produced by the apprehension of a *coup d'état*. They will not have forgotten the numerous re-unions then taking place between political men, and in which an address to the Queen was resolved upon. To that address were appended many signatures, but it was not presented. The Cortes were convoked, and some days afterward, the *Gaceta* published the projects which produced such an effect in this very Chamber that the Government suffered a serious defeat in the election of the President. The Cortes were then dissolved. The most important men of the moderate party united then in order to protest against that measure; the Duke of Valencia being nominated as the President of the re-union. For fear lest the Government should obstruct the re-unions, a committee was appointed, over which the Duke of Valencia was again elected to preside, and of which Messrs. Mon, Pidal, and other important personages, were the most active members. Beside the protest, the legality of the new elections was mooted in this committee. Two or three days after the Duke of Valencia's departure for Bayonne, the Bravo Murillo Cabinet retired. The Count d'Alcoy succeeded Bravo Murillo. The Opposition remained the same, and when the Cortes assembled, a manifest, drawn up by the Duke of Valencia, was handed to the Senate. The Senate dropped it, but it became then evident that the Opposition was assuming formidable proportions. The Cabinet of Count d'Alcoy was succeeded by that of Gen. Lersundi; then the Ministry of the Count of San Luis was installed. I regret being obliged to enter into certain details, but the moment has arrived of speaking of my own political relations with those who joined me in the camp of the Guards. I received, and all of us received, before the Duke of Valencia's return to Spain, one of his confidants, with whom he had had a long conversation, and to whom, while deploring the lamentable situation in which the country was placed, and uttering apprehensions as to the dangers menacing the throne and the Constitution, the Duke said that there remained one escape only—the appeal to force [Sensation]. The Sartorius Ministry authorized the return to Spain of the Duke of Valencia. He went first to Madrid, and then retired to Aranjuez. There we had a conference with him. He communicated to us his patriotic feelings, which I am ready to admire, although I am unable to support the Cabinet he actually presides over. He declared to us that the situation made an appeal to force inevitable; that, from particular motives, he could not pronounce first, but that the second sword to leave the sheath should be his; adding that, in the present state of things, the rising of two regiments of cavalry would suffice to decide the revolution. This declaration was made to us in the manner the most categorical. The Cortes were opened. Fully convinced that all legal means would be tried in vain, the Duke of Valencia, instead of entering the Senate and taking the lead of the Opposition, withdrew to Loja. Everybody knows what then occurred in the Cortes; all remember the famous vote of the 105. The Government, nevertheless, thought not fit to resign. The Cortes were dismissed, and then a régime of unheard-of persecutions was initiated. The Generals who had voted against the Cabinet, the most eminent political men, the journalists of the Opposition, were sent into exile; organic changes in every direction were announced; the forced loan was proclaimed; in one word, the Government outlawed itself. Now, I ask you, dare you affirm that in this country, where all parties, when in opposition, did always conspire, there has ever been a revolution more legitimate than that of 1854? As to myself, I left the modest abode where I had hidden myself during six months. I left it on horseback, followed by some generals and some regiments, with a view to overturning a Government that so shamefully was trampling down a constitution I had sworn to defend as a general and a senator. We arrived at Vicalvaro, where, to my great regret, the combat was engaged. There were neither victors nor vanquished. On both sides the troops fought gallantly. The garrison had to return to Madrid, while we remained at Vicalvaro. On the following day, according to what was agreed upon with the Duke of Valencia, we marched through Aranjuez in the direction of Andalusia. In the province of Jaen there sojourned Gen. Serrano, who had promised us his support. We arrived at Manzanares, where he met us, saying that those who had promised to follow him had disbanded, and that he came alone to share our lot. It was then that I published a manifest, and, as I am not used to deny my own acts, I shall tell what was at that moment preparing. By emissaries I was informed of all Madrid occurrences. All important men of the moderate party were involved in the movement. Only it happened—what is sure to happen—that on the planning a thing, you may rely on the concourse of a great number of men, the most zealous of whom disappear when the hour of action sounds. I was told that we were not likely to be seconded by the people, whom the Ministry endeavored to persuade that the movement arose out of merely personal squabbles, and lacked any fixed political principle. This was the motive of the publication of the manifest of Manzanares, which contained two important points:

"*Constitutional Reform,* such as I in my quality of President of the Cabinet, later on, proposed to her Majesty; and the

"*National Militia,* not as it was actually organized, but, as I intended making it, a true element of order.

We left Manzanares, and wrote to the Duke of Valencia a letter, signed by myself and four other generals, declaring that if he presented himself we should appoint him our commander-in-chief. The Duke sent us an aide-de-camp with the message that he had fallen sick and was narrowly watched. It has been said that we were resolved upon flying to Portugal. This is false. We had, on the contrary, resolved to withdraw to the Sierra Morena, to establish our cavalry at Barrios, to stop all the wagons loaded with provisions, and to improve the first occasion for presenting ourselves before Madrid, when suddenly the news of the fall of the Sartorius Cabinet and the appeal made by the Queen to the Duke of Vittoria was imparted to us. From that moment my mission was put an end to. Gen. San Miguel, the Minister *per interim,*[a] sent me word to return to Madrid. I obeyed, with the firm resolution of not entering the Cabinet. The Crown had removed the Duke of Vittoria, all relations with whom I had dropped since 1840. The same men who afterward accused me of having joined his Cabinet, came, on the very night of my arrival at Madrid, supplicating me to accept the War Ministry, as the only means of saving order and society. All these men belonged to the moderate party. I saw the Duke of Vittoria, and, at this point of my relation, I should feel much embarrassed if his own manifest did not warrant me in clearing myself from malignant imputations. Espartero embraced me cordially, and said that the time had arrived of dropping all dissensions between Spaniards; that it had become impossible to govern with one single party, and that it was his firm resolution to appeal to all men of influence and morality. I observed the situation at Madrid. The barricades stood still erect, the garrison was but very small, but the people, always judicious, inspired me with great confidence. My second interview with Espartero was rather

[a] In the meantime.—*Ed.*

cool; he offered me the portfolio of Foreign Affairs and of the Colonies. I made him aware that, on entering the Cabinet, I should decline every other place but that of War Minister. Then he told me that of all men I was most fit for fulfilling the functions of Captain-General of Cuba. I replied that, having already served in that quality, I should not like to return to Havana, and rather withdraw to private life; but I entreated him immediately to form a Ministry, and not any longer to abandon the nation to the dangers of a provisional state. Shortly afterward General Salanza, the originally-appointed War Minister, called upon me, in the name of Espartero, to accept the place of War Minister, and the same night I was sworn in with my colleagues. There were only two courses for me to take—either to leave the revolution to itself until its own excesses engendered a reaction, or to stop it in its march. The former part was the easier one; my honor and the interest of the country made me adopt the latter. I do not repent it. Our first discussion took place in regard to the Constituent Cortes. Mr. Collado, who sits among us, knows all our disputes on this point. Our efforts were baffled. The decree for the convocation of the Cortes was signed. The general election took place—not, as Mr. Pidal said, under governmental pressure, but with an unlimited liberty. The majority of representatives was composed of men sincerely wishing the welfare of the country. With a firm government, the Constitution would have been established in four months. But Espartero's proverbial weakness of character—not as a military man, but as a politician—rendered every governmental action impossible. I did not continue forming part of the Ministry with a view to betray my colleagues, as the Duke of Vittoria erroneously supposes. I clung to my post from the very motives which had made me canvass it. I remained in order to check the overflow of the revolution."

After a very clumsy apology for his *coup d'état,* O'Donnell concluded his speech with the declaration that he could not support the Cabinet of Marshal Narváez,

"since it had announced its intention of following a line of policy not in harmony with representative government."

Written on May 26, 1857

First published in the *New-York Daily Tribune,* No. 5038, June 12, 1857

Reproduced from the newspaper

Karl Marx

[THE NEW FRENCH BANK ACT][343]

The new French Bank act, and the resignation of Count d'Argout, the Governor of the Bank, are somewhat remarkable incidents in the financial history of the present Empire. Placed, in 1834, by Louis Philippe, at the head of the French Bankocracy, Mr. d'Argout distinguished himself by the tenacity with which, for 23 years, he clung to office, and by the circumspect prudence with which he weathered the tempests of 1848 and 1851. The revolution of 1848 was directed not only against Louis Philippe, but still more against the *haute finance*,[a] that had its center in the Bank of France. The latter institution and the unpopular personage at its head seemed, therefore, to be naturally the first objects for revolutionary assault. Count d'Argout, undervaluing the immediate chances of the moment, thought himself strong enough to frighten the middle classes into a counter-revolution by artificially aggravating the financial crisis. Accordingly, all at once he cut short the credit accommodations upon which the commerce of Paris was wont to rely; but the immense danger he had thus deliberately summoned, instead of shaking the Provisional Government, reverberated upon the Bank itself. Instead of the confidently expected counter-revolution, there occurred an unseasonable run on the Bank. If d'Argout had miscalculated the energies of the people, he discerned more keenly the capacities of the Government. Not only did he prevail upon them to give forced course to the notes of the Bank, and to humbly accept, under the most unfavorable conditions, a loan from that very same concern which they had just preserved from irretrievable ruin; he

[a] Financial aristocracy.— *Ed.*

improved the occasion to augment the Bank's sources of profit by procuring for it the privilege of issuing notes of a lower denomination, and to extend its monopoly by crushing the provincial banks of issue. The lowest denomination of notes issued by the Bank of France prior to 1847 was 500 francs; in 1848 it was authorized to issue notes of the value of 200 and of 100 francs. The places of the provincial banks—deprived of the privilege, hitherto enjoyed, of issuing notes—were filled up by new branches of the Bank of France. In consequence of these changes, its total circulation, which at the close of 1847 had only amounted to $48,000,000, reached at the end of 1855 the sum of $122,445,000; its gross transactions, which in 1847 fell short of $375,000,000, had already in 1855 risen to $940,600,000, of which $549,000,000 represented the business of the branches; and its shares, which before the Revolution were usually quoted at about 2,000 francs, now sell for 4,500 francs. Prior to 1848 the Bank of France had been a Parisian rather than a French institution. The new privileges bestowed upon it by the Revolutionary Government transformed it into a private concern of national dimensions. Thus, thanks to the clever management of d'Argout, the monopoly of the financial aristocracy, which the Revolution of February intended to break down, was extended, strengthened, reorganized, through the very instrumentality of that Revolution itself.

The second great catastrophe which d'Argout had to confront was the *coup d'état,* the success of which mainly hinged upon the forcible opening of the Bank coffers intrusted to his guardianship. The pliant Governor not only winked at Bonaparte's burglary, but contributed much to assuage the apprehensions of the commercial world, by sticking to his post at a moment when the exodus from the administration of all respectable or would-be respectable people threatened seriously to compromise the usurper. In reward for these good services, Bonaparte consented to take no advantage of the proviso in the last renewal of the Bank charter in 1840, by which its statutes might have been revised in 1855. D'Argout, like his friend the late Marshal Soult, never evinced fidelity to anything but place and salary. His resignation at this moment of the Governorship of the Bank of France can only be accounted for on the same principle that, according to popular belief, prompts rats to leave falling houses.

The history of the new Bank law marks it as one of those low jobs that distinguish the era of the present Empire. During the financial crisis which broke out in Europe at the end of 1856, the alteration of the existing Bank law was first mooted on the plausible pretext that the enormous transactions of the Bank rested on too small a capital. For more than six months, mysterious conferences were held in the presence of Napoleon III., between the representatives of the Bank on the one hand, and the great financiers of Paris, the Ministers and the Council of State, on the other. Yet the present bill was not presented to the *Corps Législatif*[344] till that body was on the eve of its final dissolution. In the preliminary discussions in the *bureaux,*[345] it was violently attacked; the Committee appointed to report upon it literally tore it to pieces; and there were even threats of rejecting the project altogether. But Bonaparte knew his creatures. He caused an intimation to reach them that Government was determined, and that they must make up their minds either to pass the bill or be turned out of their sinecures at the approaching election. To assist them in parting with the last remnants of shame, the last day of the session was singled out for the discussion of the law. It was then of course passed, with some insignificant amendments. What must be the features of a law which required so much management in order to its passage by such a body as this *Corps Législatif?*

In fact, in the time of Louis Philippe himself, when the Bank of France and the Rothschilds were notoriously enabled to lay an embargo upon all legislative projects not to their taste, no minister would have dared to propose such a complete surrender of the State to them. The Government resigns the power, still guaranteed by the Charter of 1846, of amending the new Bank Act before its expiration. The privileges of the Bank, which have still ten years to run, are benevolently prolonged for a further term of thirty years. It is allowed to lower the denomination of its notes to 50 francs, the importance of which clause will be fully understood when we consider that the introduction in 1848 of 200 and 100 franc notes enabled the Bank to replace about $30,000,000 of gold and silver by its own paper. Of the enormous profits, which are sure to accrue to the Bank from this change, no share whatever is reserved for the nation, which, on the contrary, has to pay the Bank for the credit conferred upon the latter in the name of France. The privilege of establishing branch banks in the departments in which they do not yet exist, is bestowed upon the Bank of France, not as a concession made by the Government to the Bank, but, on the contrary, as a concession made by the Bank to the Government. The permission to charge its customers more than the legal 6 per cent interest is encumbered with no other obligation but that of adding the profits thus derived to its capital and not to its yearly dividends. The reduction of the interest upon its current accounts with the Treasury from four to three per cent is more than compensated by the dropping of the clause of the act of 1840, which obliged the Bank to charge no interest at all whenever the account stood below 80,000,000, the common average of those accounts being 82,000,000. Last, not least, the newly created 91,250 shares, of the nominal value of 1,000 francs, are exclusively ascribed to the holders of the 91,250 shares actually existing; and the Bank shares being now sold on the Bourse at the price of 4,500 francs, these new shares are to be delivered to the old shareholders at the price of 1,100 francs. This act, so entirely framed in favor of the Bankocracy at the expense of the State, affords most conclusive proof of the monetary straits to which the Bonapartist Government finds itself already driven. As an equivalent for all its concessions, that Government receives the sum of $20,000,000, which the Bank is obliged to invest in three per cent *rentes,* to be created for this purpose, and the minimum price of which is fixed at 75 francs. The whole transaction seems strongly to support the notion circulated on the Continent of Europe, that Bonaparte has already drawn to a large amount on the coffers of the Bank, and is now anxious to clothe his fraudulent transactions in a more or less respectable garb.

Written on June 2, 1857

First published in the *New-York Daily Tribune,* No. 5045, June 20, 1857 as a leading article; reprinted unsigned in the *New-York Semi-Weekly Tribune,* No. 1260, June 23, 1857 under the title "The Bank of France"

Reproduced from the *New-York Daily Tribune*

Karl Marx

THE PERSIAN TREATY

London, June 12, 1857

Some time ago, when a question respecting the Persian war was addressed to Lord Palmerston in his own House of Commons, he tauntingly replied: "As soon as the *peace* is ratified the House may express its opinions on the *war*."[a] The treaty of peace signed at Paris, March 4, 1857, and ratified at Bagdad, May 2, 1857, has now been laid before the House. It consists of fifteen Articles, eight of them being freighted with the usual treaty-of-peace ballast. Article V. stipulates that the Persian troops are to withdraw from the territory and city of Herat, and from every part of Affghanistan, within three months, from the date of the exchange of the ratifications of the treaty. By Art. XIV. the British Government, on its part, engages, so soon as the above stipulation be carried into effect, "to withdraw without delay the British troops from all ports, places and islands belonging to Persia."[b]

Now it should be recollected that the evacuation of Herat by the Persian troops was spontaneously offered by Feroukh Khan, the Persian Embassador, during his protracted conferences at Constantinople with Lord Stratford de Redcliffe, and before the capture of Bushire had yet occurred. The only new profit accruing to England from this stipulation is, therefore, limited to the privilege of enchaining, during the most unhealthy season, her troops to the most pestilential spot of the Persian Empire. The

[a] Palmerston's speech in the House of Commons on May 18, 1857, *The Times*, No. 22684, May 19, 1857.—*Ed.*

[b] Here and below see "Treaty of Peace between Her Majesty the Queen of the United Kingdom of Great Britain and Ireland and His Majesty the Shah of Persia", *The Times*, No. 22704, June 11, 1857.—*Ed.*

terrible ravages the sun and swamps and the sea inflict during the summer months, even on the native population of Bushire and Mohammerah, are chronicled by old and modern writers; but why refer to them, since a few weeks ago, Sir Henry Rawlinson, a very competent judge, and a Palmerstonian too, publicly declared that the Anglo-Indian troops were sure to sink under the horrors of the climate?[a] *The London Times,* on receiving the news of the Mohammerah victory, proclaimed at once the necessity of advancing despite the treaty of peace to Shiraz, in order to save the troops.[b] The suicides, too, of the British Admiral and General,[c] placed at the head of the expedition, were due to their profound anxiety as to the probable fate of the troops, whom, by Governmental instruction, they were not to push beyond Mohammerah. A Crimean catastrophe on a smaller scale may thus be safely expected; this time proceeding neither from the necessities of war, nor from the blunders of the Administration, but from a treaty written with the sword of the victor. There occurs one phrase in the articles quoted which, if it suit Palmerston, may be worked into "a small bone of contention."

Art. XIV. stipulates the "withdrawal of the British troops from all ports, places and islands *belonging to Persia.*" Now it is a controversial matter whether or not the town of Mohammerah *does* belong to Persia. The Turks have never renounced their claims to that place, which, situated on the Delta of the Euphrates, was their only seaport on that river always accessible, the port of Bassora, being at certain seasons too shallow for ships of large burden. Thus, if Palmerston pleases, he may hold Mohammerah on the pretext of its not "belonging" to Persia, and of waiting for the final settlement of the boundary question between Turkey and Persia.

Art. VI. stipulates that Persia agrees to

> "relinquish all claims to sovereignty over the territory and city of Herat and the countries of Affghanistan;" to "abstain from all interference with the internal affairs of Affghanistan;" to "recognize the independence of Herat and the whole of Affghanistan, and never to attempt to interfere with the independence of those States;" to refer, in case of differences with Herat and Affghanistan, "for adjustment to the friendly offices of the British Government, and not to take up arms unless these friendly offices fail of effect."

---

[a] H. C. Rawlinson's speech at a meeting of the Royal Geographical Society on May 11, 1857, *The Times,* No. 22679, May 13, 1857.—*Ed.*

[b] *The Times,* No. 22681, May 15, 1857, leading article.—*Ed.*

[c] Etheridge and Stalker.—*Ed.*

The British Government, on their part, engage

"at all times to exert their influence with the States of Affghanistan to prevent any causes of umbrage being given by them," and "to use their best endeavors to compose differences in a manner just and honorable to Persia."

Now, if this article is stripped of its red tape, it means nothing beyond the acknowledgment by Persia of the independence of Herat, a concession to make which Feroukh Khan had declared himself ready at the Constantinople conferences. It is true that, by virtue of this article, the British Government is appointed the official intermeddler between Persia and Affghanistan, but that part it was, since the commencement of this century, always acting. Whether it be able or not to continue it, is a question, not of right, but of might. Besides if the Shah[a] harbors at the Court of Teheran any Hugo Grotius, the latter will point out that any stipulation by which an independent State gives a foreign Government the right of interfering with its international relations is null and void according to the *jus gentium,*[b] and that the stipulation with England is the more so, since it converts Affghanistan, a merely poetical term for various tribes and States, into a real country. The country of Affghanistan exists, in a diplomatic sense, no more than the country of Panslavia.

Art. VII., which stipulates that, in case of any violation of the Persian frontier by the Affghan States,

"the Persian Government shall have the right [...] to undertake military operations for the repression and punishment of the aggressors," but "must retire within its own territory so soon as its object is accomplished,"

is but a literal repetition of just that clause of the treaty of 1852[c] which gave the immediate occasion for the Bushire expedition.

By Art. IX. Persia admits the establishment and recognition of British Consul-General, Consuls, Vice-Consuls, and Consular Agents, to be placed on the footing of the most favorite nation; but by Art. XII. the British Government renounces

"the right of protecting hereafter any Persian subject not actually in the employment of the British mission or of British Consuls-General, Consuls, Vice-Consuls and Consular Agents."

The establishment of British Consulates in Persia being agreed to by Feroukh Khan before the commencement of the war, the

[a] Nasr-ed-Din.—*Ed.*

[b] International law.—*Ed.*

[c] A reference to *Articles convenus entre la Grande-Bretagne et la Perse relatifs à l'indépendance de la Ville de Hérat; signés à Téhéran, le 25 janvier 1853.*—*Ed.*

present treaty adds only the renunciation, on the part of England, of her right of protectorate over Persian subjects, which right formed one of the ostensible causes of the war.[346] Austria, France and other States have obtained the establishment of Consulates in Persia without recurring to any piratical expeditions.

Lastly, the treaty forces Mr. Murray back on the Court of Teheran, and prescribes the apology to be made to that gentleman, for being characterized in a letter addressed to Sadir Azim[a] by the Shah, as a "stupid, ignorant and insane man," as a "simpleton," and as the author of a "rude, unmeaning and disgusting document."[b] The apology to be made to Mr. Murray was likewise offered by Feroukh Khan, but then declined by the British Government, who insisted upon the dismissal of Sadir Azim, and Mr. Murray's solemn entry into Teheran "to the sound of cornet, flute, harp, sackbut, psaltery, dulcimer, and all manner of music."[c] By accepting, as Consul-General in Egypt, personal favors from Mons, Barrot; by sending, on his first landing at Bushire, the tobacco then presented to him in the Shah's name to the bazaars, there to be publicly sold; by acting the knight-errant of a Persian lady of dubious virtue, Mr. Murray has failed to impress on the Oriental mind very high notions of British integrity or dignity. His forced readmission at the Persian Court must, therefore, be considered a rather questionable success. On the whole, the treaty contains, beyond the offers Feroukh Khan made before the outbreak of the war, no stipulations worth the paper they are written upon, and still less the treasure spent and the blood shed. The clear profits of the Persian expedition may be summed up in the odium incurred by Great Britain throughout Central Asia; the disaffection of India, increased by the withdrawal of Indian troops, and the new burdens thrown on the Indian Exchequer; the almost inevitable recurrence of another Crimean catastrophe; the acknowledgment of Bonaparte's official mediation between England and Asiatic States; lastly, the acquisition by Russia of two strips of land of great importance—the one on the Caspian, the other on the north-coast frontier of Persia.

Written on June 12, 1857

First published unsigned in the *New-York Daily Tribune*, No. 5048, June 24, 1857

Reproduced from the newspaper

[a] Prime Minister Mirza Aga Khan.— *Ed.*

[b] Nasr-ed-Din's letter to Sadir Azim of December 1855, *The Times*, No. 22704, June 11, 1857, "The Peace with Persia".— *Ed.*

[c] Daniel 3:10.— *Ed.*

Karl Marx

THE REVOLT IN THE INDIAN ARMY[347]

The Roman *Divide et impera*[a] was the great rule by which Great Britain, for about one hundred and fifty years, contrived to retain the tenure of her Indian empire. The antagonism of the various races, tribes, castes, creeds and sovereignties, the aggregate of which forms the geographical unity of what is called India, continued to be the vital principle of British supremacy. In later times, however, the conditions of that supremacy have undergone a change. With the conquest of Scinde and the Punjaub,[348] the Anglo-Indian empire had not only reached its natural limits, but it had trampled out the last vestiges of independent Indian States. All warlike native tribes were subdued, all serious internal conflicts were at an end, and the late incorporation of Oude[349] proved satisfactorily that the remnants of the so-called independent Indian principalities exist on sufferance only. Hence a great change in the position of the East Indian Company. It no longer attacked one part of India by the help of another part, but found itself placed at the head, and the whole of India at its feet. No longer conquering, it had become *the* conqueror. The armies at its disposition no longer had to extend its dominion, but only to maintain it. From soldiers they were converted into policemen; 200,000,000 natives being curbed by a native army of 200,000 men, officered by Englishmen, and that native army, in its turn, being kept in check by an English army numbering 40,000 only. On first view, it is evident that the allegiance of the Indian people rests on the fidelity of the native army, in creating which the British rule simultaneously organized the first general center of

---

[a] Divide and rule.—*Ed.*

resistance which the Indian people was ever possessed of. How far that native army may be relied upon is clearly shown by its recent mutinies, breaking out as soon as the war with Persia had almost denuded the Presidency[350] of Bengal of its European soldiers. Before this there had been mutinies in the Indian army, but the present revolt[351] is distinguished by characteristic and fatal features. It is the first time that sepoy regiments have murdered their European officers; that Mussulmans and Hindoos, renouncing their mutual antipathies, have combined against their common masters; that

> "disturbances beginning with the Hindoos, have actually ended in placing on the throne of Delhi a Mohammedan Emperor;"[a]

that the mutiny has not been confined to a few localities; and lastly, that the revolt in the Anglo-Indian army has coincided with a general disaffection exhibited against English supremacy on the part of the great Asiatic nations, the revolt of the Bengal army being, beyond doubt, intimately connected with the Persian and Chinese wars.[352]

The alleged cause of the dissatisfaction which began to spread four months ago in the Bengal army was the apprehension on the part of the natives lest the Government should interfere with their religion. The serving out of cartridges, the paper of which was said to have been greased with the fat of bullocks and pigs, and the compulsory biting[353] of which was, therefore, considered by the natives as an infringement of their religious prescriptions, gave the signal for local disturbances. On the 22nd of January an incendiary fire broke out in cantonments a short distance from Calcutta. On the 25th of February the 19th native regiment mutinied at Berhampore the men objecting to the cartridges served out to them. On the 31st of March that regiment was disbanded; at the end of March the 34th sepoy regiment, stationed at Barrackpore, allowed one of its men[b] to advance with a loaded musket upon the parade-ground in front of the line, and, after having called his comrades to mutiny, he was permitted to attack and wound the Adjutant[c] and Sergeant-Major of his regiment. During the hand-to-hand conflict, that ensued, hundreds of sepoys looked passively on, while others participated in the struggle, and attacked the officers with the butt ends of their muskets.

---

[a] *The Times*, No. 22719, June 29, 1857, leading article.—*Ed.*

[b] Mungul Pandy.—*Ed.*

[c] Baugh.—*Ed.*

Subsequently that regiment was also disbanded. The month of April was signalized by incendiary fires in several cantonments of the Bengal army at Allahabad, Agra, Umballah, by a mutiny of the 3d regiment of light cavalry at Meerut, and by similar appearances of disaffection in the Madras and Bombay armies. At the beginning of May an émeute was preparing at Lucknow, the capital of Oude, which was, however, prevented by the promptitude of Sir H. Lawrence. On the 9th of May the mutineers of the 3d light cavalry of Meerut were marched off to jail, to undergo the various terms of imprisonment to which they were sentenced. On the evening of the following day the troopers of the 3d cavalry, together with the two native regiments, the 11th and 20th, assembled upon the parade-ground, killed the officers endeavoring to pacify them, set fire to the cantonments, and slew all the Englishmen they were able to lay hands on. Although the British part of the brigade mustered a regiment of infantry, another of cavalry, and an overwhelming force of horse and foot artillery, they were not able to move until nightfall. Having inflicted but little harm on the mutineers, they allowed them to betake themselves to the open field and to throw themselves into Delhi, some forty miles distant from Meerut. There they were joined by the native garrison, consisting of the 38th, 54th and 74th regiments of infantry, and a company of native artillery. The British officers were attacked, all Englishmen within reach of the rebels were murdered, and the heir of the late Mogul[a] [354] of Delhi proclaimed King of India. Of the troops sent to the rescue of Meerut, where order had been re-established, six companies of native sappers and miners, who arrived on the 15th of May, murdered their commanding officer, Major Frazer, and made at once for the open country, pursued by troops of horse artillery and several of the 6th dragoon guards. Fifty or sixty of the mutineers were shot, but the rest contrived to escape to Delhi. At Ferozepore, in the Punjaub, the 57th and 45th native infantry regiments mutinied, but were put down by force. Private letters from Lahore state the whole of the native troops to be in an undisguised state of mutiny. On the 19th of May, unsuccessful efforts were made by the sepoys stationed at Calcutta to get possession of Fort St. William.[355] Three regiments arrived from Bushire at Bombay were at once dispatched to Calcutta.

In reviewing these events, one is startled by the conduct of the

---

[a] Bahadur Shah II, son of Akbar II.—*Ed.*

British commander at Meerut[a] his late appearance on the field of battle being still less incomprehensible than the weak manner in which he pursued the mutineers. As Delhi is situated on the right and Meerut on the left bank of the Jumna—the two banks being joined at Delhi by one bridge only—nothing could have been easier than to cut off the retreat of the fugitives.

Meanwhile, martial law has been proclaimed in all the disaffected districts; forces, consisting of natives mainly, are concentrating against Delhi from the north, the east and the south; the neighboring princes are said to have pronounced for the English; letters have been sent to Ceylon to stop Lord Elgin and Gen. Ashburnham's forces, on their way to China; and finally, 14,000 British troops were to be dispatched from England to India in about a fortnight. Whatever obstacles the climate of India at the present season, and the total want of means of transportation, may oppose to the movements of the British forces, the rebels at Delhi are very likely to succumb without any prolonged resistance. Yet, even then, it is only the prologue of a most terrible tragedy that will have to be enacted.

Written on June 30, 1857

First published in the *New-York Daily Tribune,* No. 5065, July 15, 1857 as a leading article; reprinted in the *New-York Semi-Weekly Tribune,* No. 1267, July 17 and the *New-York Weekly Tribune,* No. 827, July 18, 1857

Reproduced from the *New-York Daily Tribune*

[a] Hewitt.—*Ed.*

Karl Marx

STATE OF EUROPE[356] [—FINANCIAL STATE OF FRANCE]

The soporific dullness which, since the conclusion of the Oriental war,[a] had characterized the physiognomy of Europe, is rapidly giving way to a lively and even feverish aspect. There is Great Britain, with her Reform movement looming in the future and her Indian difficulties. *The London Times,* it is true, tells the world that except those who have friends in India,

> "the British public, as a whole, look for the arrival of the next news from India with as much interest as we should on an overdue Australian steamer or the result of a rising at Madrid."[b]

On the same day, however, the same *Times,* in its money article, drops the mask of proud indifference, and betrays the real feelings of John Bull in the following strain:

> "A continued depression like that now prevailing in the stock market, in the face of an uninterrupted augmentation in the Bank bullion and the prospect of a great harvest, is almost unprecedented. The anxiety with regard to India overpowers all other considerations, and if any serious news were to arrive to-morrow it would most probably produce a panic."[c]

To speculate upon the course of events in India would be useless just now, when every mail may be expected to bring authentic news. But it is evident that, in case of a serious revolutionary explosion on the continent of Europe, England,

[a] The Crimean war, 1853-56.—*Ed.*

[b] *The Times,* No. 22728, July 9, 1857, leading article.—*Ed.*

[c] *The Times,* No. 22728, July 9, 1857, "Money-Market and City Intelligence".—*Ed.*

drained of her men and her ships by the Chinese war and the Indian revolts, would prove unable to reassume the proud position she occupied in 1848 and 1849. On the other hand, she cannot afford to stand aloof, since the Oriental war and the alliance with Napoleon have lately chained her to continental politics, at the same time that the complete dissolution of her traditionary political parties, and the growing antagonism between her wealth-producing classes, expose her social frame more than ever to spasmodic disturbances. In 1848-49, while her power weighed like an incubus on the European revolution, England was at first a little afraid of it, then diverted its own native ennui by its spectacle, then betrayed it a little, then coquetted a little with it, and at last took earnestly to making money out of it. Her industrial fortunes, somewhat roughly shaken by the commercial distress of 1846-47, may even be said to have, to some extent, been remade, through the agency of the revolution of 1848. However, the continental revolution will be for England neither a spectacle to enjoy, nor a distress to speculate upon, but a severe trial to pass through.

Crossing the English Channel, we find the surface of society already heaving and rocking with the movement of the subterranean fires. The Paris elections[357] are even less the foreboding than the real commencement of a new revolution. It is quite in keeping with the historical past of France that Cavaignac should give color and name to the effort against Bonaparte, in the same way that Odilon Barrot introduced that against Louis Philippe. Cavaignac, like Odilon Barrot, is only a pretext on the part of the people, though both of them serious conceptions on the part of the middle classes. The name under which a revolution is ushered in is never that borne on the banner on the day of triumph. To hold out any chances of success, revolutionary movements must, in modern society, borrow their colors, at the beginning, from those elements of the people which, although opposed to the existing government, are quite in harmony with existing society. In one word, revolutions must receive their tickets of admission to the official stage from the ruling classes themselves.

The Paris elections, and the Paris imprisonments, and the Paris prosecutions, can be read in their true light only by considering the state of the Paris Bourse, whose disturbances preceded the electoral agitation, as they have outlived it. Even during the last three months of 1856, when all Europe was laboring in a financial crisis, the Paris Bourse did not witness such a stupendous and continued depreciation of all securities as prevailed during all last

June and the beginning of July. Besides, it was now not a process of declining and rising by fits and starts, but all went down in quite a methodical way, following the ordinary laws of fall only in the last precipitate plunges. The shares of the Crédit Mobilier,[358] which, at the beginning of June, stood at about 1,300f. were sunk to 1,162f. on the 26th; to 1,095f. on July 3; to 975f. on the 4th; to 890f. on the 7th. The shares of the Bank of France, quoted at the beginning of June at above 4,000f., had, in spite of the new monopolies and privileges bestowed upon the Bank, fallen to 3,065f. on the 29th of June; to 2,890f. on the 3d of July, and on the 9th of July brought no more than 2,900f. The three per cent *rentes,* the shares of the principal railways, such as the Northern, the Lyons, the Mediterranean, the Grand Fusion lines, and all other joint-stock shares, have proportionably shared in this long downward movement.

The new Bank act,[a] while exposing the desperate situation of the Bonapartist exchequer, has at the same time shaken the public confidence in the Bank administration itself. The last report of the Crédit Mobilier,[b] while revealing the organic hollowness of that institution and the vastness of the interests involved in it, informed the public that there was a struggle going on between its Directors and the Emperor,[c] and that some financial *coup d'état* was contemplated. In fact, to make good its most pressing obligations, the Crédit Mobilier has been forced to throw on the market about twenty millions of securities held by it. At the same time, in order to pay their dividends and get the means of continuing or commencing the works undertaken, railways and other joint-stock companies have also had to sell securities, to call for fresh deposits on their old shares, or to procure capital by issuing new ones. Hence the protracted heaviness in the French stock market, which, so far from being the result of merely incidental circumstances, will recur in aggravated forms at every subsequent settling term.

The alarming features of the present disease may be inferred from the fact that Emile Pereire, the great financial quack of the second empire, has stepped forward and tendered a report to Louis Napoleon, taking for his text the words pronounced by the latter in 1850 in an address to the Council-General of Agriculture and Commerce:

---

[a] See this volume, pp. 289-92.— *Ed.*
[b] Ibid., pp. 270-77.— *Ed.*
[c] Napoleon III.— *Ed.*

"Credulity, let us not forget it, is the moral part of material interests—the spirit which animates the body—it increases tenfold by confidence the value of all productions." [a]

Mr. Pereire then goes on explaining in a manner already familiar to our readers the decrease of 980,000,000f. in the values of the country within the last five months. He winds up his lamentations with these fatal words: "The budget of fear almost equals the budget of France." If, as Mr. Pereire asserts, apart from the $200,000,000 France has to pay in taxes for maintaining the empire, she has to pay as much more for fear of losing it, the days of that expensive institution, adopted as it was with the exclusive view of saving money, are indeed numbered. If the financial disturbances of the empire have conjured up its political difficulties, the latter, in their turn, are sure to react on the former. It is from this state of the French empire that the recent outbreaks in Spain and Italy,[359] as well as the pending Scandinavian complications,[b] receive their true importance.

Written on July 10, 1857

First published in the *New-York Daily Tribune,* No. 5075, July 27, 1857 as a leading article

Reproduced from the newspaper

[a] Napoleon III's speech at the opening session of the Council-General of Agriculture, Commerce and Industry on April 7, 1850, *Discours et Messages de Louis-Napoléon Bonaparte...,* p. 78.—*Ed.*

[b] See this volume, pp. 334-35.—*Ed.*

Karl Marx

THE REVOLT IN INDIA

London, July 17, 1857

On the 8th of June, just a month had passed since Delhi fell into the hands of the revolted Sepoys[360] and the proclamation by them of a Mogul Emperor.[a] Any notion, however, of the mutineers being able to keep the ancient capital of India against the British forces would be preposterous. Delhi is fortified only by a wall and a simple ditch, while the hights surrounding and commanding it are already in the possession of the English, who, even without battering the walls, might enforce its surrender in a very short period by the easy process of cutting off its supply of water. Moreover, a motley crew of mutineering soldiers who have murdered their own officers, torn asunder the ties of discipline, and not succeeded in discovering a man upon whom to bestow the supreme command, are certainly the body least likely to organize a serious and protracted resistance. To make confusion more confused, the checkered Delhi ranks are daily swelling from the fresh arrivals of new contingents of mutineers from all parts of the Bengal Presidency, who, as if on a preconcerted plan, are throwing themselves into the doomed city. The two sallies which, on the 30th and 31st of May, the mutineers risked without the walls, and in both of which they were repulsed with heavy losses, seem to have proceeded from despair rather than from any feeling of self-reliance or strength. The only thing to be wondered at is the slowness of the British operations, which, to some degree, however, may be accounted for by the horrors of the season and the want of means of transport. Apart from Gen. Anson, the commander-in-chief, French letters state that about 4,000 Euro-

[a] Bahadur Shah II.—*Ed.*

pean troops have already fallen victims of the deathly heat, and even the English papers confess that in the engagements before Delhi the men suffered more from the sun than from the shot of the enemy. In consequence of its scanty means of conveyance, the main British force stationed at Umballah consumed about twenty-seven days in its march upon Delhi, so that it moved at the rate of about one and a half hours per day. A further delay was caused by the absence of heavy artillery at Umballah, and the consequent necessity of bringing over a siege-train from the nearest arsenal, which was as far off as Phillour, on the further side of the Sutlej.

With all that, the news of the fall of Delhi may be daily expected; but what next? If the uncontested possession by the rebels during a month of the traditionary center of the Indian Empire acted perhaps as the most powerful ferment in completely breaking up the Bengal army, in spreading mutiny and desertion from Calcutta to the Punjaub in the north, and to Rajpootana in the west, and in shaking the British authority from one end of India to the other, no greater mistake could be committed than to suppose that the fall of Delhi, though it may throw consternation among the ranks of the Sepoys, should suffice either to quench the rebellion, to stop its progress, or to restore the British rule. Of the whole native Bengal army, mustering about 80,000 men—composed of about 28,000 Rajpoots, 23,000 Brahmins,[361] 13,000 Mahometans, 5,000 Hindoos of inferior castes, and the rest Europeans—30,000 have disappeared in consequence of mutiny, desertion, or dismission from the ranks. As to the rest of that army, several of the regiments have openly declared that they will remain faithful and support the British authority, excepting in the matter in which the native troops are now engaged: they will not aid the authorities against the mutineers of the native regiments, and will, on the contrary, assist their "bhaies" (brothers). The truth of this has been exemplified in almost every station from Calcutta. The native regiments remained passive for a time; but, as soon as they fancied themselves strong enough, they mutinied. An Indian correspondent of *The London Times* leaves no doubt as to the "loyalty" of the regiments which have not yet pronounced, and the native inhabitants who have not yet made common cause with the rebels.

"If you read," he says, "that *all is quiet,* understand it to mean that the native troops have not yet risen in open mutiny; that the discontented part of the inhabitants are not yet in open rebellion; that they are either too weak, or fancy themselves to be so, or that they are waiting for a more fitting time. Where you read of the 'manifestation of loyalty' in any of the Bengal native regiments, cavalry or infantry, understand it to mean that one half of the regiments thus favorably mentioned only are really faithful; the other half are but acting a part, the better to find the Europeans off their guard, when the proper time arrives, or, by warding off suspicion, have it the more in their power to aid their mutinous companions."[a]

In the Punjaub, open rebellion has only been prevented by disbanding the native troops. In Oude, the English can only be said to keep Lucknow, the residency,[362] while everywhere else the native regiments have revolted, escaped with their ammunition, burned all the bungalows to the ground, and joined with the inhabitants who have taken up arms. Now, the real position of the English army is best demonstrated by the fact that it was thought necessary, in the Punjaub as well as the Rajpootana, to establish flying corps. This means that the English cannot depend either on their Sepoy troops or on the natives to keep the communication open between their scattered forces. Like the French during the Peninsular war,[363] they command only the spot of ground held by their own troops, and the next neighborhood domineered by that spot; while for communication between the disjoined members of their army they depend on flying corps, the action of which, most precarious in itself, loses naturally in intensity in the same measure that it spreads over a greater extent of space. The actual insufficiency of the British forces is further proved by the fact that, for removing treasures from disaffected stations, they were constrained to have them conveyed by Sepoys themselves, who, without any exception, broke out in rebellion on the march, and absconded with the treasures confided to them. As the troops sent from England will, in the best case, not arrive before November, and as it would be still more dangerous to draw off European troops from the presidencies of Madras and Bombay—the Tenth regiment of Madras Sepoys, having already shown symptoms of disaffection—any idea of collecting the regular taxes throughout the Bengal presidency must be abandoned, and the process of decomposition be allowed to go on. Even if we suppose that the Burmese will not improve the occasion, that the Maharajah of Gwalior[b] will continue supporting the English, and the Ruler of Nepaul,[c] commanding the finest Indian army, remain quiet; that disaffected Peshawur will not combine with the restless Hill tribes, and that the Shah of Persia[d] will not be silly enough to evacuate

---

[a] "Agra, June 3", *The Times,* No. 22733, July 15, 1857.—*Ed.*
[b] Sindhia.—*Ed.*
[c] Jung Bahadur.—*Ed.*
[d] Nasr-ed-Din.—*Ed.*

Herat—still, the whole Bengal presidency must be reconquered, and the whole Anglo-Indian army remade. The cost of this enormous enterprise will altogether fall upon the British people. As to the notion put forward by Lord Granville in the House of Lords, of the East India Company[364] being able to raise, by Indian loans, the necessary means,[a] its soundness may be judged from the effects produced by the disturbed state of the north-western provinces on the Bombay money market. An immediate panic seized the native capitalists, very large sums were withdrawn from the banks, Government securities proved almost unsalable, and hoarding to a great extent commenced, not only in Bombay but in its environs also.

Written on July 17, 1857

First published unsigned in the *New-York Daily Tribune,* No. 5082, August 4, 1857

Reproduced from the newspaper

[a] Lord Granville's speech in the House of Lords on July 16, 1857, *The Times,* No. 22735, July 17, 1857.—*Ed.*

Karl Marx

THE INDIAN QUESTION

London, July, 28 1857

The three hours' speech delivered last night in "The Dead House,"[365] by Mr. Disraeli, will gain rather than lose by being read instead of being listened to.[a] For some time, Mr. Disraeli affects an awful solemnity of speech, an elaborate slowness of utterance and a passionless method of formality, which, however consistent they may be with his peculiar notions of the dignity becoming a Minister in expectance, are really distressing to his tortured audience. Once he succeeded in giving even commonplaces the pointed appearance of epigrams. Now he contrives to bury even epigrams in the conventional dullness of respectability. An orator who, like Mr. Disraeli, excels in handling the dagger rather than in wielding the sword, should have been the last to forget Voltaire's warning, that "Tous les genres sont bons excepté le genre ennuyeux."[b]

Beside these technical peculiarities which characterize Mr. Disraeli's present manner of eloquence, he, since Palmerston's accession to power, has taken good care to deprive his parliamentary exhibitions of every possible interest of actuality. His speeches are not intended to carry his motions, but his motions are intended to prepare for his speeches. They might be called self-denying motions, since they are so constructed as neither to harm the adversary, if carried, nor to damage the proposer, if lost. They mean, in fact, to be neither carried nor lost, but simply to be

---

[a] Here and below Disraeli's speech in the House of Commons on July 27, 1857, *The Times,* No. 22744, July 28, 1857.— *Ed.*

[b] "All genres are good except the boring ones (F. M. A. Voltaire, *L'enfant prodigue,* Preface).— *Ed.*

dropped. They belong neither to the acids nor to the alkalis, but are born neutrals. The speech is not the vehicle of action, but the hypocrisy of action affords the opportunity for a speech. Such, indeed, may be the classical and final form of parliamentary eloquence; but then, at all events, the final form of parliamentary eloquence must not demur to sharing the fate of all final forms of parliamentarism—that of being ranged under the category of nuisances. Action, as Aristotle said, is the ruling law of the drama.[a] So it is of political oratory. Mr. Disraeli's speech on the Indian revolt might be published in the tracts of the Society for the Propagation of Useful Knowledge, or it might be delivered to a mechanics' institution,[366] or tendered as a prize essay to the Academy of Berlin. This curious impartiality of his speech as to the place where, and the time when, and the occasion on which it was delivered, goes far to prove that it fitted neither place, time, nor occasion. A chapter on the decline of the Roman Empire which might read exceedingly well in Montesquieu or Gibbon[b] would prove an enormous blunder if put in the mouth of a Roman Senator, whose peculiar business it was to stop that very decline. It is true that in our modern parliaments, a part lacking neither dignity nor interest might be imagined of an independent orator who, while despairing of influencing the actual course of events, should content himself to assume a position of ironical neutrality. Such a part was more or less successfully played by the late M. Garnier Pagès—not the Garnier Pagès of Provisional Government memory in Louis Philippe's Chamber of Deputies; but Mr. Disraeli, the avowed leader of an obsolete faction,[367] would consider even success in this line as a supreme failure. The revolt of the Indian army afforded certainly a magnificent opportunity for oratorical display. But, apart from his dreary manner of treating the subject, what was the gist of the motion which he made the pretext for his speech? It was no motion at all. He feigned to be anxious for becoming acquainted with two official papers, the one of which he was not quite sure to exist, and the other of which he was sure not immediately to bear on the subject in question. Consequently his speech and his motion lacked any point of contact save this, that the motion heralded a speech without an object, and that the object confessed itself not worth a

[a] Aristoteles, *De Poetica*, 6.—*Ed.*

[b] [Ch.-L. de Montesquieu,] *Considérations sur les causes de la grandeur des Romains, et de leur décadance* and E. Gibbon, *The History of the Decline and Fall of the Roman Empire*.—*Ed.*

speech. Still, as the highly elaborated opinion of the most distinguished out-of-office statesman of England, Mr. Disraeli's speech ought to attract the attention of foreign countries. I shall content myself with giving in his *ipsissima verba*[a] a short analysis of his "considerations on the decline of the Anglo-Indian Empire".

"Does the disturbance in India indicate a military mutiny, or is it a national revolt? Is the conduct of the troops the consequence of a sudden impulse, or is it the result of an organized conspiracy?"

Upon these points Mr. Disraeli asserts the whole question to hinge. Until the last ten years, he affirmed, the British empire in India was founded on the old principle of *divide et impera*—but that principle was put into action by respecting the different nationalities of which India consisted, by avoiding to tamper with their religion, and by protecting their landed property. The Sepoy army served as a safety-valve to absorb the turbulent spirits of the country. But of late years a new principle has been adopted in the government of India—the principle of destroying nationality. The principle has been realized by the forcible destruction of native princes, the disturbance of the settlement of property, and the tampering with the religion of the people. In 1848 the financial difficulties of the East India Company had reached that point that it became necessary to augment its revenues one way or the other. Then a minute in Council[368] was published, in which was laid down the principle, almost without disguise, that the only mode by which an increased revenue could be obtained was by enlarging the British territories at the expense of the native princes. Accordingly, on the death of the Rajah of Sattara,[b] his adoptive heir was not acknowledged by the East India Company, but the Raj absorbed in its own dominions. From that moment the system of annexation was acted upon whenever a native prince died without natural heirs. The principle of adoption—the very corner-stone of Indian society—was systematically set aside by the Government. Thus were forcibly annexed to the British Empire the Rajs of more than a dozen independent princes from 1848-54. In 1854 the Raj of Berar, which comprised 80,000 square miles of land, a population from 4,000,000 to 5,000,000, and enormous treasures, was forcibly seized. Mr. Disraeli ends the list of forcible annexations with Oude, which brought the East India Government in collision not only with the Hindoos, but also with the

[a] Very words.—*Ed.*
[b] Appa Sahib.—*Ed.*

Mohammedans. Mr. Disraeli then goes on showing how the settlement of property in India was disturbed by the new system of government during the last ten years.

"The principle of the law of adoption," he says, "is not the prerogative of princes and principalities in India, it applies to every man in Hindostan who has landed property, and who professes the Hindoo religion."

I quote a passage:

"The great feudatory, or jaguedar, who holds his lands by public service to his lord; and the enamdar, who holds his land free of all land-tax, who corresponds, if not precisely, in a popular sense, at least, with our freeholder[369]—both of these classes—classes most numerous in India—always, on the failure of their natural heirs, find in this principle the means of obtaining successors to their estates. These classes were all touched by the annexation of Sattara, they were touched by the annexation of the territories of the ten inferior but independent princes to whom I have already alluded, and they were more than touched, they were terrified to the last degree, when the annexation of the Raj of Berar took place. What man was safe? What feudatory, what freeholder who had not a child of his own loins was safe throughout India? [Hear, hear]. These were not idle fears; they were extensively acted upon and reduced to practice. The resumption of jagheers and of inams commenced for the first time in India. There have been, no doubt, impolitic moments when attempts have been made to inquire into titles but no one had ever dreamt of abolishing the law of adoption; therefore no authority, no Government had ever been in a position to resume jagheers and inams the holders of which had left no natural heirs. Here was a new source of revenue; but while all these things were acting upon the minds of these classes of Hindoos, the Government took another step to disturb the settlement of property, to which I must now call the attention of the House. The House is aware, no doubt, from reading the evidence taken before the Committee of 1853, that there are great portions of the land of India which are exempt from the land-tax. Being free from land-tax in India is far more than equivalent to freedom from the land-tax in this country, for, speaking generally and popularly, the land-tax in India is the whole taxation of the State.

"The origin of these grants is difficult to penetrate, but they are undoubtedly of great antiquity. They are of different kinds. Beside the private freeholds, which are very extensive, there are large grants of land free from the land-tax with which mosques and temples have been endowed."

On the pretext of fraudulent claims of exemption, the British Governor General[a] took upon himself to examine the titles of the Indian landed estates. Under the new system, established in 1848,

"That plan of investigating titles was at once embraced, as a proof of a powerful Government, vigorous Executive, and most fruitful source of public revenue. Therefore commissions were issued to inquire into titles to landed estates in the Presidency of Bengal and adjoining country. They were also issued in the Presidency of Bombay, and surveys were ordered to be made in the newly-settled provinces, in order that these commissions might be conducted, when the surveys

[a] Dalhousie.—*Ed.*

were completed, with due efficiency. Now there is no doubt that, during the last nine years, the action of these commissions of Inquiry into the freehold property of landed estates in India has been going on at an enormous rate, and immense results have been obtained."

Mr. Disraeli computes that the resumption of estates from their proprietors is not less than £500,000 a year in the Presidency of Bengal; £370,000 in the Presidency of Bombay; £200,000 in the Punjaub, &c. Not content with this one method of seizing upon the property of the natives, the British Government discontinued the pensions to the native grandees, to pay which it was bound by treaty.

"This," says Mr. Disraeli, "is confiscation by a new means, but upon a most extensive, startling and shocking scale."

Mr. Disraeli then treats the tampering with the religion of the natives, a point upon which we need not dwell. From all his premises he arrives at the conclusion that the present Indian disturbance is not a military mutiny, but a national revolt, of which the Sepoys are the acting instruments only. He ends his harangue by advising the Government to turn their attention to the internal improvement of India, instead of pursuing its present course of aggression.

Written on July 28, 1857 — Reproduced from the newspaper

First published unsigned in the *New-York Daily Tribune,* No. 5091, August 14, 1857

Karl Marx

INDIAN NEWS[370]

London, July 31, 1857

The last Indian mail, conveying news from Delhi up to the 17th June, and from Bombay up to the 1st of July, realizes the most gloomy anticipations. When Mr. Vernon Smith, the President of the Board of Control,[371] first informed the House of Commons of the Indian revolt, he confidently stated that the next mail would bring the news that Delhi had been razed to the ground.[a] The mail arrived, but Delhi was not yet "wiped out of the pages of history." It was then said that the battery train could not be brought up before the 9th of June, and that the attack on the doomed city must consequently be delayed to that date. The 9th of June passed away without being distinguished by any remarkable incident. On the 12th and 15th June some events occurred, but rather in the opposite direction, Delhi being not stormed by the English, but the English being attacked by the insurgents, the repeated sorties of whom were, however, repulsed. The fall of Delhi is thus again postponed, the alleged cause being now no longer the sole want of siege-artillery, but General Barnard's resolution to wait upon re-enforcements, as his forces—about 3,000 men—were totally inadequate to the capture of the ancient capital defended by 30,000 Sepoys, and possessed of all the military stores. The rebels had even established a camp outside the Ajmer gate. Until now, all military writers were unanimous in considering an English force of 3,000 men quite sufficient for crushing a Sepoy army of 30,000 or 40,000 men; and if such was

[a] V. Smith's speech in the House of Commons on June 29, 1857, *The Times*, No. 22720, June 30, 1857.—*Ed.*

not the case, how could England—to use an expression of *The London Times*—ever be able to "reconquer" India?[a]

The British army in India amounts actually to 30,000 men. The utmost number they can dispatch from England within the next half year cannot exceed 20,000 or 25,000 men, of whom 6,000 men are to fill up vacancies among the European ranks in India, and of whom the additional force of 18,000 or 19,000 men will be reduced by loss from the voyage, by loss from the climate, and by other casualties to about 14,000 troops able to appear on the theater of war. The British army must resolve upon meeting the mutineers in very disproportionate numbers, or it must renounce meeting them at all. Still we are at a loss to understand the slowness of the concentration of their forces around Delhi. If at this season of the year, the heat proves an invincible obstacle, which it did not in the days of Sir Charles Napier, some months later, on the arrival of the European troops, the rains will afford a still more conclusive pretext for a standstill. It should never be forgotten that the present mutiny had, in fact, already begun in the month of January, and that the British Government had thus received ample warning for keeping its powder dry and its forces ready.

The prolonged hold of Delhi by the Sepoys in face of an English besieging army has, of course, produced its natural result. The mutiny was spreading to the very gates of Calcutta, fifty Bengal regiments had ceased to exist, the Bengal army itself had become a myth of the past, and the Europeans, dispersed over an immense extent of land, and blocked up in insulated spots, were either butchered by the rebels, or had taken up position of desperate defense. At Calcutta itself the Christian inhabitants formed a volunteer guard, after a plot, said to have been most complete in its detail, for surprising the seat of the Government, had been discovered, and the native troops there stationed had been disbanded. At Benares, an attempt at disarming a native regiment was resisted by a body of Sikhs[372] and the Thirteenth irregular cavalry. This fact is very important, as it shows that the Sikhs, like the Mohammedans, were making common cause with the Brahmins, and that thus a general union against the British rule, of all the different tribes, was rapidly progressing. It had been an article of faith with the English people, that the Sepoy army constituted their whole strength in India. Now, all at once, they feel quite satisfied that that very army constitutes their sole

[a] *The Times*, No. 22740, July 23, 1857, leading article.—*Ed.*

danger. During the last Indian debates, Mr. Vernon Smith, the President of the Board of Control, still declared that

"the fact cannot be too much insisted upon that there is no connection whatever between the native princes and the revolt."[a]

Two days later the same Vernon Smith had to publish a dispatch containing this ominous paragraph:

"On the 14th of June the ex-King of Oude,[b] implicated in the conspiracy by intercepted papers, was lodged in Fort William,[373] and his followers disarmed."[c]

By and by there will ooze out other facts able to convince even John Bull himself that what he considers a military mutiny is in truth a national revolt.

The English press feigns to derive great comfort from the conviction that the revolt had not yet spread beyond the boundaries of the Bengal Presidency, and that not the least doubt was entertained of the loyalty of the Bombay and Madras armies. However, this pleasant view of the case seems singularly to clash with the fact conveyed by the last mail of a mutiny of the Nizam's[d] cavalry having broken out at Aurungabad. Aurungabad being the capital of the district of the same name which belongs to the Bombay Presidency, the truth is that the last mail announces a commencement of revolt of the Bombay army. The Aurungabad mutiny is, indeed, said to have been at once put down by General Woodburn. But was not the Meerut mutiny said to have been put down at once? Did not the Lucknow mutiny, after having been quenched by Sir H. Lawrence, make a more formidable reappearance a fortnight later? Will it not be recollected that the very first announcement of mutiny in the Indian army was accompanied with the announcement of restored order? Although the bulk of the Bombay and Madras armies is composed of low caste men, there are still mixed to every regiment some hundred Rajpoots,[374] a number quite sufficient to form the connecting links with the high caste rebels of the Bengal army. The Punjaub is declared to be quiet, but at the same time we are informed that "at

---

[a] V. Smith's speech in the House of Commons on July 27, 1857, *The Times*, No. 22744, July 28, 1857.—*Ed.*

[b] Wajid Ali Shah.—*Ed.*

[c] Dispatch from the British Vice-Consul at Trieste, *The Times*, No. 22746, July 30, 1857.—*Ed.*

[d] Ruler of the Hyderabad Principality.—*Ed.*

Ferozepore, on the 13th of June, military executions had taken place,"[a] while Vaughan's corps—5th Punjaub Infantry—is praised for "having behaved admirably in pursuit of the 55th Native Infantry."[a] This, it must be confessed, is a very queer sort of "quiet."

Written on July 31, 1857

First published unsigned in the *New-York Daily Tribune,* No. 5091, August 14, 1857

Reproduced from the newspaper

---

[a] Reprint from *The Morning Post* of July 30, *The Times,* No. 22747, July 31, 1857.—*Ed.*

Karl Marx

STATE OF THE INDIAN INSURRECTION

London, August 4, 1857

On the arrival at London of the voluminous reports conveyed by the last Indian mail, the meagre outlines of which had been anticipated by the electric telegraph, the rumor of the capture of Delhi was rapidly spreading and winning so much consistency as to influence the transactions of the Stock Exchange. It was another edition of the capture of Sevastopol hoax,[375] on a reduced scale. The slightest examination of the dates and contents of the Madras papers, from which the favorable news was avowedly derived, would have sufficed to dispel the delusion. The Madras information professed to rest upon private letters from Agra dated June 17, but an official notification, issued at Lahore, on the 17th of June, announces that up to 4 o'clock in the afternoon of the 16th, all was quiet before Delhi, while *The Bombay Times*, dated July 1, states that

> "General Barnard was waiting for re-enforcements on the morning of the 17th, after having repelled several sorties."[a]

This much, as to the date of the Madras information. As to its contents, these are evidently made up of General Barnard's bulletin, dated June 8, on his forcible occupation of the hights of Delhi, and of some private reports relating to the sallies of the besieged on the 12th and 14th June.

A military plan of Delhi and its cantonments has at last been compiled by Captain Lawrence, from the unpublished plans of the

[a] "(From *The Bombay Times* of July 1)", *The Times*, No. 22748, August 1, 1857.— *Ed.*

East India Company. Hence we see that Delhi is not quite so weakly fortified as was at first asserted, nor quite so strongly as is now pretended. It possesses a citadel, to be taken by escalade or by regular approaches. The walls, being more than seven miles in extent, are built of solid masonry, but of no great hight. The ditch is narrow and not very deep, and the flanking works do not properly enfilade the curtain. Martello towers[376] exist at intervals. They are semi-circular in form, and loopholed for musketry. Spiral staircases lead from the top of the walls down through the towers to chambers, on a level with the ditch, and those are loopholed for infantry fire, which may prove very annoying to an escalading party crossing the ditch. The bastions defending the curtains are also furnished with banquettes for riflemen, but these may be kept down by shelling. When the insurrection broke out, the arsenal in the interior of the city contained 900,000 cartridges, two complete siege trains, a large number of field guns and 10,000 muskets. The powder-magazine had been long since removed, at the desire of the inhabitants, from the city to the cantonments outside Delhi, and contained not less than 10,000 barrels. The commanding hights occupied by Gen. Barnard on the 8th of June are situated in a north-westerly direction from Delhi, where the cantonments outside the walls were also established.[a]

From the description, resting on authentic plans, it will be understood that the stronghold of the revolt must have succumbed before a single *coup de main*, if the British force now before Delhi had been there on the 26th of May, and they could have been there if supplied with sufficient carriage. A review of the list published in *The Bombay Times*, and republished in the London papers, of the number of regiments that had revolted, to the end of June, and of the dates on which they revolted,[b] proves conclusively that, on the 26th of May, Delhi was yet occupied by 4,000 to 5,000 men only; a force which could not one moment have thought of defending a wall seven miles in extent. Meerut being only forty miles distant from Delhi, and having, since the commencement of 1853, always served as the headquarters of the Bengal artillery, possessed the principal laboratory for military scientific purposes, and afforded the parade ground for exercise in the use of field and siege ordnance; it becomes the more

[a] H. [W.] Barnard's bulletin of June 8 on the occupation of the hights of Delhi, *The Times*, No. 22748, August 1, 1857.—*Ed.*

[b] "(From *The Bombay Times* of July 1)", *The Times*, No. 22748, August 1, 1857.— *Ed.*

incomprehensible that the British commander was in want of the means necessary for the execution of one of those *coups de main* by which the British forces in India always know how to secure their supremacy over the natives. First we were informed that the siege train was waited for[a]; then that re-enforcements were wanted; and now *The Press*, one of the best informed London papers, tells us,

> "It is known by our Government for a fact that General Barnard is deficient in stores and ammunition, and that his supply of the latter is limited to 24 rounds a man."

From General Barnard's own bulletin on the occupation of the hights of Delhi, which is dated the 8th of June, we see that he originally intended assailing Delhi on the following day. Instead of being able to follow up this plan, he was, by one accident or the other, confined to taking up the defensive against the besieged.

At this very moment it is extremely difficult to compute the forces on either part. The statements of the Indian press are altogether self-contradictory; but we think some reliance may be put upon an Indian correspondence of the Bonapartist *Pays*, which seems to emanate from the French Consul at Calcutta.[b] According to his statement, the army of Gen. Barnard was, on the 14th of June, composed of about 5,700 men, which was expected to be doubled (?) by the re-enforcements expected on the 20th of the same month. His train was composed of 30 heavy siege guns, while the forces of the insurgents were estimated at 40,000 men, badly organized, but richly furnished with all the means of attack and defense.

We remark *en passant*, that the 3,000 insurgents encamped without the Ajmer gate, probably in the Gazee Khan's tombs, are not, as some London papers imagine, fronting the English force, but, on the contrary, separated from them by the whole breadth of Delhi; the Ajmer gate being situated on one extremity of the south-western part of modern Delhi to the north of the ruins of ancient Delhi. On that side [of] the town nothing can prevent the insurgents from establishing some more such camps. On the north-eastern, or river side of the city, they command the ship bridge, and remain in continued connection with their countrymen, able to receive uninterrupted supplies of men and stores. On

---

[a] See this volume, p. 314.— *Ed.*

[b] De Valbezen.— *Ed.*

a smaller scale Delhi offers the image of a fortress, keeping (like Sevastopol) open its lines of communication with the interior of its own country.

The delay in the British operations has not only allowed the besieged to concentrate large numbers for the defense, but the sentiment of having held Delhi during many weeks, harassed the European forces through repeated sallies, together with the news daily pouring in of fresh revolts of the entire army, has, of course, strengthened the *morale* of the Sepoys. The English, with their small forces, can, of course, not think of investing the town, but must storm it. However, if the next regular mail bring not the news of the capture of Delhi, we may almost be sure that, for some months, all serious operations on the part of the British will have to be suspended. The rainy season will have set in in real earnest, and protect the north-eastern face of the city by filling the ditch with "the deep and rapid current of the Jumna," while a thermometer ranging from 75 to 102,[a] combined with an average fall of nine inches of rain, would scourge the Europeans with the genuine Asiatic cholera. Then would be verified the words of Lord Ellenborough,

> "I am of opinion that Sir H. Barnard cannot remain where he is—the climate forbids it. When the heavy rains set in he will be cut off from Meerut, from Umballah and from the Punjaub; he will be imprisoned in a very narrow strip of land, and he will be in a situation, I will not say of peril, but in a situation which can only end in ruin and destruction. I trust that he will retire in time."[b]

Everything, then, as far as Delhi is concerned, depends on the question whether or not Gen. Barnard found himself sufficiently provided with men and ammunition to undertake the assault of Delhi during the last weeks of June. On the other hand, a retreat on his part would immensely strengthen the moral force of the insurrection, and perhaps decide the Bombay and Madras armies upon openly joining it.

Written on August 4, 1857

First published unsigned in the *New-York Daily Tribune*, No. 5094, August 18, 1857; reprinted in the *New-York Semi-Weekly Tribune*, No. 1277, August 21, 1857

Reproduced from the *New-York Daily Tribune*

---

[a] Fahrenheit (24° to 39° Celsius).—*Ed.*

[b] Lord Ellenborough's speech in the House of Lords on July 31, 1857, *The Times*, No. 22748, August 1, 1857.—*Ed.*

Karl Marx

THE ORIENTAL QUESTION

London, Aug. 11, 1857

The Oriental question, which some fourteen months ago was said to have been settled by a peace at Paris,[377] is now fairly reopened by a diplomatic strike at Constantinople. There the embassies of France, Russia, Prussia and Sardinia have hauled down their flags, and broken off their relations with the Porte. The Embassadors of England and Austria,[a] backing the resistance of the Divan against the demands of the Four Powers, simultaneously declared they should not shun any responsibility likely to arise out of the conflict.

These events occurred on the 6th of the present month. The story of the drama is the old one, but the *dramatis personae* have shifted parts, and the plot is made to bear some air of novelty, through the contrivance of a new *mise en scène.* It is now not Russia, but France, that occupies the vanguard. M. Thouvenel, her Embassador at Constantinople, in a somewhat affected, Menchikoff strain, imperiously called upon the Porte to annul the Moldavian elections, because Vogorides, the Kaimakam[b] of Moldavia, by unfair interference, and in violation of the treaty of Paris, had contrived to give the Anti-Unionists a majority of representatives.[378] The Porte demurred to this dictation, but declared itself willing to summon the Kaimakam to Constantinople, there to answer the accusations brought forward against his administration. This proposal M. Thouvenel haughtily rejected, insisting on the inquiry into the electoral operations being

---

[a] Stratford Canning Stratford de Redcliffe and Anton von Prokesch-Osten.—*Ed.*

[b] Lieutenant.—*Ed.*

handed over to the European Commission of reorganization installed at Bucharest. Since the majority of that Commission is formed of the Commissioners of France, Russia, Prussia and Sardinia, the very parties working for the union of the Danubian Provinces, and charging Vogorides with the crime of illegal interference, the Porte, pushed on by the Embassadors of Great Britain and Austria, of course declined making its avowed antagonists the judges in their own cause. Then the catastrophe took place.

The real point in question is evidently the same that gave origin to the Russian war, viz., the virtual separation of the Danubian Provinces from Turkey, this time attempted not in the form of a "material guarantee," but in the form of a union of the Principalities under the sway of a European puppet-prince. Russia, in her calm, circumspect, patient way, never swerves from her settled purpose. Already she has succeeded in arraying, in an affair in which she alone is interested, some of her enemies against the rest, and may thus expect to subdue the one by the other. As to Bonaparte, he is actuated by various motives. He hopes to find a safety-valve against disaffection at home by complication abroad. He is immensely flattered that Russia deigns to figure in a French mask, and allows him to lead the dance. His empire of fictions must content itself with theatrical triumphs, and, in the depths of his soul, he may delude himself with the notion of putting, with the aid of Russia, a Bonaparte on the mock throne of a Roumania extemporized by protocols. Since the famous Warsaw Conference of 1850,[379] and the march of an Austrian army to the northern confines of Germany, Prussia pants for some little revenge to be wreaked on Austria, if it be allowed at the same time to keep out of harm's way. Sardinia rests all her hopes on a conflict with Austria, to be no longer waged by the dangerous alliance with Italian revolutions, but in the rear of the despotic powers of the continent.

Austria is as earnest in counteracting the union of the Danubian Principalities as Russia is in forwarding it. She knows the prime motive of that scheme, which is still more immediately aimed at her own power than that of the Porte. Palmerston at last, the principal stock in trade of whose popularity consists of a spurious Anti-Russianism, must of course feign to share the real terrors of Francis Joseph. He, by all means, must appear to side with Austria and the Porte, and not to give way to Russian pressure unless constrained by France. Such is the position of the respective parties. The Rouman people are but a pretext, a thing quite out of the question. Even the most desperate enthusiasts will scarcely be able to muster a sufficient quantity of credulity to believe in Louis Napoleon's sincere zeal for the purity of popular elections, or in Russia's ardent desire to strengthen the Rouman nationality, the destruction of which has never ceased to form an object of her intrigues and her wars since the days of Peter the Great.

A paper started at Brussels by certain self-styled Rouman patriots, and called *L'Etoile du Danube*, has just published a series of documents relating to the Moldavian elections, the substantial part of which I propose to translate for *The Tribune*. It consists of letters addressed to Nicholas Vogorides, the Kaimakam of Moldavia, by Stephen Vogorides, his father; by Musurus, his brother-in-law, and the Turkish Embassador at London; by A. Vogorides, his brother, and the Secretary to the Turkish Embassy at London; by M. Fotiades, another brother-in-law of his, and the Chargé d'Affaires of the Moldavian Government at Constantinople; and, lastly, by Baron Prokesch, the Austrian Internuncio[380] at the Sublime Porte. This correspondence was some time since stolen from the Jassy Palace of the Kaimakam, and the *Etoile du Danube* now boasts of the possession of the original letters. The *Etoile du Danube* considers burglary quite a respectable road to diplomatic information, and in this view of the case seems backed by the whole of the official European press.

SECRET CORRESPONDENCE RELATING TO THE MOLDAVIAN ELECTIONS, PUBLISHED BY THE *ÉTOILE DU DANUBE*[a]

Fragment of a Letter of M. C. Musurus, the Ottoman Embassador at London, to the Kaimakam Vogorides

London, April 23, 1857

"I tell you confidentially that Lord Clarendon approves your reply to the Consuls of France and Russia[b] concerning the press. He has found it honorable, just and legal. I have recommended to his Excellency the wisdom of your conduct in the actual circumstances. I write to the Porte, and endeavor to secure your success in the brilliant career you show yourself so worthy of. You will save this fine country from the danger into which traitors unworthy the name of Moldavians try to drag it. Stimulated by material interests and rewards, they push their perversity to the point of contributing to transform Moldavia, their fatherland, into

[a] "Extraits de lettres confidentielles adressées au caïmacam de Moldavie par différents personnages politiques", *L'Étoile du Danube*, No. 50, August 8, 1857.—*Ed.*

[b] Victor Place and Popoff.—*Ed.*

a simple appendage to Wallachia, and to wipe it out from the map of self-governing peoples. On the pretext of founding some fabulous Roumania, they want to reduce Moldavia and the Moldavians to the state of Ireland and the Irish, little caring for the maledictions of generations present and to come. You fulfill the duty of an honest and virtuos patriot in detesting such rubbish, which is not ashamed of calling itself the National party. The Unionist party may call itself the National party in Wallachia, where it aims at the aggrandizement of the fatherland; but from the same reason it cannot be designated in Moldavia but by the name of the anti-national party. There the only national party is that which resists the union... The English Government is hostile to the union. Do not doubt that. I tell you confidentially that instructions in this sense have been recently sent to the English Commissioner at Bucharest[a] (who is my friend), and your Excellency will shortly see the results of these instructions. The answer you have given to the Consuls of France and Russia in regard to the Press was a proper one... It was your duty, as the chief of a self-governing Principality, to beat back the scandalous and illegal intervention of foreigners in internal affairs. Yours is not the fault, if those two Consuls have placed themselves in a false position, from which their Governments can but enable them to withdraw by recalling them... I fear not less the Porte, constrained by foreign intervention, be placed in the unpleasant situation to involuntarily withhold from you, in its correspondence with you, all the satisfaction it derives from and all the praise it bestows upon your moderate and prudent conduct. The Kaimakam of Moldavia, you must certainly submit to the supreme Government; but, at the same time, the chief of that independent Principality, and a Moldavian Boyar, too, you have to fulfill your duty toward your country, and, if need be, to represent to the Porte that the first of the privileges *ab antiquo*[b] of the Principalities is the existence of Moldavia as a distinct, self-governing Principality."

A. Vogorides, Secretary to the Turkish Embassy at London, to the Kaimakam Vogorides

"I hasten to inform you that your brother-in-law has just seen Lord Palmerston. He has brought important news as to the disposition of his Lordship against the union of the Principalities. Lord Palmerston is a thorough adversary of the union; he considers it as subversive of the rights of our sovereign, and consequently analogous instructions will be sent to Sir Henry Bulwer, the Commissioner of Great Britain in the Principalities. Thus, as I wrote you before, it is necessary for you to strain every nerve for preventing the Moldavians from expressing any wishes in favor of the union and for showing you worthy of the benevolence of the Porte, or the support of England and Austria. The three Powers being decided upon obstructing the union, you need not care about what the French intend or threaten to do, whose journals treat you like a Greek."

The Same to the Same

London April 15, 1857

"I am advising you to blindly follow in everything the Austrian Consul,[c] even if he behaved still more fastidiously, and in spite of all his faults. You must consider

[a] William Henry Lytton Earle Bulwer.— *Ed.*
[b] Time-honoured.— *Ed.*
[c] Oscar de Goedel Lannoy.— *Ed.*

that that man acts only according to the instructions of his Government. Austria agrees with the ideas of the Sublime Porte and Great Britain, and it is for this reason that, when Austria is content, Turkey and England will be so. I repeat, therefore, that you must comply with the counsels and wishes of the Austrian Consul, and without the least objection, employ all the persons he may propose to you, without informing you whether the persons recommended be perverse or ill-famed. It suffices that these men be sincerely against the union. That suffices; for, if the union should be proclaimed by the Moldavian Divan, Austria would accuse you of being responsible, because of having resisted the advice of her Consul, so active in the opposition to the union. As to England, she will never allow the union to be realized, even if all the Divans pronounced for it. Nevertheless, it is desirable that you prevent the Moldavian Divan from pronouncing for the union, because then the difficulties of the three Powers will be less with respect to France and Russia, and thus they will owe you their gratitude... You were quite right in not granting the liberty of the press which Moldavian madcaps, friends of Russia under a French mask, would misuse for bringing about a popular move in favor of the union... Do prevent maneuvers of that sort. I feel sure that, if the *Etoile du Danube* and the like bad publications were published in France, the Government would not fail to immediately dispatch their authors to Cayenne.[381] France, which longs for liberty-clubs and political reunions in Moldo-Wallachia, should commence by admitting them at home, instead of inflicting banishment and warnings upon all journalists who dare speak a little freely. *Charité bien ordonnée*, as the French proverb says, *commence par soi-même.*[a] The Paris Treaty does not speak of the union of the Principalities; it simply says that the Divans shall pronounce themselves on the internal reorganization of the country; but the madcaps who make the union their watchword, altogether forgetting the clause of the treaty, instead of pondering over internal reforms, are exclusively bent on a new international organization, meditate independence under foreign princes... England, quite agreed with Austria, is completely opposed to the union and will, in concert with the Sublime Porte, never allow it to be carried out. If the French Consul tells you the contrary, do not believe him, because he lies."

Written on August 11, 1857

First published unsigned in the *New-York Daily Tribune*, No. 5102, August 27, 1857

Reproduced from the newspaper

[a] "Charity well directed should begin at home" (Montluc, *La Comédie des Proverbes*, Act III, 7).— *Ed.*

Karl Marx

THE INDIAN INSURRECTION

London, Aug. 14, 1857

When the Indian news, conveyed by the Trieste telegraph on the 30th of July, and by the Indian mail on the 1st of August, first arrived,[a] we showed at once, from their contents and their dates, that the capture of Delhi was a miserable hoax, and a very inferior imitation of the never-to-be-forgotten fall of Sevastopol.[382] Yet such is the unfathomable depth of John Bull's gullibility, that his ministers, his stock-jobbers and his press had, in fact, contrived to persuade him that the very news which laid bare General Barnard's merely defensive position contained evidence of the complete extermination of his enemies. From day to day this hallucination grew stronger, till it assumed at last such consistency as to induce even a veteran hand at similar matters, General Sir de Lacy Evans, to proclaim on the night of the 12th of August, amid the cheering echoes of the House of Commons, his belief in the truth of the rumor of the capture of Delhi. After this ridiculous exhibition, however, the bubble was ripe for bursting, and the following day, the 13th of August, brought successive telegraphic dispatches from Trieste and Marseilles, anticipating the Indian mails, and leaving no doubt as to the fact that on the 27th of June Delhi still stood where it had stood before,[b] and that General Barnard, still confined to the defensive, but harassed by frequent furious sorties of the besieged, was very glad to have been able to hold his ground to that time.

In our opinion the next mail is likely to impart the news of the retreat of the English army, or at least facts foreshadowing such a

[a] A reference to the report of the capture of Delhi, which proved false, see this volume, p. 318.— *Ed.*

[b] *The Times*, No. 22758, August 13, 1857.— *Ed.*

retrograde movement. It is certain that the extent of the walls of Delhi forbids the belief that the whole of them can be effectively manned, and, on the contrary, invites to *coups de main* to be executed by concentration and surprise. But Gen. Barnard seems imbued with European notions of fortified towns and sieges and bombardments, rather than prone to those bold eccentricities by which Sir Charles Napier knew how to thunderstrike Asiatic minds. His forces are, indeed, said to have been increased to about 12,000 men, 7,000 Europeans and 5,000 "faithful natives"; but on the other hand, it is not denied that the rebels were daily receiving new reinforcements, so that we may fairly assume that the numerical disproportion between besiegers and besieged has remained the same. Moreover, the only point by the surprise of which General Barnard might insure certain success is the Mogul's Palace, which occupies a commanding position, but the access to which from the river side must become impracticable from the effect of the rainy season, which will have set in, while an attack on the palace between the Cashmere gate and the river would inflict on the assailants the greatest risk in case of failure. Finally, the setting in of the rains is sure to make the securing of his line of communication and retreat the principal object of the General's operations. In one word, we see no reason to believe that he, with his still inadequate forces, should venture upon risking, at the most impracticable period of the year, what he shrunk from undertaking at a more seasonable time. That in spite of the judicial blindness by which the London press contrives to fool itself, there are entertained serious misgivings in the highest quarters, may be seen from Lord Palmerston's organ, *The Morning Post*. The venal gentlemen of that paper inform us:

"We doubt whether even by the next mail after this, we shall hear of the capture of Delhi; *but* we do expect that, as *soon* as the troops now on their march to join the besiegers shall have arrived, with a *sufficiency of large guns*, [which it seems are still missing,] we shall receive intelligence of the fall of the stronghold of the rebels."[a]

It is evident that, by dint of weakness, vacillation, and direct blunders, the British generals have contrived to raise Delhi to the dignity of the political and military center of the Indian revolt. A retreat of the English army, after a prolonged siege, or a mere staying on the defensive, will be regarded as a positive defeat, and

---

[a] *The Morning Post*, No. 26090, August 13, 1857, leading article. Italics and words in brackets belong to Marx.—*Ed.*

give the signal to a general outbreak. It would moreover expose the British troops to a fearful mortality, from which till now they have been protected by the great excitement inherent to a siege full of sorties, encounters, and a hope of soon wreaking a bloody vengeance on their enemies. As to the talk about the apathy of the Hindoos, or even their sympathy with British rule, it is all nonsense. The princes, like true Asiatics, are watching their opportunity. The people in the whole Presidency of Bengal, where not kept in check by a handful of Europeans, are enjoying a blessed anarchy; but there is nobody there against whom they could rise. It is a curious *quid pro quo* to expect an Indian revolt to assume the features of a European revolution.

In the Presidencies of Madras and Bombay, the army having not yet pronounced, the people of course do not stir. The Punjaub, at last, is to this moment the principal central station of the European forces, while its native army is disarmed. To rouse it, the neighboring semi-independent princes must throw their weight into the scale. But that such a ramification of conspiracy as exhibited by the Bengal army could not have been carried on on such an immense scale without the secret connivance and support of the natives, seems as certain as that the great difficulties the English meet with in obtaining supplies and transports—the principal cause of the slow concentration of their troops—do not witness to the good feelings of the peasantry.

The other news conveyed by the telegraphic dispatches are so far important as they show us the revolt rising on the extreme confines of the Punjaub, in Peshawur, and on the other hand striding in a southern direction from Delhi to the Presidency of Bombay, through the stations of Jhansi, Saugor, Indore, Mhow, till we arrive at last at Aurungabad, only 180 miles north-east of Bombay. With respect to Jhansi in Bundelcund, we may remark that it is fortified and may thus become another center of armed rebellion. On the other hand, it is stated that Gen. Van Cortlandt has defeated the mutineers at Sirsah, on his road from the north-west to join Gen. Barnard's force before Delhi, from which he was still 170 miles distant. He had to pass by Jhansi, where he would again encounter the rebels. As to the preparations made by the Home Government, Lord Palmerston seems to think that the most circuitous line is the shortest, and consequently sends his troops round the Cape, instead of through Egypt. The fact that some thousand men destined for China have been intercepted at Ceylon and directed to Calcutta, where the Fifth Fusileers actually arrived on the 2d of July, has afforded him the occasion for breaking a bad joke on those of his obedient Commons who still dared doubt that his Chinese war was quite a "windfall."[a]

Written on August 14, 1857

First published unsigned in the *New-York Daily Tribune,* No. 5104, August 29, 1857; reprinted in the *New-York Semi-Weekly Tribune,* No. 1280, September 1, 1857

Reproduced from the *New-York Daily Tribune*

[a] Palmerston's speech in the House of Commons on August 11, 1857, *The Times,* No. 22757, August 12, 1857.—*Ed.*

Karl Marx

[POLITICAL SITUATION IN EUROPE]

The last sitting but one of the Commons before their prorogation was seized upon by Lord Palmerston to allow them to take some faint glimpses at the entertainments he keeps in store for the English public during the interregnum between the session that has passed away and the session that is to come.[a] The first item of his programme is the announcement of the revival of the Persian war, which as he had stated some months ago, was definitely terminated by a peace concluded on the 4th of March.[b] General Sir de Lacy Evans having expressed the hope that Col. Jacob was ordered back to India with his forces now stationed on the Persian Gulf,[c] Lord Palmerston stated plainly that until Persia had executed the engagements contracted by the treaty, Col. Jacob's troops could not be withdrawn. Herat, however, had not yet been evacuated. There were, on the contrary, rumors afloat affirming that additional forces had been sent by Persia to Herat. This, indeed, had been denied by the Persian Embassador at Paris[d]; but great doubts were justly entertained of the good faith of Persia, and consequently the British forces under Col. Jacob would continue to occupy Bushire. On the day following Lord Palmerston's statement, the news was conveyed by telegraphic dispatch of the categorical demand pressed upon the Persian Government by Mr. Murray for the evacuation of Herat—a

[a] Palmerston's speech in the House of Commons on August 20, 1857, *The Times*, No. 22765, August 21, 1857.—*Ed.*

[b] See this volume, pp. 293-96.—*Ed.*

[c] Sir de Lacy Evans' speech in the House of Commons on August 20, 1857, *The Times*, No. 22765, August 21, 1857.—*Ed.*

[d] Ferrukh Khan.—*Ed.*

demand which may be fairly considered the forerunner of a new declaration of war. Such is the first international effect of the Indian revolt.

The second item of Lord Palmerston's programme makes good for its want of details by the wide perspective it unrolls. When he first announced the withdrawal of large military forces from England to be dispatched to India, he answered his opponents, accusing him of denuding Great Britain of her defensive power, and thus affording foreign countries an opportunity to take advantage of her weakened position, that

"the people of Great Britain would never tolerate any such proceeding, and that men would be raised suddenly and rapidly, sufficient for any contingency that would arrive."[a]

Now, on the eve of the prorogation of Parliament, he speaks in quite a different strain. To the advice of Gen. de Lacy Evans to send out to India the troops in screw line-of-battle ships, he did not reply, as he had done before, by asserting the superiority of the sail to the screw-propeller, but on the contrary, admitted that the General's plan appeared in the first instance highly advantageous. Yet, the House ought to bear in mind, that

"there were other considerations to be kept in view, in regard to the propriety of keeping up sufficient military and naval forces at home... Certain circumstances pointed out the inexpediency of sending out of the country a greater naval force than was absolutely necessary. The steam line-of-battle ships were, no doubt, lying in ordinary, and were of no great use at present; but if any such events as had been alluded to took place, and they wanted their naval forces to put to sea, how could they meet *the danger which threatened,* if they allowed their line-of-battle ships to do the duty of transports to India? They should be falling into a grave error if they sent to India the fleet which *circumstances occurring in Europe* might render it necessary to arm *for their own defense at a very short notice.*"[b]

Lord Palmerston, it will not be denied, plants John Bull on the horns of a very fine dilemma. If he uses the adequate means for a decisive suppression of the Indian revolt, he will be attacked at home; and if he allows the Indian revolt to consolidate, he will, as Mr. Disraeli said,

---

[a] Palmerston's speech in the House of Commons on August 11, 1857, *The Times,* No. 22757, August 12, 1857.—*Ed.*

[b] Palmerston's speech in the House of Commons on August 20, 1857, *The Times,* No. 22765, August 21, 1857 (Marx gives the quotation in his own rendering).—*Ed.*

"find other characters on the stage, with whom to contend, beside the princes of India."[a]

Before casting a glance at the "European circumstances" so mysteriously alluded to, it may not be amiss to gather up the confessions made during the same sitting of the Commons in regard to the actual position of the British forces in India. First, then, all sanguine hopes of a sudden capture of Delhi were dropped as if by mutual agreement, and the highflying expectations of former days came down to the more rational view that they ought to congratulate themselves, if the English were able to maintain their posts until November, when the advance of the re-enforcements sent from home was to take place. In the second instance, misgivings oozed out as to the probability of their losing the most important of those posts, Cawnpore, on the fate of which, as Mr. Disraeli said, everything must depend, and the relief of which he considered of even greater import than the capture of Delhi.[b] From its central position on the Ganges, its bearing on Oude, Rohilcund, Gwalior, and Bundelcund, and its serving as an advanced fort to Delhi, Cawnpore is, in fact, in the present circumstances, a place of prime importance. Lastly, Sir F. Smith, one of the military members of the House, called its attention to the fact that, actually, there were no engineers and sappers with their Indian army, as all of them had deserted, and were likely "to make Delhi a second Saragossa.[383]"[c] On the other hand, Lord Palmerston had neglected to forward from England either any officers or men of the engineer corps.

Returning now to the European events said to be "looming in the future," we are at once astonished at the comment *The London Times* makes on Lord Palmerston's allusions. The French Constitution, it says, might be overthrown, or Napoleon disappear from the scene of life, and then there would be an end to the French alliance, upon which the present security rests.[d] In other words, *The Times*, the great organ of the British Cabinet, while considering a revolution in France an event not unlikely to occur any day, simultaneously proclaims the present alliance to be

---

[a] B. Disraeli's speech in the House of Commons on August 11, 1857, *The Times*, No. 22757, August 12, 1857.—*Ed.*

[b] B. Disraeli's speech in the House of Commons on August 20, 1857, *The Times*, No. 22765, August 21, 1857.—*Ed.*

[c] J. M. F. Smith's speech in the House of Commons on August 20, 1857, *The Times*, same issue.—*Ed.*

[d] *The Times*, same issue, leading article.—*Ed.*

founded not on the sympathies of the French people, but on mere conspiracy with the French usurper. Beside a revolution in France, there is the Danubian quarrel.[384] By the annulling of the Moldavian elections,[a] it has not been made to subside, but only to enter on a new phase. There is, above all, the Scandinavian North, which, at a period not distant, is sure to become the theater of great agitation, and, perhaps, may give the signal to an international conflict in Europe. Peace is still kept in the North, because two events are anxiously waited for—the death of the King of Sweden[b] and the abdication of his throne by the present King of Denmark. At a late meeting of naturalists at Christiania, the hereditary Prince of Sweden[c] declared emphatically in favor of a Scandinavian union. Being a man in the prime of life, of a resolute and energetic character, the Scandinavian party, mustering in its ranks the ardent youth of Sweden, Norway and Denmark, will consider his accession to the throne as the opportune moment for taking up arms. On the other hand, the weak and imbecile King of Denmark, Frederick VII., is said to have been at last allowed by the Countess Danner, his morganatic consort, to withdraw to private life, a permission hitherto refused him. It was on her account that Prince Ferdinand, the King's uncle, and the presumptive heir of the Danish throne, was induced to retire from State affairs, to which he afterward returned in consequence of an arrangement brought about by the other members of the royal family. Now, at this moment, the Countess Danner is said to be disposed to change her residence at Copenhagen for one at Paris, and even to prompt the King to bid farewell to the storms of political life by resigning his scepter into the hands of Prince Ferdinand. This Prince Ferdinand, a man about 65 years of age, has always occupied the same position toward the Court of Copenhagen, which the Count of Artois—afterward Charles X.—held toward the Court of the Tuileries. Obstinate, severe and ardent in his conservative faith, he has never condescended to feign adherence to the Constitutional system. Yet the first condition of his accession to the throne would be the acceptance on oath of a Constitution he openly detests. Hence the probability of international troubles, which the Scandinavian party, both in Sweden and Denmark, are firmly resolved upon turning to their own profit. On the other hand, the conflict between

---

[a] See this volume, pp. 322-26.— *Ed.*
[b] Oscar I.— *Ed.*
[c] Carl Ludvig Eugène.— *Ed.*

Denmark and the German Duchies of Holstein and Schleswig, supported in their claims by Prussia and Austria,[385] would still more embroil matters, and entangle Germany in the agitations of the North; while the London treaty of 1852,[a] guaranteeing the throne of Denmark to Prince Ferdinand,[386] would involve Russia, France and England.

Written on August 21, 1857

First published in the *New-York Daily Tribune*, № 5110, September 5, 1857 as a leading article

Reproduced from the newspaper

---

[a] "Traité signé à Londres, le 8 mai 1852, entre le Danemark d'une part, et l'Autriche, la France, la Grande-Bretagne, la Russie et la Suède de l'autre part, relatif à l'ordre de succession dans la monarchie danoise."—*Ed.*

Karl Marx

[INVESTIGATION OF TORTURES IN INDIA][387]

Our London correspondent, whose letter with regard to the Indian revolt we published yesterday,[a] very properly referred to some of the antecedents which prepared the way for this violent outbreak. We propose to-day to devote a moment to continuing that line of reflections, and to showing that the British rulers of India are by no means such mild and spotless benefactors of the Indian people as they would have the world believe. For this purpose, we shall resort to the official Blue Books[388] on the subject of East-Indian torture, which were laid before the House of Commons during the sessions of 1856 and 1857.[b] The evidence, it will be seen, is of a sort which cannot be gainsayed.

We have first the report of the Torture Commission at Madras,[c] which states its "belief in the general existence of torture for revenue purposes." It doubts whether

> "anything like an equal number of persons is annually subjected to violence on criminal charges, as for the fault of non-payment of revenue."

It declares that there was

> "one thing which had impressed the Commission even more painfully than the conviction that torture exists; it is the difficulty of obtaining redress which confronts the injured parties."

---

[a] See this volume, pp. 353-56.—*Ed.*

[b] *East India (Torture).—Ed.*

[c] "Report of the Commission for the Investigation of Alleged Cases of Torture at Madras."—*Ed.*

The reasons for this difficulty given by the Commissioners are: 1. The distances which those who wish to make complaints personally to the Collector[389] have to travel, involving expense and loss of time in attending upon his office; 2. The fear that applications by letter

"will be returned with the ordinary indorsement of a reference to the Tahsildar"

the district police and revenue officer—that is, to the very man who, either in his person or through his petty police subordinates, has wronged him; 3. The inefficient means of procedure and punishment provided by law for officers of Government, even when formally accused or convicted of these practices. It seems that if a charge of this nature were proved before a magistrate, he could only punish by a fine of fifty rupees, or a month's imprisonment. The alternative consisted of handing over the accused

"to the criminal Judge to be punished by him, or committed for trial before the Court of the Circuit."

The report adds that

"these seem to be tedious proceedings, applicable only to one class of offenses, abuse of authority—namely, in police charges, and totally inadequate to the necessities of the case."

A police or revenue officer, who is the same person, as the revenue is collected by the police, when charged with extorting money, is first tried by the Assistant Collector; he then can appeal to the Collector; then to the Revenue Board. This Board may refer him to the Government or to the civil courts.

"In such a state of the law, no poverty-stricken ryot[390] could contend against any wealthy revenue officer; and we are not aware of any complaints having been brought forward under these two regulations (of 1822 and 1828) by the people."

Further, this extorting of money applies only to taking the public money, or forcing a further contribution from the ryot for the officer to put into his own pocket. There is, therefore, no legal means of punishment whatever for the employment of force in collecting the public revenue.

The report from which these quotations are made applies only to the Presidency of Madras; but Lord Dalhousie himself, writing, in September, 1855, to the Directors,[a] says that

"he has long ceased to doubt that torture in one shape or other is practiced by the lower subordinates in every British province."

The universal existence of torture as a financial institution of British India is thus officially admitted, but the admission is made in such a manner as to shield the British Government itself. In fact, the conclusion arrived at by the Madras commission is that the practice of torture is entirely the fault of the lower Hindoo officials, while the European servants of the Government had always, however unsuccessfully, done their best to prevent it. In answer to this assertion, the Madras Native Association presented, in January, 1856, a petition to Parliament, complaining of the torture investigation on the following grounds: 1. That there was scarcely any investigation at all, the Commission sitting only in the City of Madras, and for but three months, while it was impossible, except in very few cases, for the natives who had complaints to make to leave their homes; 2. That the Commissioners did not endeavor to trace the evil to its source; had they done so, it would have been discovered to be in the very system of collecting the revenue; 3. That no inquiry was made of the accused native officials as to what extent their superiors were acquainted with the practice.

"The origin of this coercion," say the petitioners, "is not with the physical perpetrators of it, but descends to them from the officials immediately their superiors, which latter again are answerable for the estimated amount of the collection to their European superiors, these also being responsible on the same head to the highest authority of the Government."

Indeed, a few extracts from the evidence on which the Madras Report professes to be founded, will suffice to refute its assertion that "no blame is due to Englishmen." Thus, Mr. W. D. Kohlhoff, a merchant, says:

"The modes of torture practiced are various, and suitable to the fancy of the tahsildar or his subordinates, but whether any redress is received from higher authorities, it is difficult for me to tell, *as all complaints are generally referred to the tahsildars* for investigation and information."

Among the cases of complaint from natives, we find the following:

[a] Court of Directors of the East India Company.—*Ed.*

"Last year, as our peasanum (principal paddy or rice crops) failed for want of rain, we were unable to pay as usual. When the jamabundy[391] was made, we claimed a remission on account of the losses, according to the terms of the agreement entered into in 1837, by us, when Mr. Eden was our collector. As this remission was not allowed, we refused to take our puttahs.[392] The tahsildar then commenced to compel us to pay with great severity, from the month of June to August. I and others were placed in charge of persons who used to take us in the sun. There we were made to stoop and stones were put on our backs, and we were kept in the burning sand. After 8 o'clock, we were let to go to our rice. Suchlike ill treatment was continued during three months, during which we sometimes went to give our petitions to the collector, who refused to take them. We took these petitions and appealed to the Sessions Court, who transmitted them to the collector. Still we got no justice. In the month of September, a notice was served upon us, and twenty-five days after, our property was distrained, and afterward sold. Beside what I have mentioned, our women were also ill treated; the kittee was put upon their breasts."

A native Christian states in reply to questions put by the Commissioners:

"When a European or native regiment passes through, all the ryots are pressed to bring in provisions, &c., *for nothing*, and should any of them ask for the price of the articles, they are severely tortured."

There follows the case of a Brahmin, in which he, with others of his own village and of the neighboring villages, was called on by the Tahsildars to furnish planks, charcoal, firewood, &c., gratis, that he might carry on the Coleroon bridge work; on refusing, he is seized by twelve men and maltreated in various ways. He adds:

"I presented a complaint to the Sub-Collector, Mr. W. Cadell, but he made no inquiry, and tore my complaint. As he is desirous of completing cheaply the Coleroon bridge work at the expense of the poor and of acquiring a good name from the Government, whatever may be the nature of the murder committed by the Tahsildar, he takes no cognizance of it."

The light in which illegal practices, carried to the last degree of extortion and violence, were looked upon by the highest authority, is best shown by the case of Mr. Brereton, the Commissioner in charge of the Loodhiana District in the Punjaub in 1855. According to the Report of the Chief Commissioner for the Punjaub,[a] it was proved that

"in matters under the immediate cognizance or direction of the Deputy-Commissioner, Mr. Brereton himself, the houses of wealthy citizens had been

[a] John Laird Mair Lawrence.—*Ed.*

causelessly searched; that property seized on such occasions was detained for lengthened periods; that many parties were thrown into prison, and lay there for weeks, without charges being exhibited against them; and that the laws relating to security for bad character had been applied with sweeping and indiscriminating severity. That the Deputy-Commissioner had been followed about from district to district by certain police officers and informers, whom he employed wherever he went, and that these men had been the main authors of mischief."

In his minute on the case, Lord Dalhousie says:

"We have irrefragable proof—proof, indeed, undisputed by Mr. Brereton himself—that that officer has been guilty of each item in the heavy catalogue of irregularities and illegalities with which the chief Commissioner has charged him, and which have brought disgrace on one portion of the British administration, and have subjected a large number of British subjects to gross injustice, to arbitrary imprisonment and cruel torture."

Lord Dalhousie proposes "to make a great public example," and, consequently, is of opinion that

"Mr. Brereton cannot, *for the present*, be fitly intrusted with the authority of a Deputy Commissioner, but ought to be removed from that grade to the grade of a first class Assistant."

These extracts from the Blue Books may be concluded with the petition from the inhabitants of Talook[a] in Canara, on the Malabar coast, who, after stating that they had presented several petitions to the Government to no purpose, thus contrast their former and present condition:

"While we were cultivating wet and dry lands, hill tracts, low tracts and forests, paying the light assessment fixed upon us, and thereby enjoying tranquillity and happiness under the administration of 'Ranee,'[b] Bhadur and Tippoo, the then Circar[c] servants, levied an additional assessment, but we never paid it. We were not subjected to privations, oppressions or ill-usages in collecting the revenue. On the surrender of this country to the Honorable Company,[d] they devised all sorts of plans to squeeze out money from us. With this pernicious object in view, they invented rules and framed regulations, and directed their collectors and civil judges to put them in execution. But the then collectors and their subordinate native officials paid for some time due attention to our grievances, and acted in consonance with our wishes. On the contrary, the present collectors and their subordinate officials, *desirous of obtaining promotion on any account whatever,* neglect the welfare and interests of the people in general, turn a deaf ear to our grievances, and subject us to all sorts of oppressions."

[a] Region.—*Ed.*
[b] Hindoo queen.—*Ed.*
[c] Government.—*Ed.*
[d] The East India Company.—*Ed.*

— We have here given but a brief and mildly-colored chapter from the real history of British rule in India. In view of such facts, dispassionate and thoughtful men may perhaps be led to ask whether a people are not justified in attempting to expel the foreign conquerors who have so abused their subjects. And if the English could do these things in cold blood, is it surprising that the insurgent Hindoos should be guilty, in the fury of revolt and conflict, of the crimes and cruelties alleged against them?

Written on August 28, 1857

First published in the *New-York Daily Tribune,* No. 5120, September 17, 1857 as a leading article

Reproduced from the newspaper

Karl Marx

[THE REVOLT IN INDIA]

The mail of the *Baltic* reports no new events in India, but has a mass of highly interesting details, which we proceed to condense for the instruction of our readers. The first point to be noticed is that so late as the 15th of July the English had not got into Delhi. At the same time, the cholera had made its appearance in their camp, the heavy rains were setting in, and the raising of the siege and the withdrawal of the besiegers appeared to be a question of time only. The British press would fain make us believe that the pest, while carrying off Gen. Sir H. Barnard, had spared his worse fed and harder worked men. It is, therefore, not from explicit statements, communicated to the public, but only by way of inference from avowed facts, that we can arrive at some idea of the ravages of this terrible disease in the ranks of the besieging army. An officer in the camp before Delhi, writes, July 14:

> "We are doing nothing toward taking Delhi, and are merely defending ourselves against sorties of the enemy. We have parts of five European regiments, but can muster only 2,000 Europeans, for any effective attack; large detachments from each regiment having been left to protect Jullindur, Loodhiana, Subathoo, Dugshale, Kussowlie, Umballah, Meerut and Phillour. In fact, small detachments only of each regiment have joined us. The enemy are far superior to us in artillery."

Now this proves that the forces arriving from the Punjaub found the great northern line of communication from Jullindur down to Meerut in a state of rebellion, and were consequently obliged to diminish their numbers by leaving detachments at the main posts. This accounts for the arrivals from the Punjaub not mustering their anticipated strength, but it does not explain the reduction of the European force to 2,000 men. The Bombay correspondent of *The London Times,* writing on July 30, attempts to explain in another way the passive attitude of the besiegers. He says:

> "The re-enforcements, indeed, have reached our camp—one wing of the 8th (King's), one of the 61st, a company of foot artillery, and two guns of a native troop, the 17th Irregular Cavalry regiment (escorting a large ammunition train), the 2d Punjaub Cavalry, the 1st Punjaub Infantry and the 4th Sikh Infantry; but the native portion of the troops thus added to the besieging force are not entirely and uniformly trustworthy, brigaded though they are with Europeans. The cavalry regiments of the Punjaub force contain many Mussulmans and high-caste Hindoos, from Hindostan proper, and Rohilcund, while the Bengal Irregular Cavalry are mainly composed of such elements. These men are, as a class, utterly disloyal, and their presence with the force in any numbers must be embarrassing—and so it has proved. In the 2d Punjaub Cavalry, it has been found necessary to disarm some 70 Hindostan men and to hang three, one a superior native officer. Of the 9th Irregulars, which have been some time with the force, several troopers have deserted, and the 4th Irregulars have, I believe, murdered their adjutant, while on detachment duty." [a]

Here another secret is revealed. The camp before Delhi, it seems, bears some likeness to the camp of Agramante,[393] and the English have to struggle not only with the enemy in their front, but also with the ally in their lines. Still, this fact affords no sufficient cause for there being only 2,000 Europeans to be spared for offensive operations. A third writer, the Bombay correspondent of *The Daily News,* gives an explicit enumeration of the forces assembled under Gen. Read, Barnard's successor, which seems trustworthy, as he reckons up singly the different elements of which they are composed. According to his statement, about 1,200 Europeans and 1,600 Sikhs, irregular horse, etc., say altogether about 3,000 men, headed by Brigadier-Gen. Chamberlain, reached the camp before Delhi from the Punjaub between June 23 and July 3. On the other hand, he estimates the whole of the forces now assembled under Gen. Read at 7,000 men, artillery and siege-train included, so that the army of Delhi, before the arrival of the Punjaub re-enforcements, could not have exceeded 4,000 men. *The London Times* of August 13 stated that Sir H. Barnard had collected an army of 7,000 British and 5,000 natives.[b] Although this was a flagrant exaggeration, there is every reason to believe that the European forces then amounted to

---

[a] The letter of the Bombay correspondent, dated July 30, *The Times,* No. 22773, August 31, 1857.—*Ed.*

[b] *The Times,* No. 22758, August 13, 1857, leading article.—*Ed.*

about 4,000 men, backed by a somewhat smaller number of natives. The original force, then, under Gen. Barnard, was as strong as the force now collected under Gen. Read. Consequently, the Punjaub re-enforcements have only made up for the wear and tear which have reduced the strength of the besiegers almost one-half, an enormous loss, proceeding partly from the incessant sorties of the rebels, partly from the ravages of the cholera. Thus we understand why the British can muster only 2,000 Europeans for "any effective attack."

So much for the strength of the British forces before Delhi. Now for their operations. That they were not of a very brilliant character may be fairly inferred from the simple fact that, since June 8, when Gen. Barnard made his report on the capture of the hight opposite Delhi,[a] no bulletin whatever has been issued from headquarters. The operations, with a single exception, consist of sallies made by the besieged and repulsed by the besiegers. The besiegers were attacked now in front and then in the flanks, but mostly in the right rear. The sorties took place on the 27th and 30th of June, on the 3d, 4th, 9th and 14th of July. On the 27th of June, fighting was confined to outpost skirmishes, lasting some hours, but toward the afternoon was interrupted by a heavy fall of rain, the first of the season. On the 30th of June, the insurgents showed themselves in force among the inclosures on the right of the besiegers, harassing their pickets and supports. On the 3d of July, the besieged made early in the morning a feint attack on the right rear of the English position, then advanced several miles to that rear along the Kurnaul road as far as Alipore, in order to intercept a train of supplies and treasure under convoy to the camp. On their way, they encountered an outpost of the 2d Punjaub irregular horse, which gave way at once. On their return to the city, on the 4th, the rebels were attacked by a body of 1,000 infantry and two squadrons of cavalry dispatched from the English camp to intercept them. They contrived, however, to effect their retreat with little or no loss and saving all their guns. On the 8th of July, a party was sent from the British camp to destroy a canal bridge at the village of Bussy, some six miles from Delhi, which in the former sallies had afforded the insurgents facilities for attacking the extreme British rear, and interfering with the British communications with Kurnaul and Meerut. The bridge was destroyed. On the 9th of July, the insurgents came out again in force and attacked the right rear of the British position. In the

[a] See this volume, pp. 319, 320.— *Ed.*

official accounts telegraphed to Lahore on the same day, the loss of the assailants is estimated at about one thousand killed; but this account seems much exaggerated, since we read in a letter of July 13 from the camp:

"Our men buried and burnt two hundred and fifty of the enemy's dead, and large numbers were removed by themselves into the city."

The same letter, published in *The Daily News,* does not pretend that the British forced back the Sepoys, but, on the contrary, that "the Sepoys forced back all our working parties and then retired." The loss of the besiegers was considerable, amounting, as it did, to two hundred and twelve, killed and wounded. On the 14th of July, in consequence of another sortie, another fierce fight took place, the details of which have not yet arrived.

The besieged had, meanwhile, received strong re-enforcements. On the 1st of July, the Rohilcund mutineers from Bareily, Muradabat and Shahjehanpore, consisting of four regiments of infantry, one of irregular cavalry, and one battery of artillery, had contrived to effect their junction with their comrades at Delhi.

"It had been hoped," says the Bombay correspondent of *The London Times,* "that they would find the Ganges impassable; but the anticipated rise of the river not taking place, it was crossed at Gurmukteser, the Doab was traversed and Delhi was attained. For two days, our troops had the mortification of watching the long train of men, guns, horses and beasts of burden of all kinds (for there was a treasure with the rebels, say £50,000) streaming across the bridge of boats into the city, without a possibility of preventing or in any way annoying them." [a]

This successful march of the insurgents through the whole breadth of Rohilcund proves all the country east of the Jumna up to the hills of Rohilcund to be closed against the English forces, while the untroubled march of the insurgents from Neemuch to Agra, if connected with the revolts at Indore and Mhow, proves the same fact for all the country south-west of the Jumna and up to the Vindhya Mountains. The only successful—in fact, the only—operation of the English in regard to Delhi is the pacification of the country to its north and its north-west by Gen. Van Cortlandt's Punjaub Sikh forces. Throughout the district between Loodhiana and Sirsah, he had mainly to encounter the robber-tribes inhabiting villages sparsely scattered over a wild and sandy desert. On the 11th of July, he is said to have left Sirsah for

[a] *The Times,* No. 22773, August 31, 1857.—*Ed.*

Futtehabad, thence to march on Hissar, thus opening up the country in the rear of the besieging force.

Beside Delhi, three other points in the North-Western Provinces—Agra, Cawnpore and Lucknow—had become centers of the struggle between the natives and the English. The affair of Agra bears this peculiar aspect, that it shows for the first time the mutineers setting out on a deliberate expedition over about 300 miles of ground with the intention of attacking a distant English military station. According to *The Mofussilite,* a journal printed at Agra, the Sepoy regiments of Nusserabad and Neemuch, about 10,000 strong, (say 7,000 infantry, 1,500 cavalry and 8 guns), approached Agra at the end of June, encamped in the beginning of July on a plain in the rear of the village of Sussia, about 20 miles from Agra, and on the 4th of July seemed preparing an attack on the city. On this news, the European residents in the cantonments before Agra took refuge in the fort. The Commander at Agra[a] dispatched at first the Kotah contingent of horse, foot and artillery to serve as an advanced post against the enemy, but, having reached their place of destination, one and all bolted to join the ranks of the rebels. On July 5, the Agra garrison, consisting of the 3d Bengal Europeans, a battery of artillery and a corps of European volunteers, marched out to attack the mutineers, and are said to have driven them out of the village into the plain behind it, but were evidently themselves in their turn forced back, and, after a loss of 49 killed and 92 wounded, of a total force of 500 men engaged, had to retire, being harassed and threatened by the cavalry of the enemy with such activity as to prevent their "getting a shot at them," as *The Mofussilite* says.[b] In other words, the English took to downright flight and shut themselves up in their fort, while the Sepoys, advancing to Agra, destroyed nearly all the houses in the cantonment. On the following day, July 6, they proceeded to Bhurtpore, on the way to Delhi. The important result of this affair is the interruption by the mutineers of the English line of communication between Agra and Delhi, and their probable appearance before the old city of the Moguls.

At Cawnpore, as was known from the last mail, a force of about 200 Europeans, under the command of Gen. Wheeler, having with them the wives and children of the 32d foot, was shut up in a

[a] John Colin.—*Ed.*

[b] Quoted in *The Times,* No. 22773, August 31, 1857.—*Ed.*

fortified work and surrounded by an overwhelming mass of rebels, headed by Nena Sahib of Bithoor. Different assaults on the fort took place on the 17th and between the 24th and 28th of June, in the last of which, Gen. Wheeler was shot through the leg and died of his wounds. On June 28, Nena Sahib invited the English to surrender on the condition of being allowed to depart on boats down the Ganges to Allahabad. These terms were accepted, but the British had hardly put out into the middle of the stream when guns opened upon them from the right bank of the Ganges. The people in the boats that tried to escape to the opposite bank were caught and cut down by a body of cavalry. The women and children were made captives. Messengers having been dispatched several times from Cawnpore to Allahabad with pressing demands for relief, on July 1 a column of Madras fusiliers and Sikhs started, under Major Renaud, on the way to Cawnpore. Within four miles of Futteypore it was joined, on July 13 at daybreak, by Brig.-Gen. Havelock, who, at the head of about 1,300 Europeans of the 84th and 64th, the 13th irregular horse, and the remnant of Oude Irregulars, reached Allahabad from Benares, July 3, and then followed up Major Renaud by forced marches. On the very day of his junction with Renaud, he was forced to accept battle before Futteypore, whither Nena Sahib had led his native forces. After an obstinate engagement, Gen. Havelock, by a move in the flank of the enemy, succeeded in driving him out of Futteypore in the direction of Cawnpore, where twice he had to encounter him again on the 15th and 16th of July. At the latter date, Cawnpore was recaptured by the English, Nena Sahib retreating to Bithoor, situated on the Ganges, twelve miles distant from Cawnpore, and said to be strongly fortified. Before undertaking his expedition to Futteypore, Nena Sahib had murdered all the captive English women and children. The recapture of Cawnpore was of the highest importance to the English, as it secured their Ganges line of communication.

At Lucknow, the capital of Oude, the British garrison found themselves nearly in the same plight which had proved fatal to their comrades at Cawnpore—shut up in a fort, surrounded by overwhelming forces, straitened for provisions, and deprived of their leader. The latter, Sir H. Lawrence, died July 4, of tetanus, from a wound in the leg, received on the 2d, during a sortie. On the 18th and 19th of July, Lucknow was still holding out. Its only hope of relief rested on Gen. Havelock's pushing forward his forces from Cawnpore. The question is whether he would dare to do so with Nena Sahib in his rear. Any delay, however, must prove fatal to Lucknow, since the periodical rains would soon render field operations impossible.

The examination of these events forces the conclusion upon us that, in the north-west provinces of Bengal, the British forces were gradually drifting into the position of small posts planted on insulated rocks amid a sea of revolution. In lower Bengal, there had occurred only partial acts of insubordination at Mirzapore, Dinapore and Patna, beside an unsuccessful attempt made by the roving Brahmins of the neighborhood to recapture the holy city of Benares. In the Punjaub, the spirit of rebellion was forcibly kept down, a mutiny being suppressed at Sealkote, another at Jelum, and the disaffection of Peshawur successfully checked. Emeutes had already been attempted in Gujerat, at Punderpoor in Sattara, at Nagpore and Saugor in the Nagpore territory, at Hyderabad in the Nizam's territory, and, lastly, as far south as Mysore, so that the calm of the Bombay and Madras Presidencies must be understood as by no means perfectly secure.

Written on September 1, 1857

First published in the *New-York Daily Tribune,* No. 5118, September 15, 1857 as a leading article; reprinted in the *New-York Semi-Weekly Tribune,* No. 1284, September 15, 1857, entitled "India", and the *New-York Weekly Tribune,* No. 836, September 19, 1857

Reproduced from the *New-York Daily Tribune*

Karl Marx

[BRITISH INCOMES IN INDIA]

The present state of affairs in Asia suggests the inquiry, What is the real value of their Indian dominion to the British nation and people? Directly, that is in the shape of tribute, of surplus of Indian receipts over Indian expenditures, nothing whatever reaches the British Treasury. On the contrary, the annual outgo is very large. From the moment that the East India Company[394] entered extensively on the career of conquest—now just about a century ago—their finances fell into an embarrassed condition, and they were repeatedly compelled to apply to Parliament, not only for military aid to assist them in holding the conquered territories, but for financial aid to save them from bankruptcy. And so things have continued down to the present moment, at which so large a call is made for troops on the British nation, to be followed, no doubt, by corresponding calls for money. In prosecuting its conquests hitherto, and building up its establishments, the East India Company has contracted a debt of upward of £50,000,000 sterling, while the British Government has been at the expense, for years past, of transporting to and from and keeping up in India, in addition to the forces, native and European, of the East India Company, a standing army of thirty thousand men. Such being the case, it is evident that the advantage to Great Britain from her Indian empire must be limited to the profits and benefits which accrue to individual British subjects. These profits and benefits, it must be confessed, are very considerable.

First, we have the stockholders in the East India Company, to the number of about 3,000 persons, to whom under the recent charter[395] there is guaranteed, upon a paid-up capital of six millions of pounds sterling, an annual dividend of ten and a half per cent, amounting to £630,000 annually. As the East India stock is held in transferable shares, anybody may become a stockholder who has money enough to buy the stock, which, under the existing charter, commands a premium of from 125 to 150 per cent. Stock to the amount of £500, costing say $6,000, entitles the holder to speak at the Proprietors' meetings, but to vote he must have £1,000 of stock. Holders of £3,000 have two votes, of £6,000 three votes, and of £10,000 or upward four votes. The proprietors, however, have but little voice, except in the election of the Board of Directors, of whom they choose twelve, while the Crown appoints six; but these appointees of the Crown must be qualified by having resided for ten years or more in India. One third of the Directors go out of office each year, but may be re-elected or reappointed. To be a Director, one must be a proprietor of £2,000 of stock. The Directors have a salary of £500 each, and their Chairman and Deputy Chairman twice as much; but the chief inducement to accept the office is the great patronage attached to it in the appointment of all Indian officers, civil and military—a patronage, however, largely shared, and, as to the most important offices, engrossed substantially, by the Board of Control. This Board consists of six members, all Privy Councilors, and in general two or three of them Cabinet Ministers—the President of the Board being always so, in fact a Secretary of State for India.

Next come the recipients of this patronage, divided into five classes—civil, clerical, medical, military and naval. For service in India, at least in the civil line, some knowledge of the languages spoken there is necessary, and to prepare young men to enter their civil service, the East India Company has a college at Haileybury. A corresponding college for the military service, in which, however, the rudiments of military science are the principal branches taught, has been established at Addiscombe, near London. Admission to these colleges was formerly a matter of favor on the part of the Directors of the Company, but under the latest modifications of the charter it has been opened to competition in the way of a public examination of candidates. On first reaching India, a civilian is allowed about $150 a month, till having passed a necessary examination in one or more of the native languages (which must be within twelve months after his arrival), he is attached to the service with emoluments which vary from $2,500 to near $50,000 per annum. The latter is the pay of the members of the Bengal Council; the members of the Bombay and Madras Councils[396] receive about $30,000 per annum. No person not a member of Council can receive more than about $25,000 per annum, and, to obtain an appointment worth $20,000 or over, he must have been a resident in India for twelve years. Nine years' residence qualifies for salaries of from $15,000 to $20,000, and three years' residence for salaries of from $7,000 to $15,000. Appointments in the civil service go nominally by seniority and merit, but really to a great extent by favor. As they are the best paid, there is great competition to get them, the military officers leaving their regiments for this purpose whenever they can get a chance. The average of all the salaries in the civil service is stated at about $8,000, but this does not include perquisites and extra allowances, which are often very considerable. These civil servants are employed as Governors, Councilors, Judges, Embassadors, Secretaries, Collectors of the Revenue,[397] &c.—the number in the whole being generally about 800. The salary of the Governor-General of India is $125,000, but the extra allowances often amount to a still larger sum. The Church service includes three bishops and about one hundred and sixty chaplains. The Bishop of Calcutta has $25,000 a year; those of Madras and Bombay half as much; the chaplains from $2,500 to $7,000, beside fees. The medical service includes some 800 physicians and surgeons, with salaries of from $1,500 to $10,000.

The European military officers employed in India, including those of the contingents which the dependent princes are obliged to furnish, number about 8,000. The fixed pay in the infantry is, for ensigns, $1,080; lieutenants, $1,344; captains, $2,226; majors, $3,810; lieutenant colonels, $5,520; colonels, $7,680. This is the pay in cantonment. In active service, it is more. The pay in the cavalry, artillery and engineers, is somewhat higher. By obtaining staff situations or employments in the civil service, many officers double their pay.

Here are about ten thousand British subjects holding lucrative situations in India, and drawing their pay from the Indian service. To these must be added a considerable number living in England, whither they have retired upon pensions, which in all the services are payable after serving a certain number of years. These pensions, with the dividends and interest on debts due in England, consume some fifteen to twenty millions of dollars drawn annually from India, and which may in fact be regarded as so much tribute paid to the English Government indirectly through its subjects. Those who annually retire from the several services carry with them very considerable amounts of savings from their salaries, which is so much more added to the annual drain on India.

Beside those Europeans actually employed in the service of the Government, there are other European residents in India, to the number of 6,000 or more, employed in trade or private speculation. Except a few indigo, sugar and coffee planters in the rural districts, they are principally merchants, agents and manufacturers, who reside in the cities of Calcutta, Bombay and Madras, or their immediate vicinity. The foreign trade of India, including imports and exports to the amount of about fifty millions of dollars of each, is almost entirely in their hands, and their profits are no doubt very considerable.

It is thus evident that individuals gain largely by the English connection with India, and of course their gain goes to increase the sum of the national wealth. But against all this a very large offset is to be made. The military and naval expenses paid out of the pockets of the people of England on Indian account have been constantly increasing with the extent of the Indian dominion. To this must be added the expense of Burmese,[398] Affghan, Chinese and Persian[399] wars. In fact, the whole cost of the late Russian war[a] may fairly be charged to the Indian account, since the fear and dread of Russia, which led to that war, grew entirely out of jealousy as to her designs on India. Add to this the career of endless conquest and perpetual aggression in which the English are involved by the possession of India, and it may well be doubted whether, on the whole, this dominion does not threaten to cost quite as much as it can ever be expected to come to.

Written at the beginning of September 1857

First published in the *New-York Daily Tribune,* No. 5123, September 21, 1857 as a leading article

Reproduced from the newspaper

[a] The Crimean war, 1853-56.—*Ed.*

Karl Marx

THE INDIAN REVOLT

London, Sept. 4, 1857

The outrages committed by the revolted Sepoys in India are indeed appalling, hideous, ineffable—such as one is prepared to meet only in wars of insurrection, of nationalities, of races, and above all of religion; in one word, such as respectable England used to applaud when perpetrated by the Vendeans on the "Blues", by the Spanish guerrillas on the infidel Frenchmen, by Servians on their German and Hungarian neighbors, by Croats on Viennese rebels, by Cavaignac's Garde Mobile or Bonaparte's Decembrists on the sons and daughters of proletarian France.[400] However infamous the conduct of the Sepoys, it is only the reflex, in a concentrated form, of England's own conduct in India, not only during the epoch of the foundation of her Eastern Empire, but even during the last ten years of a long-settled rule. To characterize that rule, it suffices to say that torture formed an organic institution of its financial policy.[a] There is something in human history like retribution; and it is a rule of historical retribution that its instrument be forged not by the offended, but by the offender himself.

The first blow dealt to the French monarchy proceeded from the nobility, not from the peasants. The Indian revolt does not commence with the Ryots, tortured, dishonored and stripped naked by the British, but with the Sepoys, clad, fed, petted, fatted and pampered by them. To find parallels to the Sepoy atrocities, we need not, as some London papers pretend, fall back on the middle ages, nor even wander beyond the history of cotemporary England. All we want is to study the first Chinese war,[401] an event,

---

[a] See this volume, pp. 336-41.—*Ed.*

so to say, of yesterday. The English soldiery then committed abominations for the mere fun of it; their passions being neither sanctified by religious fanaticism nor exacerbated by hatred against an overbearing and conquering race, nor provoked by the stern resistance of a heroic enemy. The violations of women, the spittings of children, the roastings of whole villages, were then mere wanton sports, not recorded by Mandarins, but by British officers themselves.

Even at the present catastrophe it would be an unmitigated mistake to suppose that all the cruelty is on the side of the Sepoys, and all the milk of human kindness flows on the side of the English. The letters of the British officers are redolent of malignity. An officer writing from Peshawur gives a description of the disarming of the 10th irregular cavalry for not charging the 55th native infantry when ordered to do so. He exults in the fact that they were not only disarmed, but stripped of their coats and boots, and after having received 12d. per man, were marched down to the river side, and there embarked in boats and sent down the Indus, where the writer is delighted to expect every mother's son will have a chance of being drowned in the rapids. Another writer informs us that, some inhabitants of Peshawur having caused a night alarm by exploding little mines of gunpowder in honor of a wedding (a national custom), the persons concerned were tied up next morning, and

"received such a flogging as they will not easily forget."

News arrived from Pindee that three native chiefs were plotting. Sir John Lawrence replied by a message ordering a spy to attend to the meeting. On the spy's report, Sir John sent a second message, "Hang them." The chiefs were hanged.[a] An officer in the civil service, from Allahabad, writes:

"We have power of life and death in our hands, and we assure you we spare not."[b]

Another, from the same place:

"Not a day passes but we string up from ten to fifteen of them (non-combatants)."

---

[a] From a letter of an artillery officer, dated Peshawur, June 26, *The Times*, No. 22766, August 22, 1857.—*Ed.*

[b] "Allahabad, June 28", *The Times*, No. 22768, August 25, 1857.—*Ed.*

One exulting officer writes:

"Holmes is hanging them by the score, like a 'brick.'"[a]

Another, in allusion to the summary hanging of a large body of the natives:

"Then our fun commenced."

A third:

"We hold court-martials on horseback, and every nigger we meet with we either string up or shoot."

From Benares we are informed that thirty Zemindars[402] were hanged on the mere suspicion of sympathizing with their own countrymen, and whole villages were burned down on the same plea. An officer from Benares, whose letter is printed in *The London Times,* says:

"The European troops have become fiends when opposed to natives."[b]

And then it should not be forgotten that, while the cruelties of the English are related as acts of martial vigor, told simply, rapidly, without dwelling on disgusting details, the outrages of the natives, shocking as they are, are still deliberately exaggerated. For instance, the circumstantial account first appearing in *The Times,* and then going the round of the London press, of the atrocities perpetrated at Delhi and Meerut, from whom did it proceed?[c] From a cowardly parson residing at Bangalore, Mysore, more than a thousand miles, as the bird flies, distant from the scene of action. Actual accounts of Delhi evince the imagination of an English parson to be capable of breeding greater horrors than even the wild fancy of a Hindoo mutineer. The cutting of noses, breasts, &c., in one word, the horrid mutilations committed by the Sepoys, are of course more revolting to European feeling than the throwing of red-hot shell on Canton dwellings by a Secretary of the Manchester Peace Society,[d] or the roasting of Arabs pent up in a cave by a French Marshal,[403] or the flaying alive of British

[a] Letter from Tirhoot, dated June 26, *The Times,* No. 22763, August 19, 1857.— *Ed.*

[b] R. H. Bartrum, "Benares, July 13", *The Times,* No. 22775, September 2, 1857.— *Ed.*

[c] "Bangalore, July 4", *The Times,* No. 22768, August 25, 1857.— *Ed.*

[d] John Bowring. See this volume, pp. 158-63 and 232-35.— *Ed.*

soldiers by the cat-o'-nine-tails under drum-head court-martial, or any other of the philanthropical appliances used in British penitentiary colonies. Cruelty, like every other thing, has its fashion, changing according to time and place. Caesar, the accomplished scholar, candidly narrates how he ordered many thousand Gallic warriors to have their right hands cut off.[a] Napoleon would have been ashamed to do this. He preferred dispatching his own French regiments, suspected of republicanism, to St. Domingo, there to die of the blacks and the plague.

The infamous mutilations committed by the Sepoys remind one of the practices of the Christian Byzantine Empire, or the prescriptions of Emperor Charles V.'s criminal law,[404] or the English punishments for high treason, as still recorded by Judge Blackstone.[b] With Hindoos, whom their religion has made virtuosi in the art of self-torturing, these tortures inflicted on the enemies of their race and creed appear quite natural, and must appear still more so to the English, who, only some years since, still used to draw revenues from the Juggernaut festivals, protecting and assisting the bloody rites of a religion of cruelty.[405]

The frantic roars of the "bloody old *Times,*" as Cobbett used to call it—its playing the part of a furious character in one of Mozart's operas, who indulges in most melodious strains in the idea of first hanging his enemy, then roasting him, then quartering him, then spitting him, and then flaying him alive[c]—its tearing the passion of revenge to tatters and to rags—all this would appear but silly if under the pathos of tragedy there were not distinctly perceptible the tricks of comedy. *The London Times* overdoes its part, not only from panic. It supplies comedy with a subject even missed by Molière, the Tartuffe of Revenge. What it simply wants is to write up the funds and to screen the Government. As Delhi has not, like the walls of Jericho, fallen before mere puffs of wind,[406] John Bull is to be steeped in cries for revenge up to his very ears, to make him forget that his Government is responsible for the mischief hatched and the colossal dimensions it has been allowed to assume.

Written on September 4, 1857

First published unsigned in the *New-York Daily Tribune,* No. 5119, September 16, 1857

Reproduced from the newspaper

---

[a] Gaius Julius Caesar, *Commentarii de bello Callico,* Libr. VIII, cap. XLIV.—*Ed.*

[b] [W. Blackstone,] *Commentaries on the Laws of England.*—*Ed.*

[c] W. A. Mozart, *Die Entführung aus dem Serail,* Act III, Scene 6, Osmin's aria.—*Ed.*

Karl Marx

[THE FRENCH CRÉDIT MOBILIER]

The downward movement of the Crédit Mobilier, as we anticipated some months ago, when examining its flowery Report for 1856,[a] has again set in, this time filling the monetary mind of Europe with considerable alarm. In the course of a few days the shares of the concern declined from 950 francs to about 850, this latter quotation being far from the lowest point to which they are likely to ebb. The rise and subsidence of the primeval waters affords no subject of greater interest to the geologist than the ascent and declension of the Crédit Mobilier shares to the politician. There are different epochs to be distinguished in the oscillations of the latter. Their first issue in 1852 was cleverly managed. The shares were divided into three series, the holders of the first series being entitled to the second and third series at par. The consequence was that the fortunate possessors of the first series had all the advantage of a limited supply of shares in a highly excited market, and also of the exaggerated anticipations of the large premium to be quickly attained by the stock of the society. With 250 francs paid on the first issue, the market price of the shares rose at once to 1,775 francs. Their oscillations during the years 1852, '53 and '54 are of minor political interest, since they indicate the different phases through which the forming enterprise had to run rather than the trials of the full-grown concern. In 1855 the Crédit Mobilier had reached its apogee, the momentary quotation at 1,900 francs of its shares marking its greater distance from common earthly business. Since that time the oscillations in the prices of the Crédit Mobilier shares, if

[a] See this volume, pp. 270-77.— *Ed.*

closely considered, and if the average of periods, say of 4 months, be taken, exhibit a downward movement, regulated, in spite of accidental deviations, by a constant and unerring law. The law is this, that from the highest point reached in each of those periods the prices subside to a lowest average point, which, in its turn, becomes the highest starting point for the subsequent period. Thus the figures of 1,400 francs, 1,300 francs, 1,100 francs, mark successively the lowest average point of one period and the highest average point of the other. During the whole of the present Summer, the shares were unable to reach, for any more protracted time, the hight of 1,000 francs; and the present crisis, if it does not result in worse consequences, will bring down the highest average price of the shares to about 800 francs, thence to sink down, in due course of time, to a still lower average level. This process can, of course, not go on *ad infinitum,* nor is it compatible with the organic laws of the Crédit Mobilier that its stocks should be reduced to their nominal quotation of 500 francs. An immense disproportion between capital and operations, hence the realization of extraordinary profits, and, consequently, an unusual elevation of the market price of its shares over their original amount, are conditions for the Crédit Mobilier not of prosperity, but of life. We need the less dwell on this point, as we have sufficiently elucidated it when examining the reduction of its profits from 40 per cent in 1855 to 23 per cent in 1856.[a]

The present depreciation of the Crédit Mobilier shares is connected with circumstances likely to be mistaken for causes, although they are only effects. Mr. A. Thurneyssen, one of the most "respectable" directors of the Crédit Mobilier, has been declared a bankrupt in consequence of the law tribunals pronouncing him liable for a debt of 15,000,000 francs, contracted by his nephew, Mr. Charles Thurneyssen, who fraudulently decamped from France in May last. That the mere bankruptcy of an individual director cannot at all account for the present state of the Crédit Mobilier, will be understood at once by referring to the bankruptcy of Mr. Place, which passed away without shaking to any sensible degree the Bonapartist bulwark. The public mind, however, is more apt to be struck by the sudden downfall of an individual than to trace the slow decline of an institution. Panic seizes the masses only when danger assumes a gross and palpable form. For instance, Law's shares and bank notes went on enjoying

---

[a] See this volume, p. 270.— *Ed.*

the superstitious confidence of France as long as the Regent[a] and his counselors contented themselves with depreciating the metallic money which the notes pretended to represent. The public did not understand that when the mint coined the mark[b] of silver in double the original number of livres, the bank note representing a given amount of silver livres was depreciated one half. But the very moment the notes themselves became, by order of council, depreciated in their official denomination, and a note of 100 livres was to be exchanged for a note of 50 livres, the process was at once understood, and the bubble burst. Thus the fall of almost 50 per cent in the profits of the Crédit Mobilier did not for a moment attract the attention even of the English money-article writers, while the whole press of Europe is now full of din and bustle about Mr. A. Thurneyssen's bankruptcy. The latter, in fact, is accompanied by aggravating circumstances. When Mr. Charles Thurneyssen defaulted in May last Mr. Isaac Pereire, with more than his usual display of virtuous indignation, started forward in the London press to solemnly deny all connection on the part of Mr. A. Thurneyssen and the Crédit Mobilier with the wretched defaulter.[c] The present decision of the French law tribunals has, therefore, given a flat contradiction to that high-sounding gentleman.

Moreover, panic seems to reign in the Crédit Mobilier itself. Mr. Ernest Andrée, one of the Directors, has thought fit to publicly free himself from all future liability, and to renounce all connection with the institution by legal methods. Others—among them the house of Hottinguer—are also said to be beating the retreat. When the pilots themselves take to the life-boat, the passengers may justly consider the vessel lost. Lastly, the intimate connection of the Thurneyssens with the St. Petersburg banking-house of Stieglitz and the great Russian railway scheme may well afford food for thought to the European monetary mind.

If the Directors of the Crédit Mobilier condescend to "create credit in France," to "foster the productive powers of the nation," and to prop up stock gambling all over the world, it would be a stupendous mistake to suppose that they did so for nothing. Over and above the average interest of about 25 per cent annum on the capital represented by their shares, they regularly received a bonus

---

[a] Philip II, Duke of Orleans.—*Ed.*

[b] Denomination of weight for silver, usually 8 oz (about 240 gr.)—*Ed.*

[c] I. Péreire's communication regarding the failure of M. Charles Thurneyssen, "Paris, May 25", *The Times*, No. 22692, May 28, 1857.—*Ed.*

of 5 per cent on the gross profits, say the sum of 275,000 francs or $55,000 each for the first five years of the institution. Then, those Railway Companies and other public works which especially enjoyed the patronage of the Crédit Mobilier, are invariably found to be somehow or other mixed up with the private affairs of the Directors. Thus the Pereires were known to be largely interested in the new shares of the French Southern Railways. Now, in perusing the published accounts, we find the Company in its aggregate capacity to have subscribed not less than 623,000,000 francs to these identical railways. But not only did the fifteen Directors use to direct the operations of the Company according to their private interests; they were also able to regulate their private speculations, in conformity with the foreknowledge they possessed of the great *coups de bourse*[a] the Company was about to execute; and, finally, to enlarge their own credit in proportion to the immense sums officially passing through their hands. Hence the miraculously rapid enrichment of these Directors; hence the nervous anxiety of the European public in regard to financial reverses occurring among them; hence, too, the intimate connection between their private fortunes and the public credit of the Company, although some of the former are sure to be so managed as to outlive the latter.

Written on September 8, 1857

First published in the *New-York Daily Tribune,* No. 5128, September 26, 1857 as a leading article

Reproduced from the newspaper

[a] Stock-exchange speculations.—*Ed.*

Karl Marx

[THE REVOLT IN INDIA]

The news from India, which reached us yesterday, wears a very disastrous and threatening aspect for the English, though, as may be seen in another column, our intelligent London correspondent regards it differently.[407] From Delhi we have details to July 29, and a later report, to the effect that, in consequence of the ravages of the cholera, the besieging forces were compelled to retire from before Delhi and take up their quarters at Agra.[a] It is true, this report is admitted by none of the London journals, but we can, at the very utmost, only regard it as somewhat premature. As we know from all the Indian correspondence, the besieging army had suffered severely in sorties made on the 14th, 18th and 23rd of July. On those occasions the rebels fought with more reckless vehemence than ever, and with a great advantage from the superiority of their cannon.

"We are firing," writes a British officer, "18 pounders and 8-inch howitzers, and the rebels are replying with twenty-fours and thirty-twos." "In the eighteen sallies," says another letter, "which we have had to stand, we have lost one-third of our numbers in killed and wounded."[b]

Of re-enforcements all that could be expected was a body of Sikhs under Gen. Van Cortlandt. Gen. Havelock, after fighting several successful battles, was forced to fall back on Cawnpore, abandoning, for the time, the relief of Lucknow. At the same time "the rains had set in heavily before Delhi," necessarily adding to

---

[a] "Alexandria, Sept. 11", *The Times,* No. 22789, September 18, 1857.— *Ed.*

[b] The letter from an officer employed on the staff at Delhi, *The Times,* No. 22777, September 4, 1857.— *Ed.*

the virulence of the cholera. The dispatch which announces the retreat to Agra and the abandonment, for the moment, at least, of the attempt to reduce the capital of the Great Mogul, must, then, soon prove true, if it is not so already.

On the line of the Ganges the main interest rests on the operations of Gen. Havelock, whose exploits at Futteypore, Cawnpore and Bithoor have naturally been rather extravagantly praised by our London cotemporaries. As we have stated above, after having advanced twenty-five miles from Cawnpore, he found himself obliged to fall back upon that place in order not only to deposit his sick, but to wait for re-enforcements. This is a cause for deep regret, for it indicates that the attempt at a rescue of Lucknow has been baffled. The only hope for the British garrison of the place is now in the force of 3,000 Goorkas[408] sent from Nepaul to their relief by Jung Bahadoor. Should they fail to raise the siege, then the Cawnpore butchery will be re-enacted at Lucknow. This will not be all. The capture by the rebels of the fortress of Lucknow, and the consequent consolidation of their power in Oude, would threaten in the flank all British operations against Delhi, and decide the balance of the contending forces at Benares, and the whole district of Bihar. Cawnpore would be stripped of half its importance and menaced in its communications with Delhi on the one side, and with Benares on the other, by the rebels holding the fortress of Lucknow. This contingency adds to the painful interest with which news from that locality must be looked for. On the 16th of June the garrison estimated their powers of endurance at six weeks on famine allowance. Up to the last date of the dispatches, five of these weeks had already elapsed. Everything there now depends on the reported, but not yet certain re-enforcements from Nepaul.

If we pass lower down the Ganges, from Cawnpore to Benares and the district of Bihar, the British prospect is still darker. A letter in *The Bengal Gazette*,[a] dated Benares, August 3, states

"that the mutineers from Dinapore, having crossed the Sone, marched upon Arrah. The European inhabitants, justly alarmed for their safety, wrote to Dinapore for re-enforcements. Two steamers were accordingly dispatched with detachments of her Majesty's 5th, 10th and 37th. In the middle of the night one of the steamers grounded in the mud and stuck fast. The men were hastily landed, and pushed forward on foot, but without taking due precautions. Suddenly they were assailed on both sides by a close and heavy fire, and 150 of their small force, including several officers, put *hors de combat*.[b] It is supposed that all the Europeans at the station, about 47 in number, have been massacred."

---

[a] Presumably a reference to *The Calcutta Gazette*.—*Ed.*

[b] Out of fight, disabled.—*Ed.*

Arrah, in the British district of Shahabad, Presidency of Bengal, is a town on the road from Dinapore to Ghazepore, twenty-five miles west of the former, seventy-five east of the latter. Benares itself was threatened. This place has a fort constructed upon European principles, and would become another Delhi if it fell into the hands of the rebels. At Mirzapore, situated to the south of Benares, and on the opposite bank of the Ganges, a Mussulman conspiracy has been detected; while at Berhampore, on the Ganges, some eighteen miles distant from Calcutta, the 63rd Native Infantry had been disarmed. In one word, disaffection on the one side and panic on the other were spreading throughout the whole Presidency of Bengal, even to the gates of Calcutta, where painful apprehensions prevailed of the great fast of the Mohurran,[409] when the followers of Islam, wrought up into a fanatical frenzy, go about with swords ready to fight on the smallest provocation, being likely to result in a general attack upon the English, and where the Governor-General[a] has felt himself compelled to disarm his own body-guard. The reader will, then, understand at once that the principal British line of communications, the Ganges line, is in danger of being interrupted, intersected and cut off. This would bear on the progress of the re-enforcements to arrive in November, and would isolate the British line of operations on the Jumna.

In the Bombay Presidency, also, affairs are assuming a very serious aspect. The mutiny at Kolapore of the 27th Bombay Native Infantry is a fact, but their defeat by the British troops is a rumor only. The Bombay native army has broken out into successive mutinies at Nagpore, Aurungabad, Hyderabad, and, finally, at Kolapore. The actual strength of the Bombay native army is 43,048 men, while there are, in fact, only two European regiments in that Presidency. The native army was relied upon not only to preserve order within the limits of the Bombay Presidency, but to send re-enforcements up to Scinde in the Punjaub, and to form the columns moved on Mhow and Indore, to recover and hold those places, to establish communications with Agra, and relieve the garrison at that place. The column of Brigadier Stuart, charged with this operation, was composed of 300 men of the 3d Bombay European Regiment, 250 men of the 5th Bombay Native Infantry, 1,000 of the 25th Bombay Native Infantry, 200 of the 19th Bombay Native Infantry, 800 of the 3d Cavalry Regiment of the Hyderabad Contingent. There are with this force, amounting

[a] Charles John Canning.— *Ed.*

to 2,250 native soldiers, about 700 Europeans, composed chiefly of the Queen's 86th Foot and the 14th Queen's Light Dragoons. The English had, moreover, assembled a column of the native army at Aurungabad to intimidate the disaffected territories of Khandeish and Nagpore, and at the same time form a support for the flying columns acting in Central India.

In that part of India we are told that "tranquillity is restored,"[a] but on this result we cannot altogether rely. In fact it is not the occupation of Mhow which decides that question, but the course pursued by the Holkar and Scindiah, the two Mahratta princes.[410] The same dispatch which informs us of Stuart's arrival at Mhow adds that, although the Holkar still remained staunch, his troops had become unmanageable.[a] As to the Scindiah's policy, not a word is dropped. He is young, popular, full of fire, and would be regarded as the natural head and rallying point for the whole Mahratta nation. He has 10,000 well disciplined troops of his own. His defection from the British would not only cost them Central India, but give immense strength and consistency to the revolutionary league. The retreat of the forces before Delhi, the menaces and solicitations of the malcontents may at length induce him to side with his countrymen. The main influence, however, on the Holkar as well as the Scindiah, will be exercised by the Mahrattas of the Deccan, where, as we have already stated,[b] the rebellion has at last decidedly raised its head. It is here, too, that the festival of the Mohurran is particularly dangerous. There is, then, some reason to anticipate a general revolt of the Bombay army. The Madras army, too, amounting to 60,555 native troops, and recruited from Hyderabad, Nagpore, Malwa, the most bigoted Mohammedan districts, would not be long in following the example. Thus, then, if it be considered that the rainy season during August and September will paralyze the movements of the British troops and interrupt their communications, the supposition seems rational that in spite of their apparent strength, the re-enforcements sent from Europe, arriving too late, and in driblets only, will prove inadequate to the task imposed upon them. We may almost expect, during the following campaign, a rehearsal of the Affghanistan disasters.[411]

Written on September 18, 1857

First published in the *New-York Daily Tribune*, No. 5134, October 3, 1857 as a leading article

Reproduced from the newspaper

[a] "Alexandria, Sept. 8", *The Times*, No. 22786, September 15, 1857.—*Ed.*

[b] See this volume, p. 348.—*Ed.*

Karl Marx

[THE REVOLT IN INDIA][412]

The news received from India by the *Atlantic* yesterday has two prominent points, namely, the failure of Gen. Havelock to advance to the relief of Lucknow, and the persistence of the English at Delhi. This latter fact finds a parallel only in British annals, and in the Walcheren expedition.[413] The failure of that expedition having become certain toward the middle of August, 1809, they delayed re-embarking until November. Napoleon, when he learned that an English army had landed at that place, recommended that it should not be attacked, and that the French should leave its destruction to the disease sure to do them more injury than the cannon, without its costing one centime to France. The present Great Mogul,[a] even more favored than Napoleon, finds himself able to back the disease by his sallies and his sallies by the disease.

A British Government dispatch, dated Cagliari, Sept. 27, tells us that

> "the latest dates from Delhi are to the 12th of August, when that city was still in possession of the rebels; but that an attack was expected to be made shortly, as Gen. Nicholson was within a day's march with considerable re-enforcements."[b]

If Delhi is not taken till Wilson and Nicholson attack it with their present strength, its walls will stand till they fall of themselves. Nicholson's considerable forces amount to about 4,000 Sikhs—a re-enforcement absurdly disproportionate for an attack upon Delhi, but just large enough to afford a new suicidal pretext for not breaking up the camp before the city.

---

[a] Bahadur Shah II.—*Ed.*

[b] "Rear-Admiral at Malta to the Secretary of the Admiralty, London. Sept. 25, 6 p.m.", *The Times*, No. 22798, September 29, 1857.—*Ed.*

After Gen. Hewitt had committed the fault, and one may even in a military point of view say the crime, of permitting the Meerut rebels to make their way to Delhi, and after the two first weeks had been wasted, allowing an irregular surprise of that city, the planning of the siege of Delhi appears an almost incomprehensible blunder. An authority which we shall take the liberty of placing even above the military oracles of *The London Times,* Napoleon, lays down two rules of warfare looking almost like commonplaces: lst. That "only what can be supported ought to be undertaken, and only what presents the greatest number of chances of success;" and 2dly. That "the main forces should be employed only where the main object of war, the destruction of the enemy, lies." In planning the siege of Delhi, these rudimental rules have been violated. The authorities in England must have been aware that the Indian Government itself had recently repaired the fortifications of Delhi so far that that city could be captured by a regular siege only, requiring a besieging force of at least 15,000 to 20,000 men, and much more, if the defense was conducted in an average style. Now, 15,000 to 20,000 men being requisite for this enterprise, it was downright folly to undertake it with 6,000 or 7,000. The English were further aware that a prolonged siege, a matter of course in consequence of their numerical weakness, would expose their forces in that locality, in that climate, and at that season, to the attacks of an invulnerable and invisible enemy, spreading the seeds of destruction among their ranks. The chances of success, therefore, were all against a siege of Delhi.

As to the object of the war, it was beyond doubt the maintenance of English rule in India. To attain that object, Delhi was a point of no strategical significance at all. Historical tradition, in truth, endowed it in the eyes of the natives with a superstitious importance, clashing with its real influence, and this was sufficient reason for the mutinous Sepoys to single it out as their general place of rendezvous. But if, instead of forming their military plans according to the native prejudices, the English had left Delhi alone and isolated it, they would have divested it of its fancied influence; while, by pitching their tents before it, running their heads against it, and concentrating upon it their main force and the attention of the world, they cut themselves off from even the chances of retreat, or rather gave to a retreat all the effects of a signal defeat. They have thus simply played into the hands of the mutineers who wanted to make Delhi the object of the campaign. But this is not all. No great ingenuity was required to convince the English that for them it was of prime importance to create an active field army, whose operations might stifle the sparks of disaffection, keep open the communications between their own military stations, throw the enemy upon some few points, and isolate Delhi. Instead of acting upon this simple and self-evident plan, they immobilize the only active army at their disposal by concentrating it before Delhi, leave the open field to the mutineers, while their *own* garrisons hold scattered spots, disconnected, far distant from each other, and blocked up by overwhelming hostile forces allowed to take their own time.

By fixing their main mobile column before Delhi, the English have not choked up the rebels, but petrified their own garrisons. But, apart from this fundamental blunder at Delhi, there is hardly anything in the annals of war to equal the stupidity which directed the operations of these garrisons, acting independently, irrespectively of each other, lacking all supreme leadership, and acting not like members of one army, but like bodies belonging to different and even hostile nations. Take, for instance, the case of Cawnpore and Lucknow. There were two adjacent places, and two separate bodies of troops, both very small and disproportionate to the occasion, placed under separate commands, though they were only forty miles apart, and with as little unity of action between them as if situated at the opposite poles. The simplest rules of strategy would have required that Sir Hugh Wheeler, the military commander at Cawnpore, should be empowered to call Sir H. Lawrence, the chief Commissioner of Oude, with his troops, back to Cawnpore, thus to strengthen his own position while momentarily evacuating Lucknow. By this operation, *both* garrisons would have been saved, and by the subsequent junction of Havelock's troops with them, a little army been created able to check Oude and to relieve Agra. Instead of this, by the independent action of the two places, the garrison of Cawnpore is butchered, the garrison of Lucknow is sure to fall with its fortress, and even the wonderful exertions of Havelock, marching his troops 126 miles in eight days, sustaining as many fights as his march numbered days, and performing all this in an Indian climate at the hight of the Summer season—even his heroic exertions are baffled. Having still more exhausted his overworked troops in vain attempts at the rescue of Lucknow, and being sure to be forced to fresh useless sacrifices by repeated expeditions from Cawnpore, executed on a constantly decreasing radius, he will, in all probability, have at last to retire upon Allahabad, with hardly any men at his back. The operations of his troops, better than anything else, show what even the small English army before

Delhi would have been able to do if concentrated for action in the field, instead of being caught alive in the pestilential camp. Concentration is the secret of strategy. Decentralization is the plan adopted by the English in India. What they had to do was to reduce their garrisons to the smallest possible number, disencumber them at once of women and children, evacuate all stations not of strategical importance, and thus collect the greatest possible army in the field. Now, even the driblets of re-enforcements, sent up the Ganges from Calcutta, have been so completely absorbed by the numerous isolated garrisons that not one detachment has reached Allahabad.

As for Lucknow, the most gloomy previsions inspired by the recent previous mails[a] are now confirmed. Havelock has again been forced to fall back on Cawnpore; there is no possibility of relief from the allied Nepaulese force; and we must now expect to hear of the capture of the place by starvation, and the massacre of its brave defenders with their wives and children.

Written on September 29, 1857

First published in the *New-York Daily Tribune,* No. 5142, October 13, 1857 as a leading article

Reproduced from the newspaper

[a] See this volume, p. 362.— *Ed.*

Karl Marx

[THE REVOLT IN INDIA]

We yesterday received files of London journals up the 7th inst.[414] In discussing the State of the Indian revolt they are full of the same optimism which they have cultivated from the beginning. We are not only told that a successful attack upon Delhi was to take place, but that it was to take place on the 20th of August. The first thing to ascertain is, of course, the present strength of the besieging force. An artillery officer, writing from the camp before Delhi on the 13th of August, gives the following detailed statement of the effective British forces on the 10th of that month:

	British Officers.	British Troops.	Native Officers.	Native Troops.	H'ses.
Staff	30	...	...	...	...
Artillery	39	598	...	...	...
Engineers	26	39	...	...	...
Cavalry	18	570	...	...	520
1st BRIGADE.					
Her Majesty's 75th Regt.	16	502	...	...	...
Hon. Co.'s 1st Fusileers	17	487	...	...	...
Kumaon Battalion	4	...	13	435	...
2nd BRIGADE.					
Her Majesty's 60th Rifles	15	251	...	...	...
Hon. Co.'s 2d Fusileers	20	493	...	...	...
Sirmoor Battalion	4	...	9	319	...
3d BRIGADE.					
Her Majesty's 8th Regt.	15	153	...	...	...
Her Majesty's 61st Regt.	12	249	...	...	...

	British Officers.	British Troops.	Native Officers.	Native Troops.	H'ses.
4th Sikhs	4	...	4	365	...
Guide Corps	4	...	4	196	...
Coke's Corps	5	...	16	709	...
Total	229	3,342	46	2,024	520[a]

The total effective British force in the camp before Delhi amounted, therefore, on the 10th of August to exactly 5,641 men. From these we must deduct 120 men (112 soldiers and 8 officers), who, according to the English reports, fell on the 12th of August during the attack upon a new battery which the rebels had opened outside the walls, in front of the English left. There remained, then, the number of 5,521[b] fighting men when Brigadier Nicholson joined the besieging army with the following forces from Ferozepore, escorting a second-class siege train: the 52d light infantry (say 900 men), a wing of the 61st (say 4 companies, 360 men), Bourchier's field battery, a wing of the 6th Punjaub regiment (say 540 men), and some Moultan horse and foot; altogether a force of about 2,000 men, of whom somewhat more than 1,200 were Europeans.[c] Now, if we add this force to the 5,521 fighting men who were in the camp on the junction of Nicholson's forces, we obtain a total of 7,521 men. Further re-enforcements are said to have been dispatched by Sir John Lawrence, the Governor of the Punjaub, consisting of the remaining wing of the 8th foot, three companies of the 24th, with three horse-artillery guns of Captain Paton's troops from Peshawur, the 2d Punjaub infantry, the 4th Punjaub infantry, and the other wing of the 6th Punjaub. This force, however, which we may estimate at 3,000 men, at the utmost, and the bulk of which consists altogether of Sikhs, had not yet arrived. If the reader can recall the arrival of the Punjaub re-enforcements under Chamberlain about a month earlier,[d] he will understand that, as the latter were only sufficient to bring Gen. Reed's army up to the original number of Sir H. Barnard's forces, so the new re-enforcements are only sufficient to bring Brigadier Wilson's army up to the

---

[a] A letter from an officer of the Bengal Artillery of August 13, 1857, *The Times,* No. 22803, October 5, 1857.—*Ed.*

[b] Here and below the *New-York Daily Tribune* has "5,529".—*Ed.*

[c] A letter from the *Times* special correspondent at Bombay of August 31, 1857, *The Times,* No. 22800, October 1, 1857.—*Ed.*

[d] See this volume, p. 343.—*Ed.*

original strength of Gen. Reed; the only real fact in favor of the English being the arrival, at last, of a siege train. But suppose even the expected 3,000 men to have joined the camp, and the total English force to have reached the number of 10,000, the loyalty of one-third of which is more than doubtful, what are they to do? They will invest Delhi, we are told. But leaving aside the ludicrous idea of investing with 10,000 men a strongly-fortified city, more than seven miles in extent, the English must first turn the Jumna from its regular course before they can think of investing Delhi. If the English entered Delhi in the morning, the rebels might leave it in the evening, either by crossing the Jumna and making for Rohilcund and Oude, or by marching down the Jumna in the direction of Mattra and Agra. At all events, the investment of a square, one of whose sides is inaccessible to the besieging forces, while affording a line of communication and retreat to the besieged, is a problem not yet solved.

"All agree," says the officer from whom we have borrowed the above table, "that taking Delhi by assault is out of the question."

He informs us, at the same time, what is really expected in the camp, viz:

"to shell the town for several days and make a decent breach."

Now, this officer himself adds that,

"at a moderate calculation, the enemy must muster now nearly forty thousand men beside guns unlimited and well worked; their infantry also fighting well."

If the desperate obstinacy with which Mussulmans are accustomed to fight behind walls be considered, it becomes a great question indeed whether the small British army, having rushed in through "a decent breach," would be allowed to rush out again.

In fact, there remains only one chance for a successful attack upon Delhi by the present British forces—that of internal dissensions breaking out among the rebels, their ammunition being spent, their forces being demoralized, and their spirit of self-reliance giving way. But we must confess that their uninterrupted fighting from the 31st of July to the 12th of August seems hardly to warrant such a supposition. At the same time, a Calcutta letter gives us a broad hint why the English generals had resolved, in the teeth of all military rules, upon keeping their ground before Delhi.

"When," it says, "a few weeks ago it became a question whether our force should retreat from before Delhi, because it was too much harassed by daily fighting to support overwhelming fatigues much longer, that intention was strenuously resisted by Sir John Lawrence, who plainly informed the Generals that their retreat would be the signal for the rising of the populations around them, by which they must be placed in imminent danger. This counsel prevailed, and Sir John Lawrence promised to send them all the re-enforcements he could muster."

Denuded as it has been by Sir John Lawrence, the Punjaub itself may now rise in rebellion, while the troops in the cantonments before Delhi are likely to be laid on their backs and decimated by the pestilential effluvia rising from the soil at the close of the rainy season. Of Gen. Van Cortlandt's forces, reported four weeks ago to have reached Hissar, and to be pushing forward to Delhi,[a] no more is heard. They must, then, have encountered serious obstacles, or have been disbanded on their route.

The position of the English on the Upper Ganges is, in fact, desperate. Gen. Havelock is threatened by the operations of the Oude rebels, moving from Lucknow via Bithoor and trying at Futteypore, to the south of Cawnpore, to cut off his retreat; while simultaneously the Gwalior contingent is marching on Cawnpore from Calpee, a town situated on the right bank of the Jumna. This concentric movement, perhaps directed by Nena Sahib, who is said to wield the supreme command at Lucknow, betrays for the first time some notion of strategy on the part of the rebels, while the English seem anxious only to exaggerate their own foolish method of centrifugal warfare. Thus we are told that the 90th foot and the 5th fusileers dispatched from Calcutta to re-enforce Gen. Havelock have been intercepted at Dinapore by Sir James Outram, who has taken it into his head to lead them via Fyrzabad to Lucknow. This plan of operation is hailed by *The Morning Advertiser* of London as the stroke of a master mind, because, it says, Lucknow will thus have been placed between two fires, being threatened on its right from Cawnpore and on its left from Fyrzabad.[b] According to the ordinary rules of war, the immensely weaker army, which, instead of trying to concentrate its scattered members, cuts itself up into two portions, separated by the whole breadth of the hostile army, has spared the enemy the pains of annihilating it. For Gen. Havelock, the question, in fact, is no longer to save Lucknow, but to save the remainder of his own and Gen. Neill's little corps. He will very likely have to fall back upon Allahabad. Allahabad is indeed a position of decisive importance, forming, as it does, the point of junction between the Ganges and

[a] See this volume pp. 345-46.

[b] "Our present position in India," *The Morning Advertiser*, No. 20686, October 5, 1857.— *Ed.*

the Jumna, and the key to the Doab,[415] situated between the two rivers.

On the first glance at the map, it will be seen that the main line of operations for an English army attempting the reconquest of the North-Western provinces runs along the valley of the lower Ganges. The positions of Dinapore, Benares, Mirzapore, and, above all, of Allahabad, from which the real operations must commence, will therefore have to be strengthened by the withdrawal to them of the garrisons of all the smaller and strategically indifferent stations in the province of Bengal Proper. That this main line of operations itself is seriously threatened at this moment may be seen from the following extract from a Bombay letter addressed to *The London Daily News:*

"The late mutiny of three regiments at Dinapore has cut off communications (except by steamers on the river) between Allahabad and Calcutta. The mutiny at Dinapore is the most serious affair that has happened lately, inasmuch as the whole of the Bihar district, within 200 miles of Calcutta, is now in a blaze. Today a report has arrived that the Santhals[416] have again risen, and the state of Bengal, overrun with 150,000 savages, who delight in blood, plunder and rapine, would be truly terrible."

The minor lines of operation, as long as Agra holds out, are those for the Bombay army, via Indore and Gwalior to Agra, and for the Madras army, via Saugor and Gwalior to Agra, with which latter place the Punjaub army, as well as the corps holding Allahabad, require to have their lines of communication restored. If, however, the wavering princes of Central India should openly declare against the English, and the mutiny among the Bombay army assume a serious aspect, all military calculation is at an end for the present, and nothing will remain certain but an immense butchery from Cashmere to Cape Comorin. In the best case, all that can be done is to delay decisive events until the arrival in November of the European forces. Whether even this be effected will depend upon the brains of Sir Colin Campbell of whom, till now, nothing is known but his personal bravery. If he is the man for his place, he will, at any expense, whether Delhi fall or not, create a disposable force, however small, with which to take the field. Yet, the ultimate decision, we must repeat, lies with the Bombay army.

Written on October 6, 1857

First published in the *New-York Daily Tribune,* No. 5151, October 23, 1857 as a leading article

Reproduced from the newspaper

Karl Marx

[THE REVOLT IN INDIA]

The mail of the *Arabia* brings us the important intelligence of the fall of Delhi. This event, so far as we can judge from the meager details at hand, appears to have resulted upon the simultaneous occurrence of bitter dissensions among the rebels, a change in the numerical proportions of the contending parties, and the arrival on Sept. 5 of the siege train which was expected as long ago as June 8.

After the arrival of Nicholson's re-enforcements, we had estimated the army before Delhi at a total of 7,521 men,[a] an estimate fully confirmed since. After the subsequent accession of 3,000 Cashmere troops, lent to the English by the Rajah Ranbeer Singh, the British forces are stated by *The Friend of India* to have amounted in all to about 11,000 men. On the other hand, *The Military Spectator* of London affirms that the rebel forces had diminished in numbers to about 17,000 men, of whom 5,000 were cavalry; while *The Friend of India* computes their forces at about 13,000, including 1,000 irregular cavalry. As the horse became quite useless after the breach was once effected and the struggle within the town had begun, and, consequently, on the very entrance of the English they made their escape, the total forces of the Sepoys, whether we accept the computation of *The Military Spectator* or of *The Friend of India,* could not be estimated beyond 11,000 or 12,000 men. The English forces, less from increase on their side than from a decrease on the opposite one, had, therefore, become almost equal to those of the mutineers; their slight numerical inferiority being more than made up by the moral

[a] See this volume, pp. 370-71.—*Ed.*

effect of a successful bombardment and the advantages of the offensive enabling them to choose the points on which to throw their main strength, while the defenders were obliged to disperse their inadequate forces over all the points of the menaced circumference.

The decrease on the part of the rebel forces was caused still more by the withdrawal of whole contingents in consequence of internal dissensions than by the heavy losses they suffered in their incessant sorties for a period of about ten days. While the Mogul specter himself, like the merchants of Delhi, had become averse to the rule of the Sepoys, who plundered them of every rupee they had amassed, the religious dissensions between the Hindoo and Mohammedan Sepoys, and the quarrels between the old garrison and the new re-enforcements, sufficed to break up their superficial organization and to insure their downfall. Still, as the English had to cope with a force but slightly superior to their own, without unity of command, enfeebled and dispirited by dissensions in their own ranks, but who yet, after 84 hours' bombardment, stood a six days' cannonade and street-fight within the walls, and then quietly crossed the Jumna on the bridge of boats, it must be confessed that the rebels at last, with their main forces, made the best of a bad position.

The facts of the capture appear to be, that on Sept. 8 the English batteries were opened much in advance of the original position of their forces and within 700 yards of the walls. Between the 8th and the 11th the British heavy ordnance guns and mortars were pushed forward still nearer to the works, a lodgment being effected and batteries established with little loss, considering that the Delhi garrison made two sorties on the 10th and 11th, and made repeated attempts to open fresh batteries, and kept up an annoying fire from rifle-pits. On the 12th the English sustained a loss of about 56 killed and wounded. On the morning of the 13th the enemy's magazine, on one bastion, was blown up, as also the wagon of a light gun, which enfiladed the British batteries from the Talwara suburbs; and the British batteries effected a practicable breach near the Cashmere gate. On the 14th the assault was made on the city. The troops entered at the breach near the Cashmere gate without serious opposition, gained possession of the large buildings in its neighborhood, and advanced along the ramparts to the Moree bastion and Cabul gate, when the resistance grew very obstinate, and the loss was consequently severe. Preparations were being made to turn the guns from the captured bastions on the city, and to bring up other guns and mortars to commanding points. On the 15th the Burn bastions and Lahore bastions were played upon by the captured guns on the Moree and Cabul bastions, while a breach was made in the magazine and the palace began to be shelled. The magazine was stormed at daylight, Sept. 16, while on the 17th the mortars continued to play upon the palace from the magazine inclosure.[a]

At this date, owing, it is said by *The Bombay Courier,* to the plunder of the Punjaub and Lahore mails on the Scinde frontier, the official accounts of the storm break off. In a private communication addressed to the Governor of Bombay,[b] it is stated that the entire city of Delhi was occupied on Sunday, the 20th, the main forces of the mutineers leaving the city at 3 a.m. on the same day, and escaping over the bridges of boats in the direction of Rohilcund. Since a pursuit on the part of the English was impracticable until after the occupation of Selimgurh, situated on the river front, it is evident that the rebels, slowly fighting their way from the extreme north end of the city to its south-eastern extremity, kept, until the 20th, the position necessary for covering their retreat.

As to the probable effect of the capture of Delhi, a competent authority, *The Friend of India,* remarks that

> "it is the condition of Bengal, and not the state of Delhi, that ought at this time to engage the attention of Englishmen. The long delay that has taken place in the capture of the town has actually destroyed any prestige that we might have derived from an early success; and the strength of the rebels and their numbers are diminished as effectually by maintaining the siege as they would be by the capture of the city."

Meanwhile, the insurrection is said to be spreading north-east from Calcutta, through Central India up to the north-west; while on the Assam frontier, two strong regiments of Poorbeahs,[c] openly proposing the restoration of the ex-Rajah Parandur Singh, had revolted; the Dinapore and Ranghur mutineers, led by Kooer Singh, were marching by Banda and Nagode in the direction of Subbulpore, and had forced, through his own troops, the Rajah of Rewah to join them. At Subbulpore itself the 52d Bengal Native Regiment had left their cantonments, taking with them a British officer as a hostage for their comrades left behind. The Gwalior mutineers are reported to have crossed the Chumbul, and are

[a] *The Times,* Nos. 22823 and 22824, October 28 and 29, 1857, "India", "India and China", "The Fall of Delhi".— *Ed.*

[b] John Elphinstone.— *Ed.*

[c] *Poorbeah* means "eastern"; here the reference is to the regiments in eastern Bengal.— *Ed.*

encamped somewhere between the river and Dhalapore. The most serious items of intelligence remain to be noticed. The Todhpore Legion has, it appears, taken service with the rebel Rajah of Arwah, a place 90 miles south-west of Beawar. They have defeated a considerable force which the Rajah of Todhpore had sent against them, killing the General and Captain Monck Mason, and capturing three guns. Gen. G. St. P. Lawrence made an advance against them with some of the Nusserabad force, and compelled them to retreat into a town, against which, however, his further attempts proved unavailing.[a] The denuding of Scinde of its European troops had resulted in a widely extended conspiracy, attempts at insurrection being made at no less than five different places, among which figure Hyderabad, Kurrachee and Sikarpore. There is also an untoward symptom in the Punjaub, the communication between Moultan and Lahore having been cut off for eight days.[b]

In another place our readers will find a tabular statement of the forces dispatched from England since June 18; the days of arrival of the respective vessels being calculated by us on official statements, and therefore in favor of the British Government.[417] From that list it will be seen that, apart from the small detachments of artillery and engineers sent by the overland route, the whole of the army embarked amounts to 30,899 men, of whom 24,739 belong to the infantry, 3,826 to the cavalry, and 2,334 to the artillery. It will also be seen that before the end of October no considerable re-enforcements were to be expected.

Troops for India

The following is a list of the troops which have been sent to India from England since June 18, 1857

Date of arrival	Total	Calcutta	Ceylon	Bombay	Kurrachee	Madras
September 20	214	214	...	...	...	...
October 1	300	300	...	...	...	...
October 15	1,906	124	1,782	...	...	...
October 17	288	288	...	...	...	...
October 20	4,235	3,845	390	...	...	...
October 30	2,028	479	1,549	...	...	...
Total for Oct.	8,757	5,036	3,721			

[a] *The Times,* Nos. 22823 and 22824, October 28 and 29, 1857, "India", "The Fall of Delhi".— *Ed.*

[b] "Trieste, Monday, Oct. 26", "Alexandria, Oct. 20", *The Times,* No. 22822, October 27, 1857.— *Ed.*

Date of arrival	Total	Calcutta	Ceylon	Bombay	Kurrachee	Madras
November 1	3,495	1,234	1,629	...	632	...
November 5	879	879	...	...	...	...
November 10	2,700	904	340	400	1,056	...
November 12	1,633	1,633	...	...	...	...
November 15	2,610	2,132	478	...	...	...
November 19	234	...	...	...	234	...
November 20	1,216	...	278	938	...	...
November 24	406	...	406	...	...	...
November 25	1,276	...	...	...	...	1,276
November 30	666	...	462	204	...	...
Total for Nov.	15,115	6,782	3,593	1,542	1,922	1,276
December 1	354	...	...	354	...	...
December 5	459	...	...	201	...	258
December 10	1,758	...	607	...	1,151	...
December 14	1,057	...	...	1,057	...	...
December 15	948	...	...	647	301	...
December 20	693	185	...	300	208	...
December 25	624	...	...	...	624	...
Total for Dec.	5,893	1,851	607	2,559	2,284	258
January 1	340	...	...	340	...	...
January 5	220	...	...	...	...	220
January 15	140	...	...	...	...	140
January 20	220	...	...	...	...	220
Total for Jan.	920	...	...	340	...	580
Sept. till Jan. 20	30,899	12,217	7,921	4,441	4,206	2,114

Troops dispatched by the overland route:

	Total	Calcutta	Ceylon	Bombay	Kurrachee	Madras
October 2	235 R.E.	117	...	...	118	...
October 12	221 Art.	221	...	...	...	...
October 14	224 R.E.	122	...	...	122	...
Total for Oct.	700	460	...	...	240	...

Total 31,599

Men en route from Cape, partly arrived 4,000

Grand total 35,599

Written on October 30, 1857

First published in the *New-York Daily Tribune,* No. 5170, November 14, 1857 as a leading article

Reproduced from the newspaper

Karl Marx

[THE BANK ACT OF 1844 AND THE MONETARY CRISIS IN ENGLAND][418]

On the 5th inst. the Bank of England raised its minimum rate of discount from 8 per cent, at which it was fixed on October 19, to 9 per cent. This enhancement, unprecedented as it is in the history of the Bank since the resumption of its cash payments, has, we presume, not yet reached its highest point. It is brought about by a drain of bullion, and by a decrease in what is called the reserve of notes. The drain of bullion acts in opposite directions—gold being shipped to this country[a] in consequence of our bankruptcy, and silver to the East, in consequence of the decline of the export trade to China and India, and the direct Government remittances made for account of the East India Company. In exchange for the silver thus wanted, gold must be sent to the continent of Europe.

As to the reserve of notes and the influential part it plays in the London money market, it is necessary to refer briefly to Sir Robert Peel's Bank act of 1844,[419] which affects not only England, but also the United States, and the whole market of the world. Sir Robert Peel, backed by the banker Lloyd, now Lord Overstone, and a number of influential men beside, proposed by his act to put into practice a self-acting principle for the circulation of paper money, according to which the latter would exactly conform in its movements of expansion and contraction to the laws of a purely metallic circulation; and all monetary crises, as he and his partisans affirmed, would thus be warded off for all time to come. The Bank of England is divided into two departments—the issuing department and the banking department; the former being

[a] The United States of America.—*Ed.*

a simple manufactory of notes and the latter the real bank. The issuing department is by law empowered to issue notes to the amount of fourteen millions sterling, a sum supposed to indicate the lowest point, beneath which the actual circulation will never fall, the security for which is found in the debt due by the British Government to the Bank. Beyond these fourteen millions, no note can be issued which is not represented in the vaults of the issuing department by bullion to the same amount. The aggregate mass of notes thus limited is made over to the banking department, which throws them into circulation. Consequently, if the bullion reserve in the vaults of the issuing department amounts to ten millions, it can issue notes to the amount of twenty-four millions, which are made over to the banking department. If the actual circulation amounts to twenty millions only, the four millions remaining in the till of the banking department forms its reserve of notes, which, in fact, constitutes the only security for the deposits confided by private individuals, and by the State to the banking department.

Suppose now that a drain of bullion sets in, and successively abstracts various quantities of bullion from the issuing department, withdrawing, for instance, the amount of four millions of gold. In this case four millions of notes will be cancelled; the amount of notes issued by the issuing department will then exactly equal the amount of notes in circulation, and the reserve of disposable notes in the till of the banking department will have altogether disappeared. The banking department, therefore, will not have a single farthing left to meet the claims of its depositors, and consequently will be compelled to declare itself insolvent; an act affecting its public as well as its private deposits, and therefore involving the suspension of the payment of the quarterly dividends due to the holders of public funds. The banking department might thus become bankrupt, while six millions of bullion were still heaped up in the vaults of the issuing department. This is not a mere supposition. On October 30, 1847, the reserve of the banking department had sunk to £1,600,000 while the deposits amounted to £13,000,000. With a few more days of the prevailing alarm, which was only allayed by a financial *coup d'état* on the part of the Government, the Bank reserve would have been exhausted and the banking department would have been compelled to stop payments, while more than six millions of bullion lay still in the vaults of the issuing department.

It is self-evident then that the drain of bullion and the decrease of the reserve of notes act mutually on each other. While the withdrawal of bullion from the vaults of the issuing department directly produces a decrease in the reserve of the banking department, the directors of the Bank, apprehensive lest the banking department should be driven to insolvency, put on the screw and raise the rate of discount. But the rise in the rate of discount induces part of the depositors to withdraw their deposits from the banking department, and lend them out at the current high rate of interest, while the steady decrease of the reserve intimidates other depositors, and induces them to withdraw their notes from the same department. Thus the very measures taken to keep up the reserve, tend to exhaust it. From this explanation the reader will understand the anxiety with which the decrease of the Bank reserve is watched in England, and the gross fallacy propounded in the money article of a recent number of *The London Times.* It says:

"The old opponents of the Bank Charter Act are beginning to bustle in the storm, and it is impossible to feel certain on any point. One of their great modes of creating fright is by pointing to the low state of the reserve of unemployed notes, as if when that is exhausted the Bank would be obliged to cease discounting altogether."

As a bankrupt, under the existing law it would be. in fact, obliged to do so.

"But the fact is that the Bank could, under such circumstances, still continue the discounts on as great a scale as ever, since their bills receivable each day of course, on the average, bring in as large a total as they are ordinarily asked to let out. They could not increase the scale, but no one will suppose that, with a contraction of business in all quarters, any increase can be required. There is, consequently, not the shadow of a pretext for government palliatives."[a]

The sleight-of-hand on which this argument rests is this: that the depositors are deliberately kept out of view. It needs no peculiar exertion of thought to understand that if the banking department had once declared itself bankrupt in regard to its lenders, it could not go on making advances by way of discounts or loans to its borrowers. Taken all-in-all, Sir Robert Peel's much vaunted Bank law does not act at all in common times; adds in difficult times a monetary panic created by law to the monetary panic resulting from the commercial crisis; and at the very moment when, according to its principles, its beneficial effects

---

[a] "The Bank of England have to-day raised their charge...", *The Times,* No. 22831, November 6, 1857.—*Ed.*

should set in, it must be suspended by Government interference. In ordinary times, the maximum of notes which the Bank may legally issue is never absorbed by the actual circulation—a fact sufficiently proved by the continued existence in such periods of a reserve of notes in the till of the banking department. You may prove this truth by comparing the reports of the Bank of England from 1847 to 1857, or even by comparing the amount of notes which actually circulated from 1819 till 1847, with that which might have circulated according to the maximum legally fixed. In difficult times, as in 1847, and at present by the arbitrary and absolute division between the two departments of the same concern, the effects of a drain of bullion are artificially aggravated, the rise of interest is artificially accelerated, the prospect of insolvency is held out not in consequence of the real insolvency of the Bank, but of the fictitious insolvency of one of its departments.

When the real monetary distress has thus been aggravated by an artificial panic, and in its wake the sufficient number of victims has been immolated, public pressure grows too strong for the Government, and the law is suspended exactly at the period for the weathering of which it was created, and during the course of which it is alone able to produce any effect at all. Thus, on Oct. 23, 1847, the principal bankers of London resorted to Downing street, there to ask relief by a suspension of Peel's Act. Lord John Russell and Sir Charles Wood consequently directed a letter to the Governor and Deputy Governor of the Bank of England,[a] recommending them to enlarge their issue of notes, and thus to exceed the legal maximum of circulation, while they took upon themselves the responsibility for the violation of the law of 1844, and declared themselves prepared to propose to Parliament, on its meeting, a bill of indemnity.[420] The same farce will be again enacted this time, after the state of things has come up to the standard of the week ending on Oct. 23, 1847, when a total suspension of all business and of all payments seemed imminent. The only advantage, then, derived from the Peel Act is this: that the whole community is placed in a thorough dependence on an aristocratic Government—on the pleasure of a reckless individual like Palmerston, for instance. Hence the Ministerial predilections for the act of 1844; investing them with an influence on private fortunes they were never before possessed of.

---

[a] J. Russell's and Ch. Wood's letter to James Morris and H. J. Prescott of October 25, 1847 in Th. Tooke's *A History of Prices, and of the State of Circulation...*, p. 449.—*Ed.*

We have thus dwelt on the Peel Act, because of its present influence on this country,[a] as well as its probable suspension in England; but if the British Government has the power of taking off the shoulders of the British public the difficulties fastened upon them by that Government itself, nothing could be falser than to suppose that the phenomena we shall witness on the London money market—the rise and the subsiding of the monetary panic—will constitute a true thermometer for the intensity of the crisis the British commercial community have to pass through. That crisis is beyond Government control.

When the first news of the American crisis reached the shores of England, there was set up by her economists a theory which may lay claim, if not to ingenuity, to originality at least. It was said that English trade was sound, but that, alas! its customers, and, above all, the Yankees, were unsound. The sound state of a trade, the healthiness of which exists on one side only, is an idea quite worthy of a British economist.[b] Cast a glance at the last half-yearly return issued by the English Board of Trade for 1857, and you will find that of the aggregate export of British produce and manufactures, 30 per cent went to the United States, 11 per cent to East India, and 10 per cent to Australia.[c] Now, while the American market is closed for a long time to come, the Indian one, glutted for two years past, is to a great extent cut off by the insurrectionary convulsions, and the Australian one is so overstocked that British merchandise of all sorts is now sold cheaper at Adelaide, Sydney and Melbourne, than at London, Manchester or Glasgow. The general soundness of the British industrialists, declared bankrupt in consequence of the sudden failure of their customers, may be inferred from two instances. At a meeting of the creditors of a Glasgow calico printer, the list of debts exhibited a total of £116,000, while the assets did not reach the modest amount of £7,000. So, too, a Glasgow shipper, with liabilities of £11,800, could only show assets to meet them of £789. But these are merely individual cases; the important point is that British manufactures have been stretched to a point which must result in a general crash under contracted foreign markets, with a consequent revulsion in the social and political state of Great

---

[a] The United States of America.—*Ed.*

[b] See Marx's letter to Engels, October 20, 1857, present edition, Vol. 40, p. 191.—*Ed.*

[c] "An Account of the Declared Value of British and Irish Produce...", *The Economist.* No. 732, September 5, 1857.—*Ed.*

Britain. The American crisis of 1837 and 1839 produced a decline in British exports from £12,425,601, at which they stood in 1836, down to £4,695,225 in 1837, to £7,585,760 in 1838, and £3,562,000 in 1842. A similar paralysis is already setting in in England. It cannot fail to produce the most important effects before it is over.

Written on November 6, 1857

First published in the *New-York Daily Tribune*, No. 5176, November 21, 1857 as a leading article

Reproduced from the newspaper

Karl Marx

THE BRITISH REVULSION[421]

The British commercial revulsion seems to have worn throughout its immense development the three distinct forms of a pressure on the money and produce markets of London and Liverpool, a bank panic in Scotland, and an industrial breakdown in the manufacturing districts. The facts were stated at length in our pages on Friday,[a] in the form of copious extracts from the British journals, but their importance and prospective consequences require a still further exposition.

Though, as we anticipated in a former article,[b] the Government was finally compelled to suspend the Bank Act of 1844, this was not done till after the Bank had bravely swamped a host of its customers in the endeavor to save itself. But finally, on the evening of Nov. 11, the chiefs of the Bank held a war council, which resulted in an appeal to the Government for help, which was answered by the suspension of the provisions of the Act. This ordinance of the Ministry will at once be submitted to Parliament for approval, that body having been convoked to meet at the close of the month. The effect of the suspension must be one of comparative relief, as we have previously shown. It does away with an artificial stringency, which the Act adds to the natural stringency of the money market in times of commercial revulsion.[422]

In the progress of the present crisis the Bank had five times raised its rate of discount, in the vain hope of checking the rush of the current which was sweeping all away. On the 8th ult. the rate

---

[a] November 27, 1857.—*Ed.*

[b] See this volume, pp. 382-83.—*Ed.*

was advanced to 6 per cent; on the 12th to 7; on the 22d to 8; on the 5th inst. to 9; and on the 9th to 10.[a] The rapidity of this movement offers a remarkable contrast to that which attended the crisis of 1847. Then the minimum rate of discount was raised to 5 per cent in April; to 5 1/2 in July; and to 8, its highest point, on the 23d of October. Thence it sank to 7 per cent on Nov. 20; to 6 on Dec. 4; and to 5 on Dec. 25. The five years next following form an epoch of continual decline in the rate, as regular, indeed, as if guided by a sliding scale. Thus, on June 26, 1852, it had reached its lowest point—being 2 per cent. The next five years, from 1852 to 1857, exhibit an opposite movement. On January 8, 1853, the rate stood at 2 1/2 per cent; on October 1, 1853, it was 5 per cent, whence, through many successive variations, at last it has attained its present elevation. So far, the oscillations of the rate of interest during the period of ten years now concluded have exhibited only the phenomena usual to the recurring phases of modern commerce. These phases are, briefly, an utter contraction of credit in the year of panic, followed by a gradual expansion, which reaches its maximum when the rate of interest sinks to its lowest point; then again a movement in the opposite direction, that of gradual contraction, which reaches its highest point when the interest has risen to its maximum, and the year of panic has again set in. Yet, on a closer examination, there will be discovered in the second part of the present period some phenomena which broadly distinguish it from all its predecessors. During the years of prosperity from 1844 till 1847, the rate of interest in London fluctuated between 3 and 4 per cent, so that the whole period was one of comparatively cheap credit. When the rate of interest reached 5 per cent, on April 10, 1847, the crisis had already set in and its universal explosion was, by a series of stratagems, put off for a few months only. On the other hand, the rate of interest which on May 6, 1854, had already mounted to 5 1/2 per cent, went down again successively to 5 per cent, 4 1/2 per cent, 4 per cent, and 3 1/2 per cent at which latter figure it continued to stand from June 16, 1855, to September 8, 1855. Then it ran again through the identical variations in the opposite direction, increasing to 4 per cent, 4 1/2 per cent, 5 per cent, until, in October, 1855, it had reached the very point from which it had started in May, 1854, namely, 5 1/2 per cent. Two weeks later, on October 20, 1855, it

[a] Here and below Marx used figures from "Dates and Duration of Bank of England Minimum Rates of Discount from 1844", *The Economist,* No. 741, November 7, 1857.—*Ed.*

rose to 6 per cent for short bills, and to 7 per cent for long ones. But again a reaction set in. During the course of 1856 it went down and up until in October, 1856, it had anew reached 6 and 7 per cent, the points from which it had started in the October of the previous year. On November 15, 1856, it rose to 7 per cent, but with irregular and often interrupted fluctuations of decline, which brought it for three months as low as 5 1/2 per cent. It did not recover the original hight of 7 per cent till October 12 of the present year, when the American crisis had begun to bear upon England. From that moment its movement of increase was rapid and constant, resulting at last in an almost complete stoppage of discount.

In other words, during the second half of the period from 1848 to 1857, the vicissitudes in the rate of interest were intensified at more frequently recurring intervals, and from October, 1855 to October, 1857, two years of dear money elapsed, when its fluctuations were circumscribed between the limits of 5 1/2 to 7 per cent. At the same time, in the face of this high rate of interest, production and exchange went on unabated at a pace never before thought of. On the one hand these exceptional phenomena may be traced back to the opportune arrivals of gold from Australia and the United States, which allowed the Bank of England to relax its grip at intervals; while on the other hand it is evident that the crisis was already due in October, 1855, that it was shifted off through a series of temporary convulsions, and that, consequently, its final explosion, as to the intensity of symptoms as well as the extent of contagion, will exceed every crisis ever before witnessed. The curious fact of the recurrence of the rate of 7 per cent on Oct. 20, 1855, on Oct. 4, 1856, and on Oct. 12, 1857, would go far to prove the latter proposition, if we did not know besides that, in 1854, a premonitory collapse had already taken place in this country, and that on the continent of Europe all the symptoms of panic had already repeated themselves in October, 1855 and 1856. On the whole, however, leaving these aggravating circumstances out of view, the period of 1848 to 1857 bears a striking resemblance to those of 1826 to 1836, and of 1837 to 1847.

It is true we were told that British Free Trade would change all this, but if nothing else is proved it is at least clear that the Free-Trade doctors are nothing but quacks. As in former periods, a series of good harvests has been followed by a series of bad ones. In spite of the Free-Trade panacea in England the average price of wheat and all other raw produce has ruled even higher from

1853 to 1857 than from 1820 to 1853; and, what is still more remarkable, while industry took an unprecedented start in the face of the high prices of corn, now, as if to cut off every possible subterfuge, it has suffered an unprecedented collapse in the face of a plentiful harvest.

Our readers will of course understand that this Bank of England rate of 10 per cent is merely nominal, and that the interest really paid by first-class paper in London, greatly exceeds that figure.

"The rates charged in the open market," says *The Daily News,* "are considerably above those of the Bank."

"The Bank of England itself," says *The Morning Chronicle,* "does not discount at the rate of 10 per cent, except in a very few cases—the exception, not the rule; while out of doors charges are notoriously disproportionate to the alleged quotation."

"The inability of second and third-class paper to obtain accommodation on any terms," says *The Morning Herald,* "is already producing immense mischief."

"In consequence of this," as says *The Globe,* "affairs are being brought to a deadlock; firms are falling whose assets exceed their liabilities; and there seems to be a general mercantile revolution."

What with this pressure on the money market, and with the influx of American products, all articles in the produce market have gone down. In the course of a few weeks cotton has fallen at Liverpool 20 to 25 per cent, sugar 25 per cent, corn 25 per cent, and coffee, saltpeter, tallow, leather, and the like, have followed in the wake.

"Discounts and advances upon produce," says *The Morning Post,* "are almost unattainable." [a]

"In Mincing Lane,[423]" says *The Standard,* "business has been turned inside out. It is no longer possible to sell any goods except in the shape of barter, money being out of the question."

All this distress, however, would not have so soon brought the Bank of England to her knees if the Bank panic in Scotland had not occurred. At Glasgow, the fall of the Western Bank was followed by that of the City of Glasgow Bank, producing in its turn a general run of depositors among the middle class and of noteholders among the working classes, and finally resulting in riotous disturbances which induced the Lord Provost of Glasgow to obtain the aid of bayonets. The City of Glasgow Bank, which

---

[a] "The market for the English funds has fluctuated...", *The Morning Post,* No. 26168, November 12, 1857.—*Ed.*

had the honor of being governed by no less a personage than the Duke of Argyll, had a paid-up capital of one million sterling, a reserved fund of £90,595, and ninety-six branches spread through the country. Its authorized issues amounted to £72,921, while those of the Western Bank of Scotland were £225,292, making together £298,213 sterling, or nearly one-tenth of the entire authorized circulating medium of Scotland. The capital of these Banks was to a great extent furnished in small sums by the agricultural population.

The Scotch panic naturally recoiled on the Bank of England; and £300,000 were taken from its vaults on Nov. 11, and £600,000 to £700,000 on the 12th, for transmission to Scotland. Other sums were also withdrawn on behalf of the Irish Banks, while large deposits were called in by the Provincial English Banks; so that the Banking Department of the Bank of England found itself driven to the very verge of bankruptcy. It is probable that for the two Scotch Banks above named the general crisis merely afforded a pretext for effecting a decent exit, they having long been rotten to the core. Still, the fact remains that the celebrated Scotch Banking system which in 1825-26, 1836-37, and in 1847 weathered the hurricanes that swept away the English and Irish Banks, for the first time, under the auspices of Peel's Bank Act, which was forced upon Scotland in 1845, has met with a general run; that for the first time the cry of "gold against paper" has been heard there; and that at Edinburgh, for the first time, even Bank of England notes have been refused. The idea of the defenders of Peel's Act, that if it was unable to ward off monetary crises in general, it would at least secure the convertibility of the notes in circulation, has now been exploded, the noteholders sharing the fate of the depositors.

The general state of the British manufacturing districts cannot be better described than by two extracts, the one from a Manchester trade circular, printed in *The Economist,* the latter from a private letter from Macclesfield in the *The London Free Press.* The Manchester circular, after giving a comparative statement of the cotton trade for the last five years, proceeds as follows:

"Prices have this week been falling with, day by day, more summary acceleration. For numerous descriptions, no prices can be given, because none could find a buyer, and generally where prices are given, they depend more on the position or apprehensions of the holder than on demand. *No current demand exists.* The home trade have laid in more stock than Winter prospects now give hope of clearing."

That foreign markets have been overstocked, the circular does, of course, not say.

"Short time has now been currently adopted as a necessity; the amount of its adoption is computed at present to *exceed one-fifth of the whole production.* The exceptions to extending its adoption are daily becoming less, and *the expediency is now debated of rather closing the mills for a time wholly.*"[a]

The Macclesfield writer tells us:

"At least 5,000 persons, consisting of skilled artisans and their families, who get up each morning and know not where to get food to break their fast, have applied for relief to the Union, and as they come under the class of able-bodied paupers, the alternative is of either going to break stones at about four pence per day, or going into the House, where they are treated like prisoners, and where unhealthy and scanty food is given to them through a hole in the wall; and as to the breaking of stones, to men that have hands only capable of handling the finest of materials, viz: silk, [that] is a complete refusal."[b]

What English writers consider an advantage of their present crisis, as compared with that of 1847—that there is no paramount channel of speculation, like the railways, for instance, absorbing their capital—is by no means a fact. The truth is the English have very largely participated in speculations abroad, both on the Continent of Europe and in America, while at home their surplus capital has been mainly invested in factories, so that, more than ever before, the present convulsion bears the character of an industrial crisis, and therefore strikes at the very roots of the national prosperity.

On the Continent of Europe the contagion has spread from Sweden to Italy in one direction, and from Madrid to Pesth in the other. Hamburg, forming the great commercial center of the exports and imports of the Zollverein,[424] and the general money market of Northern Germany, has had, of course, to bear the first shock. As to France, the Bank of France has screwed up its rate of discount to the English standard; the decrees for the prohibition of the export of corn have been revoked[425]; all the Paris papers have received confidential warnings to beware of gloomy views; the bullion dealers are being frightened by gens d'armes, and

[a] "Markets of the manufacturing districts. Manchester, Thursday Evening, Nov. 5", *The Economist,* No. 741, November 7, 1857.—*Ed.*

[b] "Macclesfield, November 5th, 1857", *The Free Press,* No. 20, November 11, 1857.—*Ed.*

Louis Bonaparte himself, in a rather coxcombical letter,[a] condescends to inform his subjects that he does not feel himself prepared for a financial *coup d'état,* and that, consequently, "the evil only exists in the imagination." [426]

Written on November 13, 1857

First published unsigned in the *New-York Daily Tribune,* No. 5183, November 30, 1857

Reproduced from the newspaper

---

[a] Napoléon III, "Lettre à S. Exc. le ministre des finances. Le 10 novembre 1857", *Le Moniteur universel,* No. 315, November 11, 1857.—*Ed.*

Frederick Engels

[THE CAPTURE OF DELHI][427]

We will not join in the noisy chorus which, in Great Britain, is now extolling to the skies the bravery of the troops that took Delhi by storm. No people, not even the French, can equal the English in self-laudation, especially when bravery is the point in question. The analysis of the facts, however, very soon reduces, in ninety-nine cases out of a hundred, the grandeur of this heroism to very commonplace proportions; and every man of common sense must be disgusted at this overtrading in other people's courage, by which the English paterfamilias who lives quietly at home, and is uncommonly averse to anything that threatens him with the remotest chance of obtaining military glory, attempts to pass himself off as a participator in the undoubted, but certainly not so very extraordinary, bravery shown in the assault on Delhi.

If we compare Delhi with Sevastopol, we of course agree that the Sepoys were no Russians; that none of their sallies against the British cantonment was anything like Inkermann[428]; that there was no Todtleben in Delhi, and that the Sepoys, bravely as every individual man and company fought in most instances, were utterly without leadership, not only for brigades and divisions, but almost for battalions; that their cohesion did not therefore extend beyond the companies; that they entirely lacked the scientific element without which an army is now-a-days helpless, and the defense of a town utterly hopeless. Still, the disproportion of numbers and means of action, the superiority of the Sepoys over the Europeans in withstanding the climate, the extreme weakness to which the force before Delhi was at times reduced, make up for many of these differences, and render a fair parallel between the two sieges (to call these operations sieges) possible. Again we do not consider the storming of Delhi as an act of uncommon or extra-heroic bravery, although as in every battle individual acts of high spirit no doubt occurred on either side, but we maintain that the Anglo-Indian army before Delhi has shown more perseverance, force of character, judgment and skill, than the English army when on its trial between Sevastopol and Balaklava.[429] The latter, after Inkermann, was ready and willing to re-embark, and no doubt would have done so if it had not been for the French. The former, when the season of the year, the deadly maladies consequent upon it, the interruption of the communications, the absence of all chance of speedy re-enforcements, the condition of all Upper India, invited a withdrawal, did indeed consider the advisability of this step, but for all that, held out at its post.

When the insurrection was at its highest point, a movable column in Upper India was the first thing required. There were only two forces that could be thus employed—the small force of Havelock, which soon proved inadequate, and the force before Delhi. That it was, under these circumstances, a military mistake to stay before Delhi, consuming the available strength in useless fights with an unassailable enemy; that the army in motion would have been worth four times its value when at rest; that the clearing of Upper India, with the exception of Delhi, the re-establishing of the communications, the crushing of every attempt of the insurgents to concentrate a force, would have been obtained, and with it the fall of Delhi as a natural and easy consequence, are indisputable facts. But political reasons commanded that the camp before Delhi should not be raised. It is the wiseacres at headquarters who sent the army to Delhi that should be blamed—not the perseverance of the army in holding out when once there. At the same time we must not omit to state that the effect of the rainy season on this army was far milder than was to be anticipated, and that with anything like an average amount of the sickness consequent upon active operations at such a period, the withdrawal or the dissolution of the army would have been unavoidable. The dangerous position of the army lasted till the end of August. The re-enforcements began to come in, while dissensions continued to weaken the rebel camp. In the beginning of September the siege train arrived, and the defensive position was changed into an offensive one. On the 7th of September the first battery opened its fire, and on the evening of the 13th two practicable breaches were opened. Let us now examine what took place during this interval.

If we were to rely, for this purpose, on the official dispatch of

Gen. Wilson,[a] we should be very badly off indeed. This report is quite as confused as the documents issued from the English headquarters in the Crimea ever were. No man living could make out from that report the position of the two breaches, or the relative position and order in which the storming columns were arranged. As to the private reports, they are, of course, still more hopelessly confused. Fortunately one of those skillful scientific officers who deserve nearly the whole credit of the success, a member of the Bengal Engineers and Artillery, has given a report of what occurred, in *The Bombay Gazette*, as clear and business-like as it is simple and unpretending.[b] During the whole of the Crimean war not one English officer was found able to write a report as sensible as this. Unfortunately he got wounded on the first day of the assault, and then his letter stops. As to later transactions, we are, therefore, still quite in the dark.

The English had strengthened the defenses of Delhi so far that they could resist a siege by an Asiatic army. According to our modern notions, Delhi was scarcely to be called a fortress, but merely a place secured against the forcible assault of a field force. Its masonry wall, 16 feet high and 12 feet thick, crowned by a parapet of 3 feet thickness and 8 feet hight, offered 6 feet of masonry beside the parapet, uncovered by the glacis and exposed to the direct fire of the attack. The narrowness of this masonry rampart put it out of the question to place cannon anywhere, except in the bastions and martello towers.[430] These latter flanked the curtain but very imperfectly, and a masonry parapet of three feet thickness being easily battered down by siege guns (field pieces could do it), to silence the fire of the defense, and particularly the guns flanking the ditch, was very easy. Between wall and ditch there was a wide berm or level road, facilitating the formation of a practicable breach, and the ditch, under these circumstances, instead of being a *coupe-gorge*[c] for any force that got entangled in it, became a resting place to re-form those columns that had got into disorder while advancing on the glacis.

To advance against such a place, with regular trenches, according to the rules of sieges, would have been insane, even if the first condition had not been wanting, viz, a force sufficient to invest the place on all sides. The state of the defenses, the

---

[a] [A. Wilson,] "Despatch from General Wilson", *The Times*, No. 22839, November 16, 1857.— *Ed.*

[b] *The Times*, same issue, "India".— *Ed.*

[c] Cut-throat place.— *Ed.*

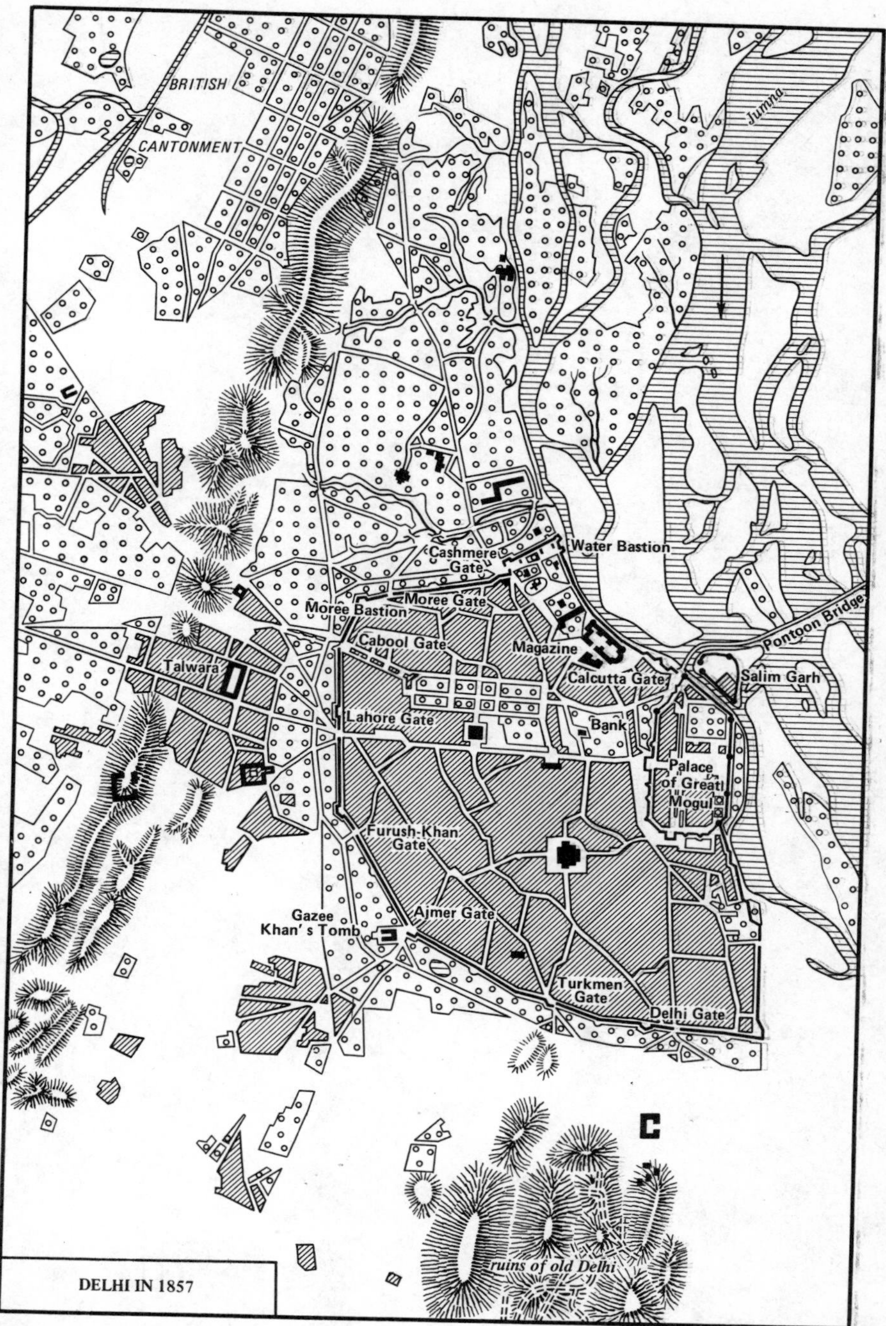

DELHI IN 1857

disorganization and sinking spirit of the defenders, would have rendered every other mode of attack than the one pursued an absolute fault. This mode is very well known to military men under the name of the forcible attack *(attaque de vive force).* The defenses, being such only as to render an open attack impossible without heavy guns, are dealt with summarily by the artillery; the interior of the place is all the while shelled, and as soon as the breaches are practicable the troops advance to the assault.

The front under attack was the northern one, directly opposite to the English camp. This front is composed of two curtains and three bastions, forming a slightly re-entering angle at the central (the Cashmere) bastion. The eastern position, from the Cashmere to the Water bastion, is the shorter one, and projects a little in front of the western position, between the Cashmere and the Moree bastions. The ground in front of the Cashmere and Water bastions was covered with low jungle, gardens, houses, &c, which had not been leveled down by the Sepoys, and afforded shelter to the attack. (This circumstance explains how it was possible that the English could so often follow the Sepoys under the very guns of the place, which was at that time considered extremely heroic, but was in fact a matter of little danger so long as they had this cover.) Besides, at about 400 or 500 yards from this front, a deep ravine ran in the same direction as the wall, so as to form a natural parallel for the attack. The river, besides, giving a capital basis to the English left, the slight salient formed by the Cashmere and Water bastions was selected very properly as the main point of attack. The western curtain and bastions were simultaneously subjected to a simulated attack, and this maneuver succeeded so well that the main force of the Sepoys was directed against it. They assembled a strong body in the suburbs outside the Cabool gate, so as to menace the English right. This maneuver would have been perfectly correct and very effective, if the western curtain between the Moree and Cashmere bastions had been the most in danger. The flanking position of the Sepoys would have been capital as a means of active defense, every column of assault being at once taken in flank by a movement of this force in advance. But the effect of this position could not reach as far eastward as the curtain between the Cashmere and Water bastions; and thus its occupation drew away the best part of the defending force from the decisive point.

The selection of the places for the batteries, their construction and arming, and the way in which they were served, deserve the greatest praise. The English had about 50 guns and mortars, concentrated in powerful batteries, behind good solid parapets. The Sepoys had, according to official statements, 55 guns on the attacked front, but scattered over small bastions and martello towers, incapable of concentrated action, and scarcely sheltered by the miserable three-feet parapet. No doubt a couple of hours must have sufficed to silence the fire of the defense, and then there remained little to be done.

On the 8th, No. 1 battery, 10 guns, opened fire at 700 yards from the wall. During the following night the ravine aforesaid was worked out into a sort of trench. On the 9th, the broken ground and houses in front of this ravine were seized without resistance; and on the 10th, No. 2 battery, 8 guns, was unmasked. This latter was 500 or 600 yards from the wall. On the 11th, No. 3 battery, built very boldly and cleverly at 200 yards from the Water bastion in some broken ground, opened fire with six guns, while ten heavy mortars shelled the town. On the evening of the 13th the breaches—one in the curtain adjoining the right flank of the Cashmere bastion, and the other in the left face and flank of the Water bastion—were reported practicable for escalade, and the assault was ordered. The Sepoys on the 11th had made a counter-approach on the glacis between the two menaced bastions, and threw out a trench for skirmishers about three hundred and fifty yards in front of the English batteries. They also advanced from this position outside the Cabool gate to flank attacks. But these attempts at active defense were carried out without unity, connection or spirit, and led to no result.

At daylight on the 14th five British columns advanced to the attack. One, on the right, to occupy the force outside the Cabool gate and attack, in case of success, the Lahore gate. One against each breach, one against the Cashmere gate, which was to be blown up, and one to act as a reserve. With the exception of the first, all these columns were successful. The breaches were but slightly defended, but the resistance in the houses near the wall was very obstinate. The heroism of an officer and three sergeants of the Engineers (for here there *was* heroism) succeeded in blowing open the Cashmere gate, and thus this column entered also. By evening the whole northern front was in the possession of the English. Here Gen. Wilson, however, stopped. The indiscriminate assault was arrested, guns brought up and directed against every strong position in the town. With the exception of the storming of the magazine, there seems to have been very little actual fighting. The insurgents were dispirited and left the town in masses. Wilson advanced cautiously into the town, found scarcely any resistance after the 17th, and occupied it completely on the 20th.

Our opinion on the conduct of the attack has been stated. As to the defense—the attempt at offensive counter movements, the flanking position at the Cabool gate, the counter-approaches, the rifle-pits, all show that some notions of scientific warfare had penetrated among the Sepoys; but either they were not clear enough, or not powerful enough, to be carried out with any effect. Whether they originated with Indians, or with some of the Europeans that are with them, is of course difficult to decide; but one thing is certain: that those attempts, though imperfect in execution, bear a close resemblance in their ground-work to the active defense of Sevastopol and that their execution looks as if a correct plan had been made for the Sepoys by some European officer, but that they had not been able to understand the idea fully, or that disorganization and want of command turned practical projects into weak and powerless attempts.

Written on November 16, 1857

First published in the *New-York Daily Tribune,* No. 5188, December 5, 1857 as a leading article

Reproduced from the newspaper

Karl Marx

[THE TRADE CRISIS IN ENGLAND]

While on this side of the ocean we were indulging in our little prelude to that great symphonious crash of bankruptcy which has since burst upon the world, our eccentric cotemporary *The London Times* was playing triumphant rhetorical variations, with the "soundness" of British commerce as its theme. Now, however, it tunes another and a sadder chord. In one of its latest impressions, that of Nov. 26, brought to these happy shores by the *Europa* yesterday, that journal declares "the trading classes of England to be unsound to the core." Then proceeding to work itself up to the highest pitch of moral indignation, it exclaims:

> "It is the demoralizing career pursued through eight or ten years of prosperity, before the consummation arrives, that works the deepest ruin. It is in calling into existence gangs of reckless speculators and fictitious bill drawers, and elevating them as examples of successful British enterprise, so as to discourage reliance upon the slow profits of honest industry, that the poison is infused. [...] Each point of corruption thus created forms an ever-extending circle." [a]

We shall not now inquire whether the English journalists who, for a decade, propagated the doctrine that the era of commercial convulsions was finally closed with the introduction of Free Trade, are now warranted in turning all at once from sycophantic encomiasts into Roman censors of modern money-making. The following statements submitted to recent meetings of creditors in Scotland, may serve, however, as matter-of-fact comment on the "soundness" of British commerce.

---

[a] *The Times,* No. 22848, November 26, 1857, "Money-Market and City Intelligence".— *Ed.*

John Monteith & Co., liabilities in excess of the assets	£430,000
D. & T. Macdonald	334,000
Godfrey, Pattison & Co	240,000
William Smith & Co	104,000
T. Trehes, Robinson & Co	75,000
Total	£1,183,000

"It appears from this statement", as *The North British Mail* says, "that on the bankrupts' own showing, £1,183,000 have been lost to the creditors of five houses."

Still the very recurrence of crises despite all the warnings of the past, in regular intervals, forbids the idea of seeking their final causes in the recklessness of single individuals. If speculation toward the close of a given commercial period appears as the immediate forerunner of the crash, it should not be forgotten that speculation itself was engendered in the previous phases of the period, and is therefore, itself a result and an accident, instead of the final cause and the substance. The political economists who pretend to explain the regular spasms of industry and commerce by speculation, resemble the now extinct school of natural philosophers who considered fever as the true cause of all maladies.

The European crisis has so far maintained its center in England, and in England herself, as we anticipated,[a] it has changed aspects. If the first reaction on Great Britain of our American collapse manifested itself in a monetary panic, attended by a general depression in the produce market, and followed more remotely by manufacturing distress, the industrial crisis now stands at the top and the monetary difficulty at the bottom. If London was for a moment the focus of the conflagration, Manchester is so now. The most serious convulsion which English industry ever sustained, and the only one which produced great social changes, the industrial distress from 1838 to 1843, was, for a short period during 1839, accompanied by a contraction of the money market, while during the greater part of the same epoch the rate of interest ruled low, and even sunk down to $2^{1}/_{2}$ and 2 per cent. We make this remark, not because we consider the relative improvement of the London money market as a symptom of its final recovery, but only to note the fact, that in a manufacturing country like England, the fluctuations of the money market are far

---

[a] See this volume, p. 390.— *Ed.*

from indicating either the intensity or the extent of a commercial crisis. Compare, for instance, the London and the Manchester papers of the same date. The former, watching but the efflux and influx of bullion, are all brightness when the Bank of England, by a new purchase of gold, has "strengthened its position." The latter are all gloom, feeling that strength has been bought at their expense, by a rise in the rate of interest and a fall in the price of their products. Hence, even Mr. Tooke, the writer of the *History of Prices,* well as he handles the phenomena of the London money and colonial markets, has proved unable not only to delineate, but even to comprehend, the contractions in the heart of English production.

As to the English money market, its history during the week ending Nov. 27 shows, on the one hand, a continuous alternation between a day of failures and a day marked by the absence of failures; on the other hand, the recovery of the Bank of England and the downfall of the Northumberland and Durham District Bank. The latter bank, founded 21 years ago, numbering 408 shareholders, and disposing of a paid-up capital of £562,891, had its head office at Newcastle and its branch establishments at Alnwick, Berwick, Hexham, Morpeth, North and South Shields, Sunderland and Durham. Its liabilities are stated to amount to three millions sterling, and the weekly wages alone, paid through its instrumentality, to £35,000. The stoppage of the great collieries and iron-works carried on by the advances of this bank will, of course, be the first consequence of its collapse. Many thousand workingmen will thus be thrown out of employment.

The Bank of England is stated to have increased her metallic reserve by about £700,000, an influx of bullion to be accounted for partly by the cessation of the drain to Scotland, partly by shipments from this country[a] and from Russia, and lastly by the arrival of Australian gold. There is nothing remarkable in this movement, since it is perfectly understood that the Bank of England, by screwing up the rate of interest, will curtail imports, force exports, draw back a portion of the British capital invested abroad, and consequently turn the balance of trade and effect an influx of bullion to a certain amount. It is no less sure that on the least relaxation of the terms of discount gold will again begin to flow abroad. The only question is how long the Bank will be able to maintain these terms.

[a] The United States of America.—*Ed.*

The official reports of the Board of Trade for October,[a] a month during which the minimum rate of discount was successively advanced to 6, 7, and 8 per cent, prove evidently that the first effect of that operation was not to stop manufactures, but to force their products into foreign markets and to curtail the importation of foreign produce.

In spite of the American crisis, the exports for October, 1857, exhibit a surplus of £318,838, as compared with October, 1856, while the considerable decrease in the consumption of all articles of food and luxuries exhibited by the same returns proves that this surplus manufacture was far from being remunerative, or the natural consequence of thriving industry. The recoil of the crisis on English industry will become apparent in the next Board of Trade returns. A comparison of the returns for the single months from January, 1857, to October, 1857, will show that English production attained its maximum in the month of May, when the surplus export over that of May, 1856, amounted to £2,648,904. In June, consequent upon the first news of the Indian mutinies, the total production sank down beneath that of the corresponding month in 1856, and exhibited a relative decrease in the exports of £30,247. In July, despite the contraction of the Indian market, the production had not only recovered the standard of the corresponding month in 1856, but exceeded it by no less a sum than £2,233,306. It is, therefore, clear that in that month the other markets had to absorb beyond their ordinary consumption not only the portion usually sent to India, but a great surplus over the usual English production. In that month, therefore, the foreign markets seem to have been so far overstocked that the increase in the exports was successively forced down from about two and one third millions to £885,513 in August, £852,203 in September, and £318,838 in October. The study of the English trade reports affords the only trustworthy clue to the mystery of the present convulsion in that country.

Written on November 27, 1857

First published in the *New-York Daily Tribune*, No. 5196, December 15, 1857 as a leading article

Reproduced from the newspaper

[a] Here and below Marx used the data from *The Economist*, Nos. 718, 722, 727, 731, 736, 740, 744; May 30, June 27, August 1, August 29, October 3, October 31, November 28, 1857.—*Ed.*

Karl Marx

[THE FINANCIAL CRISIS IN EUROPE]

The arrival yesterday morning[a] of the mails of the *Canada* and the *Adriatic* puts us in possession of a week's history of the European financial crisis. This history may be summed up in a few words. Hamburg still formed the center of the convulsion, which reacted more or less severely on Prussia, and was gradually reducing the English money market to the unsettled state which it seemed to be recovering from. Some distant echoes of the storm had reverberated from Spain and Italy. Through the whole of Europe the palsy of industrial activity and the consequent distress of the laboring classes are rapidly spreading. On the other hand, the comparative resistance which France still opposed to the contagion puzzled the political economists as a riddle harder to be solved than the general crisis itself.

The Hamburg crisis was thought to have passed its climax after Nov. 21, upon the establishment of the Guaranteed Discount Association, the total subscriptions for which amounted to 12,000,000 marks banco, destined to secure the circulation of such bills and notes as should receive the stamp of the Association. Still, some days later, the recurrence of some failures, and events like the suicide of the bill broker Gowa, foreshadowed new disasters. On Nov. 26, the panic again had full swing; and as at first the Discount Association, so now the Government itself stepped forward to stem its current. On the 27th, the Senate proposed, and obtained leave from the freehold burgesses of the city, to issue securities bearing interest (exchequer notes), to the amount of 15,000,000 marks banco, for the purpose of making advances

[a] December 3, 1857.—*Ed.*

upon goods of a permanent description, or upon State securities—such advances to amount to from 50 to $66^{2}/_{3}$ per cent of the respective value of the pawned commodities. This second effort to right the course of commerce foundered like the first—both resembling the vain cries of distress which precede a shipwreck. The guaranty of the Discount Association itself was found to need another guaranty in its turn, and the advances of the State, limited in their amount as well as the description of commodities to which they applied, became, moreover, by dint of the very conditions under which they were made, relatively useless, at the same ratio that prices were going down. To uphold prices, and thus ward off the active cause of the distress, the State must pay the prices ruling before the outbreak of the commercial panic, and realize the value of bills of exchange which had ceased to represent anything but foreign failures. In other words, the fortune of the whole community, which the Government represents, ought to make good for the losses of private capitalists. This sort of communism, where the mutuality is all on one side, seems rather attractive to the European capitalists.

On November 29, twenty great commercial Hamburg firms, beside numerous Altona houses, broke down, the discount of bills had ceased, the prices of merchandise and securities became nominal, and all business arrived at a dead lock.[a] From the list of failures it appears that five of them occurred in banking operations with Sweden and Norway—the liabilities of Messrs. Ullberg & Cramer, amounting to 12,000,000 marks banco, five in the Colonial produce trade, four in the Baltic produce trade, two in the export of manufactures, two in insurance agencies, one in the Stock Exchange, one in the ship-building trade. Sweden depends so entirely on Hamburg as her exporter, bill-broker and banker, that the history of the Hamburg market is that of the Stockholm market. Consequently, two days after the collapse a telegram[b] announced that the failures in Hamburg had led to failures in Stockholm, and that there too Government support had proved unavailable. What in this respect holds good for Sweden is still more true for Denmark, whose commercial center, Altona, is but a suburb of Hamburg. On the 1st of December extensive stoppages occurred, including two very old firms, viz.: Conrad

[a] Here and below Marx used the reports from Hamburg of November 30 and December 1, 1857. See *The Times,* Nos. 22854, 22855, December 3, 4, 1857.—*Ed.*

[b] A telegram from Hamburg, dated the 2nd of December, was published in *The Times,* No. 22855, December 4, 1857.—*Ed.*

Warneke, in the Colonial trade, especially sugar, with a capital of 2,000,000 marks banco, and extensively connected with Germany, Denmark and Sweden; and Lorent am Ende & Co., carrying on business with Sweden and Norway. One ship-owner and general merchant committed suicide in consequence of his embarrassments.

The general extent of Hamburg commerce may be inferred from the fact that at this very moment about 500,000,000 m. b. in goods of all kinds are held in warehouses and in port, on account of its merchants. The republic is now recurring to the only remedy against the crisis, that of relieving its citizens from the duty of paying their debts. A law granting a respite of one month on all bills payable at maturity is likely to be passed. As to Prussia, the distress of the manufacturing districts of the Rhine and Westphalia is hardly noticed by the public papers, since it has not yet resulted in extensive failures, the latter having been limited to the corn exporters at Stettin and Dantzig, and to about forty manufacturers at Berlin. The Prussian Government has interfered by authorizing the Berlin Bank to advance loans on goods deposited and by suspending the usury laws.[a] The former measure will prove as vain at Berlin as at Stockholm and Hamburg, and the latter puts Prussia only on a footing of equality with other commercial countries.

The Hamburg collapse is a conclusive answer to those imaginative minds which presume the present crisis to have originated in prices artificially enhanced by a paper currency. In regard to currency, Hamburg forms the opposite pole to this country. There, there is no money but silver. There exists no paper circulation at all, but a medium of exchanges purely metallic is boasted of. Still the present panic not only rages there most severely, but since the appearance of general commercial crises—the discovery of which is not so old as that of the comets—Hamburg has been their favorite arena. Twice during the last third of the eighteenth century it exhibited the same spectacle as at present; and if it is distinguished by one characteristic feature from other great commercial centers of the world, it is by the frequency and violence of the fluctuations in the rate of interest.

Turning from Hamburg to England, we find that the tone of the London money market was progressively improving from

[a] See the reports from Berlin of November 28 and 29 in *The Times,* No. 22853, December 2, 1857.—*Ed.*

Nov. 27 to Dec. 1, when again an opposite current set in. On November 28 the price of silver had actually declined, but after Dec. 1 it again recovered and will probably advance, large amounts being required for Hamburg. In other words, gold will again be withdrawn from London to buy Continental silver, and this renewed drain of bullion will call for the renewed action of the Bank of England screw. Beside the sudden demand at Hamburg, there is looming in a not remote future the Indian loan, which the Government, however it may try to shift off the evil day, must necessarily resort to. The occurrence of fresh failures had also contributed after the 1st inst. to dispel the delusion that the money market had seen its worst. As Lord Overstone (the banker Lloyd) remarked in the opening session of the House of Lords:

"The next occasion of pressure upon the Bank will probably occur before the exchanges are rectified, and then the crisis will be greater than that which we have shrunk from meeting on the present occasion. There are serious and formidable difficulties hanging over this country." [a]

The catastrophe at Hamburg has not yet been felt at London. The greater easiness of the loan market had favorably affected the produce market; but, irrespective of the eventual new contraction of money, it is evident that the great fall in the prices of produce in Stettin, Dantzig and Hamburg cannot but bring down the London quotations. The French decree rescinding the prohibition of the export of corn and flour [431] immediately compelled the London millers to reduce their quotations by three shillings per 280 pounds, in order to stem the influx of flour from France. Several failures in the corn-trade have been reported, but they have been confined to smaller houses and operators in grain for distant delivery.

The English manufacturing districts exhibit no novelty, except that cotton goods adapted to the Indian demand, such as brown shirtings, jaconets, madapolams, as well as yarns suitable for the same market, fetch, for the first time since 1847, remunerative prices in India. Since 1847, the profits made by the Manchester manufacturers in that trade have been derived, not from the price realized on the sale of their goods in East India, but only on the sale in England of their East Indian returns. The almost total suppression of Indian export since June, 1857, occasioned by the revolt, has allowed the Indian market to absorb the floating

[a] S. Overstone's speech in the House of Lords, December 3, 1857, *The Times*, No. 22855, December 4, 1857.— *Ed.*

English goods and even to open itself for new supplies at enhanced prices.[a] Under ordinary circumstances such an event would have given extraordinary liveliness to the Manchester trade. At present, as we are informed by private letters, it has hardly raised the prices of the privileged articles, while it turned such an amount of employment seeking productive power to the manufacture of these particular articles as would suffice to overstock three Indias on the shortest notice. Such has been the general enlargement of productive power in the British manufacturing districts during the last ten years, that even the reduction of labor to less than two-thirds its previous amount can only be sustained by the mill-owners accumulating in their warehouses a large surplus stock of fabrics. Messrs. Du Fay & Co., in their monthly Manchester trade report, say that "there was a pause in business during the month; very few transactions took place, and prices were altogether nominal. Never before was the sum total of a month's transactions so small as in November."

It is, perhaps, proper here to call attention to the fact that in the year 1858 the repeal of the British Corn Laws[432] will first be put to a serious test. What with the influence of Australian gold and industrial prosperity, what with the natural results of bad harvests, the average price of wheat during the epoch from 1847 to 1857 ruled higher than during the epoch from 1826 to 1836. A keen competition of foreign agriculture and produce will now have to be sustained concurrently with a decline in the home demand; and agricultural distress, which seemed buried in the annals of British history from 1815 to 1832, is likely to appear again. It is true that the advance in the price of French wheat and flour, following upon the Imperial decrees, has proved but temporary, and vanished even before any extensive export to England took place. But with a further pressure on the money market of France she will be forced to throw her corn and flour into England, which will be at the same time assailed by forced sales of German produce. Then in the spring the shipments from the United States will come forward, and give the British corn market its finishing blow. If, as the whole history of prices warrants us in supposing, several good harvests are now to follow each other in succession, we shall see fully worked out the true consequences of the repeal of the Corn Laws for the agricultural laborers in the first instance,

---

[a] See Engels's letter to Marx of November 15, 1857 (present edition, Vol. 40, pp. 200-04).— *Ed.*

the farmers in the second, and the whole framework of British landed property in the last.

Written on December 4, 1857

First published in the *New-York Daily Tribune,* No. 5202, December 22, 1857 as a leading article

Reproduced from the newspaper

Karl Marx

[THE CRISIS IN EUROPE][433]

The mails of the *Niagara* reached us yesterday, and a careful examination of our files of British journals only confirms the views we have lately had to express with regard to the probable course of the crisis in England.[a] The London money market is decidedly improving; that is to say, gold is accumulating in the vaults of the Bank of England; the demand for discount at the Bank is decreasing; first-class paper may be discounted in Lombard street[434] at $9^1/_2$ to $9^3/_4$ per cent; the public funds are firm, and the share market participates to some degree in this movement. This agreeable aspect of things is, however, badly impaired by great failures, recurring every two or three days in London; by daily dispatches, sad messengers of provincial disasters; and by the thunder of *The London Times,* inveighing more than ever against the general and helpless corruption of the British mercantile classes. In fact, the comparative easiness with which unexceptionable paper is discounted, seems to be more than balanced by the growing difficulty of finding paper which can pass as unexceptionable. Consequently, we are told in the London money articles of the latest date, that at Threadneedle street[435] the applications are extremely "limited," and that at Lombard street but little business is doing. Still, as the supply on the part of the Bank and the discount houses is increasing—while the pressure upon them, the demand on the part of their customers, is decreasing—the money market must be said to be comparatively easy. Nevertheless the Bank of England Directors have not yet dared to lower the rate of discount, convinced as it would appear

[a] See this volume, pp. 406-09.—*Ed.*

that the renewal of the monetary crisis is not a question of time, but of percentage, and that, consequently, as the rate of discount sinks, the monetary crisis is sure to rise again.

While the London money market, one way or the other, has thus got more easy, the stringency of the English produce market is increasing in intensity, a continuous fall in prices not being able to overcome the growing disinclination to purchase. Even such articles as tallow, for instance, which had previously formed an exception to the general rule, have now, by dint of forced sales, been obliged to give way. On comparing the price current of the week ending December 18 with the weekly price current of November, it appears that the extreme depression in prices which prevailed in the latter month has again been reached; this time, however, not in the shape of a panic, but the methodic form of a sliding scale. As to the manufacturing markets, an earnest of the industrial crisis which we predicted[a] has now been given in half a dozen failures of spinners and weavers in Lancashire, of three leading houses in the woolen trade in the West Riding, and an important firm in the carpet trade of Worcester.

Since the phenomena of this double crisis, in the produce market and among the manufacturing classes, will by and by become more palpable, we shall content ourselves, for the present, with quoting the following passage of a private letter from Manchester, which has been communicated for our columns:

> "Of the continuous pressure on the market and its disastrous effects you can hardly form any notion. No one can sell. Every day you hear of lower quotations. Things are come to that pass that respectable people prefer not to offer their commodities at all. Spinners and weavers are weighed down by utter despondency. No yarn commissioners sell yarn to the weavers except on cash or double securities. It is impossible for this state of things to go on without ending in a frightful collapse."[b]

The Hamburg crisis has scarcely abated.[c] It is the most regular and classical example of a monetary crisis that ever existed. Everything except silver and gold had become worthless. Firms of old standing have broken down, because they are unable to pay in cash some single bill that had fallen due, although in their tills

---

[a] See this volume, pp. 390, 401-02.— *Ed.*

[b] Marx paraphrases Engels's letter to him of December 17, 1857 (present edition, Vol. 40, pp. 222-23). In this article he also uses other data from that letter.— *Ed.*

[c] See this volume, pp. 404-06.— *Ed.*

there lay bills to a hundred times its value, which, however, for the moment were valueless, not because they were dishonored, but because they could not be discounted. Thus, we are informed that the old and wealthy firm of Ch. M. Schröder, before its bankruptcy, had offered to it two millions in silver, on the part of L. H. Schröder, the brother, of London, but replied by telegraph: "Three millions or nothing." The three millions did not come forward, and Ch. M. Schröder went to the wall. A different instance is that of Ullberg & Co., a firm much spoken of in the European press, which, with liabilities amounting to 12,000,000 marks banco, including 7,000,000 of bills of exchange, had, as now appears, a capital of only 300,000 marks banco as the basis of such enormous transactions.[a]

In Sweden, and especially in Denmark, the crisis has rather increased in violence.[b] The revival of the evil after it appeared to have passed away is to be explained by the dates on which the great demands on Hamburg, Stockholm and Copenhagen fall due. During December, for instance, nine millions of bills drawn on Hamburg by Rio de Janeiro houses for coffee fell due, were all protested, and this mass of protests created a new panic. In January the drafts for the cargoes of sugar shipped from Bahia and Pernambuco will probably meet with a similar fate, and cause a similar revival of the crisis.

Written on December 18, 1857

First published in the *New-York Daily Tribune,* No. 5213, January 5, 1858 as a leading article, and reprinted in the *New-York Semi-Weekly Tribune,* No. 1316, January 5, 1858

Reproduced from the *New-York Daily Tribune*

---

[a] For the description of the Hamburg bankruptcies Marx used the facts cited by Engels in his letter of December 7, 1857 (present edition, Vol. 40, pp. 212-13).— *Ed.*

[b] See this volume, pp. 405-06.— *Ed.*

Karl Marx

THE FRENCH CRISIS[436]

The successive reduction by the Bank of France of its rate of discount from 10 per cent, at which it stood after Nov. 12, to 9 per cent on Nov. 26, 8 per cent on Dec. 5, and 6 per cent on Dec. 17,[a] is, of course, pointed out by the Imperialist organs as irrefutable proof that the commercial revulsion has entered its decreasing stage, and that "France will go through the severe trial without any catastrophe." The financial system of Napoleon III. is said to have created "this evident superiority of the commercial state of France over that of all other nations," and to insure the fact that France is, and always will be, "less injured in a time of crisis than the countries competing with it." Now, 6 per cent is a rate of bank discount which, since the beginning of the present century, has never occurred in France save in February, 1800, some days after the foundation of the Bank by the uncle,[b] until under the nephew,[c] in the critical period of 1855 and 1856. But if the Bank of France continues to lower its rate of interest, say to 4 per cent, what then? The rate of discount was reduced to 4 per cent on Dec. 27, 1847, when the general crisis still lasted and the French crisis had not yet reached its climax. Then, as now, the Government congratulated France on its privilege of escaping general crisis with nothing but scratches, and those not skin deep. Two months later the financial earthquake had overturned the throne and the wise man who sat upon it.[d]

---

[a] Marsaud, "Banque de France", *Le Moniteur universel,* No. 352, December 18, 1857.— *Ed.*

[b] Napoleon I.— *Ed.*

[c] Napoleon III.— *Ed.*

[d] Louis Philippe.— *Ed.*

We do certainly not contest the fact that thus far the crisis has had less influence on French commerce than was expected. The reason is simply that in transactions with the United States, Great Britain, and the Hanseatic towns, the balance of trade is, and has been for a long time, in favor of France. Thus, in order that the disasters occurring in those countries should directly recoil on France, large credits must have been given to them, or commodities for export to them have been speculatively accumulated. Nothing of the sort has happened. The American, English and Hanseatic events could, consequently, produce no drain of bullion from France; and if its Bank for some weeks raised the rate of interest to the English standard, it did this only for fear lest French capital should seek more profitable employment abroad.

But it cannot be denied that the general crisis has, even in its present phase, told on France in a form agreeable to the commercial relations of that country with the United States, England and the Hanseatic towns, viz.: in the chronic form of distress. It has forced Bonaparte—who, in his letter of November 10, declared "the evil to exist in the imagination only"[a]—to come out with another official message to the effect that "in spite of the prudence of French trade and the vigilance of the Government, the commercial crisis has obliged many branches of industry, if not to suspend work, at any rate to shorten their time or lower their wages," so that "many workmen suffer from forced idleness."[b] He has consequently opened a credit of a million francs for the relief of the necessitous and finding them means of employment; he has ordered military precautions to be taken at Lyons; and, through his journals, has appealed to private charity. The withdrawals from the savings banks have begun by far to exceed the deposits. Heavy losses from failures in America and England have been sustained by many manufacturers, production is contracting to a disastrous degree at Paris, Lyons, Mühlhausen, Roubaix, Rouen, Lille, Nantes, St. Etienne, and other industrial centers, while serious embarrassments prevail at Marseilles, Havre and Bordeaux.

The general stagnation of trade throughout the country is most evident from the last monthly report of the Bank of France, which shows for the month of December a decrease in circulation of

---

[a] Napoléon III, "Lettre à S. Exc. le ministre des finances...", *Le Moniteur universel,* No. 315, November 11, 1857.—*Ed.*

[b] A. Billault, "Rapport à l'Empereur", *Le Moniteur universel,* No. 346, December 12, 1857.—*Ed.*

73,040,000 francs, as compared with October, and of 48,955,900 francs as compared with November; while the aggregate of discounts has fallen about 100,000,000 francs, if compared with October, and 77,067,059 francs compared with November.[a] In the present state of the French press it is, of course, not possible to ascertain the exact state of the failures occurring in provincial towns, but the Paris bankruptcies, although certainly not yet serious, exhibit a tendency to grow not only in quantity, but also in the quality of the concerns involved. In the fortnight from Nov. 17 to Dec. 1 thirty-four Paris bankruptcies only occurred, of which not fewer than twenty-four were of dealers in second-hand clothes, milk-dealers, tailors, artificial flower-makers, cabinet-makers, reticule-makers, gilders, leather dealers, jewelers, fringe-makers, vinegar-makers, cap-makers, fruiterers, &c. From the 1st of December up to the 8th the bankruptcies were no fewer than thirty-one, and from the 9th to the 15th the number amounted to thirty-four, including some of greater importance, such as Messrs. Bourdon, Dubuch & Co., bankers; the General Company of *voitures de remise,*[b] a Company for Jacquard looms, an oil Company,[c] &c. On the other hand, Bonaparte's attempt at checking the ruinous fall in the prices of wheat and flour by the abrogation of the prohibition decrees, has proved a failure, prices having progressively sunk from the 26th November to the 21st of December, and despite a fair margin of profit on sales in London, no more than 3,000 sacks (of 110 kilogrammes) being shipped thither up to the 22d of December.

If, however, the balance of trade is in favor of France in her dealings with the United States, England, and the Hanseatic towns, it is against her in her commerce with Southern Russia, the Zollverein,[437] Holland, Belgium, the Levant and Italy. As to Switzerland, the temporary balance of trade is always against her, but France is so deeply indebted to her—most of the Alsatian manufactures being carried on by Swiss capital—that in times of monetary scarcity she may always heavily pull upon the French money market. At this period, as at every former one, there will be no active French crisis before the commercial difficulties in those countries have reached a certain hight. That Holland cannot tide over the present storm, will be understood on the simple

[a] "Situation de la Banque de France et de ses succursales", *Le Moniteur universel,* Nos. 282, 317 and 345, October 9, November 13 and December 11 1857.—*Ed.*

[b] Hired carriages.—*Ed.*

[c] *The Economist,* No. 747, December 19, 1857.—*Ed.*

consideration that her still large commerce is almost limited to that description of produce which has undergone and is progressively undergoing the most fatal depreciation. In the industrial centers of the Zollverein the premonitory symptoms of the crisis are already visible. Apprehensions of a crash in the Black Sea and Levantine trade are announcing themselves in the Trieste papers, and its first precursory flashes have sufficed to bring down some large houses at Marseilles. In Italy, finally, the monetary panic, at the very moment that it seems subsiding in the North of Europe, has burst out ablaze, as will be seen from the following extract from the *Opinione* of Milan, of Dec. 18:

"The difficulties of the present time are very, very great; failures are occurring on a frightful scale, and after those of Palleari, of Ballabio and Co., of Cighera, of Redaelli, of Wechler and Mazzola, after the *contre-coup* of foreign cities, after the suspension of payments by the best houses of Verona, Venice, Udine and Bergamo, our strongest firms also begin to waver, and to make up their accounts. And the accounts are very sad. Let it suffice to remark that among our great silk houses there is not one that has in warehouse a less quantity than 50,000 pounds of silk, whence it is easy to calculate that at present prices every one of them must lose from half a million to two millions of francs—the stock of some of them exceeding 150,000 lb. The firm of Brambilla Brothers was supported by a loan of one million and a half of francs; Battista Gavazzi is liquidating, and others are doing the same. Every man asks himself what we have to look forward to; so many fortunes vanished, so many reduced by one-half; so many families, lately in easy circumstances, now at their last shift; so many workmen without work or bread, or means of subsistence of any kind."[a]

When the French crisis, consequent upon the growing pressure from these countries, comes to maturity, it will have to grapple with a nation of gamblers, if not of commercial adventurers, and with a Government that has played the same part in France as private commerce has done in this country,[b] in England and Hamburg. It will fall severely upon the stock market and endanger the supreme security of that market—the State itself. The natural result of the contraction of French commerce and industry is to place money at the disposition of the Bourse, especially as the Bank of France is bound to make advances upon public funds and railway securities. Instead of checking stock gambling, the present stagnation of French commerce and industry has favored it. Thus we see from the last monthly report of the Bank of France, that its advances on railway shares have increased simultaneously with the decrease in discounts and

---

[a] Quoted according to the report from Turin of December 19, 1857, published in *The Times*, No. 22871, December 23, 1857.—*Ed.*

[b] The United States of America.—*Ed.*

circulation. Thus, in spite of the heavy decrease in the receipts of most of the French railways, their quotations are looking up, the receipts of the Orleans line, for instance, having decreased by 22 1/2 per cent toward the close of November, as compared with the corresponding period of last year; yet Orleans was quoted on Dec. 22 at 1,355, while it stood on 1,310 francs only on Oct. 23.[a]

When the depression of trade set in upon France some railway companies were at once compelled to interrupt their works, and a similar fate threatened almost all of them. To mend this the Emperor forced the Bank of France into a treaty with the companies, by dint of which it becomes in fact the real railway contractor. It has to advance the money upon the new bonds which the companies are authorized by the settlement of Nov. 30, 1856, to emit in 1858; and on that part which remained still to be issued for 1857; the authorized issue of bonds for 1858 amounting to forty-two and a half millions. The Crédit Mobilier[438] seemed also destined to succumb before the first shock, and had on the 3d of December to sell at an enormous sacrifice part of its immense amount of securities. There is now a project afloat of amalgamating it with the Crédit Foncier and the Comptoire d'Escompte,[439] in order to make it share in the privilege granted to those institutions of having their bills discounted and their securities received by the Bank of France. Thus the plan evidently is to weather the storm by making the Bank of France responsible for all these concerns—a maneuver which of course exposes the Bank itself to wreck. But what even Napoleon III cannot think of, is to make the Bank pay the calls the private shareholders of the different joint-stock companies will have to encounter. Excluding petty affairs, the calls to be met toward the close of December were: Mercantile and Industrial Company of Madrid (Messrs. Rothschild), $30 per share; Franco-American Navigation Company, $10 per share; Victor Emmanuel Railway Company, $30 per share; Herserange Iron Works Company, $20 per share; the Mediterranean, $30 per share; the Austrian Railway, $15; the Saragossa, $10; the Franco-Swiss, $10; the Société Générale de Tanneries, $10; the Companie de la Carbonisation de Houilles[b] $10, &c. At the beginning of the year there is a payment of $20 per share on the

[a] "Bourse du mardi 22 décembre 1857", *Le Moniteur universel,* No. 357, December 23, 1857; "Bourse du vendredi 23 octobre 1857", *Le Moniteur universel,* No. 297, October 24, 1857. The sum given in *Le Moniteur* is 1,320 francs.—*Ed.*

[b] Company of the Carbonisation of Coal.—*Ed.*

Chimay and Marienburg Railway, of $12\frac{1}{2}$ on the Lombard-Venetian Railways, and $20 on the Belgian and South American Steam Navigation Company. According to the settlement of Nov. 30, 1856, the calls for French railways alone will, in 1858, amount to about $50,000,000. There is certainly a great danger that France may founder on these heavy engagements in 1858, as England did in 1846-47. Moreover, capitalists in Germany, Switzerland and the Netherlands, are large holders of French securities, the greater part of which, at the progress of the crisis in those countries, will be thrown upon the Paris Bourse to be turned into money at any price.

Written on December 25, 1857

First published in the *New-York Daily Tribune,* No. 5219, January 12, 1858 as a leading article

Reproduced from the newspaper

Frederick Engels

[THE SIEGE AND STORMING OF LUCKNOW][440]

The last mails from Calcutta brought some details, which have made their way to this country through the London journals, from which it is possible to form a judgment as to Sir Colin Campbell's performance at Lucknow. As the British press assert that this feat of arms stands forth in unrivaled glory in the history of warfare, the subject may as well be a little more closely examined.

The town of Lucknow is situated on the right bank of the River Goomtee, which at that locality runs in a south-easterly direction. At a distance of from two to three miles from the river a canal runs nearly parallel to it, intersects the town, and below it approaches the river, which it then joins about a mile further down. The banks of the river are not occupied by crowded streets, but by a succession of palaces, with gardens and insulated public buildings. At the junction of the canal and river, but on the right or southern bank of both, are situated, close together, a school, called La Martinière, and a hunting-palace and park, called Dilkhoosha. Crossing the canal, but remaining on the southern side of the river, and close to its bank, the first palace and garden is that of Secunderbagh; further west come barracks and Mess-house, and then the Motee Mahal (Pearl Palace), which is but a few hundred yards from the Residency.[441] This latter building is erected on the only high ground in the neighborhood; it commands the town, and consists of a considerable inclosure with several palaces and out-houses within it. To the south of this line of buildings is the compact portion of the town, and two miles south of this is the park and palace of Alumbagh.

The natural strength of the Residency at once explains how it was possible for the English to hold out in it against far superior numbers; but this very fact at once shows also what class of fighters the Oudians are. In fact, men who, partly drilled under European officers and provided plentifully with artillery, have never yet been able to overcome a single miserable inclosure defended by Europeans—such men are, militarily speaking, no better than savages, and a victory over them cannot add much to the glory of any army, however great the odds may be in favor of the natives. Another fact which classes the Oudians with the most contemptible opponents to be met with, is the manner in which Havelock forced his way through the very thickest portion of the town, in spite of barricades, loopholed houses, and the like. His loss, indeed, was great; but compare such an engagement with even the worst-fought street-battle of 1848![a] Not one man of his weak column could have made good his way had there been any real fighting. The houses cannot have been defended at all; it would have required weeks to take as many of them as would have secured a clear passage. As to the judgment displayed by Havelock in thus taking the bull by the horns, we cannot form an opinion; it is said he was compelled to do so from the great strait to which the Residency was reduced, and other motives are mentioned; however, nothing authentic is known.

When Sir Colin Campbell arrived he had about 2,000 European and 1,000 Sikh infantry; 350 European and 600 Sikh cavalry; 18 horse-artillery guns, 4 siege guns, and 300 sailors with their heavy shipguns; in all, 5,000 men, among which were 3,000 Europeans. This force was about as strong in numbers as a very fair average of most Anglo-Indian armies that have accomplished great exploits; indeed, the field-force with which Sir C. Napier conquered Sinde[442] was scarcely half as large, and often less. On the other hand, its large admixture of the European element and the circumstance that all its native portion consisted of the best fighting nation of India, the Sikhs, give it a character of intrinsic strength and cohesion far superior to the generality of Anglo-Indian armies. Its opponents, as we have seen, were contemptible, for the most part rough militia instead of trained soldiers. True, the Oudians pass for the most warlike race of Lower Hindostan, but this is the case merely in comparison with the cowardly Bengalees, whose *morale* is utterly broken down by the most relaxing climate of the world and by centuries of oppression. The way in which they submitted to the "filibustering" annexation of their country to the Company's dominions, and the whole of their

---

[a] The reference is to the revolution of 1848-49.—*Ed.*

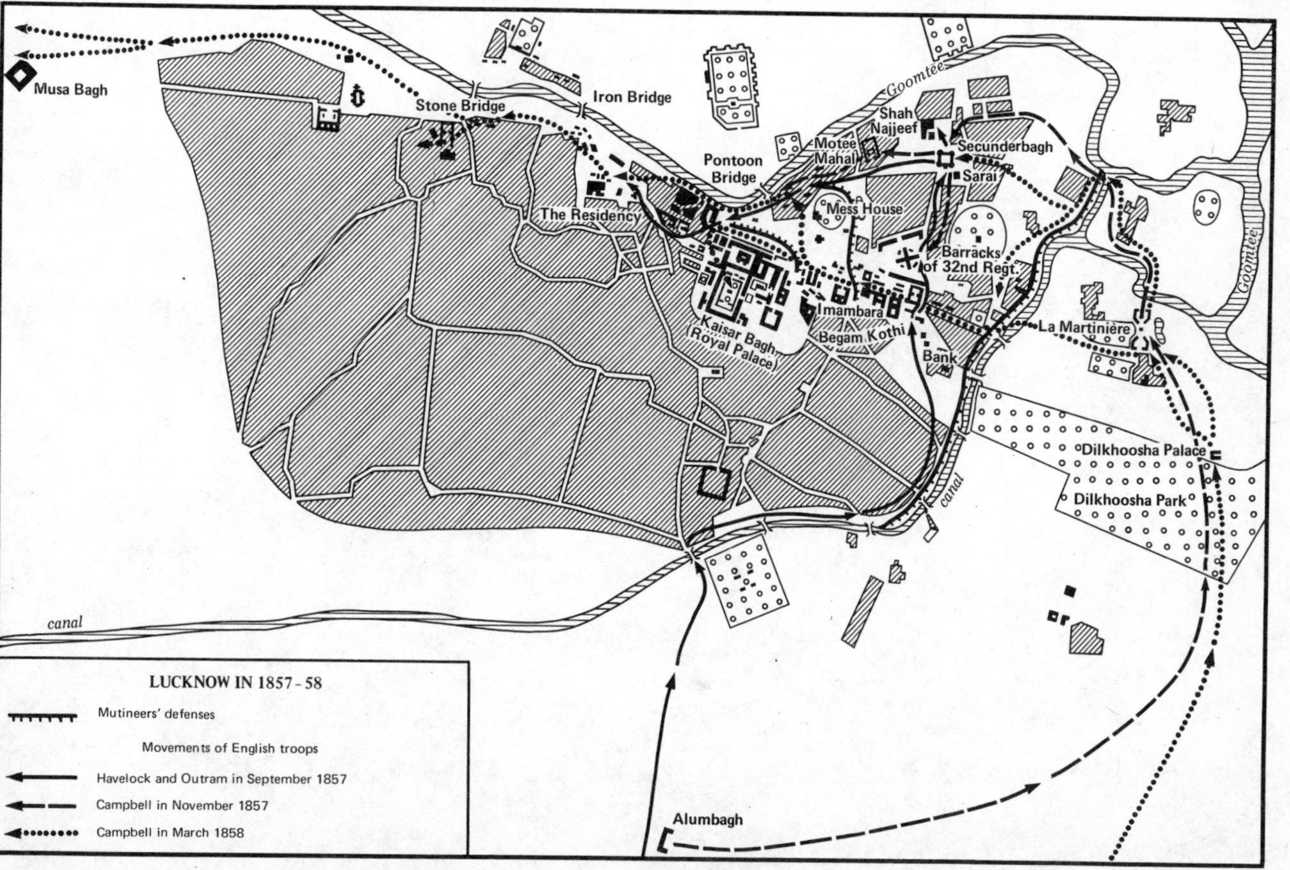
Musa Bagh
Stone Bridge
Iron Bridge
Goomtee
Shah Najjeef
Secunderbagh
Motee Mahal
Pontoon Bridge
Sarai
Mess House
The Residency
Barracks of 32nd Regt.
Imambara
Kaisar Bagh (Royal Palace)
Begam Kothi
Bank
La Martinière
Goomtee
Dilkhoosha Palace
Dilkhoosha Park
canal
canal
Alumbagh
LUCKNOW IN 1857–58
Mutineers' defenses
Movements of English troops
Havelock and Outram in September 1857
Campbell in November 1857
Campbell in March 1858

behavior during the insurrection, certainly places them below the level of the Sepoys, as far as courage and intelligence are concerned. We are, indeed, informed that quantity made up for quality. Some letter-writers say there were as many as 100,000 in the town. They were, no doubt, superior to the British in the proportion of four or six to one, perhaps more; but with such enemies that makes little difference. A position can only be defended by a certain number, and if these are determined to run away it matters little whether four or five times that number of similar heroes are within half a mile. There is no doubt that many instances of individual bravery have been seen, even among these Oudians. Some among them may have fought like lions; but of what avail were these in a place which they were too weak to defend after the mere rabble among the garrison had run away? There appears to have never been among them any attempt at bringing the whole under a single command; their local chiefs had no authority except over their own men, and would not submit to anybody else.

Sir Colin Campbell advanced first on Alumbagh; then, instead of forcing his way through the town as Havelock had done, he profited by the experience gained by that General and turned toward Dilkhoosha and La Martinière.[a] The ground in front of these inclosures was cleared of the Oudian skirmishers on Nov. 13. On the 15th the attack commenced. So neglectful had the enemy been that the preparations for intrenching the Dilkhoosha were not yet completed even then; it was taken at once, and without much resistance, and so was the Martinière. These two positions secured to the English the line of the canal. The enemy advanced once more across this obstacle to retake the two posts, lost in the morning, but they were soon routed, with heavy loss. On the 16th the British crossed the canal and attacked the Secunderbagh Palace. The intrenchments here were in a little better order, consequently Gen. Campbell wisely attacked the place with artillery. After the defenses had been destroyed, the infantry charged and took the place. The Samuck, another fortified position, was next cannonaded for three hours and then taken, "after one of the severest fights ever witnessed," says Sir C. Campbell[b]—and, adds a wise correspondent from the seat of

---

[a] Here and below Engels draws on "The Relief of Lucknow", *The Times*, No. 22876, December 29, 1857.—*Ed.*

[b] C. Campbell's words were cited by G. F. Edmonstone in the telegram published in *The Times*, No. 22876, December 29, 1857.—*Ed.*

war, "few men have seen more of hard fighting than he." We should like to know where he saw it. Surely not in the Crimea, where, after the battle of the Alma,[443] he had a very quiet life of it at Balaklava, only one of his regiments being engaged at the battle of Balaklava[444] and none at Inkermann.[445]

On the 17th the artillery was pointed on the barracks and Mess-house which formed the next position toward the Residency. This cannonade lasted till 3 o'clock, after which the infantry took the place by storm. The flying enemy was hotly pursued. One more position remained between the advancing army and the Residency—the Motee Mahal. Before dusk this, too, was carried, and the communication with the garrison was fully established.

Campbell should be praised for the judgment with which he took the easier route and with which he used his heavy artillery to reduce the intrenched positions before he launched his columns. But the British fought with all the advantages of skilled soldiers obeying one chief over half savages commanded by nobody; and, as we see, they fully availed themselves of these advantages. They did not expose their men more than was absolutely necessary. They used artillery as long as there was anything to be battered down. No doubt they fought with valor; but what they deserve credit for is discretion. The best proof of this is in the number of the killed and wounded. It has not yet been published as far as the men are concerned; but there were five officers killed and thirty-two wounded. The army must have had, with 5,000 men, at least 250 to 300 officers. The English officers are certainly never sparing of their lives. To show an example of bravery to their men is in too many cases the part of their duty which they only know. And when in three days' consecutive fighting, under circumstances and in positions which are known to cost more lives than any other to conquer, the loss is only one in eight or nine, it is out of the question to call it hard fighting. To take an example from British history alone, what is all this Indian fighting put together against the single defense of Hougoumont and La Haye Sainte at Waterloo?[446] What would these writers who now turn every little skirmish into a pitched battle say of contests like Borodino, where one army lost one-half and the other one-third of its combatants?[447]

Written on January 4, 1858

First published in the *New-York Daily Tribune,* No. 5235, January 30, 1858 as a leading article

Reproduced from the newspaper

Karl Marx

BRITISH COMMERCE

During the late extraordinary session of the British Parliament, Lord Derby declared in the House of Lords that, for the last three years the value of British imports had exceeded that of British exports to the amount of £160,000,000.[a] This statement gave rise to a controversy, out of doors, some private individuals applying to Lord Stanley of Alderley, President of the Board of Trade, for information as to the correctness of Lord Derby's statement. The President of the Board of Trade, in a letter addressed to his interrogators, replied:

"The assertion made by Lord Derby in the House of Lords, that the value of our imports during the last three years had exceeded that of our exports by £160,000,000, is incorrect, and arises from Lord Derby having taken the total value of our imports, including our imports from the Colonies and foreign countries, while he has excluded the re-export of merchandize which has been received from the Colonies and foreign countries. Thus Lord Derby's calculation shows:

"Importations	£468,000,000
Exports	308,000,000
Difference	£160,000,000

"Whereas it should be:

Importations	£468,000,000
Exports	371,000,000,
Difference	£97,000,000"[b]

---

[a] E. G. Derby's speech in the House of Lords, December 3, 1857, *The Times*, No. 22855, December 4, 1857.—*Ed.*

[b] J. Johnson's inquiry, made on the instructions of the Foreign Affairs Association, and J. G. Fanshawe's reply on behalf of the President of the Board of Trade were published in *The Free Press*, No. 26, December 23, 1857.—*Ed.*

The President of the Board of Trade substantiates this assertion by adding to it a comparative statement of the value of the exports and imports of the United Kingdom during the years 1855, 1856 and 1857. This highly interesting document, which is not to be found in the London newspapers, we reprint below.[a] First it will be seen that the case might be put in a shape confirmatory of Lord Derby's assertion, viz.:

Total imports	£468,000,000
British exports	308,000,000
Excess of imports over British exports	£160,000,000
Re-exports of foreign produce	63,000,000
Balance of trade against Great Britain	£97,000,000

Thus, there is actually an excess of foreign imports over British exports of 160,000,000, and after the re-export of 63,000,000 of foreign productions, there remains a balance of trade against Great Britain, as stated by the President of the Board of Trade himself, of 97,000,000, or more than 32,000,000 for the average of the three years, 1855, 1856, and 1857. Hence, the recent complaint of *The London Times:*

"The actual losses sustained by the nation have been going on for the last five or six years, and it is only now that we have found them out."[b]

These losses, however, arise not from the excess of imports over exports, but from the specific character of a great part of the exports.

The fact is, one-half the re-exports consists of foreign raw materials used in manufactures serving to increase foreign rivalry against the British industrial interests, and, to some extent, returned to the Britishers in manufactured goods for their home consumption. The decisive point, however, to be kept in view, is this, that the large re-exports of raw materials, resulting from the competition of Continental manufactures, enhanced the price of the raw material so much as almost to absorb the profit left to the British manufacturer. On a former occasion, we made some statements in this sense with respect to the British Cotton industry.

[a] See this volume, pp. 428-29.— *Ed.*

[b] *The Times,* No. 22869, December 21, 1857 "Money-Market and City Intelligence".— *Ed.*

As at the present moment the industrial crisis rages most violently in the British Woolen districts, where failure follows upon failure, anxiously concealed from the general public by the London press, it may be opportune to give at this place some figures showing into what effective competition for raw wool the manufacturers of the European Continent were entering with the British ones—a competition which led to the unparalleled enhancement in the price of that raw material, ruinous to the manufacturer, and fostering the now blown-up speculations in that article. The following statement comprises the first nine months of each of the last five years[a]:

Imports.

Year.	Foreign.	Colonial.	Total.
1853	£37,586,199	£46,277,276	£83,863,475
1854	27,006,173	50,187,692	77,193,865
1855	17,293,842	53,896,173	71,190,015
1856	22,377,714	62,148,467	84,526,181
1857	27,604,364	63,053,100	90,657,464

Exports.

Year.	Foreign.	Colonial.	Total.
1853	£2,480,410	£5,243,166	£7,723,576
1854	5,993,366	13,117,102	19,110,468
1855	8,860,904	12,948,561	21,809,465
1856	5,523,345	14,433,958	19,957,303
1857	4,561,000	25,068,787	29,629,787

The quantities of foreign and colonial wools returned for British home consumption appear, therefore, to have been, in the years:

Year	*Wool.*	Pounds
1853	....	76,139,899
1854	....	58,083,397
1855	....	49,380,550
1856	....	64,568,878
1857	....	61,027,677

---

[a] Here and below Marx quotes from "The Supply and Consumption of Wool", *The Economist,* No. 741, November 7, 1857.—*Ed.*

On the other hand, the quantities of British home-grown wool exported were:

1853	lb 4,755,443
1854	9,477,396
1855	13,592,756
1856	11,539,201
1857	13,492,386

By deducting from the quantity of foreign wools imported into the United Kingdom, first the quantity re-exported and next the quantities of English wools exported, we find the following real quantities of foreign wool available for British home consumption:

1853	lb 71,384,456
1854	48,606,001
1855	35,787,794
1856	53,029,677
1857	47,535,291

While, therefore, the import into the United Kingdom of colonial wool increased from 46,277,276 lbs. in the first nine months of 1853 to 63,053,100 lbs. in the same period of 1857, and the total imports of all kinds from 83,863,475 lbs. to 90,657,464 lbs. during the same respective periods, such, in the mean time, had been the increase in the demand for the European Continent, that, in regard to the foreign and colonial wools, the quantities returned for British consumption diminished in the five years from 76,139,899 lbs. in 1853 to 61,027,677 lbs. in 1857; and taking into account the quantities of English wools exported, there took place an aggregate reduction from 71,384,456 lbs. in 1853 to 47,535,291 lbs. in 1857. The significance of these statements will be better understood when attention is called to the fact avowed by *The London Times,* in a money article, that, simultaneously with this increase in the export of wool from the United Kingdom, the import of Continental woolen manufactures, especially French ones, was increasing.

From the figures furnished by Lord Stanley of Alderley we have abstracted the following tabular statement, showing the degree in which the balance of trade with Great Britain was favorable or unfavorable to different countries:

Balance of Trade against England
for 1855, 1856, 1857.

1. United States	£28,571,764
2. China	22,675,433
3. East Indies	19,605,742

4. Russia	16,642,167
5. Prussia	12,842,488
6. Egypt	8,214,941
7. Spain	7,146,917
8. Br. West Indies	6,906,314
9. Peru	6,282,382
10. Sweden	5,027,934
11. Cuba & Porto Rico	4,853,484
12. Mauritius	4,672,090
13. New-Brunswick	3,431,303
14. Denmark	3,391,144
15. Ceylon	3,134,575
16. France	2,696,291
17. Canada	1,808,454
18. Norway	1,686,962
19. Africa (Western)	1,432,195
20. Portugal	1,283,075
21. Two Sicilies	1,030,139
22. Chili	693,155
23. Buenos Ayres	107,676

Balance of Trade in favor of England for 1855, 1856, 1857.

1. Hanse Towns	18,883,428
2. Australia	17,761,889
3. Turkey	6,947,220
4. Brazil	7,131,160
5. Belgium	2,214,207
6. Holland	1,600,904
7. Cape of G. Hope	59,661

The simple fact of the excess of British imports over exports, amounting in three years to £97,000,000 would by no means warrant the cry now raised by the Britishers "of carrying on their trade at a yearly sacrifice of £33,000,000," and benefiting by that trade foreign countries only. The enormous and increasing amount of British capital invested in all parts of the world must be paid for in interest, dividends and profits, all of which are to be remitted to a great extent in the form of foreign produce, and consequently go to swell the list of British imports. Beyond the imports corresponding to their exports, there must be a surplus of imports, remitted not in payment for commodities, but as revenue of capital. Generally speaking, the so-called balance of trade must, therefore, always be in favor of the world against England, because the world has yearly to pay to England not only for the commodities it purchases from her, but also the interest of the debt it owes her. The really disquieting feature for England of the statements above made is this, that she is apparently at a loss to find at home a sufficient field of employment for her unwieldy capital; that she must consequently lend on an increasing scale, and similar, in this point, to Holland, Venice and Genoa, at the epoch of their decline, forge herself the weapons for her competitors. She is forced, by giving large credits, to foster speculation in other countries in order to find a field of employment for her surplus capital, and thus to hazard her acquired wealth in order to augment and conserve it. By being obliged to give large credits to foreign manufacturing countries, such as the Continent of Europe, she forwards herself the means to her industrial rivals to compete with her for the raw produce, and thus is herself instrumental in enhancing the raw material of her own fabrics. The small margin of profit thus left to the British manufacturer, still reduced by the constant necessity for a country the very existence of which is bound up with the monopoly of forming the workshop of the world, constantly to undersell the rest of the world, is then compensated for by curtailing the wages of the laboring classes and creating home misery on a rapidly-enlarging scale. Such is the natural price paid by England for her commercial and industrial supremacy.

A Comparative Statement
of the Value of the Imports and Exports of the United Kingdom
from and to the Principal Foreign Countries
and British Possessions in 1854, 1855, and 1856.[a]

		IMPORTS.	VALUE OF EXPORTS.		
Countries.	Years.	Computed real value of Imports.	Declared Value of Produce of the United Kingdom.	Computed Real Value of Foreign & Colonial Produce.	Total.
		£	£	£	£
Foreign.					
Russia	1854	4,252,288	54,301	19,738	74,039
	1855	478,169	...	...	...
	1856	11,561,924	1,595,237	1,775,617	3,370,854

[a] The data given here and below are taken from *The Free Press*, No. 26, December 23, 1857.—*Ed.*

Countries.	Years.	IMPORTS. Computed real value of Imports.	VALUE OF EXPORTS. Declared Value of Produce of the United Kingdom.	Computed Real Value of Foreign & Colonial Produce.	Total.
		£	£	£	£
Sweden	1854	2,509,539	334,518	249,792	584,310
	1855	2,325,171	545,384	279,515	824,899
	1856	2,031,861	629,697	300,795	930,492
Norway	1854	1,369,440	402,290	106,244	508,534
	1855	1,099,642	487,400	102,551	589,951
	1856	947,934	488,489	143,080	631,569
Denmark	1854	2,706,186	758,228	230,010	988,238
	1855	3,086,979	756,967	260,624	1,017,591
	1856	2,201,831	1,033,142	352,173	1,385,315
Prussia	1854	9,055,503	798,434	1.717,285	2,515,719
	1855	10,242,862	1,100,021	2,016,650	3,116,671
	1856	4,534,815	933,715	624,908	1,558,623
Hanse Towns	1854	6,221,524	7,413,715	2,720,274	10,133,989
	1855	4,816,298	8,350,228	3,344,416	11,694,644
	1856	5,302,739	10,134,813	3,260,543	13,395,356
Holland	1854	6,731,141	4,573,034	2,320,877	6,893,911
	1855	6,460,932	4,558,210	2,611,767	7,169,977
	1856	7,433,442	5,728,253	2,434,278	8,162,531
Belgium	1854	3,631,161	1,406,932	1,948,740	3,355,672
	1855	2,533,732	1,707,693	2,239,514	3,947,207
	1856	2,936,796	1,689,975	2,323,042	4,013,017
France	1854	10,447,774	3,175,290	3,216,175	6,391,465
	1855	9,146,418	6,012,658	4,409,223	10,421,881
	1856	10,386,522	6,432,650	4,038,427	10,471,077
Spain	1854	3,594,501	1,270,464	165,642	1,436,106
	1855	4,799,728	1,158,800	135,192	1,293,992
	1856	3,645,083	1,734,483	377,820	2,112,303
Cuba and Porto Rico	1854	3,369,444	1,073,861	4,727	1,078,588
	1855	2,332,753	1,077,745	22,933	1,100,678
	1856	2,654,580	1,398,837	25,190	1,424,027

Countries.	Years.	IMPORTS. Computed real value of Imports.	VALUE OF EXPORTS. Declared Value of Produce of the United Kingdom.	Computed Real Value of Foreign & Colonial Produce.	Total.
		£	£	£	£
Portugal	1854	2,101,126	1,370,603	148,997	1,519,600
	1855	1,962,044	1,350,791	184,580	1,535,371
	1856	2,164,090	1,455,754	433,470	1,889,224
Two Sicilies	1854	1,411,457	563,033	109,258	672,291
	1855	1,281,940	921,220	175,221	1,096,441
	1856	1,505,582	1,202,183	197,925	1,400,108
Turkey Proper	1854	2,219,298	2,758,605	317,476	3,076,081
	1855	2,294,571	5,639,898	419,119	6,059,017
	1856	2,383,029	4,416,029	291,991	4,708,020
Egypt	1854	3,355,928	1,253,353	113,895	1,367,248
	1855	3,674,682	1,454,371	117,235	1,571,606
	1856	5,753,518	1,587,682	43,151	1,630,833
United States (including California)	1854	29,795,302	21,410,369	923,034	22,333,403
	1855	25,741,752	17,318,086	744,517	18,062,603
	1856	36,047,773	21,918,105	698,772	22,616,877
Brazil	1854	2,083,589	2,891,840	119,982	3,011,822
	1855	2,273,819	3,312,728	128,550	3,441,278
	1856	2,229,048	4,084,537	179,979	4,264,516
Buenos Ayres	1854	1,285,186	1,267,125	32,565	1,299,690
	1855	1,052,033	742,442	26,383	768,825
	1856	981,193	998,329	43,892	1,042,221
Chili	1854	1,380,563	1,421,855	43,589	1,465,444
	1855	1,925,271	1,330,385	56,688	1,387,073
	1856	1,700,776	1,396,446	64,492	1,460,938
Peru	1854	3,138,527	949,289	22,236	971,525
	1855	3,484,288	1,285,160	60,278	1,345,438
	1856	3,048,694	1,046,010	26,154	1,072,164
China (including Hong Kong)	1854	9,125,040	1,000,716	26,400	1,027,116
	1855	8,746,590	1,277,944	26,052	1,303,996
	1856	9,421,648	2,216,123	70,611	2,286,734

Countries.	Years.	IMPORTS. Computed real value of Imports.	VALUE OF EXPORTS. Declared Value of Produce of the United Kingdom.	Computed Real Value of Foreign & Colonial Produce.	Total.
		£	£	£	£
W. C. of Africa (exclusive of Br. & Fr. Pos.)	1854	1,528,896	646,868	174,073	820,941
	1855	1,516,729	839,831	219,827	1,059,658
	1856	1,657,375	666,374	223,842	890,216
Total Foreign Countries	1854	118,239,554	63,800,605	15,645,612	79,446,217
	1855	109,959,539	69,524,475	18,710,749	88,235,224
	1856	129,517,568	83,327,154	20,035,442	103,362,596
British Possessions					
Canada	1854	4,007,052	3,957,085	180,569	4,137,654
	1855	2,296,277	1,515,823	90,298	1,606,121
	1856	3,779,741	2,418,250	123,591	2,541,841
New-Brunswick	1854	2,079,674	863,704	40,273	903,977
	1855	4,379,041	370,560	27,718	398,278
	1856	1,891,707	572,542	34,322	606,864
British West India Islands	1854	3,977,271	1,870,674*	166,690	2,037,364
	1855	3,978,278	1,389,992	136,022	1,526,014
	1856	4,157,098	1,462,156	180,799	1,642,955
British Guiana	1854	1,636,267		31,779	31,779
	1855	1,491,935	421,398	35,189	456,587
	1856	1,418,264	411,241	41,248	452,489
British Settlements in Australia	1854	4,301,868	11,931,352	1,474,634	13,405,986
	1855	4,500,200	6,278,966	942,659	7,221,625
	1856	5,736,043	9,912,575	1,759,814	11,672,389
British East Indies	1854	10,672,862	9,127,556	493,154	9,620,710
	1855	12,668,732	9,949,154	404,321	10,358,475
	1856	17,262,851	10,546,190	478,328	11,024,518
Ceylon	1854	1,506,646	382,276	31,228	413,504
	1855	1,474,251	305,576	20,321	325,897
	1856	1,304,174	388,435	22,660	411,095

* Including British Guiana.
** Included with West Indies.

Countries.	Years.	IMPORTS. Computed real value of Imports.	VALUE OF EXPORTS. Declared Value of Produce of the United Kingdom.	Computed Real Value of Foreign & Colonial Produce.	Total.
		£	£	£	£
Mauritius	1854	1,677,533	383,210	17,936	401,146
	1855	1,723,807	303,173	14,772	317,945
	1856	2,427,007	420,180	16,977	437,157
Cape of Good Hope & Brit. Pos. in S. Afr'a	1854	691,352	921,957	63,309	985,266
	1855	949,640	791,313	45,437	836,750
	1856	1,502,828	1,344,338	73,127	1,417,465
Total of British Possessions	1854	34,149,499	33,384,121	2,990,754	36,374,875
	1855	33,583,311	26,163,610	2,292,466	28,456,076
	1856	43,026,586	32,499,794	3,357,963	35,857,757
Total Foreign Countries and Br. Posses'ns.	1854	152,389,053	97,184,726	18,636,366	115,821,092
	1855	143,542,850	95,688,085	21,003,215	116,691,300
	1856	172,544,154	115,826,948	23,393,405	139,220,353

Written on about January 7, 1858

First published unsigned in the *New-York Daily Tribune,* No. 5238, February 3, 1858

Reproduced from the newspaper

Frederick Engels

THE RELIEF OF LUCKNOW[448]

We have at last before us the official dispatch of Sir Colin Campbell on the relief of Lucknow. It confirms in every respect the conclusions we drew from the first non-official reports on this engagement.[a] The contemptible character of the resistance offered by the Oudians is even more apparent from this document, while on the other hand Campbell himself appears to take more pride in his skillful generalship than in any uncommon bravery displayed either by him or his troops. The dispatch states the strength of the British troops at about 5,000, of whom some 3,200 were infantry, and 700 cavalry, the rest artillery, naval brigade, engineers, &c. The operations commenced, as stated, with the attack on Dilkhoosha. This garden was taken after a running fight. "The loss was very trifling; the enemy's loss, too, was trifling, owing to the suddenness of retreat."[b] There was, indeed, no chance of displaying heroism on this occasion. The Oudians retreated in such a hurry that they crossed at once through the grounds of La Martinière without availing themselves of the new line of defense offered by this post. The first symptom of a more obstinate resistance was shown at the Secunderbagh, a high-walled, loop-holed inclosure 120 yards square, flanked by a loop-holed village about 100 yards distant. There Campbell at once displayed his less dashing but more sensible mode of warfare. The heavy and field artillery concentrated their efforts on the main inclosure, while

---

[a] See this volume, pp. 419-24.— *Ed.*

[b] Here and below see C. Campbell, "From His Excellency the Commander-in-Chief to the Right Hon. the Governor-General", *The Times,* No. 22889, January 13, 1858.— *Ed.*

one brigade attacked the barricaded village, and another drove back whatever bands of the enemy attempted the open field. The defense was lamentable. Two intrenched positions like those described flanking each other by their fire, in the hands of indifferent soldiers, or even of plucky undisciplined insurgents, would require a deal of fighting to take. But here there appears to have been neither pluck, nor concert, nor even a shadow of sense. We do not hear of any artillery used in the defense. The village (evidently a small cluster of houses) was taken at the first onset. The troops in the field were scattered without an effort. Thus in a few moments the Secunderbagh was quite isolated, and when, after an hour's cannonading, the walls gave way in one point, the Highlanders stormed the breach and killed every soul in the place; 2,000 natives are said by Sir C. Campbell to have been found dead in it.

The Shah Nujjeef was the next post—a walled inclosure prepared for defense, with a mosque for a reduit; again one of those positions which a commander of brave but half-disciplined troops would exactly wish for. This place was stormed after a three hours' cannonade had opened the walls. On the next day, Nov. 17, the Mess-house was attacked. This was a group of buildings inclosed by a mud rampart and a scarped ditch twelve feet wide—in other words, a common field redoubt with a slight ditch and a parapet of problematical thickness and hight. For some cause or other, this place appeared rather formidable to Gen. Campbell, for he at once resolved to give his artillery full time to batter it down before he stormed it. The cannonade accordingly lasted the whole morning, till 3 o'clock p. m., when the infantry advanced and took the position with a rash. No sharp fighting here, at all events. The Motee Mahal, the last post of the Oudians on the line toward the Residency,[449] was cannonaded for an hour; several breaches were made and then taken without difficulty, and this ended the fighting for the relief of the garrison.

The character of the whole engagement is that of an attack by well-disciplined, well-officered European troops, inured to war and of average courage, upon an Asiatic rabble, possessing neither discipline nor officers, nor the habits of war, nor even adequate arms, and whose courage was broken by the consciousness of the double superiority possessed by their opponents, as soldiers over civilians and as Europeans over Asiatics. We have seen that Sir Colin Campbell nowhere appears to have been opposed by artillery. We shall see, further on, that Brigadier Inglis's report leads to the conclusion that the great bulk of the insurgents must have been without fire-arms;[a] and if it is true that 2,000 natives were massacred in the Secunderbagh, it is evident they must have been very imperfectly armed, otherwise the greatest cowards would have defended the place against *one* assaulting column.

On the other hand, the conduct of the fight by Gen. Campbell deserves the highest praise for tactical skill. From the want of artillery in his opponents, he must have known that his progress could not be resisted; accordingly he used this arm to its full extent, clearing first the way for his columns before he launched them. The attack upon Secunderbagh and its flanking defenses is a very excellent specimen of the mode of conducting such an affair. At the same time, having once ascertained the despicable nature of the defense, he did not treat such opponents with any unnecessary formality; as soon as there was a gap in the walls, the infantry advanced. Altogether, Sir C. Campbell ranks from the day of Lucknow as a general; hitherto he was known as a soldier only.

By the relief of Lucknow we are at last put in possession of a document describing the occurrences which took place during the siege of the Residency. Brigadier Inglis, the successor in command of Sir H. Lawrence, has made his report to the Governor-General[b]; and, according to Gen. Outram and the *unisono* of the British press, here is a conspicuous case of heroism, indeed[c]—for such bravery, such perseverance, such endurance of fatigue and hardships, have never been seen at any time, and the defense of Lucknow stands unparalleled in the history of sieges. The report of Brigadier Inglis informs us that on the 30th of June the British made a sortie against the natives, who were then just concentrating, but were repulsed with such heavy loss that they had at once to confine themselves to the defense of the Residency, and even to abandon and blow up another group of buildings in the vicinity, containing 240 barrels of powder and 6,000,000 musket cartridges. The enemy at once invested the Residency, taking possession of and fortifying the buildings in its immediate vicinity, some within 50 yards of the defenses, and which, against the advice of the engineers, Sir H. Lawrence had refused to raze. The British parapets were still partly unfinished, and only two batteries

---

[a] Here and below Engels used the report "From Brigadier Inglis, Commanding Garrison of Lucknow, to the Secretary to Government, Military Department, Calcutta", published in *The Times*, No. 22889, January 13, 1858.— *Ed.*

[b] Charles John Canning.— *Ed.*

[c] *The Times*, No. 22889, January 13, 1858, leading article.— *Ed.*

were in working order, but, in spite of the terrific and incessant fire "kept up by" 8,000 men firing "at one time into the position," they were enabled to complete them very soon, and have 30 guns in battery. This terrific fire must have been a very wild and random kind of firing, not at all deserving the name of sharp-shooting with which Gen. Inglis adorns it; how otherwise could a man have lived in the place, defended as it was by perhaps 1,200 men? The instances related to show the terrific nature of this fire, that it killed women and children, and wounded men in places considered well sheltered, are very poor examples, as they occur never oftener than when the enemy's fire, instead of being aimed at different objects, is directed toward the fortification at large, and consequently never hits the actual defenders. On the 1st of July Lawrence was mortally wounded, and Inglis took the command. The enemy had by this time 20 or 25 guns in position, "planted all round our post." Very lucky for the defense, for if they had concentrated their fire on one or two places of the ramparts, the position would in all likelihood have been taken. Some of these guns were posted in places "where our own heavy guns could not reply to them." Now, as the Residency is on commanding ground, these places can only have been so situated that the guns of the attack could not fire at the rampart, but merely at the tops of the buildings inside; which was very fortunate for the defense, as that did no great harm, and the same guns might have been far more usefully employed in firing at the parapet or barricades. Upon the whole, the artillery on both sides must have been miserably served, as otherwise a cannonade at such short range must have been very shortly put a stop to by the batteries mutually dismounting each other; and that this did not take place, is still a mystery.

On July 20, the Oudians exploded a mine under the parapet, which, however, did no damage. Two main columns immediately advanced to an assault, while sham attacks were attempted at other places; but the mere effect of the garrison's fire drove them back. On the 10th of August another mine exploded, and opened a breach,

> "through which a regiment could have advanced in perfect order. A column charged this breach, flanked by the subordinate attacks; but at the breach only a few of the enemy advanced with the utmost determination."

These few were soon disposed of by the flank fire of the garrison, while at the flank attacks hand-grenades and a little firing drove the undisciplined masses back. The third mine was sprung on the 18th August; a new breach was formed, but the assault was even more spiritless than before, and was easily repelled. The last explosion and assault took place on the 5th September, but again hand-grenades and musketry drove them back. From that time to the arrival of relief, the siege appears to have been converted into a mere blockade, with a more or less sustained fire of muskets and artillery.

This is, indeed, an extraordinary transaction. A mob of 50,000 men or more, composed of the inhabitants of Lucknow and the surrounding country, with perhaps 5,000 or 6,000 drilled soldiers among them, blockade a body of some 1,200 or 1,500 Europeans in the Residency of Lucknow and attempt to reduce them. So little order reigned among the blockading body, that the supplies of the garrison appear never to have been completely cut off, though their communications with Cawnpore were. The proceedings of what is called "the siege" are distinguished by a mixture of Asiatic ignorance and wildness, with here and there a glimpse of some military knowledge introduced by European example and rule. There were evidently some artillerymen and sappers among the Oudians who knew how to construct batteries; but their action appears to have been confined to the construction of shelter from the enemy's fire. They even appear to have brought this art of sheltering themselves to great perfection, so much so that their batteries must have been very safe, not only for the gunners but also for the besieged; no guns could have been worked in them with any effect. Nor were they; or how is this unparalleled fact to be explained, that 30 guns inside and 25 outside worked against each other at exceedingly short ranges, some not more than 50 yards, and yet we hear nothing of dismounted guns or one party silencing the artillery of the other? As to the musketry fire, we first have to ask how it is possible that eight thousand natives could take position within musket range from the British batteries without being sent to the right about by the artillery? And if they did, how is it possible that they did not kill and wound every soul on the place? Still we are told that they did hold their own, and did fire day and night, and that in spite of all this the 32d Regiment, which could at the very outside count 500 men after June 30, and had to bear the brunt of the whole siege, still was 300 strong at its end? If this is not an exact counterpart of the "last surviving ten of the Fourth (Polish) Regiment," which marched into Prussia 88 officers and 1,815 rank and file strong, what then is it? The British are perfectly right that such fighting was never seen as there was at Lucknow—indeed it was not. In spite of the unassuming, apparently simple tone of Inglis's report, yet his queer observation about guns placed so that they could not be fired at, about 8,000 men firing day and night, without effect, about 50,000 insurgents blockading him, about the hardships of bullets going into places where they had no business to go, and about assaults carried out with the utmost determination, yet repulsed, without any effort—all these observations compel us to acknowledge the whole of this report is full of the most glaring exaggerations, and will not stand cool criticism for a moment.

But then surely the besieged underwent uncommon hardships? Listen:

> "The want of native servants has also been a source of *much privation*. Several ladies have had to tend their children, and even to wash their own clothes as well as to cook their scanty meals entirely unaided."

Pity the sorrows of a poor Lucknow lady! True, in these times of ups and downs, when dynasties are made and unmade in a day, and revolutions and commercial crashes combine to render the permanency of all creature comforts most splendidly insecure, we are not called upon to show any great sympathy if we hear of some ex-queen having to darn her own stockings, and even to wash them, not to speak of her cooking her own mutton-chop. But an Anglo-Indian lady, one of that vast number of sisters, cousins, or nieces to half-pay officers, Indian Government writers, merchants, clerks, or adventurers, who are, or rather were, before the mutiny, sent out every year, fresh from the boarding-school, to the large marriage-market in India, neither more nor less ceremoniously, and often far less willingly, than the fair Circassians that go to the Constantinople market—the very idea of one of these ladies having to wash her own clothes and cook her scanty meals entirely unaided—entirely! One's blood boils at it. Completely without "native servants"—ay, having actually to tend their own children! It is revolting—Cawnpore would have been preferable![a]

The rabble investing the Residency may have counted 50,000 men; but then the large majority cannot have had any firearms. The 8,000 "sharp-shooters" may have had firearms; but of what description both arms and men were, the effect of their fire is there to tell. The twenty-five guns in the battery have been proved to have been most despicably served. The mining was as much at random as the firing. The assaults do not deserve the name even of reconnaissances. So much for the besiegers.

The besieged deserve full credit for the great strength of character with which they have held out for nearly five months,

---

[a] See this volume, pp. 346-47.— *Ed.*

the greater portion of which time they were without any news whatever from the British forces. They fought, and hoped against hope, as it behooves men to do when they have their lives to sell as dearly as they can, and women and children to defend against Asiatic cruelty. Again, full credit do we give them for their watchfulness and perseverance. But, after the experiences of Wheeler's surrender at Cawnpore, who would not have done the same?

As to the attempt to turn the defense of Lucknow into a piece of unparalleled heroism, it is ridiculous, especially after the clumsy report of Gen. Inglis.[450] The privations of the garrison were confined to scanty shelter and exposure to the weather (which, however, did not produce any serious disease), and as to provisions, the very worst they had consisted in "coarse beef and still coarser flour!" far more comfortable fare than besieged soldiers are accustomed to in Europe! Compare the defense of Lucknow against a stupid and ignorant barbarian rabble with that of Antwerp, 1832, and the Fort of Malghera near Venice, in 1848 and '49,[451] not to speak of Todtleben at Sevastopol,[452] who had far greater difficulties to contend with than Gen. Inglis. Malghera was attacked by the best engineers and artillerymen of Austria, and defended by a weak garrison of raw levies; four-fifths of them had no bomb-proof shelter; the low soil created malaria more dangerous than an Indian climate; a hundred guns played upon them, and during the last three days of the bombardment, forty rounds were fired every minute; still the fort held out a month, and would have held out longer, if the Austrians had not taken hold of a position necessitating their retreat. Or take Dantzig, where Rapp, with the sick remnants of the French regiments returned from Russia, held out eleven months.[453] Take in fact any respectable siege of modern days, and you will find that more skill, more spirit, and quite as much pluck and endurance were shown against quite as great odds as in this Lucknow affair.

The Oude insurgents, however, though contemptible in the field, proved, immediately after the arrival of Campbell, the strength of a national insurrection. Campbell saw at once that he could neither attack the City of Lucknow with his forces, nor hold his own. This is quite natural, and will appear so to any one who has attentively read the French invasion of Spain under Napoleon. The strength of a national insurrection does not lie in pitched battles, but in petty warfare, in the defense of towns, and in the interruption of the enemy's communications. Campbell accordingly prepared for the retreat with the same skill with which he had arranged the attack. A few more positions about the Residency were carried. They served to deceive the enemy as to Campbell's intentions, and to cover the arrangements for the retreat. With a daring perfectly justified in front of such an opponent, the whole army, a small reserve excepted, was employed to occupy an extensive line of outposts and pickets, behind which the women, the sick and wounded, and the baggage were evacuated. As soon as this preliminary operation was performed the outlying pickets fell back, concentrating gradually into more solid masses, the foremost of which then retreated through the next line, again to form as a reserve to the rear. Without being attacked, the whole of this maneuver was carried out with perfect order; with the exception of Outram and a small garrison left at Alumbagh (for what purposes we do not at present see), the whole army marched to Cawnpore, thus evacuating the Kingdom of Oude.

In the mean time unpleasant events had taken place at Cawnpore. Windham, the "hero of the Redan,"[454] another of those officers of whose skill we are told that they have proved it by being very brave, had on the 26th defeated the advanced guard of the Gwalior contingent, but on the 27th he had been severely beaten by them, his camp taken and burned, and he himself compelled to retreat into Wheeler's old intrenchment at Cawnpore. On the 28th they attacked this post, but were repulsed, and on the 6th Campbell defeated them with scarcely any loss, taking all their guns and train, and pursuing them for fourteen miles. The details of all these affairs are so far but scanty; but this much is certain, that the Indian Rebellion is as yet far from being quelled, and that, although most or all British re-enforcements have now landed, yet they disappear in an almost unaccountable manner. Some 20,000 men have landed in Bengal, and still the active army is no larger than when Delhi was taken. There is something wrong here. The climate must make terrible havoc among the newcomers.

Written on January 14, 1858

First published unsigned in the *New-York Daily Tribune,* No. 5236, February 1, 1858

Reproduced from the newspaper

Karl Marx

THE APPROACHING INDIAN LOAN

London, Jan. 22, 1858

The buoyancy in the London money market, resulting from the withdrawal of an enormous mass of capital from the ordinary productive investments, and its consequent transfer to the security markets, has, in the last fortnight, been somewhat lessened by the prospects of an impending *Indian loan* to the amount of eight or ten million pounds sterling. This loan, to be raised in England, and to be authorized by Parliament immediately on its assembling in February, is required to meet the claims upon the East India Company by its home creditors, as well as the extra expenditure for war materials, stores, transport of troops, &c., necessitated by the Indian revolt. In August 1857, the British Government had, before the prorogation of Parliament, solemnly declared in the House of Commons that no such loan was intended, the financial resources of the Company being more than sufficient to meet the crisis. The agreeable delusion thus palmed on John Bull was, however, soon dispelled when it oozed out that by a proceeding of a very questionable character, the East India Company had laid hold on a sum of about £3,500,000 sterling, intrusted to them by different companies, for the construction of Indian railways; and had, moreover, secretly borrowed £1,000,000 sterling from the Bank of England, and another million from the London Joint Stock banks. The public being thus prepared for the worst, the Government did no longer hesitate to drop the mask, and by semi-official articles in *The Times, Globe,* and other governmental organs, avow the necessity of the loan.

It may be asked why a special act on the part of the legislative power is required for launching such a loan, and then, why such an event does create the least apprehension, since, on the contrary, every vent for British capital, seeking now in vain for profitable investment, should, under present circumstances, be considered a windfall, and a most salutary check upon the rapid depreciation of capital.

It is generally known that the commercial existence of the East India Company was terminated in 1834, when its principal remaining source of commercial profits, the monopoly of the China trade, was cut off.[a] [455] Consequently, the holders of East India stock having derived their dividends, nominally, at least, from the trade-profits of the Company, a new financial arrangement with regard to them had become necessary. The payment of the dividends, till then chargeable upon the commercial revenue of the Company, was transferred to its political revenue. The proprietors of East India stocks were to be paid out of the revenues enjoyed by the East India Company in its governmental capacity, and, by act of Parliament, the Indian stock, amounting to £6,000,000 sterling, bearing ten per cent interest,[b] was converted into a capital not to be liquidated except at the rate of £200 for every £100 of stock. In other words, the original East India stock of £6,000,000 sterling was converted into a capital of £12,000,000 sterling, bearing five per cent interest, and chargeable upon the revenue derived from the taxes of the Indian people. The debt of the East India Company was thus, by a Parliamentary sleight of hand, changed into a debt of the Indian people. There exists, besides, a debt exceeding £50,000,000 sterling, contracted by the East India Company in India, and exclusively chargeable upon the State revenues of that country; such loans contracted by the Company in India itself having always been considered to lay beyond the district of Parliamentary legislation, and regarded no more than the debts contracted by the Colonial Governments in Canada or Australia for instance.

On the other hand, the East India Company was prohibited from contracting interest-bearing debts in Great Britain herself, without the especial sanction of Parliament. Some years ago, when the Company set about establishing railways and electric telegraphs in India, it applied for the authorization of Indian Bonds in the London market, a request which was granted to the amount of £7,000,000 sterling to be issued in Bonds bearing 4 per cent

---

[a] *An Act for effecting an Arrangement with the East India Company...*—*Ed.*

[b] Here and below Marx draws on "The financial obligations of the East India Company", *The Economist,* No. 749, January 2, 1858.—*Ed.*

interest, and secured only on the Indian State revenues. At the commencement of the outbreak in India, this bond-debt stood at £3,894,400 sterling,[a] and the very necessity of again applying to Parliament shows the East India Company to have, during the course of the Indian insurrection, exhausted its legal powers of borrowing at home.

Now it is no secret that before recurring to this step, the East India Company had opened a loan at Calcutta, which, however, turned out a complete failure. This proves, on the one hand, that Indian capitalists are far from considering the prospects of British supremacy in India in the same sanguine spirit which distinguishes the London press; and, on the other hand, exacerbates the feelings of John Bull to an uncommon pitch, since he is aware of the immense hoardings of capital having gone on for the last seven years in India, whither, according to a statement recently published by Messrs. Haggard & Paxley, there has been shipped in 1856 and 1857, from the port of London alone, bullion to the amount of £21,000,000. *The London Times,* in a most persuasive strain, has taught its readers that

> "of all the incentives to the loyalty of the natives, that of making them our creditors was the least doubtful; while, on the other hand, among an impulsive, secretive and avaricious people no temptation to discontent or treachery could be stronger than that created by the idea that they were annually taxed to send dividends to wealthy claimants in other countries."[b]

The Indians, however, appear not to understand the beauty of a plan which would not only restore English supremacy at the expense of Indian capital, but at the same time, in a circuitous way, open the native hoards to British commerce. If, indeed, the Indian capitalists were as fond of British rule as every true Englishman thinks it an article of faith to assert, no better opportunity could have been afforded them of exhibiting their loyalty and getting rid of their silver. The Indian capitalists shutting up their hoards, John Bull must open his mind to the dire necessity of defraying himself in the first instance, at least, the expenses of the Indian insurrection, without any support on the part of the natives. The impending loan constitutes, moreover, a precedent only, and looks like the first leaf in a book, bearing the title Anglo-Indian Home Debt. It is no secret that what the East India Company wants are not eight millions, or ten millions, but

[a] "Indian loans", *The Economist,* No. 750, January 9, 1858.—*Ed.*

[b] *The Times,* No. 22883, January 6, 1858, "Money-Market and City Intelligence".—*Ed.*

twenty-five to thirty millions pounds, and even these as a first installment only, not for expenses to be incurred, but for debts already due. The deficient revenue for the last three years amounted to £5,000,000; the treasure plundered by the insurgents up to the 15th October last, to £10,000,000, according to the statement of the *Phoenix,* an Indian governmental paper; the loss of revenue in the Northeastern provinces, consequent upon the rebellion, to £5,000,000, and the war expenses to at least £10,000,000.

It is true that successive loans by the Indian Company, in the London Money Market, would raise the value of money and prevent the increasing depreciation of capital; that is to say, the further fall in the rate of interest; but such a fall is exactly required for the revival of British industry and commerce. Any artificial check put upon the downward movement of the rate of discount is equivalent to an enhancement in the cost of production and the terms of credit, which, in its present weak state, English trade feels itself unable to bear. Hence the general cry of distress at the announcement of the Indian loan. Though the Parliamentary sanction adds no imperial guarantee to the loan of the Company, that guarantee, too, must be conceded, if money is not to be obtained on other terms; and despite all fine distinctions, as soon as the East India Company is supplanted by the British Government its debt will be merged into the British debt. A further increase of the large national debt seems, therefore, one of the first financial consequences of the Indian Revolt.

Written on January 22, 1858

First published unsigned in the *New-York Daily Tribune,* No. 5243, February 9, 1858

Reproduced from the newspaper

Frederick Engels

WINDHAM'S DEFEAT[456]

While during the Crimean war all England was calling for a man capable of organizing and leading her armies, and while incapables like Raglan, Simpson and Codrington were intrusted with the office, there was a soldier in the Crimea endowed with the qualities required in a general. We mean Sir Colin Campbell, who is now daily showing in India that he understands his profession with a master's mind. In the Crimea, after having been allowed to lead his brigade at the Alma[457] where from the rigid line-tactics of the British army, he had no chance to show his capacities, he was cooped up in Balaklava and never once allowed to participate in the succeeding operations. And yet, his military talents had been clearly established in India long before, by no less an authority than the greatest general England has produced since Marlborough, by Sir Charles James Napier. But Napier was an independent man, too proud to stoop to the reigning oligarchy—and his recommendation was enough to make Campbell marked and distrusted.

Other men, however, gained distinctions and honors in that war. There was Sir William Fenwick Williams of Kars, who now finds it convenient to rest on the laurels acquired by impudence, self-puffing, and by defrauding Gen. Kmetty of his well-earned fame. A baronetcy, a thousand a year, a comfortable berth at Woolwich, and a seat in Parliament, are quite sufficient to prevent him risking his reputation in India. Unlike him, "the hero of the Redan,"[458] Gen. Windham, has set out to command a division against the Sepoys, and his very first act has settled him forever. This same Windham, an obscure colonel of good family connections, commanded a brigade at the assault of the Redan, during which operation he behaved extremely phlegmatically, and at last, no re-enforcement arriving, twice left his troops to shift for themselves, while he went to inquire about them himself. For this very questionable act, which in other services would have been inquired into by a court-martial, he was forthwith made a General, and shortly afterward called to the post of Chief of the Staff.

When Colin Campbell advanced to Lucknow, he left the old intrenchments, the camp and the town of Cawnpore, together with the bridge over the Ganges, in charge of General Windham and a force sufficient for the purpose. There were five regiments of infantry, whole or in part, many guns of position, 10 field guns and two naval guns, beside 100 horse; the whole force above 2,000. While Campbell was engaged at Lucknow, the various bodies of rebels hovering about the Doab[459] drew together for an attack on Cawnpore. Beside a miscellaneous rabble, collected by insurgent Zemindars,[460] the attacking force counted of drilled troops (disciplined they cannot be called), the remainder of the Dinapore Sepoys and a portion of the Gwalior contingent. These latter were the only insurgent troops, the formation of which can be said to go beyond that of companies, as they had been officered by natives almost exclusively, and thus, with their field-officers and captains, retained something like organized battalions. They were consequently regarded with some respect by the British. Windham had strict orders to remain on the defensive, but getting no replies to his dispatches from Campbell, the communication being interrupted, he resolved to act on his own responsibility. On the 26th November, he advanced with 1,200 infantry, 100 horse and 8 guns to meet the advancing insurgents. Having easily defeated their vanguard, he saw the main column approaching and retired close to Cawnpore. Here he took up a position in front of the town, the 34th Regiment on the left, the Rifles (5 companies) and two companies of the 82d on the right. The line of retreat lay through the town, and there were some brick-kilns in rear of the left. Within four hundred yards from the front, and on various points still nearer to the flanks, were woods, and jungle, offering excellent shelter to the advancing enemy. In fact, a worse position could not well have been chosen—the British exposed in the open plain, while the Indians could approach under shelter to within three or four hundred yards! To bring out Windham's "heroism" in a still stronger light, there was a very decent position close by, with a plain in front and rear, and with the canal as an obstacle before the front; but, of course, the worse position was insisted on. On the 27th November, the enemy opened a cannonade, bringing up his guns to the edge of the cover afforded by the jungle. Windham, who, with the modesty inherent in a hero, calls this a "bombardment," says his troops stood it for five hours; but after this time, there happened some things which neither Windham, nor any man present, nor any Indian or British newspaper, has as yet dared to relate. From the moment the cannonade was turned into a battle, all our direct sources of information cease, and we are left to draw our own conclusions from the hesitating, prevaricating and incomplete evidence before us. Windham confines himself to the following incoherent statement:

"In spite of the heavy bombardment of the enemy, my troops resisted the attack [rather novel to call a cannonade against field-troops an *attack*] for five hours, and still held the ground, until I found from the number of men bayoneted by the 88th, that the mutineers had fully penetrated the town; *having been told* that they were attacking the fort, I directed Gen. Dupuis to fall back. The whole force retired into the fort, with all our stores and guns, shortly before dark. Owing to the flight of the camp-followers, I was unable to carry off my camp equipage and some of the baggage. Had not an error occurred in the conveyance of an order issued by me, I am of opinion that I could have held my ground, at all events until dark." [a]

Gen. Windham, with that instinct shown already at the Redan, moves off to the reserve (the 88th occupying the town, as we must conclude), and finds, not the enemy alive and fighting, but a great number of the enemy bayoneted by the 88th. This fact leads him to the conclusion that the enemy (he does not say whether dead or alive) has fully penetrated the town! Alarming as this conclusion is both to the reader and to himself, our hero does not stop here. He is told that the fort is attacked. A common general would have inquired into the truth of this story, which of course turned out to be false. Not so Windham. He orders a retreat, though his troops could have held the position at least until dark, had not an error been committed in the conveyance of one of Windham's orders! Thus, first you have Windham's heroic conclusion, that where there are many dead Sepoys there must be many live ones; secondly, the false alarm respecting the attack on the fort; and thirdly, the error committed in the conveyance of an order; all of which mishaps combined made it possible for a very numerous rabble of natives to defeat the hero of the Redan and to beat the indomitable British pluck of his soldiers.

Another reporter, an officer present, says:

"I do not believe any one can accurately describe the fight and retreat of this forenoon. A retreat was ordered. Her Majesty's 34th foot being directed to fall

---

[a] C. A. Windham, "Major-General C. A. Windham to the Commander-in-Chief", *The Times*, No. 22904, January 30, 1858.—*Ed.*

back behind the brick kiln, neither officers nor men knew where to find it! The news flew rapidly about the cantonments that our force was worsted and on the retreat, and an overwhelming rush was made at the inner intrenchments, as resistless as the mass of water at the Falls of Niagara. Soldiers and Jacks, Europeans and natives, men, women and children, horses, camels and oxen, poured in in countless numbers from 2 p. m. By nightfall the intrenched camp, with its motley assemblage of men and beasts, baggage, luggage, and ten thousand nondescript incumbrances, rivaled the chaos that existed before the fiat of creation went forth."[a]

Finally, *The Times*'s Calcutta correspondent states that evidently the British suffered on the 27th "what almost amounts to a repulse,"[b] but that from patriotic motives the Anglo-Indian press covers the disgrace with the impenetrable vail of charity. Thus much, however, is also admitted, that one of Her Majesty's regiments, composed mostly of recruits, one moment got into disorder, without however giving way, and that at the fort the confusion was extreme, Windham having lost all control over his men, until in the evening of the 28th Campbell arrived and "with a few haughty words" brought everybody to his place again.

Now, what are the evident conclusions from all these confused and prevaricating statements? No other than that, under the incapable direction of Windham, the British troops were completely, though quite unnecessarily defeated; that when the retreat was ordered, the officers of the 34th Regiment, who had not even taken the trouble to get in any way acquainted with the ground they had fought on, could not find the place they were ordered to retreat to; that the regiment got into disorder and finally fled; that this led to a panic in the camp, which broke down all the bounds of order and discipline, and occasioned the loss of the camp-equipage and part of the baggage; that finally, in spite of Windham's assertion about the stores, 15,000 Minié cartridges, the Paymaster's chests, and the shoes and clothing for many regiments and new levies, fell into the hands of the enemy.

English infantry, when in line or column, seldom run away. In common with the Russians, they have a natural cohesion which generally belongs to old soldiers only, and which is in part explained by the considerable admixture of old soldiers in both services, but it in part also evidently belongs to national character. This quality, which has nothing whatever to do with "pluck," but is on the contrary rather a peculiar development of the instinct of self-preservation, is still very valuable, especially in defensive

---

[a] "Cawnpore, Dec. 7", *The Times,* No. 22902, January 28, 1858.—*Ed.*
[b] *The Times,* No. 22902, January 28, 1858.—*Ed.*

positions. It also, in common with the phlegmatic nature of Englishmen, prevents panic; but it is to be remarked that when Irish troops are once disordered and brought to panic, they are not easy to rally. Thus it happened to Windham on Nov. 27. He will figure henceforth among that not very large but distinguished list of English generals who have succeeded in making their troops run away under a panic.

On the 28th the Gwalior contingent were re-enforced by a considerable body from Bithoor, and closed up to within four hundred yards of the British intrenched outposts. There was another engagement, conducted on the part of the assailants without any vigor whatever. During it an example of real pluck occurred on the part of the soldiers and officers of the 64th, which we are glad to relate, although the exploit itself was as foolish as the renowned Balaklava charge.[461] The responsibility of it, too, is shifted upon a dead man—Col. Wilson of that regiment. It appears that Wilson advanced with one hundred and eighty men against four guns of the enemy, defended by far superior numbers. We are not told who they were; but the result leads to the conclusion that they were of the Gwalior troops. The British took the guns with a rush, spiked three of them, and held out for some time, when, no re-enforcement arriving, they had to retreat, leaving sixty men and most of their officers on the ground. The proof of the hard fighting is in the loss. Here we have a small force, which, from the loss they suffered, must have been pretty well met, holding a battery till one-third of their numbers are down. This is hard fighting indeed, and the first instance of it we have since the storming of Delhi. The man who planned this advance, however, deserves to be tried by court-martial and shot. Windham says it was Wilson. He fell in it, and cannot reply.

In the evening the whole British force was pent up in the fort, where disorder continued to reign, and the position with the bridge was in evident danger. But then Campbell arrived. He restored order, drew over fresh troops in the morning, and so far repelled the enemy as to secure the bridge and fort. Then he made all his wounded, women, children and baggage cross, and held a defensive position until all these had a fair start on the road to Allahabad. As soon as this was accomplished, he attacked the Sepoys on the 6th, and defeated them, his cavalry and artillery following them up for fourteen miles the same day. That there was little resistance offered is shown from Campbell's report; he merely describes the advance of his own troops, never mentioning any resistance or maneuvers on the part of the enemy; there was no check, and it was not a battle, but a *battue.* Brigadier Hope Grant, with a light division, followed the fugitives, and caught them on the 8th in the act of passing a river; thus brought to bay, they turned round and suffered severe loss. With this event Campbell's first campaign, that of Lucknow and Cawnpore, is brought to a close, and a fresh series of operations must begin, whose first developments we may expect to hear of within a fortnight or three weeks.

Written on about February 2, 1858

First published in the *New-York Daily Tribune,* No. 5253, February 20, 1858 as a leading article

Reproduced from the newspaper

Karl Marx

THE ATTEMPT UPON THE LIFE OF BONAPARTE[462]

Quos deus vult perdere prius dementat[a] seems the judgment pretty generally passed in Europe on the French usurper, whom, but a few weeks ago, the numberless sycophants of success in all countries, and of all languages, concurred to magnify into a kind of sublunary providence. Now, all at once, on the first approach of real danger, the demi-god is supposed to have run mad. To those, however, who are not to be carried away by first impressions, nothing will appear more evident than that the hero of Boulogne[463] is to-day what he was yesterday—simply a gambler. If he stakes his last card and risks all, it is not the man that has changed, but the chances of the game. There had been attempts on Bonaparte's life before without producing any visible effect on the economy of the Empire. Why did the quicksilver which exploded on the 14th of January[464] not only kill persons, but a state of things? It is with the hand-grenades of the Rue Lepelletier as it was with the greased cartridges dealt out at Barrackpore.[b] They have not metamorphosed an empire, but only rent the veil which concealed a metamorphosis already accomplished.

The secret of Bonaparte's elevation is to be found on the one hand in the mutual prostration of the antagonist parties, and on the other in the coincidence of his *coup d'état* with the entrance of the commercial world upon a period of prosperity. The commercial crisis, therefore, has necessarily sapped the material basis of the Empire, which never possessed any moral basis, save the

---

[a] "Those whom the gods wish to destroy they first make mad" (Sophocles, *Antigone*, 620).— *Ed.*

[b] See this volume, p. 298.— *Ed.*

temporary demoralization of all classes and all parties. The working classes reassumed their hostile attitude to the existing Government the very moment they were thrown out of employment. A great part of the commercial and industrial middle classes were placed by the crisis in exactly the same position which spurred Napoleon to hasten his *coup d'état;* it being well known that the fear of the debtors' prison at Clichy put an end to his vacillations. The same motive hurried the Paris bourgeois to the barricades in 1848, and would make him regard a political convulsion at this moment as a godsend. It is now perfectly understood that, at the hight of the panic, the Bank of France, on Government order, renewed all bills due—an accommodation which, by the by, it was again compelled to afford on the 31st of January; but this suspense in the liquidation of debts, instead of restoring commercial activity, has only imparted a chronic character to panic. Another very large portion of the Paris middle classes, and a very influential one too—the *petits rentiers,* or men of small fixed incomes—have met with wholesale ruin, consequent upon the enormous fluctuations of the Bourse, which were fostered by, and contributed to enrich, the Imperial dynasty and its adventurous retainers. That portion, at least, of the French higher classes which pretends to represent what is called French civilization never accepted the Empire, except as a necessary makeshift, never concealed their profound hostility to the "nephew of his uncle,"[a] and of late have seized upon every pretext to show their anger at the attempt to transform a mere expedient, as they considered it, into a lasting institution. Such was the general state of feeling to which the attempt of the Rue Lepelletier afforded an occasion of manifesting itself. This manifestation, on the other hand, has roused the pseudo Bonaparte to a sense of the gathering storm, and compelled him to play out his last card. Much has been said in the *Moniteur* as to the shouts and cries and the "public enthusiasm"[b] lavished on the Imperial party at their exit from the Opera. The value of this street enthusiasm is shown by the following anecdote emanating from a chief actor in the scene and the authenticity of which is vouched for by a highly respectable English paper:

"On the night of the 14th a person high in the Imperial household, but not that night on service, was crossing the Boulevards, when he heard the explosions, and saw people running toward the Opera. He ran thither also, and was present at the whole scene. Being recognized directly, one of the persons most nearly concerned

---

[a] Napoleon III, Napoleon I.—*Ed.*

[b] "Paris, le 14 janvier", *Le Moniteur universel,* No. 15, January 15, 1858.—*Ed.*

in all that had occurred said, 'Oh, Mr.—, for God's sake, find some one belonging to the Tuileries, and send off for fresh carriages. If you can find none, go yourself.' The person thus addressed set to work immediately to find some of the household servants, which was no easy task—all, from high to low, chamberlains to footmen, having, with one or two admirable exceptions, taken to their heels with incredible alacrity. However, at the end of a quarter of an hour, he laid hands on a messenger, and sent him post-haste to the palace with the necessary orders. About five and twenty minutes or half an hour had elapsed, when he returned to the Rue Lepelletier, and made his way back to the peristyle of the theater with great difficulty, on account of the crowd. The wounded were still lying about on all sides, and apparently disorder reigned everywhere. At a little distance the gentleman alluded to espied M. Pietri, the Prefect of Police, and called to him, in order to attract his attention, and prevent him from going away until he could rejoin him. When he did so, he instantly exclaimed, 'Let me implore of you to get the street closed without loss of time. The fresh carriages will be here soon, and they cannot drive up to the door. Besides, see what confusion ensues. Let me entreat of you, get the streets cleared.' M. Pietri looked at him with surprise. 'The street cleared!' he echoed; 'why, the street is cleared; it was cleared in five minutes.' His interlocutor stared at him. 'But, then, what is all that crowd? What is that dense mass of men that one cannot elbow one's way through?' 'Those are all my people,' was M. Pietri's reply; 'there is not a stranger at this moment in this portion of the Rue Lepelletier; all those you see belong to me.'"

If such was the secret of the street enthusiasm paraded by the *Moniteur,* its paragraphs on the "spontaneous illuminations of the Boulevards after the attempt"[a] could certainly not mislead the Parisians who had witnessed that illumination, which was limited to the shops of the tradespeople employed by the Emperor and the Empress. Even these individuals were not backward in saying that half an hour after the explosion of the "infernal machine," police agents paid them a visit, to suggest the propriety of instantly illuminating, in order to prove how enchanted they were at the Emperor's escape.

Still more the character of the congratulatory addresses and the public protestations of devotion to the Emperor bears witness to his complete isolation. There is not a single man who signed them who does not, one way or the other, belong to the Administration, that ubiquitous parasite feeding on the vitals of France, and put in motion like a mannikin by the touch of the Minister of the Interior.[b] The *Moniteur* was obliged, day after day, to register these monotonous congratulations, addressed by the Emperor to the Emperor, as so many proofs of the unbounded love of the people for the *coup d'état.*[c] Some efforts were, indeed, made to

---

[a] "Paris, le 14 janvier", *Le Moniteur universel,* No. 15, January 15, 1858.—*Ed.*

[b] Adolphe Billault.—*Ed.*

[c] "Adresses présentées à l'Empereur", *Le Moniteur universel,* No. 17, January 17, 1858; see also the following issues.—*Ed.*

obtain an address from the Paris population, and for that purpose an address was carried about by the agents of the police; but as it was found that the mass of signatures would not be sufficiently imposing, the plan was abandoned. Even the Paris shopkeepers dared to decline signing the address, on the pretext that the police was not the proper source for it to emanate from. The attitude of the Paris press, as far as it depends on the public, and not on the public purse, entirely responded to the attitude of the people. Either, like the unfortunate *Spectateur*, it muttered some half-suppressed words on hereditary rights, or, like the *Phare de la Loire,* quoted semi-official papers as its authorities for the reported enthusiasm, or, like the *Journal des Débats,* kept its congratulations within the rigid bounds of conventional courtesy, or limited itself to reprinting the articles of the *Moniteur.* In one word, it became evident that if France was not just yet prepared to take up arms against the Empire, it was certainly resolved to get rid of it on the first occasion.

"According to my informants," writes the Vienna correspondent of *The London Times,* "who have recently arrived from Paris, the *general opinion* in that city is, *that the present dynasty is nodding to its fall.*"[a] [465]

Bonaparte himself, till then the only man in France believing in the final victory of the *coup d'état,* became at once aware of the hollowness of his delusions. While all public bodies and the press were swearing that the crime of the Rue Lepelletier, perpetrated as it was by Italians solely, but served to put in relief the love of France for Louis Napoleon, Louis Napoleon himself hastened to the Corps Législatif,[466] there publicly to declare that the conspiracy was a national one, and that France consequently wanted new "repressive laws" to keep her down.[b] Those laws already proposed, at the head of which figure the *lois des suspects,*[467] are nothing but a repetition of the identical measures employed in the first days of the *coup d'état.* Then, however, they were announced as temporary expedients, while they are now proclaimed as organic laws. Thus it is declared by Louis Napoleon himself, that the Empire can be perpetuated only by the very infamies through which it was produced; that all its pretensions to the more or less respectable forms of a regular Government must be dropped, and that the time of the sullen acquiescence of the

---

[a] See the report from Vienna of January 29 in *The Times,* No. 22906, February 2, 1858.—*Ed.*

[b] Napoleon III's speech at the opening of the Corps Législatif, January 18, 1858, published in *Le Moniteur universel,* No. 19, January 19, 1858.—*Ed.*

nation in the rule of the Society of the perjured usurper[468] has definitively passed away.

Shortly before the execution of the *coup d'état,* Louis Napoleon contrived to gather from all departments, and principally from the rural districts, addresses leveled at the National Assembly, and expressive of unlimited confidence in the President. This source being now exhausted there remained nothing but to appeal to the army. The military addresses, in one of which the Zouaves[469] "almost regret not to have had an opportunity to manifest in a striking manner their devotion to the Emperor,"[a] are simply the undisguised proclamation of pretorian rule[470] in France. The division of France into five great military pashalics, with five marshals at their head, under the supreme control of Pelissier as marshal general,[471] is a simple consequence of that premise. On the other hand, the installation of a Privy Council, which is at the same time to act as Council during the eventual Regency of a Montijo, composed of such grotesque fellows as Fould, Morny, Persigny, Baroche and the like, shows France at the same time what sort of regime the newly-installed statesmen have in store for her. The installation of this Council, together with the family reconciliation, denoted to the astounded world by Louis Napoleon's letter in the *Moniteur,* by virtue of which Jerome, the ex-King of Westphalia, is nominated President of the State Councils in the Emperor's absence[b]—all this, it has been justly remarked, "looks like the pilgrim about to set out on a perilous journey."[c] On what new adventure is the hero of Strasbourg then to embark?[472] Some say that he means to relieve himself by a campaign in Africa; others that he intends an invasion of England. As to the first plan, it reminds one of his former notion of going to Sevastopol[473]; but now, as then, his discretion might prove the better part of his valor.[d] As to any hostility against England, it would only reveal to Bonaparte his isolation in Europe, as the attempt of the Rue Lepelletier revealed his isolation in France. Already the threats held out to England in the addresses of the soldiery have put the final extinguisher upon the Anglo-French

---

[a] "Le régiment de zouaves de la garde imperiale", *Le Moniteur universel,* No. 26, January 26, 1858.—*Ed.*

[b] Napoleon III's decree on the appointment of Prince Jerome President of the State Council, February 1, 1858, *Le Moniteur universel,* No. 34, February 3, 1858.—*Ed.*

[c] J. Bunyan, *The Pilgrim's Progress.*—*Ed.*

[d] Shakespeare, *King Henry IV,* Part I, Act V, Scene IV.—*Ed.*

alliance, long since struggling in *articulo mortis.*[a] Palmerston's Alien bill[474] will only contribute to exasperate the already wounded pride of John Bull. Whatever step Bonaparte may take—and he must try to restore his prestige in some way or other—will only precipitate his ruin. He approaches the end of his strange, wicked and pernicious career.

Written on February 5, 1858

First published in the *New-York Daily Tribune,* No. 5254, February 22, 1858 as a leading article

Reproduced from the newspaper

[a] At the point of death.— *Ed.*

Karl Marx

[THE ECONOMIC CRISIS IN FRANCE]

No argument can be required to prove that the precarious tenure of power by which Louis Napoleon still calls himself the Emperor of the French, must be seriously affected by the culmination in France of the commercial crisis which has already spent its fury in other parts of the world. The symptoms of this culmination are now chiefly to be found in the condition of the Bank of France and of the French markets for agricultural produce. The returns of the Bank, for the second week of February, as compared with those of the last week in January, exhibit the following features[a]:

Decrease of circulation	francs	8,766,400
Decrease in deposits		29,018,024
Decrease of discounts at the Bank		47,746,641
Decrease of discounts at the Branches		23,264,271
Total decrease in discounts		71,010,912
Increase in bills overdue		2,761,435
Increase in bullion		31,508,278
Increase in premium on purchases of gold and silver		3,284,691

Throughout the whole of the commercial world the metallic reserve of the banks has increased as the activity of trade has diminished. At the same ratio that industrial life has grown fainter, the position of the banks has, generally, grown stronger;

[a] Here and below see "Situation de la Banque de France et de ses succursales", *Le Moniteur universel,* Nos. 15 and 43, January 15 and February 12, 1858.— *Ed.*

and so far the bullion increase in the vaults of the Bank of France would seem but one more instance of an economical phenomenon observed here in New-York as well as in London and Hamburg. Yet there is one feature distinctive of the bullion movement in France, viz.: the increase to the amount of 3,284,691 francs of the premium on purchases of gold and silver, while the total sum spent in this way by the Bank of France for the month of February reaches the figure of 4,438,549 francs. The gravity of this fact becomes evident from the following comparison:

Premiums paid by the Bank of France on purchases of gold and silver.

February, 1858	francs	4,438,549
January, 1858		1,153,858
December, 1857		1,176,029
November, 1857		1,327,443
October, 1857		949,656
1st January to 30th June, 1856		3,100,000
1st July to 11th December, 1856		3,250,000
1st July to 31st December, 1855		4,000,000

Thus we see that the premium paid in February to procure temporary artificial additions to the bullion reserve of the Bank amounts to a sum almost equal to that expended for the same purpose during the four months from October, 1857, to January, '58, and exceeds the aggregate half-yearly premiums paid during the years 1856 and 1855; while the total amount of premiums paid from October, 1857, to February, 1858, reaching the figure of 9,045,535f., exceeds the premium paid during the whole year of 1856 by almost one-half. Despite this apparent plethora, the metallic reserve of the Bank is, consequently, really weaker than for the last three years. So far from the Bank being incumbered with bullion, the influx is only artificially raised to its necessary level. This single fact proves at once that in France the commercial crisis has not yet entered the phase already passed in the United States, England, and the North of Europe. In France, a general depression of commerce exists, as is shown by the simultaneous decrease in circulation and discounts; but the crash is still impending, as is shown by the decrease of deposits simultaneously with an increase of premium on bullion bought, and of bills overdue.

The Bank has also been forced to announce that a great part of its own new shares, on which the installments have not been duly paid up, will be sold. It has also been converted by the

Government into the general railway contractor of France, and compelled to make within fixed periods large advances to the railway companies—advances which for January and February alone amounted to the sum of 50,000,000 francs. It is true that in return for these advances it has received the bonds of the companies, which it may sell when it can. The present moment, however, is peculiarly unfavorable to such a sale, and the weekly railway returns, testifying to a constant falling off in receipts, are far from warranting any sanguine expectations in this line. For the month of January, for instance, the Orleans presented a decline of 21 per cent, the Eastern of 18 per cent, the Lyons of about 11 per cent, and the Western of 14 per cent, compared with the corresponding receipts in 1857.[a]

It is a well-known fact that the resistance, on the side of the seller or the buyer, against a change from low prices to high ones, and still more from high prices to low, is always very considerable; and that frequently there occur intervals, of longer or shorter duration, during which sales are heavy and prices nominal, until at last the tendency of the market declares itself one way or the other with irresistible force. Such a transitory struggle between the holders and buyers of merchandise is nothing extraordinary; but the protracted contest, lasting from the beginning of November to the present day, between French merchants and French consumers, is perhaps unparalleled in the history of prices. While French industry is stagnant, great numbers of workmen unemployed, and the means of everybody stinted, prices, which have elsewhere declined on an average from 30 to 40 per cent, are still maintained in France at the speculative range of the period preceding the general crisis. If we are asked by what means this economical miracle has been worked, the answer is simply that the Bank of France, under Government pressure, has twice been obliged to renew the bills and loans which had fallen due, and that thus, more or less directly, the means of the French people, accumulated in the Bank vaults, have been employed to keep up inflated prices against that very people. The Government seems to imagine that by this exceedingly simple process of distributing bank notes wherever they are wanted, the catastrophe can be definitively warded off. Yet the real result of this contrivance has been, on the one hand, an aggravation of distress on the part of the consumers, whose diminished means have not been met by diminished prices; on the other hand, an enormous accumulation

---

[a] *The Economist*, No. 754, February 6, 1858.—*Ed.*

of commodities in the Customs entrepots, which, when ultimately, as they must be, they are forced upon the market, will collapse under their own weight. The following statement, extracted from an official French paper, of the comparative quantities of merchandise stored up in the French Customs entrepots at the end of December, 1857, 1856 and 1855, will leave no doubt as to the violent self-adjustment of prices still looming in the future for France[a]:

	1857 Metrical qtls.[b]	1856 Metrical qtls.	1855 Metrical qtls.
Cocoa	19,419	17,799	10,188
Coffee	210,741	100,758	57,644
Cotton	156,006	76,322	28,766
Copper	15,377	1,253	3,197
Tin	4,053	1,853	1,811
Cast-Iron	132,924	102,202	76,337
Oleaginous Seeds	253,596	198,982	74,537
Tallow	25,299	15,292	11,276
Indigo	5,253	2,411	3,783
Wool	72,150	31,560	38,146
Pepper	23,448	18,442	10,682
Sugar (colonial)	170,334	56,735	55,387
Sugar (foreign)	89,607	89,807	71,913

In the trade in bread-stuffs, however, the contest has already terminated with disastrous consequences for the holders. Still their losses are of far less importance than the general state of the agricultural population of France at the present juncture. At a recent meeting of French agriculturists it was stated that the average price of wheat for all France was 31fr. 94c. the hectolitre (about $2^3/_4$ bushels) at the end of January, 1854; 27fr. 24c. at the same epoch in 1855; 32fr. 46c. in January, 1856; 27fr. 9c. in January, 1857, and 17fr. 38c. in January, 1858. The unanimous conclusion arrived at was that

"this state of prices must prove ruinous to French agriculture, and that at 17fr. 38c. the present average price, the producers in some parts of France have an extremely narrow margin of profit left them, while in others they sustain a serious loss."[c]

---

[a] *The Economist,* No. 754, February 6, 1858. (The Paris correspondent said that the information had been taken by him "from an official paper".)— *Ed.*

[b] Metrical quintal—a unit of weight equal to 100 kilograms.— *Ed.*

[c] *The Economist,* No. 755, February 13, 1858.— *Ed.*

One would think that in a country like France, where the greater part of the soil belongs to the cultivators themselves, and but a relatively small portion of the aggregate produce finds its way to market, a superabundance of grain ought to be considered a blessing instead of a bane. Yet, as Louis XVIII. told us in a crown speech on Nov. 30, 1821: "No law can prevent the distress resulting from a superabundant harvest."[a] The fact is that the large majority of the French peasantry are owners in name only—the mortgagees and the Government being the real proprietors. Whether the French peasant be able to meet the heavy engagements weighing on his narrow strip of soil depends not on the quantity, but on the price of his produce.

This agricultural distress, taken together with the depression of trade, the stagnation of industry, and the commercial catastrophe still in suspense, must tend to bring the French people into that state of mind in which they are wont to embark in fresh political ventures. With the disappearance of material prosperity and its regular appendage of political indifference, every pretext for the prolongation of the second Empire also disappears.

Written on February 12, 1858

First published in the *New-York Daily Tribune*, No. 5270, March 12, 1858 as a leading article

Reproduced from the newspaper

---

[a] Louis XVIII's speech in the Chamber of Deputies on November 30, 1821, *Le Moniteur universel*, No. 335, December 1, 1821.—*Ed.*

Karl Marx

THE RULE OF THE PRETORIANS

Paris, Feb. 22, 1858

"When is Gérard the lion-killer to be named Minister of Public Instruction?" Such is the cant phrase current in the faubourgs of Paris since the appointment of Gen. Espinasse of Dobrudja memory[475] as Minister of the Interior and Public Safety. In Russia, it is well known, a general of cavalry presides over the Holy Synod.[a] Why not Espinasse over the French Home-Ministry, since France has become the home of Pretorians only?[476] By such apparent incongruities the rule of the naked sword is proclaimed in most unmistakable terms, and Bonaparte wants France to clearly understand that the imperial rule does rest not on her will but on 600,000 bayonets. Hence the Pretorian addresses cut out by the colonels of the different regiments, after a pattern supplied from the Tuileries—addresses in which the slightest allusion to the so-called "will of the people" is anxiously shunned; hence the parceling out of France into five pashalics[477]; hence the transformation of the Home-Ministry into an appendage of the Army. Here the change is not to stop. About 60 prefects are said to be on the eve of being disgraced, and to be replaced, for the most part, by military men. Prefectorial administration is to devolve upon half-pay colonels and lieutenant-colonels. The antagonism between the Army and the population is to be organized as the guarantee of "Public Safety," viz: the safety of the hero of Satory[478] and his dynasty.

A great modern historian has told us that, disguise the fact as you like, France, since the days of the Great Revolution, has been

[a] A. P. Tolstoi.—*Ed.*

always disposed of by the army. There have certainly ruled different classes under the Empire, the Restoration, Louis Philippe, and the Republic of 1848. Under the first the peasantry, the offspring of the revolution of 1789, predominated; under the second, the great landed property; under the third, the *bourgeoisie;* and the last, not in the intention of its founders but in fact, proved an abortive attempt at dividing dominion in equal shares among the men of the legitimate monarchy and the men of the monarchy of July. Still, all these regimes rested alike on the army. Has not even the Constitution of the Republic of 1848 been elaborated and proclaimed under a state of siege—that is, the rule of the bayonet? Was that Republic not personated by Gen. Cavaignac? Was it not saved by the army in June, 1848, and again saved in June, 1849, to be finally dropped by the same army in December, 1851? What then forms the novelty in the regime now openly inaugurated by Louis Bonaparte? That he rules by the instrumentality of the army? So did all his predecessors since the days of Thermidor.[479] Yet, if in all the bygone epochs the ruling class, the ascendency of which corresponded to a specific development of French society, rested its *ultima ratio*[a] against its adversaries upon the army, it was nevertheless a specific social interest that predominated. Under the second Empire the interest of the army itself is to predominate. The army is no longer to maintain the rule of one part of the people over another part of the people. The army is to maintain its own rule, personated by its own dynasty, over the French people in general.

It is to represent the *State* in antagonism to the *society*. It must not be imagined that Bonaparte is not aware of the dangerous character of the experiment he tries. In proclaiming himself the chief of the Pretorians, he declares every Pretorian chief his competitor. His own partisans, with Gen. Vaillant at their head, demurred against the division of the French Army into five Marshalships, saying that if it was good for the cause of order, it was not so for that of the Empire, and would one day end in civil war. The treacheries of Napoleon's Marshals, with Berthier at their head, were ransacked by the Palais Royal,[480] which feels extremely vexed at the new turn of Imperial policy.

The future conduct of the five Marshals, who hate each other cordially, at a critical juncture, may be best judged from their past. Magnan betrayed Louis Philippe; Baraguay d'Hilliers betrayed Napoleon; Bosquet betrayed the Republic, to which he owed

[a] Final reason or argument.—*Ed.*

his advancement, and to the principles of which he is known to be partial. Castellane has not even awaited a real catastrophe to betray Louis Bonaparte himself. During the Russian War[a] a telegraphic dispatch reached him to this effect: "The Emperor is dead." He instantly drew up a proclamation in favor of Henri V. and sent it to be printed. The Préfet of Lyons had received the real dispatch, which ran thus: "The Emperor of Russia[b] is dead." The proclamation was hushed, but the story got abroad. As to Canrobert, he may be an Imperialist, but then he is but a fraction, and, above all, lacks the capability of being a whole number. The five Marshals themselves, feeling the arduous task they were called upon to undertake, hesitated so considerably at accepting their respective commands that nothing could be settled with their consent; which seeing, Bonaparte wrote out himself the names of their separate destinations, gave the note to Mr. Fould to be filled up and sent to the *Moniteur,* and thus they were all gazetted at last, whether they would or not.[c] Bonaparte, on the other hand, dared not complete his plan by Pelissier's nomination of Marshal-General. Of his pentarchy of Marshals, we may say what Prince Jérôme Napoleon is stated to have answered to Fould, sent by Bonaparte to present his uncle with his nomination to the first place in the Council of Regency. After having declined the offer in most impolite terms, the ex-King of Westphalia, as Paris gossip has it, bowed Mr. Fould out with the words, "*Du reste,*[d] your Council of Regency is so framed as for you all to have but one object; that, namely, of arresting each other as promptly as possible." We repeat that it is impossible to suppose Louis Bonaparte ignorant of the dangers with which his new-fangled system is fraught. But he has no choice left. He understands his own situation and the impatience of French society to get rid of him and his Imperial mummeries. He knows that the different parties have recovered from their paralysis, and that the material basis of his stock-jobbing regime has been blown up by the commercial earthquake. Consequently, he is not only preparing for war against French society, but loudly proclaims the fact. It tallies with his resolution to take up a warlike attitude against France that he confounds the most heterogeneous parties. Thus,

---

[a] The Crimean war, 1853-56.— *Ed.*

[b] Nicholas I.— *Ed.*

[c] Napoleon III's decree on the nomination of the five Marshals, February 13, 1858, *Le Moniteur universel,* No. 45, February 14, 1858.— *Ed.*

[d] However.— *Ed.*

when Cassagnac, in the *Constitutionnel*,[a] denounced Mr. Villemain as a "provoker of hatred" to the Empire, and accused the *Journal des Débats* of "complicity" in the *attentat* "through its silence," this was at first considered to be an act of foolish zeal on the part of the man whom Guizot has described as the *roi des drôles*.[b] Soon, however, it oozed out that the article had been imposed upon the *Constitutionnel* by Mr. Rouland, the Minister of Public Instruction, who had himself corrected the proofs of it. This explanation, by the by, was given to Mr. De Sacy of the *Débats* by Mr. Mirès, the proprietor of the *Constitutionnel*, who did not choose to bear the responsibility of the article. The denunciation of *all parties* as his personal enemies enters, therefore, into the game of Bonaparte. It forms part of his system. He tells them, in so many words, that he indulges no delusion as to the general aversion his rule is the subject of, but that he is ready to encounter it with grape and musketry.

Written on February 22, 1858

First published unsigned in the *New-York Daily Tribune*, No. 5270, March 12, 1858

Reproduced from the newspaper

[a] A. Granier de Cassagnac, "La palinodie des honnêtes gens", *Le Constitutionnel*, No. 31, January 31, 1858.—*Ed.*

[b] King of fools. The description has been cited by E. Dupont in "Chronique de l'Intérieur", *La Voix du Proscrit*, No. 8, December 15, 1850.—*Ed.*

Karl Marx

THE DERBY MINISTRY.— PALMERSTON'S SHAM RESIGNATION[481]

If Orsini did not kill Louis Napoleon,[482] he certainly killed Palmerston. Made dictator of England by a Chinese Mandarin at Canton,[a] it is historically appropriate that this political gamester should finally be ruined by an Italian Carbonaro at Paris.[483] But that he should be succeeded by Lord Derby is something above the range of mere historical propriety, and approaches the dignity of a historical law. It is in accordance with the traditional working of the British Constitution. Pitt was followed by Fox; Fox by Perceval, a weaker Pitt; Wellington by Grey, a weaker Fox; Grey by Wellington; Wellington by Melbourne, a weaker Grey; Melbourne by Wellington again, under the name of Peel; Peel by Melbourne again, under the name of Russell; Russell by Derby, the substitute of Peel; Derby again by Russell. Why should not Palmerston, the usurper of Russell's place, be followed by Derby in his turn?

If there be in England any new force able to put an end to the ancient routine exemplified by this last change of places between right honorable gentlemen on one side of the House and right honorable gentlemen on the other side; if there be any man or body of men able to confront and supplant the traditional governing class, the world has not yet found it out. But of one thing there can be no doubt; and that is that a Tory Administration is far more favorable to every kind of progress than any other. For the last fifty years, all popular movements have either been initiated or consummated under Tory rule. It was a Tory Ministry which passed the Catholic Emancipation

[a] Yeh Ming-chin.—*Ed.*

bill.[484] It was under a Tory Ministry that the Reform movement grew irresistible.[485] The imposition of an Income tax, which, however incongruous in its present state, contains the germs of proportional taxation, is the work of a Tory Ministry. The Anti-Corn-Law League,[486] weak and timid under the Whig Administration, assumed revolutionary dimensions under the Tories; and while Russell, in his most audacious flights, never ventured beyond the limit of a fixed duty, as moderate as himself, Peel could not but consign the Corn Laws to the grave of all the Capulets.[a] So, too, it is the Tories who have, so to say, popularized the aristocracy by bringing plebeian vigor and talent to re-enforce its energies. Through the Tories, Canning, the son of an actress,[b] lorded it over the old landed aristocracy of England; so did Peel, the son of a parvenu cotton spinner,[c] who had originally been a hand-loom weaver; so does Disraeli, the son of a simple literary man,[d] and a Jew into the bargain. Lord Derby himself converted the son of a small shopkeeper[e] of Lewes into a Lord High Chancellor of England, under the name of Lord St. Leonards. The Whigs, on the other hand, have always proved strong enough to bury their plebeian tools in vain decorations, or to drop them by dint of haughty insult. Brougham, the soul of the Reform movement, was nullified by being made over to the Lords; and Cobden, the chief of the Anti-Corn-Law League, was offered the place of Vice President of the Board of Trade by the very Whigs he had reinstalled in office.[487]

In point of mere intellectual ability, the new Cabinet can easily bear comparison with its predecessor. Men like Disraeli, Stanley, and Ellenborough, suffer no harm when matched against people of the stamp of Mr. Vernon Smith, late of the Board of Control,[488] of Lord Panmure, a War Minister, whom nothing but his "Take care of Dowb,"[489] can ever make immortal, and of Sir G. C. Lewis, of *Edinburgh Review* dullness, or even against such moral grandeurs as Clanricarde of the Privy Seal. In fact Palmerston had not only replaced the Ministry of all parties by a Ministry of no party, but also the Cabinet of all the talents[490] by a Cabinet of no talent except his own.

There can be no question that Palmerston had no idea of the finality of his ruin. He believed Lord Derby would decline the

---

[a] Shakespeare, *Romeo and Juliet.—Ed.*

[b] Mary Anne Castello.—*Ed.*

[c] Robert Peel.—*Ed.*

[d] Isaac D'Israeli.—*Ed.*

[e] Richard Sugden.—*Ed.*

Premiership now as he had done during the Crimean war. Russell would then have been summoned to the Queen[a]; but with the bulk of his own troops serving under Palmerston, and the bulk of the hostile army arrayed under Disraeli, he would have despaired of forming a Cabinet, especially as he, a Whig, could not resort to the "ultimate reason" of dissolving a Parliament elected under the Whig banners. Palmerston's return to office, after a week's oscillation, would thus have become inevitable. This fine bit of calculation has been nullified by Derby's acceptance. The Tory Ministry may hold office for a longer or shorter period. They may go on for several months before they are compelled to resort to a dissolution—a measure they are sure to employ before they finally resign their power. But we may be certain of two things, namely: that their career will be marked by the introduction of exceedingly liberal measures in regard to social reforms (Lord Stanley's course thus far, and Sir John Pakington's education bill, are a pledge of this); and above all, that in foreign policy they bring with them a most beneficial and cheering change. It is true, many shallow thinkers and writers argue that Palmerston's fall is not a damaging blow to Louis Napoleon, because several of the new Tory Ministry are personally on good terms with the French despot, and England [is] in no condition to wage war with a giant Continental power. But it is precisely because England is in no state to embark in a new war that we deem the answer given by Great Britain to the bullying menaces and exactions of Louis Napoleon's satraps most significant. It was not because Malmesbury and Disraeli were to come into the Ministry that the independent Liberals in Parliament, reflecting the undoubted and emphatic sentiment of the Nation, answered the dispatch of Walewski[b] by throwing out Palmerston's Conspiracy bill.[491] Lord Derby may stumble and fall, but the vote which carried Milner Gibson's amendment[492] will live and bear fruit, nevertheless.

We do not believe in any cordial and lasting alliance between British Toryism and French Bonapartism. The instincts, traditions, aspirations of both parties revolt at it. We do not believe it possible that the new Cabinet will take up and press Palmerston's Conspiracy bill, as the Paris journals so confidently anticipate. If they do, it will not be till after they shall have answered Walewski and De Morny, and answered them in the spirit of Pitt and

---

[a] Victoria.—*Ed.*

[b] A. Walewski's dispatch to the French Ambassador in London of January 20, 1858, *Le Constitutionnel*, No. 41, February 10, 1858.—*Ed.*

Castlereagh. Toryism, with all its faults, must have changed its nature to be ready to change the laws of England at the beck of a Bonaparte.

But the significance of the late vote is unaffected by any presumption of speedy feud between the two Governments. It is as a proclamation to Europe that Britain has ceased to play second to French Imperialism that we deem it most important. Thus it is understood at Brussels, at Turin, and even at Vienna; thus it will soon be understood at Berlin, at Madrid, at St. Petersburg. England, so long the jailer of the first Napoleon, has pointedly refused to be longer the jackal of his successor.[493]

Written on February 26, 1858

First published in the *New-York Daily Tribune,* No. 5272, March 15, 1858 as a leading article; reprinted in the *New-York Semi-Weekly Tribune,* No. 1337, March 19, 1858, under the title "The End of Palmerston"

Reproduced from the *New-York Daily Tribune*

Karl Marx

PORTENTS OF THE DAY

Paris, March 11, 1858

At Chalons-sur-Saone, on the night of Saturday, March 6, there was a Republican outbreak on a small scale; on Wednesday night, March 10, there was a seditious gathering in this city; since the 24th of February, the tenth anniversary of the Revolution of February, wholesale arrests have been carried on in such an Algerian razzia style[494] that, as *The London Punch* says, there will soon be left but two classes in France, prisoners and jailers[a]; there has appeared a semi-official pamphlet, "Napoleon III. and England,"[b] and at the same time the *Moniteur* published extracts from the correspondence of Napoleon I[c]; and, lastly, half Paris has been on its legs to make sure of places to witness Orsini's execution, which has not yet taken place. Commencing with the concluding article in this Imperial bill of fare, it ought to be remarked that by a concurrence of circumstances, not generally known, the question of Orsini's "launching into eternity," as the cynical Cockney phrase runs, has assumed proportions more fatal than even the execution of the Buzançais rioters in Louis Philippe's time.[495] In the latter case, a storm of popular indignation was roused because that bloody act, although judicial and in accordance with all the formalities of French law, laid bare the most disgusting features of Louis Philippe's hypocritical reign. The Duke of Praslin had poison administered to him, in order to spare him the ignominy of a felon's death,[496] while these *émeutiers*

[a] "A Bad Look Out", *Punch*, March 13, 1858.—*Ed.*

[b] [A. La Guéronnière,] *L'Empereur Napoléon III et l'Angleterre.*—*Ed.*

[c] Napoléon I, "Correspondance de Napoléon Ier", *Le Moniteur universel*, Nos. 66, 70, 71, 73 and 78, March 7, 11, 12, 14 and 19, 1858.—*Ed.*

of famine, half-starved peasants who had committed manslaughter in an affray caused by the export of grain, were mercilessly surrendered to the executioner. Orsini, on his part, has manfully avowed his participation in the attempt, and taken all the responsibility upon himself.[a] He has been condemned according to law, and whatever sympathy the mass of the Paris population may feel for him, there can be nothing in his doom, considered in itself, particularly damaging to the second Empire. Yet the whole face of the affair is completely changed by the circumstances accompanying it. Throughout the whole of the judicial proceedings, the curiosity of Paris was stirred by their exceptional management, unheard of in the annals of French political trials.

In the act of accusation, mild and moderate expressions were used. The facts elicited by the Juge d'Instruction were only vaguely alluded to, while the long and repeated interrogatories of the police authorities, which used to play a principal part in that sort of trials, were altogether dropped. The less you say of them the better, seemed the prevailing notion.[b] For the first time, a prisoner was decently treated in an Imperial court of justice. There was, as an eye-witness says, "little or no bullying, brow-beating or attempt at declamation." Jules Favre, Orsini's advocate, was not even called to order when he ventured to give vent to this sentence:

> "I hate force when not devoted to the service of right. If a nation existed miserable enough to be in the hands of a despot, the poniard would not sever its chains. God, who counts them, knows the hours of the despot's weakness, and reserves to tyrants catastrophes more inevitable than the dagger of the assassin."[c]

Neither did the low murmur which approved this passage afford occasion for a legal ebullition on the part of Mr. Delangle, the President. This was not all. It oozed out that the letter written to the Emperor by Orsini[d] was carried to the Tuileries by Jules Favre himself, examined by the Emperor, who is said to have struck out two phrases of it, and allowed to be published. Hardly, however, had sentence been passed on Orsini, when the extremest

---

[a] F. Orsini's testimony at the court session on February 25, 1858, *Le Moniteur universel,* No. 57, February 26, 1858.— *Ed.*

[b] "Cour d'assises de la Seine. Audience du 25 février 1858. Attentat du 14 janvier. Acte d'accusation", *Le Moniteur universel,* No. 57, February 26, 1858.— *Ed.*

[c] J. Favre's speech before the Jury on February 26, 1858, *Le Moniteur universel,* No. 58, February 27, 1858.— *Ed.*

[d] F. Orsini, "À Napoléon III, Empereur des Français, 11 février 1858," *Le Moniteur universel,* same issue.— *Ed.*

severity was shown to him, and, on his asking permission to "set his papers in order," he was answered by the immediate application of the *camisole de force.*[a]

It thus becomes evident that an infernal double game was here played. Orsini had revelations to make, and had made them to Piétri, relating to Napoleon's participation in Carbonarism, and the positive pledges which, even after the *coup d'état,* when still undecided in the course to follow, he had given to the Italian patriots.[497] In order to give Orsini an interest in his own moderation, and thus prevent a great public scandal, promises of pardon were held out to him which were never meant to be kept. This manner of proceeding is no novelty in the annals of the second Empire. The reader will perhaps recollect the trial of Berryer, the son of the celebrated French advocate and legitimist. The question then at issue was frauds committed in regard to a joint-stock company enterprise—the *Docks Napoléoniens.* Well, Berryer, the father, had his hands full of documents proving Prince Napoleon and Princess Mathilde to have been the gainers largely by the same swindling tricks that had dragged his son to the criminal's bench. If Berryer, the greatest artist in the French way of oratory—a way altogether dependent on the action, the tone, the eye, and the gesticulation of the performer, which turn words, that appear dull when glanced at in print, into speaking flames, into electric strokes when heard—if he had produced these documents and commented upon them, the Imperial throne would have tottered. Accordingly he was induced to abstain from so doing, by the interference of those nearest about the Emperor, who offered him his son's certain acquittal as the price of his silence. He yielded; his son was condemned, and father and son were duped. The same maneuver has been repeated, and with the same success, in Orsini's case. But this is not all. He was not only induced to spare Bonaparte a fearful scandal, but to break his silence and commit himself in Bonaparte's interest. He received intimations of the Emperor's secret leanings for Italian liberty, and was thus instigated to write his letter. Then the scene with Jules Favre was enacted. Orsini's letter was inserted in the *Moniteur.* Austria was to be frightened into compliance with Bonaparte's demands by showing her, unmistakably, how Bonaparte might still wield the patriotic aspirations of the Italians. She was even offended. Orsini's head is to soothe her anger, and in payment for it she is to make herself still more detested in Italy, and to stifle

---

[a] Straight jacket.— *Ed.*

the feeble germs of the liberty of the press at Vienna. Such, whether true or false, is the general interpretation put on the case of Orsini.

As to the Chalons *émeute,* it is but a premonitory symptom. If even all manhood was extinct in France, from a mere sense of self-preservation, men would resort to insurrection. To die in a street fight, or to rot at Cayenne,[498] is the alternative left to them. The pretexts on which the imprisonments are carried on—and every arrest may lead to Cayenne, as every road leads to Rome—may be exemplified by one single instance. It is known that some time ago three Paris lawyers were arrested.[a] The bar, or rather the council of the advocates, took up the business, and applied to the Minister of Justice[b]; the answer was, that no explanations could be given, but that these three gentlemen were taken up for "intrigues and maneuvers" during the late Paris elections, ten months back. If the Chalons *émeute* appears, therefore, fully due in the natural course of things, the behavior, on that occasion, of the officers of the garrison hardly tallies with the frantic addresses which the French army was ordered to send to the *Moniteur.*[c] The barracks are situated on the right bank of the Saone, while the officers mostly live in lodgings on the left bank, where the rising took place. Instead of rushing to the head of their men in defense of the Empire, they cautiously adopted some diplomatic movements in order to ascertain whether or not the Republic was proclaimed at Paris. Even the *Moniteur* dares not altogether suppress the fact. It says:

> "The *officers of the garrison, who had hastened to the sub-prefecture to obtain some information* relative to the rumors already in circulation, forced their passage sword in hand."[d]

The *Patrie* tries to turn the awkward incident that way, saying that those curious officers wanted "to arrest the sub-prefect, in case he should side with the Republic;"[e] but the fact is that they ran to the sub-prefect to ask him if it was true that the Republic was proclaimed at Paris. It was only on his denial that they thought fit to exhibit their professional zeal. Castellane has already

---

[a] "(Correspondance particulière de *L'Indépendance belge.*) Paris, 4 mars", *L'Indépendance belge,* No. 65, March 6, 1858.—*Ed.*

[b] Paul de Royer.—*Ed.*

[c] See addresses of the French army men, *Le Moniteur universel,* Nos. 26 and 27, January 26 and 27, 1858, and also the following issues.—*Ed.*

[d] "À Châlon-sur-Saône, dans la soirée...", *Le Moniteur universel,* No. 68, March 9, 1858.—*Ed.*

[e] Quoted from *L'Indépendance belge,* No. 71, March 12, 1858.—*Ed.*

started from Lyons to investigate their behavior. In one word, the army shows symptoms of disaffection. The manner in which it was paraded in the *Moniteur,* and made the laughing-stock of Europe, then to be simply thrown overboard out of deference to John Bull; Bonaparte's breaking it up into five armies, for fear of abdicating its supreme command into Pelissier's hands,[499] who has now become cold toward his master; the disdainful letters in which Changarnier and Bedeau have declined the permission to return to France[a]; the raising of L'Espinasse, generally detested in the barracks since the Dobrodja affair,[500] to a post of exceptional trust; and lastly, that dark presentiment of an impending turn in the tide which has always distinguished the "intelligent bayonets"[501] of France; all this has contributed to estrange the calculating chiefs of the army. Beside the Chalons affair, there is Gen. M'Mahon's conduct in the French Senate to bear witness to this strange and rather unexpected change. His remarks on the *loi des suspects*[502] were most outspoken, and his was the one adverse vote among Bonaparte's embroidered liverymen.[b]

Written on March 11, 1858

First published unsigned in the *New-York Daily Tribune,* No. 5285, March 30, 1858; reprinted in the *New-York Semi-Weekly Tribune,* No. 1341, April 2, 1858

Reproduced from the *New-York Daily Tribune*

[a] Changarnier's letter to the editor of *L'Indépendance belge* of March 1, 1858, *L'Indépendance belge,* No. 61, March 2, 1858; Bedeau's letter to the editor of *L'Indépendance belge* of March 3, 1858, *L'Indépendance belge,* No. 65, March 6, 1858.— *Ed.*

[b] MacMahon's speech in the French Senate on February 25, 1858. *Le Moniteur universel,* No. 57, February 26, 1858; also quoted in *L'Indépendance belge,* No. 59, February 28, 1858.— *Ed.*

Karl Marx

BONAPARTE'S PRESENT POSITION [503]

Paris, March 18, 1858

"Risorgero nemico ognor piu crudo
Cenere anco sepolto e spirto ignudo."

(I shall revive from the dead a still more cruel foe, though but buried ash and a naked spirit.) These two lines of Tasso's *Jerusalem*,[a] which Orsini, after Favre's speech,[b] with a strange smile, whispered to his defender, are already beginning to be fulfilled. The attitude of the crowd witnessing the death of the Italian patriot is thus described by an eye-witness:

"Such had been the alarm of the Government that an entire division was had out, under the personal command of a general officer, who assisted at the execution. Fifteen thousand soldiers were ready to act on the slightest signal, and every issue and outlet was guarded as in times of insurrection. In my estimation, between 90,000 and 100,000 men of the Faubourgs, workmen in blouses, were assembled in the spaces and in the streets near the Place de la Roquette;, but they were so grouped by the way in which the troops were stationed, that they could see little or nothing. When the dead, dull sound of the falling of the knife upon Orsini was heard, it was responded to by an immense but smothered reply of '*Vive la République*.' I cannot properly describe this; it was like a gigantic mutter; it was not a cry or a shout, but it sounded like the breath or the sigh of thousands of human beings. It was well appreciated by the authorities, for, on the instant, the soldiers raised the most disorderly clatter imaginable, struck their horses, so as to make them plunge and kick, shook their arms, and contrived that the popular whisper should be stifled without being literally put down. But the words '*Vive la République*' must have been clearly audible to every one. I purposely went home on foot, threading my way slowly through the groups wherever I found them thickest. I am bound to admit that everywhere I heard expressions of sympathy and admiration for Orsini, whose crime seems utterly forgotten, while only the effect produced by his courage and generosity toward his associates remains. Pieri's name I did not hear once. The attitude of the populace was, I should say, extremely menacing, for it had the marks of a hate and a thirst for vengeance

---

[a] Torquato Tasso, *Gerusalemme liberata*, canto nono, stanza XCIX.—*Ed.*

[b] J. Favre's speech before the Jury on February 26, 1858, *Le Moniteur universel*, No. 58, February 27, 1858.—*Ed.*

seated too deep for words. All the remarks I heard were made in an undertone, as though a police spy were dreaded at every instant."

It seems, then, that the measures of "general safety" intended to weed out the Republican element, the wholesale imprisonments and transportation, prove no more successful than the *cités ouvrières,*[a] the newly-established workshops, and other attempts to purchase the conscience of the French working classes. The circumstances dwelt upon on a former occasion,[b] which accompanied Orsini's trial, have now become the general topic of Paris conversation. It has even oozed out that when the voluminous correspondence of Orsini and Pieri came to be examined, letters written by Louis Napoleon, and signed by himself, dated many years ago, came to light. If the French *Constitutionnel* was still in the agreeable position it held in Mr. Guizot's time, we should, day after day, be treated with the solemn phrase, *"L'horizon politique s'obscurcit."*[c 504] And so it does, indeed. Great was the consternation at the Tuileries on ascertaining the conduct of the officers of the garrison at Chalons, and excessive the anger at the naïveté of the *Moniteur* informing France and Europe that, instead of on the instant laughing at the whole affair, ordering out their men, or declaring that, even were the Republic proclaimed in Paris, they would fight against it for the Empire, the officers at Chalons first ran to the sub-prefect[d] and declined to risk their skins and their commissions for the Emperor, before having made sure whether or not the Republic was proclaimed. The fact proves that the mass of the army cannot be relied upon. Save its heads, which are too deeply compromised or have received too brilliant rewards to separate their destinies from that of the Empire, there is perhaps but one single portion of it altogether trustworthy, namely, the Guards. This corps is indeed very strong, and must be aware that, under any other government, it would be merged into the line, or altogether disbanded. Its infantry force consists of four regiments of grenadiers, two regiments of voltigeurs, one regiment of gens d'armes, one regiment of Zouaves[505] and one battalion of chasseurs—altogether seventeen battalions of infantry. It musters, besides, two regiments of cuirassiers, two regiments of dragoons, one regiment of mounted grenadiers, one regiment of hussars,

---

[a] Workers' settlements.—*Ed.*

[b] See this volume, pp. 474-76.—*Ed.*

[c] The political horizon darkens.—*Ed.*

[d] "À Châlon-sur-Saône, dans la soirée...", *Le Moniteur universel,* No. 68, March 9, 1858. See this volume, p. 475.—*Ed.*

and one regiment of chasseurs, or twenty-one squadrons of cavalry; its artillery, too, being rather strong. Its whole numerical force amounts to about 20,000 men, with 40 to 50 cannons, a nucleus sufficiently powerful to counteract the tendencies to vacillation which might prevail in the line in the case of a serious struggle with the Paris people. Moreover, everything is provided for a sudden concentration of the troops from the provinces, as the most superficial glance at a railway map of France will prove, so that a movement which should not take the Government by surprise is sure to find arrayed against it the formidable force of from 60,000 to 80,000 men. But the very measures Bonaparte has taken to suppress an armed revolt make it quite improbable that it should occur except on some great unforeseen occasion, when the decidedly anti-Bonapartist attitude of the bourgeoisie, the secret societies undermining the lower strata of the army, the petty jealousies, venal treacheries and Orleanist or Legitimist[506] leanings dividing its superior layers, are likely to turn the scale in favor of the revolutionary masses. The worst thing that could happen to the latter would be a successfull attempt on Bonaparte's life. In that case the answer given by Morny, at the beginning of the Russian war, to Bonaparte's question, what they intended doing on his sudden death:

> "*Nous commencerions de jeter tous les Jerômes par la fenêtre, et puis nous tâcherions de nous arranger tant bien que mal avec les Orléans,*" [We shall begin by throwing all the Jeromes out of the window, and then we shall arrange matters as well as we can with the Orleans family,]

would perhaps turn out a prophecy. Before the men of the faubourgs could have decided upon the course to take, Morny might execute his palace-revolution, proclaim the Orleans, and thus draw over the middle classes to the anti-revolutionary camp.

Meanwhile Bonaparte's disappointments in the field of foreign policy vastly contribute to urge him on in his system of domestic terrorism. Every check he sustains from without, by betraying the weakness of his position, and giving new life to the aspirations of his antagonists, is necessarily followed up by new displays of what is called "governmental vigor." And these foreign miscarriages have rapidly accumulated during the last weeks. There was first the great failure with regard to England.[507] Then even Switzerland, although she had made very cowardly concessions, took courage to demur at the further steps urged upon her in the most unceremonious manner. It was formally declared to the Confederation that, if necessary, regiments of French infantry would enter and perform those police duties which the police of Switzerland could not do for themselves. At this point even Mr. Kern found it necessary to demand his passports, and the French Government to draw off. Belgium, having altered its law at Bonaparte's dictation,[508] declined to comply with the demand for Gen. Changarnier's expulsion. The Commission of the Piedmontese Chamber charged with the duty of examining the bill[a] to assimilate the Sardinian institutions to the *Idées Napoléoniennes,*[b] by a majority of five against two, proposed the pure and simple rejection of the Bonapartist project. Austria, fully aware that Orsini's execution has bound over to her, hand and foot, the hero of Strasbourg,[509] and that he can no longer alarm her through Italy, shows him the cold shoulder.

To expose itself to ridicule is the surest way for a French Government to annihilate itself. Bonaparte is conscious of the grotesque luster which his last baffled attempts at playing the dictator of Europe have shed upon him. The more contemptible his European position grows, the more keenly he feels the necessity of appearing formidable to France. Consequently, the reign of terror is progressively extending. Gen. Espinasse, at the head of the Ministry of the Interior, is now backed by Mr. Boitelle, a former colonel in the hussars, at the head of the Prefecture of Police. The system adopted by these military myrmidons of the second Empire is thus described in *The Continental Review*:

"They have taken the old lists of individuals who, after the troubles of 1848 and 1851, were designated by the police as dangerous, and they have arrested these persons *en masse,* both in Paris and in the departments. All this was done without the slightest inquiry being made as to whether or not these persons had since that period given ground of complaint, and the most cruel effects have ensued. Thus, honest citizens, who, being carried away in 1848 by the whirlwind which agitated the whole nation, professed advanced ideas, but who have since abandoned politics, and many of whom are now fathers of families and industrious tradesmen, were carried off by the police from the midst of their affairs and from their families. These are known facts which show how little ground there was for the arrests, and with what an absence of even the semblance of legality or necessity these measures of terrorism were carried out. Among the persons whom the agents of the police attempted to arrest, there were some individuals who had been no less than six years out of France, and who consequently could not have committed any offense, but who, if they had been in France at the present moment, would inevitably have been thrown into prison on pretense of 'public safety.' Nay, more, the police went to the houses of several persons who had been dead for some years, for the

[a] The bill submitted to the Turin Chamber of Deputies on February 17, 1858, *Le Moniteur universel,* No. 54, February 23, 1858.—*Ed.*

[b] An allusion to Louis Bonaparte's book *Des idées napoléoniennes.*—*Ed.*

purpose of arresting them. Their names figured on the lists of persons formerly arrested (and many of these simply because they were among the crowd in the streets, and that was their only crime). It is therefore clear that it is not against the guilty that the police war, but against the suspected; and the manner in which the law is executed is of itself a justification of the title conferred upon it by public opinion. In the departments matters proceed pretty much as in Paris. The lists of the suspected were drawn up by the administrative authorities, and woe to those who, in the elections of June last, ventured to oppose the candidates supported by the Prefect, and who, looking on the Constitution, the electoral law and the circulars of the Minister of the Interior as serious realities, have believed that they might take measures for the election of the candidates of their choice. These latter are considered as the worst of culprits, and they must be either very rich, very influential, or very well protected by their friends, to escape the vengeance of those officials whose paths they had crossed. Among the persons arrested in the provinces appears the name of Gen. Courtais, who, after having played a part in 1848 as Commander-in-Chief of the National Guard of Paris, lived for the last nine years in the greatest retirement in a country house in the department of the Allier, removed from society, and altogether a stranger to politics or public affairs."

What with this system of "general safety," what with the pangs of a commercial crisis that has become chronic, the French middle classes will soon be worked up to the point where they will consider a revolution necessary for the "restoration of confidence."

Written on March 18, 1858

First published unsigned in the *New-York Daily Tribune*, No. 5287, April 1, 1858; reprinted in the *New-York Semi-Weekly Tribune*, No. 1341, April 2, 1858 and in the *New-York Weekly Tribune*, No. 864, April 3, 1858

Reproduced from the *New-York Daily Tribune*

Karl Marx

PELISSIER'S MISSION TO ENGLAND

Paris, March 27, 1858

Of all governmental positions, the most trying is that of a civilian at the head of a despotic military state. In the Orient, the difficulty is more or less met by transforming the despot into a god, theocratic attributes not allowing the ruler to be reduced to a measure common to himself and to his swordsmen. In Imperial Rome, the deification of the Emperors, while not affording the same defense, grew out of the same necessity. Now, Louis Bonaparte is a civilian, although he was the editor of a history of cannon,[a] but he cannot adopt the Roman expedient. Hence the accumulating perplexities of his position. At the same rate that France grows impatient of the yoke of the army, the army waxes bolder in its purpose of yoking Bonaparte. After the 10th of December,[510] Bonaparte could flatter himself that he was the elect of the peasantry, that is, the mass of the French nation. Since the attempt of the 14th January,[511] he knows that he is at the mercy of the army. Having been compelled to avow that he rules through the army, it is quite natural that the latter should seek to rule through him.

The parceling out of France into five pashalics,[512] therefore, but preceded the installation of Espinasse as Minister of the Interior. The latter step was followed by making over the police of Paris to M. Boitelle, who was a non-commissioned officer in 1830, serving with M. de Persigny in the same regiment at La Fere and trying, when the revolution of July broke out, to make his comrades cry "Vive Napoleon II." The glorification of Boitelle is backed by the nomination of Pelissier Duc de Malakoff, as his Imperial Majesty's representative at the Court of St. James's. This appointment means flattery to the army and menace to England. It is true that the *Moniteur* pretends to turn it into a compliment to John

[a] Napoléon-Louis Bonaparte, *Histoire du canon dans les armées modernes.—Ed.*

Bull,[a] but Veuillot of the *Univers*, who is known to have his *petites* and *grandes entrées*[b] at the Tuileries, foreshadowed the event in a fierce article containing this significant phrase:

"The pride of England is wounded. The wound is an old one. The wound was inflicted in the Crimea at the Alma, at Inkermann, at the *Malakoff*, everywhere where the French were the first at the field and penetrated the deepest into the enemy's ranks. St. Arnaud, Bosquet, Canrobert, Pelissier, McMahon—these are the men who wounded the pride of England.'[c]

In one word, Napoleon III. has sent his Menchikoff to London, of whom, by-the-by, he is rather glad to get rid for a time, since Pelissier has taken up the attitude of a frondeur from the moment his appointment as Commander-in-Chief of the five pashalics was rescinded. The Paris Bourse, on the news becoming known, went down at once.

Pelissier has more than one grudge to avenge upon England. In 1841, before his electors at Tiverton, Palmerston publicly branded him as a monster,[d] and gave the signal to his general abuse by the London Press. After the Crimean campaign, General de Lacy Evans, in the House of Commons, more than hinted at Pelissier as the principal cause of the disgrace that had befallen the English army before Sevastopol. He was also roughly handled by the British Press, expatiating upon the intimations of Gen. Evans. Lastly, at a banquet given to the Crimean Generals, Pelissier simply appropriated the whole Crimean glory, such as it is, to the eagles of France, not even condescending to recollect John Bull's cooperation. Again, the London Press, by way of reprisal, dissected Pelissier. Moreover, his temper is known to unfit him altogether for the part of that mythological Greek personage who alone was able to heal the wounds it had inflicted.[e] Still we cannot share the opinion of those London papers which, working themselves up to a Roman state of mind, warn the Consuls to take care "*ne republica detrimenti capiat.*"[f] Pelissier means intimidation,

---

[a] "Voici en quels termes les principaux organes...", *Le Moniteur universel*, No. 86, March 27, 1858.—*Ed.*

[b] The right of informal and official entrance.—*Ed.*

[c] "Le journal la Patrie publie...", *L'Indépendance belge*, No. 86, March 27, 1858.—*Ed.*

[d] Palmerston's speech before the electors at Tiverton on June 28, 1841, *The Times*, No. 1773, July 3, 1841.—*Ed.*

[e] The reference is to Achilles, who, as the Greek myth has it, was the only one able to heal the wounds he had inflicted to Telephus, Heracles' son.—*Ed.*

[f] That the state suffer no harm (the *decretum ultimum* passed by the Roman senate in times of national peril, which gave the chief magistrates, the consuls, full powers to use any means to save the commonwealth).—*Ed.*

but he does not mean war. This appointment is a mere *coup de théâtre.*

The broad ditch that separates *perfide* Albion[513] from *la belle France,* is her Lacus Curtius,[514] but Bonaparte is not the romantic youth to close the yawning chasm by plunging himself into the gulf, and disappearing. Of all men in Europe, he knows best that his frail tenure of power hinges upon the alliance with England; but this is a truth fatal to the revenger of Waterloo,[515] and which he must do his best to conceal from his armed myrmidons[516] by pulling hard on John Bull, and clothing the very alliance in the garbs of a vassalage, imposed by France, and accepted by England.

Such is his game, a most dangerous one, likely to hasten the issue it aims to put off. If Pelissier fails in his bullying mission, as he is sure to do, the last card has been played, the theatrical performances must make room for real ones, or Bonaparte will stand before his army a confessed impostor, hiding behind his Napoleonic airs the sorry figure of the London constable of the 10th of April, 1848.[517]

In point of fact, it was but the alliance with England which enabled the nephew for a time to mimic the uncle. The close connection of England and France, while giving the death-blow to the Holy Alliance[518] and putting at nought the balance of European power, naturally invested Bonaparte, the Continental representative of that alliance, with the appearance of the arbiter of Europe. So long as the Russian war and the internal state of France allowed him to do so, he was but too glad to content himself with this symbolical rather than real supremacy. All this has changed since peace reigns in Europe and the army reigns in France. He is now called upon by the army to show that, like a real Napoleon, he holds the dictature of Europe, not in trust for England, but in spite of England. Hence his perplexities. On the one hand he bullies John Bull, on the other hand he insinuates to him that he means no harm. He rather implores him to look frightened, out of courtesy, at the mock-menaces of his "august ally." This is the very way of stiffening John Bull, who feels that he risks nothing in giving himself heroical airs.

Written on March 26, 1858 Reproduced from the newspaper

First published unsigned in the *New-York Daily Tribune,* No. 5299, April 15, 1858

Karl Marx

MAZZINI AND NAPOLEON

M. Mazzini has recently addressed a letter to the French Emperor,[a] which, in a literary point of view, must hold, perhaps, the first place among his productions. There are but few traces left of that false sublimity, puffy grandeur, verbosity and prophetic mysticism so characteristic of many of his writings, and almost forming the distinctive features of that school of Italian literature of which he is the founder. An enlargement of views is also perceptible. He has, till now, figured as the chief of the Republican formalists of Europe. Exclusively bent on the political forms of the State, they have had no eye for the organization of society on which the political superstructure rests. Boasting of a false idealism, they have considered it beneath their dignity to become acquainted with economical realities. Nothing is easier than to be an idealist on behalf of other people. A surfeited man may easily sneer at the materialism of hungry people asking for vulgar bread instead of sublime ideas. The Triumvirs of the Roman Republic of 1848,[519] leaving the peasants of the Campagna in a state of slavery more exasperating than that of their ancestors of the times of imperial Rome, were quite welcome to descant on the degraded state of the rural mind.

All real progress in the writing of modern history has been effected by descending from the political surface into the depths of social life. Dureau de la Malle, in tracing the different phases of the development of landed property in ancient Rome, has afforded a key to the destinies of that world-conquering city, beside which Montesquieu's considerations on its greatness and

[a] G. Mazzini, *To Louis Napoléon.—Ed.*

decline[a] appear almost like a schoolboy's declamation. The venerable Lelewel, by his laborious research into the economical circumstances which transformed the Polish peasant from a free man into a serf,[b] has done more to shed light on the subjugation of his country than the whole host of writers whose stock in trade is simple denunciation of Russia. M. Mazzini, too, does not now disdain to dwell on social realities, the interests of the different classes, the exports and imports, the prices of necessaries, house-rent, and other such vulgar things, being struck, perhaps, by the great if not fatal shock given to the second Empire, not by the manifestoes of Democratic Committees, but by the commercial convulsion which started from New-York to encompass the world. It is only to be hoped that he will not stop at this point, but, unbiased by a false pride, will proceed to reform his whole political catechism by the light of economical science. His letter commences with this vigorous apostrophe to Louis Napoleon:

"The fullness of time approaches; the Imperial tide is visibly rolling back. You too feel it. All the measures you have been enacting, since the 14th of January,[520] in France—all the diplomatic notes and requests you have been, since the fatal day, scattering to the four winds abroad, are bespeaking the restlessness of terror. There is a Macbeth feeling of intense agony preying upon your soul, and betraying itself through all that you say or do. There is at work within a presentiment that *summa dies et ineluctabile fatum*[c] are impending. The 'Thane of Glamis, Thane of Cawdor, and King'—the Pretender, President and Usurper—are doomed. The spell is broken. The conscience of mankind is aroused; it gazes sternly on you; it confronts you; it sifts your acts, and calls to account your promises. From this moment, your fate is sealed. You may now live months; years you cannot."[d]

Having thus announced the doom of the second Empire, Mazzini contrasts the present economical state of France with Napoleon's glowing promises of general prosperity:

"You promised, when you unlawfully conquered power, and as an atonement for its origin, that you would rule restless, perturbed, perturbing France to peace. Is imprisoning, gagging, transporting, *ruling*? Is the gendarme a teacher? Is the spy an apostle of morality and mutual trust? You told the French uneducated peasant that a new era was, with your empire, dawning for him, and that the burdens under which he groans would all, one by one, disappear. Has *any* disappeared? Can you point out a single amelioration to his fate—a single element of taxation removed? Can you explain how it is that the peasant is now enlisting in the *Marianne*[521]? Can you deny that the absorption of the funds, once naturally

[a] A. Dureau de la Malle, *Economie politique des Romains;* Ch. Montesquieu, *Considérations sur les causes de la grandeur des Romains et de leur décadence.*—*Ed.*

[b] J. Lelevel, *Considérations sur l'état politique de l'ancienne Pologne et sur l'histoire de son peuple.*—*Ed.*

[c] The last day and the ineluctable hour (cf. Virgil, *Aeneid,* II, 325).—*Ed.*

[d] G. Mazzini, *To Louis Napoléon,* p. 3.—*Ed.*

devoted to the agricultural element, into the channels of industrial speculation opened by you, has deprived the laborer of the possibility of finding advances for the purchase of working implements and the improvement of the land? You allured the misguided working man by declaring that you would be the *Empereur du peuple*, a sort of remodeled Henry IV., and procure to him perennial work, high wages, and *la poule au pot*.[a] Is not *la poule au pot* somewhat dear just now in France? Is not house-rent, are not some of the first necessaries of life, still dearer? You have opened new streets—drawn for your strategic, repressive purposes new lines of communication—destroyed and rebuilt. But do the bulk of the working classes belong to the benefited building branch? Can you overturn Paris and the main provincial towns, indefinitely, for the sake of creating for the *prolétaire* a source of work and earnings? Can you ever dream of making of such a factitious, temporary remedy a substitute for regular normal progress, and requited production? Is the demand for production now in a satisfactory state? Are not three-fifths of the cabinet-makers, of the carpenters, of the mechanicians, out of employment now in Paris? You whispered to the easily frightened, easily fascinated bourgeoisie fantastic dreams, hopes of a redoubled industrial activity, new sources of profits, El Dorados of stimulated exportation, and international intercourse. Where are they? Stagnation hovers over your French productive life; orders to commerce are diminishing; capital is beginning to retreat. You have, like the barbarian, cut the tree to pluck the fruit. You have artificially over-stimulated wild, immoral, all-promising and never-fulfilling speculation; you have, by self-puffing, gigantic, swollen schemes, attracted the savings of the small capitalists from the four corners of France to Paris, and diverted them from the only true permanent sources of national wealth, agriculture, trade and industry. These savings have been engulfed and disappeared in the hands of some dozens of leading speculators; they have been squandered in boundless unproductive luxuries; or they are quietly and prudently—I might quote members of your family—transferred to safe foreign countries. The half of these schemes have sunk into oblivious nonentity. Some of their inventors are traveling, as a precautionary measure, in foreign countries. You find yourself before a dissatisfied bourgeoisie, with all normal resources dried up, with the incubus of some five hundred millions of francs spent, throughout the principal towns of France, in unproductive public works, with a deficit of three hundred millions visible in your last budget, with an extensively indebted city of Paris, with no remedy to propose except a new loan of one hundred and sixty millions to be opened—not in your name, it would not succeed—but in the name of the City Council itself, and to meet the burden of interest, a widening of the barriers, therefore, of the hated octroi,[b] to the extent of the outward fortifications. The remedy will weigh heavy on the working class, and embitter against you the hitherto devoted suburbs. Your artificial contrivances are at an end; henceforth, everything you do to meet the financial difficulty of your position, will mark a step in the fatal descent. You have hitherto lived on an indefinite series of loans and credit; but where is your guaranty for prolonged credit? Rome and Napoleon were ransacking a world; you have only France to ransack. Their armies lived on conquest; yours cannot. You may dream of conquest; you cannot, do not dare to venture on it. The Roman dictators and your uncle were leading the conquering armies; however fond of gilt parade uniforms, I doubt your being able to lead a few combined battalions."[c]

---

[a] A fowl in his pot.—*Ed.*

[b] A tax on articles (for sale) entering a town.—*Ed.*

[c] Here and below G. Mazzini, *To Louis Napoléon*, pp. 3-8 and 13.—*Ed.*

From the material prospect of the second Empire, Mazzini turns to the moral, and, of course, is somewhat perplexed in summing up the evidence for the proposition that liberty wears no Bonapartist livery. Liberty, not only in its bodily forms, but in its very soul, its intellectual life, has shriveled at the coarse touch of these resurrectionists of a bygone epoch. Consequently, the representatives of intellectual France, by no means distinguished by too nice a delicacy of political conscience, never failing to gather around every regime, from the Regent[a] to Robespierre—from Louis XIV. to Louis Philippe—from the first Empire to the second Republic—have, for the first time in French history, seceded in mass from an established government.

"From Thiers to Guizot, from Cousin to Villemain, from Michelet to Jean Reynaud, intellectual France shrinks from your polluting contact. Your men are Veuillot, the upholder of the St. Bartholomew[522] and of the Inquisition, Granier de Cassagnac, the patron of negro slavery, and such like. To find a man worth indorsing your pamphlet addressed to England, you have to look for one who is an apostate from Legitimism, and an apostate from Republicanism."

Mazzini then hits on the true meaning of the affair of the 14th of January by stating that the missiles which missed the Emperor pierced the Empire, and laid bare the hollowness of its boasts:

"You boasted to Europe, only a short while ago, that the heart of France was yours, hailing you as her savior, calm, happy, undisturbed. A few months have elapsed, a crash has been heard in the rue Lepelletier, and through your wild, alarmed, repressive measures—through your half-threatening, half-imploring appeals to Europe—through your military division of the country, with a saber in the Ministry of the Interior, you declare now, after seven years of unlimited sway—with an overwhelming concentrated army—with the national ranks cleared of all the dreaded leading men—that you cannot live and rule unless France is converted into a huge Bastille, and Europe into a mere Imperial police-office.... Yes; the Empire has proved a lie. You shaped it, Sir, to your own image. No man, during the last half century, has lied in Europe, Talleyrand excepted, so much as you have; and *that* is the secret of your temporary power."

The falsehoods of the savior of society are then recapitulated from 1831, when he joined the insurrectionary movement of the Roman population against the Pope[523] as "a sacred cause;" to 1851, a few days before the coup d'état, when he said to the army, "I shall ask nothing from you beyond my right, recognized by the Constitution;" to the 2d of December itself, the final result of the usurping schemes still pending, when he proclaimed that "his duty was to protect the Republic." Finally, he tells Napoleon roundly

[a] Philip II of Orleans.—*Ed.*

that but for England he would have been already conquered by the Revolution. Then, having disposed of Napoleon's claim to have inaugurated the alliance between France and England, he concludes with the words:

> "You stand now, Sir, whatever self-mouthed, self-disguising diplomacy may say, alone in Europe."

Written on March 30, 1858

First published unsigned in the *New-York Daily Tribune,* No. 5321, May 11, 1858

Reproduced from the newspaper

Karl Marx

THE FRENCH TRIALS IN LONDON[524]

Paris, April 4, 1858

When Victor Hugo marked the nephew as Napoleon the Little, he acknowledged the uncle as Napoleon the Great. The title of his celebrated pamphlet[a] meant an antithesis, and,to some degree, did homage to that very Napoleon-worship on which the son of Hortense Beauharnais contrived to raise the bloody fabric of his fortune. What is more useful to impress on the present generation is that Napoleon the Little represents in fact the littleness of Napoleon the Great. The plainest illustration of this fact is afforded by the recent "painful misconceptions" between England and France, and the criminal proceedings against refugees and printers which they have led to on the part of the English Government. A short historical review will prove that during the whole of this miserable melo-drama Napoleon the Little has only re-enacted with anxious minuteness the shabby part invented and played before by Napoleon the Great.

It was only during the short interval separating the peace of Amiens[525] (March 25, 1802) from the new declaration of war on the part of Great Britain (May 18, 1803) that Napoleon could indulge his desire for interference with the internal state of Great Britain. He lost no time. Even while the peace negotiations were still pending, the *Moniteur* emitted his venom on all the London papers venturing to question "the moderation and sincerity of Bonaparte's views," and gave no very unintelligible hint that "such disbelief might ere long be followed with chastisement."[b] Nor did

[a] V. Hugo, *Napoléon le petit.* (Originally this epithet was used by the author of the pamphlet in his speech in the Legislative Assembly in 1851.).— *Ed.*

[b] "Paris, le 22 ventôse", "Paris, le 25 ventôse", *Gazette nationale, ou Le Moniteur universel,* Nos. 173, 176, 23, 26 ventôse an 10 de la République française.— *Ed.*

the Consul confine himself to a censorship over the language and sentiments of the British press. The *Moniteur* abused Lord Grenville and Mr. Windham for the part they took in the discussions on peace.[a] Mr. Elliot, a Member of Parliament, was called to account in the House of Commons by Perceval, the Attorney-General, for expressing his doubts as to Bonaparte's intentions.[b] Lord Castlereagh and Pitt himself pitched the key of submission, by inculcating, what had never been done on any former occasions, forbearance of language in debate as respecting the Consul of France.[c] About six weeks had passed from the conclusion of the peace, when Talleyrand, on June 3, 1802, informed Mr. Merry, the British Plenipotentiary at Paris, that Bonaparte, out of consideration for England, had resolved to replace Mr. Otto, the French Plenipotentiary at London, by a real Embassador in the person of Gen. Andréossy; but that before the arrival of that exalted personage at London, it was the First Consul's sincere wish

> "to see such obstacles removed which stood very much in the way of the perfect reconciliation between the two countries and their Governments."

What he demanded, was simply the removal out of the British dominions of

> "all the French princes and their adherents, together with the French bishops and other French individuals whose political principles and conduct must necessarily occasion great jealousy of the French Government.... The protection and favor which all the persons in question continued to meet with, in a country so close a neighbor to France, must alone be always considered as an encouragement to the disaffected here, even without those persons themselves being guilty of any acts leading to foment fresh disturbances in this country; but that the Government here possessed proofs of the abuse which they were now making of the protection which they enjoyed in England, and of the advantage they were taking of their vicinity to France, by being really guilty of such acts, since several printed papers had lately been intercepted, which it was known they had sent, and caused to be circulated in France, and which had for their object to create an opposition to the Government."[d]

There existed at that time an alien law[526] in England, which, however, was framed strictly with a view to the protection of the

---

[a] "Paris, le 10 nivôse an 11", *Gazette nationale, ou Le Moniteur universel,* No. 101, 11 nivôse an 11 de la République française.— *Ed.*

[b] W. Elliot's speech in the House of Commons on November 4, 1801, *Cobbett's Annual Register,* Vol. II, col. 1187.— *Ed.*

[c] R. St. Castlereagh's and W. Pitt's speeches in the House of Commons on November 3, 1801, *Cobbett's Annual Register,* Vol. II, col. 1133-34, 1144.— *Ed.*

[d] Ch. M. Talleyrand's conversation with A. Merry on the 3rd of June 1802, *Cobbett's Annual Register,* Vol. III, col. 998.— *Ed.*

British Government. In answer to Talleyrand's demand, Lord Hawkesbury, the then Foreign Minister, replied that

"His Majesty the King[a] certainly expected that all foreigners who might reside within his dominions, should not only hold a conduct conformable to the laws of the country, but abstain from all acts hostile to the Government of any country with which his Majesty might be at peace. As long, however, as they conduct themselves according to these principles, his Majesty would feel it inconsistent with his dignity, with his honor, and with the common laws of hospitality, to deprive them of that protection which individuals resident in his dominions can only forfeit by their own misconduct. The greater part of the persons to whom allusion has been made in Mr. Talleyrand's conversation, are living in retirement."[b]

In delivering Lord Hawkesbury's dispatch to Talleyrand, Mr. Merry was by no means sparing of assurances calculated to "soothe, tranquilize and satisfy the First Consul."[c] Talleyrand, however, insisted upon his pound of flesh,[d] stating that the First Consul had solicited no more than the British Government itself had demanded of Louis XIV., when the Pretender[e] was in France, that he could not see any humiliation in the measure intimated, and that he must repeat

"that the adoption of it would be in the highest degree agreeable and satisfactory to the First Consul," and be considered by him as "the most convincing proof of his Majesty's disposition to see a cordial good understanding established between the two countries."[f]

On July 25, 1802, Mr. Otto, from his residence at Portman Square, addressed a letter to Lord Hawkesbury, requesting, in a very categorical way, nothing less than the suppression of the liberty of the English press, as far as Bonaparte and his Government were concerned.

"I transmitted," he says, "some time ago, to Mr. Hammond, a number of Peltier, containing the most gross calumnies against the French Government, and against the whole nation; and I observed, that I should probably receive an order to demand a punishment of such an abuse of the press. That order is actually arrived, and I cannot conceal from you, my Lord, that the reiterated insults of a small number of foreigners, assembled in London to conspire against the French Government, have produced the most unfavorable effects on the good understand-

---

[a] George III.—*Ed.*

[b] R. Hawkesbury's dispatch to A. Merry, dated June 10, 1802, *Cobbett's Annual Register*, Vol. III, col. 999-1000.—*Ed.*

[c] A. Merry's dispatch to R. Hawkesbury, dated Paris, June 17, 1802, *Cobbett's Annual Register*, Vol. III, col. 1000-02.—*Ed.*

[d] Shakespeare, *The Merchant of Venice*, Act I, Scene 3.—*Ed.*

[e] James II.—*Ed.*

[f] Ch. M. Talleyrand's conversation with A. Merry, *Cobbett's Annual Register*, Vol. III, col. 1000-01.—*Ed.*

ing between the two nations.... It is not to Peltier alone, but to the editor of the *Courrier Français de Londres* (Reynaud), to Cobbett, and to other writers who resemble them, that I have to direct the attention of his Majesty's Government.... The want of positive laws against these sorts of offenses cannot palliate the violation of the laws of nations, according to which peace should put a stop to all species of hostilities; and doubtless those which wound the honor and reputation of a Government, and which tend to create a revolt of the people whose interests are confided to that Government, are the most apt to lessen the advantages of peace and to keep up national resentments."[a]

Instead of meeting these first reproaches of Bonaparte's interference on the subject of the press with a firm and dignified reply, Lord Hawkesbury, in a letter to M. Otto on July 28, made a paltry apology for the existence of the liberty of the press. He says that it is

"impossible his Majesty's Government could peruse Peltier's article without the greatest displeasure, and without an anxious desire that a person who published it should suffer the punishment he so justly deserves."

Then, after lamenting the "inconveniences" of prosecutions for libel, and the "difficulty" of obtaining judgment against the offenders, he concludes by stating that he has referred the matter to the King's Attorney-General[b] "for his opinion whether it is or is not a libel."[c]

While the British Government was thus preparing a crusade against the liberty of the press, in order to soothe the susceptibility of its great and new ally, there appeared suddenly, on August 9, a menacing article in the *Moniteur*, in which England was not only accused of receiving French robbers and assassins, of harboring them at Jersey, and of sending them to make predatory excursions on the coasts of France, but in which the English King himself was represented as a rewarder and instigator of assassination:

"*The Times*, which is said to be under Ministerial inspection, is filled with perpetual invectives against France. Two of its four pages are every day employed in giving currency to the grossest calumnies. All that imagination can depict, that is low, vile and base, is by that miserable paper attributed to the French Government. What is its end? Who pays it? What does it effect? A French journal,[d] edited by some miserable emigrants, the remnant of the most impure, a vile refuse, without country, without honor, sullied with crimes which it is not in the power of any amnesty to wash away, outdoes even *The Times*." "Eleven Bishops, presided over

---

[a] L. G. Otto's letter to R. Hawkesbury, dated July 25, 1802, *Cobbett's Annual Register*, Vol. III, col. 1002.—*Ed.*

[b] Spencer Perceval.—*Ed.*

[c] R. Hawkesbury's letter to L. G. Otto, dated July 28, 1802, *Cobbett's Annual Register*, Vol. III, col. 1003.—*Ed.*

[d] *L'Ambigu, variétés atroces et amusantes.*—*Ed.*

by the atrocious *Bishop of Arras,* rebels to their country and to the Church, have assembled in London. They print libels against the Bishops and the French clergy." "The Isle of Jersey is full of brigands, condemned to death by the tribunals, committed subsequent to the peace for assassination, robberies, and the practices of an incendiary. Georges[a] wears openly at London his red ribbon, as a recompense for the infernal machine which destroyed a part of Paris, and killed thirty women and children, or peaceable citizens.[b] This special protection authorizes a belief that if he had succeeded, he would have been honored with the Order of the Garter." "Either the English Government authorizes and tolerates those public and private crimes, in which case it cannot be said that such conduct is consistent with British generosity, civilization and honor; or it cannot prevent them, in which case it does not deserve the name of a Government, above all, if it does not possess the means of repressing assassination and calumny and protecting social order."[c]

When the menacing *Moniteur* arrived late at night in London, it produced such an irritation that *The True Briton,* the Ministerial paper, was compelled to declare,

"That article could not have been inserted in the *Moniteur* with the knowledge or consent of the French Government."[d]

In the House of Commons Dr. Laurence called upon Mr. Addington (afterward Lord Sidmouth) as to the French libels on his Majesty.[e] The Minister replied that

"he wished he could show to the learned gentleman the satisfactory explanations which had taken place on that head."[f]

It was replied that while the British Government made a public matter of a jest on Bonaparte and his wife, and Mr. Peltier was, for his jokes upon those people, to be brought into the Court of King's Bench[527] and to be arraigned as a criminal; in the other case, when the British nation was libeled and its royal master, in the official gazette of France, styled the rewarder of assassins, the matter was to be settled by an "explanation", and that explanation so secret, too, as not to admit of being communicated to Parliament. Encouraged by the apparent vacillation of the English

---

[a] Georges Cadoudal.— *Ed.*

[b] The reference is to the attempt on the life of Napoleon Bonaparte on December 24, 1800 in the rue Saint-Nicaise.— *Ed.*

[c] "Paris, le 19 thermidor", *Gazette nationale, ou Le Moniteur universel,* No. 320, 20 thermidor an 10 de la République française. (The last sentence of this passage was quoted by Marx in his letter to Engels of February 14, 1858. See present edition, Vol. 40, p. 266.).— *Ed.*

[d] *The True Briton's* declaration, *Cobbett's Annual Register,* Vol. II, col. 130.— *Ed.*

[e] Fr. Laurence's speech in the House of Commons on December 9, 1802, *Cobbett's Annual Register,* Vol. II, col. 1774-76.— *Ed.*

[f] H. Addington's speech in the House of Commons on December 9, 1802, *Cobbett's Annual Register,* Vol. II, col. 1776-77.— *Ed.*

Ministry, Otto, on Aug. 17, 1802, came out with a most impudent note to Lord Hawkesbury, in which the demand is formally put to adopt effectual measures for putting down all the unbecoming and seditious publications of the English prints, to send out of Jersey certain individuals, to expel the French bishops, to transport Georges and his adherents to Canada, and to send the French princes to Warsaw. With reference to the alien law M. Otto insists that the Ministry must possess

> "a legal and sufficient power to restrain foreigners, without having recourse to the courts of law;"

and he adds,

> "The French Government, which offers on this point a perfect reciprocity, thinks it gives a new proof of its pacific intentions, by demanding that those persons should be sent away whose machinations uniformly tend to sow discord between the two nations."[a]

Lord Hawkesbury's answer, dated Aug. 28, sent in the form of a dispatch to the English Plenipotentiary at Paris, has during the late quarrel with Bonaparte III. been quoted by the London press as a model of statesmanlike dignity; but it must be confessed that in spite of the terms of virtuous indignation in which it is couched, promises are held out of sacrificing the French emigrants to the jealous fears of the First Consul.[b]

In the beginning of the year 1803 Napoleon took upon himself to regulate the proceedings of Parliament and to restrain the liberty of speech among its members. With respect to the ex-Ministers, Mr. Windham, Lord Grenville, and Lord Minto, he intimated literally in his *Moniteur*,

> "It would be a patriotic and wise law which should ordain that displaced Ministers should not, for the first seven years after their dismissal, be competent to sit in the English Parliament. Another law, not less wise, would be that every member who should insult a friendly people and power should be condemned to silence for two years. When the tongue offends, the tongue must suffer punishment."[c]

At the same time Gen. Andréossy, who had meanwhile arrived at London, complained in a note to Lord Hawkesbury that the despicable pamphleteers and libelers of the British press

---

[a] L. G. Otto's note to R. Hawkesbury, dated August 17, 1802, *Cobbett's Annual Register*, Vol. III, col. 1103.—*Ed.*

[b] R. Hawkesbury's dispatch to A. Merry, dated August 28, 1802, *Cobbett's Annual Register*, Vol. III, col. 1007-13.—*Ed.*

[c] "Paris, le 10 nivôse an 11", *Gazette nationale, ou Le Moniteur universel*, No. 101, 11 nivôse an 11 de la République française.—*Ed.*

"have found themselves invariably supported in their insolent observations by particular phrases, taken from the speeches of some leading Members of Parliament."

Of these speeches it is said that

"every reasonable Englishman must be humiliated by such unheard-of licentiousness."

In the name of the First Consul he expresses the wish

"that means should be adopted to prevent in future any mention being made of what is passing in France, either in the official discussions or in the polemical writings in England, as in like manner, in the French official discussions and polemical writings, no mention should be made of what is passing in England."[a]

While Bonaparte in this tone of mingled hypocrisy and arrogance privately addressed the British Government, the *Moniteur* teemed with insults against the British people, and also published an official report of Col. Sebastiani, containing the most injurious charges against the British army in Egypt.[b] On Feb. 5, 1803, the French *Commissaire de Relation Commerciale* at Jersey, though acknowledged in no public capacity, had the insolence to prefer a complaint against some printers for inserting paragraphs from the London papers offensive to Bonaparte, and to threaten that if the practice was not punished, Bonaparte would certainly revenge himself upon Jersey. This threat had the desired effect. Two of the printers were brought before the Royal Court, and the positive injunction was laid on them not to publish in future anything offensive to France, even from the London papers.[c] On Feb. 20, 1803, one day before Peltier's trial, Lord Whitworth, the English Embassador at Paris, was summoned into the presence of the great man himself. Being received in his cabinet, Whitworth was desired to sit down after Bonaparte had sat down himself on the other side of the table. He enumerated the several provocations which he pretended to have received from England.

"He adverted to the abuse thrown out about him in the English prints, but this he said he did not so much regard as that which appeared in the French papers published in London. This he considered as much more mischievous, since it was meant to excite his country against him and his Government. He complained of the protection given to Georges and others of his description; [...] he acknowledged that the irritation he felt against England increased daily, because every wind which

---

[a] A. Fr. Andréossy's note to R. Hawkesbury, dated March 29, 1803, *Cobbett's Annual Register*, Vol. III, col. 1053-57.—*Ed.*

[b] H. Sebastiani, "Rapport fait au Premier Consul", *Gazette nationale, ou Le Moniteur universel*, No. 130, 10 pluviôse an 11 de la République française.—*Ed.*

[c] "Summary of Politics", *Cobbett's Annual Register*, Vol. III, col. 315.—*Ed.*

blew from England brought nothing but enmity and hatred against him.... As a proof of his desire to maintain peace, he wished to know what he had to gain by going to war with England. A descent was the only means of offense he had, and that he was determined to attempt, by putting himself at the head of the expedition. He acknowledged that there were one hundred chances to one against him, but still he was determined to attempt it if war should be the consequence of the present discussion; and that such was the disposition of the troops that army after army would be found for the enterprise.... To preserve peace the treaty of Amiens must be fulfilled, the abuse in the public prints, if not totally suppressed, at least kept within bounds and confined to the English papers, and the protection so openly given to his bitterest enemies must be withdrawn."[a]

On Feb. 21, Peltier was tried before Lord Ellenborough and a special Jury, for libeling Bonaparte and "intending to excite the people of France to assassinate their ruler."[b] Lord Ellenborough had the meanness to terminate his address to the Jury with the following words:

"Gentlemen, I trust your verdict will strengthen the relations by which the interests of this country are connected with those of France, and that it will illustrate and justify in every quarter of the world the conviction that has been long and universally entertained of the unsullied purity of British judicature."[c]

The Jury, without retiring from their box, immediately returned the verdict of Guilty. In consequence of the subsequent rupture between the two countries, Mr. Peltier was, however, not called upon to receive judgment, and the prosecution thus stopped. Having goaded the British Ministry into these persecutions of the press, and wrung from them Peltier's condemnation, the truthful and heroic *Moniteur*, March 2, 1803, published the following commentary:

"A person of the name of Peltier has been found guilty, before a court of justice at London, of printing and publishing some wretched libels against the First Consul. It is not easy to imagine why the English Ministry should affect to make this a matter of so much éclat. As it has been said in the English newspapers that the trial was instituted at the demand of the French Government, and that the French Embassador was even in the Court when the Jury gave in their verdict, we have authority to deny that any such things did ever take place. The First Consul was even ignorant of the existence of Peltier's libels till they came to his knowledge in the public accounts of the proceedings at his trial.... Yet it is to be acknowledged that these proceedings, however useless in other respects, have afforded an occasion to the Judges who presided at the trial to evince, by their wisdom and

---

[a] Napoleon I's conversation with Lord Whitworth, dated February 20, 1803, *Cobbett's Annual Register*, Vol. III, col. 1034.—*Ed.*

[b] Cited according to "Trial of Mr. Peltier", *Cobbett's Annual Register*, Vol. III, col. 276-83.—*Ed.*

[c] E. L. Ellenborough's speech at the trial of J. G. Peltier on February 21, 1803, *Cobbett's Annual Register*, Supplement to Vol. III, col. 1232.—*Ed.*

impartiality, that they are truly worthy to administer justice in a nation so enlightened, and estimable in so many respects."[a]

While the *Moniteur* in the same article insisted that the duty weighed on all "civilized nations in Europe" reciprocally to put down the barbarians of the press, M. Reinhard, the French Plenipotentiary at Hamburg, summoned together the Hamburg Senate, in order to consider a requisition from the First Consul to insert in the *Hamburger Correspondent* an article most offensive to the British Government. It was the wish of the Senate at least to be allowed to omit or qualify the most offensive passages; but M. Reinhard said his orders were positive for the full and exact insertion of the whole. The article appeared consequently in its original coarseness. The French Minister desired that the same should be published in the papers at Altona; but the Danish magistrates said that they could not possibly permit it without an express order from their Government. In consequence of this refusal, M. D'Aguesseau, the French Minister at Copenhagen, received from his colleague at Hamburg a copy of the article, with the request that he would solicit permission for its publication in the Danish papers. When called upon with respect to this libel by Lord Whitworth, M. Talleyrand declared that

"the British Ministers could not be more surprised than the First Consul had been at seeing such an article inserted by authority; that an immediate explanation had been required of M. Reinhard, etc."[b]

Such was Napoleon the Great.

Written on April 4, 1858

First published unsigned in the *New-York Daily Tribune*, No. 5309, April 27, 1858

Reproduced from the newspaper

[a] "Paris, le 11 ventôse", *Gazette nationale, ou Le Moniteur universel*, No. 162, 12 ventôse an 11 de la République française.— *Ed.*

[b] Ch. M. Talleyrand's conversation with Lord Whitworth, *Cobbett's Annual Register*, Vol. III, col. 1066.— *Ed.*

Karl Marx

[THE FINANCIAL STATE OF FRANCE]

Paris, April 13, 1858

By mere force of circumstances the restored Empire finds itself more and more compelled to throw up its adventitious graces and show its real features in their native hideousness. The hour of confessions has broken in upon it unexpectedly. It had already dropped every pretense of being a regular Government, or the offspring of the "*suffrage universel.*" It had proclaimed itself the régime of the upstart, the informer and the 12-pounder.[528] It goes now a step further, and avows itself the régime of the swindler. The *Moniteur* of April 11 contains a note stating that certain journals have announced prematurely the fixation of the dividend upon the shares of certain *railway companies* and *other industrial societies,* and have attributed to this dividend a lower figure than that which has been since determined by the Councils of Administration.

"These are maneuvers against which the industry and the capital of the country must be protected. *The editors of the journals referred to have been called before the Procureur Impérial,* and warned that such facts will for the future be sent before the tribunals, as constituting the offense of publishing false views. The duty of the press is to enlighten the public, and not deceive it."[a]

In other words, it is the duty of the press writers, at the peril of being transported to Cayenne,[529] to bolster up the *Crédit Mobilier,*[530] instead of warning the public of the impending breaking up of that monster imposture, as they have done of late, although in very timid and subdued tones. The Crédit Mobilier is to hold its general annual meeting April 29 and declare its dividend for the past year. While its directors shrouded themselves

[a] "Paris, le 10 avril", *Le Moniteur universel,* No. 101, April 11, 1858.—*Ed.*

in impenetrable mystery, most disastrous reports were circulated as to the way in which the expected dividend was to be "cooked," and one paper dared to hint at the fact that at the meeting of one company, connected with the Crédit Mobilier, held some time before, the manager coolly announced that though he could only declare a dividend of 8 per cent, *the company was in a far better position* than the year before, when he gave 25. The writer ventured upon expressing his suspicion whether *any* dividend of this "and other" companies were not paid out of the capital rather than the profits realized. Hence the wrath of the *Moniteur*. The shares of the Crédit Mobilier, quoted from 957 to 960 frs. on Feb. 10, from 820 to 860 frs. on March 10, had fallen to from 715 to 720 frs. on April 10, and even this latter quotation was merely nominal. There was no means of concealing the ugly fact that Austrian and Prussian holders had resolved upon selling no fewer than 6,000 shares, and that the "Maritime *Générale Compagnie,*" one of the fantastic creations of the Péreires, was *in articulo mortis,*[a] from having engaged in speculations anything but "maritime."[b] It is a fine notion, quite worthy of a political economist of the force of General Espinasse, to imagine that menaces in the *Moniteur* will enforce credit as well as silence. The warning will act, but quite in the opposite direction, the more so since it emanates from a Government whose financial frauds have become a topic of general conversation. It is known that the budget drawn up by M. Magne, the Minister of Finance, represented a surplus, but, by the indiscretion of some member of the *Cour de Révision,* it oozed out that it showed in fact a deficit of some 100,000,000 francs.[c] When summoned to the "savior of property"[d][531] for an explanation, M. Magne had the grave impudence to tell his master that knowing his predilections for a "surplus," he had "cooked up" a budget, as the Ministers of Louis Philippe had done before him. There the matter rested, but the notoriety given to this incident drove the Government into a confession. Having pompously announced in the *Moniteur*[e] that an augmentation had taken place in the customs receipts for the month of February, it dared not stand by its own statement. The

---

[a] At the point of death.—*Ed.*

[b] *The Economist,* No. 756, February 20, 1858, "Foreign Correspondence".—*Ed.*

[c] P. Magne, "Rapport à l'Empereur. Paris, le 29 octobre, 1857", *Le Moniteur universel,* No. 303, October 30, 1857.—*Ed.*

[d] Napoleon III.—*Ed.*

[e] "Paris, le 11 mars", *Le Moniteur universel,* No. 71, March 12, 1858.—*Ed.*

monthly customs returns, published at the end of March,[a] show the import duties in February last to be, even in the official version, but 13,614,251 francs, while they amounted, in the corresponding month of 1857, to 14,160,013 francs; and to be for the months of January and February united only 25,842,256 francs, against 28,044,478 for the same months of 1857. Such is the official meaning of "protecting the industry and the capital of the country against maneuvers," and of "enlightening the public," instead of "deceiving it."

The re-enactment of the *coup d'état* on an enlarged scale, the wholesale transportations, the parceling out of France into Praetorian camps, the rumors of war, the complications without and the conspiracies within—in one word, the convulsive spasms of the lesser Empire since the attempt of Jan. 14,[532] have somewhat distracted the general attention from the financial state of France. Otherwise the public would have become aware that during that same epoch the factitious prosperity of the Bonapartist régime has already resolved itself into its elementary principles of peculation and jobbery. In proof of this proposition, I will content myself with enumerating such facts as have from time to time found their way into the European press. There is first M. Prost, the chief of the *Compagnie Générale de Caisses d'Escompte*, which not only engaged in all sorts of Bourse speculations, but took upon itself to establish banks of discount all over France. The capital was $6,000,000, in 60,000 shares. It had effected an amalgamation with the Portuguese Crédit Mobilier, and was *magna pars*[b] of the Crédit Mobilier of Madrid. All the capital is gone, and the liabilities amount to about $3,000,000.[c] M. Damonieu, of the *Compagnie Parisienne des Equipages de grandes Remises,* was condemned by the tribunal of *police correctionelle* for having swindled his shareholders out of $100,000 in cash and shares, having plunged them into debt to the amount of $400,000, and squandered all the capital, amounting to $1,600,000.[d] The manager of another company—the *Lignéenne*—professing to make paper from wood, has also been condemned for embezzling the capital of $800,000. Two other Bonapartist "saviors of property" were convicted for having entered into an arrangement with some

[a] "Direction générale des douanes et des contributions indirectes", *Le Moniteur universel,* No. 80, March 21, 1858.— *Ed.*

[b] An important part.— *Ed.*

[c] *The Economist*, No. 756, February 20, 1858, "Foreign Correspondence".— *Ed.*

[d] Here and below *The Economist,* No. 760, March 20, 1858, "Foreign Correspondence".— *Ed.*

bankers to palm off on the public, for $10,000,000 or $15,000,000, some forests and mines far off on the banks of the Danube, which they had purchased for $200,000. In another case, it appeared that the managers of a mining company near Aix-la-Chapelle had sold to their shareholders for $500,000 mines which they were afterward obliged to admit were worth only $200,000. In consequence of these and other similar revelations, the shares of the *Messageries Générales,* once quoted at 1,510 francs, fell to about 500 francs. The shares of the *Compagnie des Petites Voitures,* shortly after their issue maneuvered up to 210 francs, have sunk to 40 francs. The shares of the Union Company have dwindled down from 500 to 65 francs. The shares in the Franco-American Navigation Company, once at 750 francs, may now be had at 30 francs. The Amalgamated Gas Company shares have receded from 1,120 francs to 720 francs. The shareholders of the *Caisse des Actionnaires* have been told by M. Millaud, their director, one of the mushroom millionaires of the lesser Empire, that

> "the operations of the last half-year have produced no profits at all, so that it would not be possible to declare a dividend, nor even to pay the ordinary half-year's interest, but that he would pay this interest out of his *own pocket.*" [a]

Thus the social ulcers of the lesser Empire are breaking up. The ridiculous conferences of Louis Bonaparte with the principal stock-jobbers as to the remedies to be applied to French commerce and industry have, of course, resulted in nothing. The Bank of France finds itself in a bad plight, since it is unable to sell the bonds of the railway companies, on the security of which it has been obliged to provide them with the money for carrying out their works. Nobody wants to buy these bonds at a moment when all railway property is rapidly depreciating in France, and the weekly railway returns exhibit a continuous falling off in receipts.

> "With respect to the state of French trade," remarks the Paris correspondent of *The London Economist,* "it remains what it was; that is to say manifesting a tendency to improve, but not improving." [b]

Meanwhile, Bonaparte clings to his old way of sinking capital in unproductive works, but which, as Mr. Hausmann, the Prefect of

---

[a] M. Millaud's report to the shareholders of the *Caisse des Actionnaires* of February 10, 1858 was published in *The Economist,* No. 756, February 20, 1858, and also in the *Allgemeine Zeitung,* No. 45, February 14, 1858, supplement. Italics by Marx.— *Ed.*

[b] *The Economist,* No. 763, April 10, 1858, "Foreign Correspondence". — *Ed.*

the Seine, has the frankness to impart to the Paris people, are important in "a strategical point of view," and calculated to guard against "unforeseen events which may always arise to put society in danger." Thus Paris is condemned to erect new boulevards and streets, the cost of which is estimated at 180,000,000 francs, in order to protect it from its own ebullitions. The opening of the continuation of the boulevard of Sevastopol was quite in keeping with this "strategical point of view." Originally intended to be a purely civil and municipal ceremony, it was all of a sudden converted into a military demonstration, it being pretended that a fresh plot for the assassination of Bonaparte had been discovered. To explain away this *quid pro quo* the *Moniteur* says:

> "It was quite right that a muster of troops should mark the inauguration of such an artery of the capital, and, after the Emperor, our soldiers were the first who ought to have trodden a soil bearing the name of so glorious a victory."[a]

Written on April 13, 1858 — Reproduced from the newspaper

First published unsigned in the *New-York Daily Tribune,* No. 5312, April 30, 1858

[a] "Paris, le 5 avril", *Le Moniteur universel,* No. 95-96, April 5-6, 1858.—*Ed.*

Frederick Engels

THE FALL OF LUCKNOW[533]

The second critical period of the Indian insurrection has been brought to a close. The first found its center in Delhi, and was ended by the storming of that city; the second centered in Lucknow, and that place, too, has now fallen. Unless fresh insurrections break out in places hitherto quiet, the revolt must now gradually subside into its concluding, chronic period, during which the insurgents will finally take the character of dacoits or robbers, and find the inhabitants of the country as much their enemies as the British themselves.

The details of the storming of Lucknow are not yet received, but the preliminary operations and the outlines of the final engagements are known. Our readers recollect[a] that after the relief of the residency of Lucknow, Gen. Campbell blew up that post, but left Gen. Outram with about 5,000 men in the Alumbagh, an intrenched position a few miles from the city. He himself, with the remainder of his troops, marched back to Cawnpore, where Gen. Windham had been defeated by a body of rebels; these he completely beat, and drove them across the Jumna at Calpee. He then awaited at Cawnpore the arrival of re-enforcements and the heavy guns, arranged his plans of attack, gave orders for the concentration of the various columns destined to advance into Oude, and especially turned Cawnpore into an intrenched camp of strength and proportions requisite for the immediate and principal base of operations against Lucknow. When all this was completed, he had another task to perform before he thought it safe to move—a task the attempting of which

[a] See this volume, pp. 441-42.—*Ed.*

at once distinguishes him from almost all preceding Indian commanders. He would have no women loitering about the camp. He had had quite enough of the "heroines" at Lucknow, and on the march to Cawnpore; they had considered it quite natural that the movements of the army, as had always been the case in India, should be subordinate to their fancies and their comfort. No sooner had Campbell reached Cawnpore than he sent the whole interesting and troublesome community to Allahabad, out of his way; and immediately sent for the second batch of ladies, then at Agra. Not before they had reached Cawnpore, and not before he had seen them safely off to Allahabad, did he follow his advancing troops toward Lucknow.

The arrangements made for this campaign of Oude were on a scale hitherto unprecedented in India. In the greatest expedition ever undertaken by the British there, the invasion of Afghanistan,[534] the troops employed never exceeded 20,000 at a time, and of these the great majority were natives. In this campaign of Oude, the number of Europeans alone exceeded that of all the troops sent into Afghanistan. The main army, led by Sir Colin Campbell personally, consisted of three divisions of infantry,[a] one of cavalry, and one of artillery and engineers. The first division of infantry, under Outram, held the Alumbagh. It consisted of five European and one native regiment. The second (four European and one native regiment) and third (five European and one native regiment), the cavalry division under Sir Hope Grant (three European and four or five native regiments) and the mass of the artillery (forty-eight field-guns, siege trains and engineers), formed Campbell's active force, with which he advanced on the road from Cawnpore. A brigade concentrated under Brigadier Franks at Juanpore and Azimghur, between the Goomtee and the Ganges, was to advance along the course of the former river to Lucknow. This brigade numbered three European regiments and two batteries, beside native troops, and was to form Campbell's right wing. Including it, Campbell's force in all amounted to—

	Infantry.	Cavalry.	Artillery and Eng'rs.	Total.
Europeans	15,000	2,000	3,000	20,000
Natives	5,000	3,000	2,000	10,000

[a] Here and below Engels used the material from *The Times*, Nos. 22954, 22959 and 22963, March 30, April 5 and 9, 1858.—*Ed.*

or in all 30,000 men; to whom must be added the 10,000 Nepaulese Ghoorkas advancing under Jung Bahadoor from Goruckpore on Sultanpore, making the total of the invading army 40,000 men, almost all regular troops. But this is not all. On the south of Cawnpore, Sir H. Rose was advancing with a strong column from Saugor upon Calpee and the lower Jumna, there to intercept any fugitives that might escape between the two columns of Franks and Campbell. On the north-west, Brigadier Chamberlain crossed toward the end of February the upper Ganges, entering the Rohilcund, situated north-north-west of Oude, and, as was correctly anticipated, the chief point of retreat of the insurgent army. The garrisons of the towns surrounding Oude must also be included in the force directly or indirectly employed against that kingdom, so that the whole of this force is certainly from 70,000 to 80,000 combatants, of which, according to the official statements, at least 28,000 are British. In this is not included the mass of Sir John Lawrence's force, which occupies at Delhi a sort of flank position, and which consists of 5,500 Europeans at Meerut and Delhi, and some 20,000 or 30,000 natives of the Punjaub.

The concentration of this immense force is the result partly of Gen. Campbell's combinations, but partly also of the suppression of the revolt in various parts of Hindostan, in consequence of which the troops naturally concentrated toward the scene of action. No doubt Campbell would have ventured to act with a smaller force; but while he was waiting for this, fresh resources were thrown, by circumstances, on his hands; and he was not the man to refuse to avail himself of them, even against so contemptible an enemy as he knew he would meet at Lucknow. And it must not be forgotten that, imposing as these numbers look, they still were spread over a space as large as France; and that at the decisive point at Lucknow he could only appear with about 20,000 Europeans, 10,000 Hindoos, and 10,000 Ghoorkas—the value of the last, under native command, being at least doubtful. This force, in its European components alone, was certainly more than enough to insure a speedy victory, but still its strength was not out of proportion to its task; and very likely Campbell desired to show the Oudians, for once, a more formidable army of white faces than any people in India had ever seen before, as a sequal to an insurrection which had been based on the small number and wide dispersion of the Europeans over the country.

The force in Oude consisted of the remnants of most of the mutinous Bengal regiments and of native levies from the country itself. Of the former, there cannot have been more than 35,000 or 40,000 at the very outside. The sword, desertion and demoralization must have reduced this force, originally 80,000 strong, at least one half; and what was left was disorganized, disheartened, badly appointed, and totally unfit to take the field. The new levies are variously stated at from 100,000 to 150,000 men; but what their numbers may have been is unimportant. Their arms were but in part firearms, of inferior construction; most of them carried arms for close encounter only—the kind of fighting they were least likely to meet with. The greater part of this force was at Lucknow, engaging Sir J. Outram's troops; but two columns were acting in the direction of Allahabad and Juanpore.

The concentric movement upon Lucknow began about the middle of February. From the 15th to the 26th the main army and its immense train (60,000 camp followers alone) marched from Cawnpore upon the capital of Oude, meeting with no resistance. The enemy, in the mean time, attacked Outram's position, without a chance of success, on February 21 and 24. On the 19th Franks advanced upon Sultanpore, defeated both columns of the insurgents in one day, and pursued them as well as the want of cavalry permitted. The two defeated columns having united, he beat them again on the 23d, with the loss of 20 guns and all their camp and baggage. Gen. Hope Grant, commanding the advanced guard of the main army, had also, during its forced march, detached himself from it, and making a point to the left had, on the 23d and 24th, destroyed two forts on the road from Lucknow to Rohilcund.

On March 2 the main army was concentrated before the southern side of Lucknow. This side is protected by the canal, which had to be passed by Campbell in his previous attack on the city; behind this canal strong intrenchments had been thrown up. On the 3d, the British occupied the Dilkhoosha Park, with the storming of which the first attack also had commenced. On the 4th, Brig. Franks joined the main army, and now formed its right flank, his right supported by the River Goomtee. Meantime, batteries against the enemy's intrenchments were erected, and two floating bridges were constructed, below the town, across the Goomtee; and as soon as these were ready, Sir J. Outram, with his division of infantry, 1,400 horse, and 30 guns, moved across to take position on the left or north-eastern bank. From here he could enfilade a great part of the enemy's line along the canal, and many of the intrenched palaces to its rear; he also cut off the enemy's communications with the whole north-eastern part of

Oude. He met with considerable resistance on the 6th and 7th, but drove the enemy before him. On the 8th, he was again attacked, but with no better success. In the mean time, the batteries on the right bank had opened their fire; Outram's batteries, along the river-bank, took the position of the insurgents in flank and rear; and on the 9th the 2d division, under Sir E. Lugard, stormed the Martiniere, which, as our readers may recollect,[a] is a college and park situated on the south side of the canal, at its junction with the Goomtee, and opposite the Dilkhoosha. On the 10th, the Bank-House was breached and stormed, Outram advancing further up the river, and enfilading with his guns every successive position of the insurgents. On the 11th, two Highland regiments (42d and 93d) stormed the Queen's Palace, and Outram attacked and carried the stone-bridges leading from the left bank of the river into the town. He then passed his troops across and joined in the attack against the next building in front. On March 13, another fortified building, the Imambarrah, was attacked, a sap being resorted to in order to construct the batteries under shelter; and on the following day, the breach being completed, this building was stormed. The enemy, flying to the Kaiserbagh or King's Palace, was so hotly pursued that the British entered the place at the heels of the fugitives. A violent struggle ensued, but by 3 o'clock in the afternoon the palace was in the possession of the British. This seems to have brought matters to a crisis; at least, all spirit of resistance seems to have ceased, and Campbell at once took measures for the pursuit and interception of the fugitives. Brigadier Campbell, with one brigade of cavalry and some horse artillery, was sent to pursue them, while Grant took the other brigade round to Seetapore, on the road from Lucknow to Rohilcund, in order to intercept them. While thus the portion of the garrison which took to flight was provided for, the infantry and artillery advanced further into the city, to clear it from those who still held out. From the 15th to the 19th, the fighting must have been mainly in the narrow streets of the town, the line of palaces and parks along the river having been previously carried; but on the 19th, the whole of the town was in Campbell's possession. About 50,000 insurgents are said to have fled, partly to Rohilcund, partly toward the Doab and Bundelcund. In this latter direction they had a chance of escaping, as Gen. Rose, with his column, was still sixty miles at least from the Jumna, and was said to have 30,000 insurgents in front of him. In the direction of

[a] See this volume, p. 419.— *Ed.*

Rohilcund there was also a chance of their being able to concentrate again; Campbell would not be in a position to follow them very fast, while of the whereabouts of Chamberlain we know nothing, and the province is large enough to afford them shelter for a short time. The next feature of the insurrection, therefore, will most likely be the formation of two insurgent armies in Bundelcund and Rohilcund, the latter of which, however, may soon be destroyed by concentric marches of the Lucknow and Delhi armies.

The operations of Sir C. Campbell in this campaign, as far as we can now judge, were characterized by his usual prudence and vigor. The dispositions for his concentric march on Lucknow were excellent, and the arrangements for the attack appear to have taken advantage of every circumstance. The conduct of the insurgents, on the other hand, was as contemptible, if not more so, than before. The sight of the redcoats struck them everywhere with panic. Franks's column defeated twenty times its numbers, with scarcely a man lost; and though the telegrams talk of "stout resistance" and "hard fighting,"[a] as usual, the losses of the British appear, where they are mentioned, so ridiculously small that we fear there was no more heroism needed and no more laurels to be gathered this time at Lucknow than when the British got there before.[b]

Written on April 15, 1858

First published in the *New-York Daily Tribune,* No. 5312, April 30, 1858 as a leading article; reprinted in the *New-York Semi-Weekly Tribune,* No. 1350, May 4, 1858

Reproduced from the *New-York Daily Tribune*

---

[a] "The Siege of Lucknow", *The Times,* No. 22966, April 13, 1858.— *Ed.*

[b] See this volume, pp. 419-24 and 435-42.— *Ed.*

Karl Marx

MR. DISRAELI'S BUDGET

London, April 20, 1858

Mr. Disraeli's speech on the Budget in the Commons, on April 19,[a] fills about ten columns of *The London Times,* but, at all events, it is pleasant to read, perhaps rather more so than the *Young Duke* of the same author. As to lucidity of analysis, simplicity of composition, skillful arrangement and easy handling of details, it stands in happy contrast with the cumbersome and circumlocutory lucubrations of his Palmerstonian predecessor.[b] Neither does it contain or pretend to any striking novelty. Mr. Disraeli found himself in the happy position of a Minister of Finance who has to deal with a deficit not of his own making, but bequeathed by a rival. His part was that of the doctor, not of the patient. On the one hand, then, he had to meet a deficit; on the other, all serious restriction of expenditure was put out of the question by the ventures England had embarked in under the auspices of Lord Palmerston. Mr. Disraeli roundly told the House that, if they wanted a policy of invasion and aggression, they must pay for it, and that their loud cry for economy was a mere mockery, blended, as it was, with an unscrupulous readiness for expenditure. According to his statement, the charges devolving upon the financial year 1858-59 would be:

Charge on the funded debt.................................	£28,400,000
Permanent charge on the consolidated fund	1,900,000
Army estimates...	11,750,000
Charge for the navy, including packet service	9,860,000
Civil service	7,000,000

[a] *The Times,* No. 22972, April 20, 1858.—*Ed.*

[b] G. C. Lewis.—*Ed.*

Revenue department	4,700,000
Exchequer bonds to be liquidated in May, '58	2,000,000
War sinking fund	1,500,000
Total charge	£67,110,000

The revenue of the year 1858-59 was estimated as follows:

Customs	£23,400,000
Excise	18,000,000
Stamp duty	7,550,000
Land & assessed taxes	3,200,000
Post-Office	3,200,000
Property and income tax	6,100,000
Crown lands	270,000
Miscellaneous	1,300,000
Total revenue	£63,020,000

A comparison between the estimated expenditure and the estimated income shows, despite the rather sanguine views taken by Mr. Disraeli of the eventual produce of the customs, the excise and the post-office, a clear deficit of £4,000,000. How was it to be met? The Palmerstonians had chuckled at the mere idea that Mr. Disraeli would be forced to suspend the decline in the next year of the income tax from 7d. to 5d. in the pound, a proposition which, when made by Sir Cornewall Lewis, he and Mr. Gladstone had distinguished themselves by opposing. Then the cry of factious opposition would have been raised, and the unpopularity of the tax turned to good account. In one word, the income tax was the rock which it was confidently predicted the Derby state ship must split upon. Mr. Disraeli, however, was too old a fox to be ensnared in such a trap. He told the House, on the contrary, that John Bull, during the last five years, had "behaved" like a good boy in financial matters; had borne the public burdens with great spirit, and should, therefore, under his present distressed circumstances, not be grieved by a tax he had always felt a peculiar aversion to, especially since, by the arrangement of the year 1853,[535] resolved upon by an immense majority of the House, the good boy had been promised the progressive diminution of the tax, and its final extinction at the end of a certain number of years. Mr. Disraeli's own prescriptions for meeting the deficit, and securing even a small margin of surplus income, amount to this: Postpone the liquidation of two millions of Exchequer bonds to a later period; do not pay the £1,300,000 for the war sinking fund until there is a *bona fide* surplus to be sunk in it; equalize the

English and Irish duties on spirits, by raising the latter from 6s. 10d. to 8s. per gallon, which equalization would give an increase of £500,000 to the Exchequer; and, lastly, put a penny stamp on bankers' checks, which would produce to the revenue a surplus of £300,000.

Now as to the trifling new taxes imposed by Mr. Disraeli, no serious objection can be raised against them. Though the representatives of Paddy felt it, of course, their duty to protest, any check put upon the spirit consumption in Ireland must be considered a curative measure. In proposing it, the Chancellor of the Exchequer could not withstand the temptation of poking some fun at his Irish friends. "In the most cordial spirit" he asked "the high-spirited Irishmen" to concur in the proposition for taxing "Irish spirit," and mingle their "spirits" with those of Englishmen and Scotchmen, &c. The penny stamp on bankers' checks was fiercely attacked by Mr. Glyn,[a] the representative of the London banking and stock-jobbing interest. That unfortunate penny, he felt sure, would prevent the monetary circulation of the country from performing its duties; but, whatever terror Mr. Glyn might feel or feign to feel at the audacity of imposing a trifling duty on bankers and stock-jobbers, his feelings are not likely to find an echo among the mass of the British people.

The serious feature of Mr. Disraeli's budget is the stopping of the operation of the artificial sinking fund, that great financial sham reintroduced by Sir Cornewall Lewis, on occasion of the debts contracted during the Russian war.[b] The genuine British sinking fund is one of those monster delusions which obscure the mental faculties of a whole generation, and the gist of which the following one is hardly able to understand. It was first in the year 1771, that Dr. Richard Price, in his observations on reversionary payments, revealed to the world the mysteries of compound interest and the sinking fund.

"Money," he said, "bearing compound interest, increases at first slowly; but, the rate of increase being continually accelerated, it becomes in some time so rapid as to mock all the powers of imagination. One penny, put out at our Savior's birth at five per cent interest, would, before this time, have increased to a greater sum than would be contained in 150 millions of earths, all solid gold. But, if put out at simple interest, it would in the same time have amounted to no more than 7s. 4 1/2d. Our Government has hitherto chosen to improve money in the last rather

[a] G. G. Glyn's speech in the House of Commons on April 19, 1858, *The Times*, No. 22972, April 20, 1858.—*Ed.*

[b] The Crimean war of 1853-56.—*Ed.*

than the first of these ways.[a] A State need never be under any difficulties; for, with the smallest savings, it may, in as little time as its interest can require, pay off the largest debts. On this plan, it is of little importance what interest the State is obliged to give for money; for the higher the interest the sooner will such a fund pay off the principal."[b]

Consequently he proposed,

"an annual saving, to be applied invariably, together with the interest of all the sums redeemed by it, to the purpose of discharging the public debt; or, in other words, the establishment of a sinking fund."[c]

This fantastic scheme, rather less ingenious than the financial plan of the fool in one of Cervantes' novels,[d] who proposed to the whole Spanish people to abstain for only two weeks from eating and drinking, in order to get the means of discharging the public debt, nevertheless caught the imagination of Pitt. It was avowedly on this basis that he built up his sinking fund in 1786, allotting a fixed sum of 5,000,000 sterling, to be paid every year "without fail," for this purpose. The system was not abandoned until 1825, when the Commons passed a resolution that only the *bona fide* surplus revenue of the country was to be applied in payment of the national debt. The whole system of public credit had been thrown into confusion by this curious sort of sinking fund. Between what was borrowed from necessity, and what was borrowed from amusement; between loans that were to increase the debt, and loans that were to pay it off, there arose a tumultuous medley. Interest and compound interest, debt and redemption, danced before men's eyes in such perpetual succession; there was such a phantasmagoria of consols and bonds, of debentures and exchequer bills, of capital without interest and interest without capital, that the strongest understanding became bewildered. Dr. Price's principle was that the State should borrow money at simple interest in order to improve it at compound interest. In fact, the United Kingdom contracted a debt of 1,000 millions sterling, for which it nominally received about 600 millions, 390 millions of this sum being, however, destined not for the payment of the debt, but to keep up the sinking fund. This glorious institution, which marks the golden era of stock-jobbers and speculators, the Palmerstonian Chancellor of the Exchequer

---

[a] R. Price, *An Appeal to the Public on the Subject of the National Debt*, pp. 18 and 19.—*Ed.*

[b] R. Price, *Observations on Reversionary Payments...*, pp. XIV and 140.—*Ed.*

[c] Ibid., p. 139.—*Ed.*

[d] M. de Cervantes Saavedra, *Novelas exemplares.*—*Ed.*

had attempted to saddle again on the shoulders of John Bull. Mr. Disraeli has given it the *coup de grâce*.

Written on April 20, 1858

First published unsigned in the *New-York Daily Tribune*, No. 5318, May 7, 1858

Reproduced from the newspaper

Karl Marx

THE ENGLISH ALLIANCE

Paris, April 22, 1858

The Anglo-French alliance has taken a new turn since Dr. Bernard's acquittal[a][536] and the public enthusiasm that cheered it. In the first instance, being shrewd enough to understand that the "heart of England" spoke not "in the starched compliments with which the municipality of Dover overwhelmed the frank nature of the Duke of Malakoff", but rather "in the infamous huzzas raised by the people in the Court of Old Bailey," the *Univers* proclaimed England not only a "den of assassins," but a people of assassins, juries and judges included.[b] The original proposition of the colonels[537] is thus affirmed on a broader basis. At the heels of the *Univers*, in steps the *Constitutionnel* with an article appearing at the head of its columns, and signed by M. Renée,[c] the son-in-law of Mr. Macquard, who in his turn is the known amanuensis, confidant, and factotum of Bonaparte. If the *Univers* had taken up the colonels' definition of the English people, while enlarging its meaning, the *Constitutionnel* repeats their menaces, only that it tries to back the exasperation of the barracks by the alleged indignation of the "towns and rural districts." Affecting that tone of wounded moral sensibility so peculiar to the meretricious literature of the second Empire, it exclaims:

"We will not dwell at any length on such an acquittal, which throws an unheard-of scandal on public morality; for what man of honor in France or England could entertain a doubt of Bernard's guilt? We will only inform those of

[a] "Trial and acquittal of Simon Bernard...", *The Times*, No. 22971, April 19, 1858.—*Ed.*

[b] *The Times*, No. 22973, April 21, 1858, "France".—*Ed.*

[c] Am. Renée, "L'acquittement de Bernard a causé...", *Le Constitutionnel*, No. 111, April 21, 1858.—*Ed.*

our neighbors who desire *the maintenance of good relations between the two countries,* that if, by misfortune, the address pronounced by Bernard's counsel—that address which was *allowed* to teem with calumny and insult against the Emperor, against the nation which elected him, against the army, and against our institutions—was circulated in the towns, barracks, and rural districts of France" (a curious position this, of the barracks, between the towns and rural districts!) *"it would be difficult for Government, with the best intention, to stay the consequences of public indignation."*

So far so good. On the mere chance whether or not Mr. James's speech,[a] advertised by the *Constitutionnel* itself,[b] be or be not circulated in France, it will then depend whether or not France shall rush upon England. But after this quasi-declaration of war, there follows, a day later, a curious and startling winding-up in the *Patrie.* The French invasion is to be averted, but only by a new turn to be given to the Anglo-French alliance. Bernard's acquittal has revealed the rising power of anarchy in British society. Lord Derby is to save society in England in the same way as Bonaparte has saved it in France. Such is the upshot of the alliance, and such is its *conditio sine qua non.*[c] The Earl of Derby, it is added, is a "man of immense talent, and of almost royal alliances," and consequently the man to save society in England![d] The English daily papers cling to the weakness, tergiversation, and infirmity of purpose, betrayed in this alternation of rage, menace and sophism. The Paris correspondent of *The Daily News* imagines himself to have solved the riddle of these dissolving views exhibited in the *Univers,* the *Constitutionnel,* and the *Patrie,* by dwelling upon the well-known fact that Bonaparte has a double set of advisers—the drunken revelers of the evening, and the sober counselors of the morning. He smells in the articles of the *Univers* and the *Constitutionnel* the fumes of Chateau Maryaux and cigars, and in the article of the *Patrie* the showers of the cold water bath. But the same double set acted during Bonaparte's duel with the French Republic. The one, after January, 1849, threatened, in its little evening journals, with a *coup d'état,* while the other, in the heavy columns of the *Moniteur,* gave them the lie direct. Still it was not in the "starched" articles of the *Moniteur,* but in the drunken "huzzas" of the *Pouvoir,* that the shadow of coming events was traced. We are, however, far from believing that Bonaparte is

---

[a] E. James' speech at the court hearing of S. Bernard's case on April 16, 1858, *The Times,* No. 22970, April 17, 1858.—*Ed.*

[b] "Affaire Simon Bernard.—Complicité dans l'attentat du 14 janvier", *Le Constitutionnel,* No. 108, April 18, 1858.—*Ed.*

[c] Indispensable condition.—*Ed.*

[d] *The Times,* No. 22975, April 23, 1858, "France".—*Ed.*

possessed of the means of successfully crossing the "broad ditch."[a] The comical lucubrations in that line, which *The N. Y. Herald* had taken upon itself to publish, are sure to raise a smile on the lips even of mere tyros in military science. But we are decidedly of opinion that Bonaparte, a civilian, it ought never to be forgotten, at the head of a military Government, has, in the *Patrie*, put the last and the only possible interpretation on the Anglo-French alliance which will satisfy his "colonels." He finds himself in a situation at once the most grotesque and the most dangerous. To impose upon foreign Governments, he must clap on the sword. To soothe the sword-bearers, and prevent them from taking his rhodomontades in real good earnest, he must recur to such impossible *fictiones juris* as that the Anglo-French alliance means the saving of society in England in the approved Bonapartist fashion. Of course, facts must clash with his doctrines, and the upshot, if his reign is not, as we are inclined to think, cut short by a revolution, will be that his fortune is engulfed, as it has been raised, in mad-brain adventures in some *expédition de Boulogne*[538] on an enlarged scale. The Emperor will subside into the adventurer, as the adventurer has been converted into the Emperor.

In the mean time, while the *Patrie* has spoken the last word Bonaparte can utter as to the meaning of the Anglo-French alliance, it is worth the while to direct attention to the manner in which this alliance is now spoken of among the governing classes of England. In this respect an article of *The London Economist*, entitled *"The French Alliance, its character, its value and its price,"*[b] claims peculiar notice. It is written with studied pedantry, such as fits the position of an ex-Secretary of the Treasury under Palmerston's Administration, and an expounder of the economical views of English capitalists. Mr. Wilson sets out with the thesis that "the thing gained may not be exactly the thing bargained for." "Scarcely," he says, "any estimate of the value of a real alliance between France and England can be too high;" but then there exist different sorts of alliances, real ones and artificial ones, genuine alliances and alliances of a hot-house growth, "natural" ones and "governmental" ones, "governmental" alliances and "personal" alliances. In the first place, *The Economist* gives full swing to his "imagination;" and it may be remarked with respect to *The Economist*, what has been said with respect to lawyers, that

---

[a] The Channel.—*Ed.*

[b] Here and below *The Economist*, No. 763, April 10, 1858.—*Ed.*

the more prosaic the man the more tricks imagination is able to play with him. He can scarcely trust his

"imagination to dwell on the influence which a real alliance between the two great peoples which stand at the head of modern civilization would exercise on the destinies of Europe and the fortune and felicity of all other lands."

Still he is forced to admit that, although he hopes and believes the two nations to be "ripening" for a genuine alliance, they "are not *ripe* for it yet." If, then, England and France are not yet ripe for a genuine, national alliance, the question will naturally arise, of what sort is the present Anglo-French alliance?

"Our alliance of late," confesses the ex-member of the Palmerston Administration and the oracle of English capitalists, "has been to a great extent, we admit, unavoidably with the Government rather than with the nation—with the Emperor rather than the Empire—with Louis Bonaparte rather than with France; and further, in the value we have set upon the alliance and the price we have paid for it, we have somewhat lost sight of this material and weighty fact."

Bonaparte, of course, is the chosen of the French nation, and all that bosh, but, unfortunately,

"he represents only the numerical and not the intellectual majority of the French people. By mischance, it so happens that the classes which stand aloof from him comprise precisely those parties whose opinions on nearly all the great questions of civilization, are analogous to our own."

Having thus in most cautious and civil language, and in circumlocutory sentences which we will not discomfort the reader with, laid down the axiom that the present so-called Anglo-French alliance is rather governmental than national, *The Economist* goes the length of confessing that it is more *personal* even than purely *governmental*.

"Louis Napoleon," he says, "has hinted more plainly than became the head of a great nation that *he* was our especial friend in France—that he, rather than his people, desired and sustained the English alliance; and it may be that *we* have acquiesced in this view of the matter more readily and fully than was perfectly *prudent* and *sincere*." [a]

Take it all in all, the Anglo-French alliance is a spurious, adulterated article—an alliance with Louis Bonaparte, but not an alliance with France. The question, therefore, naturally arises, whether that spurious article was worth the price paid for it? Here *The Economist* beats his own bosom and cries, in the name of the English governing classes, *Pater, peccavi!*[b] In the first place,

---

[a] Here and below *The Economist*, No. 764, April 17, 1858.—*Ed.*

[b] "Father, I have sinned", Luke 15:18.—*Ed.*

England is a constitutional country, while Bonaparte is an autocrat.

> "We owed to ourselves that our frank and loyal courtesy toward the *de facto* sovereign of France should be allowed to ripen and to warm into cordial and affectionate admiration only as far and as fast as his policy turned out such as we could honestly and righteously approve."

Instead of applying thus a sliding scale to their Bonapartism, the English people, a constitutional people,

> "have lavished on an Emperor who had destroyed the constitutional liberties of his subjects, attentions such as were never before bestowed on a constitutional king who had granted and respected them. And when he was angry and irritated, we have stooped to soothe him by language of fulsome adulation which sounded marvelous from English lips. Our proceedings and our language have alienated all those sections of the French people in whose eyes Louis Napoleon is either a usurper or a military despot. It has especially irritated and disgusted the Parliamentary party in France, whether Republican or Orleanist."

The Economist discovers at last that this prostration before a lucky usurper was far from prudent.

> "It is impossible," he says, "to believe that the existing régime in France can be the permanent one under which that energetic and restless nation will consent to live.... Is it wise, therefore, so to ally ourselves with a *passing phase of government in France* as to excite the enmity of its future and more permanent development?"

Moreover, the English alliance was more necessary to Bonaparte than his alliance to England. In 1852, he was an adventurer—a successful one, but still an adventurer.

> "He was not recognized in Europe; it was questionable whether he would be recognized. But England promptly and unhesitatingly accepted him; acknowledged his title deeds at once; admitted him to the circle of royal exclusiveness, and gave him thus currency among the courts of Europe." "Nay, more, by the exchange of visits and cordial coalitions, our Court allowed acquaintanceship to ripen into intimacy.... Those enterprising moneyed and commercial classes, by whom it was especially important to him to be supported, saw at once how vast was the strength he gained by the closeness and cordiality of the alliance with England."

That alliance was necessary for him, and he "would have bought it at almost *any price*." Did the English Government prove their commercial acumen and wonted sharpness in fixing that price? They asked no price at all; they insisted upon no condition whatever; but, like Oriental satraps, crawled in the dust while handing to him the gift of the alliance. No infamy on his part was colossal enough to make them halt for one moment in their race "of thriftless generosity," as *The Economist* calls it—of reckless flunkeyism, as we should call it.

"It would be hard to prove," confesses the English sinner, "that of all his various measures for discountenancing Protestantism, for repressing thought, for destroying municipal action, for reducing Senates and Chambers to a mockery, we have manifested our dissatisfaction with a single one by even so much as a passing coolness or a casual frown." "Whatever he has done, whomsoever he has proscribed, how many journals he has seized or repressed, whatever the flimsy pretexts on which he has dismissed honorable and eminent professors from their posts—our language has still been the same; he has still been this great man, this wise and sagacious statesman, this eminent and firm ruler."

Not only have the English thus fostered, supported and promoted his abominable domestic policy, but, as *The Economist* avows, allowed him to hamper, modify, emasculate and degrade their foreign policy.

"To continue longer in such a false position," concludes *The Economist*, "may redound neither to our honor nor to our profit, nor to the benefit of the commonwealth of nations."

Compare this declaration with that of the *Patrie*, and there can remain no doubt that the Anglo-French alliance is gone, and with it the only international prop of the second Empire.

Written on April 22, 1858

First published unsigned in the *New-York Daily Tribune*, No. 5319, May 8, 1858

Reproduced from the newspaper

Karl Marx

IMPORTANT BRITISH DOCUMENTS

London, April 30, 1858

There have been recently issued on the part of the British Government several statistical papers—the Board of Trade returns for the first quarter of 1858,[a] a comparative statement of Pauperism for January, 1857 and 1858,[b] and lastly, the half-yearly reports of the Inspectors of Factories. The Board of Trade returns, as was to be expected, show a considerable falling off in exports as well as imports during the first three months of 1858, if compared with the same quarter of the previous year. The total declared value of all articles exported, which during the latter period amounted to £28,827,493, had fallen for the first three months of this year to £23,510,290, so that the aggregate decrease in British exports may be rated at about 19 per cent. The table of the values of the principal articles of import, given only up to the end of February, shows a decline, as compared with the first two months of 1857, from £14,694,806 to £10,117,920, the downward movement in imports being thus more marked still than that in exports. The comparative state of the export trade from the United Kingdom to the United States during the first three months of 1857 and 1858 may be ascertained from the following extract:

---

[a] "Accounts Relating to Trade and Navigation for the Three Months Ended March 31", "The Board of Trade Returns", *The Economist*, No. 765, April 24, 1858.—*Ed.*

[b] Presumably a reference to *Monthly Comparative Return of Paupers relieved in each month in each year* [1857, 1858].—*Ed.*

Exports from the United Kingdom to the United States.

	Quantities		Declared Val.	
	1857	1858	1857	1858
Beer and Ale (bbls.)	9,504	6,581	£40,893	£29,269
Coal and Culm (tuns)	19,972	44,299	11,975	24,818
Cottons (yards)	61,198,140	35,371,538	1,128,453	618,540
Hardw's & Cutlery (cwt.)	44,096	14,623	301,275	104,668
Linens (yards)	18,373,022	8,757,750	527,076	265,536
Iron, Pig (tuns)	10,172	6,569	39,927	20,344
Iron, Bar (tuns)	70,877	6,417	610,124	54,602
Iron, Cast (tuns)	207	2,362	4,659	14,475
Wrought of all sorts	12,578	2,097	151,602	29,218
Steel, unwrought	3,607	1,118	128,178	43,666
Copper (cwt.)	11,075	1,954	69,286	10,595
Lead (tuns)	941	60	21,793	1,324
Oil Seed (gals.)	400,200	42,790	62,576	5,768
Salt (tuns)	66,022	35,205	33,169	16,990
Silk manufactures (lb)	66,973	22,920	82,280	25,212
Woolens, Cloth (pieces)	106,519	30,624	351,911	110,096
Woolens, mixed stuffs (ps) ..	9,030,643	6,368,551	401,249	232,202
Worsted stuffs (pieces)	212,763	80,601	249,013	106,913
Earthenware & Porcel'n	...	...	155,700	70,998
Haberdashery & Millin'y	...	...	614,825	288,752
Tin Plates	...	...	273,409	105,847[a]

With some trifling exceptions, this list exhibits a general and heavy falling off; but what strikes us is that in most instances the decline in the value of exports hardly keeps pace with the diminution in their quantity. The United States proves in this respect a far better market than other countries whence the Britishers for an increased quantity fetched in return a smaller value. Thus, for instance, of wool there were exported to Holland, in 1858, 277,342 lbs. against 254,593 lbs. in 1857; but the former realized but a value of £24,949, while the latter had brought £25,563; and for 1,505,621 lbs. exported to France in 1858, as against 1,445,322 lbs. exported in 1857, the value returned amounts but to £103,235, while for the smaller export of 1857 it reached the sum of £108,412. Moreover, if we compare the

[a] Here and below "Accounts Relating to Trade and Navigation...", III.—Exports of the Principal and Other Articles of British and Irish Produce and Manufactures...—*Ed.*

returns for the whole of the first quarter of 1858 with those for the month of March, a tendency to recovery in the British export trade to the United States will be discovered. Thus, in worsted stuffs the falling off between March, 1857, and March, 1858, is only from £66,617 to £54,376, while on the whole quarter it is from £249,013 to £106,913. The only country, however, which forms an exception to the general rule, and shows a considerably increased instead of diminished absorption of British manufactures, is India, as will appear from the following figures:

	Quantities.		Declared Val.	
	1857	1858	1857	1858
Beer and ale, bbls	24,817	51,913	£77,845	£166,567
Cotton, yards	120,092,475	151,463,533	1,385,888	1,787,943
Hardw's & Cut'ry, cwt.	10,642	16,776	42,849	67,287
Cotton yarn, yards	5,145,044	10,609,434	276,469	531,567
Iron bar, tuns	20,674	26,266	191,528	217,539
Cop'r sh'ts & rails, cwt.	18,503	23,313	115,927	132,156
Woolens, cloth	12,123	19,571	63,846	90,584
Earthware & porcel'n	...	...	9,989	19,631
Haberd'y & millinery	...	...	21,350	31,427
Steam engines	...	...	31,408	36,019

The increase in the British exports to India may, for some items, woolens for instance, be accounted for by the war demand. Generally, however, the rationale of that ascending movement is not to be sought in that direction. The case is simply this, that the insurrection for some months had shut up the Indian market altogether, thus causing the commodities floating in the market to be absorbed and creating a vacuum now again filled up. With respect to Australia, the returns show also considerable increase in some articles of British export, but the letters received from Sidney and Melbourne leave no doubt as to the merely speculative character of those shipments which, instead of selling at their declared value, will have to be disposed of at a heavy discount.

The comparative statement of Paupers in England and Wales,[539] who received official relief in the fifth week of January, 1857 and 1858, shows their number, from 920,608, to which it amounted in the former period, to have increased to 976,773 in the latter one, thus exhibiting an aggregate increase of 6.10 per cent. For the North Midland, North-Western and York divisions, however, that is, for the industrial districts, the increase in the percentage of paupers rose respectively by 20.52, 44.87, and 23.13 per cent. Besides, it must be kept in view that a very considerable portion of the working classes stubbornly prefer starvation to enrollment in the workhouses. The following extract from the official returns is curious, because it proves how small a percentage even in England the strictly manufacturing population bears to the aggregate people:

Industrial Statistics.

		Ratio per cent of persons aged 20 years and upward, occupied in			
Divisions.	No. of persons aged 20 years and upward.	Mechanical Arts, Trade and Domestic Service.	Agriculture.	Manufactures.	Mining and Mineral Works.
1. The Metropolis	1,394,963	47.6	1.1	6.0	3.5
2. South-Eastern	887,134	30.7	20.8	2.5	2.4
3. South Midland	660,775	28.8	25.4	7.1	2.4
4. Eastern	603,720	27.4	26.5	4.0	2.3
5. South-Western	978,025	28.6	23.3	4.6	5.6
6. West Midland	1,160,387	29.1	15.5	5.2	12.6
7. North Midland	654,679	31.8	21.7	6.4	5.3
8. North-Western	1,351,830	29.8	8.3	21.5	5.4
9. York	961,945	25.2	14.3	17.5	7.3
10. Northern	521,460	27.7	16.1	4.2	12.4
11. Welsh	641,680	21.8	25.7	2.5	12.4
England and Wales	9,816,597	31.0	16.1	8.4	6.3

The reports of the Inspectors of Factories, extending only to the end of October, 1857, are deprived of their usual interest, because, as the Inspectors unanimously state, the closing of mills, the working of short time, the numerous bankruptcies among mill-owners, and the general depression of trade, which set in at the very time when they drew up their returns, prevented them from collecting that reliable information, which on former occasions allowed them to prepare a statement of the number of new factories, of factories that had added to their motive power, and of those which had ceased to work. The industrial statistics, therefore, illustrating the effects of the crisis, must be looked for in their next reports. The only new feature exhibited in the present publication is limited to some revelations as to the treatment of children and young persons in printing works. It was not until 1845 that the British Legislature extended their interference from textile fabrics to print-works. The Print-Works act follows the provisions of the Factory acts in all those details relating to powers of inspectors, the mode of their dealing with offenders, and the various difficulties which might arise in the administration of the law, which are to be found in the Factory acts.[a] It provides, in the same manner as in factories, for the registration of the persons employed: for the examination by certifying surgeons of the younger hands prior to their permanent employment; and for insuring regularity in the observance of the times of beginning and ending daily labor by a public clock. It adopts also the nomenclature of the Factory acts in the division of the hands into classes, but differs widely from those acts in the definition of what persons shall constitute each class, and, consequently, in the amount of protection afforded by the restrictions upon labor.

The three classes under the Factory acts are: 1. Males over 18 years of age, whose labor is unrestricted; 2. Males between 13 and 18 years of age, and females above 13 years of age, whose labor is restricted; 3. Children between 8 and 13 years of age, whose labor is restricted, and who are required to attend school *daily*.

The corresponding classes in print-works are: 1. Males above 13 years of age, whose labor is unrestricted; 2. Females above 13 years of age, whose hours of labor are restricted; 3. Children of both sexes, between the ages of 8 and 13, whose labor is restricted, and who are required to attend school *periodically*. The Print-Works act differs essentially from the Factory acts, in containing no provisions of any kind for either of the following purposes: For setting apart times for meals; for the Saturday holiday; for the cessation from work on Christmas day and Good Friday; for periodical half-holidays; for the secure fencing of dangerous machinery; for the reporting of accidents, and compensation of injured persons; for the periodical lime-washing of the premises. The hours of labor in factories are now assimilated to the ordinary hours of work of mechanics and general laborers, i.e., from 6 a. m. to 6 p. m., with intervals of one hour and a half for meals. The hours of labor in print-works may practically be considered to be unrestricted, notwithstanding the existence of statutory limitation. The only restriction upon labor is contained in §22 of the Print-Works act (8 and 9 Vict., 29), which enacts that no child between the ages of 8 and 13 years, and no female, shall be

[a] Here and below [A. Redgrave,] "Report of Alexander Redgrave, Esq., Inspector of Factories, for the Half Year Ended the 31st October 1857", *Reports of the Inspectors of Factories...*, pp. 38, 39, 41, 43.—*Ed.*

employed during the night, which is defined to be between 10 p. m. and 6 a. m. of the following morning. Children, therefore, of the age of 8 years, may be and are lawfully employed in a labor analogous in many respects to factory labor, mostly in rooms in which the temperature is oppressive, continuously and without any cessation from work for rest or refreshment, from 6 a. m. till 10 p. m.; and a boy, having attained the age of 13, may, and is often, lawfully employed day and night for any number of hours, without any restriction whatever. The school attendance of children employed in print-works is thus provided for: Every child, before being employed in a print-work, must have attended school for at least thirty days and not less than one hundred any fifty hours during the six months immediately preceding such first day of employment, and during the continuance of its employment in the print-work must attend for a like period of thirty days and one hundred and fifty hours during every successive period of six months. The attendance at school must be between 8 a. m. and 6 p. m. No attendance of less than two hours and a half nor more than five hours, on any one day, shall be reckoned as part of the one hundred and fifty hours. The philanthropy of the master-printers shines peculiarly in the method of executing these regulations. Sometimes a child would attend school for the number of hours required by law at one period of the day, sometimes at another period, but never regularly; for instance, the attendance on one day might be from 8 a. m. to 11 a. m., on another day from 1 p. m. to 4 p. m., and the child might not appear at school again for several days, when it would attend perhaps from 3 p. m. to 6 p. m.; then it might attend for three or four days consecutively or for a week; then it would not appear in school for three weeks or a month after that, upon some odd days at some odd hours when the employer chose to spare it. Thus the child is as it were buffeted from school to work, and from work to school, until the tale of one hundred and fifty hours is told.

Written on April 30, 1858

First published unsigned in the *New-York Daily Tribune,* No. 5329, May 20, 1858

Reproduced from the newspaper

Frederick Engels

[DETAILS OF THE ATTACK ON LUCKNOW]

At last we are in possession of detailed accounts of the attack and fall of Lucknow. The principal sources of information, in a military point of view, the dispatches of Sir Colin Campbell, have not yet, indeed, been published; but the correspondence of the British press, and especially the letters of Mr. Russell in *The London Times*,[a] the chief portions of which have been laid before our readers, are quite sufficient to give a general insight into the proceedings of the attacking party.

The conclusions we drew from the telegraphic news, as to the ignorance and cowardice displayed in the defense,[b] are more than confirmed by the detailed accounts. The works erected by the Hindoos, formidable in appearance, were in reality of no greater consequence than the fiery dragons and grimacing faces painted by Chinese "braves" on their shields or on the walls of their cities. Every single work exhibited an apparently impregnable front, nothing but loopholed and embrasured walls and parapets, difficulties of access of every possible description, cannon and small-arms bristling everywhere. But the flanks and rear of every position were completely neglected, a mutual support of the various works was never thought of, and even the ground between the works, as well as in front of them, had never been cleared, so that both front and flank attacks could be prepared without the knowledge of the defense, and could approach under perfect shelter to within a few yards from the parapet. It was just such a

---

[a] Here and below [W. H. Russell,] "The Fall of Lucknow", *The Times*, No. 22986, May 6, 1858.— *Ed.*

[b] See this volume, pp. 435-37, 506-09.— *Ed.*

conglomerate of intrenchments as might be expected from a body of private sappers deprived of their officers, and serving in an army where ignorance and indiscipline reigned supreme. The intrenchments of Lucknow are but a translation of the whole method of Sepoy warfare into baked clay walls and earthen parapets. The mechanical portion of European tactics had been partially impressed upon their minds; they knew the manual and platoon drill well enough; they could also build a battery and loophole a wall; but how to combine the movements of companies and battalions in the defense of a position, or how to combine batteries and loopholed houses and walls, so as to form an intrenched camp capable of resistance—of this they were utterly ignorant. Thus, they weakened the solid masonry walls of their palaces by over-loopholing them, heaped tier upon tier of loopholes and embrasures, placed parapeted batteries on their roofs, and all this to no purpose whatever, because it could all be turned in the easiest possible manner. In the same way, knowing their tactical inferiority, they tried to make up for it by cramming every post as full of men as possible, to no other purpose than to give terrible effect to the British artillery and to render impossible all orderly and systematic defense as soon as the attacking columns fell upon this motley host from an unexpected direction. And when the British, by some accidental circumstance, were compelled to attack even the formidable front of the works, their construction was so faulty that they could be approached, breached and stormed almost without any risk. At the Imambarrah this was the case. Within a few yards from the building stood a pucka (sun-baked clay) wall. Up to this the British made a short sap (proof enough that the embrasures and loopholes on the higher part of the building had no plunging fire upon the ground immediately in front), and used this very wall as a breaching battery, prepared for them by the Hindoos themselves! They brought up two 68-pounders (naval guns) behind this wall. The lightest 68-pounder in the British service weighs 87 cwt., without the carriage; but supposing even that an 8-inch gun for hollow shot only is alluded to, the lightest gun of that class weighs 50 cwt., and with the carriage at least three tuns. That such guns could be brought up at all in such proximity to a palace several stories high, with a battery on the roof, shows a contempt of commanding positions and an ignorance of military engineering which no private sapper in any civilized army could be capable of.

Thus much for the science against which the British had to contend. As to courage and obstinacy, they were equally absent from the defense. From the Martinière to the Mousabagh, on the part of the natives, there was but one grand and unanimous act of bolting, as soon as a column advanced to the attack. There is nothing in the whole series of engagements that can compare even with the massacre (for fight it can scarcely be called) in the Secunderbagh during Campbell's relief of the Residency. No sooner do the attacking parties advance, than there is a general helter-skelter to the rear, and where there are but a few narrow exits so as to bring the crowded rabble to a stop, they fall pell-mell, and without any resistance, under the volleys and bayonets of the advancing British. The "British bayonet" has done more execution in any one of these onslaughts on panic-stricken natives than in all the wars of the English in Europe and America put together. In the East, such bayonet-battles, where one party is active and the other abjectly passive, are a regular occurrence in warfare; the Burmese stockades in every case furnished an example.[540] According to Mr. Russell's account, the chief loss suffered by the British was caused by Hindoos cut off from retreat, and barricaded in the rooms of the palaces, whence they fired from the windows upon the officers in the court-yards and gardens.

In storming the Imambarra and the Kaiserbagh, the bolting of the Hindoos was so rapid, that the place was not taken, but simply marched into. The interesting scene, however, was now only commencing; for, as Mr. Russell blandly observes, the conquest of the Kaiserbagh on that day was so unexpected that there was no time to guard against indiscriminate plunder. A merry scene it must have been for a true, liberty-loving John Bull to see his British grenadiers helping themselves freely to the jewels, costly arms, clothes, and all the toggery of his Majesty of Oude. The Sikhs, Ghoorkas and camp-followers were quite ready to imitate the example, and a scene of plunder and destruction followed which evidently surpassed even the descriptive talent of Mr. Russell. Every fresh step in advance was accompanied with plunder and devastation. The Kaiserbagh had fallen on the 14th; and half an hour after, discipline was at an end, and the officers had lost all command over their men. On the 17th, Gen. Campbell was obliged to establish patrols to check plundering, and to remain in inactivity "until the present license ceases." The troops were evidently completely out of hand. On the 18th, we hear that there is a cessation of the *grosser* sort of plunder, but devastation is still going on freely. In the city, however, while the vanguard were fighting against the natives' fire from the houses, the rearguard plundered and destroyed to their hearts' content. In the evening, there is another proclamation against plundering; strong parties of every regiment to go out and fetch in their own men, and to keep their camp-followers at home; nobody to leave the camp except on duty. On the 20th, a recapitulation of the same orders. On the same day, two British "officers and gentlemen", Lieuts. Cape and Thackwell, "went into the city *looting,* and were murdered in a house;" and on the 26th, matters were still so bad that the most stringent orders were issued for the suppression of plunder and outrage; hourly roll-calls were instituted; all soldiers strictly forbidden to enter the city; camp-followers, if found armed in the city, to be hanged; soldiers not to wear arms except on duty, and all non-combatants to be disarmed. To give due weight to these orders, a number of triangles for flogging were erected "at proper places."

This is indeed a pretty state of things in a civilized army in the nineteenth century; and if any other troops in the world had committed one-tenth of these excesses, how would the indignant British press brand them with infamy! But these are the deeds of the British army, and therefore we are told that such things are but the normal consequences of war. British officers and gentlemen are perfectly welcome to appropriate to themselves any silver spoons, jeweled bracelets, and other little memorials they may find about the scene of their glory; and if Campbell is compelled to disarm his own army in the midst of war, in order to stop wholesale robbery and violence, there may have been military reasons for the step; but surely nobody will begrudge these poor fellows a week's holiday and a little frolic after so many fatigues and privations.

The fact is, there is no army in Europe or America with so much brutality as the British. Plundering, violence, massacre—things that everywhere else are strictly and completely banished—are a time-honored privilege, a vested right of the British soldier. The infamies committed for days together, after the storming of Badajos and San Sebastian,[541] in the Peninsular war, are without a parallel in the annals of any other nation since the beginning of the French Revolution; and the medieval usage, proscribed everywhere else, of giving up to plunder a town taken by assault, is still the rule with the British. At Delhi imperious military considerations enforced an exception; but the army, though bought off by extra pay, grumbled, and now at Lucknow they have made up for what they missed at Delhi. For twelve days and nights there was no British army at Lucknow—nothing but a lawless, drunken, brutal rabble, dissolved into bands of robbers, far more lawless, violent and greedy than the Sepoys who had just been driven out of the place. The sack of Lucknow in 1858 will remain an everlasting disgrace to the British military service.

If the reckless soldiery, in their civilizing and humanizing progress through India, could rob the natives of their personal property only, the British Government steps in immediately afterward and strips them of their real estate as well. Talk of the first French Revolution confiscating the lands of the nobles and the church! Talk of Louis Napoleon confiscating the property of the Orleans family! Here comes Lord Canning, a British nobleman, mild in language, manners and feelings, and confiscates, by order of his superior, Viscount Palmerston, the lands of a whole people, every rood, perch and acre, over an extent of ten thousand square miles.[542] A very nice bit of *loot* indeed for John Bull! And no sooner had Lord Ellenborough, in the name of the new Government, disapproved of this hitherto unexampled measure,[a] than up rise *The Times* and a host of minor British papers to defend this wholesale robbery, and break a lance for the right of John Bull to confiscate everything he likes. But then, John is an exceptional being, and what is virtue in him, according to *The Times,* would be infamy in others.[b]

Meanwhile—thanks to the complete dissolution of the British army for the purpose of plunder—the insurgents escaped, unpursued, into the open country. They concentrate in Rohilcund, while a portion carry on petty warfare in Oude, and other fugitives have taken the direction of Bundelcund. At the same time, the hot weather and the rains are fast approaching; and it is not to be expected that the season will be so uncommonly favorable to European constitutions as last year. Then, the mass of the European troops were more or less acclimated; this year, most of them are newly arrived. There is no doubt that a campaign in June, July and August will cost the British an immense number of lives, and what with the garrisons that have to be left in every conquered city, the active army will melt down very rapidly. Already are we informed that re-enforcements of 1,000 men per month will scarcely keep up the army at its effective strength; and as to garrisons, Lucknow alone requires at least 8,000 men, over one-third of Campbell's army. The force organizing for the

[a] E. L. Ellenborough's speech in the House of Lords on May 7, 1858, *The Times,* No. 22988, May 8, 1858.—*Ed.*

[b] "On Monday it will be exactly a twelvemonth since...", *The Times,* same issue.—*Ed.*

campaign of Rohilcund will scarcely be stronger than this garrison of Lucknow. We are also informed that among the British officers the opinion is gaining ground that the guerrilla warfare which is sure to succeed the dispersion of the larger bodies of insurgents, will be far more harassing and destructive of life to the British than the present war with its battles and sieges. And, lastly, the Sikhs are beginning to talk in a way which bodes no good to the English. They feel that without their assistance the British would scarcely have been able to hold India, and that, had they joined the insurrection, Hindostan would certainly have been lost to England, at least for a time. They say this loudly, and exaggerate it in their Eastern way. To them the English no longer appear as that superior race which beat them at Moodka, Ferozepore and Aliwal.[543] From such a conviction to open hostility there is but a step with Eastern nations; a spark may kindle the blaze.

Altogether, the taking of Lucknow has no more put down the Indian insurrection than the taking of Delhi. This Summer's campaign may produce such events that the British will have, next Winter, to go substantially over the same ground again, and perhaps even to reconquer the Punjaub. But in the best of cases, a long and harassing guerrilla warfare is before them—not an enviable thing for Europeans under an Indian sun.

Written on May 8, 1858

First published in the *New-York Daily Tribune,* No. 5333, May 25, 1858 as a leading article; reprinted in the *New-York Semi-Weekly Tribune,* No. 1357, May 28, 1858 and the *New-York Weekly Tribune,* No. 872, May 29, 1858

Reproduced from the *New-York Daily Tribune*

Karl Marx

THE ANNEXATION OF OUDE[544]

About eighteen months ago, at Canton, the British Government propounded the novel doctrine in the law of nations that a State may commit hostilities on a large scale against a Province of another State, without either declaring war or establishing a state of war against that other State.[545] Now the same British Government, in the person of the Governor-General of India, Lord Canning, has made another forward move in its task of upsetting the existing law of nations. It has proclaimed that

"the proprietary right in the soil of the Province of Oude is confiscated to the British Government, which will dispose of that right in such manner as it may seem fitting."[a]

When, after the fall of Warsaw in 1831, the Russian Emperor[b] confiscated "the proprietary right in the soil" hitherto held by numerous Polish nobles,[546] there was one unanimous outburst of indignation in the British press and Parliament. When, after the battle of Novara,[547] the Austrian Government did not confiscate, but merely sequestered, the estates of such Lombard noblemen as had taken an active part in the war of independence, that unanimous outburst of British indignation was repeated. And when, after the 2d December, 1851, Louis Napoleon confiscated the estates of the Orleans family, which, by the common law of France, ought to have been united to the public domain on the accession of Louis Philippe, but which had escaped that fate by a

[a] Here and below Ch. J. Canning, "Proclamation", *The Times*, No. 22986, May 6, 1858.— *Ed.*

[b] Nicholas I.— *Ed.*

legal quibble, then British indignation knew no bounds, and *The London Times* declared that by this act the very foundations of social order were upset, and that civil society could no longer exist.[a] All this honest indignation has now been practically illustrated. England, by one stroke of the pen, has confiscated not only the estates of a few noblemen, or of a royal family, but the whole length and breadth of a kingdom[548] nearly as large as Ireland, "the inheritance of a whole people," as Lord Ellenborough himself terms it.[b]

But let us hear what pretexts—grounds we cannot call them—Lord Canning, in the name of the British Government, sets forth for this unheard-of proceeding: First, "The army is in possession of Lucknow." Second, "The resistance, begun by a mutinous soldiery, has found support from the inhabitants of the city and of the province at large." Third, "They have been guilty of a great crime, and have subjected themselves to a just retribution." In plain English: Because the British army have got hold of Lucknow, the Government has the right to confiscate all the land in Oude which they have not yet got hold of. Because the native soldiers in British pay have mutinied, the natives of Oude, who were subjected to British rule by force, have not the right to rise for their national independence. In short, the people of Oude have rebelled against the legitimate authority of the British Government, and the British Government now distinctly declares that rebellion is a sufficient ground for confiscation. Leaving, therefore, out of the question all the circumlocution of Lord Canning, the whole question turns upon the point that he assumes the British rule in Oude to have been legitimately established.

Now, British rule in Oude was established in the following manner: When, in 1856, Lord Dalhousie thought the moment for action had arrived, he concentrated an army at Cawnpore which, the King of Oude[c] was told, was to serve as a corps of observation against Nepaul. This army suddenly invaded the country, took possession of Lucknow, and took the King prisoner. He was urged to cede the country to the British, but in vain. He was then carried off to Calcutta, and the country was annexed to the territories of the East India Company. This treacherous invasion was based

---

[a] "If Louis Napoleon had proceeded to exercise with judgment...", *The Times*, No. 21021, January 26, 1852.—*Ed.*

[b] E. L. Ellenborough's speech in the House of Lords on May 7, 1858, *The Times*, No. 22988, May 8, 1858.—*Ed.*

[c] Wajid Ali Shah.—*Ed.*

upon article 6 of the treaty of 1801,[a] concluded by Lord Wellesley.[549] This treaty was the natural consequence of that concluded in 1798 by Sir John Shore.[b] According to the usual policy followed by the Anglo-Indian Government in their intercourse with native princes, this first treaty of 1798 was a treaty of offensive and defensive alliance on both sides. It secured to the East India Company a yearly subsidy of 76 lacs[c] of rupees ($3,800,000); but by articles 12 and 13 the King was obliged to reduce the taxation of the country. As a matter of course, these two conditions, in open contradiction to each other, could not be fulfilled by the King at the same time. This result, looked for by the East India Company, gave rise to fresh complications, resulting in the treaty of 1801, by which a cession of territory had to make up for the alleged infractions of the former treaty; a cession of territory which, by the way, was at the time denounced in Parliament as a downright robbery, and would have brought Lord Wellesley before a Committee of Inquiry, but for the political influence then held by his family.

In consideration of this cession of territory, the East India Company, by article 3, undertook to defend the King's remaining territories against all foreign and domestic enemies; and by article 6 guaranteed the possession of these territories to him and his heirs and successors forever. But this same article 6 contained also a pit-fall for the King, viz: The King engaged that he would establish such a system of administration, to be carried into effect by his own officers, as should be conducive to the prosperity of his subjects, and be calculated to secure the lives and property of the inhabitants. Now, supposing the King of Oude had broken this treaty; had not, by his government, secured the lives and property of the inhabitants (say by blowing them from the cannon's mouth, and confiscating the whole of their lands), what remedy remained to the East India Company? The King was, by the treaty, acknowledged as an independent sovereign, a free agent, one of the contracting parties. The East India Company, on declaring the treaty broken and thereby annulled, could have but two modes of action: either by negotiation, backed by pressure, they might have come to a new arrangement, or else they might have declared war against the King. But to invade his territory without declaration of

---

[a] "Treaty between the Honorable East India Company and His Excellency the Nabob Vizier-ul-Momalik..., 10th November 1801".—*Ed.*

[b] "Treaty with the Nabob Vizier Saadet Ali Khan Behauder, 21st February 1798".—*Ed.*

[c] Lac=100,000.—*Ed.*

war, to take him prisoner unawares, dethrone him and annex his territory, was an infraction not only of the treaty, but of every principle of the law of nations.

That the annexation of Oude was not a sudden resolution of the British Government is proved by a curious fact. No sooner was Lord Palmerston, in 1831, Foreign Secretary, than he sent an order to the then Governor-General[a] to annex Oude. The subordinate at that time declined to carry out the suggestion. The affair, however, came to the knowledge of the King of Oude,[b] who availed himself of some pretext to send an embassy to London. In spite of all obstacles, the embassy succeeded in acquainting William IV., who was ignorant of the whole proceeding, with the danger which had menaced their country. The result was a violent scene between William IV. and Palmerston, ending in a strict injunction to the latter never to repeat such *coups d'état* on pain of instant dismissal. It is important to recollect that the actual annexation of Oude and the confiscation of all the landed property of the country took place when Palmerston was again in power. The papers relating to this first attempt at annexing Oude, in 1831, were moved for, a few weeks ago, in the House of Commons, when Mr. Baillie, Secretary of the Board of Control, declared that these papers had disappeared.[c]

Again, in 1837, when Palmerston, for the second time, was Foreign Secretary, and Lord Auckland Governor-General of India, the King of Oude[d] was compelled to make a fresh treaty with the East India Company.[e] This treaty takes up article 6 of the one of 1801, because "it provides no remedy for the obligation contained in it" (to govern the country well); and it expressly provides, therefore, by article 7,

"that the King of Oude shall immediately take into consideration, in concert with the British Resident, the best means of remedying the defects in the police, and in the judicial and revenue administrations of his dominions; and that if his Majesty should neglect to attend to the advice and counsel of the British Government, and if gross and systematic oppression, anarchy and misrule should prevail within the Oude dominions, such as seriously to endanger the public tranquillity, the British Government reserves to itself the right of appointing its

[a] W. C. Bentinck.— *Ed.*

[b] Nazir-ed-Din.— *Ed.*

[c] H. J. Baillie's speech in the House of Commons on March 16, 1858, *The Times*, No. 22943, March 17, 1858.— *Ed.*

[d] Mohammed Ali Shah.— *Ed.*

[e] "Treaty between the Honorable East India Company and His Majesty ... Mohammud Ali Shah..., 11th September 1837".— *Ed.*

own officers to the management of whatsoever portions of the Oude territory, either to a small or great extent, in which such misrule shall have occurred, for so long a period as it may deem necessary; the surplus receipts in such case, after defraying all charges, to be paid into the King's Treasury, and a true and faithful account rendered to his Majesty of the receipts and expenditure."

By article 8, the treaty further provides:

"That in case the Governor-General of India in Council should be compelled to resort to the exercise of the authority vested in him by article 7, he will endeavor so far as possible to maintain, with such improvements as they may admit of, the native institutions and forms of administration within the assumed territories, so as to facilitate the restoration of these territories to the Sovereign of Oude, when the proper period for such restoration shall arrive."

This treaty professes to be concluded between the Governor-General of British India in Council,[550] on one hand, and the King of Oude on the other. It was, as such, duly ratified, by both parties, and the ratifications were duly exchanged. But when it was submitted to the Board of Directors of the East India Company, it was annulled (April 10, 1838) as an infraction of the friendly relations between the Company and the King of Oude, and an encroachment, on the part of the Governor-General, on the rights of that potentate. Palmerston had not asked the Company's leave to conclude the treaty, and he took no notice of their annulling resolution. Nor was the King of Oude informed that the treaty had ever been canceled. This is proved by Lord Dalhousie himself (minute Jan. 5, 1856):

"It is very probable that the King, in the course of the discussions which will take place with the Resident, may refer to the treaty negotiated with his predecessor in 1837; the Resident is aware that the treaty was not continued in force, having been annulled by the Court of Directors as soon as it was received in England. The Resident is further aware that, although the King of Oude was informed at the time that certain aggravating provisions of the treaty of 1837, respecting an increased military force, would not be carried into effect, the *entire abrogation of it was never communicated to his Majesty*. The effect of this reserve and want of full communication is felt to be embarrassing to-day. It is the more embarrassing that the canceled instrument was still included in a volume of treaties which was published in 1845, by the authority of Government."

In the same minute, sec. 17, it is said:

"If the King should allude to the treaty of 1837, and should ask why, if further measures are necessary in relation to the administration of Oude, the large powers which are given to the British Government by the said treaty should not now be put in force, his Majesty must be informed that the treaty has had no existence since it was communicated to the Court of Directors, by whom it was wholly annulled. His Majesty will be reminded that the Court of Lucknow was informed at the time that certain articles of the treaty of 1837, by which the payment of an additional military force was imposed upon the King, were to be set aside. It must be presumed that it was not thought necessary at that time to make any communication to his Majesty regarding those articles of the treaty which were not of immediate operation, and that the subsequent communication was inadvertently neglected."

But not only was this treaty inserted in the official collection of 1845, it was also officially adverted to as a subsisting treaty in Lord Auckland's notification to the King of Oude, dated July 8, 1839; in Lord Hardinge's (then Governor-General) remonstrance to the same King, of November 23, 1847, and in Col. Sleeman's (Resident at Lucknow) communication to Lord Dalhousie himself, of the 10th December, 1851. Now, why was Lord Dalhousie so eager to deny the validity of a treaty which all his predecessors, and even his own agents, had acknowledged to be in force in their communications with the King of Oude? Solely because, by this treaty, whatever pretext the King might give for interference, that interference was limited to an assumption of government by British officers *in the name of the King of Oude,* who was to receive the surplus revenue. That was the very opposite of what was wanted. Nothing short of annexation would do. This denying the validity of treaties which had formed the acknowledged base of intercourse for twenty years; this seizing violently upon independent territories in open infraction even of the acknowledged treaties; this final confiscation of every acre of land in the whole country; all these treacherous and brutal modes of proceeding of the British toward the natives of India are now beginning to avenge themselves, not only in India, but in England.

Written on May 14, 1858

First published in the *New-York Daily Tribune,* No. 5336, May 28, 1858 as a leading article; reprinted in the *New-York Semi-Weekly Tribune,* No. 1358, June 1, 1858, under the title "Confiscation in Oude"

Reproduced from the *New-York Daily Tribune*

Karl Marx

A CURIOUS PIECE OF HISTORY[551]

Manchester (Eng.), May 18, 1858

A very short time after the close of the last Russian war[a] the public was informed that a certain Mohammed Bey, Colonel in the Turkish army, alias M. Bangya, ex-Colonel of the Hungarian army, had left Constantinople for Circassia along with a number of Polish volunteers. On his arrival, he at once became a sort of chief of the staff to Sefer Pasha, the Circassian chief. Those who knew the antecedents of this Hungarian liberator of Circassia could have no doubt that he had gone to that country for one purpose only: to sell it to Russia. The man had been, openly and unmistakably, proved to have been, in London and Paris, a spy in the pay both of the French and the Prussian police.[b] Accordingly, about a month ago, the European papers contained the news that Bangya-Mohammed Bey had actually been detected in treasonable correspondence with the Russian General, Philipson, and that a Court-martial, held upon him, had sentenced him to death. Bangya, however, a short time after, appeared all at once in Constantinople, and, with his usual impudence, declared all these stories about treachery, courts-martial, &c., to be pure inventions of his enemies, and tried to pass himself off as the victim of an intrigue.

We happen to be in possession of the most important documents relating to this curious incident of the Circassian war, and shall now give some extracts from them. These papers were brought to Constantinople by Sub-Lieutenant Franz Stock of the Polish battalion in Circassia, and one of the members of the

[a] The Crimean war of 1853-56.—*Ed.*

[b] See this volume, pp. 236-37.—*Ed.*

Court-martial which convicted Bangya. The public may then judge for themselves.[a]

Extracts from the Minutes of the Council of War held at Aderbi, Circassia, on Mohammed Bey, alias J. Bangya of Illosfalva.

[No. 1]—Sitting of January 9, 1858.—Deposition of Mustapha, native of the Province of Natkhouatz.

"... When the Colonel, Mohammed Bey, came to Shepsohour, he asked me to forward a letter to the Commander of the Cossack of the Black Sea, General Philipson. On my observing that I could not do so without informing Sefer Pasha, or without his permission, Mohammed Bey informed me that as Envoy and Lieutenant of the Padishah and Military Commandant in Circassia he had the right to exchange letters with the Russians; that Sefer Pasha was acquainted with the subject, and that his object was to mislead the Russians.... When Sefer Pasha and the National Assembly forwarded to me the manifesto of Circassia, addressed to the Czar,[b] Mohammed Bey gave me also a letter for Gen. Philipson. I did not find Gen. Philipson at Anapa, and I delivered the letter to the Major commanding at Anapa. The Major promised to forward the manifesto, but would not accept the letter, which was without address or signature. I brought back the letter, but feeling suspicious of the frequent correspondence of Mohammed Bey, and fearing myself to get compromised, I communicated the whole affair to the authorities...."

[No. 2.]—Deposition of Achmet Effendi, formerly Turkish Secretary to Mohammed Bey.

"... Mohammed Bey was very irate against Tefik Bey (Col. Lapinski) and spoke very ill of him, adding that he would block his path very long. The second night after our arrival at Aderbi ... it was early dawn when I was roused by Mohammed Bey's groom. Mohammed Bey himself told me that a great noise of guns was heard in the direction of Ghelendjeek. He was up and seemed uneasy.... The report that Col. Lapinski had been captured with all his party arrived at Aderbi, I know not how, even before the roar of the guns had ceased. I heard Mohammed Bey talk of it. When later news came that neither the Colonel nor his men had been made prisoners, Mohammed Bey said, very angrily,

"'That probably he had sold his guns to the Russians.'..."

[No. 3.]—Deposition of the Officers and Soldiers of the Polish Detachment stationed at Aderbi.

"One day before Ghelendjeek was surprised, Mohammed Bey came to the camp and said he had received letters from Constantinople, informing him that it was entirely Col. Lapinski's fault if they got no assistance anywhere.... He caused spirits to be distributed to the soldiers, and made them all sorts of promises if they would

[a] Here and below Marx used the material from *The Free Press*, No. 16, May 12, 1858, pp. 121-25.—*Ed.*

[b] Alexander II.—*Ed.*

abandon their Colonel and follow him.... When afterward the news (of the supposed capture of Lapinski) turned out false, Mohammed Bey came in person to the camp and harangued the detachment to induce them to refuse obedience to the Colonel. But when the Colonel came back, he pretended to know nothing about the matter, and abandoned several individuals who had attached themselves to him, and allowed them to be punished without interfering in their favor. Later, during the absence of the Colonel, Mohammed Bey endeavored to lead the troops into rebellion by the means of several Hungarians. The Hungarians drew up an act of accusation against the Colonel and endeavored to get the men to sign. With the exception of three men, who admit that they were seduced to sign, all the others declared on their oath that their signatures had been forged.... This forgery was the easier since in the detachment only a few soldiers knew how to write."

[No. 4.]—Confession of Bangya before the Court-Martial.[a]

"Tired of so long interrogatory, I present to the Commission this confession, written by my hand and signed by me. I hope that my judges, to whom I spare by so doing a long and difficult task, will be the more disposed to remember that with my fate is tied up also the fate of my innocent family.* Formerly my name was John Bangya of Illosfalva; my name now is Mohammed Bey; my age is forty; my religion was the Roman Catholic, but in 1853 I embraced Islamism.... My political action ... was dictated by the ancient chief of my country, Louis Kossuth.... Provided with letters of introduction from my political chief, I came to Constantinople on the 22d of December, 1853.... I entered the Turkish army with the rank of Colonel. At this time I was frequently receiving from Kossuth letters and instructions concerning the interest of my country. At the same epoch Kossuth addressed to the Ottoman Government a missive, in which he warmly recommends the Turks to beware of the French, English or Austrian alliance, and advised them to link themselves rather with the revolutionary Italians and Hungarians.... My instructions recommended me to get attached in some way or other to the troops destined to act on the Circassian shores.... Arrived in Circassia, I contented myself for a time with studying the state of affairs in the country, and communicating my observations to my political friends.... I tried to attach myself to Sefer Pasha.... My instructions recommended me to prevent any offensive steps on the part of the Circassians, and to oppose all foreign influence in the country. A very short time previous to my departure from Constantinople Col. Türr, who receives his instructions from the same quarters as myself, and with whom I have been for years in political relation, received orders to join the Greek insurrection. Gen. Stein (Ferhad Pasha), who also belongs to our party, was directed to proceed to Anatolia. As for the plan of getting attached to Sefer Pasha, it succeeded, and very soon I gained his entire confidence. His confidence once acquired, it was easy for me to follow and execute my instructions.... I persuaded Sefer Pasha that after the war

* By this he alludes to the Bangya family No. 3. He has one wife living in Hungary and another in Paris, beside the Islamic family he has in Constantinople. [This footnote is missing in *The Free Press*. It is not established whether it belongs to Marx or the *NYDT* editors.—*Ed.*]

[a] Marx also used "Extract from the Minutes of the Council of War, held at Aderbi" and especially "Confession of Bangya" in his *Herr Vogt* (see present edition, Vol. 17).—*Ed.*

Circassia would be restored to the Sultan's rule.... To the Turkish commanders I represented that all offensive measures with their troops would be dangerous, since the Circassians ... would desert them in the hour of danger. The circumstances were favorable for me, and although the Russians had sent their troops to the theater of war, and left unprotected their frontiers, they had not to suffer from any serious incursions of the Circassians. I forwarded regular reports of my secret action to my political chiefs.... At the same time I found on my way men and circumstances just contrary to my plans. I allude to the arrival at Anapa of Mr. Longworth, British Consul. Mr. Longworth's instructions ordered him to induce Sefer Pasha to organize 6,000 Circassians at the expense of Great Britain and to dispatch them to the Crimea.... I received similar orders from the Turkish authorities, but at the same time my secret chiefs sent me the most positive order to do all in my power to annihilate the mission of the Consul.... In a conversation which I had with Mr. Longworth ... I asked for a post in the British army with the rank of Colonel, or for the capital sum of £10,000.... Mr. Longworth thought to gain me by an offer of 50,000 piasters.... My intrigue succeeded. Prince Sefer, so often deceived by vain promises, became suspicious and roundly refused to the Consul what he wanted of his people.... At this time I made an enemy in the person of Prince Ibrahim Karabatir, the son of Sefer Pasha, who had been named to command the 6,000 Circassians....

"The 21st of March, 1856, Sefer Pasha informed me that it had been decided in the General Assembly to send a deputation to the Turkish, French and British Governments to ask these Powers to reincorporate Circassia with Turkey. I induced Sefer Pasha to send me with this deputation.... On my arrival in Constantinople ... I addressed to my political friends and to Kossuth a detailed account of the state of Circassia.... I received in reply instructions ordering me to communicate with Col. Türr and Gen. Stein, and to conduct the affairs in common with them, and to engage in it as many Hungarians as possible. At the same time I entered into communication with Ismail Pasha, Postmaster of the Ottoman Empire, a Circassian by birth, who appeared to me patriotic and able to make sacrifices for his country. I consulted with him on the manner in which it might be possible for us to send into Circassia arms, ammunition, tools for artificers, good officers and artisans. *But the real plan of the expedition was arranged between Gen. Stein, Col. Türr and myself. Capt. Franchini, military secretary to the Russian Minister, was present at several of our conferences. The object was to gain over Circassia to Russian interests in a peaceable, slow, but certain manner....*[a] When once Circassia should have submitted to the direction of Gen. Stein and myself, our plan would be:

"I. To choose some native Prince who would bring the whole country under his rule;

"II. To persuade the Circassians that they are not to expect any assistance either from the Sultan or from any other Power;

"III. To demoralize the mountaineers by dint of defeats on the field of battle—defeats studied and prepared beforehand;

"IV. To bring them to recognize the Czar as their nominal sovereign without paying any tribute, but admitting garrisons into the country.... The Hungarians imported into Circassia would be placed about the Prince; the more capable would be intrusted with the important posts.... Capt. Franchini assured me that Russia required nothing more than apparent submission; ... the marks of Imperial favor, money and Russian orders would do the rest....

"The 22d of September, 1856, Ismail Pasha recommended me to engage for Circassia several hundred Poles who were barracked in Scutari, and who had

[a] Italics by Marx.—*Ed.*

formed part of the legion under Zamoyski.... This proposal did not agree with our plans, but it was difficult to reject it.... I had formerly known M. Lapinski, who had served with distinction in Hungary.... He was living at Scutari.... We agreed with Gen. Stein that the best plan would be to engage Col. Lapinski, who had absolute confidence in me.... On Sept. 24 I notified in writing to Col. Lapinski that he was called upon by the Circassian patriots to form a Polish corps in Circassia. The Colonel, in reply, demanded arms and equipments for 700 Poles.... We afterward consulted together—*Gen. Stein, Türr, Franchini and myself*[a]—and it was decided that Türr should proceed to England to purchase tools and machines for making cartridges, but that he would delay sending any arms. We wanted to be sure of the Poles before we gave them any arms.... The serious remonstrances of Col. Lapinski ... obliged me to hurry the departure, although I had not the means of taking with me the Hungarian officers I had engaged.... In the month of January, 1857, I received letters and instructions from Kossuth and from my other political friends. My plan was approved.... A short time before my departure an apparent coolness was simulated between me and Gen. Stein. I still wanted to delay my departure to render possible that of a few Hungarians with me, *but Capt. Franchini declared that there was not a day to be lost,*[a] because the expedition had become the talk of all Constantinople, and *if the Russian Embassy did not interfere it might be accused of complicity.*[a] On the 15th of February Col. Lapinski embarked on board the English steamer *Kangaroo.* I embarked also.... On my arrival at Dob (Kabardinsk of the Russians) I addressed letters to Sefer Pasha, to the Naïb,[b] and to the other chiefs of the tribes; and in those letters I announced myself as sent by his Imperial Majesty the Sultan to command the military forces of Circassia.... The conduct of Col. Lapinski was not very reassuring for me.... A few weeks after the arrival of the Polish detachment at Shepsohour (Fort Tenginsk of the Russians), the residence of Sefer Pasha, Mr. Römer arrived at Dob with the brig laden with arms and ammunition which we had left in the Bosphorus.... The irruption of the Russians by Attakum, in the month of May, brought together thousands of Circassian warriors from all parts of the country. For the first time the Circassians saw artillery of their own attacking with advantage the Russian artillery. This engagement, of little consequence in itself, gave importance to the Polish detachment and to me.... I took advantage of this disposition of the people to act my part; I presented myself in public as the Envoy of the Sultan[c]; I exacted obedience.... I afterward learned that Col. Lapinski was working with all his might to upset my plans.... I endeavored to gain partisans among the officers and men of his detachment, and the situation of the corps being precarious, I attributed this to the fault of their commander.... The capture by a Russian vessel of a few sandals, in the ports of Sudjak and Ghelendjeek, gave me an occasion to remove the Colonel to a distance from the seat of war, near Attakum, and to isolate him completely.... A few days later I received from Col. Lapinski a letter, by which he announced that there were no troops at Ghelendjeek, and that his position was not tenable.... I went myself to Ghelendjeek, and on the spot Col. Lapinski represented to me the danger of his position and the imminence of an attack from the Russians. Nine days afterward his prediction was realized....

"The agitation which I kept up among the officers and soldiers at Aderbi, during and after the catastrophe at Ghelendjeek, was simply the consequence of the resolution which I had taken to sow discord between the detachment and Col.

---

[a] Italics by Marx.—*Ed.*
[b] Mohammed-Amin.—*Ed.*
[c] Abdul Mejid.—*Ed.*

Lapinski.... Through emissaries I was circulating among the Circassians reports that he had sold the guns to the Russians.... I allowed myself to be taken in by the simulated sincerity of the Colonel, who was observing me with greater vigilance than ever....

"In conformity with my instructions I was to form relations with the Russian General.[a] ... My anonymous letter, which is actually in the hands of the Commission, was to be the introduction to a regular correspondence, but by the stupidity of the Russian commander it has fallen into your hands....

"All of a sudden Col. Lapinski threw off the mask, and abruptly declared to me at Sefer Pasha's that he did not recognize me either as his superior or as military commandant in Circassia, broke off all intercourse with me, ... addressed also a general order in this sense to the Polish detachment. I tried to depose him by another order of the day addressed to the soldiers, but my efforts were vain....

"(Signed.)

Mohammed Bey."

[No. 5.]—Letter of John Bangya to General Philipson.

"Would it not be in the interest of Russia to pacify Circassia? It might be possible to conquer the plains of Circassia momentarily by dint of enormous sacrifices, but the mountains and natural fastnesses will never be conquered. The Russian guns have lost their influence. The Circassian artillery will reply to the Russian with satisfactory results. The Circassians are not what they were five years ago; supported by a small regular force, they fight as well as the Russian troops, and for their religion and their country they will fight to the last man. Would it not be better to allow the Circassians a sort of mock liberty? to place Circassia under a national prince, and take this prince under the protection of the Russian Czar? In a word, to make of Circassia another Georgia, or something of the kind? Once Circassia intimately allied to Russia, the roads of Anatolia and of India are open to the Russians. *Sapienti sat.*[b] It might be possible to open negotiations on this basis. Reflect and answer."

[No. 6.]—Sentence, January 20, 1858.

"After the reading of the confession of Col. Mohammed Bey, read at the sittings of the 2d, 3d, 4th, 5th, 6th, 7th and 11th of January; after having heard the depositions of the witnesses at the sitting of the 9th of January, the Court-Martial declares, at the sitting of this day, Mohammed Bey, by his confession and by the depositions of the witnesses, convicted of treachery to the country, and secret correspondence with the enemy; declares him infamous, deprived of his rank in this country, and condemns him to death—unanimously.

"Signed: *Jacob Beckert,* soldier; *Philipp Terteltaub,* bombardier; *Mathias Bedneizek,* sergeant; *Otto Linovski,* gunner; *Franz Stock,* sub-lieutenant; *Anton Krysciewicz,* sub-lieutenant; *Michael Marecki,* lieutenant; *Leon Zawadski,* gunner; *Stanislas Tanckowski,* lance-corporal; *John Hamaniski,* sergeant;

[a] G. I. Philipson.—*Ed.*

[b] Enough for the wise. Terence, *Phormio,* III, 3, 8.—*Ed.*

Alexander Michicki, sergeant-major; *Casimir Wystocki,* sub-lieutenant; *Josef Aranoski,* lieutenant; *Peter Stankiewicz,* captain; *Theophil Lapinski,* colonel."

To the above documents we have merely to add that Sefer Pasha was loth to have the sentence of death executed upon a man who held the rank of Colonel in the Sultan's army, and that he consequently had him escorted to Trebizond. The Hungarians in Constantinople declared Mohammed Bey's treachery to be a pure calumny, but the Polish officers at once protested against this assertion and threatened an eventual publication of the documents relating to this affair. We now publish them, in extract, as they form by far the most interesting contribution to the history of the Circassian war.

With regard to the conduct of the Russian Embassy during this affair, we may add the following facts: It was generally known in Constantinople that the *Kangaroo* was chartered to take troops and stores to Circassia. The Russian Embassy, however, did not drop one word with respect to that expedition to the Porte; but the very day the *Kangaroo* got clear of the Bosphorus, the Russian Embassador[a] addressed a protest to the Porte, and caused an inquiry to be made to discover the promoters of the expedition. They strained every nerve to implicate Count Zamoyski, who was at Constantinople at the time; but they signally failed in this. Then, on the ostensible demand of Russia, Gen. Stein and Ismail Pasha were sent into exile for having been mixed up with the affair. After a banishment of some months, on the occasion of a festal day in the Russian Imperial family, at the request again of the Russian Embassy, Gen. Stein and Ismail Pasha were allowed to return to Constantinople.

Critical remarks on the documents were written on May 18, 1858

First published unsigned in the *New-York Daily Tribune,* No. 5352, June 16, 1858; reprinted in the *New-York Semi-Weekly Tribune,* No. 1363, June 18, 1858

Reproduced from the *New-York Daily Tribune*

[a] A. P. Butenev.—*Ed.*

Karl Marx

[LORD CANNING'S PROCLAMATION AND LAND TENURE IN INDIA]

Lord Canning's proclamation in relation to Oude,[a] some important documents in reference to which we published on Saturday,[b] has revived the discussion as to the land tenures of India—a subject upon which there have been great disputes and differences of opinion in times past, and misapprehensions in reference to which have led, so it is alleged, to very serious practical mistakes in the administration of those parts of India directly under British rule.[552] The great point in this controversy is, what is the exact position which the zemindars, talookdars or sirdars, so called,[553] hold in the economical system of India? Are they properly to be considered as landed proprietors or as mere tax-gatherers?

It is agreed that in India, as in most Asiatic countries, the ultimate property in the soil rests [with] the Government; but while one party to this controversy insists that the Government is to be looked upon as a soil proprietor, letting out the land on shares to the cultivators, the other side maintain that in substance the land in India is just as much private property as in any other country whatever—this alleged property in the Government being nothing more than the derivation of title from the sovereign theoretically acknowledged in all countries, the codes of which are based on the feudal law and substantially acknowledged in all countries whatever in the power of the Government to levy taxes

---

[a] *The Times*, No. 22986, May 6, 1858.—*Ed.*

[b] The words "some important documents ... on Saturday" belong to the *NYDT* editors who refer to "The Oude Proclamation. The Correspondence between the Governor-General and the Commissioner of Oude" published in the newspaper, No. 5343, June 5, 1858.—*Ed.*

on the land to the extent of the needs of the Government, quite independent of all considerations, except as mere matter of policy, of the convenience of the owners.

Admitting, however, that the lands of India are private property, held by as good and strong a private title as land elsewhere, who shall be regarded as the real owners? There are two parties for whom this claim has been set up. One of these parties is the class known as zemindars and talookdars, who have been considered to occupy a position similar to that of the landed nobility and gentry of Europe; to be, indeed, the real owners of the land, subject to a certain assessment due to the Government, and, as owners, to have the right of displacing at pleasure the actual cultivators, who, in this view of the case, are regarded as standing in the position of mere tenants at will, liable to any payment in the way of rent which the zemindars may see fit to impose. The view of the case which naturally fell in with English ideas, as to the importance and necessity of a landed gentry as the main pillar of the social fabric, was made the foundation of the famous landed settlement of Bengal seventy years ago, under the Governor-Generalship of Lord Cornwallis[554]—a settlement which still remains in force, but which, as it is maintained by many, wrought great injustice alike to the Government and to the actual cultivators. A more thorough study of the institutions of Hindostan, together with the inconveniences, both social and political, resulting from the Bengal settlement, has given currency to the opinion that by the original Hindoo institutions, the property of the land was in the village corporations, in which resided the power of allotting it out to individuals for cultivation, while the zemindars and talookdars were in their origin nothing but officers of the Government, appointed to look after, to collect, and to pay over to the prince the assessment due from the village.

This view has influenced to a considerable degree the settlement of the landed tenures and revenue made of late years in the Indian provinces, of which the direct administration has been assumed by the English. The exclusive proprietary rights claimed by the talookdars and zemindars have been regarded as originating in usurpations at once against the Government and the cultivators, and every effort has been made to get rid of them as an incubus on the real cultivators of the soil and the general improvement of the country. As, however, these middlemen, whatever the origin of their rights might be, could claim prescription in their favor, it was impossible not to recognize their claims as to a certain extent legal, however inconvenient, arbitrary and oppressive to the people. In Oude, under the feeble reign of the native princes, these feudal landholders had gone very far in curtailing alike the claims of the Government and the rights of the cultivators; and when, upon the recent annexation of that kingdom,[555] this matter came under revision, the Commissioners charged with making the settlement soon got into a very acrimonious controversy with them as to the real extent of their rights. Hence resulted a state of discontent on their part which led them to make common cause with the revolted Sepoys.

By those who incline to the policy above indicated—that of a system of village settlement—looking at the actual cultivators as invested with a proprietary right in the land, superior to that of the middlemen, through whom the Government receives its share of the landed produce—the proclamation of Lord Canning is defended as an advantage taken of the position in which the great body of the zemindars and talookdars of Oude had placed themselves, to open a door for the introduction of much more extensive reforms than otherwise would have been practicable—the proprietary right confiscated by that proclamation being merely the zemindarree or talookdarree right, and affecting only a very small part of the population, and that by no means the actual cultivators.

Independently of any question of justice and humanity, the view taken on the other hand by the Derby Ministry of Lord Canning's proclamation, corresponds sufficiently well with the general principles which the Tory or Conservative party maintain on the sacredness of vested rights and the importance of upholding an aristocratic landed interest. In speaking of the landed interest at home, they always refer rather to the landlords and rent-receivers than to the rent-payers and to the actual cultivators; and it is, therefore, not surprising that they should regard the interests of the zemindars and talookdars, however few their actual number, as equivalent to the interests of the great body of the people.

Here indeed is one of the greatest inconveniences and difficulties in the Government of India from England, that views of Indian questions are liable to be influenced by purely English prejudices or sentiments, applied to a state of society and a condition of things to which they have in fact very little real pertinency. The defense which Lord Canning makes in his dispatch, published to-day,[a] of the policy of his proclamation

[a] "The Correspondence between the Governor-General and the Commissioner of Oude", *The Times*, No. 23000, May 22, 1858.—*Ed.*

against the objections of Sir James Outram, the Commissioner of Oude, is very plausible, though it appears that he so far yielded to the representations of the Commissioner as to insert into the proclamation the mollifying sentence, not contained in the original draft sent to England, and on which Lord Ellenborough's dispatch[a] was based.[556]

Lord Canning's opinion as to the light in which the conduct of landholders of Oude in joining in the rebellion ought to be viewed does not appear to differ much from that of Sir James Outram and Lord Ellenborough. He argues that they stand in a very different position not only from the mutinous Sepoys, but from that of the inhabitants of rebellious districts in which the British rule had been longer established. He admits that they are entitled to be treated as persons having provocation for the course they took; but at the same time insists that they must be made to understand that rebellion cannot be resorted to without involving serious consequences to themselves. We shall soon learn what the effect of the issue of the proclamation has been, and whether Lord Canning or Sir James Outram was nearer right in his anticipation of its results.

Written on May 25, 1858

First published in the *New-York Daily Tribune,* No. 5344, June 7, 1858 as a leading article

Reproduced from the newspaper

---

[a] [E. L. Ellenborough,] "The Secret Committee of the Court of Directors of the East India Company to the Governor-General of India in Council. April 19, 1858", *The Times,* No. 22989, May 10, 1858.—*Ed.*

Karl Marx

[BONAPARTE'S FINANCIAL MANEUVERS. —MILITARY DESPOTISM][557]

Paris, May 27, 1858

The dilapidated state of the Bonapartist Exchequer cannot longer be said to form a matter of dispute. It has been openly proclaimed by the "savior of property"[558] himself. In no other way is it possible to account for General Espinasse's circular to the French Prefects,[a] calling upon them to use their influence, and, "if need be, their authority," in order to induce the trustees of hospitals and other charitable institutions to convert the real property from which they derive their revenues into three per cent consols. That property amounts to $100,000,000, but, as Bonaparte, in the name of the poor, bewails, does not report an income of more than $2^1/_2$ per cent. If invested in the Funds the revenue would improve by at least one half. In his paternal solicitude Bonaparte had recently bid the Council of State to initiate a law for this conversion of the landed property of the charitable establishments into funded property, but, strange to say, his own Council of State doggedly declined to take the hint. What he thus failed in effecting in the legislative way he now tries to get at in the "executive way," by a military *ordre du jour*. There are some people silly enough to fancy that he only intends increasing the funds by the maneuver. Nothing can be further off the mark. If the above-named landed property was sold at its nominal value of $100,000,000, a great part of that purchase money would of course be forthcoming from capital till now invested in consols and other public securities, so that the artificially created demand for the funds would be met by heaps of them thrown into the

[a] [Ch. M. E. Espinasse,] "La circulaire au sujet des biens immeubles...", *Le Moniteur universel*, No. 142, May 22, 1858.—*Ed.*

open market. The operation might even result in a further depression of the security market. However, Bonaparte's scheme is of a much sounder and more intelligible character. For the 100,000,000 of landed property he intends creating 100,000,000 of new *Rentes.* With the one hand he wants to seize the property of the charitable establishments, and with the other to indemnify them by drawing a cheque upon the *"grand livre"*[a] of the nation. On a former occasion, when examining the French Bank act of 1857,[b] we dwelt upon the enormous privileges Bonaparte had bestowed upon the Bank, at the cost of the State, with a view to secure himself a miserable loan of $20,000,000.[c] We considered that Bank act as a financial cry of distress on the part of the savior of society, but since that time the disasters overwhelming French commerce, industry and agriculture have rebounded upon the Exchequer, while its expenses were increasing at an awful ratio. The different ministries for 1858 actually require 79,804,004 francs more than they did in 1855; the expense for the army alone amounting to 51 per cent of the total receipts of the country. The *Crédit Mobilier,*[559] unable to pay a dividend to its own shareholders, and whose last report,[d] if closely scrutinized, shows a considerable surplus of liabilities over assets, cannot, as it did in 1854 and 1855, come to the rescue, and help raise loans on "democratic" principles. There remains, then, nothing for Bonaparte but to return, in financial matters, as he has been forced to do in political ones, to the original principles of the *coup d'état.* The financial policy initiated by the theft from the Bank cellars of 25,000,000 francs, continued in the confiscation of the Orleans estates, is now to receive a further development in the confiscation of the property of the charitable establishments.

The latter operation, however, would cost Bonaparte one of his armies, his army of priests, who administer by far the greatest portion of the charitable establishments. Already, for the first time since the *coup d'état,* the *Univers* dares openly dissent from the savior of society, and even implores the *Siècle* to make common cause against this intended encroachment upon "private property."

---

[a] "Debt register".—*Ed.*

[b] See this volume, pp. 289-92.—*Ed.*

[c] Napoléon III, "Loi portant prorogation du privilège de la Banque de France", *Le Moniteur universel,* No. 162, June 11, 1857.—*Ed.*

[d] I. Péreire, "Rapport présenté au nom du Conseil d'administration [29 avril 1858]", *Le Moniteur universel,* No. 120, April 30, 1858.—*Ed.*

While the "eldest son of the Church"[a] is placed in this rather equivocal position toward his holy army, his most profane army simultaneously threatens to become unmanageable. If he should interfere, in real good earnest, with the amusements of such heroes as Messrs. De Mercy, Léaudais and Hyenne, he will lose his hold on the only portion of the army on which he can rely. If, on the contrary, he allows that pretorian corruption[560] which he has so systematically fostered since the days of the Camp of Satory[561] boldly to show its front, all discipline will be at an end, and the army prove unable to withstand any shock from without. Another such event as the assassination of the *rédacteur,* of the *Figaro,*[b] and that shock will take place. The general exasperation prevailing may be inferred from the one fact, that when the account of the duel got to Paris about 5,000 young men flocked to the *bureaux* of the *Figaro,* requesting to be inscribed upon a list, as ready to fight with any sub-lieutenant who might be forthcoming. The *Figaro,* of course, is itself a Bonapartist creation, heading that literature of scandal and *chantage* and private slander which suddenly shot up after the violent extinction of the political press, and found in the soil and atmosphere of the lesser Empire all the conditions for a luxuriant growth. It is a fine trait of historical irony that the signal for the impending conflict should be given by the murderous quarrel between the literary and the military representatives of the Bonapartist swell mob.

Written on May 27, 1858

Reproduced from the newspaper

First published unsigned in the *New-York Daily Tribune,* No. 5348, June 11, 1858

---

[a] Napoleon III.—*Ed.*

[b] For details on the duel of Henri de Pène and the Sub-Lieutenant Hyenne in which the former was wounded see *The Times,* No. 23000, May 22, 1858.—*Ed.*

Frederick Engels

[THE REVOLT IN INDIA]

In spite of the great military operations of the English in the capture first of Delhi and then of Lucknow, the successive headquarters of the Sepoy rebellion, the pacification of India is yet very far from being accomplished. Indeed, it may be almost said that the real difficulty of the case is but just beginning to show itself. So long as the rebellious Sepoys kept together in large masses, so long as it was a question of sieges and pitched battles on a great scale, the vast superiority of the English troops for such operations gave them every advantage. But with the new character which the war is now taking on, this advantage is likely to be in a great measure lost. The capture of Lucknow does not carry with it the submission of Oude; nor would even the submission of Oude carry with it the pacification of India. The whole Kingdom of Oude bristles with fortresses of greater or less pretensions; and though perhaps none would long resist a regular attack, yet the capture of these forts one by one will not only be a very tedious process, but it will be attended with much greater proportional loss than operations against such great cities as Delhi and Lucknow.

But it is not alone the Kingdom of Oude that requires to be conquered and pacified. The discomfited Sepoys dislodged from Lucknow have scattered and fled in all directions. A great body of them have taken refuge in the hill districts of Rohilcund to the north, which still remains entirely in possession of the rebels. Others fled into Goruckpore on the east—which district, though it had been traversed by the British troops on their march to Lucknow, it has now become necessary to recover a second time. Many others have succeeded in penetrating southward into Bundelcund.

Indeed, a controversy seems to have arisen as to the best method of proceeding, and whether it would not have been better to have first subdued all the outlying districts which might have afforded the rebels a shelter, before directing operations against their main body collected at Lucknow. Such is said to have been the scheme of operations preferred by the military; but it is difficult to see how, with the limited number of troops at the disposal of the English, those surrounding districts could have been so occupied as to exclude the fugitive Sepoys, when finally dislodged from Lucknow, from entering into them, and, as in the case of Goruckpore, making their reconquest necessary.

Since the capture of Lucknow, the main body of the rebels appear to have retired upon Bareilly. It is stated that Nena Sahib was there. Against this city and district, upward of a hundred miles north-west from Lucknow, it has been judged necessary to undertake a Summer campaign, and at the latest accounts Sir Colin Campbell was himself marching thither.[a]

Meanwhile, however, a guerrilla warfare seems to be spreading in various directions. While the troops are drawn off to the North, scattered parties of rebel soldiery are crossing the Ganges into the Doab, interrupting the communication with Calcutta, and by their ravages disabling the cultivators to pay their land tax, or at least affording them an excuse for not doing so.

Even the capture of Bareilly, so far from operating to remedy those evils, will be likely, perhaps, to increase them. It is in this desultory warfare that the advantage of the Sepoys lies. They can beat the English troops at marching to much the same extent that the English can beat them at fighting. An English column cannot move twenty miles a day; a Sepoy force can move forty, and, if hard pushed, even sixty. It is this rapidity of movement which gives to the Sepoy troops their chief value, and this, with their power of standing the climate and the comparative facility of feeding them, makes them indispensable in Indian warfare. The consumption of English troops in service, and especially in a Summer campaign, is enormous. Already, the lack of men is severely felt. It may become necessary to chase the flying rebels from one end of India to the other. For that purpose, European troops would hardly answer, while the contact of the wandering rebels with the native regiments of Bombay and Madras, which have hitherto remained faithful, might lead to new revolts.

Even without any accession of new mutineers, there are still in

[a] *The Times*, No. 23008, June 1, 1858, "India".—*Ed.*

the field not less than a hundred and fifty thousand armed men, while the unarmed population fail to afford the English either assistance or information.

Meanwhile, the deficiency of rain in Bengal threatens a famine—calamity unknown within this century, though in former times, and even since the English occupation, the source of terrible sufferings.

Written at the end of May 1858

First published in the *New-York Daily Tribune*, No. 5351, June 15, 1858 as a leading article

Reproduced from the newspaper

Frederick Engels

[THE BRITISH ARMY IN INDIA][562]

Our indiscreet friend, Mr. William Russell of *The London Times*, has recently been induced, by his love of the picturesque, to illustrate, for the second time, the sack of Lucknow, to a degree which other people will not think very flattering to the British character.[a] It now appears that Delhi, too, was "looted" to a very considerable extent, and that besides the Kaiserbagh, the city of Lucknow generally contributed to reward the British soldier for his previous privations and heroic efforts. We quote from Mr. Russell:

"There are companies which can boast of privates with thousands of pounds worth in their ranks. One man I heard of who complacently offered to lend an officer 'whatever sum he wanted if he wished to buy over the Captain.' Others have remitted large sums to their friends. [...] Ere this letter reaches England, many a diamond, emerald and delicate pearl will have told its tale in a very quiet, pleasant way, of the storm and sack of the Kaiserbagh. *It is as well that the fair wearers ... saw not how the glittering baubles were won, or the scenes in which the treasure was trove....* Some of these officers have made, literally, *their fortunes....* There are certain small caskets in battered uniform cases which contain *estates in Scotland and Ireland*, and snug fishing and shooting boxes in every game-haunted or salmon-frequented angle of the world."[b]

This, then, accounts for the inactivity of the British army after the conquest of Lucknow. The fortnight devoted to plunder was well spent. Officers and soldiers went into the town poor and debt-ridden, and came out suddenly enriched. They were no longer the same men; yet they were expected to return to their

[a] Here and below see W. H. Russell, "Lucknow, April 5", *The Times*, No. 23007, May 31, 1858.—*Ed.*

[b] Italics by Engels.—*Ed.*

former military duty, to submission, silent obedience, fatigue, privation and battle. But this is out of the question. The army, disbanded for the purpose of plunder, is changed for ever; no word of command, no prestige of the General, can make it again what it once was. Listen again to Mr. Russell:

"It is curious to observe how riches develop disease; how one's liver is affected by loot, and what tremendous ravages in one's family, among the nearest and dearest, can be caused by a few crystals of carbon.... The weight of the belt round the private's waist, full of rupees and gold mohurs, assures him the vision" (of a comfortable independency at home) "can be realized, and it is no wonder he resents the 'fall in, there, fall in!' ... Two battas, two shares of prize-money, the plunder of two cities, and many 'pickings by the way', have made some of our men too rich for easy soldiering."

Accordingly, we hear that above 150 officers have sent in their resignations to Sir Colin Campbell—a very singular proceeding indeed in an army before the enemy, which in any other service would be followed up in twenty-four hours by cashiering and severest punishment otherwise, but which, we suppose, is considered in the British army as a very proper act for "an officer and a gentleman" who has suddenly made his fortune. As to the private soldiers, with them the proceeding is different. Loot engenders the desire for more; and if no more Indian treasures are at hand for the purpose, why not loot those of the British Government? Accordingly, says Mr. Russell:

"There has been a suspicious upsetting of two treasure tumbrils under a European guard, in which some few rupees were missing, and *paymasters exhibit a preference for natives in the discharge of the delicate duty of convoy!*"[a]

Very good, indeed. The Hindoo or Sikh is better disciplined, less thieving, less rapacious than that incomparable model of a warrior, the British soldier! But so far we have seen the individual British only employed. Let us now cast a glance at the British army, "looting" in its collective capacity:

"Every day adds to the prize property, and it is estimated that the sales will produce £600,000. [...] *The town of Cawnpore is said to be full of the plunder of Lucknow,* and if the damage done to public buildings, the destruction of private property, the deterioration in value of houses and land, and the results of depopulation could be estimated, it would be found that *the capital of Oude has sustained a loss of five or six millions sterling.*"[a]

The Calmuck hordes of Jenghiz Khan and Timur, falling upon a city like a swarm of locusts, and devouring everything that came

[a] Italics by Engels.—*Ed.*

in their way, must have been a blessing to a country, compared with the irruption of these Christian, civilized, chivalrous and gentle British soldiers. The former, at least, soon passed away on their erratic course; but these methodic Englishmen bring along with them their prize-agents, who convert loot into a system, who register the plunder, sell it by auction, and keep a sharp look-out that British heroism is not defrauded of a tittle of its reward. We shall watch with curiosity the capabilities of this army, relaxed as its discipline is by the effects of wholesale plunder, at a time when the fatigues of a hot weather campaign require the greatest stringency of discipline.

The Hindoos must, however, by this time be still less fit for regular battle than they were at Lucknow, but that is not now the main question. It is far more important to know what shall be done if the insurgents, after a show of resistance, again shift the seat of war, say to Rajpootana, which is far from being subdued. Sir Colin Campbell must leave garrisons everywhere; his field army has melted down to less than one-half of the force he had before Lucknow. If he is to occupy Rohilcund what disposable strength will remain for the field? The hot weather is now upon him, in June the rains must have put a stop to active campaigning, and allowed the insurgents breathing time. The loss of European soldiers through sickness will have increased every day after the middle of April, when the weather became oppressive; and the young men imported into India last Winter must succumb to the climate in far greater numbers than the seasoned Indian campaigners who last Summer fought under Havelock and Wilson. Rohilcund is no more the decisive point than Lucknow was, or Delhi. The insurrection, it is true, has lost most of its capacity for pitched battles; but it is far more formidable in its present scattered form, which compels the English to ruin their army by marching and exposure. Look at the many new centers of resistance. There is Rohilcund, where the mass of the old Sepoys are collected; there is Northeastern Oude beyond the Gogra, where the Oudians have taken up position; there is Calpee, which for the present serves as a point of concentration for the insurgents of Bundelcund. We shall most likely hear in a few weeks, if not sooner, that both Bareilly and Calpee have fallen. The former will be of little importance, inasmuch as it will serve to absorb nearly all, if not the whole of Campbell's disposable forces. Calpee, menaced now by General Whitlock, who has led his column from Nagpoor to Banda, in Bundelcund, and by General Rose, who approaches from Jhansi, and has defeated the advanced guard of the Calpee forces, will be a more important conquest; it will free Campbell's base of operations, Cawnpore, from the only danger menacing it, and thus perhaps enable him to recruit his field forces to some extent by troops set at liberty thereby. But it is very doubtful whether there will be enough to do more than to clear Oude.

Thus, the strongest army England ever concentrated on one point in India is again scattered in all directions, and had more work cut out than it can conveniently do. The ravages of the climate, during the Summer's heats and rains, must be terrible; and whatever the moral superiority of the European over the Hindoos, it is very doubtful whether the physical superiority of the Hindoos in braving the heat and rains of an Indian Summer will not again be the means of destroying the English forces. There are at present but few British troops on the road to India, and it is not intended to send out large re-enforcements before July and August. Up to October and November, therefore, Campbell has but that one army, melting down rapidly as it is, to hold his own with. What if in the mean time the insurgent Hindoos succeed in raising Rajpootana and Mahratta country in rebellion? What if the Sikhs, of whom there are 80,000 in the British service, and who claim all the honor of the victories for themselves, and whose temper is not altogether favorable to the British, were to rise?

Altogether, one more Winter's campaign, at least, appears to be in store for the British in India, and that cannot be carried on without another army from England.

Written on about June 4, 1858

First published in the *New-York Daily Tribune,* No. 5361, June 26, 1858 as a leading article

Reproduced from the newspaper

Karl Marx

THE STATE OF BRITISH COMMERCE

London, June 8, 1858

The trade and navigation tables just published by the British Board of Trade[a] comprise an account of the declared value of the exports of the United Kingdom in the three months ending 31st March, 1858, compared with the corresponding period of the year 1857; an account of the number and tunnage of vessels entered inward and cleared outward, with cargoes, in the four months ending 30th April, 1858, compared with the corresponding period of the years 1856 and 1857; and, lastly, an account of the principal exports and imports for the four months ending 30th April, 1858. The amount of the exports for the month of April, 1858, is £9,451,000, against £9,965,000 in 1857, and £9,424,000 in 1856,[b] while for the four months there is a reduction of nearly £6,000,000 in the year 1858. Accordingly the British exports of the month of April, 1858, would appear not only to have risen above the level of 1856, but closely to approach that reached in 1857, some months prior to the commercial explosion in the United States. Hence it might be inferred that the last traces of the crisis are rapidly disappearing, and that British commerce, at least, is again entering a new epoch of expansion. Such a conclusion, however, would be altogether erroneous. In the first place, it must be considered that the official statistics, as far as they relate to declared value, do not show the actual returns, but the returns as anticipated by the exporters. Moreover, a closer

---

[a] "Accounts Relating to Trade and Navigation for the Four Months ended April 30", *The Economist*, No. 770, May 29, 1858, supplement.— *Ed.*

[b] "The Board of Trade Tables", *The Economist*, No. 770, May 29, 1858, p. 592.— *Ed.*

examination of the tables of exports proves that the apparent recovery of British commerce is mainly due to an over-importation of East India, which must lead to a violent contraction of that market. Already we read in the last commercial circular of Messrs. George Frazer & Company:

> "The later advices from the East show symptoms of reaction from the extraordinary high range of prices which have been current in Bombay and in Calcutta during the period when supplies there were so short. A not inconsiderable decline has already been submitted to upon the arrival out of cargoes which were shipped not later than December. The supplies since then have been to both markets most liberal, if not excessive; and it seems very probable, therefore, that for some time to come we must look for less support to prices from the great activity of the Eastern demand than has been so far experienced since the beginning of January."

Beside India, those European and other countries which till now had not been reached by the effects of the commercial crisis, have been blocked up by British merchandise, not in consequence of increased demand, but by way of experiment. The countries thus blessed were Belgium, Spain and its dependencies, some Italian States—principally the Two Sicilies—Egypt, Mexico, Central America, Peru, China, and some minor markets. At the very time when the most disastrous news was arriving from Brazil and put a check upon the aggregate export to that country, some branches of British industry, compelled to find an outlet for their exuberant produce, did not only not curtail, but actually augment their shipments for that market. Thus, during the month of April, linens, earthenware and porcelain, destined for Brazil, were increasing in quantity as well as declared value. Nobody can consider this bona fide exports. The same remark holds true with respect to Australia, which had acted as so elastic a center of absorption during the first months of the crisis. Australia was then and is still overstocked; a sudden reaction took place; the aggregate exports thither were diminished, but again some branches of British industry, instead of contracting, have actually expanded—speculatively, of course—their supplies in spite of the warnings of all the Australian local papers. The export tables of the month of April, therefore, must be considered not as the bona fide standard of the recovery of British industry, but as mere feelers thrown out in order to ascertain what pressure the markets of the world are again able to bear. The following table contains an account of the declared value of the British and Irish exports in the three months ending 31st of March, 1858, compared with the corresponding period of the year 1857:

Foreign Countries to which Exported.[a]

	1857.	1858.
Russia, Northern Ports	£3,015	£8,853
Russia, Southern Ports	72,777	42,493
Sweden	48,007	3,717
Norway	30,217	5,911
Denmark	92,046	40,148
Prussia	133,000	78,917
Mecklenburg	9,502	3,099
Hanover	288,648	236,669
Oldenburg	3,520	1,957
Hanse Towns	2,318,260	1,645,419
Holland	1,305,606	975,428
Belgium	515,175	546,033
France	1,631,672	1,035,096
Portugal proper	380,160	356,178
Azores	10,793	12,581
Madeira	9,955	16,245
Spain	496,788	584,287
Canary Islands	18,817	8,475
Sardinia	290,131	293,138
Tuscany	189,534	257,508
Papal States	69,953	123,059
Two Sicilies	284,045	375,177
Austrian Territories	253,042	323,086
Greece	40,860	69,570
Turkey	969,288	821,204
Wallachia and Moldavia	111,052	98,135
Syria and Palestine	199,070	81,874
Egypt (ports on the Mediterranean)	449,497	483,516
Tunis	865	2,323
Algeria	4,790	4,831
Morocco	55,826	37,206
Western Coast of Africa (foreign)	235,527	196,484
Eastern Coast of Africa	301	1,927
African Ports on the Red Sea	1,130	567
Cape Verde Islands	2,419	3,965
Java	234,071	149,493

[a] Here and below "An Account of the Declared Value of British and Irish Produce and Manufactures...," *The Economist*, No. 770, May 29, 1858.—*Ed.*

	1857	1858
Philippine Islands	144,992	212,942
China (exclusive of Hong Kong)	290,441	389,647
South Sea Islands	...	585
Foreign West Indies	620,022	521,435
United States (Ports on the Atlantic)	6,231,501	2,565,566
California	50,219	94,147
Mexico	112,277	151,890
Central America	22,453	46,201
New Granada	88,502	117,411
Venezuela	105,417	62,685
Ecuador	2,099	...
Brazil	1,292,325	826,583
Uruguay	145,481	177,281
Buenos Ayres	285,187	279,913
Chili	336,309	270,176
Peru	209,889	299,725
Total to foreign countries	£20,636,473	£14,940,756

British Possessions.

Channel Islands	£136,071	£120,431
Gibraltar	152,926	210,575
Malta	116,821	131,238
Ionian Islands	66,148	52,849
West Coast of Africa (British)	135,452	62,343
Cape of Good Hope	442,796	403,579
Natal	26,605	23,106
Ascension	3,832	2,308
St. Helena	3,837	8,416
Mauritius	142,303	164,042
Aden	11,263	11,996
British Territories in the East Indies (exclusive of Singapore and Ceylon)	2,822,009	3,502,664
Singapore	101,535	308,545
Ceylon	98,817	153,090
Hong Kong	133,743	242,757
West Australia	15,515	13,813
South Australia	180,123	249,162
New South Wales	706,337	682,265

	1857.	1858.
Victoria	£1,427,248	£1,056,537
Tasmania	67,550	82,942
New Zealand	96,893	93,768
British North American Colonies	818,560	439,433
British West India Islands	334,024	426,421
British Guiana	122,249	95,385
Honduras (British Settlements)	28,363	31,869
Total to British Possessions	£8,191,020	£8,569,534
Total to Foreign Countries and British Possessions	28,827,493	23,510,290

The Economist thinks that, from an accurate analysis of these figures,

> "the curious fact is disclosed that the entire decrease has taken place in the British trade to foreign countries as contrasted with the *colonial* possessions."[a]

In fact, the above tables may be condensed as follows:

Exports for three months.

	1857.	1858.
To foreign countries	£20,636,473	£14,940,756
To British possessions	8,191,020	8,569,534
Total	£28,827,493	£23,510,290

Yet the conclusion arrived at by *The Economist* seems a fallacy. According to the condensed statement there would appear to have taken place a reduction in the trade to foreign countries to the amount of £5,695,717, simultaneously with an increase of £378,514 in the colonial trade. However, if we deduct the increase in the trade of British smuggling places such as Gibraltar, Malta, Hong Kong, and of mere depots for foreign countries, such as Singapore, a decrease in the aggregate colonial trade becomes evident; and if we deduct India, the decrease appears very considerable. Of the decrease in the trade to foreign countries, the main percentage falls upon the following countries:

[a] Here and below "The Board of Trade Tables", *The Economist*, No. 770, May 29, 1858 (italics by Marx).—*Ed.*

	1857.	1858.
United States	£6,231,501	£2,565,566
Brazil	1,292,325	826,583
Hanse Towns	2,318,260	1,645,410
France	1,631,672	1,035,096
Holland	1,305,606	975,428

The accounts relating to navigation show a slight increase in the number as well as tunnage of the British vessels entered inward, but a decrease in the number and tunnage of the vessels cleared outward. Of foreign countries, the navigation of the United States continues to maintain the first rank. The following figures show the movement of their vessels to and from the British ports:

	1856.		1857.		1858.	
	Ships.	Tunnage.	Ships.	Tunnage.	Ships.	Tunnage.
Entered Inward.						
United States...	382	383,255	367	366,407	366	366,650
Cleared Outward.						
United States...	414	395,102	440	427,221	343	321,015

According to the same accounts, Norway, Denmark and Russia seem the countries upon whose navigation the commercial crisis told with the most disastrous effect.

Written on June 8, 1858

First published unsigned in the *New-York Daily Tribune*, No. 5356, June 21, 1858

Reproduced from the newspaper

Karl Marx

[POLITICAL PARTIES IN ENGLAND.— SITUATION IN EUROPE]

England offers at this moment the curious spectacle of dissolution appearing at the summit of the State, while at the base of society all seems immovable. There is no audible agitation among the masses, but there is a visible change among their rulers. Shall we believe that the upper strata are liquefying, while the lower remain in the same dull solidity? We are, of course, not alluding to the cynical attempts of Palmerston and his compeers to "loot" the Treasury.[563] The battles between the exiles and their proscribers form no more a standing feature in the medieval annals of Italian towns than the conflicts between the Ins and Outs in the Parliamentary history of England. But now we have the Tory leader in the House of Commons winding up a speech with the ominous declaration that

> "There is one bond of union between us [the Radicals and the Tories] in this House and in this country; and that is, that we shall not any longer be the tools or the victims of an obsolete oligarchy!"[a]

There is the House of Lords passing one point of the People's Charter—the abolition of the property qualification for the members of the Commons[564]; there is Lord Grey, the descendant of the Whig Reformer,[b] warning his noble compeers that they are drifting to "a total revolution in the whole system of their Government and in the character of their Constitution;"[c] there is

[a] B. Disraeli's speech in the House of Commons on May 31, 1858, *The Times*, No. 23008, June 1, 1858.—*Ed.*

[b] Charles Grey.—*Ed.*

[c] H. G. Grey's speech in the House of Lords on June 10, 1858, *The Times*, No. 23017, June 11, 1858.—*Ed.*

the Duke of Rutland frightened out of his senses by the vista of having to swallow "the whole hog of the five points of the Charter, and something more."[a] And then *The London Times* in sinister accents one day cautions the middle classes that Disraeli and Bulwer wish them no good, and, in order to master them, may ally themselves with the vile multitude[b]; and then, the very next day, it warns the landed aristocracy that they are to be swamped by the shopocracy, to be enthroned through Locke King's bill, which has just passed through its second reading in the Lower House, for the extension of the elective franchise to the £10 occupiers in the counties.[c]

The fact is that the two ruling oligarchic parties of England were long ago transformed into mere factions, without any distinctive principles. Having in vain tried first a coalition and then a dictatorship, they are now arrived at the point where each of them can only think of obtaining a respite of life by betraying their common interest into the hands of their common foe, the radical middle-class party, who are powerfully represented in the Commons by John Bright. Till now, the Tories have been aristocrats ruling in the name of the aristocracy, and the Whigs aristocrats ruling in the name of the middle class; but the middle class having assumed to rule in their own name, the business of the Whigs is gone. In order to keep the Whigs out of office, the Tories will yield to the encroachments of the middle-class party until they have worried out Whig patience and convinced these oligarchs that, in order to save the interests of their order, they must merge in the conservative ranks and forsake their traditionary pretensions to represent the liberal interest or form a power of their own. Absorption of the Whig faction into the Tory faction, and their common metamorphosis into the party of the aristocracy, as opposed to the new middle-class party, acting under its own chiefs, under its own banners, with its own watchwords—such is the consummation we are now witnessing in England.

If we consider this state of internal affairs in England, and couple with it the fact that the Indian war will continue to drain her of men and money, we may feel sure that she will be disabled

---

[a] Ch. C. J. Rutland's speech in the House of Lords on June 10, 1858, *The Times*, No. 23017, June 11, 1858.—*Ed.*

[b] "In those sad days of Ireland's history...," *The Times*, No. 23016, June 10, 1858.—*Ed.*

[c] "There was a time within the memory...", *The Times*, No. 23017, June 11, 1858.—*Ed.*

from clogging, as she did in 1848, the European Revolution that draws visibly nearer. There is another great power which, ten years ago, most powerfully checked the revolutionary current. We mean Russia. This time, combustible matter has accumulated under her own feet, which a strong blast from the West may suddenly set on fire. The symptoms of a servile war are so visible in the interior of Russia, that the Provincial Governors feel themselves unable otherwise to account for the unwonted fermentation than by charging Austria with propagating through secret emissaries Socialist and revolutionary doctrines all over the land. Think only of Austria being not only suspected but publicly accused of acting as the emissary of revolution! The Galician massacres[565] have, indeed, fully proved to the world that the Cabinet of Vienna knows, in case of need, how to teach serfs a socialism of its own. Austria, however, angrily retorts the charge, by the statement that her eastern provinces are overrun and poisoned through Russian Panslavist agents, while her Italian subjects are wrought upon by the combined intrigues of Bonaparte and the Czar.[a] Prussia, finally, is keenly awake to the dangers of the situation; but she is bound hand and foot, and interdicted from moving in any direction. The royal power is, in fact, broken by the insanity of the King,[b] and the want of full powers on the part of the Regent.[c] The strife between the camarilla of the King, who refuses to resign, and the camarilla of the Prince, who dares not to reign, has opened a floodgate for the popular torrent.

Everything, then, depends upon France, and there the commercial and agricultural distress, financial *coup d'état,* and the substitution of the rule *of* the army for rule *by* the army, are hastening the explosion. Even the French press at length admits that all hopes of a return of prosperity must be abandoned for the present. "We believe that it would be foolish to tantalize the public with the chimerical hope of an immediate reaction," says the *Constitutionnel.*[d] "The stagnation continues, and in spite of the existing favorable elements, we must not expect any immediate modification," says the *Patrie.*

The *Union* and the *Univers* re-echo these complaints.[e] "It is

---

[a] Alexander II.—*Ed.*

[b] Frederick William IV.—*Ed.*

[c] William, Prince of Prussia.—*Ed.*

[d] "Bulletin hebdomadaire de la Bourse de Paris", *Le Constitutionnel,* No. 158, June 7, 1858.—*Ed.*

[e] "Paris, Monday, June 7, 6 p.m.", *The Times,* No. 23015, June 9, 1858.—*Ed.*

generally admitted that there has not been more commercial distress experienced in Paris since the Revolution of 1848 than at the present moment," says the Paris correspondent of *The London Times*[a]; and the shares of the Crédit Mobilier,[566] have sunk down to something like 550 frs., that is, below the nominal price at which they were sold to the general public. On the other hand, the emptiness of the Imperial exchequer forces Napoleon to insist on his plan of confiscation.[b] "The only thing to be asked is," says a clerical paper appearing at Anjou, "whether or not property is to be respected." Property indeed! The only thing to be asked at this moment, answers Bonaparte, is how to make sure of the army? and he solves this question in his habitual way. The whole army is to be bought anew. He has ordered a general increase of its wages.[c] Meanwhile England is alarmed and Austria in terror. On all hands, war is believed to be imminent. Louis Napoleon has no other means of escaping speedy destruction. The beginning of the end is at hand.

Written on June 11, 1858

First published in the *New-York Daily Tribune*, No. 5359, June 24, 1858 as a leading article; reprinted unsigned in the *New-York Semi-Weekly Tribune*, No. 1365, June 25, 1858 under the title "The European Revolution"

Reproduced from the *New-York Daily Tribune*

[a] *The Times*, No. 23014, June 8, 1858.—*Ed.*

[b] See this volume, pp. 550-52.—*Ed.*

[c] Napoléon III, "Loi relative à la création d'une dotation de l'armée, an rengagement, au remplacement et aux pensions militaires".—*Ed.*

Karl Marx

THE BRITISH GOVERNMENT AND THE SLAVE-TRADE

London, June 18, 1858

In the sitting of the House of Lords on June 17, the question of the slave-trade was introduced by the Bishop of Oxford, who presented a petition against that trade from the Parish of St. Mary in Jamaica.[a] The impression these debates are sure to produce upon every mind not strongly prejudiced is that of great moderation on the part of the present British Government, and its firm purpose of avoiding any pretext of quarrel with the United States. Lord Malmesbury dropped altogether the "right of visit," as far as ships under the American flag are concerned, by the following declaration:

"The United States say that on no account, for no purpose, and upon no suspicion shall a ship carrying the American flag be boarded except by an American ship, unless at the risk of the officer boarding or detaining her. I have not admitted the international law as laid down by the American Minister for Foreign Affairs,[b] until that statement had been approved and fortified by the law officers of the Crown. But having admitted that, I have put it as strong as possible to the American Government that if it is known that the American flag covers every iniquity, every pirate and slaver on earth will carry it and no other; that this must bring disgrace on that honored banner, and that instead of vindicating the honor of the country by an obstinate adherence to their present declaration the contrary result will follow; that the American flag will be prostituted to the worst of purposes. I shall continue to urge that it is necessary in these civilized times, with countless vessels navigating the ocean, that there should be a police on the ocean; that there should be, if not a right by international law, an agreement among nations how far they would go to verify the nationality of vessels, and ascertain their right to bear a particular flag. From the language I have used, from the conversations which I had with the American Minister resident in this country,[c]

[a] *The Times*, No. 23023, June 18, 1858. Speeches by the members of the House of Lords quoted below are to be found in the same issue.—*Ed.*

[b] L. Cass.—*Ed.*

[c] J. M. Dallas.—*Ed.*

and from the observations contained in a very able paper drawn up by Gen. Cass on this subject, I am not without strong hope that some arrangement of this kind may be made with the United States, which, with the orders given to the officers of both countries, may enable us to verify the flags of all countries, without running the risk of offense to the country to which a ship belongs."

On the Opposition benches there was also no attempt made at vindicating the right of visit on the part of Great Britain against the United States, but, as Earl Grey remarked,

"The English had treaties with Spain and other powers for the prevention of the slave-trade, and if they had reasonable grounds for suspecting that a vessel was engaged in this abominable traffic, and that she had for the time made use of the United States flag, that she was not really an American ship at all, they had a right to overhaul her and to search her. If, however, she produced the American papers, even though she be full of slaves, it was their duty to discharge her, and to leave to the United States the disgrace of that iniquitous traffic. He hoped and trusted that the orders to their cruisers were strict in this respect, and that any excess of that discretion which was allowed their officers under the circumstances would meet with proper punishment."

The question then turns exclusively upon the point, and even this point seems abandoned by Lord Malmesbury, whether or not vessels suspected of usurping the American flag may not be called upon to produce their papers. Lord Aberdeen directly denied that any controversy could arise out of such a practice, since the instructions under which the British officers were to proceed on such an occurrence—instructions drawn up by Dr. Lushington and Sir G. Cockburn—had been communicated at the time to the American Government and acquiesced in by Mr. Webster, on the part of that Government.[a] If, therefore, there had been no change in these instructions, and if the officers had acted within their limits, "the American Government could have no ground of complaint." There seemed, indeed, a strong suspicion hovering in the minds of the hereditary wisdom, that Palmerston had played one of his usual tricks by effecting some arbitrary change in the orders issued to the British cruisers. It is known that Palmerston, while boasting of his zeal in the suppression of the slave-trade, had, during the eleven years of his administration of foreign affairs, ending in 1841, broken up all the existing slave-trade treaties, had ordered acts which the British law authorities pronounced criminal, and which actually subjected one of his instruments to legal procedure and placed a slave-dealer under the protection of the law of England against its own Government.

[a] "Annex (B) to the treaty between Great Britain, Austria...; signed at London, the Twentieth Day of December in the Year One Thousand Eight Hundred and Forty-One. Instructions to Cruisers."—*Ed.*

He chose the slave-trade as his field of battle, and converted it into a mere instrument of provoking quarrels between England and other States. Before leaving office in 1841 he had given instructions[a] which, according to the words of Sir Robert Peel, "must have led, had they not been countermanded, to a collision with the United States." In *his own words,* he had enjoined the naval officers "to have no very nice regard to the law of nations." Lord Malmesbury, although in very reserved language, intimated that "by sending the British squadrons to the Cuban waters, instead of leaving them on the coast of Africa," Palmerston removed them from a station where, before the outbreak of the Russian war, they had almost succeeded in extinguishing the slave-trade, to a place where they could be good for little else than picking up a quarrel with the United States. Lord Woodhouse, Palmerston's own late Embassador to the Court of St. Petersburg, concurring in this view of the case, remarked that,

"No matter what instructions had been given, if the Government gave authority to the British vessels to go in such numbers into the American waters, a difference would sooner or later arise between us and the United States."

Yet, whatever may have been Palmerston's secret intentions, it is evident that they are baffled by the Tory Government in 1858, as they had been in 1842, and that the war cry so lustily raised in the Congress and in the press is doomed to result in "much ado about nothing."

As to the question of the slave-trade itself, Spain was denounced by the Bishop of Oxford, as well as Lord Brougham, as the main stay of that nefarious traffic. Both of them called upon the British Government to force, by every means in its power, that country into a course of policy consonant to existing treaties. As early as 1814 a general treaty was entered into between Great Britain and Spain, by which the latter passed an unequivocal condemnation of the slave-trade. In 1817 a specific treaty was concluded, by which Spain fixed the abolition of the slave-trade, on the part of her own subjects, for the year 1820, and, by way of compensation for the losses her subjects might suffer by carrying out the contract, received an indemnity of £400,000. The money was pocketed, but no equivalent was tendered for it. In 1835 a new treaty[b] was entered into, by which Spain bound herself formally to bring in a

[a] "Lettre adressée le 18 mai 1841, par le département des affaires étrangères aux lords de l'amirauté, au sujet de la poursuite des bâtimens américains..."—*Ed.*

[b] "Treaty between His Majesty and the Queen Regent of Spain ... signed in Madrid, June 28, 1835."—*Ed.*

sufficiently stringent penal law to make it impossible for her subjects to continue the traffic. The procrastinating Spanish proverb, *"A la mañana,"*[a] was again strictly adhered to. It was only ten years later that the penal law was carried; but, by a singular mischance, the principal clause contended for by England was left out, namely, that of making the slave-trade piracy. In one word, nothing was done, save that the Captain-General of Cuba,[b] the Minister at home,[c] the Camarilla, and, if rumor speaks truth, royal personages themselves, raised a private tax upon the slavers, selling the license of dealing in human flesh and blood at so many doubloons per head.

"Spain," said the Bishop of Oxford, "had not the excuse that this traffic was a system which her Government was not strong enough to put down, because Gen. Valdez had shown that such a plea could not be urged with any show of truth. On his arrival in the island he called together the principal contractors, and, giving them six months' time to close all their transactions in the slave-trade, told them that he was determined to put it down at the end of that period. What was the result? In 1840, the year previous to the administration of Gen. Valdez, the number of ships which came to Cuba from the coast of Africa with slaves was 56. In 1842, while Gen. Valdez was Captain-General, the number was only 3. In 1840 no less than 14,470 slaves were landed at the island; in 1842 the number was 3,100."

Now what shall England do with Spain? Repeat her protests, multiply her dispatches, renew her negotiations? Lord Malmesbury himself states that they could cover all the waters from the Spanish coast to Cuba with the documents vainly exchanged between the two Governments. Or shall England enforce her claims, sanctioned by so many treaties? Here it is that the shoe pinches. In steps the sinister figure of the "august ally," now the acknowledged guardian angel of the slave-trade. The third Bonaparte, the patron of Slavery in all its forms, forbids England to act up to her convictions and her treaties. Lord Malmesbury, it is known, is strongly suspected of an undue intimacy with the hero of Satory. Nevertheless, he denounced him in plain terms as the general slave-dealer of Europe—as the man who had revived the infamous traffic in its worst features under the pretext of "free emigration" of the blacks to the French colonies. Earl Grey completed this denunciation by stating that "wars had been undertaken in Africa for the purpose of making captives, who were to be sold to the agents of the French Government." The

---

[a] "Leave it till tomorrow."—*Ed.*

[b] Leopoldo O'Donnel y Jorris.—*Ed.*

[c] P. J. Pidal.—*Ed.*

Earl of Clarendon added that "both Spain and France were rivals in the African market, offering a certain sum per man; and there was not the least difference in the treatment of these negroes, whether they were conveyed to Cuba or to a French colony."

Such, then, is the glorious position England finds herself in by having lent her help to that man in overthrowing the Republic. The second Republic, like the first one, had abolished Slavery. Bonaparte, who acquired his power solely by truckling to the meanest passions of men, is unable to prolong it save by buying day by day new accomplices. Thus he has not only restored Slavery, but has bought the planters by the renewal of the slave-trade. Everything degrading the conscience of the nation, is a new lease of power granted to him. To convert France into a slave-trading nation would be the surest means of enslaving France, who, when herself, had the boldness of proclaiming in the face of the world: Let the colonies perish, but let principles live! One thing at least has been accomplished by Bonaparte. The slave-trade has become a battle-cry between the Imperialist and the Republican camps. If the French Republic be restored to-day, to-morrow Spain will be *forced* to abandon the infamous traffic.

Written on June 18, 1858

First published in the *New-York Daily Tribune,* No. 5366, July 2, 1858; reprinted unsigned in the *New-York Semi-Weekly Tribune,* No. 1367, July 2, 1858

Reproduced from the *New-York Daily Tribune*

Karl Marx

[TAXATION IN INDIA]

According to the London journals, Indian stock and railway securities have of late been distinguished by a downward movement in that market, which is far from testifying to the genuineness of the sanguine convictions which John Bull likes to exhibit in regard to the state of the Indian guerrilla war; and which, at all events, indicates a stubborn distrust in the elasticity of Indian financial resources. As to the latter, two opposite views are propounded. On the one hand, it is affirmed that taxes in India are onerous and oppressive beyond those of any country in the world; that as a rule throughout most of the presidencies, and through those presidencies most where they have been longest under British rule, the cultivators, that is, the great body of the people of India, are in a condition of unmitigated impoverishment and dejection; that, consequently, Indian revenues have been stretched to their utmost possible limit, and Indian finances are therefore past recovery. A rather discomfortable opinion this at a period when, according to Mr. Gladstone,[a] for some years to come, the extraordinary Indian expenditure alone will annually amount to about £20,000,000 sterling. On the other hand, it is asserted—the asseveration being made good by an array of statistical illustrations—that India is the least taxed country in the world; that, if expenditure is going on increasing, revenue may be increased too; and that it is an utter fallacy to imagine that the Indian people will not bear any new taxes. Mr. Bright, who may be considered the most arduous and influential representative of

[a] W. E. Gladstone's speech in the House of Commons on June 7, 1858, *The Times*, No. 23014, June 8, 1858.—*Ed.*

the "discomfortable" doctrine, made, on the occasion of the second reading of the new Government of India bill,[567] the following statement:

"The Indian Government had cost more to govern India than it was possible to extort from the population of India, although the Government had been by no means scrupulous either as to the taxes imposed, or as to the mode in which they had been levied. [...] It cost more than £30,000,000 to govern India, for that was the gross revenue, and there was always a deficit, which had to be made up by loans borrowed at a high rate of interest. [...] The Indian debt now amounted to £60,000,000, and was increasing; while the credit of the Government was falling, partly because they had not treated their creditors very honorably on one or two occasions, and now on account of the calamities which had recently happened in India. [...] He had alluded to the gross revenue; but as that included the opium revenue, which was hardly a tax upon the people of India, he would take the taxation which really pressed upon them at £25,000,000. Now, let not this £25,000,000 be compared with the £60,000,000 that was raised in this country. Let the House recollect that in India it was possible to purchase twelve days' labor for the same amount of gold or silver that would be obtained in payment for one in England. This £25,000,000 expended in the purchase of labor in India would buy as much as an outlay of £300,000,000 would procure in England. [...] He might be asked how much was the labor of an Indian worth? Well, if the labor of an Indian was only worth 2d. a day, it was clear that we could not expect him to pay as much taxation as if it was worth 2s. [...] We had 30,000,000 of population in Great Britain and Ireland; in India there were 150,000,000 inhabitants. [...] We raised here £60,000,000 sterling of taxes; in India, reckoning by the days' labor of the people of India, we raised £300,000,000 of revenue, or five times a greater revenue than was collected at home. Looking at the fact that the population of India was five times greater than that of the British Empire, a man might say that the taxation per head in India and England was about the same, and that therefore there was no great hardship inflicted. But in England there was an incalculable power of machinery and steam, of means of transit, and of everything that capital and human invention could bring to aid the industry of a people. In India there was nothing of the kind. They had scarcely a decent road throughout India."[a]

Now, it must be admitted that there is something wrong in this method of comparing Indian taxes with British taxes. There is on the one side the Indian population, five times as great as the British one, and there is on the other side the Indian taxation amounting to half the British. But, then, Mr. Bright says, Indian labor is an equivalent for about one-twelfth only of British labor. Consequently £30,000,000 of taxes in India would represent £300,000,000 of taxes in Great Britain, instead of the £60,000,000 actually there raised. What then is the conclusion he ought to have arrived at? That the people of India in regard to their numerical strength pay the *same* taxation as the people in Great Britain, if allowance is made for the comparative poverty of the people in

[a] J. Bright's speech in the House of Commons on June 24, 1858, *The Times*, No. 23029, June 25, 1858.—*Ed.*

India, and £30,000,000 is supposed to weigh as heavily upon 150,000,000 Indians as £60,000,000 upon 30,000,000 Britons. Such being his supposition, it is certainly fallacious to turn round and say that a poor people cannot pay so much as a rich one, because the comparative poverty of the Indian people has already been taken into account in making out the statement that the Indian pays as much as the Briton. There might, in fact, another question be raised. It might be asked, whether a man who earns say 12 cents a day can be fairly expected to pay 1 cent with the same ease with which another, earning $12 a day, pays $1? Both would relatively contribute the same aliquot part of their income, but still the tax might bear in quite different proportions upon their respective necessities. Yet, Mr. Bright has not yet put the question in these terms, and, if he had, the comparison between the burden of taxation, borne by the British wages' laborer on the one hand, and the British capitalist on the other, would perhaps have struck nearer home than the comparison between Indian and British taxation. Moreover, he admits himself that from the £30,000,000 of Indian taxes, the £5,000,000 constituting the opium revenue must be subtracted, since this is, properly speaking, no tax pressing upon the Indian people, but rather an export duty charged upon Chinese consumption. Then we are reminded by the apologists of the Anglo-Indian Administration that £16,000,000 of income is derived from the land revenue, or rent, which from times immemorial has belonged to the State in its capacity as supreme landlord, never constituted part of the private fortune of the cultivator, and does, in fact, no more enter into taxation, properly so called, than the rent paid by the British farmers to the British aristocracy can be said to enter British taxation. Indian taxation, according to this point of view, would stand thus:

Aggregate sum raised	£30,000,000
Deduct for opium revenue	5,000,000
Deduct for rent of land	16,000,000
Taxation proper	£9,000,000

Of this £9,000,000, again, it must be admitted that some important items, such as the post-office, the stamp duties, and the customs duties, bear in a very minute proportion on the mass of the people. Accordingly, Mr. Hendriks, in a paper recently laid before the British Statistical Society on the Finances of India,[a] tries

[a] *The Economist,* No. 772, June 12, 1858.—*Ed.*

to prove, from Parliamentary and other official documents, that of the total revenue paid by the people of India, not more than one-fifth is at present raised by taxation, i. e., from the real income of the people; that in Bengal 27 per cent only, in the Punjaub 23 per cent only, in Madras 21 per cent only, in the North-West Provinces 17 per cent only, and in Bombay 16 per cent only of the total revenue is derived from taxation proper.

The following comparative view of the average amount of taxation derived from each inhabitant of India and the United Kingdom, during the years 1855-56, is abstracted from Mr. Hendriks's statement:

Bengal, per head, Revenue	£0	5	0...Taxation proper.	£0	1	4
North-West Provinces		3	5...Taxation proper.		0	7
Madras		4	7...Taxation proper.		1	0
Bombay		8	3...Taxation proper.		1	4
Punjaub		3	3...Taxation proper.		0	9
United Kingdom		-	-...Taxation proper.	1	10	0

For a different year the following estimate of the average paid by each individual to the national revenue is made by Gen. Briggs[a]:

In England, 1852	£ 1	19	4
In France	1	12	0
In Prussia	0	19	3
In India, 1854	0	3	8 1/2

From these statements it is inferred by the apologists of the British Administration that there is not a single country in Europe, where, even if the comparative poverty of India is taken into account, the people are so lightly taxed. Thus it seems that not only opinions with respect to Indian taxation are conflicting, but that the facts from which they purport to be drawn are themselves contradictory. On the one hand, we must admit the nominal amount of Indian taxation to be relatively small; but on the other, we might heap evidence upon evidence from Parliamentary documents, as well as from the writings of the greatest authorities on Indian affairs, all proving beyond doubt that this apparently light taxation crushes the mass of the Indian people to the dust, and that its exaction necessitates a resort to such infamies as torture, for instance. But is any other proof wanted beyond the constant and rapid increase of the Indian debt and the accumula-

---

[a] *The Economist*, No. 772, June 12, 1858.—*Ed.*

tion of Indian deficits? It will certainly not be contended that the Indian Government prefers increasing debts and deficits because it shrinks from touching too roughly upon the resources of the people. It embarks in debt, because it sees no other way to make both ends meet. In 1805 the Indian debt amounted to £25,626,631[a]; in 1829 it reached about £34,000,000[b]; in 1850 £47,151,018[c]; and at present it amounts to about £60,000,000. By the by, we leave out of the count the East Indian debt contracted in England, which is also chargeable upon the East Indian revenue.

The annual deficit, which in 1805 amounted to about two and a half millions, had, under Lord Dalhousie's administration, reached the average of five millions. Mr. George Campbell of the Bengal Civil Service, and of a mind strongly biased in favor of the Anglo-Indian administration, was obliged to avow, in 1852, that:

> "Although no Oriental conquerors have ever obtained so complete an ascendency, so quiet, universal and undisputed possession of India as we have, yet all have enriched themselves from the revenues of the country, and many have out of their abundance laid out considerable sums on works of public improvements. ...From doing this we are debarred. ...The quantity of the whole burden is by no means diminished" (under the English rule), *"yet we have no surplus."*[d]

In estimating the burden of taxation, its nominal amount must not fall heavier into the balance than the method of raising it and the manner of employing it. The former is detestable in India, and in the branch of the land-tax, for instance, wastes perhaps more produce than it gets. As to the application of the taxes, it will suffice to say that no part of them is returned to the people in works of public utility, more indispensable in Asiatic countries than anywhere else, and that, as Mr. Bright justly remarked, nowhere so extravagant is a provision made for the governing class itself.[e]

Written on June 29, 1858

First published in the *New-York Daily Tribune*, No. 5383, July 23, 1858 as a leading article

Reproduced from the newspaper

---

[a] G. Campbell, *Modern India: a Sketch of the System of Civil Government*, p. 412.—*Ed.*

[b] Ibid., p. 414.—*Ed.*

[c] Ibid., p. 417.—*Ed.*

[d] Ibid., p. 406. Italics by Marx.—*Ed.*

[e] J. Bright's speech in the House of Commons on June 24, 1858, *The Times*, No. 23029, June 25, 1858.—*Ed.*

Frederick Engels

THE INDIAN ARMY[568]

The war in India is gradually passing into that stage of desultory guerrilla warfare, to which, more than once, we have pointed[a] as its next impending and most dangerous phase of development. The insurgent armies, after their successive defeats in pitched battles, and in the defense of towns and entrenched camps, gradually dissolve into smaller bodies of from two to six or eight thousand men, acting, to a certain degree, independently of each other, but always ready to unite for a short expedition against any British detachment which may be surprised singly. The abandonment of Bareilly without a blow, after having drawn the active field force of Sir C. Campbell some eighty miles away from Lucknow, was the turning point, in this respect, for the main army of the insurgents; the abandonment of Calpee had the same significance for the second great body of natives. In either case, the last defensible central base of operations was given up, and the warfare of an army thereby becoming impossible, the insurgents made eccentric retreats by separating into smaller bodies. These movable columns require no large town for a central base of operations. They can find means of existence, of re-equipment, and of recruitment in the various districts in which they move; and a small town or a large village as a center of reorganization may be as valuable to each of them as Delhi, Lucknow, or Calpee to the larger armies. By this change, the war loses much of its interest; the movements of the various columns of insurgents cannot be followed up in detail and appear confused in the accounts; the operations of the British commanders, to a great

---

[a] See this volume, pp. 441, 532, 553-55.—*Ed.*

extent, escape criticism, from the unavoidable obscurity enveloping the premises on which they are based; success or failure remain the only criterion, and they are certainly of all the most deceitful.

This uncertainty respecting the movements of the natives is already very great. After the taking of Lucknow, they retreated eccentrically—some south-east, some north-east, some north-west. The latter were the stronger body, and were followed by Campbell into Rohilcund. They had concentrated and re-formed at Bareilly; but when the British came up, they abandoned the place without resistance, and again retreated in different directions. Particulars of these different lines of retreat are not known. We only know that a portion went toward the hills on the frontiers of Nepaul, while one or more columns appear to have marched in the opposite direction, toward the Ganges and the Doab (the country between the Ganges and the Jumna). No sooner, however, had Campbell occupied Bareilly, than the insurgents, who had retreated in an easterly direction, effected a junction with some bodies on the Oude frontier and fell upon Shahjehanpore, where a small British garrison had been left; while further insurgent columns were hastening in that direction. Fortunately for the garrison, Brigadier Jones arrived with re-enforcements as early as the 11th of May, and defeated the natives; but they, too, were re-enforced by the columns concentrating on Shahjehanpore, and again invested the town on the 15th. On this day, Campbell, leaving a garrison in Bareilly, marched to its relief; but it was not before the 24th of May that he attacked them and drove them back, the various columns of insurgents which had cooperated in this maneuver again dispersing in different directions.

While Campbell was thus engaged on the frontiers of Rohilcund, Gen. Hope Grant marched his troops backward and forward in the South of Oude, without any result, except losses to his own force by fatigue under an Indian Summer's sun. The insurgents were too quick for him. They were everywhere but where he happened to look for them, and when he expected to find them in front, they had long since again gained his rear. Lower down the Ganges, Gen. Lugard was occupied with a chase after a similar shadow in the district between Dinapore, Jugdespore and Buxar. The natives kept him constantly on the move, and, after drawing him away from Jugdespore, all at once fell upon the garrison of that place. Lugard returned, and a telegram reports his having gained a victory on the 26th.[a] The identity of

[a] "Alexandria, June 23", "From the India-House", *The Times*, No. 23032, June 29, 1858.—*Ed.*

the tactics of these insurgents with those of the Oude and Rohilcund columns is evident. The victory gained by Lugard will, however, scarcely be of much importance. Such bands can afford to be beaten a good many times before they become demoralized and weak.

Thus, by the middle of May, the whole insurgent force of Northern India had given up warfare on a large scale, with the exception of the army of Calpee. This force, in a comparatively short time, had organized in that town a complete center of operations; they had provisions, powder and other stores in profusion, plenty of guns, and even founderies and musket manufactories. Though within 25 miles of Cawnpore, Campbell had left them unmolested; he merely observed them by a force on the Doab or western side of the Jumna. Generals Rose and Whitlock had been on the march to Calpee for a long while; at last Rose arrived, and defeated the insurgents in a series of engagements in front of Calpee. The observing force on the other side of the Jumna, in the mean time, had shelled the town and fort, and suddenly the insurgents evacuated both, breaking up this their last large army into independent columns. The roads taken by them are not at all clear, from the accounts received; we only know that some have gone into the Doab, and others toward Gwalior.[a]

Thus the whole district from the Himalaya to the Bihar and Vindhya mountains, and from Gwalior and Delhi to Joruckpore and Dinapore, is swarming with active insurgent bands, organized to a certain degree by the experience of a twelve months war, and encouraged, amid a number of defeats, by the indecisive character of each, and by the small advantages gained by the British. It is true, all their strongholds and centers of operations have been taken from them; the greater portion of their stores and artillery are lost; the important towns are all in the hands of their enemies. But on the other hand, the British, in all this vast district, hold nothing but the towns, and of the open country, nothing but the spot where their movable columns happen to stand; they are compelled to chase their nimble enemies without any hope of attaining them; and they are under the necessity of entering upon this harassing mode of warfare at the very deadliest season of the year. The native Indian can stand the mid-day heat of his Summer with comparative comfort, while mere exposure to the rays of the sun is almost certain death to the European; he can march forty

[a] Here and below "Bombay, June 4", *The Times*, No. 23037, July 5, 1858.—*Ed.*

miles in such a season, where ten break down his northern opponent; to him even the hot rains and swampy jungles are comparatively innocuous, while dysentery, cholera, and ague follow every exertion made by Europeans in the rainy season or in swampy neighborhoods. We are without detailed accounts of the sanitary condition of the British army; but from the comparative numbers of those struck by the sun and those hit by the enemy in Gen. Rose's army, from the report that the garrison of Lucknow is sickly, that the 38th regiment arrived last Autumn above 1,000 strong, now scarcely numbers 550, and from other indications we may draw the conclusion that the Summer's heat, during April and May, has done its work among the newly-imported men and lads who have replaced the bronzed old Indian soldiers of last year's campaign. With the men Campbell has, he cannot undertake the forced marches of Havelock nor a siege during the rainy season like that of Delhi. And although the British Government are again sending off strong re-enforcements, it is doubtful whether they will be sufficient to replace the wear and tear of this Summer's campaign against an enemy who declines to fight the British except on terms most favorable to himself.

The insurgent warfare now begins to take the character of that of the Bedouins of Algeria against the French[569]; with the difference that the Hindoos are far from being so fanatical, and that they are not a nation of horsemen. This latter is important in a flat country of immense extent. There are plenty of Mohammedans among them who would make good irregular cavalry; still the principal cavalry nations of India have not joined the insurrection so far. The strength of their army is in the infantry, and that arm being unfit to meet the English in the field, becomes a drag in guerrilla warfare in the plain; for in such a country the sinew of desultory warfare is irregular cavalry. How far this want may be remedied during the compulsory holiday the English will have to take during the rains, we shall see. This holiday will, altogether, give the natives an opportunity of reorganizing and recruiting their forces. Beside the organization of cavalry, there are two more points of importance. As soon as the cold weather sets in, guerrilla warfare alone will not do. Centers of operation, stores, artillery, intrenched camps or towns, are required to keep the British busy until the cold season is over; otherwise the guerrilla warfare might be extinguished before the next Summer gives it fresh life. Gwalior appears to be, among others, a favorable point, if the insurgents have really got hold of it. Secondly, the fate of the insurrection is dependent upon its being able to expand. If the dispersed columns cannot manage to cross from Rohilcund into Rajpootana and the Mahratta country; if the movement remains confined to the northern central district, then, no doubt, the next Winter will suffice to disperse the bands, and to turn them into dacoits, which will soon be more hateful to the inhabitants than even the palefaced invaders.

Written on July 6, 1858

First published in the *New-York Daily Tribune,* No. 5381, July 21, 1858 as a leading article

Reproduced from the newspaper

Karl Marx

THE INDIAN BILL[570]

The latest India bill has passed through its third reading in the House of Commons,[a] and since the Lords swayed by Derby's influence, are not likely to show fight, the doom of the East India Company appears to be sealed. They do not die like heroes, it must be confessed; but they have bartered away their power, as they crept into it, bit by bit, in a business-like way. In fact, their whole history is one of buying and selling. They commenced by buying sovereignty, and they have ended by selling it. *They have fallen,* not in a pitched battle, but under the hammer of the auctioneer, into the hands of the highest bidder. In 1693 they procured from the Crown a charter for twenty-one years by paying large sums to the Duke of Leeds and other public officers. In 1767 they prolonged their tenure of power for two years by the promise of annually paying £400,000 into the Imperial exchequer. In 1769 they struck a similar bargain for five years; but soon after, in return for the Exchequer's foregoing the stipulated annual payment and lending them £1,400,000 at 4 per cent, they alienated some parcels of sovereignty, leaving to Parliament in the first instance the nomination of the Governor-General and four Councilors, altogether surrendering to the Crown the appointment of the Lord Chief Justice and his three Judges, and agreeing to the conversion of the Court of Proprietors from a democratic into an oligarchic body.[571] In 1858, after having solemnly pledged themselves to the Court of Proprietors to resist by all constitutional "means" the transfer to the Crown of the governing powers of the

---

[a] See *The Times,* No. 23036, July 3, 1858.—*Ed.*

East India Company,[a] they have accepted that principle, and agreed to a bill penal as regards the Company, but securing emolument and place to its principal Directors. If the death of a hero, as Schiller says, resembles the setting of the sun,[b] the exit of the East India Company bears more likeness to the compromise effected by a bankrupt with his creditors.

By this bill the principal functions of administration are intrusted to a Secretary of State in Council,[572] just as at Calcutta the Governor-General in Council manages affairs. But both these functionaries—the Secretary of State in England and the Governor-General in India—are alike authorized to disregard the advice of their assessors and to act upon their own judgment. The new bill also invests the Secretary of State with all the powers at present exercised by the President of the Board of Control, through the agency of the Secret Committee—the power, that is, in urgent cases, of dispatching orders to India without stopping to ask the advice of his Council. In constituting that Council it has been found necessary, after all, to resort to the East India Company as the only practicable source of appointments to it other than nominations by the Crown. The elective members of the Council are to be elected by the Directors of the East India Company from among their own number.

Thus, after all, the name of the East India Company is to outlive its substance. At the last hour it was confessed by the Derby Cabinet that their bill contains no clause abolishing the East India Company, as represented by a Court of Directors, but that it becomes reduced to its ancient character of a company of stockholders, distributing the dividends guaranteed by different acts of legislation.[c] Pitt's bill of 1784 virtually subjected their government to the sway of the Cabinet under the name of the Board of Control. The act of 1813 stripped them of their monopoly of commerce, save the trade with China. The act of 1834 destroyed their commercial character altogether, and the act of 1854 annihilated their last remnant of power, still leaving them in possession of the Indian administration. By the rotation of history the East India Company, converted in 1612 into a joint-stock company, is again clothed in its primitive garb, only that it represents now a trading partnership without trade, and a

---

[a] *The Times*, No. 22896, January 21, 1858.—*Ed.*

[b] Schiller, *Die Räuber*, Act III, Scene II.—*Ed.*

[c] H. Cairns' speech in the House of Commons on July 8, 1858, *The Times*, No. 23041, July 9, 1858.—*Ed.*

joint-stock company which has no funds to administer, but only fixed dividends to draw.

The history of the Indian bill is marked by greater dramatic changes than any other act of modern Parliamentary legislation. When the Sepoy insurrection broke out, the cry of Indian reform rang through all classes of British society. Popular imagination was heated by the torture reports; the Government interference with the native religion was loudly denounced by Indian general officers and civilians of high standing; the rapacious annexation policy of Lord Dalhousie, the mere tool of Downing street; the fermentation recklessly created in the Asiatic mind by the piratical wars in Persia and China—wars commenced and pursued on Palmerston's private dictation—the weak measures with which he met the outbreak, sailing ships being chosen for transport in preference to steam vessels, and the circuitous navigation around the cape of Good Hope instead of trasportation over the Isthmus of Suez—all these accumulated grievances burst into the cry for Indian Reform—reform of the Company's Indian administration, reform of the Government's Indian policy. Palmerston caught at the popular cry, but resolved upon turning it to his exclusive profit. Because both the Government and the Company had miserably broken down, the Company was to be killed in sacrifice, and the Government to be rendered omnipotent. The power of the Company was to be simply transferred to the dictator of the day, pretending to represent the Crown as against the Parliament, and to represent Parliament as against the Crown, thus absorbing the privileges of the one and the other in his single person. With the Indian army at his back, the Indian treasury at his command, and the Indian patronage in his pocket, Palmerston's position would have become impregnable.

His bill passed triumphantly through the first reading, but his career was cut short by the famous Conspiracy bill,[573] followed by the advent of the Tories to power.

On the very first day of their official reappearance on the Treasury benches, they declared that, out of deference for the decisive will of the Commons, they would forsake their opposition to the transfer from the Company to the Crown of the Indian Government.[a] Lord Ellenborough's legislative abortion seemed to hasten Palmerston's restoration, when Lord John Russell, in order to force the dictator into a compromise, stepped in, and saved the

[a] E. G. Derby's speech in the House of Lords on March 1, 1858, *The Times*, No. 22930, March 2, 1858.—*Ed.*

Government by proposing to proceed with the Indian bill by way of Parliamentary resolution, instead of by a governmental bill.[a] Then Lord Ellenborough's Oude dispatch, his sudden resignation, and the consequent disorganization in the Ministerial camp, were eagerly seized upon by Palmerston. The Tories were again to be planted in the cold shade of opposition, after they had employed their short lease of power in breaking down the opposition of their own party against the confiscation of the East India Company. Yet it is sufficiently known how these fine calculations were baffled. Instead of rising on the ruins of the East India Company, Palmerston has been buried beneath them. During the whole of the Indian debates, the House seemed to indulge the peculiar satisfaction of humiliating the *Civis Romanus*.[574] All his amendments, great and small, were ignominiously lost; allusions of the most unsavory kind, relating to the Afghan war,[575] the Persian war,[576] and the Chinese war,[577] were continually flung at his head; and Mr. Gladstone's clause, withdrawing from the Indian Minister the power of originating wars beyond the boundaries of India,[b] intended as a general vote of censure on Palmerston's past foreign policy, was passed by a crushing majority, despite his furious resistance. But although the man has been thrown overboard, his principle, upon the whole, has been accepted. Although somewhat checked by the obstructive attributes of the Board of Council, which, in fact, is but the well-paid specter of the old Court of Directors, the power of the executive has, by the formal annexation of India, been raised to such a degree that, to counterpoise it, democratic weight must be thrown into the Parliamentary scale.

Written on July 9, 1858

First published in the *New-York Daily Tribune,* No. 5384, July 24, 1858 as a leading article; reprinted in the *New-York Semi-Weekly Tribune,* No. 1374, July 27, 1858

Reproduced from the *New-York Daily Tribune*

[a] J. Russell's speech in the House of Commons on April 12, 1858, *The Times,* No. 22966, April 13, 1858.—*Ed.*

[b] W. E. Gladstone's speech in the House of Commons on July 6, 1858, *The Times,* No. 23039, July 7, 1858.—*Ed.*

Karl Marx

TO THE EDITOR OF THE *NEUE ZEIT*[578]

[London, not later than July 12, 1858]

How a German "man of the people" and "poet" succeeds in combining the Pleasant with the Useful.

Four weeks ago Dr Kinkel inserted the following advertisement in *The Manchester Guardian:*

"**Tour through the English Lakes.** *Reading German Litterature.* A Professor of German at one of the most distinguished educational establishments in this country will read to a Party composed of Ladies and Gentlemen: Schiller's Gedichte, 'Don Carlos', Auerbach's 'Dorfgeschichten' and Hauff's 'Bettlerin vom Pont des Arts'. This Party being a select one, care will be taken to keep it so, and to connect by these means sociable and pleasant intercourse with instructive and entertaining reading. The Party to start from Kendall, Monday, July 5th. Early applications will oblige, as none will be received after June 19th. Address to the Publisher of this paper for Dr. K."[a]

For the edification of such of our German readers who have not completely mastered the English tongue, I append a translation of this concoction which is a curiosity if only by reason of its style.[b]

..."This Party being a select one" (how republican and how grammatical!)... "by these means" (how?)...

If desired, I can provide a cutting of the original advertisement.

Anti-Humbug

First published in *Die Neue Zeit,* London, No. 4, July 17, 1858

Published according to the newspaper

Published in English for the first time

---

[a] Quoted by Marx in English.—*Ed.*

[b] In the original there follows a German rendering with comments in brackets by Marx. Only these have been retained, preceded by the particular words to which they refer.—*Ed.*

Frederick Engels

TRANSPORT OF TROOPS TO INDIA[579]

London, July 27, 1858

At the beginning of the Anglo-Indian war, two curious questions were mooted—the one relating to the respective superiority of steamers or sailing vessels, the other as to the use of the overland route for the transport of troops. The British Government having decided in favor of sailing vessels against steamers, and for the voyage round the Cape of Good Hope against the overland route, the House of Commons, on the motion of Sir De Lacy Evans, ordered, on the 4th of February, 1858, a Committee to be appointed, under the chairmanship of the veteran General, which was to inquire "concerning the measures resorted to."[a] The formation of this Committee was completely altered by the intervening change of Ministry, consequent upon which three Palmerstonians were substituted for Lord Stanley and Sir John Pakington. The report of the Committee proving, on the whole, favorable to the late Administration, Gen. Sir De Lacy Evans had a protest printed and circulated, in which he asserts the conclusion arrived at to be at utter variance with the premises from which it pretended to be drawn, and quite inconsistent with the facts and evidence laid before them. An examination of the evidence itself must oblige all impartial persons to fully concur in this view of the case.

The decisive importance of a short line of communication between an army in the field and its base of communication needs no demonstration. During the American War of Independence[580] the principal obstacle England had to grapple with was a sea line

[a] G. de Lacy Evans' speech in the House of Commons on February 4, 1858, *The Times*, No. 22909, February 5, 1858.—*Ed.*

of 3,000 miles over which she had to convey her troops, stores and re-enforcements. From Great Britain to the mouths of the Indus and Ganges, to Calcutta, Madras, Kurrachee and Bombay, the distance, according to past arrangements, may be reckoned at about 14,000 miles; but the use of steam offered the means of shortening it considerably. Hitherto on all occasions it had been the practice to effect the relief of regiments in India, by this long sea voyage in sailing vessels. This was considered a sufficient reason on the part of the late British Administration, for declaring at the beginning of the Indian troubles, that sailing vessels would still be preferred to steamers for the conveyance of troops. Up to the 10th of July, 1857, of 31 vessels taken up, nearly the whole were sailing ships. Meanwhile, public censure in England and unfavorable news from India effected so much that in the interval from the 10th of July to the 1st of December, among the 59 ships taken up for troops, 29 screw steamers were admitted. Thus a rough test was afforded of the relative qualities of steamers and sailing vessels in accomplishing the transit. According to the return furnished by the Marine Department of the East India Company, giving names of transports and length of passages to the four principal ports of India, the following may be considered the average results as between steamers and sailing vessels.

From England to Calcutta.

	Days.
From August 6 to October 21, 1857, average of steamers, omitting fractions	82
Average of 22 sailing vessels, from June 10 to August 27, 1857	116
Difference in favor of steamers	34

To Madras.

Average of 2 steamers	90
Average of 2 sailing ships	131
Difference in favor of steamers	41

To Bombay.

Average of 5 steamers	76
Average of 9 sailing ships	118
Difference in favor of steamers	42

To Kurrachee.

Average of 3 steamers	91
Average of 10 ships	128
Difference in favor of steamers	37
Average of the whole of the 19 passages by steamers to the four ports of India	83
Average passage of 43 sailing ships	120
Difference between averages of steam and sailing vessels	37

The same official return, dated Feb. 27, 1858, gives the following details:

	Men.
To Calcutta were conveyed by steamers	6,798
By sailing ships	9,489
Total to Calcutta	16,287
To Madras, by steamers	2,089
By sailing ships	985
Total to Madras	3,074
To Bombay, by steamers	3,906
By sailing ships	3,439
Total to Bombay	7,345
To Kurrachee, by steamers	1,351
By sailing ships	2,321
Total to Kurrachee	3,672

It appears, then, from the above that 27 steamers carried to the four ports of disembarkation in India 14,144 men, averaging, therefore, 548 men in each ship; that in 55 sailing ships were conveyed 16,234 men, averaging 289 men in each. Now, by the same official statement of averages, it appears that the 14,144 men conveyed in steamers arrived at their respective places of destination on an average of 37 days sooner than the 16,234 men embarked on sailing ships. On the part of the British Admiralty and the other ministerial departments no arguments were adduced in favor of the traditionary transport but precedent and routine, both dating from an epoch when steam navigation was utterly unknown. Lord Palmerston's principal plea, however, for the delay was expense, the cost of steamers in most of the above cases amounting to perhaps treble that of sailing ships. Apart from the fact that this great enhancement of charge for steamers must have gradually diminished after the first unusual demand, and that in so vital an emergency expense ought not to be admitted as an element of calculation, it is evident that the increased cost of transport would have been more than compensated for by the lessened chances of the insurrection.

Still more important than the question of superiority as between steamers and sailing vessels, seems the controversy respecting the voyage round the Cape on the one hand and the overland route on the other; Lord Palmerston affirming the general impracticability of the latter route. A controversy in regard to it between his Board of Control and the East India Directors, appears to have commenced cotemporaneously with the first information of the Indian revolt reaching England. The question had, in fact, been solved as long ago as the beginning of this century. In the year 1801, when there were no steam navigation company's agents to aid the military arrangements, and when no railway existed, a large force under Sir David Baird proceeded from India and landed at Kosseir in May and June; crossed in nine days the desert of Kherie,[a] on the Nile; proceeded down that river, garrisoned Alexandria, and in the following year, 1802, several regiments returned to India by Suez and the Red Sea, in the month of June. That force, amounting to 5,000 men, consisted of a troop of horse-artillery, six guns and small arms, ammunition, camp equipage, baggage, and 126 chests of treasure. The troops generally were very healthy. The march across the Suez Desert, from the lake of St. Pilgrims,[b] near Grand Cairo to Suez, was performed in four days with the greatest ease, marching by night and encamping during the day. In June the ships proceeded to India, the wind at that season blowing down the Red Sea. They made a very quick passage. Again, during the late Russian war,[c] in the summer of 1854, the 10th and 11th regiments of Dragoons (1,400 horses, 1,600 men) arrived in Egypt from India, and were forwarded thence to the Crimea. These corps, though their transfer took place during the hot months, or monsoon, and though they had to remain some time in Egypt, are known to have

[a] Wadi Karim.—*Ed.*
[b] Now non-existent.—*Ed.*
[c] The Crimean war, 1853-56.—*Ed.*

been remarkably healthy and efficient, and to have continued so throughout their Crimean service. In the last instance there is the experience of the actual Indian war. After the waste of nearly four months, some thousand troops were dispatched by Egypt with extraordinary advantage as to economy of time, and with perfect preservation of health. The first regiment that was conveyed by this line passed from Plymouth to Bombay in thirty-seven days. Of the first regiment sent from Malta, the first wing arrived at Bombay in sixteen and the second wing in eighteen days. An overwhelming mass of evidence, from numerous trustworthy witnesses, attest the peculiar facilities, especially in periods of emergency, afforded by the overland route transport. Col. Poeklington, Deputy Quartermaster-General, appointed in October, 1857, to direct and superintend the transit of the troops, and who, expressly prepared by order of the War Department a report for the Committee of Inquiry, states:

"The advantages of the overland route are very considerable, and the trajet is most simple. A thousand men per week can be conveyed across the isthmus by the Transit administration of Egypt without interference with the ordinary passenger traffic. Between 300 and 400 men can move at a time, and perform the distance from ship to ship in 26 hours. The transit by rail is completed to within almost twenty miles of Suez. This last portion of the journey is performed by the soldiers on donkeys in about six hours. There can be no doubt as to the experiment having succeeded."

The time occupied by troops from England to India is, by the overland route, from 33 to 46 days. From Malta to India, from 16 to 18 or 20 days. Compare these periods with the 83 by steamers, or the 120 by sailing ships, on the long sea route, and the difference will appear striking. Again, during the longer route, Great Britain will have from 15,000 to 20,000 troops, in effect *hors de combat*,[a] and beyond counter orders for a period annually, of from 3 to 4 months, while, with the shorter line, it will be but for the brief period of some 14 days, during the transit from Suez to India, that the troops will be beyond reach of recall, for any unexpected European contingency.

In resorting to the overland route only 4 months after the outbreak of the Indian war, and then only for a mere handful of troops, Palmerston set at naught the general anticipation of India and Europe. The Governor-General in India[b] assumed that the Home Government would dispatch troops by the way of Egypt. The following is a passage from the Governor-General in Council's

[a] Out of action.— *Ed.*
[b] Charles John Canning.— *Ed.*

letter to the Home Government, dated Aug. 7, 1857:

"We are also in communication with the Peninsular and Oriental Steam Navigation Company for the conveyance from Suez of the troops that may possibly have been dispatched to India by that route."

On the very day of the arrival at Constantinople of the news of the revolt, Lord Stratford de Redcliffe telegraphed to London to know whether he should apply to the Turkish Government to allow the British troops to pass through Egypt, on their way to India. The Sultan[a] having meanwhile offered and transmitted a firman to that effect on the 2d of July, Palmerston replied by telegraph, that it was not his intention to send troops by that route. It being in France likewise assumed, as a matter of course, that the acceleration of the military re-enforcements must at that moment form the paramount object of British policy, Bonaparte spontaneously tendered permission for the passage over France of British troops, to enable their being embarked, if deemed desirable, at Marseilles, for Egypt. The Pasha of Egypt[b] lastly, when, at length, Mr. Holton, the Superintendent of the Peninsular and Oriental Company in Egypt, was authorized to reply on the subject, answered immediately,

"It would be a satisfaction to him to give facility to the passage of not only 200 men, as in the present instance, but to that of 20,000, if necessary, and not *en bourgeois*[c] but in uniform, and with their arms, if required."

Such were the facilities recklessly thrown away, the proper use of which might have prevented the Indian war from assuming its formidable dimensions. The motives by which Lord Palmerston was prompted in preferring sailing vessels to steamers, and a line of communication extending over 14,000 miles to one limited to 4,000 miles, belong to the mysteries of cotemporaneous history.

Written between July 16 and 20, 1858

First published unsigned in the *New-York Daily Tribune,* No. 5401, August 13, 1858

Reproduced from the newspaper

---

[a] Abdul Mejid.—*Ed.*

[b] Said Pasha.—*Ed.*

[c] In civilian clothes.—*Ed.*

Karl Marx

IMPRISONMENT OF LADY BULWER-LYTTON

London, July 23, 1858

The great Bulwer scandal, which *The London Times* thought to be "fortunately" hushed up by an amicable family arrangement, is far from having subsided into a state of quiescence. It is true that, despite the great party interest involved, the metropolitan press, with some trifling exceptions, did everything in its power to hush the case by a conspiracy of silence—Sir Edward Bulwer being one of the chiefs of the literary coterie which lords it more despotically over the heads of the London journalists than even party connection, and to openly affront whose wrath literary gentlemen generally lack the necessary courage. *The Morning Post* first informed the public that Lady Bulwer's friends intended insisting upon legal investigation[a]; *The London Times* reprinted the short paragraph of *The Morning Post*,[b] and even *The Advertiser*, although it certainly has no literary position to hazard, did not venture beyond some meager extracts from *The Somerset Gazette*. Even Palmerston's influence proved for the moment unavailing to extort anything from his literary retainers, and on the appearance of the flippantly apologetical letter of Bulwer's son,[c] all these public guardians of the liberty of the subject, while declaring themselves highly satisfied, deprecated any further indelicate intrusion upon the "painful matter." The Tory press, of course, has long since spent all its virtuous indignation on Lord Clanricarde's behalf, and the Radical press, which more or less receives its inspirations from

---

[a] *The Morning Post*, No. 26369, July 5, 1858.—*Ed.*

[b] *The Times*, No. 23038, July 6, 1858.—*Ed.*

[c] Here and below R. B. Lytton, "To the Editor of the *Observer*", *The Times*, No. 23049, July 19, 1858.—*Ed.*

the Manchester school,[581] anxiously avoids creating any embarrassment to the present Administration. Yet, along with the respectable or would-be respectable press of the metropolis, there exists an irrespectable press, absolutely swayed by its political patrons with no literary standing to check them, always ready to coin money out of its privilege of free speech, and anxious to improve an opportunity of appearing in the eyes of the public as the last representatives of manliness. On the other hand, the moral instincts of the bulk of the people once awakened, there will be no need of further maneuvering. The public mind once worked into a state of moral excitement, even *The London Times* may throw off its mask of reserve, and, with a bleeding heart of course, stab the Derby Administration by passing the sentence of "public opinion" on such a literary chieftain even as Sir Edward Bulwer-Lytton.

This is exactly the turn things are now taking. That Lord Palmerston, as we hinted at first,[582] is the secret manager of the spectacle is now *un secret qui court les rues,*[a] as the French say.

> "*On dit,*"[b] says a London weekly, "that Lady Bulwer-Lytton's best friend in this affair has been Lady Palmerston. We all remember how the Tories took up the cudgels for Mr. Norton when Lord Melbourne was in trouble about that gentleman's wife. Tit for tat is fair play. But on reflection it is rather sad at this time of day to find a Secretary of State using the influence of his position to commit acts of oppression, and the wife of a Minister playing off the wife of another Minister against an Administration."

It is often by the crooked ways of political intrigue only that truth becomes smuggled into some corner of the British press. The apparently generous horror at a real outrage is after all but a calculated grimace; and public justice is only appealed to in order to cherish private malice. For aught the chivalrous knights of the inkhorn would care about it, Lady Bulwer might have remained forever in a lunatic asylum, at London; she might have been disposed of more quietly than at St. Petersburg or Vienna; the conventionalities of literary decorum would have debarred her from any means of redress but for the happy circumstance of Palmerston's keen eye singling her out as the thin end of the wedge wherewith possibly to split a Tory Administration.

A short analysis of the letter, addressed by Bulwer's son to the London journals, will go far to elucidate the true state of the case. Mr. Robert B. Lytton sets out by asserting that his "simple assertion" must be "at once believed in," because he is "the son of

---

[a] A secret known to everybody.—*Ed.*
[b] It is said.—*Ed.*

Lady Bulwer-Lytton, with the best right to speak on her behalf, and obviously with the best means of information." Now, this very tender son had neither cared for his mother, nor corresponded with her, nor seen her, for nearly seventeen years, until he met her at the hustings at Hertford on the occasion of his father's re-election. When Lady Bulwer left the hustings and visited the Mayor of Hertford in order to apply for the use of the Town Hall as a lecturing room, Mr. Robert B. Lytton sent a physician into the Mayor's house with the mission of taking cognizance of the state of the maternal mind. When, afterward, his mother was kidnapped in London, at the house of Mr. Hale Thompson, Clarges street, and her cousin Miss Ryves ran out into the street, and seeing Mr. Lytton waiting outside, entreated him to interfere and procure assistance to prevent his mother being carried off to Brentford, Mr. Lytton coolly refused to have anything to do with the matter. Having acted first as one of the principal agents in the plot laid by his father, he now shifts sides and presents himself as the natural spokesman of his mother. The second point pleaded by Mr. Lytton is, that his mother "was never for a moment taken to a lunatic asylum," but, on the contrary, into the "private house" of Mr. Robert Gardiner Hill, surgeon. This is a mere quibble. As the "Wyke House," conducted by Mr. Hill, does legally not belong to the category of "asylums," but to that of "Metropolitan Licensed Houses," it is literally true that Lady Bulwer was thrown, not into a "lunatic asylum," but into a lunatic house.

Surgeon Hill, who trades upon his own account in "lunacy," has also come out with an apology, wherein he states that Lady Bulwer had never been locked in, but, on the contrary, had enjoyed the use of a brougham and driven almost every evening during her detention to Richmond, Acton, Hanwell or Isleworth. Mr. Hill forgets to tell the public that this "improved treatment of the insane," adopted by him, exactly corresponds to the official recommendation of the Commissioners in Lunacy. The friendly grimaces, the smiling forbearance, the childish coaxing, the oily twaddle, the knowing winks and the affected serenity of a band of trained attendants may drive a sensitive woman mad as well as douches, straight waistcoats, brutal keepers and dark wards. However that may be, the protests on the part of Mr. Surgeon Hill and Mr. Lytton amount simply to this, that Lady Bulwer was treated as a lunatic indeed, but after the rules of the new instead of the old system.

"I," says Mr. Lytton, in his letter, "put myself in constant communication with my mother, ... and I carried out the injunctions of my father, who confided to me implicitly every arrangement ... and enjoined me to avail myself of the advice of Lord Shaftesbury in whatever was judged best and kindest to Lady Lytton."

Lord Shaftesbury, it is known, is the commander-in-chief of the host who have their head-quarters at Exeter Hall. To deodorise a dirty affair by his odor of sanctity might be considered a *coup de théâtre* worthy of the inventive genius of a novel writer. More than once, in the Chinese business, for instance, and in the Cambridge House conspiracy, Lord Shaftesbury has been employed in that line. Yet Mr. Lytton admits the public only to a half confidence, otherwise he would have plainly declared that on the kidnapping of his mother an imperious note from Lady Palmerston upset Sir Edward's plans, and induced him to "avail himself of the advice of Lord Shaftesbury," who, by a particular mischance, happens to be at once Palmerston's son-in-law and the Chairman of the Commissioners in Lunacy. In his attempt at mystification, Mr. Lytton proceeds to state:

"From the moment my father felt compelled to authorize those steps which have been made the subject of so much misrepresentation, his anxiety was to obtain the opinion of the most experienced and able physicians, in order that my mother should not be subject to restraint for one moment longer than was strictly justifiable. Such was his charge to me."

From the evasive wording of this studiously awkward passage it appears, then, that Sir Edward Bulwer felt the necessity of authoritative medical advice, not for sequestrating his wife as insane, but for setting her free as *mentis compos*.[a] In fact, the medical men upon whose consent Lady Bulwer was kidnapped were anything but "most experienced and able physicians." The fellows employed by Sir Edward were one Mr. Ross, a city apothecary, whom, it seems, his license for trading in drugs has all at once converted into a psychological luminary, and one Mr. Hale Thompson, formerly connected with the Westminster Hospital, but a thorough stranger to the scientific world. It was only after gentle pressure from without had set in, when Sir Edward felt anxious to retrace his steps, that he addressed himself to men of medical standing. Their certificates are published by his son—but what do they prove? Dr. Forbes Winslow, the editor of "The Journal of Psychological Medicine," who had previously been consulted by Lady Bulwer's legal advisers, certifies that, "having examined Lady B. Lytton as to her state of mind," he found it such as "to justify her liberation from restraint."[b] The thing to be

[a] Being in her right mind.—*Ed.*

[b] F. Winslow, "To Edwin James, Esq., Q. C.", *The Times*, No. 23049, July 19, 1858.—*Ed.*

proved to the public was, not that Lady Bulwer's liberation, but on the contrary, that her restraint was justified. Mr. Lytton dares not touch upon this delicate and decisive point. Would not a constable, accused of illegal imprisonment of a free-born Briton, be laughed at for pleading that he had committed no wrong in setting his prisoner at large? But is Lady Bulwer really set at large?

> "My mother," continues Mr. Lytton, *"is now with me,* free from all restraint, and about, at her own wish, to travel for a short time, in company with myself and a female friend and relation, of her own selection."

Mr. Lytton's letter is dated "No. 1 Park lane," that is, from the town residence of his father. Has, then, Lady Bulwer been removed from her place of confinement at Brentford to a place of confinement at London, and been bodily delivered up to an exasperated foe? Who warrants her being "free from all restraint?" At all events, when signing the proposed compromise, she was not free from restraint, but smarting under Surgeon Hill's improved system. The most important circumstance is this: While Sir Edward has spoken, Lady Bulwer has kept silence. No declaration on her part, given as she is to literary exercise, has met the public eye. An account written by herself, of her own treatment, has been cleverly withdrawn from the hands of the individual to whom it was addressed.

Whatever may be the agreement entered upon by the husband and the wife, the question for the British public is whether, under the cloak of the lunacy act, *lettres de cachet*[a] may be issued by unscrupulous individuals able to pay tempting fees to two hungry practitioners. Another question is, whether a Secretary of State will be allowed to condone for a public crime by a private compromise. It has now oozed out that during the present year, while investigating into the state of a Yorkshire asylum, the Lunacy Commissioners discovered a man, in the full possession of his mental faculties, who, for several years, had been immured and secreted in a cellar. On a question being put in the House of Commons by Mr. Fitzroy, in regard to this case, Mr. Walpole answered that he had found "no record of the fact," an answer which denies the record but not the fact. That things will not be allowed to rest at this point, may be inferred from Mr. Tite's notice that "on an early day next session he would move for

[a] Warrants for arrest and imprisonment.—*Ed.*

a select committee to inquire into the operation of the Lunacy act."[a]

Written on July 23, 1858

First published unsigned in the *New-York Daily Tribune,* No. 5393, August 4, 1858 and reprinted in the *New-York Semi-Weekly Tribune,* No. 1377, August 6, 1858, and also in the *New-York Weekly Tribune,* No. 882, August 7, 1858

Reproduced from the *New-York Daily Tribune*

---

[a] *The Times,* No. 23053, July 23, 1858.—*Ed.*

Karl Marx

[THE INCREASE OF LUNACY IN GREAT BRITAIN]

There is, perhaps, no better established fact in British society than that of the corresponding growth of modern wealth and pauperism. Curiously enough, the same law seems to hold good with respect to lunacy. The increase of lunacy in Great Britain has kept pace with the increase of exports, and has outstripped the increase of population. Its rapid progress in England and Wales during the period extending from 1852 to 1857, a period of unprecedented commercial prosperity, will become evident from the following tabular comparison of the annual returns of paupers, lunatics and idiots for the years 1852, 1854 and 1857[a]:

Date.	Population.	Patients in County or Borough Asylums.	In licensed houses.	In Workhouses.	With friends or elsewhere.	Total of Lunatics and Idiots.	Proportion to population.
Jan. 1, 1852	17,927,609	9,412	2,584	5,055	4,107	21,158	1 in 847
Jan. 1, 1854	18,649,849	11,956	1,878	5,713	4,940	24,487	1 in 762
Jan. 1, 1857	19,408,464	13,488	1,908	6,800	5,497	27,693	1 in 701

The proportion of acute and curable cases to those of a chronic and apparently incurable kind was, on the last day of 1856,

[a] Here and below *Sixth, Eighth* and *Eleventh Annual Reports of the Commissioners in Lunacy to the Lord Chancellor. 1852, 1854, 1857.—Ed.*

estimated to be somewhat less than 1 in 5, according to the following summary of official returns:

	Patients of all classes in Asylums.	Deemed curable.
In County and Borough Asylums	14,393	2,070
In Hospitals	1,742	340
In Metropolitan licensed Houses	2,578	390
In Provincial licensed Houses	2,598	527
Total	21,311	3,327
Deemed curable	3,327	
Deemed incurable	17,984	

There exist in England and Wales, for the accommodation of lunatics and idiots of all sorts and of all classes, 37 public asylums, of which 33 are county and 4 borough asylums; 15 hospitals; 116 private licensed houses, of which 37 are metropolitan and 79 provincial; and lastly, the workhouses. The public asylums, or lunatic asylums properly so called, were, by law, exclusively destined for the reception of the lunatic poor, to be used as hospitals for the medical treatment, not as safe places for the mere custody of the insane. On the whole, in the counties at least, they may be considered well regulated establishments, although of too extensive a construction to be properly superintended, overcrowded, lacking the careful separation of the different classes of patients, and yet inadequate to the accommodation of somewhat more than one-half of the lunatic poor. After all, the space afforded by these 37 establishments, spreading over the whole country, suffices for the housing of over 15,690 inmates. The pressure upon these costly asylums on the part of the lunatic population may be illustrated by one case. When, in 1831, Hanwell (in Middlesex) was built for 500 patients, it was supposed to be large enough to meet all the wants of the county. But, two years later, it was full; after another two years, it had to be enlarged for 300 more; and at this time (Colney Hatch having been meanwhile constructed for the reception of 1,200 lunatic paupers belonging to the same county) Hanwell contains upward of 1,000 patients. Colney Hatch was opened in 1851; within a period of less than five years, it became necessary to appeal to the rate-payers for further accommodation; and the latest returns show that at the close of 1856 there were more than 1,100 pauper lunatics belonging to the county unprovided for in either of its asylums. While the existing asylums are too large to be properly conducted, their number is too small to meet rapid spread of mental disorders. Above all, the asylums ought to be separated into two distinct categories: asylums for the incurable, hospitals for the curable. By huddling both classes together, neither receives its proper treatment and cure.

The private licensed houses are, on the whole, reserved for the more affluent portion of the insane. Against these "snug retreats," as they like to call themselves, public indignation has been lately raised by the kidnapping of Lady Bulwer into Wyke House, and the atrocious outrages committed on Mrs. Turner in Acomb House, York. A Parliamentary inquiry into the secrets of the trade in British lunacy being imminent, we may refer to that part of the subject hereafter. For the present let us call attention only to the treatment of the 2,000 lunatic poor, whom, by way of contract, the Boards of Guardians and other local authorities let out to managers of private licensed houses. The weekly consideration per head for maintenance, treatment and clothing, allotted to these private contractors, varies from five to twelve shillings, but the average allowance may be estimated from 5s. to 8s. 4d. The whole study of the contractors consists, of course, in the one single point of making large profits out of these small receipts, and consequently of keeping the patient at the lowest possible expense. In their latest report[a] the Commissioners of Lunacy state that even where the means of accommodation in these licensed houses are large and ample, the actual accommodation afforded is a mere sham, and the treatment of the inmates a disgrace.

It is true that a power is vested in the Lord Chancellor of revoking a license or preventing its renewal, on the advice of the Commissioners in Lunacy; but, in many instances, where there exists no public asylum in the neighborhood, or where the existing asylum is already overcrowded, no alternative was left the Commissioners but to prevent the license to continue, or to throw large masses of the insane poor into their several workhouses. Yet, the same Commissioners add that great as are the evils of the licensed houses, they are not so great as the danger and evil combined of leaving those paupers almost uncared for in workhouses. In the latter about 7,000 lunatics are at present confined. At first the lunatic wards in workhouses were restricted to the reception of such pauper lunatics as required little more than ordinary accommodation, and were capable of associating with the other inmates. What with the difficulty of obtaining

[a] *Return of Lunatic Asylums in England and Wales....*— *Ed.*

admission for their insane poor into properly regulated asylums, what with motives of parsimony, the parochial boards are more and more transforming the workhouses into lunatic asylums, but into asylums wanting in the attendance, the treatment and the supervision which form the principal safeguard of patients detained in asylums regularly constituted. Many of the larger workhouses have lunatic wards containing from 40 to 120 inmates. The wards are gloomy and unprovided with any means for occupation, exercise or amusement. The attendants for the most part are pauper inmates totally unfitted for the charge imposed upon them. The diet, essential above everything else to the unhappy objects of mental disease, rarely exceeds in any case that allowed for the healthy and able-bodied inmates. Hence, it is a natural result that detention in workhouses not only deteriorates the cases of harmless imbecility for which it was originally intended, but has the tendency to render chronic and permanent cases that might have yielded to early care. The decisive principle for the Boards of Guardians is economy.

According to law, the insane pauper should come at first under the care of the district parish surgeon, who is bound to give notice to the relieving officers, by whom communication is to be made to the magistrate, upon whose order they are to be conveyed to the asylum. In fact, these provisions are disregarded altogether. The pauper lunatics are in the first instance hurried into the workhouses, there to be permanently detained, if found to be manageable. The recommendation of the Commissioners in Lunacy, during their visits to the workhouses, of removing to the asylums all inmates considered to be curable, or to be exposed to treatment unsuited to their state, is generally outweighed by the report of the medical officer of the Union, to the effect that the patient is "harmless." What the workhouse accommodation is, may be understood from the following illustrations described in the last Lunacy Report as "faithfully exhibiting the general characteristics of workhouse accommodation."

In the Infirmary Asylum of Norwich the beds of even the sick and feeble patients were of straw. The floors of thirteen small rooms were of stone. There were no water-closets. The nightwatch on the male side had been discontinued. There was a great deficiency of blankets, of toweling, of flannels, of waistcoats, of washing basins, of chairs, of plates, of spoons and of dining accommodation. The ventilation was bad. We quote:

"Neither was there any faith to be put in what, to outward appearance, might have been taken for improvement. It was discovered, for example, that in reference to a considerable number of beds occupied by dirty patients, the practice exists of removing them in the morning and of substituting, merely for show during the day, clean beds of a better appearance, by means of sheets and blankets placed on the bedsteads, which were regularly taken away at night and the inferior beds replaced."

Take, as another example, the Blackburn Workhouse:

"The day rooms on the ground floor, occupied by the men, are small, low, gloomy and dirty, and the space containing 11 patients is much taken up by several heavy chairs, in which the patients are confined by means of straps, and a large, projecting fire-guard. Those of the women, on the upper floor, are also much crowded, and one, which is used also as a bedroom has a large portion boarded off as a privy; and the beds are placed close together, without any space between them. A bedroom containing 16 male patients was close and offensive. The room is 29 feet long, 17 feet 10 inches wide, and 7 feet 5 inches high, thus allowing 2,39 cubic feet for each patient. The beds throughout are of straw, and no other description is provided for sick or bed-ridden patients. The cases were generally much soiled and marked by the rusty iron laths of the bedsteads. The care of the beds seems to be chiefly left to the patients. A large number of the patients are dirty in their habits, which is mainly to be attributed to the want of proper care and attention. Very few chamber utensils are provided, and a tub is stated to be placed in the center of the large dormitory for the use of the male patients. The graveled yards in which the patients walk are two for each sex, surrounded by high walls, and without seats. The largest of these is 74 feet long, by 30 feet 7 inches wide, and the smallest 32 feet by 17 feet 6 inches. A cell in one of the yards is occasionally used for secluding excited patients. It is entirely built of stone, and has a small, square opening for the admission of light, with iron bars let in to prevent the escape of the patient, but without either shutter or casement. A large straw bed was on the floor, and a heavy chair in one corner of the room. Complete control of the department is in the hands of an attendant and the nurse: the master seldom interferes with them, nor does he inspect this as closely as he does the other parts of the workhouse."

It would be too loathsome even to give extracts from the Commissioners' report on the St. Pancras Workhouse at London, a sort of low Pandemonium. Generally speaking, there are few English stables which, at the side of the lunatic wards in the workhouses, would not appear boudoirs, and where the treatment received by the quadrupeds may not be called sentimental when compared to that of the poor insane.

Written on July 30, 1858 — Reproduced from the newspaper

First published in the *New-York Daily Tribune,* No. 5407, August 20, 1858 as a leading article

Frederick Engels

[THE REVOLT IN INDIA]

The campaign in India has been almost completely suspended during the hot and rainy summer months. Sir Colin Campbell having secured, by a vigorous effort in the beginning of summer, all the important positions in Oude and Rohilcund, very wisely put his troops into quarters, leaving the open country in the possession of the insurgents, and limiting his efforts to maintaining his communications. The only episode of interest which occurred during this period in Oude, was the excursion of Sir Hope Grant to Shahgunge for the relief of Maun Singh, a native chief, who, after a deal of tergiversation, had lately made his peace with the British, and was now blockaded by his late native allies. The excursion proved a mere military promenade, though it must have caused great loss to the British by sun-stroke and cholera. The natives dispersed without showing fight, and Maun Singh joined the British. The easy success of this expedition, though it cannot be taken as an indication of an equally easy subjection of the whole of Oude, shows that the insurgents have lost heart completely. If it was the interest of the British to rest during the hot weather, it was the interest of the insurgents to disturb them as much as possible. But instead of organizing an active guerrilla warfare, intercepting the communications between the towns held by the enemy, of waylaying small parties, harassing the foragers, of rendering impassable the supply of victuals, without which no large town held by the British could live—instead of this, the natives have been satisfied with levying revenue and enjoying the leisure left to them by their opponents. Better still, they appear to have squabbled among themselves. Neither do they appear to have profited by the few quiet weeks to reorganize their forces, to refill their ammunition stores, or to replace the lost artillery. The bolt at Shahgunge shows a still greater want of confidence in themselves and their leaders than any previous defeat. In the mean time, a secret correspondence is carried on between the majority of the chiefs and the British Government, who have after all found it rather impracticable to pocket the whole of the soil of Oude, and are quite willing to let the former owners have it again on reasonable terms. Thus, as the final success of the British is now beyond all doubt, the insurrection in Oude bids fair to die out without passing through a period of active guerrilla warfare. As soon as the majority of the landholders come to terms with the British, the insurgent bodies will be broken up, and those who have too much to fear from the Government will turn robbers (dacoits), in the capture of whom the peasantry will gladly assist.

South-west of Oude the Jugdispore jungles appear to offer a center for such dacoits. These impenetrable forests of bamboo and underwood are held by a party of insurgents under Ummer Singh, who shows rather more activity and knowledge of guerrilla warfare; at all events, he attacks the British whenever he can, instead of quietly waiting for them. If, as it is feared, part of the Oude insurgents should join him before he can be expelled from his stronghold, the British may expect rather harder work than they have had of late. These jungles have now for nearly eight months served as a retreat to insurgent parties, who have been able to render very insecure the Grand Trunk Road from Calcutta to Allahabad, the main communication of the British.

In Western India, the Gwalior insurgents are still followed up by Gen. Roberts and Col. Holmes. At the time of the capture of Gwalior, it was a question of much consequence, what direction the retreating army might take; for the whole of the Mahratta country and part of Rajpootana appeared ready for a rising as soon as a sufficiently strong body of regular troops arrived there to form a nucleus for the insurrection. A retreat of the Gwalior force in a south-westerly direction then seemed the most likely maneuver to realize such a result. But the insurgents, from reasons which we cannot guess at from the reports before us, have chosen a north-westerly direction. They went to Jeypore, thence turning south toward Oodeypore, trying to gain the road to the Mahratta country. But this roundabout marching gave Roberts an opportunity of coming up with them, and defeating them totally without any great effort. The remnants of this body, without guns, without organization and ammunition, without leaders of repute, are not the men who are likely to induce fresh risings. On the contrary, the immense quantity of plunder which they carry along with them, and which hampers all their movements, appears already to have excited the avidity of the peasantry. Every straggling Sepoy is killed and eased of his load of gold mohurs. If it has come to that, Gen. Roberts may safely leave the final dispersion of these Sepoys to the country population. The loot of Scindiah's treasures by his troops saves the British from a renewal of the insurrection in a quarter more dangerous than Hindostan; for a rising in the Mahratta country would put the Bombay army upon a rather severe trial.

There is a fresh mutiny in the neighborhood of Gwalior. A small vassal of Scindiah, Maun Singh (not the Maun Singh of Oude) has joined the insurgents, and got hold of the small fortress of Paoree. This place, is, however, already invested by the British, and must soon be captured.

In the mean time, the conquered districts are gradually pacified. The neighborhood of Delhi, it is said, has been so completely tranquillized by Sir J. Lawrence that a European may travel about with perfect safety, unarmed, and without an escort. The secret of the matter is, that the people of every village have been made collectively responsible for any crime or outrage committed on its ground; that a military police has been organized; and, above all, that the summary justice of the Court-Martial, so peculiarly impressive upon Orientals, is everywhere in full swing. Still, this success appears to be the exception, as we do not hear anything of the kind from other districts. The complete pacification of Rohilcund and Oude, of Bundelcund and many other large provinces, must yet require a very long time and give plenty of work yet to British troops and Court-Martials.

But while the insurrection of Hindostan dwindles down to dimensions which deprive it of almost all military interest, there has occurred an event far off, at the utmost frontiers of Afghanistan, which is big with the threat of future difficulties. A conspiracy to murder their officers and to rise against the British has been discovered among several Sikh regiments at Dera Ismael Khan. How far this conspiracy was ramified, we cannot tell. Perhaps it was merely a local affair, arising among a peculiar class of Sikhs; but we are not in a position to assert this. At all events, this is a highly dangerous symptom. There are now nearly 100,000 Sikhs in the British service, and we have heard how saucy they are; they fight, they say, to-day for the British, but may fight to-morrow against them, as it may please God. Brave, passionate, fickle, they are even more subject to sudden and unexpected impulses than other Orientals. If mutiny should break out in earnest among them, then would the British indeed have hard work to keep their own. The Sikhs were always the most formidable opponents of the British among the natives of India; they have formed a comparatively powerful empire[583]; they are of a peculiar sect of Brahminism, and hate both Hindoos and Mussulmans. They have seen the British "raj" in the utmost peril; they have contributed a great deal to restore it, and they are even convinced that their own share of the work was the decisive one. What is more natural than that they should harbor the idea that the time has come when the British raj shall be replaced by a Sikh raj, that a Sikh Emperor is to rule India from Delhi or Calcutta? It may be that this idea is still far from being matured among the Sikhs, it may be that they are so cleverly distributed that they are balanced by Europeans, so that any rising could be easily put down; but that this idea exists among them must be clear, we presume, to everybody who has read the accounts of the behaviour of the Sikhs after Delhi and Lucknow.

Still, for the present, the British have reconquered India. The great rebellion, stirred up by the mutiny of the Bengal army, is indeed, it appears, dying out. But this second conquest has not increased England's hold upon the mind of the Indian people. The cruelty of the retribution dealt out by the British troops, goaded on by exaggerated and false reports of the atrocities attributed to the natives, and the attempt at confiscating the Kingdom of Oude, both wholesale and retail, have not created any particular fondness for the victors. On the contrary, they themselves confess that among both Hindoos and Mussulmans, the hereditary hatred against the Christian intruder is more fierce than ever. Impotent as this hatred may be at present, it is not without its significance and importance, while that menacing cloud is resting over the Sikh Punjaub. And this is not all. The two great Asiatic powers, England and Russia, have by this time got hold of one point between Siberia and India, where Russian and English interests must come into direct collision. That point is Pekin. Thence westward a line will ere long be drawn across the breadth of the Asiatic Continent, on which this collision of rival interests will constantly take place. Thus the time may indeed not be so very distant when "the Sepoy and the Cossack will meet in the plains of the Oxus,"[a][584] and if that meeting is to take place, the

[a] Amu Darya.—*Ed.*

anti-British passions of 150,000 native Indians will be a matter of serious consideration.

Written on about September 17, 1858

First published in the *New-York Daily Tribune*, No. 5443, October 1, 1858 as a leading article

Reproduced from the newspaper

FROM THE PREPARATORY MATERIALS

Karl Marx

VENICE[585]

Venice and Genoa. (Trieste was linked with their Mediterranean trade...) *Genoa. Latter half of the 13th century:* Very substantial privileges accorded the Genoese in consequence of their support of the Greeks against the Catholic monarchs (privileges in Constantinople—Galata and Pera).[586] Superior to the Venetians here; (in Constantinople and the Black Sea[a]) *Venetians* favoured by the Catholic monarchs, commercial supremacy in Dalmatia, the Morea,[b] Asia Minor, Cyprus, Syria, etc.

Causes of decline. Since the beginning of the 15th century, conquest of the Greek empire by the Turks; notably Constantinople in *1453.* Italians lost their privileges there and their settlements in Constantinople, Syria, Armenia, on the Black Sea, etc. Accorded privileges by the sultans of Egypt, etc.

From the end of the 15th century the Portuguese sailing round the Cape of Good Hope. Market for Indian goods shifted to Lisbon. Very marked *decline from mid-16th century.* Moreover the *discovery of America* was of less use to them than to other states, etc. Venice severely handicapped since Constantinople no longer centre for trade and goods traffic from Asia.

Towards the end of the 18th century under French rule; war with England; *trade declined in all* Italian *maritime towns.*

Treaty *of 1815* restored only small proportion of trade enjoyed even *before the French Revolution;* most of it went to *Trieste,* much favoured by the Austrian government. *Trieste*'s volume of trade was three times greater than that of Venice. Trieste especially

[a] The words "Black Sea" are in English in the original.—*Ed.*
[b] Peloponnesus.—*Ed.*

favoured by the growing prosperity of the *Russian ports*, particularly *Odessa*, on the Black Sea. Captured the grain trade which had still been conducted by Venice as recently as the final decades of the 18th century.

Trieste. (1838) 1,700 houses, 52,000 inhabitants; on the Gulf of Trieste; also hemmed in by steep Karst Hills; 1,000 merchants; 700 brokers; English, French, German, Greek, Armenian, Jewish business houses.

Prior to the treaty of Campoformio of 17 October 1797 Napoleon had already dissolved the Venetian Republic in favour of the Cisalpine Republic consisting of Milan, Mantua, etc., the Valtellina, Romagna, etc. The *greater part of the Venetian Free State as far as the Adige was annexed to Austria.*

Treaty of Luneville 9 February 1801[587]: The Adige thalweg became the boundary between Austria and the Cisalpine Republic; she acquired Venice with the greater part of the former Venetian Free State as far as the Adige thalweg, together with Istria, Venetian Dalmatia, the islands belonging thereto, and the Bocche di Cattaro.

1805. 26 September: Treaty of Pressburg.[588] Austria loses her share of Venice to Italy.

1807. 10 October. Austria compelled to cede the county of Monfalcone to Italy,[589] the result being that the Isonzo thalweg became her boundary.

14 October 1809 Treaty of Vienna[590]: Napoleon created the so-called Illyrian Provinces out of the Villach District in Carinthia, the duchy of Carniola, the Trieste district, the county of Gorizia, Friuli, that part of Croatia on the right bank of the Sava including Fiume, as well as the Hungarian littoral and Austrian Istria, and annexed them to Istria, Dalmatia and Ragusa; he reserved these for himself and handed them over to a special governor-general.

Convention Money[591]
About 1844 Trieste's Volume of Trade

1842-3

Imports: 58,400,000 (*Hamburg,* 1843, *Total value:* 215,500,000)
Exports: 40,500,000 (*Havre,* 1842, *Total value:* 168,700,000)

Total: 98,900,000

Florins C. M.

Austria's Mercantile Marine

1 Jan. 1840	*Vessels*	*Tonnage*
	1,590	176,696

Austrian Commerce

(Figures in millions)

Sea-borne Trade	1838		1841		1842	
	Imp.	Exp.	Imp.	Exp.	Imp.	Exp.
Via *Fiume*	0.2	1.7	0.2	1.6	0.2	1.7
Trieste	32.2	14.4	22.3	11.2	24.9	11.9
Venice	9.0	5.3	8.5	3.1	11.5	3.4
Other Maritime Towns	8.0	2.0	5.3	1.9	5.1	2.6
	49.4	23.4	36.3	17.8	41.7	19.6

1839

Commerce of Trieste and Venice.

Imports into Venice: into Trieste =1:2.84
Exports =1:3.8

Commerce of Trieste

(Value in fl. C. M.)

1832		1836		1840	
Imp.	Exp.	Imp.	Exp.	Imp.	Exp.
57,000,000	44,000,000	77,000,000	54,000,000	49,000,000	37,000,000

Shipping Traffic of Trieste

1835		1836		1837		1838	
Entered	Cleared	Ent.	Cl.	Ent.	Cl.	Ent.	Cl.
988	1,069	1,146	1,117	1,094	1,132	1,154	1,118

1839

Foreign vessels entering

	Trieste	*Venice*	
	1,217	271	Number of vessels entering Venice:
Austrian			
	10,375	3,147	Number entering Trieste=1:4
combined	11,592	3,418	

Tonnage of foreign vessels	133,343	20,254
Austrian	330,404	196,135
	463,747	216,389

Value in Turkish Piastres
Smyrna: Imp. and Exp. 1835-9

	Imports	
At the forefront	*England.*	126,313,146
	(*Malta.*	2,979,040)
Then	*Trieste.*	93,500,456
Then	*America, etc.*	57,329,165
	Exports	
	England.	44,618,032
	(*Malta.*	3,361,185)
	Trieste.	52,477,765
	America.	46,608,320

Egypt: Imports and Exports (1837) *fcs.*

	Imp.	*Exp.*
1) *Austria* (Trieste)	13,858,000	14,532,000
2) *Turkey*	12,661,000	12,150,000
3) *France*	10,702,000	11,463,000
4) *England and Malta*	15,158,000	5,404,000

Compiled in November 1856

First published in: Marx and Engels, *Works*, Second Russian Edition, Vol. 44, Moscow, 1977

Printed according to the manuscript

Published in English for the first time

SUPPLEMENT

Karl Marx

REVOLUTIONARY SPAIN

[NINTH ARTICLE][592]

M. de Chateaubriand, in his *Congrès de Vérone,* accuses the Spanish Revolution of 1820-23 of having been nothing but a servile parody of the first French Revolution, performed on the Madrid stage, and in Castilian costumes.[a] He forgets that the struggles of different peoples emerging from the feudal state of society, and moving toward middle class civilization, cannot be supposed to differ in anything but the peculiar coloring derived from race, nationality, language, stage customs and costumes. His censure reminds us of the foolish old woman who strongly suspected all enamored girls of mimicking her own better days.

A whole library has been written *pro* and *con* upon the Constitution of 1812,[593] the proclamation of which, in 1820, gave rise to a three years' struggle between the prejudices and interests of the old society and the wants and aspirations of the new one. The Constitution of 1812 had strongly impressed upon it that same stamp of impracticability which characterizes all charters originally drawn up by modern nations at the epoch of their regeneration. At the revolutionary epoch, to which they owe their origin, they are impracticable, not in consequence of this or that paragraph, but simply because of their constitutional nature. At the Constitutional epoch they are out of place, because of their being impregnated with the generous delusions, inseparable from the dawn of social regeneration. The French Constitution of 1791,[594] for instance, at its own time justly considered to be reactionary, would have been found guilty of Jacobinism in 1830. Why so? In 1791 the royal power and the ruling forces of the

[a] F. R. Chateaubriand, *Congrès de Vérone,* T. I, pp. 33-34, 37.—*Ed.*

ancient society it represented, had not yet undergone those transformations which were to enable them to enter into combination with, and to take place within the elements of the new society. What was then wanted was revolutionary action to break down the resistance of the old society, and not a Constitution sanctioning an impossible compromise with it. In 1830, on the contrary, when limited monarchy had become possible, it was generally understood that it meant the rule of the bourgeoisie instead of the emancipation of the people. The Constitution of 1791 must then have appeared an incendiary anachronism. The same argument holds good for the Spanish Constitution of 1812, but there is still that distinction to be drawn between France in 1791, and Spain in 1820, that the Constitution of 1791 only pretended to make a halt, in a two years' revolutionary march, while the Constitution of 1812 was to supersede revolution altogether. Spain, the day before an Oriental despotism,[595] was to be a day later—a democracy with a monarch at its head. Such sudden changes belong exclusively to Spanish history. Ferdinand VII, when restored to absolute power, in 1823, as well as in 1814, expunged, by one stroke of the pen, all that had been done in the revolutionary interregnum.[596] The Revolutionists, on their part, acted in the same manner. In 1854, the Spanish people began with Espartero, with whom they ended in 1843.[597] In 1814 the revolution was terminated by Ferdinand's refusing to swear to the Cadiz Constitution. In 1820, it began with forcing upon him the oath to that same Constitution. He reassembled the same Cortes he had dissolved two years before, and made the very men Ministers he had banished or imprisoned in 1814. All parties in Spain, with equal obstinacy, tear out all those leaves from the book of their national history which they have not written themselves. Hence these sudden changes, these monstrous exactions, this endless, uninterrupted series of contests. Hence, also, that indelible perseverance which may be defeated, but can never be disheartened or discouraged.

The first Constitutional Ministry, as the chief of which Don Augustin Arguelles may be considered, was, as we have seen, formed of the martyrs of 1814. Martyrs are, on the whole, very dangerous political characters, deflowered, as it were, by the consciousness of their past failures; inflated by exaggerated notions of their past merits; inclined to attribute to themselves the greater capacities because of their damped courage; prone to declare the era of revolution closed with their arrival in the government; from the very fact of their restoration likely to assume the character of revolutionary legitimists or of legitimate revolutionists; overjealous of the new men whom they are astonished to find their rivals; constantly vacillating between the fear of counter-revolution and the apprehension of anarchy; by the very force of circumstances induced to compromise with the former, in order not to be swept away by the latter, or to see overthrown what they used to call the true boundaries of progress. Such was the Ministry of Arguelles. During the four months which elapsed from its formation till the meeting of the Cortes, all public authority was, in fact, suspended. Juntas in the provinces and in the capital, public clubs backed by secret societies, for the first time a popular and unbridled press, stormy petitions, patriotic songs, the erection of constitutional monuments, demonstrations of effervescence natural with a nation on the recovery of its liberty, but yet no acts of vengeance, no crimes committed, and a magnanimity displayed which was not to be expected from southern natures wont to abandon themselves to the impetuosity of their passions.

The Cortes at last opened their first session on July 9, 1820. They made Don José Espiga, Archbishop of Seville, their president. Ferdinand VII swore before them, as he had done before the Ayuntamientos,[598] on the Gospel, to observe the Cadiz Constitution.

> "So soon", he said, "as the excess of undeserved suffering brought the long-suppressed wishes of the people to a distinct expression, I hastened to pursue the course they indicated, and professed the oath of fidelity to the Constitution of the Cortes of 1812. From this moment the king and the people entered on their legitimate rights. *My resolution was free and voluntary.*"[a]

Ferdinand VII, a despotic coward, a tiger with the heart of a hare, a man as greedy of authority as unfit to exercise it, a prince pretending to absolute power in order to be enabled to renounce it into the hands of his footmen,[599] proud, however, of one thing, namely, his perfect mastery in hypocrisy. He enjoyed a sort of satisfaction in exaggerating his own self humiliation before a victorious enemy, resolved, as he was, to avenge, at the opportune moment, his abjection by still more astounding perfidy. When a prisoner of Napoleon,[600] he humbly thanked him for the refuge he had afforded him, and begged for the hand of a princess of the Bonaparte family. When Bonaparte negotiated with him for his restoration to the Spanish throne, he protested, in an adulatory

---

[a] Marx quotes Ferdinand VII's speech of July 9, 1820 from his notes on H. Davis' book *The War of Ormuzd and Ahriman in the Nineteenth Century*.—*Ed.*

letter, that he should be the meanest of mortals, and become a byword in Europe, if he ever proved ungrateful to his imperial benefactor, simultaneously writing a secret letter to the Regency at Madrid, informing them that, once set at liberty, his first act would be to betray the French Emperor.[601] When, on July 9, 1820, he swore anew to the Constitution, declaring that his "resolution was free and voluntary," the Count of Espagne[a] and Mr. Pons were already negotiating in his name, at Paris, with the Pavillon Marsan[602]—viz., the Count of Artois (afterward Charles X) and his coterie—on the means of subverting that same Constitution.

There were some moments in his political life, as for instance the decree of September 30, 1823,[603] when he made false promises in the most solemn manner, for no other possible purpose than the mere pleasure of breaking them. The serious work of counter-revolution, he committed entirely to the partisans of the ancient *régime*, reserving to himself to encourage their efforts in every possible way, but with the mental reservation of disowning them if unfortunate, and quietly delivering them to the resentment of their enemies if beaten. No mortal ever bore others' sufferings with more stoical apathy. For his own official part he limited himself to showing his disgust at the Constitution by playing the fool with it. One night,[b] for instance, he writes to the head of the Cabinet, a letter to the effect that he had appointed Gen. Contador as War Minister. The Ministers, at a loss to find a Contador in the army list, are astonished at discovering at length that Contador was the ex-chief of a squadron, 84 years old, long since disabled for any kind of service. The Ministers so insolently mocked, tendered their resignation. Ferdinand, having succeeded in composing the difference, proposes to replace Contador by Gen. Martinez Rodriguez, as unknown as his predecessor. New troublesome researches having taken place, it appears that Martinez had been dangerously hurt in the head at Badajoz,[604] by the explosion of a powder barrel, and had never recovered his senses since that accident. A sort of virtuoso in the art of passive audacity and active cowardice, Ferdinand VII never shrunk from provoking a catastrophe, resolved, as he was, to be beforehand with the danger.

The majority of the Cortes was composed of deputies to the Cadiz Cortes,[605] the authors of the Constitution and their

---

[a] Presumably Count of Casa Irujo.—*Ed.*

[b] Presumably on August 23, 1821, the day R. Contador was appointed War Minister.—*Ed.*

adherents, while the minority consisted of men who had conspired to reestablish the Constitution. The majority considering the proclamation of the Constitution as the final term of the revolution, while the minority considered it as its beginning; the former having laid hold of the Government, while the latter were still striving to seize it; a schism between the Liberals of 1812 and the Liberals of 1820, between the Moderados and the Exaltados,[606] became inevitable. If the influence of the Liberals of 1812 was preponderant in the Cortes, the Liberals of 1820 were the stronger in the clubs,[607] the press, and the streets. If the former disposed of the Administration, the latter relied upon the army of the Isla,[608] which, strengthened by some regiments that had not participated in the military revolt, was still concentrated in Andalusia, and placed under the supreme command of Riego, Quiroga having been sent as a deputy to the Cortes. In order to break the stronghold of the Exaltados, the Marquis de Las Amarillas, Minister-of-War, disbanded the army of the Isla, Riego having before been removed from his troops on the pretext of being installed as Captain-General of Galicia. Hardly was the army of the Isla disbanded—the only military corps in Spain that deserved the name of an army—when the first Bands of the Faith[609] were seen to appear in Castile and in the North of Spain.

Riego, secretly summoned by his partisans, on the 31st August suddenly appeared at Madrid, where he became the idol of the people, who received him with turbulent ovations and with an overflow of enthusiasm, which the Ministry viewed as a general calamity. They resolved upon exiling him to Oviedo—several other Isla officers being also banished to different places. Although Riego did not resist this arbitrary act of proscription, the Ministers, apprehending an insurrection as likely to break out upon his nocturnal departure from Madrid, called the garrison to arms, occupied the principal places, filled the streets of Madrid with artillery, while on the following day, Arguelles proposed in the Cortes that measures should be taken against popular assemblies, which was warmly supported by Toreno and Martínez de la Rosa. From this day, (Sept. 7, 1820), is to be dated the open rupture between the two Liberal fractions and the retrogression of the revolutionary movement. The same fanaticism of order, the same complaints of incessant agitation, and the same angry impatience at every symptom of popular effervescence, which Europe witnessed during the first weeks after the Revolution of 1848, now possessed at once the Liberal aristocracy and the higher ranks of the middle classes in the Peninsula.

The first session of the Cortes being closed on November 9, 1820, Ferdinand VII, who had retired to the Escorial, with Victor Sáez, his confessor, thought the moment opportune for putting out his feelers. In spite of the Constitution, he nominated, by a royal decree, without the counter-signature of a responsible minister, Gen. Carvajal as Captain-General of New-Castile and Commandant of Madrid,[610] in the place of Gen. Vigodet, who, however, refused to resign his place into the hands of Carvajal. The Ministry, believing themselves lost, now appealed to the very party they had commenced by persecuting. They applied to the directors of the Clubs, and received, in the most gracious manner, the violent address of the Madrid Ayuntamiento, which insisted upon the King's return to Madrid. A similar address was drawn up by the permanent Commission, who represented the Cortes during their absence. The garrison and the militia were put under arms; the sittings of the Clubs became permanent; the populace burst forth into insulting menaces against the King; insurrection was openly preached by the daily papers, and a mass expedition to the Escorial, to fetch the King, seemed imminent. Bending before the storm, Ferdinand revoked his offensive decree, dismissed his anti-liberal confessor, and returned, with his whole family, to Madrid, where he arrived on Nov. 21, 1820. His entry resembled that of Louis XVI, and his family, on their forced return from Versailles to Paris on October 6, 1789.[611]

The Ministry had not obtained the support of the Liberals of 1820 without giving them due reparation, by removing the Marqués de las Amarillas, who afterward openly professed himself a zealous partisan of absolute monarchy, from the War Ministry, and by raising the Isla officers to separate commands. Riego was appointed Captain-General of Aragon, Mina, Captain-General of Galicia, and Velasco, Captain-General of Estremadura. The Ministry of the Martyrs,[612] irresolutely floating between fear of reaction and alarm at anarchy, contrived to become equally discredited with all parties. As to the royal family, its position—to quote the words of a thorough Legitimist—"continued precarious, owing to the indiscreet zeal of the Royalists, which it became impossible to control."[a]

At the opening of the second session, (March 1, 1821), the King acted his part quite in the tone and with the gestures of a stump-orator. Not content with simply reciting the speech drawn

[a] Marx quotes from his notes on W. Walton, *The Revolutions of Spain,* Vol. I, London, 1837, p. 249.—*Ed.*

up by his Cabinet, he puzzled the ministers, by altering their text in a revolutionary sense, and laying higher colors upon the most decisive passages, such as that relating to the invasion of Naples by Austria.[613] For a moment they fancied they had made a convert of him, but were soon disabused. Ferdinand terminated his speech[a] with a fulminant accusation of his own ministers, who had suffered him to be exposed to menace and insults, which would not have taken place, if the Government had displayed that energy and vigor required by the Constitution and desired by the Cortes.

The King's constitutional speech was only the forerunner of the dismissal of the Ministry, and the nomination of a Cabinet which, to the great astonishment of the nation, contained not a single individual attached to the new institutions, or who had not figured as an agent of despotism in the former Government.

The chief of the new Cabinet, M. Felix,[b] formerly a sub-lieutenant in a militia regiment of Lima, and Deputy to the Cortes of 1812 for Peru, was, even at the epoch of the Cadiz Cortes, known as a venal and subtle intriguer. Bardaji, the Minister of Foreign Affairs, was a former diplomatist connected with the heads of the absolutist Cabinets, and Pelegrín, formerly a member of the Council of Castile, boasted that he was entirely devoted to the Holy Alliance. The avowed aim of this Ministry, which could not even pretend to any influence in the Cortes, was "to restore order and suppress anarchy."[c] Accordingly, the Exaltados were again removed from their commands, and full sway was given to the servile party;[614] the most important places were intrusted to men known for their hatred of the prevailing system, a vail being cast upon all the royalist conspiracies that had burst forth in the Peninsula, and their authors, nearly all imprisoned by the people, being set at liberty by the Government. Gen. Morillo, Count of Carthagena, had just arrived from Terra Firma,[d] where he had rendered himself notorious for his ferocity, dictatorial manners, want of probity, and a six years fratricidal war,[615] which he carried on with fanatical enthusiasm. On his return, he staid a few days at Paris, where he connected himself with the intrigues of the

---

[a] Marx gives the contents of Ferdinand VII's speech of March 1, 1822 according to the excerpts from Marliani's *Historia politica de la España moderna,* pp. 70-71.—*Ed.*

[b] The reference is to R. Feliu.—*Ed.*

[c] Marx quotes from his notes on the book. *Examen critique des révolutions d'Espagne de 1820 à 1823 et de 1836.—Ed.*

[d] i.e. the Continent, in contrast to Spanish island possessions in Latin America.—*Ed.*

Pavillon Marsan, the ultra journals at Paris signalizing him as the man who was to restore the King to his ancient rights, and destroy the influence of the Cortes. When he arrived at Madrid, the Ministry lavished on him the strongest expressions of deference and respect, and appointed him Commander of the City and Province of Madrid. It was apparently this nomination which the servile party waited for to execute a coup d'état. The Brigadier Don José Martinez San Martin, a man of inflexible energy and strong Legitimist opinions, was joined to Morillo in the quality of *Jefe Politico*[a] of the capital. While Madrid seemed overawed by the terror of Morillo's name, Catalonia and Galicia became the scenes of passionate contests. Cadiz, Seville and Badajoz broke out in open revolt, refused to admit the Government officers, and disclaimed acknowledging any royal orders unless the Ministry were dismissed. In a message dated Nov. 25, 1821, the King summoned the Cortes to check these disorders.[b] The Cortes, in their answer, drawn up by Don José María Calatrava, blamed the conduct of Cadiz and Seville, but insisted upon the dismissal of the Ministry, who had lost the confidence of the country, and "the moral force to carry on Government."[c] Notwithstanding this vote of distrust, Ferdinand did not think fit to appoint another Ministry[616] till forty-eight hours before the opening of the new Cortes on March 1, 1822.

The elections to the new Cortes having taken place at the moment when the popular passions were exaggerated by the counter revolutionary course of the Government, by the news of Austria's armed interference to suppress the Spanish Constitution proclaimed at Naples,[617] and by the plundering expeditions of the Bands of the Faith at different points of the Peninsula, the Liberals of 1820, then called Exaltados, had, of course, a large majority. "The large majority of the new Legislature," says a Moderado "being possessed of nothing, had nothing to lose."[d] They belonged almost exclusively to the plebeian ranks of the middle-class and the army. The difference between them and their predecessors may be understood from the single fact that, while the latter had appointed the Archbishop of Seville[e] as their

[a] Governor.—*Ed.*

[b] Marx renders Ferdinand VII's message of November 25, 1821 according to the excerpts from *Examen critique des révolutions d'Espagne de 1820 à 1823 et de 1836.—Ed.*

[c] Marx quotes from his notes on *Examen critique des révolutions d'Espagne de 1820 à 1823 et de 1836.—Ed.*

[d] Ibid.—*Ed.*

[e] Don José Espiga.—*Ed.*

President, they, on their part, called to the presidential chair the hero of Las Cabezas[618]—Don Rafael del Riego.

The new Ministry, consisting of Ex-Deputies to the Cortes of 1820, was formed by Martinez de la Rosa, who accepted the Ministry of Foreign Affairs. Martinez de la Rosa—who has since acted an important part under the reign of the innocent Isabella; formerly a Deputy to the short-lived Madrid Cortes of 1814; persecuted during the period of reaction; a Moderado *par excellence*; one of the most elegant Spanish poets and prose-writers—has proved at all epochs a true partisan of the doctrinaire school[619] of the Guizots, the moderation of which gentlemen consists in their fixed notion that concessions to the mass of mankind can never be of too moderate a character. They exult in the erection of a liberal Aristocracy and the supreme rule of the Bourgeoisie, blended with the greatest possible amount of the abuses and traditions of the ancient *régime*. Martinez de la Rosa—overwhelmed with politeness, courted and flattered by the successive French Embassadors at Madrid—the Prince Laval de Montmorency and the Count Lagarde—aimed to modify the Constitution of 1812, by establishing a House of Peers—giving the King an absolute veto, introducing a property qualification for the Lower House, and laying restrictions upon the press. From 1834 to 1836 this incorrigible doctrinaire had the pleasure of witnessing the introduction and the downfall of the abortive Constitution he had hatched in 1822. The French diplomatists made him understand that the Court of the Tuileries would approve of institutions similar to those which then existed in France, while he flattered himself that the King would not be averse to a charter which had enabled Louis XVIII to do what he liked.[620] The King, on his part, cajoled the self-conceited Moderado, whom he intended, as was afterward proved, to send directly from the palace to the scaffold.

According to the plan concocted between the Camarilla and the Ministry, all conspiracies were to be winked at, and confusion was to be suffered to reign, so as, afterward, by the assistance of France, to introduce order, and give the nation a moderate Charter, capable of perpetuating power and influence in its original promoters, and winning over the privileged classes to the new system. Consequently, in opposition to the secret societies of the Liberals, a secret society was founded on moderate principles—the Society of the Anillo, the members of which were to act conjointly with the Ministry. Money was plentifully scattered among the Royal Life Guards, but these distributions being denounced to the Ministry by members of the municipal police, they ridiculed them, treating the information as a symptom of radicalism and republicanism. The regiment of the Royal Cuirassiers, cantoned in Andalusia, was completely seduced; alarming reports were spread in the different provinces whither were sent, as Political Chiefs, members of the Society of the Anillo. At the same time the tribunals received secret instructions to treat with great indulgence all conspiracies that might fall under their judicial powers. The object of these proceedings was to excite an explosion at Madrid, which was to coincide with another at Valencia.[621] Gen. Elío, the traitor of 1814, then a prisoner in that town, was to put himself at the head of the counter-revolution in the eastern part of Spain, the garrison of Valencia being composed of only one regiment, greatly attached to Elío, and hostile, therefore, to the Constitutional system. The Deputy Bertrán de Lys,[a] in the Assembly of the Cortes, entreated the Ministers to withdraw this body of soldiers from Valencia, and when they remained inflexible, brought in a motion of impeachment. The day appointed for the explosion was the last day of May (1822), the feast of St. Ferdinand. The Court was then at Aranjuez. On a given signal the guards rushed into the streets and, backed by the Aranjuez mob, assembled in the front of the palace, shouting cries of "Long live our absolute monarch! Down with the Constitution."[b] This riot was, however, instantly suppressed by Gen. Zayas, and the simultaneous revolt of the regiment of Valencia proved, after a bloody combat between the militia and the soldiers, no more successful. The failures of Aranjuez and Valencia served only to exasperate the Liberals. On all sides parties prepared for self-defense. The agitation becoming universal, the Ministers alone remained passive spectators in the midst of the confusion that announced an approaching storm.

Written on November 14, 1854

First published in the *New-York Daily Tribune* No. 4345, March 23, 1855

Reproduced from the newspaper

[a] Presumably this refers to Manuel Bertrán de Lis.— *Ed.*

[b] Marx quotes from his notes on *The Last Days of Spain. By an Eye-Witness*, London, 1823.— *Ed.*

NOTES
AND
INDEXES

NOTES

[1] Besides *The People's Paper*, Marx also sent this article to the *New-York Daily Tribune*, which published it without title and signature. In the *Tribune* certain passages were omitted.

The People's Paper was founded in May 1852 as a weekly of the revolutionary Chartists. Marx contributed to it and helped Ernest Jones, its chief editor, with the editing and organisational matters, especially in its early years. Between October 1852 and December 1856, besides publishing the articles Marx wrote specially for it, the paper reprinted the most important articles by him and Engels from the *New-York Daily Tribune*. At the beginning of 1856 Marx's contributions to *The People's Paper* became especially frequent. However, towards the end of that year Marx and Engels temporarily broke off relations with Jones and stopped contributing to his weekly because of Jones' increasing association with bourgeois radicals. The paper ceased publication in September 1858.

The *New-York Daily Tribune* was founded in 1841 and was published until 1924. Prior to the mid-1850s it was a left-wing paper and then it became the organ of the Republican Party. Among its contributors were prominent American writers and journalists. Charles Dana, who was strongly influenced by the ideas of utopian socialism, was one of its editors from the late 1840s. Marx contributed to the newspaper from August 1851 to March 1862. His contacts with the newspaper ceased entirely during the US Civil War. p. 3

[2] *Guelphs and Ghibellines*—political parties in Italy formed in the twelfth century in the period of strife between the popes and the German emperors. The *Ghibellines* included mostly feudal lords who supported the emperors and violently opposed the papal party of the *Guelphs*, which represented the upper trade and artisan strata of Italian towns. The parties existed till the fifteenth century. p. 3

[3] Marx is referring to the wars of the Spanish (1701-14) (see Note 236) and the Austrian (1740-48) Succession. As a result of the first war, under the Treaty of Utrecht (1713) Savoy obtained Sicily, Montferrato and part of the duchy of Milan. The Duke of Savoy became King of Sicily. In 1720 Savoy, Piedmont and Sardinia, which had been ceded to Savoy in compensation for Sicily seized by Spain in 1718, formed the Kingdom of Sardinia ruled by the kings of the Savoy dynasty.

The War of the Austrian Succession ended with the Peace Treaty of Aachen (1748) under which the Kingdom of Sardinia received from Austria part of the Principality of Pavia and some other Austrian possessions in Italy. p. 3

4 In conformity with a secret article of a treaty concluded between France and Austria on May 30, 1814 the Republic of Genoa was placed under the aegis of the Savoy dynasty.

This treaty also determined the future of Venice and Lombardy, officially fixed in Article 93 of the Final Act of the Congress of Vienna on June 9, 1815. p. 3

5 The *Holy Alliance*—an association of European monarchs founded in September 1815 on the initiative of the Russian Tsar Alexander I and the Austrian Chancellor Metternich to suppress revolutionary movements and preserve feudal monarchies in the European countries. p. 3

6 There was vague information about the Sardinian memorandum in the press (see *The Times*, No. 22330, April 1, 1856). Presumably this refers to the Note by Count Cavour, the Prime Minister and Minister of Foreign Affairs of Piedmont, of March 27, 1856, which he sent to the French Minister of Foreign Affairs Count Walewski and the British Foreign Secretary Lord Clarendon. The Note concerned the situation in the Papal States, occupied by Austrian and French troops, and in the Kingdom of Naples.

The Italian question was discussed at a session of the Congress of Paris on April 8, 1856. Cavour used the text of the Note as the basis of his speech in which he came out against the Austrian domination in Italy and tried to persuade the audience to resolve the Italian question in favour of the Sardinian monarchy.

The domestic policy of King Ferdinand II of Naples was subjected to harsh criticism by Cavour and other speakers in the course of the discussion on April 8. On April 16, 1856, at the closing session of the Congress, the Piedmontese plenipotentiaries handed another memorandum on the same issue to Britain and France which Marx cites in this article.

The discussion of the Italian question did not lead to any decisions. However, it promoted the supremacy of the Kingdom of Sardinia in the Italian national liberation movement. p. 3

7 On December 2, 1851 Louis Bonaparte accomplished a coup d'état by dissolving the Legislative Assembly. p. 3

8 During the 1848-49 revolution, the Whig government, of which Lord Palmerston was Foreign Secretary, supported only in word the liberal movement in Italy which strove for moderate reforms and constitutional changes. In fact, however, Britain did not help Piedmont in its struggle against Austrian rule in Northern Italy either in 1848 or in 1849. p. 3

9 Marx is referring to the dispatch of an expeditionary corps to Italy in April 1849 under the pretext of defending the Roman Republic. Initiated by the President of the French Republic, Louis Bonaparte, this invasion of the Roman Republic aimed at restoring the Pope's temporal power (see K. Marx, *The Class Struggles in France. 1848-1850*, present edition, Vol. 10, pp. 91-94). p. 5

10 The reference is to the brutal suppression of the Irish uprising in the summer of 1848 by Clarendon, Lord-Lieutenant of Ireland (1847-52), which broke out as a result of the famine caused by the potato crop failure in 1845-47. p. 5

[11] Marx means Louis Napoleon whose advent to power resulted in mass arrests of republicans and participants in the 1848-49 revolution.

Cayenne—a reference to French Guiana, where political prisoners were sent for penal servitude.

Lambessa (Lambèse)—a French penal colony founded on the ruins of the ancient Roman town of Lambessa in North Africa; from 1851 to 1860 it was a place of exile for political prisoners.

Belle Isle—an island in the Bay of Biscay, where political prisoners were detained in 1849-57, among others, workers who took part in the Paris uprising in June 1848 were imprisoned there. p. 5

[12] It was Charles Albert, King of Sardinia, who abdicated after the defeat of the Piedmontese army at Novara on March 23, 1849, during the Austro-Italian war of 1848-49. His son Victor Emmanuel II, the new king, concluded an armistice with the Austrians on March 26, and on August 6 a peace treaty was signed restoring Austrian rule in Northern Italy and the Austrian protectorate over a number of states of Central Italy. p. 5

[13] Marx is apparently referring to Napoleon III's plans to marry his cousin Prince Napoleon nicknamed Plon-Plon to Clotilde, the daughter of King Victor Emmanuel II of Sardinia. The wedding took place in 1859. p. 6

[14] The *Delphic oracle*—Apollo's oracle at Delphi reputed for its prophecies about political and religious events which enabled Delphi to conduct and support certain conservative tendencies in politics. The knowledge of the situation in different Greek states influenced the prophecies of the oracle's medium, the Pythia.

The *Trophonian oracle* was in a cave at a temple near the town of Lebadea, Boeotia. Its prophecies were of a more private nature and concerned the human destinies in the main, and so it was much less important than the Delphic oracle.

Marx thought that M. P.'s speeches lacked originality and merely reflected Palmerston's policy. p. 6

[15] The *Crédit Mobilier* is short for the *Société générale du Crédit Mobilier*—a French joint-stock bank founded in 1852 by the Péreire brothers. The bank was closely connected with the Government of Napoleon III and, protected by it, engaged in speculation. It went bankrupt in 1867 and was liquidated in 1871.

The first article on *Crédit Mobilier* was published by Marx in *The People's Paper* without any indication that it was "to be continued". The editors of the *New-York Daily Tribune* who published the subsequent articles on the subject printed them as a series and defined them by ordinal numbers.

In this volume the numbers of articles are put in square brackets as subtitles. p. 8

[16] Louis Bonaparte was nicknamed "the Little" by Victor Hugo in a speech in the Legislative Assembly in November 1851; the nickname became popular after the publication of Hugo's pamphlet *Napoléon le Petit* (1852). p. 11

[17] In May 1852 Louis Bonaparte's presidential powers were to expire and, according to the Constitution of the French Republic of 1848, new elections were to be held on the second Sunday in May. In view of this the Bonapartists began to prepare a coup d'état in the second half of 1851. They launched a propaganda campaign trying to intimidate the man in the street with the possible victory of democrats and socialists and with the anarchy which, they claimed, would set in if "the red spectre" was victorious. p. 14

[18] The *Society of December 10*—a secret Bonapartist organisation founded in 1849 and consisting mainly of declassed elements, political adventurers and the military. For details see Marx's work *The Eighteenth Brumaire of Louis Bonaparte* (present edition, Vol. 11, pp. 148-51). p. 14

[19] The *Fronde*, a movement in France against the absolutist regime from 1648 to 1653, involved various social sections—from radical peasant and plebeian elements and the bourgeoisie in opposition to high-ranking officials and aristocrats—which in many cases pursued opposite aims. The defeat of the Fronde led to the strengthening of absolutism. p. 14

[20] The *Corps Législatif* was established, alongside the State Council and the Senate, under the Constitution of February 14, 1852, after the Bonapartist coup d'état of 1851. Its powers were confined to endorsing bills drawn up by the State Council. The *Corps Législatif* was an elected body. However, the elections were supervised by state officials and the police, so that a majority obedient to the government was ensured. In fact it served as a screen for Napoleon III's unlimited powers. p. 16

[21] This refers to an *Act to remove doubts respecting promissory notes of the Governor and Company of the Bank of England, for payment of sums of money under £5* of March 3, 1797 and *An Act for continuing for a limited time, the restriction contained in the minute of Council of the 26th of February, 1797, on payment of cash by the bank* of May 3, 1797 which established a compulsory rate of banknotes and gave temporary permission to the Bank to stop the exchange of banknotes for gold. In 1821 the exchange was resumed under the law of 1819. p. 24

[22] In the 1850s, while studying the foreign policies of European states and endeavouring to disclose the inner springs of these policies, Marx often turned to the history of diplomacy. Working at the British Museum, he discovered, in the collection of an English historian and writer, William Coxe, a mass of eighteenth-century documents, including letters from English ambassadors in St. Petersburg. This find served as an immediate stimulus for writing the *Revelations of the Diplomatic History of the 18th Century* which he conceived at the beginning of 1856, when the Crimean war was still in progress. Marx wrote later: "While looking through the diplomatic manuscripts in the possession of the British Museum I came across a series of English documents, going back from the end of the eighteenth century to the time of Peter the Great, which reveal the continuous secret collaboration between the Cabinets of London and St. Petersburg, and seem to indicate that this relationship arose at the time of Peter the Great" (see present edition, Vol. 17, p. 117).

Initially Marx intended to publish some of these documents, with his own comments, in the American *Putnam's Monthly Magazine*, but he then decided to develop the theme and write an extensive (about 20 printed sheets) work on the history of Anglo-Russian relations in the 18th century. However, his negotiations with the German publisher in London Nikolaus Trübner in March-May 1856 on the publication of the work were fruitless. Marx failed to find another publisher and thought of printing it in one of the newspapers published by the followers of the English conservative journalist, David Urquhart, who was in opposition to the British Government and vigorously criticised its foreign policy. Marx had occasionally contributed to these papers, though he always dissociated himself from Urquhart's anti-democratic stance (see, for example, present edition, Vol. 12, pp. 477-78; Vol. 17, p. 117). It was because of Urquhart's political approach that Marx hesitated for some time before entrusting him with his work for publication. Marx wrote to Engels on

August 1, 1856: "...Should Urquhart come out with his counter-revolutionary nonsense in such a way that collaboration with him would discredit me in the eyes of the revolutionaries here, I would be obliged ... to decide against it" (present edition, Vol. 40, p. 62).

The *Revelations of the Diplomatic History of the 18th Century,* which Marx wrote from June 1856 to March 1857, began to appear in instalments in *The Sheffield Free Press,* an Urquhartist newspaper, in late June 1856. But since the editors interfered with the text by arbitrarily making cuts without Marx's consent, he stopped publication and handed over the work to another Urquhartist periodical—the London weekly *Free Press.* The work was published from the very beginning without any abridgements, as the text was sent in by Marx, from August 16, 1856 to April 1, 1857.

The published text was, in Marx's own words, only an Introduction to a projected work that was never written. It is divided into five chapters. More than half consists of documents (reports, letters and pamphlets) concerning the history of diplomatic relations between England and Russia in the 18th century. Chapter I consists of documents and Marx's numerous comments. In chapters II and III the proportion of Marx's text proper is insignificant. The whole of Chapter IV was written by Marx; in Chapter V, where he profusely cites the pamphlet *Truth Is But Truth...* Marx gives a description of Peter I's foreign policy.

The *Revelations* was never reprinted during Marx's and Engels' lifetime. After Engels' death this work, like some other works written by Marx and Engels in the 1850s, was prepared for the press by Marx's daughter Eleanor. It appeared in London under the title *Secret Diplomatic History of the Eighteenth Century* after Eleanor's death in 1899. In this book, the pamplet *The Defensive Treaty* (see this volume, pp. 65-73) was printed as a separate chapter. Hence, as distinct from the publication during Marx's lifetime, this book contained six chapters. Moreover, in the 1899 edition the concluding part (about four pages) of the fifth (fourth in the original) chapter was omitted.

In English the *Revelations* was also published in London and New York in 1969; the French translation appeared in 1954; the German translation in 1960, 1977 and 1981; the Polish translation in 1967; the Italian translation in 1977.

All these publications, as a rule, reproduce or are based upon the 1899 edition but restore the concluding pages of the fifth (fourth in the original) chapter omitted in that edition. Commentaries in some of them are biased.

In this volume the text of the book is reproduced from *The Free Press* collated with the 1899 edition.

Some minor factual inaccuracies are silently corrected. p. 25

23 In this chapter Marx quotes letters of the British diplomats in Russia and the account of L. K. Pitt, Chaplain at the English trading station in St. Petersburg, which he discovered at the British Museum in the collection of William Coxe, an English historian and writer (see present edition, Vol. 40, p. 17). p. 27

24 This letter, as well as other reports from British diplomats in Russia in 1736-39, was published, with the permission of the British Government, in full in *Sbornik imperatorskogo russkogo istoricheskogo obshchestva* (Records of the Imperial Russian Historical Society), St. Petersburg, 1892, Vol. 80, pp. 13-19, from the original in the Public Record Office of Great Britain. p. 27

25 Marx is referring to the mediation offered by Britain and Holland in the Russo-Turkish war of 1735-39; it was rejected by Russia. p. 27

[26] An allusion to the *Union of Kalmar* (1397-1523)—a personal union of Denmark, Norway (with Iceland) and Sweden (with Finland) under Danish kings. In the fifteenth century Sweden virtually withdrew from the union. Christian II of Denmark made an attempt to restore his rule over Sweden by staging a massacre in Stockholm in November 1520 (this came to be called "the blood-bath of Stockholm"). This caused a popular uprising led by Gustavus Eriksson (Gustavus Vasa) and as a result Sweden was restored as a state. p. 28

[27] Marx is referring to a plan, drawn up by Russian diplomats in the 1760s, to unite the North-European states of Russia, Prussia, England, Denmark, Sweden and Poland. It came to be known as "the grand scheme uniting the Powers of the North" or the Northern Alliance, and was to be directed against France and Austria. Despite a number of treaties concluded by Russia (a defensive treaty with Prussia, 1764; a defensive treaty with Denmark, 1765; and a trade agreement with Great Britain, 1766), the project was not implemented because Prussia and England opposed it and Russia's foreign policy underwent some changes after the Russo-Turkish war of 1768-74. p. 29

[28] Presumably a reference to the preparation of the Russo-Prussian Treaty of Alliance which Peter III and Frederick II concluded on April 24 (May 5), 1762 during the Seven Years' War (1756-63). Frederick II received back all of his lands which had been conquered by Russian troops. Sir George Macartney's information was inaccurate: at that time Count Alexei Bestuzhev-Ryumin was relieved of his diplomatic duties. p. 29

[29] Marx is quoting the words of Horace Walpole and the statements by the Earl of Sandwich and William Pitt the Younger mentioned below according to T. S. Hughes' *The History of England, from the Accession of George III, 1760, to the Accession of Queen Victoria, 1837.* Third edition. London, 1846, Vol. I, p. 183; Vol. II, pp. 146, 261; Vol. III, p. 124. p. 30

[30] This letter was published in *Diaries and Correspondence of James Harris, First Earl of Malmesbury; containing an account of his missions to the courts of Madrid, Frederick the Great, Catherine the Second, and the Hague, and his special missions to Berlin, Brunswick, and the French Republic.* Edited by his grandson, the Third Earl. Vol. I, London, 1844, pp. 528-35. p. 31

[31] Sir James Harris writes about the moods prevailing at the Russian Court, in which the British Government was much interested since it intended to win Russia's support in the war against the North-American colonies (1775-83). p. 31

[32] The *Peace of Teshen* concluded between Austria and Prussia on May 13, 1779 ended the war of the Bavarian succession. The war had been caused by the claims of the German states to various parts of Bavaria after the death of the childless Bavarian Elector Maximilian Joseph, and also by the struggle between Austria and Prussia for domination over Germany. Under this treaty and the adjoining conventions, Prussia and Austria obtained some territories of Bavaria, while Saxony received money compensation. The Elector of the Palatinate became Elector of Bavaria. The Peace of Teshen confirmed a series of peace treaties which had previously been concluded by the German states. At first Russia and France acted as mediators between the warring countries, and in a special article of the treaty they were declared guarantor-powers. p. 31

[33] Harris presumably means the document on Spain's declaration of war on Britain in June 1779. p. 31

[34] The declaration of armed neutrality announced by Catherine II on February 28 (March 11), 1780, was directed against Britain during her war against the insurgent North-American colonies (1775-83). It proclaimed the right of neutral powers to trade freely with the belligerent countries and a series of other principles guaranteeing security to merchant shipping. The Declaration was joined in 1780-83 by Denmark, Sweden, Holland, Prussia, Austria, Portugal and the Kingdom of the Two Sicilies. p. 32

[35] In March 1781 the British Government offered Russia the Island of Minorca, an important strategic base in the Mediterranean, on the condition that Russia gave up her armed neutrality (see Note 34) and supported Britain in her war against the North-American colonies. This offer was rejected. p. 32

[36] This refers to the negotiations which ended with the signing of the Versailles Peace Treaty on September 3, 1783 between Britain and the USA with its allies—France, Spain and the Netherlands. According to this treaty, Britain recognised the USA's independence. p. 32

[37] On the initiative of Prussia, a convention on preliminary terms of partition of Poland was signed in St. Petersburg on 6 (17) February, 1772. Soon Austria also joined it. The partition undermined the national independence of Poland, which was undergoing a profound social and political crisis. p. 32

[38] This refers to the aggravation of Russo-Swedish relations after the 1772 coup d'état of Gustavus III. Having abolished the 1719 Constitution and the power of the aristocratic oligarchy, who had enjoyed the support of Britain and Russia, Gustavus virtually restored absolutism in Sweden. Russia as a guarantor of Sweden's statehood under the Peace of Nystad (1721), feared the growing influence of France which was financing Gustavus III. p. 32

[39] The *Kuchuk-Kainarji peace treaty* ended the Russo-Turkish war of 1768-74. Russia obtained part of the Black Sea shore between the South Bug and the Dnieper with the fortress of Kinburn; she also gained Azov, Kerch and Yenikale and compelled Turkey to recognise the independence of the Crimea. Russian merchant ships won free passage through the Bosphorus and Dardanelles. In conformity with the treaty the Sultan also undertook to grant certain privileges to the Greek Orthodox Church. p. 33

[40] The reference is to George III, King of Great Britain and Ireland (1760-1820), and a group of Tories supporting him. George III belonged to the Hanover royal family which held the British throne under the provisions of the Act of Settlement (1701); up to 1815 the British kings of the Hanover dynasty were also the Electors of Hanover, and up to 1837 Kings of Hanover. p. 33

[41] Marx draws a parallel here between the 18th-century events and the actions of the British Admiralty in 1854 when an attempt was made to raise a blockade of the Russian harbours on the Black Sea at the beginning of the Crimean war (1853-56). James Graham's statement, report about his dispatch of April 5, 1854 and Admiral James Dundas' replies are cited by Marx according to the material of the John Arthur Roebuck commission appointed to investigate the state of the British Army in the Crimea ("State of the Army before Sebastopol", *The Times*, No. 22054, May 15, 1855). p. 34

[42] Marx quotes George III's speech on October 26, 1775, the words of Lord Cavendish and North's statement mentioned below from T. S. Hughes' *The History of England...*, Vol. II, pp. 191, 113. p. 34

[43] Marx is referring to the Versailles Peace Treaty (see Note 36). p. 35

44 A reference to the retirement of Rockingham's ministry after his death on July 1, 1782. p. 35

45 Marx quotes Burke from T. S. Hughes' *The History of England...*, Vol. III, pp. 148-49. p. 36

46 The Shelburne ministry (1782-83) succeeded Rockingham's ministry (see Note 44). p. 36

47 [Ph. H.] Mahon, *History of England from the Peace of Utrecht to the Peace of Aix-la-Chapelle*, Vol. I, London, 1839, p. 341. p. 36

48 The reference is to the French Revolution. p. 36

49 A reference to Russia's secession from the second anti-French coalition in 1800. p. 37

50 Marx is referring to the diplomatic correspondence between Pozzo di Borgo, the Russian ambassador to France, and the Russian Chancellor Count Nesselrode; Marx got acquainted with it from a collection of diplomatic documents and material entitled *The Portfolio; or a Collection of State Papers* edited by David Urquhart and published in London from 1835 to 1837, and also from *Recueil des documents relatifs à la Russie pour la plupart secrets et inédits utiles à consulter dans la crise actuelle*, Paris, 1854. p. 38

51 A reference to the treaties on the partition of the Spanish possessions in Europe and elsewhere concluded by France with Britain, the Netherlands and Austria in 1698 and 1700 in anticipation of the death of the childless King of Spain, Charles II of Habsburg.

On October 2, 1700, Charles II made a will by which the Spanish crown was to go to Philip of Anjou, the grandson of Louis XIV of France, provided Philip renounced his right to the French crown. Despite this, in February 1701 Louis XIV made Philip of Anjou, who in 1700 became King of Spain under the name of Philip V, his heir, which led to the *War of the Spanish Succession* (1701-14). In this war, Britain, Austria, the Netherlands and some other countries fought against France and Spain. France's failures in the war resulted in the realignment of forces in Europe (see Note 236). p. 41

52 Presumably Marx means here the annexation of Cracow by Austria after the 1846 insurrection. p. 41

53 After the rout of the Swedish army at Poltava, Charles XII fled to Turkey and settled in Bendery where he stayed till 1713. Marx used the Latin text of the manifesto (Carolus, *Espèce de Manifeste du Roi de Suède contre le Roi Auguste*) published in Lamberty, *Mémoires pour servir à l'histoire du XVIII siècle, contenant les négociations, traitez, résolutions et autres documents authentiques concernant les affaires d'état*, Tome sixième, La Haye, 1728, pp. 434-36. p. 41

54 The *Glorious revolution*—the name given in English historiography to the coup d'état of 1688 which overthrew the Stuarts and established a constitutional monarchy, with William III of Orange at its head (from 1689), which was based on a compromise between the landed aristocracy and the big bourgeoisie. p. 41

55 The *Peace Treaty of Travendahl* signed on August 18, 1700, ended the war between Denmark and the duchy of Holstein. It was concluded under military pressure from England, Holland and Sweden. Denmark was forced to recognise the independence of Holstein and withdraw from the anti-Swedish coalition. p. 41

[56] Marx is presumably referring to the fact that during the Northern War (1700-21) an abortive attempt was made in 1716 to unite the Danish and Russian naval forces. p. 42

[57] An inaccuracy in the text: Count Gyllenborg calls himself the author of the pamphlet not in the letter to Baron Görtz of January 12 (23), 1717 but in a letter to his brother of October 16 (27), 1716. Marx quotes Gyllenborg's letter from *Letters which passed between Count Gyllenborg, the barons Görtz, Sparre, and others; relating to the Design of Raising a Rebellion in His Majesty's Dominions, to be supported by a Force from Sweden*, London, 1717.

The *Court of St. James's*, called so after St. James's Palace in London, the residence of British kings until the beginning of the nineteenth century. p. 43

[58] The reference is to the decisions reached at a conference held by Peter I and Danish and Saxon ministers on October 22, 1711 in the town of Crossen (Krossen), Brandenburg. The conference drew up plans for immediate military-diplomatic action by the Allies against Sweden. p. 45

[59] *Rix dollar*—continental silver coin in the sixteenth-nineteenth centuries. p. 45

[60] This passage in *The Free Press* of September 20, 1856 was preceded by the following editorial note: "Our readers may, perhaps, require to be reminded that the following is a quotation from a pamphlet published in London, in 1716, and entitled the 'Northern Crisis'. Our last number contained the recital (copied from "The Northern Crisis") of the Danish Minister's reasons for delaying the descent upon Schonen." p. 46

[61] That is, the War of the Spanish Succession (see Note 51). p. 47

[62] This refers to an episode in the first stage of the Northern War (1700-21)—the defeat of the Russian troops at Narva on November 30, 1700. p. 48

[63] A reference to the *Peace Treaty of Altranstadt* concluded on September 24, 1706 between Augustus II, King of Poland and Elector of Saxony, and Charles XII of Sweden. Under the provisions of the treaty, Augustus II was to abdicate from the Polish throne in favour of Stanislaus Leszczynski and annul the union with Russia. p. 48

[64] See Note 55. p. 49

[65] This sentence opens the next instalment in *The Free Press* on October 4, 1856. The editors of the newspaper preceded it with the following comment: "We beg to remind our readers that the following is part of a pamphlet written in—, and entitled the 'Northern Crisis', and that it is a continuation of 'Important Reflections' on the Danish Minister's 'Reasons for delaying the descent upon Schonen'". p. 50

[66] This refers to a 9,000-strong Russian detachment summoned by the Grand Duke Karl Leopold to Mecklenburg in 1716. The Duke was married to Peter I's niece Yekaterina Ivanovna. The same year the detachment was withdrawn from the duchy. p. 50

[67] A reference to what is known as the *Holy Roman Empire of the German Nation* founded in 962 when Otto I, the German King, was crowned Holy Roman Emperor. By the eighteenth century the Empire, ruled by sovereigns from the Habsburg dynasty, lost its political influence; it ceased to exist on August 6, 1806. p. 51

[68] A reference to the war waged by Austria and her ally, the Venetian Republic, against Turkey in 1716-18. p. 51

[69] Augustus II, the Elector of Saxony (1694-1733) and King of Poland (1697-1706 and 1709-33), adopted the Catholic faith to facilitate his election to the Polish throne. p. 53

[70] Marx means the pamphlet: [G. Mackenzie,] *Truth is but Truth, as it is Timed! Or, our Ministry's present Measures against the Moscovite vindicated by Plain and Obvious Reasons, Tending to Prove,* etc., London, 1719. p. 56

[71] On August 2, 1718 Britain, Austria and France concluded an alliance against Spain with a view to retaining the provisions of the Peace Treaty of Utrecht, which confirmed the results of the War of the Spanish Succession (see notes 51 and 236). On August 22 of that year the British fleet attacked and destroyed the Spanish fleet near the Cape of Passaro (Sicily). p. 57

[72] Marx took the data for his calculations from A. Anderson, *An Historical and Chronological Deduction of the Origin of Commerce, from the earliest accounts. Containing an history of great commercial interests of the British Empire,* Vols. I, III, IV, London, 1787, 1789. p. 58

[73] The *Balance of Trade doctrine*—one of the tenets of mercantilism. According to it a country's prosperity depends totally on the constant inflow of bullion from abroad, and to secure this it is necessary to attain a favourable balance of foreign trade. p. 60

[74] Marx has in mind the book: S. Puffendorf, *De Rebus gestis Friderici Wilhelmi Magni, Electoris Brandenburgici, commentariorum Libri novendecim,* Berolini, 1695. p. 60

[75] The *Russian* or *Muscovy Company* (its real name: Merchant Adventurers for the Discovery of Lands, Countries, Isles, not before known or frequented by any English)—an English trade company founded in the mid-sixteenth century which enjoyed some privileges from the Russian Government. However, the Company's intentions to get hold of the Russian market and also its plans to seize the North of Russia and the Volga route in 1612 during the period of the Polish and Swedish intervention caused dissatisfaction on the part of the Russian Government and merchants. The result of it was that in 1649 the Company virtually ceased to exist. At the beginning of the eighteenth century, during the War of the Spanish Succession (see Note 51), the Company was re-established as England was in great need of shipbuilding materials. p. 61

[76] The publication date of these petitions is not known. p. 61

[77] This refers to the fact Marx wrote about as early as June 1854 in his article "The Formation of a Special Ministry of War in Britain.—The War on the Danube.—The Economic Situation": "For the measure announced by Sir J. Graham in last Monday's House of Commons, viz.: The non-blockade of the port of Archangel, *The Morning Herald* accounts in the following laconic paragraph: 'There is a house at Archangel which bears the name of the Chancellor of the Exchequer'" (see present edition, Vol. 13, pp. 225-26). p. 61

[78] See Note 54. p. 61

[79] Marx has in mind the Polish emigrant to the USA and contributor to the *New-York Daily Tribune* Adam Gurowski, the French historian and writer Elias Regnault and the German philosopher and journalist Bruno Bauer, who wrote

a great deal on the Eastern question and European foreign policy during the Crimean war. p. 62

80 The fortress of Kars was captured by Russian troops during the Crimean war in November 1855. See K. Marx's series of articles "The Fall of Kars" (present edition, Vol. 14, pp. 621-54). p. 63

81 The *Suez Canal* was built from 1859 to 1869. Ferdinand de Lesseps, a French diplomat and engineer, obtained a concession for the building and exploitation of it on November 30, 1854. The British Government was against the project at first, fearing the expansion of French influence in Egypt and the Middle East. p. 63

82 The town of Narva was captured by the Russian troops in 1558 during the Livonian War (1558-83) fought by Russia against the Livonian Confederation, the Polish-Lithuanian state and Sweden. p. 63

83 The *Treaty of Ryswick of 1697* ended the war between France and the Augsburg League (the Netherlands, England, Spain, the German Emperor and several German princes) which lasted from 1688. It confirmed the slightly changed pre-war state boundaries. France was obliged to recognise the 1688 coup d'état in England (see Note 54). p. 64

84 Marx has drawn on the anonymous pamphlet *Reasons for the present conduct of Sweden in relation to the trade in the Baltic set forth in a letter from a gentleman at Dantzick, to his friend at Amsterdam. Translated from the French original published in Holland; and now submitted to the consideration of all just and impartial Britons,* London, 1715. p. 64

85 This is the nickname of the British statesman Robert Walpole, who habitually employed bribery to have his supporters elected to Parliament. p. 65

86 This pamphlet, which contains the text of the treaty and comments to it ("queries"), was published, as Marx supposed, in 1720. The author of the queries is unknown.

The Publishers express their gratitude to the British Museum Library for kindly granting them photocopies of this document and *Truth is but Truth,* the pamphlet Marx used in writing Chapter V (see this volume, pp. 92-96). p. 65

87 A reference to the war of the Spanish Succession (see Note 51). p. 67

88 The *Treaty of Westphalia,* signed in 1648, ended the Thirty Years' War. Sweden gained a considerable part of East Pomerania and also the Isle of Rügen, the port of Wismar and the bishoprics of Bremen and Verden, and became a member of the Holy Roman Empire (see Note 67).

The *Peace Treaty of Roskilde* ended the 1657-58 war between Denmark and Sweden. Denmark ceded her possessions in the South of the Scandinavian peninsular, the fief of Trondheim in Norway and several islands in the Baltic Sea. Besides, Denmark pledged to open negotiations with the Duke of Holstein-Gottorp on relieving him of her suzerainty, to annul the alliances and treaties directed against Sweden and to free Sweden from payment of the Sound duties.

The *Copenhagen Peace Treaty* ended the 1658-60 war between Denmark and Sweden. The war, provoked by differences connected with the implementation of the Treaty of Roskilde, was launched by Sweden with a view to completely abolishing Denmark's independence. Under the Copenhagen Treaty, the Isle of Bornholm and the fief of Trondheim were returned to Denmark.

The *Peace Treaty of Lunden* ended the 1675-79 war between Denmark and Sweden. Denmark gave up her possessions in Skåne which went to Sweden. p. 70

89 See Note 55. p. 71

90 The great *Battle of Poltava* (the Ukraine) was fought between Russian and Swedish troops on July 8, 1709, in the course of the Northern War (1700-21). The Russian troops commanded by Peter I won a decisive victory over Charles XII. p. 71

91 This refers to the *Act of Settlement* of June 12, 1701 which fixed the succession to the throne on the Hanover royal family (see Note 40) and deprived the Stuarts of the right of succeeding to the English throne. p. 72

92 The reference is to the "glorious revolution" (see Note 54). p. 72

93 In this chapter Marx tried to outline Russia's historical development from the ninth to the fifteenth centuries from the perspective of her role in international affairs, and attempted to reveal the historical roots of the foreign policy of Russian Tsarism in the nineteenth century. Marx did not intend to give a comprehensive analysis of Russian history and restricted himself to making "some preliminary remarks on the general history of Russian politics" (see p. 74). Marx's main source was *History of Russia and of Peter the Great* (London, 1829), an English translation of a very unreliable book by the French aristocrat Philippe Paul Ségur. For comments on Marx's other sources see pp. XXI and XXII. p. 74

94 Oleg, Prince of Kiev, raided Constantinople in 911. His successor Igor made war on Byzantium on two occasions, in 941 and 944, which resulted in the conclusion of a trade agreement in 944. p. 75

95 Anna, the daughter of the Byzantine Emperor Romanus II, was married to Prince Vladimir Svyatoslavich of Kiev (who after baptism adopted the name of Vasily) in 987, after her father's death, by her brother, the Byzantine Emperor Basil II (976-1025). The name of Prince Vladimir Svyatoslavich is connected with the adoption of Christianity in Kiev Russia (988-989) and the latter's growing might. p. 75

96 Presumably Marx is hinting at the so-called "Will of Peter the Great"—a spurious document, different versions of which were repeatedly published in Western Europe in the nineteenth century. Historians have since proved irrefutably that the "Will" was a complete forgery. p. 75

97 An inaccuracy in Marx's text. The third prince of the Vladimir-Suzdal principality was Andrei Bogolyubsky's brother, Vsevolod Bolshoye Gnezdo (1176-1212), during whose reign the territory of the principality was extended and its political and cultural significance grew considerably. p. 77

98 The Tartar-Mongol yoke in Russia ended in 1480 as a result of the long and heroic struggle by the Russian people (see Note 109). p. 77

99 Marx presumably means the rise of the Moscow Principality in the fourteenth century and the victories of the Russian troops under Dmitry Donskoi over the Golden Horde (battles on the Vozha River in 1378 and on Kulikovo Field in 1380). Later, in his *Chronological Notes* (1882), Marx wrote in particular: "*September 8, 1380—Battle* on the broad field of *Kulikovo;* Dmitry's complete victory; 200,000 said to be killed on both sides." p. 78

100 An inaccuracy in Marx's text: Yury Danilovich, the elder brother of Ivan I Danilovich Kalita, bore the title of Grand Prince of Vladimir from 1317; his brother inherited it in 1328. p. 78

101 The reference is to a branch of the Rurik dynasty, the princes of the Principality of Tver which existed in Russia in the thirteenth-fifteenth centuries. In the struggle for power with Prince Yury Danilovich of Moscow (see Note 100), Prince Mikhail Yaroslavich of Tver (1271-1318) was defeated and killed in the camp of Uzbek Khan. p. 78

102 The episcopal seat of the primate was finally transferred to Moscow in 1328. p. 79

103 In 1492 Ivan III sent a deed to Sultan Bajazet II containing a protest against the harassment of Russian merchants in the Turkish possessions.. Having received no answer from the Sultan (his envoy was detained in Lithuania), Ivan III sent his own man, ambassador Mikhail Pleshcheyev, to Turkey with instructions to confirm the claims contained in the 1492 deed and to "stand on his feet not knees" during the audience. Pleshcheyev's mission was successful. Sultan Bajazet II promised not to put obstacles in the way of Russian merchants within the Ottoman Empire. p. 80

104 The Golden Horde practically ceased to exist in the second quarter of the fifteenth century due to internecine strife and the liberation movement of the subject peoples, especially the Russian people (see notes 99 and 109). It was succeeded by a Tartar state, the Big Horde, which sprang up on the lower reaches of the Volga; the Nogai (Nogay) Horde, which occupied the territory from the Volga to the Irtysh River, virtually separated from the Golden Horde at the end of the fourteenth and beginning of the fifteenth century; the final separation took place in 1426-40. p. 81

105 Timour (Tamerlane) dealt crushing blows to the Golden Horde in his three big campaigns (1389, 1391, 1394-95). p. 81

106 Marx means the free Cossack communities formed on the southern and south-eastern outskirts of the Moscow state in the second half of the fifteenth century by the peasants who had fled from the landowners, and the townsmen. They were used for defence purposes. p. 81

107 The *Crimean Khanate* separated from the Golden Horde in 1443 as a result of a prolonged struggle; in 1475 it became a vassal of the Ottoman Empire. p. 81

108 Ivan III ceased paying tribute to the Big Horde (see Note 104) in 1476. p. 81

109 The disintegration of the Golden Horde (see Note 104) and especially the heroic struggle of the Russian people were the principal factors which led to the liberation of the Grand Principality of Moscow from the Tartar-Mongol yoke. The events which culminated this struggle are presented by Marx inaccurately. Khan Akhmat launched two campaigns against Moscow: in 1472 and in 1480. In 1472 he captured the town of Aleksin but was forced to retreat before the Russians. In 1480 Khan Akhmat's troops were confronted by strong Russian detachments on the River Ugra (known as "Standing on the Ugra"). Khan Akhmat was forced to retreat in October and November and on January 6, 1481 he was killed by the Nogay Khan Ivak. The "Standing on the Ugra" put an end to the 240-year Tartar-Mongol yoke over Russia.

The Crimean Khan Mengli-Ghirai defeated the Big Horde, but much later, in 1502. p. 82

110 In 1459 the Vyatka territory was subordinated to Moscow though it had enjoyed certain autonomy. The reign of Ivan III in the second half of the fifteenth century was marked by the growing separatist movement of the Vyatka boyars and merchants. However, in 1485-86 the movement was suppressed and in 1489 the Vyatka territory was incorporated into the Grand Principality of Moscow. p. 82

111 The feudal republic of Pskov existed as an independent state from 1348 to 1510. p. 82

112 A reference to the victory of the Moscow army over the Novgorodians on the banks of the River Shelon in 1471. This victory predetermined the abolition of political independence for the Novgorod feudal republic, which existed ever since the twelfth century. p. 83

113 After 1475 despite the old statutes legal proceedings on the complaints of the Novgorodians were not taken in their native city but in Moscow. p. 83

114 The final incorporation of Novgorod in the Grand Principality of Moscow took place in 1478. p. 84

115 The reference is to a kind of a republic formed by the Ukrainian Cossacks (Zaporozhye Sech) in the mid-sixteenth century. It was defeated by Peter I in 1709 and finally abolished by Catherine II in 1775. p. 84

116 The last independent Prince of Tver, Mikhail Borisovich, was married to the granddaughter of the Lithuanian Prince Casimir. Trying to throw off the growing dependence on Moscow, he entered into an alliance with Lithuania. However, Ivan III succeeded in breaking Tver's resistance and in 1485 Tver was finally annexed to Moscow. So ended the struggle of the Tver and Moscow princes for supremacy in Russia (see Note 101). p. 85

117 An inaccuracy in the text. Ivan III had four brothers, whose appanages were annexed to the possessions of the Grand Prince at different times. One of his brothers, Andrei Bolshoi, died in confinement. p. 85

118 After Casimir's death in 1492, his son Jan Albrecht succeeded to the Polish throne, and another son, Alexander, to the Lithuanian throne. p. 85

119 Elena Ivanovna, the daughter of Ivan III and Sophia Palaeologus, was married to the Lithuanian Grand Prince Alexander on the initiative of and pressure from the Lithuanian nobles who hoped by this means to win concessions from Ivan III. p. 86

120 As a result of the wars waged by Ivan III against the Grand Principality of Lithuania (1487-94 and 1500-03) western Russian towns (Chernigov, Novgorod-Seversky, Gomel, Bryansk) and the lands adjoining them were appended to Moscow. Smolensk was incorporated into Russia in 1514, after Ivan III's death. p. 86

121 The facts are inaccurate here. In an attempt to save the Byzantine Empire from the Turkish invasion the representatives of the Eastern Orthodox Church entered into union with the Catholic Church at the Council of Florence in 1439. Under the terms of the Union of Florence the Eastern Orthodox Church acknowledged the supremacy of the Pope and accepted the Catholic dogmas, while retaining its own rites. After the capture of Constantinople by the Turks

in 1453, Thomas, the brother of the last Byzantine Emperor Constantine XI Palaeologus, and his family, fled to Rome.

Pope Paul II, by planning to marry Thomas's daughter Sophia (Zoë) Palaeologus to Ivan III, and basing himself on the decisions of the Union of Florence, hoped to consolidate his power over the Russian Orthodox Church.

Ivan III married Sophia Palaeologus on November 12, 1472, under Pope Sixtus IV. Ivan III used this marriage to enhance Russia's prestige in international affairs and his own authority as a Grand Prince in Russia. p. 86

122 In this chapter, Marx drew on one of Engels' articles about Pan-Slavism, written for the *New-York Daily Tribune* in 1856, but never published. The manuscripts of these articles, which the editors of the newspaper returned to Marx, have not been traced. Soon after the ***Revelations of the Diplomatic History of the 18th Century*** had been published, Marx wrote to Engels on April 9, 1857: "In the last one I used the text of one of your articles, in which you speak of Peter I" (see present edition, Vol. 40, p. 120). p. 88

123 This refers to the Russo-Turkish wars of 1686-99 and 1710-13 and Peter I's campaign to the Persian possessions near the Caspian Sea in 1722-23. p. 89

124 Peter I assumed the title of Emperor in 1721. p. 93

125 An ironic allusion to the actions of the English fleet commanded by Charles Napier (1854) and Richard Dundas (1855) during the Crimean war (1853-56). p. 94

126 The *Peace Treaty of Stolbowa* was concluded between Russia and Sweden with Britain's mediation in 1617, after the failure of the intervention of Poland and Sweden in Russia at the beginning of the seventeenth century. Sweden returned several Russian towns to Russia, but retained the territories in Karelia and the Baltic lands, and thus cut off Russia from the Baltic Sea. The treaty envisaged the resumption of trade between Russia and Sweden. The state boundaries established by this treaty were intact till the Northern War (1700-21). p. 94

127 See Note 88. p. 95

128 See Note 55. p. 95

129 A reference to the treaty of 1711, signed during the Russo-Turkish war of 1710-13. p. 96

130 This refers to events in Madrid during the summer of 1856 which ended the fourth bourgeois revolution in Spain (1854-56). In July 1856 the conservative liberal opposition secured the resignation of the Espartero Progresista ministry and the formation of a conservative ministry headed by General O'Donnell. Disturbances organised by the left-democratic forces of the Cortes in Madrid, Barcelona, Saragossa and other towns were brutally suppressed by O'Donnell. p. 97

131 See Note 7. p. 98

132 Marx is referring to the counter-revolutionary mutiny (pronunciamiento) organised in May 1843 by generals Narváez, Conche and others against the dictatorship of Espartero, leader of the Progresistas. Some of the Progresistas, dissatisfied with the dictator's policy, supported the mutiny. On July 30, 1843, Espartero fled from the country and General Narváez, a leader of the

Moderados (see Note 136), who found support among the big landowners, became dictator. The reaction set in till the fourth revolution (1854-56). p. 98

[133] *Ayacuchos*—the name given to Espartero's followers during his Regency (1840-43), members of the pro-English military party headed by him. They were so called after the decisive battle at Ayacucho, Peru, on December 9, 1824, during the war of independence of the Spanish colonies in America. The metropolitan troops were led by Espartero and other generals. The battle was won by the insurgent army and put an end to Spain's rule in South America. See also the article "Ayacucho" by Marx and Engels (present edition, Vol. 18, pp. 170-71). p. 98

[134] A reference to Anglo-French diplomatic battles round the marriages of Queen Isabella II of Spain and her sister infanta María Luisa Fernanda. Their mother María Cristina (secretly married to Agustín Fernando Múñoz, a sergeant of the royal guards who later received the title of Duke of Riánsares; hence, Marx calls her Madame Múñoz) made an agreement with King Louis Philippe of France and, as a result, despite the intrigues of English diplomats, in October 1846 Isabella married Don Francisco de Asis of the Spanish Bourbons, and Maria Luisa Fernanda married the Duke of Montpensier,. Louis Philippe's younger son. p. 98

[135] A reference is to the second bourgeois revolution in Spain (1820-23). After an abortive attempt to overthrow the constitutional government in Madrid on July 7, 1822, King Ferdinand VII of Spain secretly appealed to the Holy Alliance (see Note 5) for help in suppressing the revolution. By decision adopted at the Congress of Verona of the Holy Alliance on October 20, 1822 France was to help Ferdinand. On April 7, 1823 a French expeditionary corps entered Spain and on October 1 the King's absolute power was restored in the country. The French troops stayed in Spain until 1828. p. 99

[136] *Moderados,* a party advocating a constitutional monarchy and representing the interests of the big bourgeoisie and liberal nobility, was organised at the beginning of the bourgeois revolution of 1820-23. In the 1840s and 1850s one of its leaders was General Narváez.

The liberal-bourgeois *Progresista* party was formed in the 1830s. The Progresistas found support among the urban middle and petty bourgeoisie, intellectuals and some officers. Their principal demand was for restriction of the powers of the monarchy. p. 99

[137] A reference to the events in Madrid in June-July 1854 which started the fourth bourgeois revolution in Spain (1854-56). In July 1854 the Cabinet reshufflings caused by an uprising in the army and disturbances in the city brought to power the Ministry of the Duke of Rivas (Ryos y Rosas also became its member). It was nicknamed "the shrapnel ministry" for the way it suppressed the uprising. The Ministry's activity led to a new uprising, and the Ministry had to resign. p. 100

[138] An allusion to the battle at Luchana bridge on December 25, 1836, during the first Carlist war (1833-40), in which the troops commanded by Espartero won a decisive victory over the Carlists and captured the town of Bilbao. Espartero was made Count of Luchana.

Below Marx alludes to Espartero's speech in Madrid in July 1854, at the beginning of the fourth Spanish revolution (1854-56): "Men of Madrid, you have summoned me to establish for ever the liberties of our land. Here I am;

and if the enemies of our most Holy liberty would snatch it from us, with the sword of Luchana I will put myself at your head, at the head of all Spaniards, and will show you the way to glory." p. 101

139 This refers to Espartero's resignation in July 1856. O'Donnell, Espartero's opponent in the government, succeeded in rallying all reactionary elements in the country, the Court and the Catholic clergy included, due to Espartero's irresolution and half-way policy. Behind Espartero's back he contacted Queen Isabella who was interested in suppressing the peasant movement which swept Spain in the spring and summer of 1856.

Unable to settle the differences in his government, Espartero chose Isabella as his arbiter. On July 13, 1856 he requested her to help him make peace between two members of the government: the radical Escosura and O'Donnell. Considering them both of great use in the government, Espartero declared that he would leave his post if one of them resigned. Therefore, when the Queen consented to Escosura's resignation, Espartero was forced to keep his promise.

On July 14, O'Donnell was appointed Prime Minister. Espartero gave up his struggle and did not head the democratic left wing of the Cortes which adopted a resolution against the new cabinet and called on the national militia and the people of Madrid to rebel. p. 103

140 *Carlism, Carlists*—a reactionary clerico-absolutist group in Spain consisting of adherents of the pretender to the Spanish throne Don Carlos, the brother of Ferdinand VII. Relying on the military and the Catholic clergy, and also making use of the support of the backward peasants in some regions of Spain, the Carlists launched in 1833 a civil war, which in fact turned into a struggle between the feudal-Catholic and liberal-bourgeois elements and led to the third bourgeois revolution (1834-43). p. 104

141 Marx is referring to the uprising of the Paris proletariat against the bourgeois regime of the Second Republic (June 23-26, 1848) and to an armed uprising which took place in Dresden on May 3-9, 1849. p. 105

142 A reference to the war of independence of the Spanish people against France (1808-14) which combined with the first bourgeois revolution in Spain. At the beginning of 1808, Napoleon I's troops entered Spain. The people answered with an uprising. Charles IV was forced to abdicate in favour of his son Ferdinand VII. Napoleon I, however, made Ferdinand VII give up his rights and proclaimed his brother Joseph King of Spain. Ferdinand VII was sent to France. A guerrilla war flared up and the organs of revolutionary power were set up. In 1810 the Cortes introduced a series of liberal reforms and in 1812 adopted the so-called Cadiz Constitution. This restricted the King's powers, and transferred legislative power to the one-chamber Cortes elected by universal suffrage. When the French troops were driven out of Spain, Ferdinand VII returned to Madrid. He refused to recognise the Constitution and restored the reactionary absolutist system. p. 106

143 A reference to the second bourgeois revolution in Spain (1820-23) which started on January 1, 1820 with a mutiny in the army directed by Rafael del Riego. It soon grew into a popular movement that swept the country. The revolution aimed at abolishing feudal relations in Spain. The Constitution of 1812 (see Note 142) which was abrogated in 1814 was reinstated. Some moderate reforms were adopted to liquidate the legal and administrative remnants of feudalism. However, an agrarian reform was not carried through, and this made the peasants withdraw from the revolution thereby facilitating its

defeat. The revolution was suppressed by the Holy Alliance in October 1823 (see Note 135). p. 106

144 On May 2, 1808 a popular uprising against the French interventionists flared up in Madrid. It was brutally suppressed by the commander-in-chief of the French army in Spain, Murat. p. 106

145 In the eighteenth and nineteenth centuries Spain and her colonies were divided into 17 military districts directed by captain-generals (hence the name Captain-Generalships). As viceroys, they possessed supreme power, both civil and military. p. 107

146 Marx is referring to the period of feudal absolutist reaction which set in after Ferdinand VII's return from France to Spain in March 1814. These years were characterised by numerous army conspiracies, and by the impotence and instability of the Spanish Government. From 1814 to 1819, 24 ministries succeeded one another.

For the *dynastic war of 1833-40* see Note 140. p. 107

147 A reference to the proclamation issued by generals O'Donnell and Dulce on July 1, 1854 after the mutiny of the Madrid garrison on June 28 with the aim of overthrowing San Luis' ministry and seizing power. On July 7 in Manzanares, La Mancha, the proclamation, known as the Manzanares programme was adopted. It envisaged the preservation of the monarchy, but the removal of the Court camarilla, the observance of the laws, formation of a national militia and other points. By adopting this programme O'Donnell and his followers sought to win the support of the masses. p. 107

148 *"The Croats of Radetzky"*—a reference to the Croatian border regiments stationed in the Military Border Area, a special militarily organised region of the Austrian Empire along the frontier with Turkey. They were used by the Austrian command to suppress the national liberation movements in the provinces, in Northern Italy in particular.

By the *"Africans of Bonaparte"* Marx means the *Zouaves*—French colonial troops first formed in 1830. Originally they were composed of Algerians and French colonists and later of Frenchmen only, while Algerians were formed into special regiments of riflemen. They were notorious for their atrocities during the colonial wars in Algeria.

In November 1848 the troops commanded by Wrangel took part in the counter-revolutionary coup in Berlin and in the dissolution of the Prussian National Assembly. The troops included many men from Pomerania, Wrangel's homeland. p. 107

149 An allusion to the methods employed by Louis Bonaparte to win supporters while preparing the coup d'état of December 2, 1851. At the receptions and military reviews he held as President of the Republic at Satory and elsewhere, army officers and men were treated to sausages, cold meat and champagne (see Marx, *The Eighteenth Brumaire of Louis Bonaparte*, present edition, Vol. 11, pp. 150, 151, 179 and 180). p. 107

150 The *Deists* recognise the idea of God as the rational creator of the universe, but deny God's interference in nature and social life. In 1624, in Paris, Edward Herbert of Cherbury composed a Deist profession of faith. p. 109

151 Marx dwelt on this subject in his letter to Engels of September 26, 1856 in the part which is devoted to the state of the European money market at the time (see present edition, Vol. 40, p. 72). p. 110

152 The *Court of Chancery*—one of England's highest courts, a division of the High Court of Justice following the Judicature Act of 1873. It was presided over by the Lord Chancellor and dealt with matters relating to inheritance, observance of contracts, joint-stock companies and similar legal problems. It was notorious for red tape and procrastination. p. 112

153 The banquets in support of the electoral reform were held in France in July 1847-January 1848 on the eve of the 1848 revolution.

The *Sonderbund*—a separatist union formed by the seven economically backward Catholic cantons of Switzerland in 1843 to resist progressive bourgeois reforms and defend the privileges of the church and the Jesuits. The decree of the Swiss Diet of July 1847 on the dissolution of the Sonderbund served as a pretext for the latter to start hostilities against the other cantons early in November. On November 23, 1847, the Sonderbund army was defeated by federal forces.

The *United Diet*—an assembly of representatives from the eight Provincial Diets of Prussia based on the estate principle. It sanctioned new taxes and loans, discussed new Bills and had the right to petition the King.

On the *Spanish marriages* see Note 134.

By decision of the Congress of Vienna (1815), the duchies of *Schleswig* and *Holstein* were incorporated into the Kingdom of Denmark, even though the majority of the population in Holstein and in Southern Schleswig were Germans. Under the impact of the March 1848 revolution in Prussia, the national liberation movement among the German population of the duchies grew in strength, becoming radical and democratic and forming part of the struggle for the unification of Germany.

Prussia and other states of the German Confederation sent federal troops to the duchies. Fearing a popular outbreak and an intensification of the revolution, the Prussian Government sought an agreement with the Danish monarchy to the detriment of overall German interests. As a result, the duchies remained part of the Kingdom of Denmark. p. 114

154 The July revolution of 1830 in France greatly influenced the social and political life of Germany. Constitutions were proclaimed in Brunswick, Saxony, Hesse, Cassel and other German states. Like the "1830 Charter" in France, which was a compromise between the topmost bourgeoisie—the finance aristocracy—and the landed aristocracy, these constitutions were a compromise between the bourgeoisie on the one hand and the king and the nobility on the other. p. 116

155 In the spring of 1856 floods occurred in the valleys of the Rhône and the Loire. Napoleon III visited a number of the affected towns and villages in a boat and personally handed out money. He also directed a message to the Minister of Public Works recommending measures to prevent such calamities. p. 119

156 Rich gold deposits were discovered in California in 1848 and Australia in 1851. Apart from their great importance for the commercial and industrial development of the European and American countries, these discoveries whipped up stock-exchange speculation there. p. 120

157 *"The Second Congress of Paris"* is Marx's scathing name for the meeting of European countries which was being prepared in Paris. It took place in March 1857 and was devoted to the peaceful settlement of the so-called Neuchâtel conflict between Prussia and Switzerland.

In September 1856 an uprising by adherents of the King of Prussia flared up in Neuchâtel. The insurgents were arrested by the Swiss troops. In answer to the King's demand to release the prisoners Switzerland suggested that the King should give up his rights to Neuchâtel. It was only under French pressure that Prussia was forced to officially renounce her claims in May 1857. p. 122

158 The *Naples question* was discussed at the Congress of Paris (1856) at the request of Piedmont's representatives, who drew the attention of the Congress to the policy of terror in the Kingdom of Naples (the Kingdom of the Two Sicilies) (see Note 6). Fearing that this policy might set off a revolutionary explosion, France and England demanded in May 1856 that King Ferdinand II of Naples should give up this policy. Convinced that Austria would support him, Ferdinand II refused to comply with the demand. After this, in October 1856, diplomatic relations with France and England were broken off. The governments of France and England put their naval squadrons in the Mediterranean on alert. However, owing to differences between these countries the Neapolitan expedition did not take place. p. 122

159 On the *Neapolitan question* see Note 158.

The Danubian question was one of the central issues at the Congress of Paris (1856). The point of discussion was the status of the Danubian principalities of Wallachia and Moldavia. All participants in the Congress guaranteed them autonomy within the Ottoman Empire. In view of the growing social movement in the principalities for unification into a single state the Congress adopted a decision to hold a referendum on this issue. It was decided to convene a special conference to finally determine the status and rights of the Danubian principalities. Marx means here complicated diplomatic struggle around that issue during preparations of the conference which was convened in 1858.

The *Bessarabian question* was directly connected with that of the Danubian principalities at the Congress of Paris (1856). Under the Paris treaty of March 30, 1856, part of the Bessarabian lands that had formerly belonged to Russia were ceded to Moldavia which was still under Turkey's protectorate.

On the new *Congress of Paris* see Note 157. p. 124

160 See Note 156. p. 124

161 Marx is referring to the war of independence of the Spanish colonies in America which lasted from 1810 to 1826. As a result of this war Spain lost Mexico and the South-American colonies which became independent republics. p. 125

162 The *British East India Company* was founded at the beginning of the seventeenth century. It had the monopoly of trade with the East Indies and played a decisive part in establishing the British colonial empire.

The East India Company's trade monopoly was abolished in 1813. The only exception was trade with China, the main articles of which were opium and tea. The Company was finally liquidated in 1858, during the popular Indian uprising of 1857-59. Marx gave a detailed description of the company in his article "The East India Company—Its History and Results" (see present edition, Vol. 12). p. 126

163 In 1850 popular unrest spread over a number of southern provinces in China and developed into a powerful peasant war. The insurgents established a state of their own over a considerable part of Chinese territory. It was called the Celestial Empire (Taiping Tankuo, hence the name of the movement—the Taiping uprising). The leaders put forward a utopian programme calling for

the existing social order to be transformed into a militarised patriarchal system based on the egalitarian principle. The movement, which was also anti-colonial in character, was weakened by internal strife and the formation of its own aristocracy in the Taiping state. It was dealt a crushing blow by the armed intervention of Britain and France. The Taiping uprising was put down in 1864. p. 126

164 Marx is referring to the manifestoes issued by Mazzini during the democratic popular movement for the liberation and unification of Italy. They had no decisive influence on the liberation struggle of the Italian people. Mazzini counted on the people as the main force of the national liberation struggle, but he did not take into account the specific interests of the Italian peasants who formed the bulk of the country's population. The conspiracies and uprisings instigated by him in the 1830s-50s were a failure because he was divorced from the masses and chose the moment for action on the impulse. Marx and Engels repeatedly criticised Mazzini's manifestoes for their vagueness, contradictoriness and bourgeois limitations (see present edition, Vol. 10, pp. 528-32). p. 129

165 The additional 45-centime tax for every franc of all direct taxes was introduced by the French Provisional Government on March 16, 1848, and it became a heavy burden, above all for the peasants who made up the majority of France's population. This measure caused the peasant masses to turn away from the revolution and to vote for Louis Napoleon Bonaparte at the presidential elections on December 10, 1848. p. 134

166 The *national workshops (ateliers)* were instituted by the Provisional Government immediately after the February revolution of 1848. By this means the government sought to discredit Louis Blanc's ideas on the "Organisation of Labour" in the eyes of the workers and, at the same time, to utilise those employed in the national workshops, organised on military lines, against the revolutionary proletariat. Revolutionary ideas, however, continued to gain ground in the national workshops. The government took steps to reduce the number of workers employed in them, to send a large number off to public works in the province and, finally, to liquidate the workshops. The government's actions precipitated a proletarian uprising in Paris in June 1848. After its suppression, the Cavaignac Government issued a decree on July 3 disbanding the national workshops.

For an assessment of the national workshops see Karl Marx, *The Class Struggles in France. 1848 to 1850* (present edition, Vol. 10, p. 63). p. 134

167 Presumably a reference to the events in Paris connected with the funeral of the well-known French sculptor David d'Angers, a republican. Many republican-minded students took part in the funeral procession in January 1856. Very popular among them was an anti-Bonapartist song ascribed to Béranger, who was also among the mourners and was greeted by the students with great enthusiasm. p. 135

168 Next comes this paragraph, inserted by the editors of the *New-York Daily Tribune:* "Of one thing, too, we in America may be perfectly assured; and that is, that when the downfall of this vast structure of swindling comes we shall go with it. We boast of our prosperity, but it is hollow. We are mere colonists and dependents of Europe. Let Napoleon tumble, and the event will be deeply felt not only in the coffers of the Wall-street gambler, but still more in the workshop and the home of the American laboring man." p. 138

169 When working on this article, Marx made a rough draft, "Venice", which is extant in his Notebook of excerpts for November 1854-beginning of 1857. It is published in this volume, in the section "From the Preparatory Materials", pp. 615-18.

The editors have no sources used by Marx for the article. p. 139

170 The *Treaty of Campo-Formio,* signed on October 17, 1797, concluded the victorious war of the French Republic against Austria, a member-country of the first anti-French coalition. Under the treaty, a large part of the Venetian Republic, including Venice, and also Istria and Dalmatia, were given to Austria in exchange for concessions made to France on the Rhine frontier.

The *Peace of Lunéville* of 1801 between France and Austria ended the war between France and the second coalition. It confirmed the provisions of the Treaty of Campo-Formio. p. 139

171 Under the *Treaty of Pressburg* concluded on December 26, 1805 between France and Austria, the latter acknowledged France's seizure of part of Italian territory (Piedmont, Genoa, Parma, Piacenza, etc.) and yielded to the Kingdom of Italy (i.e. to Napoleon I who became King of Italy) the Adriatic coast—the Venetian region, Istria and Dalmatia—keeping only Trieste.

Under the *Treaty of Vienna,* known under the name of Schönbrunn peace treaty concluded on October 14, 1809, between France and Austria, the latter ceded to France, Trieste, Craina, part of Carinthia and Croatia and also Istria. France undertook not to interfere with Austria's transit trade via Fiume. p. 139

172 The *Final (General) Act of the Congress of Vienna of June 9, 1815* annulled the Schönbrunn Peace Treaty (see Note 171). Austria acquired North-Eastern Italy (Lombardy and Venetia) and smaller Italian duchies. p. 139

173 The *Austrian Lloyd*—the name given by Marx to a maritime company founded in Trieste in 1833. Initially an insurance company, in 1836 the Austrian Lloyd became a steamship company entitled *Die Dampfschiffahrtsgesellschaft des Österreichisch-Ungarischen Lloyd.*

Many maritime insurance companies in Europe began to be named Lloyd's after Edward Lloyd, the owner of a coffee-house in London where the first English maritime insurance company was established in the late seventeenth century. p. 140

174 A reference to the *customs system* introduced by Napoleon I during the Continental Blockade of 1806-14. It included a series of strict prohibitions in customs policy and exceptionally high tariffs for colonial products imported to Europe, which was highly detrimental to trade in the Adriatic Sea's ports. p. 141

175 See Note 170. p. 146

176 See Note 171. p. 146

177 The *civil wars in Rome* reflected the class struggle between different groups in the slave-owning society in the second and first centuries B.C. They reached their peak in the 80s-40s B.C., particularly during Julius Caesar's struggle for dictatorship and in the epoch of the second triumvirate. They resulted in the substitution of an empire—a new political system—for the Roman Republic. p. 146

178 The *Uskoks* (Serbian: fugitives)—Balkan Slavs who fled to the Dalmatian coast of the Adriatic Sea following the seizure of Bosnia and Herzegovina by the

Turks in the second half of the fifteenth century. They waged a struggle against the Turks, making land and sea raids supported by local population. Their raids in the region of the Adriatic Sea also undermined Venice's maritime trade. p. 147

179 See Note 115. p. 147

180 See Note 171. p. 148

181 The *Battle of Austerlitz* on December 2 (November 20), 1805 between the Russian and Austrian forces (the third European coalition) and the French ended in a victory for Napoleon I. p. 148

182 The article is based on Marx's rough draft of an article which he entitled "Prussia ('The Military State')" and which is an annotated synopsis of A. F. Stein's *Preussisch-Brandenburgische Geschichte. Ein Handbuch zur Erinnerung und Belehrung.* p. 151

183 In the eighteenth century the Principality of Neuchâtel and Valangin (in German, Neuenburg and Vallendis) was under Prussian rule. In 1815 by decision of the Vienna Congress it was incorporated into Swiss Confederation as the 21st canton, while remaining a vassal of Prussia. In 1848 a republic was proclaimed in Neuchâtel. However, Prussia laid constant claim to Neuchâtel up to 1857, which led to a sharp conflict with Switzerland. p. 151

184 This refers to the so-called *Burgundian wars* (1474-77) waged by Charles the Bold, Duke of Burgundy, against France.

The Principality of Neuchâtel, committed to Berne by an obligation (1406), sided with the Swiss Confederation, which was France's ally and which declared war on Charles the Bold. The troops of Charles the Bold were defeated by the Allied forces at Nancy on January 5, 1477 and he himself was killed in the battle. This led to the disintegration of the Duchy of Burgundy and the strengthening of the ties of Neuchâtel and Valangin with the Swiss Confederation. p. 152

185 Under the Final Act of the Congress of Vienna (1815) Prussia received what was known as Swedish Pomerania from Denmark. p. 153

186 The *Council of Constance* (1414-18) was convened to strengthen the weakened position of the Catholic Church. It condemned the teachings of John Wycliffe and Jan Hus and ended the schism in the Catholic Church by electing a new Pope. p. 155

187 The *Teutonic Order*—a German religious Order of Knights founded in 1190 during the Crusades. The Order seized vast possessions in Germany and other countries. These were administered by dignitaries known as commandores (or comthurs). In the thirteenth century, East Prussia fell under the rule of the Order after it was overrun and the local population exterminated. In 1237 the Order amalgamated with the Livonian Order, which also had its seat in the Baltic area. The Eastern possessions of the Order became a seat of aggression against Poland, Lithuania and the adjoining Russian principalities. After the defeat at Chudskoye Lake in 1242 and in the battle at Grünwald in 1410, the Order rapidly declined and was only able to maintain a small part of its former possessions. p. 155

188 The *Hussites*—the followers of Jan Hus, a preacher, thinker and the exponent of the Bohemian Reformation. They participated in the popular movement of 1419-37 against the Catholic Church, feudal exploitation and German

domination in Bohemia. There were two trends in the Hussite movement: a moderate (the Calixtines, or Utraquists) and a radical (the Taborites—see Note 189) trend. The Hussites built up a strong army which rebuffed five crusades organised against Bohemia by the Pope and the German Emperor Sigismund I. The movement was suppressed as a result of the burghers' and knights' compromise with Sigismund I. p. 155

189 The *Taborites* (so called from their camp in the town of Tabor, Bohemia)—a radical trend in the Hussite movement. They were the revolutionary, democratic wing of the Hussites, and their demands reflected the desire of the peasantry and the urban lower classes for an end to all feudal oppression and all manifestations of social and political arbitrariness. The Taborites were the core of the Hussite army. p. 155

190 A reference to the *League of Schmalkalden* (February 27, 1531), named after the town in Thuringia where it was formed, was a union of Protestant princes and a number of Imperial towns for the protection of the Reformation against the Catholic princes headed by Emperor Charles V. From 1546 to 1548 the League and the Emperor were engaged in a war which ended in the latter's victory and the disintegration of the League. p. 156

191 The *Thirty Years' War* (1618-48)—a European war in which the Pope, the Spanish and Austrian Habsburgs and the Catholic German princes, rallied under the banner of Catholicism, fought the Protestant countries: Bohemia, Denmark, Sweden, the Republic of the Netherlands and a number of Protestant German states. The rulers of Catholic France—rivals of the Habsburgs—supported the Protestant camp. Germany was the principal battle area and the main object of plunder and territorial claims. The Treaty of Westphalia (1648) sealed the political dismemberment of Germany. p. 156

192 This refers to what is known as the *Peace of Prague,* a separate agreement concluded by the Elector of Saxony Johann Georg and the Emperor Ferdinand II of Habsburg on May 30, 1635. They were joined by the Elector of Brandenburg Georg Wilhelm and certain Protestant princes. Under this agreement the Elector of Saxony received Upper and Lower Łužica and part of Magdeburg's possessions.

The Protestant princes consolidated their hold on the lands which they had seized from the Church in the sixteenth century. p. 156

193 In 1611, the Polish Diet adopted a decision on the unification of the Duchy of Prussia with Brandenburg under Hohenzollern rule. This was done despite the opposition of a group of deputies who advocated Poland's rights to East Prussia. However, the Duchy of Prussia remained a territory held in fee by Poland. This decision was implemented in 1618 when the Elector of Brandenburg, Johann Sigismund, received the Duchy of Prussia in fee from the Polish King in exchange for his promise to take part in the war against Sweden. Under the Wielawa-Bydgoszcz Treaty of 1657 Poland finally renounced her supreme rights to the Duchy of Prussia in favour of Brandenburg. p. 156

194 On the *War of the Spanish Succession* (1701-14) see Note 51.

The Elector of Brandenburg, Friedrich III, having secured the support of the Polish nobility by bribery, and that of Emperor Leopold I by sending him Brandenburg troops for his war in Spain, announced, on January 18, 1701, the establishment of the Kingdom of Prussia and proclaimed himself King Frederick I. p. 157

195 On February 1, 1720, Prussia, a participant in the Northern War on Russia's side, concluded a peace treaty with Sweden under which it received Eastern Pomerania with the town of Stettin.

The three partitions of Poland (by Austria, Prussia and Russia) took place in 1772, 1793 and 1795.

Polish lands, including Pomorze, Great Poland, and part of Mazovia with Warsaw, went over to Prussia; Russia gained Lithuanian, Byelorussian and Ukrainian territories; Austria received the Western Ukraine and part of Smaller Poland. As a result of the third partition, Poland ceased to exist as a state.

Under the Final Act of the Congress of Vienna signed on June 9, 1815 Prussia gained Northern Saxony (almost half of Saxony's territory), Torn and Poznan, the Rhine Province and the greater part of Westphalia. p. 157

196 This refers to the incident which sparked off the Second Opium War: the seizure by the Chinese authorities of the British lorcha *Arrow* carrying contraband opium in Canton in 1856. The British Government retaliated by sending a corps of 5,000 men to China under the command of Lord Elgin. Canton was brutally bombarded in October-November 1856 by the fleet commanded by Admiral Seymour and on December 29, 1857 it was captured by the British. p. 158

197 This refers to Article 9 of the Anglo-Chinese treaty of October 8, 1843 signed to supplement the Treaty of Nanking.

The *Treaty of Nanking,* concluded between Britain and China in 1842, was the first of a series of unequal treaties imposed by the Western powers on China, reducing it to the status of a semi-colony. The Nanking Treaty made China open five of its ports to British commerce—Canton, Shanghai, Amoy, Ningpo and Fu-chou, cede the Island of Hongkong to Britain "in perpetuity" and pay a large indemnity. It introduced import and export tariffs advantageous to Britain.

The supplementary protocol of 1843 concerning the general rules for trading in the five open ports contained articles (2, 7 and 13) envisaging cooperation between the British and Chinese authorities in inspecting the goods brought to the ports and in organising their work. According to its Article 9 the Chinese who cooperated with the British were not subject to China's jurisdiction. p. 158

198 According to Article 2 of the Treaty of Nanking of 1842 (see Note 197), British subjects with their families and their property were allowed to stay in Canton "to achieve their commercial aims". However, because of resistance on the part of the Chinese population, access to Canton was postponed, first, under the agreement of 1846 for indefinite time; then, in 1847, for two more years. p. 161

199 See Note 197. p. 162

200 In the 1850s William Walker, an American adventurer, made several expeditions to Central America actually pursuing expansionist aims. In 1855, he captured Granada, the capital of Nicaragua, and soon proclaimed himself president. He tried to establish a dictatorship and restore slavery. During an expedition to Honduras in the late 1850s, Walker was taken prisoner and shot in 1860. p. 162

201 As a pretext for the First Opium War (1839-42), Britain used the confiscation by the Chinese authorities in Canton of opium stocks owned by foreign merchants. p. 163

[202] Here Marx is referring to the Taipings (see Note 163) who by the beginning of 1857 had established an Empire in the central part of China, its most fertile and rich regions along the middle reaches of the Yangtze. p. 163

[203] In the *New-York Daily Tribune* this is followed by a note from the editors: "With regard to the reported destruction of a Chinese fort by the American frigate *Portsmouth,* we are not yet sufficiently informed to express a decided opinion." p. 163

[204] Engels wrote this article for the *New-York Daily Tribune* early in January 1857 at Marx's request. In his letter to Engels of January 10, Marx informed him of the receipt of the article (see present edition, Vol. 40, p. 89).

The article was prompted by the Neuchâtel conflict (see Note 157) and the plans for the invasion of Switzerland by Prussian troops, widely discussed in the press. It consisted of two parts, the first being published in the *New-York Daily Tribune* on January 27, 1857. The editors of the *Tribune* decided not to print the second part, and Charles Dana informed Marx of this in a letter of March 5, 1857, because on January 16, 1857 the Swiss government made concessions to Prussia by releasing the arrested monarchists. "The miserable collapse of Switzerland's braggadocio"—such was Marx's appraisal of the latest events of the Neuchâtel conflict in his letter to Engels of January 20 (see present edition, Vol. 40, p. 94).

In the present edition the first part of the article is reproduced from the *New-York Daily Tribune* collated with an extant excerpt of the rough manuscript. The most important passages in the manuscript, which were omitted in the printed text, are given in the footnotes. The second part of the article is published according to the manuscript copied by Marx. p. 164

[205] In the *Battle of Sempach* (Canton of Lucerne) on July 9, 1386 the Swiss defeated the Austrian troops of Prince Leopold III.

The *Battle of Morgarten* between Swiss volunteers and the troops of Leopold of Habsburg on November 15, 1315 ended in victory for the volunteers.

At *Murten* (Canton of Freiburg) on June 22, 1476 and at *Granson* (Canton Vaud) on March 2, 1476, the Swiss defeated the troops of Charles the Bold, Duke of Burgundy. p. 164

[206] Engels is referring here to the wars of the League of Three Forest Cantons against the Habsburgs. As a result of them a Swiss Confederation consisting of eight lands was set up in 1389; the independence of Switzerland was recognised in 1499.

On the *Burgundian wars* see Note 184. p. 167

[207] The troops of the French Directory entered Switzerland in the spring of 1798 to support the economically advanced cantons which were for the abolition of the feudal relations in the country. On April 12, 1798 a Helvetian Republic was proclaimed in Switzerland, and a constitution modelled on the French constitution of 1795 was adopted. The measures introduced by the new constitution favoured the economically advanced cantons and provoked stubborn resistance from the agrarian cantons in the central and eastern parts of the country. By the insurrections of the old forest cantons Engels means their actions against the French in April, May and August 1798. The Helvetian Republic became fully dependent on France with the conclusion of a defensive-offensive union, which led to the republic's participation in the war against the Second Coalition on France's side. The coalition was formed in

1798 and included Austria, England, the Kingdom of Naples, Russia, Turkey and other countries. p. 168

208 During the war of the Second Coalition (see Note 207) against France, the Russian and Austrian forces under the command of Alexander Suvorov freed almost the whole of Northern Italy from the French in the spring and summer of 1799. At the insistence of the Austrian Government Suvorov's army was then sent to Switzerland to link up with the Russian corps of Rimsky-Korsakov, which was being pressed by the forces of the French General Masséna. After the Russian army had heroically fought its way across the Saint Gotthard and several other mountain passes it was encircled by superior French forces, which had defeated Korsakov's corps at Zurich on September 25. Under extremely hard conditions Suvorov's troops succeeded in making their way through a number of Alpine mountain passes and on October 12 reached the upper Rhine. In his work *Po and Rhine* Engels wrote: "This passage was the most impressive of all Alpine crossings in modern times" (see present edition, Vol. 16, p. 222). p. 169

209 In 1830 the French Government launched a colonial war in Algeria. The Algerian people put up a stubborn resistance to the colonialists; it took the French 40 years to turn Algeria into their colony. p. 170

210 The *Tyrolese insurrection*—the insurrection of the Tyrol peasants which broke out in April 1809 and was headed by Andreas Hofer. It was directed against the French occupants and the Bavarian authorities. Under the Treaty of Pressburg of 1805 Tyrol was annexed from Austria to Bavaria by Napoleon I. The Austrian Government used the growing discontent of the Tyrolese with the new order in its own interests and supported the insurrection which at its initial stage was successful. After the Treaty of Schönbrunn (1809) by which Austria recognised the annexation of Tyrol to Bavaria, Napoleon I moved considerable forces against the Tyrolese peasants. The insurrection was suppressed in 1810.

On the *Spanish guerrilla war* see Note 142.

On the *Carlist Basque insurrection* see Note 140. p. 171

211 A reference to the war waged by the peoples of the North Caucasus (Adyghei, Chechens, Avars, Lezghins, etc.) against the Tsarist government. In the 1820s the liberation struggle of these peoples against the Tsarist colonialists and the arbitrary rule of the local feudal lords was headed by Shamyl, who was proclaimed Imam of Daghestan in 1834. The movement reached its peak in the 1840s and was suppressed in 1859. p. 171

212 Engels is referring to the wars, which lasted from 1792 to 1815, between revolutionary and Napoleonic France and the coalitions of European states. p. 173

213 The *Landsturm*—an armed force, a second-rate militia. It was organised in Tyrol in 1809. In the nineteenth and the beginning of the twentieth centuries the *Landsturm* existed in Germany, Austria-Hungary, Holland, Switzerland and Sweden. It was called out in the event of a national emergency. In Switzerland all citizens from seventeen to fifty years of age outside the regular army or the *Landwehr* were enrolled in it. p. 175

214 This article was compiled by the editors of the *New-York Daily Tribune* from Marx's two articles on the Anglo-Persian war, as can be seen from Charles Dana's letter of March 5, 1857. He wrote: "Two articles on Persia were

condensed into one and published in that form." The rough copies of both articles are extant. The heading of the article was taken from them. p. 177

215 The *Sikhs*—a religious sect which appeared in the Punjab (North-West India) in the sixteenth century. Their teaching on the equality of people was used by the peasants who fought against the Hindu feudal lords and the Afghan invaders at the end of the seventeenth century. Subsequently a local aristocracy emerged among the Sikhs and its representatives ruled the Sikh state, which in the early nineteenth century included the Punjab and some border regions. In 1845-46 and 1848-49 Britain waged aggressive wars against the Sikhs which ended with the subjugation of the Punjab. The conquest of the Punjab completed the British colonisation of India. p. 177

216 *Sunnites (Sunni)* and *Shiites (Shiahs)*—members of the two main Islamic branches which appeared in the seventh century as a result of conflicts between the successors of Mohammed, founder of Islam.

The Shiites differ from the Sunnites in their views on the provenance of supreme power. They believe that the Caliph, as a successor of Mohammed, should not be elected by people. At their inception the Shiites, being a political party, defended the rights of Ali, Mohammed's son-in-law, and his descendants from the Prophet's daughter, to spiritual and secular guidance in the Moslem world. With the Sunnites the election of the Caliph rests on the "consent of the whole community". Subsequently, the rites and laws of the Shiites too became slightly different from those of the Sunnites. p. 178

217 The *Treaty of Ghulistan,* which ended the Russo-Persian war of 1804-13, was signed on October 24 (November 5), 1813. Under this treaty the Russian Empire acquired Daghestan, Georgia with Shuragel province, Imeretia, Guria, Mingrelia and Abkhazia, and also the khanates of Karabakh, Ganja, Sheki, Shirvan, Derbent, Kuba, Baku and Talyshin. Russia also received the exclusive right to have a fleet in the Caspian Sea. In her turn Russia undertook to support the heir to the Persian throne chosen by the Shah. This treaty was in force until 1828, when the Turkmanchai Treaty between Russia and Persia was concluded. p. 178

218 The *Treaty of Turkmanchai,* which ended the Russo-Persian war of 1826-28, was signed on February 22, 1828. Under this treaty Russia received the territories of the Erivan and Nakhichevan khanates (Eastern Armenia), and Russia's exclusive right to have a fleet in the Caspian Sea was confirmed. Persia was to pay war indemnities (see also K. Marx, *Lord Palmerston,* present edition, Vol. 12, pp. 355-56). p. 178

219 After the death of Abbas Mirza, the heir to the Shah of Persia, in October 1833 his son, Mohammed Mirza, who had been appointed the governor of Azerbaidjan was proclaimed his successor. After the death of Mohammed Mirza's grandfather, Fath Ali Shah, in October 1834 several pretenders to the throne appeared. Supported by Russia and England, Mohammed Mirza became Shah of Persia at the beginning of 1835. With a view to consolidating their position in Persia the English sent a big military mission, which stayed in Persia till 1838, and a large shipment of arms. The British officer H. Lindsay Bethune commanded the Shah's troops for some time. p. 178

220 Marx is referring to Article 9 of the Definitive Treaty of Friendship and Alliance between Great Britain and Persia, signed on November 25, 1814. p. 179

221 This was the first Anglo-Afghan war (1838-42) which began with the invasion of Afghanistan by British occupation troops in Sind. The immediate cause was Persia's attack of Herat in the autumn of 1837; the siege of it lasted till August 15, 1838. The invasion was carried out under the pretext of rendering assistance to the pretender, Emir Dost Mohammed's brother Shuja. However, a popular uprising in November 1841 against the British invaders and their puppet Shuja compelled the British, who sustained a severe defeat, to withdraw. p. 180

222 This unfinished work by Marx is devoted to the criticism of Bruno Bauer's views on foreign policy and especially his view of the role of Tsarist Russia in the destinies of European peoples. Bruno Bauer, a German idealist philosopher, was a bourgeois radical in politics. In 1854, during the Crimean war of 1853-56, he published several pamphlets in which he analysed the events of the war and the preceding history of the foreign policy of the European states. He came to the conclusion that the western powers were a failure, and that Russia was becoming the arbiter in European affairs. Back in 1855 Marx and Engels intended to come out against "its [Critical Criticism's] arrogant stupidity", i.e. against Bruno Bauer (see present edition, Vol. 39, p. 535). In the *Revelations of the Diplomatic History of the 18th Century* Marx, alluding to Bauer (this volume, p. 62 and Note 79), expressed his intention of analysing his views. Presumably, this manuscript which he wrote in January 1857 was an attempt to realise his plan. In it Marx criticised in the main Bauer's two pamphlets *La Russie et l'Angleterre* (which was published in Scharlottenburg in June 1854 and was a translation from the German edition *Russland und England*) and *Die jetzige Stellung Russlands* (also published in Scharlottenburg in October 1854).

This manuscript opens Marx's Notebook of excerpts for 1857 marked on the first page: "1. Heft A."; on the second page: "Spada. Russian Ephémérides" (this refers to Spada, *Ephémérides russes politiques, littéraires, historiques et nécrologiques ... jusqu'en 1816,* St. Petersburg, 1816) and the date "1857 (Januar)". The text of the manuscript begins on the third page. It contains six pages altogether. The title of the manuscript is preceded by figure 1).

Some passages deleted in the manuscript are given in the footnotes. The manuscript was first published in Russian, in the magazine *Letopisi marksizma,* Vol. VI, 1928. p. 181

223 *Criticism*—an ironic name given to Bruno Bauer by Marx and Engels in the first half of the 1840s (see their joint work *The Holy Family, or Critique of Critical Criticism,* present edition, Vol. 4, pp. 3-211). p. 181

224 A reference to the coup d'état of December 2, 1851 in France carried out by Louis Bonaparte, to the introduction of the reactionary constitution by Emperor Francis Joseph of Austria in March 1849, and to the constitution imposed by King Frederick William IV of Prussia on December 5, 1848, simultaneously with the publication of the order dissolving the Prussian National Assembly. p. 182

225 Marx is referring to the actions of the Russian troops on the Danube in May-September 1854 and primarily to the raising of the siege of Silistria (see present edition, Vol. 13, pp. 234-57, 276-81, 334-39, etc.). p. 182

226 This refers to the following proposition: "Europe has apportioned itself roles in the constitutional drama: the West has assumed the role of stalwart

opposition; to Russia has fallen the role of an energetic government with might." It was first used by Bauer in his *La Russie et l'Angleterre.* It also opens his pamphlet *Die jetzige Stellung Russlands.* The words "quoted above" were inserted by Marx. p. 182

227 Marx gave a detailed criticism of Proudhon's theory of "People's Bank" (Banque du Peuple) and "labour money" in his *Economic Manuscripts of 1857-58* (the first version of *Capital*), Chapter on Money (see present edition, Vol. 28). p. 185

228 In 1774 Baron A. R. J. Turgot, who became controller general of finances, introduced free trade in corn and flour. This measure and his subsequent reforms roused strong opposition on the part of the Court, high priesthood, nobility and officialdom. In 1776 Louis XVI signed his resignation.

The *Anti-Corn Law League* was founded in 1838 by the Manchester textile manufacturers and free traders Richard Cobden and John Bright. It campaigned for the repeal of the high import tariffs on corn established in 1815 and for unrestricted free trade. The League ceased to exist after the repeal of the Corn Laws (see Note 287) in 1846. p. 185

229 A reference to the Crimean war, 1853-56. p. 185

230 The Reform Bill of 1831 (passed as a law in 1832) was directed against the political monopoly of the landed and finance aristocracy. It liquidated some "rotten boroughs" (see Note 243) and admitted the industrial bourgeoisie to Parliament. In the early 1850s a movement for a new electoral reform started in England. In February 1852, Russell declared in Parliament that he intended to present a new Reform Bill. However, the Bill was not discussed. Engels analyses this Bill in his article "England" (see present edition, Vol. 11, pp. 205-09). p. 186

231 *Influence étrangère* (foreign influence)—an allusion to David Urquhart, who regarded Palmerston as a direct agent of the Tsarist Government. p. 186

232 The version that the British diplomat Robert Adair, a confidential agent of the leader of the opposition Charles James Fox, was sent to St. Petersburg so as to disrupt William Pitt's plans (see Note 233) was put forward in G. Tomline's *Memoirs of the Life of the Right Honorable William Pitt,* in 3 volumes, London, 1821. p. 187

233 Disturbed by Russia's victories in the Russo-Turkish war of 1787-91, William Pitt (the Younger) tried to wreck the Jassy Peace Treaty. Having employed the British press and entered into relations with Fox, the Russian diplomats managed to avert the rupture of diplomatic relations with Britain. Fox made a speech in the House of Commons severely criticising Pitt's policy. Having won a diplomatic victory over Pitt, Catherine II ordered a bust of Fox to be bought for her in London and installed in her palace in Tsarskoye Selo, between the statues of Demosthenes and Cicero. When writing about the "illicit liaison" Marx presumably meant these circumstances. p. 187

234 An allusion to the fact that the Marquis of Carmarthen paid £15,000 to Peter I for the monopoly of the tobacco trade in Russia. p. 187

235 Presumably Marx has in mind here the documents used by him in *Revelations of the Diplomatic History of the 18th Century* (see this volume, pp. 27-37). p. 187

236 The *Treaty of Utrecht of 1713* was one of the peace treaties concluded between

France and Spain, on the one hand, and the countries of the anti-French coalition (England, Holland, Portugal, Prussia and the Austrian Habsburgs) on the other, which ended the War of the Spanish Succession, begun in 1701 (see notes 51 and 71). Under the terms of the 1713 treaty, the Spanish throne was retained by Philip V, Louis XIV's grandson; the King of France, however, was to give up his plans to unite the French and Spanish monarchies and renounce his claims and those of his Bourbon heirs to the Spanish crown. Several French and Spanish colonies in the West Indies and North America, as well as Gibraltar, were ceded to England.

In 1716 England and France signed a secret treaty in Hanover, under which England became a guarantor country: in case Louis XV died childless, the French crown remained with the Orleans dynasty. For England the treaty was signed by Stanhope, George I's Foreign Secretary of State, and for France by Cardinal Dubois. This treaty served as a basis for the Triple Alliance between England, France, and Holland, concluded in 1717; in 1718 Austria joined it (in this way, the Quadruple Alliance was formed). Marx speaks about these events below in the text. p. 187

237 A reference to a convention signed by France, England, Spain and Portugal in London on April 22, 1834. It dealt with the problems concerning the Peninsula. p. 187

238 A reference to a convention signed by England, Russia, Austria and Prussia on July 15, 1840 on the help to the Sultan of Turkey against the Egyptian pasha Mohammed-Ali, who was supported by France. p. 187

239 The *"Captain of Eton"*—honorary title received by the students at Eton College for participating in political disputes conducted in the form of parliamentary debates. Canning was awarded this title on graduating from the college in 1788. p. 188

240 On December 12, 1826 Canning made a speech in the House of Commons in connection with the dispatch of British troops to Portugal where the civil war was waged at that time (the so-called Miguelist wars of 1823-34). He said: "The situation of England amidst the struggle of political opinions which agitates, more or less sensibly, different countries of the world, may be compared to that of the Ruler of the Winds, as described by the poet:—

"'Celsa sedet Aeolus arce,
Sceptra tenens; mollitque animus et temperat iras;
Ni faciat, maria ac terras caelumque profundum
Quippe ferant rapidi secum, verrantque per auras.'"
(Virgil, *Aeneid,* I, 55-59).

[The tyrant Aeolus,
from his airy throne,
With power imperial
curbs the struggling winds,
And sounding tempests in
dark prisons binds.
(Dryden's translation)]

p. 188

241 This refers to the anti-French policy of the British Prime Minister William Pitt (Senior), who had much to do with unleashing the Seven Years' War (1756-63),

which enabled England to capture almost all the French possessions in India and North America. p. 188

242 The independence of the Spanish colonies in America (except for Cuba and Puerto Rico) was proclaimed in 1826; the independence of the Portuguese colony—Brazil—was obtained in 1822 as a result of the war of the Spanish and Portuguese colonies in 1810-26. p. 188

243 *Rotten boroughs* (the name current in England in the eighteenth and nineteenth centuries) were sparsely populated or depopulated towns and villages which had enjoyed the right to send representatives to Parliament since the Middle Ages. The Reform Acts of 1832 (see notes 230 and 292), 1867 and 1884 deprived the rotten boroughs of their privileges. p. 188

244 See Note 54. p. 189

245 The German *"Stämme"* used by Marx has been translated as "population" here, because the term *"Stamm"* had a wider range of meanings in the 1840s and 1850s than it has now. It denoted an historical community of people descended from a common ancestor. p. 191

246 The Russo-Turkish war of 1828-29 was concluded by signing the Treaty of Adrianople in September 1829. It confirmed the autonomy of Serbia and secured the autonomy of the Danubian principalities (Moldavia and Wallachia). Their rights were to be guaranteed by Russia. Under the terms of the treaty the Organic Regulations which determined their socio-political organisation were introduced in the Danubian principalities in 1831-32. For Marx's estimation of these Regulations see also *Capital,* Vol. I (present edition, Vol. 35, Chapter X, Section 2). p. 191

247 Marx is referring to the siege of Enos on the Aegean Sea by the Russians during the Russo-Turkish war of 1828-29. Enos was taken by General Sivers' detachment on August 26, 1829. p. 192

248 The quotation from Lieven's dispatch cited by Bauer in his *La Russie et l'Angleterre* (p. 40) reads as follows: "It is in our camp that peace must be concluded; and it is only after its conclusion that Europe must know its conditions; the protests would be belated then and one must be patiently content with what could not be prevented." p. 192

249 On November 25, 1836 a Russian man-of-war captured the British merchant ship *Vixen* in the bay of Sujuk-Kale (the Caucasian coast of the Black Sea). p. 193

250 On the policy of the Frankfurt National Assembly concerning the nationalities question see Marx's and Engels' articles for the *Neue Rheinische Zeitung* (present edition, Vol. 7, pp. 109-10, 337-81). p. 193

251 This article was written by Engels on Marx's request, made by him in the letter of January 23, 1857: "I should be grateful if you should let me have by Tuesday ... a military article on *Persia*" (see present edition, Vol. 40, p. 98). There is no evidence that the article was sent on the following Tuesday, January 27. However, it must have been sent not later than February 6, because after this date Marx temporarily stopped sending articles to the *Tribune*; this can be seen from his letter to Engels of February 6, 1857 (present edition, Vol. 40, p. 99). p. 194

252 The object of the Anglo-Persian war of 1856-57 was to establish British influence in Persia, pave the way for further colonial expansion in the Middle

East and Central Asia and prevent the Shah of Persia from establishing his power over the independent principality of Herat. When Persian troops occupied Herat in October 1856, Britain used this as a pretext to open hostilities. The war took an unfavourable turn for Persia. However, the national liberation uprising that flared up in India in 1857 and continued up to 1859 compelled Britain to conclude a peace treaty with Persia in all haste. Under the terms of the treaty, signed in Paris in March 1857, Persia repudiated her claims to Herat, which, in 1863, was incorporated into the possessions of the Afghan Emir. p. 194

253 See Note 218. p. 196

254 The Khanate of Khiva acknowledged its dependence on Russia only as a result of the treaty signed by Russia and Khiva on August 12, 1873. Between 1853 and 1857 V. A. Perovsky, Military Governor of Orenburg, erected a number of fortifications on the Syr-Darya River. p. 196

255 The Russian expedition to the Khanate of Khiva in November 1839 was undertaken under General Perovsky. His 5,000-strong detachment, with artillery and a food convoy, proved unprepared for a winter march through the barren steppes and lost half its men through epidemics. Perovsky failed to reach Khiva and was forced to return to Orenburg. p. 197

256 At the *Battle of Inkermann* on November 5, 1854, during the Crimean war of 1853-56, the Anglo-French forces defeated the Russian army. Engels described the battle in detail in his article "The Battle of Inkermann" (see present edition, Vol. 13, pp. 528-35).

Sepoys—mercenary troops in the British-Indian army recruited from the Indian population and serving under British officers. They were used by the British to subjugate India and to fight the wars of conquest against Afghanistan, Burma and other neighbouring states. p. 198

257 In Marx's Notebook for 1857, in his entry for February 20, this article is entitled "The Budget of Lewis". The rough drafts which are extant consist of two parts: "The Budget of Sir G. Lewis" and "Direct and Indirect Taxation". p. 200

258 The *Free Traders* advocated removal of protective tariffs and non-intervention by the government in economic life. They were supporters of the *Manchester School*—a trend in economic thinking which reflected the interests of the industrial bourgeoisie. The centre of the Free Traders' agitation was Manchester, where the movement was headed by two textile manufacturers, Richard Cobden and John Bright, who founded the Anti-Corn Law League in 1838 (see Note 228). In the 1840s and 1850s the Free Traders were a separate political group, which later formed the Left wing of the Liberal Party. p. 201

259 This refers to the peace treaty signed in Paris in March 1856 after the end of the Crimean war. p. 202

260 A reference to Aberdeen's coalition ministry of 1852-55. The "Cabinet of All the Talents" included Whigs, Peelites (see Note 262) and representatives of the Irish faction in the British Parliament. p. 203

261 A reference to an intensive bombardment of Canton by the British in October-November 1856, which sparked off the Anglo-Franco-Chinese war of 1856-60 (known as the Second Opium War). p. 204

[262] The *Peelites*—adherents of Robert Peel, who favoured concessions to the trading and industrial bourgeoisie in the sphere of economics and the continued political supremacy of the big landowners and financial magnates. In 1846 Peel secured the repeal of the Corn Laws in the interests of the industrial bourgeoisie; this aroused great discontent among the Protectionist Tories and led to a split in the Tory Party and the formation of an independent group by the Peelites. After Peel's death in 1850, the Peelites had no definite programme. At the end of the 1850s and the beginning of the 1860s they joined the Liberal Party, which was then being formed.

In February 1852 the Peelites seconded Palmerston's amendment to the militia Bill, which led to the resignation of Lord Russell's Government. In December of that year they opposed the budget suggested by Derby. Derby's cabinet was also forced to resign. In February 1855, Aberdeen's Ministry also fell. The Peelites helped Palmerston come to power by agreeing to enter his cabinet. However, when their leaders, William Gladstone, Sidney Herbert and James Graham, resigned shortly afterwards, Palmerston immediately replaced them by Whig representatives. p. 204

[263] See Note 158. p. 205

[264] The *workhouses*—public institutions for the maintenance of paupers—first appeared in England in the seventeenth century. By the Poor Law of 1834 they were the only form of relief for the able-bodied poor. In the workhouses with a prison-like regime the workers were engaged in unproductive, monotonous and exhausting labour. The people called these workhouses "Bastilles for the poor". p. 206

[265] In Marx's Notebook for 1857 there is an entry about this article on February 26: "Chinese debates". The drafts of the first part of the article are in the Notebook of excerpts for 1857. The most important divergences are given in the footnotes. p. 207

[266] See Note 196. p. 207

[267] See Note 261. p. 208

[268] See Note 197. p. 208

[269] The *greatest happiness of the greatest number*—the principal tenet of the theory of Jeremy Bentham, the father of the English philosophy of utilitarianism. p. 209

[270] The *Peace Society*—a pacifist organisation founded by the Quakers (see Note 310) in London in 1816. The society was actively supported by the Free Traders, who thought that in conditions of peace free trade would enable England to make full use of her industrial superiority and thus gain economic and political supremacy. The society had branches in other towns. p. 209

[271] The reference is to the campaign for a second electoral reform in England in the 1850s. Its aim was to extend suffrage and finally abolish the "rotten boroughs" (see Note 243). Palmerston was against the reform. p. 212

[272] See Note 20. p. 213

[273] See Note 260. p. 213

[274] See Note 259. p. 214

[275] Marx has in mind the unsuccessful attack of the British troops on the Big

Redan (Bastion No. 3 of Sevastopol's defences) on June 6 (18) and August 27 (September 8), 1855.

Marx gave a detailed account of the battle in his report "The Mishap of June 18.—Reinforcements" and Engels described it in his articles "From Sevastopol", "The Late Repulse of the Allies", "The Fall of Sevastopol" and "The Great Event of the War" (see present edition, Vol. 14, pp. 297-301, 313-19, 328-32, 519-23 and 546-52).

Assisted by the British, the Turks had turned Kars into a bridgehead for the invasion of Transcaucasia. The successful operations by the Russian forces against the Turks in the Caucasian theatre of the Crimean war resulted in the capture of Kars on November 28, 1855 and this accelerated the conclusion of peace. p. 214

276 On the *Treaty of Paris* see Note 259.

By the "misunderstandings with the United States" Marx means the conflict that arose in 1855 because the US Government supported the American adventurer William Walker (see Note 200) who proclaimed himself President of Nicaragua. This was done with the aim of counteracting Britain in her aspirations to entrench herself on the Mosquito Coast in Central America. The conflict was settled in October 1856, when the US Government censured Walker's actions and Britain gave up her territorial claims.

On the *expedition to Naples* see Note 158.

Ostensible squabbles with Bonaparte—a reference to disagreements between England and France which arose after the Paris Congress of 1856. The rapprochement between France and Russia evident during the Congress prevented England from achieving her aims in the Crimean war. However, these disagreements had no serious consequences.

On *Persian invasion* see Note 252.

On the *Chinese massacres* see Note 261. p. 214

277 On the *Peelites* see Note 262.

On the *Manchester men* see Note 258. p. 214

278 *Old Bailey*—the London Central Criminal Court, so called because it stands in the ancient bailey of the city wall. p. 214

279 In June 1844 the Bandiera brothers, who were members of a conspiratorial organisation, landed on the Calabrian coast at the head of a small detachment of Italian patriots with the intention of sparking off an insurrection against the Bourbons of Naples and the Austrian rule. But the members of the expedition were betrayed by one of their number and taken prisoner; the Bandiera brothers were executed.

On the orders of Sir James Graham, then British Home Secretary, the letters of Italian emigrants were opened and their contents made known to the Austrian Government, which thus obtained information about the intended landing. p. 216

280 In Marx's Notebook for 1857 this article is entitled "Palmerston and the General Election". p. 219

281 The name "resurrectionists" was given in England to people who secretly exhumed corpses and sold them to dissecting rooms. In the 1820s this practice was particularly widespread; for example, there was the notorious case of William Burke, who murdered people in Edinburgh solely for this purpose and left no traces of the crime. p. 219

282 A reference to the *First Opium War* (1839-42)—an aggressive war waged by

Britain against China which started China's transformation into a semi-colony. One of the clauses of the Nanking Treaty imposed on China provided for the opening of five Chinese ports to foreign trade. See also Note 197. p. 220

283 The *Grand Cophta* was the name of the omnipotent and omniscient Egyptian priest who headed the non-existent Masonic "Egyptian Lodge" which the famous eighteenth-century impostor "Count" Cagliostro (Giuseppe Balsamo) claimed to have founded. p. 220

284 *Blue Books*—periodically published collections of documents of the British Parliament and Foreign Office. Their publication began in the seventeenth century. p. 221

285 Louis Bonaparte's appeal to the National Assembly of November 4, 1851, contained a demagogic demand for the re-establishment of universal suffrage in France. After the National Assembly's rejection of the Bill, introduced on the occasion by Bonaparte's ministry, Louis Bonaparte accomplished a coup d'état on December 2, 1851. p. 222

286 Marx is referring here to the six laws passed by the British Parliament, on Castlereagh's proposal, following the massacre (known as Peterloo) of the workers, participants in a mass meeting in support of electoral reform and in protest against the Corn Laws at St. Peter's Field, Manchester, on August 16, 1819. Known as the "gagging laws", they virtually abolished the Habeas Corpus act and restricted the freedom of the press and assembly.

The *Habeas Corpus Act* was passed by the British Parliament in 1679 and envisages the issue of a writ requiring an imprisoned person to be brought before a court or a judge within three to twenty days or to be set free. The procedure does not apply to persons accused of high treason and could be suspended by decision of Parliament. p. 222

287 On the butchery of the people at Manchester see Note 286.

The *Corn Laws* (first introduced in the fifteenth century) imposed high import duties on agricultural produce in the interests of landowners in order to maintain high prices for these products on the home market. The struggle between the industrial bourgeoisie and the landed aristocracy over the Corn Laws ended in 1846 with their repeal (see also Note 228). p. 222

288 A reference to an additional article to the Treaty of Kiakhta of 1727 dealing with the demarcation and Russo-Chinese trade, which was adopted in October 1768. It also specified the legal stipulations concerning the violation of the state borders. p. 224

289 See Note 163. p. 224

290 A reference to the Amur expedition of 1849-55 under a naval officer, Gennady Nevelskoi. Its aim was to investigate the Amur and the adjoining territories, as well as Sakhalin and the Ussuri area. The Governor-General of Eastern Siberia, Nikolai Muravyev-Amursky, took an active part in it. Poor knowledge of the Amur territories was the main reason why Russia's border with China had not been precisely defined by the Nerchinsk Treaty of 1689.

As a result of the expedition, accurate maps were drawn up and the area described, with valuable data on the geography and population of the area. It served as a basis for establishing the state border between Russia and China laid down by the Treaty of Aigun of 1858. Under this treaty the left bank of the Amur from the Argun River to its estuary was confirmed as belonging to Russia. p. 225

291 See Note 285 and also K. Marx, *The Eighteenth Brumaire of Louis Bonaparte* (present edition, Vol. 11, parts VI and VII). p. 226

292 The Reform Bill of 1832 was directed against the political monopoly of the landed and financial aristocracy and gave representatives of the industrial bourgeoisie access to Parliament. The proletariat and the petty bourgeoisie, the main forces in the struggle for the reform, received no electoral rights. p. 226

293 The *Legitimists,* supporters of the main branch of the Bourbon dynasty overthrown in 1830, expressed the interests of the big hereditary landowners and upheld the claim to the French throne of the Count of Chambord, King Charles X's grandson, who called himself Henry V. Some of the Legitimists remained outside the bloc of monarchist groups. p. 227

294 The *Orleanists* were supporters of the House of Orleans (a lateral branch of the Bourbon dynasty) overthrown by the February revolution of 1848; they represented the interests of the financial aristocracy and the big industrial bourgeoisie; their candidate for the throne was Louis Philippe Albert, Count of Paris and grandson of Louis Philippe. p. 227

295 See Note 258. p. 228

296 A reference to the talks, sponsored by Emperor Francis Joseph, between the British, French and Russian Ambassadors and Austrian Minister Buol, which opened in December 1854. Their official purpose was to work out a basis for peace negotiations between the belligerents in the Crimean war.

In mid-March 1855 representatives of Austria, Britain, France, Turkey and Russia met at a higher level at the Vienna Conference (Britain was represented by Special Envoy Lord John Russell). The conference produced no results. p. 228

297 The *Test Act* of 1673 demanded recognition of the dogmas of the Church of England by persons occupying government posts. At first directed against attempts to re-establish Catholicism, this Act was subsequently applied against various religious sects and trends which deviated from the dogmas of the Established Church. Repealed in 1828.

Under the *Corporation Act* passed by the British Parliament in 1661 persons who held elected posts (this applied mainly to municipal administration) were required to accept the dogmas of the Church of England. Repealed in 1828.

On the *Parliamentary Reform Bill* see Note 292.

The *Municipal Corporation Acts,* adopted for Scotland in 1833 and for England in 1835 introduced a single system of government in all big cities except London. In Scotland municipal corporations were elected by landlords with an annual income of no less than ten pounds; and in England by all taxpayers.

Under the *Commutation Act* of 1838, the *tithes,* which the native Catholic population of Ireland had allotted to the Anglican Church from the sixteenth century, were commuted: payment in kind was changed to a special money-rent which was part of the rent of land.

Dissenters or *Dissidents* were members of various Protestant sects and trends in England who to some degree or other rejected the dogmas of the Established Church. Under the *Dissenters' Marriage Bill* introduced by Russell into the House of Commons in 1834, the dissenters were to be allowed to conduct marriage rituals in their churches. The adoption of the Bill was postponed. p. 229

[298] *Stamp duty* and *advertisement duty* on newspapers introduced in 1712 were the sources of state revenue and a means of fighting the opposition press. In 1836 Parliament was compelled to reduce stamp duty and in 1855 to abolish it altogether. Advertisement duty was annulled in 1853.

The annulment of these duties was not in the interests of the few expensive newspapers because it encouraged the appearance of many cheap rival newspapers, thus lowering the profits of the older newspapers. p. 230

[299] See Note 228. p. 230

[300] After this comes a passage inserted by the editors of the *New-York Daily Tribune*: "For the sake of Christian and commercial intercourse with China, it is in the highest degree desirable that we should keep out of this quarrel, and that the Chinese should not be led to regard all the nations of the Western World as united in a conspiracy against them." p. 235

[301] In this article Marx used the information in Engels' letters of March 11, 20 and 31, 1857 (see present edition, Vol. 40, pp. 104, 110, 115-16). p. 238

[302] The *Whigs*—a political party in England in the seventeenth-nineteenth centuries that arose as a faction expressing the interests of the aristocracy which had become bourgeois and the big commercial and finance bourgeoisie. In the mid-nineteenth century, they united with the Peelites and began to call themselves the Liberal Party.

On the *Peelites* see Note 262. p. 238

[303] See Note 20. p. 238

[304] See Note 258. p. 238

[305] See Note 243. p. 239

[306] In his speech to the electors in the Free Trade Hall in Manchester on March 18, 1857 Cobden criticised Palmerston's home and foreign policy, in particular his aggressive policy against China and Persia. He also gave an unfavourable appraisal of Bob Lowe. p. 239

[307] See Note 228. p. 239

[308] By the "parliamentary godfathers of the penny press" Marx means the Manchester bourgeois radicals (in particular John Bright) who, both inside and outside Parliament, took an active part in the agitation for the abolition of the stamp and advertisement duties (see Note 298). p. 240

[309] The Free Traders' leaders John Bright and Richard Cobden opposed England's participation in the Crimean war, 1853-56, maintaining that by free trade alone England could use her industrial superiority substantially to strengthen her economic and political might. p. 241

[310] *Quakers* (or the *Society of Friends*)—a religious sect founded in England during the seventeenth-century revolution and later widespread in North America. They rejected the Established Church with its rites and preached pacifist ideas. p. 241

[311] The *Rump Parliament* or the *Rump*—the remnant of the Long Parliament (convened by Charles I in 1640) after the expulsion of its Presbyterian majority in December 1648. The Rump—about a hundred Independents, supporters of the Protestant Church—was dissolved by Cromwell in April 1653. p. 241

312 *"The truly British minister"*—this ironic reference to Lord Palmerston is based on a passage from Lord Russell's speech in the House of Commons on June 20, 1850, who said: "...So long as we continue the government of this country, I can answer for my noble friend that he will act not as the minister ... of any other country, but as the minister of England." p. 242

313 A reference to the bombardment of Chinese maritime towns and posts on the Yangtze and other rivers by the British naval and land forces in 1839-40, during the First Opium War (1839-42). See also Note 282. p. 243

314 See Note 197. p. 245

315 Engels is referring to the Taiping uprising in China (see Note 163). In March 1853 the Taipings captured Nanking and made it the capital of their empire. p. 246

316 On the *Peelites* see Note 262.
On the *Manchester men* see Note 258. p. 247

317 See Notes 228 and 287. p. 248

318 See Note 260. p. 248

319 A reference to the bombardment of Odessa by the British and French fleets on April 10 (22), 1854, during the Crimean war.
The ruling party of Peelites was criticised by the Parliamentary opposition for irresolute military actions. p. 249

320 See Note 296. p. 249

321 See Note 152. p. 251

322 During the bombardment of Canton in 1856 (see Note 261) the British Navy lost three men. p. 252

323 See Note 312. p. 253

324 A reference to the Act to Regulate the Labour of Children and Young Persons in the Mills and Factories of the United Kingdom (1833) and the Act to Amend the Laws Relating to Labour in Factories (1844) on the employment of children, juveniles and women in the English textile industry.
Under the 1833 law children from nine to thirteen years of age worked nine hours a day (48-hour week) and had to attend school (two hours a day). The working day for juveniles from fourteen to eighteen years of age was twelve hours a day (69-hour week).
The 1844 law forbade the employment of children under eight years of age and introduced for children from eight to thirteen years half-shift work (six and a half hours a day). It restricted for the first time the working day for women: it was the same as for juveniles under the 1833 law. p. 261

325 The title is given in accordance with an entry in Marx's Notebook for 1857: "April 17. Changes in the Russian army." p. 262

326 The *"Great Unpaid"*—magistrates or justices. p. 266

327 The title is given in accordance with the entries in Marx's Notebook for 1857: "May 12. Crédit Mobilier (I)", "May 15. Crédit Mobilier (II)". p. 270

328 For *Corps Législatif* see Note 20.
The law on the Bank of France was passed on May 28, 1857. For details, see this volume, pp. 289-92. p. 277

[329] Marx's Notebook for 1857 has the following entry: "May 22. *China-Persian (War)* (Artikel an *Tribune*)". p. 278

[330] Engels is referring to the Anglo-Persian war of 1856-57 (see Note 252) and to the Second Opium War, 1856-60 (see Note 196). p. 278

[331] A reference to what is known as the First Opium War, 1838-42 (see Note 282). p. 278

[332] The *Russo-Turkish war of 1828-29* was launched by the Tsarist government in support of the national movement of the Christian population of Greece against the Turkish yoke. The Turkish troops, partly trained by European instructors and well armed, at first offered a strong resistance to the Russian army concentrated on the Danube (at Silistria, Shumla and Varna). However, the victorious offensive of the Russians on May 30 (June 11), 1829, put the Turkish army to flight. The war was ended by the treaty of Adrianople on September 2 (14), 1829, under which Russia obtained the Danube delta including the islands, and a considerable part of the eastern Black Sea coast south of the Kuban estuary. Turkey was to recognise the autonomy of Moldavia and Wallachia and also the independence of Greece, whose only obligation to Turkey was to pay an annual tribute to the Sultan. p. 278

[333] The *Russo-Turkish war of 1806-12* broke out over the violation by Turkey of certain terms of the previously concluded Russo-Turkish treaties (in particular the abolition of free passage for Russian men-of-war and merchant ships through the Bosporus and the Dardanelles). Neither side gained the advantage for long. In 1811 the threat of Napoleon's invasion of Russia forced the Russian government to take measures to conclude the war. After Mikhail Kutuzov had been appointed commander of the Danubian army the war took a turn in favour of Russia who concluded the Treaty of Bucharest with Turkey on May 16 (28), 1812. Under its terms, Russia obtained Bessarabia and certain areas in Transcaucasia. Turkey was to grant internal autonomy to Serbia and confirm its earlier agreements with Russia, extending a measure of autonomy to Moldavia and Wallachia. p. 279

[334] At *Oltenitza* (south-east Wallachia) in the Danubian theatre of operations, the Russian and Turkish forces fought one of the first battles of the Crimean war (November 4, 1853). A Russian detachment attacked the Turkish forces which had crossed to the left bank of the Danube. The attack failed, but the Turkish troops were soon compelled to withdraw to the right bank. Engels described the battle in his article "The War on the Danube" (see present edition, Vol. 12, pp. 516-22).

The battle of *Citate,* in the Danubian theatre of operations, between the Turkish and Russian armies, took place in the early period of the Crimean war, on January 6, 1854. After a stiff fight the Russian detachment was compelled to retreat under pressure from considerable Turkish forces (about 18,000 men), but following the arrival of Russian reinforcements the Turks were forced to go over to the defensive and eventually retreated to Kalafat. For a description of these events see Engels' article "The Last Battle in Europe" (present edition, Vol. 12, pp. 579-82).

On the capture of *Kars* see Note 275. In this case, Engels is referring to the abortive assault on the fortress by the Russians on September 29, 1855. For details see present edition, Vol. 14, pp. 563-68).

In the battle on the *Inguri* in Mingrelia on October 25 (November 6), 1855 the nearly 30-thousand-strong Turkish army met the 18.5-thousand-strong Russian army, the Russians were defeated. p. 279

335 *Renegades* was the name given in the Middle Ages to Christians in Moslem Spain who adopted Islam. Among Christians in Europe the word was afterwards applied generally to Christians in the Eastern countries who became Mohammedans. p. 280

336 See Note 163. p. 282

337 A reference to dissension among the Taiping leaders in the autumn of 1856. As a result, three of the leaders were killed and many thousands of insurgents in Nanking were massacred. The discord was caused by the fact that private and group interests prevailed over class and national considerations among the insurgent leaders. This had a detrimental effect on the further progress of the Taiping uprising. p. 283

338 Marx's Notebook has the following entry concerning this article: "May 26. O'Donnell's speech in the Senate, on the 18th of May." p. 284

339 The *Polacos* was the name adopted in the mid-eighteenth century by the admirers of the de la Cruz theatre in Madrid. In the mid-nineteenth century it was applied to the coterie of the Count San Luis (former journalist Sartorius), whose government ruled Spain from September 1853 to July 1854, i.e., up to the outbreak of the fourth Spanish revolution (1854-56). p. 284

340 See Note 132. p. 284

341 Marx means the beginning of the fourth bourgeois revolution in Spain (1854-56) (see notes 137 and 147) which brought to power the Espartero government of the Progresistas and Right-wing liberals. p. 284

342 See Note 147. p. 285

343 The draft of the *Loi portant prorogation du privilége de la Banque de France* was published in *Le Moniteur universel,* No. 130, on May 10, 1857. After it was passed by the Corps Législatif on May 28, the final text appeared in the same paper, No. 162, on June 11, 1857. p. 289

344 See Note 20. p. 291

345 The *bureaux* were formed by the President of the Corps Législatif out of its deputies for the preliminary discussion of various questions. Usually there were several bureaux, their composition changing periodically. p. 291

346 A reference to the Anglo-Persian war of 1856-57 (see Note 252). The official cause for England and Persia breaking off diplomatic relations at the end of 1855 was a conflict between the British envoy to Teheran and the Persian Sadir Asam (Prime Minister): Mirza Hashim, secretary of the British mission who was a Persian subject, was accused of spying for England. p. 296

347 This title was given according to the entry in Marx's notebook for 1857. p. 297

348 *Scinde,* a province of India bordering on Afghanistan, was finally colonised by the British in 1843.

On the subjugation of the Punjab see Note 215. p. 297

349 In 1856 the British authorities in India proclaimed the ruler of Oudh (a principality in the north of India) deposed and his possessions incorporated in

the territories controlled by the East India Company (see also this volume, pp. 533-38). p. 297

350 The *Presidency*—any of the three original provinces of British India (Bengal, Madras and Bombay). The term was derived from the word "president", a title of the chief of the Council of the principal factory under the East India Company. The title of President was used until 1784, when a parliamentary act was adopted by which governors were appointed instead of presidents. p. 298

351 This refers to the major national liberation uprising of the Indian people against the British rule in 1857-59. It was caused by the indignation of broad sections of the Indian population at colonial exploitation—the exorbitantly high tax burden which led to the complete ruin of the Indian peasants and the expropriation of certain strata of feudal lords; the policy of annexing the remaining independent Indian territories; the system of torture to extort taxes and the colonial reign of terror; gross violation of time-honoured national traditions and customs. The revolt broke out in the spring of 1857 (preparations for it began in mid-1856) among the sepoy units (see Note 256) of the Bengal army quartered in Northern India. They became the military core of the revolt, which assumed wide scope and spread to large areas of Northern and Central India, chiefly Delhi, Lucknow, Cawnpore, Rohilkhand and Bundelkhand. The chief driving force were peasants and urban artisans, but the leadership was in the hands of the feudal lords, the overwhelming majority of whom betrayed the revolt after the colonial authorities promised in 1858 to leave their possessions intact. The main reasons for the defeat of the revolt were: British military and technical superiority, the lack of a single leadership and a general plan of action among the insurgents, as well as contradictory aims largely resulting from the feudal disunity of India; the ethnic heterogeneity of the population and the latter's religious and caste division. Though the revolt did not involve directly certain parts of India (the English managed to prevent its spreading to the Punjab, Bengal and the south of India), it shook the whole country and compelled the British authorities to reform the system of government there.

Marx and Engels regularly described the course of the revolt in the columns of the *New-York Daily Tribune*. p. 298

352 A reference to the Anglo-Persian war of 1856-57 (see Note 252) and the Second Opium War of 1856-60 (see this volume, pp. 158-63, 207-12, 232-35, 243-46, 278-83). p. 298

353 The Indian army was equipped with Enfield rifled guns. When loading a rifle the paper wrapping of a cartridge had to be bitten off. In January 1857 a rumour spread among the Sepoys that the cartridges were greased with the fat of bullocks and pigs. The Sepoys refused to use these cartridges because to touch them meant insult to the religious convictions of the Hindus and Moslems. p. 298

354 The *Moguls*—invaders of Turkish descent who came to India from the east of Central Asia in the early sixteenth century and in 1526 founded the Empire of the Great Moguls in Northern India. The Great Mogul was the title the Europeans gave to the rulers of the Mogul Empire who called themselves Padishahs and resided in Delhi. The Mogul Empire reached considerable power, having subjugated most of India and part of Afghanistan by the mid-seventeenth century. However, due to peasant rebellions and the growing

feudal separatist tendencies, the Empire of the Great Moguls began to decline and practically disintegrated in the first half of the eighteenth century, though formally it lasted until 1858.

Here the reference is to Bahadur Shah II, son of Akbar II. p. 299

355 *Fort William*—an English fortress built in Calcutta in 1696 and named in honour of William III of Orange, King of England at the time. After the English conquered Bengal in 1757, government institutions were quartered in that fortress and its name began to denote "the English government of India". p. 299

356 This title is given in accordance with the entry in Marx's notebook for 1857. p. 301

357 A reference to the elections to the Corps Législatif in the summer of 1857. Despite the police measures taken by the government to secure success to the official candidates, the anti-Bonapartist opposition supported by the workers managed, for the first time in the history of the Second Empire, to get five of its representatives elected to the Chamber. p. 302

358 See Note 15. p. 303

359 Marx refers here to the revolution in Spain in 1856 (see this volume, pp. 97-108) and to the events in Italy in 1857. At the end of June 1857, Mazzini, who secretly arrived in Genoa, and other supporters of revolutionary action attempted to start an uprising in Italy with a view to liberating and uniting the country. A detachment of revolutionaries led by Pisacane seized a ship bound for Tunis from Genoa and landed in the Kingdom of Naples. Attempts were also made to start uprisings in Leghorn and Genoa but, like the expedition to the South, they also failed. p. 304

360 See notes 256 and 351. p. 305

361 *Rajputs*—a higher caste and a people in India inhabiting mainly Rajputana (present Rajasthan) and also some other districts of Northern India.

Brahmins—one of the four ancient Indian castes which originally consisted mainly of privileged priests; like other Indian castes, it subsequently embraced people of different trades and social standing, including impoverished peasants and artisans.

Only Hindus belonging to higher castes were recruited to the sepoy army of Bengal (as distinct from those of Bombay and Madras) and hence Brahmins and Rajputs made up a considerable part of it. p. 306

362 The *Residency*—an official abode of a British Resident (a political counsellor in an Indian principality); in this case the Resident of Oudh. p. 307

363 A reference to the war of independence the Spanish people waged in 1808-14 against the French occupation (see Note 142). p. 307

364 See Note 162. p. 308

365 Marx is apparently referring to the fact that members of the British House of Commons often preferred personal pursuits and recreation to their parliamentary duties during the summer sessions of Parliament. For this reason, speakers often had to address an almost empty house. p. 309

366 *Mechanics' Institutions* or *Institutes* were evening schools in which workers were taught general and technical subjects. Such schools first appeared in Glasgow in 1823 and in London in 1824. In the early 1840s there were over 200 of them,

mainly in the factory towns of Lancashire and Yorkshire. The bourgeoisie used these institutions to train skilled workers for industry and to bring them under the influence of bourgeois ideas, though initially this was resisted by the working-class activists. p. 310

367 A reference to the Tories, the party of the big British landed and financial aristocracy, which was founded in the seventeenth century. With the development of capitalism in Britain, the Tories gradually lost their former political influence and their monopoly in Parliament, especially after the 1832 Electoral Reform and the repeal of the Corn Laws in 1846. The mid-1850s witnessed a process of disintegration in the Tory party. Its class composition changed, and in the late 1850s-early 1860s the British Conservative Party arose on its basis. p. 310

368 This refers to the Council under the Governor-General of India. The Council was instituted in 1773 under the Governor-General of Bengal, whom the Act of 1833 also made Governor-General of India. By the Act of 1853 the council of four, enjoying the functions of an executive body, was supplemented by a larger legislative council which included the Governor-General, the Commander-in-Chief, the Lord Chief Justice of Bengal and a judge of the Supreme Court. This statute of the Council under the Governor-General of India was in force until 1858. p. 311

369 *Jaguedar* or *jagirdar*—a Moslem feudal lord in the Great Mogul Empire (see Note 354) who received for temporary use a large estate (jagir) in return for which he rendered military service and supplied a specified contingent of troops. When the Empire began to disintegrate, the jagirdars became hereditary feudal owners.

Enamdar—an owner of an enam, a grant of land to be held in perpetuity rent free or on favourable terms. Enams were granted mainly to Hindu and Moslem priests and religious and charitable institutions, and sometimes, in Southern India, to the men at the top of the village community.

Freeholders—a category of English small landowners originating in feudal times. They paid their lord an insignificant fixed rent for plots of land which were at their complete disposal. p. 312

370 The title is given according to the entry in Marx's notebook for 1857. p. 314

371 The *Board of Control* was instituted under the 1784 Act for the better regulation and management of the affairs of the East India Company, and of the British possessions in India. The Board of Control consisted of six members appointed by the King from among the members of the Privy Council. The President of the Board of Control was a Cabinet Minister, and, in effect, the Secretary of State for India and India's supreme ruler. The decisions of the Board of Control, which sat in London, were conveyed to India by the Secret Committee, which consisted of three East India Company directors. In this way the 1784 Act established a dual system of government in India—the Board of Control (British Government) and the Court of Directors (East India Company). The Board of Control was dissolved in 1858. p. 314

372 See Note 215. p. 315

373 See Note 355. p. 316

374 See Note 361. p. 316

375 In early October 1854, when the Crimean war was at its height, a rumour spread in Paris that the Allies had captured Sevastopol. This hoax was taken up

by the official French, British, Belgian and German press. However, a few days later, the French newspapers were compelled to publish a refutation. Sevastopol did not fall until September 9, 1855. p. 318

376 *Martello towers*—circular forts armed with two or three guns—used for coastal defence. They were first thus used by the British Navy who occupied one on the Cape Mortella, Corsica, in 1794, during the wars against revolutionary France. p. 319

377 See Note 259. p. 322

378 See Note 159. p. 322

379 In 1849 and 1850 the reactionary Prussian Government, pressed by the broad sections of the German public who aspired to unification, took measures to reogranise the impotent German Confederation, seeking Prussia's victory over Austria in the struggle for supremacy over German states. In October 1850, Nicholas I, who did not want Prussia to grow stronger at Austria's expense, summoned to Warsaw Austrian Chancellor Prince Schwarzenberg and Prussian Prime Minister Count Brandenburg. Also present at the meeting, known as the *Warsaw Conference*, were Prince William of Prussia and Emperor Francis Joseph I of Austria. Nicholas I made it clear that he most decidedly supported Austria against Prussia. p. 323

380 *Internuncio*—a second-rank diplomat (envoy), Austria's representative at Constantinople. p. 324

381 See Note 11. p. 326

382 See Note 375. p. 327

383 *Sàragossa* became famous for its heroic defence during the national liberation struggle of the Spanish people against Napoleon's troops, which besieged the town twice, in 1808 and 1809. Saragossa fell only on February 20, 1809 after the second, two-month siege. p. 333

384 See Note 159. p. 334

385 The German duchies of Schleswig, Holstein and Lauenburg were under the rule of the Danish Crown for centuries. The London protocol on the integrity of the Danish monarchy signed on May 8, 1852 by Russia, Austria, Britain, France, Prussia, Sweden and the representatives of Denmark recognised the right of the duchies to self-government, but preserved the supreme power of the Danish king over them. In spite of the protocol, however, the Danish Government promulgated a Constitution in 1855 which ruled out the independence and self-government of these duchies. This caused a protest on the part of their representatives in the Danish Parliament, who were supported by Prussia and Austria. The Schleswig-Holstein question was finally solved in the Danish war of 1864 when Schleswig was incorporated into Prussia and Holstein into Austria. After the Austro-Prussian war of 1866 Holstein was annexed to Prussia. p. 335

386 An inaccuracy in the text. According to the London protocol of May 8, 1852, the childless King Frederick VII of Denmark was to be succeeded by Christian of Glücksburg (later King Christian IX). p. 335

387 This article, according to the entry "India (Torture)" in Marx's notebook for 1857, was written by him on August 28, 1857, but for some unknown reason the editors of the *New-York Daily Tribune* published it after the article "The

Indian Revolt" written on September 4 and mentioned here. In the present edition the articles are published in chronological order according to the date of their writing. p. 336

388 See Note 284. p. 336

389 *Collector*—a British governor of a district in India who had unlimited powers. He performed the duties of the main tax collector (sued those who did not pay taxes), the chief judge (sentenced them) and an administrative official (executed the sentence). p. 337

390 *Ryot*—an Indian peasant who enjoyed full rights of a community member prior to the introduction of new land taxation laws by the English colonialists in the late eighteenth and the early nineteenth century and the destruction of the Indian community by them. In districts, where the so-called Zemindari system was introduced in 1793, the ryot became a land tenant of a Zemindar (see Note 402). After the introduction of the Ryotwari land taxation system in the Presidencies of Bombay and Madras in the early nineteenth century, the ryot became a holder of state land. He paid rent-tax for his plot, the rate of which was fixed by the British Government in India at its own discretion. p. 337

391 *Jamabundy*—an annual account of land tax. p. 339

392 *Puttah*—an official document drawn up by a landowner or a tax-collector to the tenant. It defined the nature of the tenure and fixed the sum of the rent. p. 339

393 *Agramante*—the Moorish king in Lodovico Ariosto's poem *L'Orlando furioso.* At war with Charlemagne, Agramante besieged Paris, concentrating the bulk of his forces by the walls of that city. But soon dissensions began in their camp. When Marx compared the English camp near Delhi with that of Agramante he meant a line in Ariosto's poem, "There is dissent in Agramante's camp" which had become a dictum. p. 343

394 See Note 162. p. 349

395 This refers to the law of 1853 on the East India Company Charter which curtailed to some extent the Company's monopoly rights in India. The Court of Directors was placed under a greater control of the British Crown, the directors lost the right to appoint officials. Their number was reduced from 24 to 18, of whom six were appointed by the Crown. The President of the Board of Control (see Note 371) was put on a par with the Secretary of State for India. However, the Company's shareholders were guaranteed fixed dividends out of revenues from Indian taxes. p. 349

396 On the *Bengal Council* see Note 368.

Councils consisting of the senior officials of the East India Company also existed under the Governors of the Bombay and Madras Presidencies. p. 350

397 See Note 389. p. 351

398 Marx means the second Anglo-Burmese war of 1852 which resulted in the annexation of the Burmese province of Pegu to the East India Company's possessions. However, Burma did not sign a peace treaty and refused to recognise the seizure of Pegu. p. 352

399 Marx means the first Anglo-Afghan war of 1838-42 (see Note 221), the Second Opium War of 1856-60 and the Anglo-Persian war of 1856-57 (see Note 252). p. 352

400 In the Vendée (a province in western France) the royalists used the backward peasants to engineer a counter-revolutionary revolt in 1793 which was put down by the republican army. Its soldiers, like all the supporters of the Convention in general, were called the "Blues".

During the national liberation war against France in 1808-14 (see Note 142) the Spanish guerrillas, mainly the peasants, offered stubborn resistance to the conquerors.

The counter-revolutionary Austrian forces which suppressed the revolutionary movement in Austria and Hungary in 1848 and 1849 included Serbian and Croat troops (see also present edition, Vol. 7, pp. 503-06).

The *Guard Mobile* was formed by the French Provisional Government's decree of February 25, 1848 to fight the revolutionary masses. Its units consisted mainly of the lumpenproletarians and were used to crush the June uprising of the Paris workers.

Decembrists—members of the secret Bonapartist Society of December 10 (see Note 18). After the coup d'état of December 2, 1851 (see Note 7) they were active organisers of massive repressions against the republicans and especially against participants in the February 1848 revolution. p. 353

401 See Note 282. p. 354

402 *Zemindars*—in the Great Mogul Empire, feudal lords mainly from among the conquered Hindus who retained the right to hold land by heredity on condition that they paid to the government a certain share of the rent-tax they collected from the peasants. In the seventeenth and the eighteenth century the term "Zemindars" applied also to big land-revenue collectors in Bengal and some other areas. In the provinces of British India it began to denote various groups of feudal lords enjoying the rights of landed proprietors. p. 355

403 On *Peace Society* see Note 270.

During the suppression of a popular uprising against the French conquerors, in Algeria in 1845, General Pélissier, later Marshal of France, gave orders for a thousand Arab insurgents, who had hidden in mountain caves, to be suffocated by the smoke from fires. p. 355

404 *Charles V's criminal law* (*Constitutio criminalis Carolina*), adopted by the German Imperial Diet in Regensburg in 1532, was distinguished for extremely harsh punishments. p. 356

405 *Juggernaut* (*Jagannath*)—an incarnation of Vishnu. The famous place of worship was the temple in Puri near Cuttack (Eastern India). The priests of the temple enjoyed the protection of the East India Company and received large incomes from mass pilgrimages and sumptuous festivals in honour of Juggernaut. Particularly large number of pilgrims flocked to celebrate Rathayatra, when the idol of Juggernaut was carried on a chariot. Under its wheels many devotees immolated themselves. p. 356

406 At the end of the second millennium B.C., Jericho was destroyed by the Israelites who invaded Palestine. According to the Bible, the walls of Jericho fell at the blasts of the conquerors' trumpets. p. 356

407 This sentence was added by the editors of the *New-York Daily Tribune* who meant here their correspondent Ferencz Pulszki, a Hungarian writer and journalist, who emigrated to the USA after the defeat of the Hungarian revolution of 1848. They received from him mainly reviews of international affairs. p. 361

408 *Goorkas* (or *Gurkhas*)—a conventional name of peoples inhabiting central and south-western areas of the Nepal. Part of them live in India—in the State of Uttar Pradesh (former United Provinces of British India) and West Bengal districts adjoining Nepal. p. 362

409 *Mohurran* (or *Muharram*)—the first month of the Moslem calendar. During its first ten days a great fast in commemoration of Imam Hosain is held; the religious ceremonies are usually accompanied by self-torture. p. 363

410 *Mahrattas* (*Marathas*)—a people who lived in the North-Western Deccan. In the mid-seventeenth century they began an armed struggle against the Empire of the Great Moguls (see Note 354), thus contributing to its decline. In the course of the struggle the Mahrattas formed their own independent state, whose rulers soon embarked on wars of conquest. At the close of the seventeenth century their state was weakened by internal feudal strife, but early in the eighteenth century a powerful confederation of Mahratta principalities was formed under a supreme governor, the peshwa. In 1761 they suffered a crushing defeat at the hands of the Afghans in the struggle for supremacy in India. Weakened by this and by internal feudal strife, the Mahratta principalities fell prey to the East India Company which annexed a considerable part of their territories in the three Anglo-Mahratta wars (1775-82, 1803-05 and 1817-18).

The reference here is to Tukaji II Holkar and Ali Jah Jaiaji Sindhia, princes of Mahratta. p. 364

411 See Note 221. p. 364

412 When writing this article Marx drew on the information about the uprising in India contained in Engels' letter to him of September 24, 1857 (see present edition, Vol. 40, pp. 182-85). p. 365

413 Marx is referring to the British naval expedition to the mouth of the Schelde River in July 1809, during the war of the fifth European coalition against Napoleonic France, at the moment when Napoleon's main forces were drawn to the war with Austria. After seizing the island of Walcheren, the British failed to use it as a base for action against Antwerp and other French fortified points in Belgium and Holland and were forced to withdraw in December 1809 having lost from hunger and disease about a quarter of their 40,000-strong landing force. p. 365

414 This sentence was interpolated by the newspaper editors. p. 369

415 The *Doab*—here the reference is to the territory in India between the Ganges and the Jumna. p. 373

416 The *Santhals*—a people inhabiting mainly Bihar, the western areas of Bengal, and Orissa; Dravidian by origin. p. 373

417 The table compiled by Marx was sent to the *New-York Daily Tribune* presumably simultaneously with this article, but the editors published the table separately, in the same issue on p. 6. Marx quoted this table, somewhat enlarged, in his letter to Engels of October 20, 1857 (see present edition, Vol. 40, pp. 192-93). p. 377

418 Concerning this article Marx wrote to Engels on December 8, 1857: "I've had a gratifying experience with the *Tribune.* On 6 November I wrote an exposé for them of the 1844 Bank Act in which I said that the next few days would see the farce of suspension, but that not too much should be made of this monetary panic, the real *affaire* being the impending industrial crash." The

article was published on November 21 as a leader but on the 24th the *New-York Times* came out against the author's assertions, declaring the "TALK of an 'INDUSTRIAL CRASH' in England to be 'SIMPLY ABSURD'." However, "the following day the *N.Y.T.* received a telegram ... with the news that the Bank Act had been *suspended*, and likewise news of 'INDUSTRIAL DISTRESS'" (see present edition, Vol. 40, p. 215). p. 379

419 Marx is referring to *An Act to Regulate the Issue of Bank Notes, and for Giving to the Governor and Company of the Bank of England Certain Privileges for a Limited Period,* introduced by Robert Peel on July 19, 1844.

Marx analysed the Act of 1844 and its significance in a number of articles for the *New-York Daily Tribune*: "The Vienna Note.—The United States and Europe.—Letters from Shumla.—Peel's Bank Act" (see present edition, Vol. 12), "The English Bank Act of 1844" (Vol. 16). A detailed description of the Act was given by Marx later, in *Capital,* Vol. III, Chapter XXXIV (present edition, Vol. 37). p. 379

420 When describing the influence of the Bank Act of 1844 on the course of the 1847 crisis, Marx presumably drew on Th. Tooke's *A History of Prices, and of the State of the Circulation...* [Vol. IV], pp. 318-19 and 449. p. 382

421 In Marx's notebook for 1857 this article is entitled "English Monetary Crisis. Suspension of Peel's Act." p. 385

422 Here follows a sentence added by the *New-York Daily Tribune* editors: "This view of the case is confirmed by the news by the *Fulton,* reported in our columns by telegraph this morning". p. 385

423 *Mincing Lane*—a street in London, the centre of wholesale trade in colonial goods. p. 388

424 The *Zollverein,* a union of German states, which established a common customs frontier, was set up in 1834 under the aegis of Prussia. Brought into being by the need to create an all-German market, the Customs Union subsequently embraced all the German states except Austria and a few of the smaller states. p. 390

425 Napoleon III's decree of November 10, 1857 revoked the laws of September 8, 1856 and September 22, 1857 which prohibited the export of corn, flour and other food products. p. 390

426 Here the newspaper's editors added the following passage: "If we are not much mistaken, something of the same sort was put forth in this country, when philosophers like our neighbors of *The Times* and *The Independent* thought the catastrophe might be prevented, if people would only determine to be jolly, and give three cheers." p. 391

427 This and other articles by Engels on the subject published in this volume show how closely he followed the developments in India. This is also proved by his correspondence with Marx who was constantly interested to know his friend's opinion on these events, and on the military aspects of the uprising in particular. This article reflects some of Engels' ideas as expressed in his letter to Marx on September 24, 1857, namely, about the siege of Delhi from the point of view of England's *political consideration* (see also Note 412). Engels mentioned his writing of this article in the letters to Marx of November 16 and 17, 1857 (see present edition, Vol. 40, pp. 204 and 207). p. 392

428 See Note 256. p. 392

429 The *Battle of Balaklava* took place on October 25, 1854 during the Crimean war of 1853-56. Units of the Russian army tried to cut off the British and Turkish troops taking part in the siege of Sevastopol from their base in Balaklava. They succeeded in inflicting serious losses on the enemy, especially on the British cavalry, but failed to achieve their main objective. For the description of this battle see Engels' article "The War in the East" (present edition, Vol. 13, pp. 518-27). p. 395

430 See Note 376. p. 396

431 See Note 425. p. 407

432 See Note 287. p. 408

433 The title is given according to the *New-York Semi-Weekly Tribune*. p. 410

434 The big London banks and discounting houses are located in *Lombard Street* which has become a synonym for the London money market. As distinct from the Bank of England, where only banks' first class papers were discounted, all bills of exchange could be discounted in Lombard Street and the discount interest there, being called market interest, was always higher than that of the Bank of England. p. 410

435 In *Threadneedle Street* (London) the Bank of England is situated. p. 410

436 Marx's notebook for 1857 contains the entry: "December 25. Französische Krisis". Marx also expressed his ideas about the crisis in France in his letter to Engels written on the same day, December 25, 1857 (see present edition, Vol. 40, pp. 228-32). p. 413

437 See Note 424. p. 415

438 See Note 15. p. 417

439 *Crédit Foncier* (Land Credit)—a French joint-stock bank set up in 1852 on the basis of the former Paris Land Bank. It granted short- and long-term loans on security of immovable property at a definite interest and received considerable government subsidies.

Comptoir national d'Escompte de Paris (National Discount Bank of Paris) was founded in 1848 by the Provisional Government of the French Republic. Originally it discounted bills and granted credits on the security of goods stored in public warehouses. At the time of Napoleon III it became a joint-stock society (from 1853 on) and acquired the privilege of making advances on government bonds and shares of industrial and credit companies. p. 417

440 Engels wrote this article on Marx's request (see Marx's letters to Engels of December 30, 1857 and January 1, 1858, present edition, Vol. 40, pp. 233 and 237). Engels expressed his ideas about the siege of Lucknow in his letter to Marx of December 31, 1857 (see ibid., pp. 233-36) and partly in this article. p. 419

441 *Mess-house*—premises of the officers' club and dining-room of the Lucknow military garrison.

The *Residency*—see Note 362. p. 419

442 On the occupation of Scinde, see Note 348.

Sir Charles Napier was formally given command of all the troops in Scinde and was empowered to exercise control over all civil and political officials as well as military officers within his command. p. 420

443 The *Battle of the Alma* took place on September 20, 1854 during the Crimean war (1853-56). The Russian forces were commanded by A. S. Menshikov, and the numerically superior forces of the French, British and Turks by Saint-Arnaud and Raglan. It was the first battle after the Allies' landing in the Crimea (at Eupatoria) on September 14. The defeat and withdrawal of the Russian troops opened up the way to Sevastopol for the Allies. p. 424

444 See Note 429. p. 424

445 See Note 256. p. 424

446 The castle of *Hougoumont* and the farm *La Haye Sainte* on the approaches to Waterloo were used by the English and Prussian troops as strong natural fortifications. In the battle of Waterloo on June 18, 1815 the defenders of these camps put up a stubborn resistance despite their small numbers (there were 7 companies and one battalion in Hougoumont and one battalion in La Haye Sainte). All attempts of the French to capture the first point failed, and only after a heavy bombardment and a pitched battle did they take the second. p. 424

447 At *Borodino,* near Moscow, a full-scale battle was fought by the French and Russian forces on September 7, 1812. During the battle the French had 135,000 men and 587 guns, the Russians 120,000 men and 640 guns. The French lost 58,000 men killed and wounded, the Russians about 44,000. p. 427

448 Engels wrote this article on Marx's request (see Marx's letter to Engels of January 11 and Engels' reply of January 14, 1858, present edition, Vol. 40, pp. 244 and 247) who thought very highly of it. "Your article is splendid and in style and manner altogether reminiscent of the *Neue Rheinische Zeitung* in its heyday," Marx wrote to Engels on January 16, 1858 (ibid., p. 249). p. 435

449 See Note 362. p. 436

450 Informing Marx of this article in the letter of January 14, 1858, Engels wrote with irony: "The Lucknow garrison's greatest act of heroism consisted in the fact that they had to face every day the 'coarse beef' cooked by the ladies, *'entirely unaided'*. Must have been damned badly cooked" (see present edition, Vol. 40, p. 247). p. 441

451 In October 1832 the Anglo-French troops, reinforced by the Belgian artillery and engineers, under Marshal Gérard blocked the ports of the Kingdom of the Netherlands and besieged the citadel of Antwerp so as to compel the Netherlands to comply with the London treaty of 1831 on Belgium's independence and the transfer of Antwerp to it. At the end of December 1832, after the fortress was in ruins, its commandant General Chassé and his garrison surrendered.

Venice, which rose against the Austrian rule in March 1848, was besieged by the Austrian troops from land and sea for over a year. The Austrians under Marshal Haynau directed their main attack on the Fort of *Marghera* which was defended by 2,500 men under Colonel Ulloa. Only when all the fortified works were destroyed and most of the guns put out of order did the defenders abandon it on the night of May 26, 1849. p. 441

452 In his articles "Progress of the War", "From Sevastopol", "The Armies of Europe." and "Aspects of the War" dealing with the Crimean war of 1853-56 and the heroic defence of Sevastopol in particular (see present edition, Vol. 14), Engels, more than once, highly appreciated the activity of General

E. I. Todtleben, chief engineer and organiser of the defence, and said that he was "the only man in either camp who has shown a spark of genius" (ibid., p. 487). p. 441

453 The fortress of Danzig, occupied by the French garrison under General Rapp after the defeat of Napoleon's army in Russia in 1812, was besieged from land and sea by the Russian and Prussian troops in early 1813. During the eleven and a half months the fortress withstood three regular sieges. The French lost 19,000 men, the Allies 10,000. On January 2, 1814, the Allies entered the city. p. 441

454 Engels alludes to the events of the Crimean war of 1853-56. Colonel Windham commanded a British brigade during the abortive attack on Bastion No. 3 (the Great Redan) of the Sevastopol fortifications on June 18, 1855. His actions were extremely slack, moreover, during the heat of the battle, he twice left for the rear, allegedly to bring up reinforcements (see this volume, pp. 447-52). p. 442

455 The commercial existence of the East India Company was terminated by the Parliamentary Act of 1833 which abolished its monopoly of the China trade. Though the Act left the Indian possessions of the Company in its hands for a further period of twenty years, it put the Company under stricter government control through a Crown-appointed official on the Bengal Council (see also Note 368). p. 444

456 Engels' letter to Marx of January 28, 1858 testifies to his work on this article (see present edition, Vol. 40, p. 254) but he did not manage to finish it by Friday, January 29, and sent Marx only three articles for *The New American Cyclopaedia.* Nevertheless, on their receipt, Marx made the following entry in his notebook: "Windham's defeat, Berme, Blenheim, Borodino." In the letter of January 30, Engels definitely stated: "'Windham' will be ready for Tuesday" (ibid., p. 257), i.e. February 2, 1858. p. 447

457 See Note 443. p. 447

458 See Note 454. p. 447

459 See Note 415. p. 448

460 See Note 402. p. 448

461 Lord Raglan, the British commander-in-chief, gave order for a cavalry attack on the Russian batteries at the battle of Balaklava on October 25, 1854 (see Note 429) which led to the destruction of the British light cavalry under Lord Cardigan. (General command of the light and heavy cavalry was under Lord Lucan.) This event produced a grave impression on the British public. Later, trying to justify himself, Lord Raglan sought to put the blame on Lucan and Cardigan who, he alleged, had misunderstood him, and on Captain Nolan who was said to have passed the order inaccurately. There was no possibility of verifying the fact because Nolan was killed a few minutes after he had given the order. p. 451

462 This title is given according to the entry made by Marx in his notebook on February 5, 1858: "Bonaparte Attempt". p. 453

463 Marx is referring here to Louis Bonaparte who attempted a coup d'état on August 6, 1840. Profiting by a certain revival of pro-Bonapartist sentiments in France, he landed with a handful of conspirators at Boulogne and tried to raise

a mutiny among the local garrison. His attempt failed. He was sentenced to life imprisonment, but escaped to England in 1846. p. 453

464 On January 14, 1858 the Italian revolutionary Felice Orsini made an attempt on the life of Napoleon III, thus hoping to provoke revolutionary actions in Europe and intense struggle for the national unification of Italy. His attempt failed, and Orsini was executed on March 13, 1858. p. 453

465 The editors of the *New-York Daily Tribune* inserted the following paragraph here: "Or as an eminent American, now in France, writes in a letter received by the *Africa*: 'There is a frightful foreboding in the bosoms of the French themselves. I was talking with a friend the other day, a very devout and clear-headed woman, and she told me *sotto voce* that she talked with no one who did not feel a stifling fear of what was coming, of a day of vengeance too black to contemplate. She told me that the receipts of the *mont-de-piété* were falling off so much that the truth was becoming evident that the people had nothing left to dispose of, and this to her and her friends was a sure sign that the final crash was near.'" p. 456

466 See Note 20. p. 456

467 A reference to *La loi relatif à des mesures de sûreté générale* (Law on Public Security Measures) known as *La loi des suspects* (Suspects Law) adopted by the Corps législatif on February 19 and promulgated on February 28, 1858. It gave the emperor and his government unlimited power to exile to different parts of France or Algeria or to banish altogether from French territory any person suspected of hostility to the Second Empire. p. 456

468 A reference to the *Society of December 10* (see Note 18). p. 457

469 See Note 148. p. 457

470 In Ancient Rome Praetorians were privileged soldiers in the personal guard of a general or the emperor. Here Marx is referring to the French military on whom Napoleon III relied (see also this volume, pp. 464-67). p. 457

471 Under Napoleon III's decree of January 27, 1858 the whole of French territory was divided into five military districts, with Paris, Nancy, Lyons, Toulouse and Tours as their capitals and Marshals Magnan, Baraguay d'Hilliers, Bosquet, Castellane and Canrobert as their commanders. Marx calls these districts *pashaliks* (a comparison earlier used by the French republican press), to emphasise the similarity of the unlimited powers of the reactionary Marshals and the despotic power of the Turkish pashas. Pélissier's proposed appointment as marshal general in 1858 remained unrealised. p. 457

472 Marx is referring to Louis Bonaparte who, during the July monarchy, attempted to stage a coup d'état by means of a military mutiny. On October 30, 1836 he succeeded, with the help of several Bonapartist officers, in inciting two artillery regiments of the Strasbourg garrison to mutiny, but they were disarmed within a few hours. Louis Bonaparte was arrested and deported to America. p. 457

473 In March 1855 Napoleon III planned to go to the Crimea with the aim of suppressing the discontent in the army and the country, invigorating military actions and speeding up the capture of Sevastopol. His trip did not take place. p. 457

474 After Orsini's attempt on the life of Napoleon III, Count Walewski, the French Foreign Minister, sent a dispatch to the British Government on January 20,

1858 expressing dissatisfaction that England should be giving asylum to French political refugees. The dispatch served as a pretext for Palmerston to move a new Alien Bill (also called *Conspiracy to Murder Bill*) on February 8, 1858. It stipulated that any Englishman or foreigner living in the United Kingdom who became party to a conspiracy to murder a person in Britain or any other country, was to be tried by an English court and severely punished. During the second reading of the new Alien Bill on February 19, 1858 the radicals Milner Gibson and John Bright moved an amendment censuring the Palmerston Government for not giving a fitting reply to Walewski's dispatch. By a majority vote, the House of Commons adopted the amendment and rejected the Bill. The Palmerston Government was compelled to resign. p. 458

475 In July 1854, during the Crimean war (1853-56), Marshal Saint-Arnaud ordered to organise an expedition under General Espinasse against the Russian troops in Dobrudja. However, having taken no military actions (except minor skirmishes with the retreating Cossacks) and having lost over half of the expeditionary corps due to epidemics of cholera and malaria among the soldiers, Espinasse returned to Varna. p. 464

476 See Note 470. p. 464

477 See Note 471. p. 464

478 On October 10, 1850 Louis Bonaparte, then President of the French Republic, held a general review of troops on the plain of Satory (near Versailles). During this review Bonaparte, who was preparing a coup d'état, treated the soldiers and officers to sausages in order to win their support. p. 464

479 A counter-revolutionary coup d'état of the *Ninth Thermidor* (July 27-28, 1794) overthrew the Jacobin government and established the rule of the big bourgeoisie. p. 465

480 The *Palais-Royal* in Paris was the residence of Louis XIV from 1643; in 1692 it became the property of the Orlean branch of the Bourbons. During the Second Empire it was the residence of Napoleon III's uncle, ex-King of Westphalia Jérôme, and his son Joseph Bonaparte, hereditary Prince until the birth of Napoleon III's son.

Here Marx hints at the strained relations between Jérôme and Louis Bonaparte. p. 465

481 The title is given according to the entry of February 26, 1858 in Marx's Notebook: "Derby Ministry. Palmerston's sham resignation". p. 468

482 See Note 464. p. 468

483 As a result of the Anglo-Chinese conflict, which arose in October 1856 (see Note 196) and marked the beginning of the Second "Opium" War (the main role in the conflict was played by Yeh Ming-Chin, Governor-General of Kwantung and Kwangsi, who objected to the unlawful demands by the British), and the debate over it in the House of Commons of February 26-March 3, 1857, the Palmerston Government was given a vote of no confidence by 263 against 247. Making use of this, Palmerston dissolved the Parliament. The new elections brought victory to the government candidates even in the bulwark of the Opposition—Manchester and secured a majority in the House for the champions of aggression against China.

On *Palmerston's resignation in 1858*, see Note 474.

Carbonari—members of secret political societies in Italy and France in the first half of the nineteenth century. In Italy they fought for national independence, the unification of the country and liberal constitutional reforms. In France the movement was above all directed against the restored monarchy of the Bourbons (1815-30). In the first half of the nineteenth century the word "Carbonari" was synonymous with "revolutionary". p. 468

484 The *Emancipation of the Catholics*—in 1829 the British Parliament, under pressure of a mass movement in Ireland, lifted some of the restrictions curtailing the political rights of the Catholic population. Catholics were granted the right to be elected to Parliament and to hold certain government posts. Simultaneously the property qualification for electors increased fivefold. With the aid of this manoeuvre the British ruling classes hoped to win over to their side the upper crust of the Irish bourgeoisie and Catholic landowners and thus split the Irish national movement. p. 469

485 A reference to the campaign for an electoral reform carried out by the British Government in 1832 (see Note 292). p. 469

486 See Note 228. p. 469

487 Richard Cobden's campaign in 1845 for the repeal of the Corn Laws facilitated the fall of the Peel Cabinet. Lord John Russell, the leader of the Whig Party, who was charged to form a new Cabinet, offered Cobden the post of Vice-President of the Board of Trade, but the latter declined on the ground that he would be more efficient as the out-of-doors advocate of Free Trade than in an official capacity. Owing to internal dissensions among the Whig chiefs, the Cabinet was not formed, and on December 20 Peel returned to office. p. 469

488 See Note 371. p. 469

489 The phrase "Take care of Dowb" was used by British Secretary at War Panmure in a dispatch to General Simpson, appointed commander-in-chief in the Crimea in June 1855. It became widely known in England and was considered as proof that Panmure cared more for his nephew, a young officer named Dowbiggin, than for the whole British army. p. 469

490 See Note 260. p. 469

491 See Note 474. p. 470

492 See Note 474. p. 470

493 In the *New-York Daily Tribune* the article ended with the text added by the editors: "Every capital of Europe breathes more freely in consequence; every Liberal feels sure that the triumphant uprising of the People is much nearer than it was a month ago. We cite in confirmation a single passage from the speech of England's foremost orator, and one of her most promising statesmen—Mr. Gladstone, long the bosom friend of Sir Robert Peel, the representative of the University of Oxford—who, in the great debate which hurled Palmerston from office, said:

"'These times are grave for liberty. We live in the nineteenth century. We talk of progress; we believe that we are advancing; but can any man of observation who has watched the events of the last few years in Europe have failed to perceive that there is a movement, indeed, but a downward and backward movement? There are a few spots in which institutions that claim our sympathy still exist and flourish. They are secondary places, nay, they are almost the holes and corners of Europe, so far as mere material greatness is concerned, although their moral greatness will, I trust, insure them long prosperity and happiness. But in these times more than ever does responsibility center upon England; and if it does center upon England, upon her principles, upon her laws, and upon her governors, then I say that a measure passed by this House of Commons—the chief hope of freedom—which attempts to establish a moral complicity between us and those who seek safety in repressive measures, will be a blow and a discouragement to that sacred cause in every country in the world.' [Loud cheers.]

"Bear in mind that Mr. Gladstone was urged by Lord Derby to accept a very high place in his Cabinet, and that there has not recently been, and is not likely soon to be, a Premier who would not gladly share with him the gravest responsibility." p. 471

494 An allusion to the atrocities committed by the French colonialists on the Arab tribes during the war in Algeria. See also Note 403. p. 472

495 In the spring of 1847 at Buzançais (department of the Indre) the starving workers and the neighbouring villagers looted storehouses belonging to profiteers, which led to a clash between the population and troops. Four of those who took part were executed and many others sentenced to hard labour. p. 472

496 In August 1847 Altarice-Rosalba-Fanny, the Duchess of Praslin, was found murdered in her home. Suspicion fell on her husband, the Duke of Praslin, who was arrested and who poisoned himself during the investigation. p. 472

497 On *Carbonari* see Note 483.

In the latter half of the 1850s several attempts were made on the life of Napoleon III, including one by the Italian patriot Orsini (see Note 464). In European circles some of these actions were ascribed to the desire to punish Napoleon III, who was member of the Italian Carbonari organisation in 1831, for breaking his commitments to it. p. 474

498 See Note 11. p. 475

499 See Note 471. p. 476

500 See Note 475. p. 476

501 The expression *"intelligent bayonets" (baïonnettes intelligentes)* is ascribed to the French general Changarnier. When in 1849, Marrast, President of the Constituent Assembly, felt a threat on the part of the Bonapartists and requested Changarnier to call up troops for the defence of the Assembly, Changarnier refused to do that with the remark that he did not like *baïonnettes intelligentes.* In this way he made it clear that the army should not be guided by political motives in its actions. Marx is alluding ironically here to the pro-Bonapartist French army which, in fact, played a considerable part in the policy of the Second Empire. p. 476

502 See Note 467. p. 476

503 In this article Marx made use of Engels' letter to him of March 17, 1858 (see present edition, Vol. 40, pp. 289-93). p. 477

504 The phrase *"L'horizon politique s'obscurcit"* (the political horizon is darkening) appeared daily in *Le Constitutionnel* on the eve of the revolution in France in 1848. p. 478

505 See Note 148. p. 478

506 See Note 293. p. 479

507 A reference to the rejection of the Alien Bill in the House of Commons in February 1858 and the resignation of the Palmerston Government that followed (see Note 474). p. 479

508 Marx is referring to the convention signed between France and Belgium on September 22 and ratified on October 11, 1856. It restricted Belgium's right to give asylum to political emigrants accused of the attempt on the life or of assassination of foreign sovereigns or members of their family. p. 480

509 See Note 472. p. 480

510 On December 10, 1848 Louis Bonaparte was elected President of the French Republic by a majority vote. p. 482

511 See Note 464. p. 482

512 See Note 471. p. 482

513 *Albion*—an old name of the British Isles; the expression "perfide Albion", current from the time of the French Revolution, was taken from a poem by Augustin, Marquis de Ximénès. Britain was so called for its government's numerous intrigues against the French Republic and organisation of anti-French coalitions. p. 484

514 It is said that in 362 B. C. a deep gulf opened in the forum, which the seers declared would never close until Rome's most valuable possession was thrown into it. Then Curtius, recognizing that nothing was more precious than a brave citizen, leaped into the chasm, which immediately closed. The spot was afterward covered by a marsh called the *Lacus Curtius*. p. 484

515 At the *Battle of Waterloo* (June 18, 1815) Napoleon's army was defeated by British and Prussian forces commanded by the Duke of Wellington and Blücher. p. 484

516 *Myrmidons,* in Homer, the inhabitants of Phthiotis in Thessaly. A fierce and devoted followers of Achilles. In modern times their name is used to mean subordinates who carry out orders implacably. p. 484

517 An allusion to the fact that, while in emigration in England, Louis Bonaparte volunteered for the special constabulary (a police reserve consisting of civilians) which helped the regular police disperse the Chartist demonstration on April 10, 1848, organised to present a petition to Parliament for the adoption of the People's Charter. p. 484

518 The *Holy Alliance*—an association of European monarchs founded on September 26, 1815, on the initiative of the Russian Emperor Alexander I and the Austrian Chancellor Metternich, to suppress revolutionary movements and preserve feudal monarchies in European countries. p. 484

519 The *Triumvirs*—Mazzini, Saffi and Armellini—of the Roman Republic (1848-49) pursued a moderate policy. Although their measures towards peasants were progressive, in practice they neither changed agrarian relations in the countryside nor improved the hard condition of the peasants, who did not support the revolution in the greater part of the Italian states. p. 485

520 See Note 464. p. 486

521 The *Marianne,* founded in France in 1850, was a secret republican society which opposed Napoleon III during the Second Empire. p. 486

[522] A great massacre of Huguenots by Catholics took place in Paris on St. Bartholomew's Day (August 24) in 1572.

Marx calls Louis François Veuillot the upholder of St. Bartholomew's Day because he was a rabid Catholic. p. 488

[523] After the death of Pius VIII on November 20, 1830, the Holy See remained vacant until February 2, 1831. This created favourable conditions for uprisings against the Pope's secular power in a number of provinces of the Papal States—Romagna, Marca, Umbria—and also in the dukedoms of Modena and Parma. They were instigated by the Carbonari (see Note 483). Louis Bonaparte took part in the plot in Rome which was denounced by one of the conspirators. Expelled from Rome, Louis Bonaparte left for Florence. In late March 1831 the uprisings were suppressed by the Austrian troops and the government forces of small Italian states. p. 488

[524] Marx's main source for this article were *Papers relating to the Negotiations carried on between Great Britain and France, between the conclusion of the Treaty of Amiens, 25th March, 1802, and the recall of Lord Whitworth from Paris, 12th of May, 1803, including divers Papers from the English Ministers at the Hague, Berlin, Vienna, St. Petersburgh, Copenhagen, and Hamburgh; to which is added an Appendix, containing offensive Papers, published by France.* Laid before the Parliament by His Majesty's Command on the 18th of May, 1803. This material was published in *Cobbett's Annual Register,* Vol. III, from January to June 1803 and Marx informed Engels about this in his letter of February 14, 1858 (see present edition, Vol. 40, pp. 265-66). p. 490

[525] The *Peace of Amiens* signed by France on March 25 and by Britain on March 27, 1802 ended the war between France and the second European coalition. But peace did not last long. Napoleon I soon resumed the war under the pretext of Britain's failure to fulfil one of the conditions of the Amiens peace, namely to evacuate Malta, which she had occupied in 1800, and return it to the Order of St. John of Jerusalem. p. 490

[526] The *Alien Bill* was passed by the British Parliament in 1793 and renewed in 1802, 1803, 1816, 1818 and, finally, in 1848. The Bill authorised the Government to expel any foreigner from the Realm at any moment. It remained in force for one year. Subsequently conservative circles repeatedly urged its renewal. p. 491

[527] The *Court of King's (Queen's) Bench* is one of the oldest courts in England; in the nineteenth century (up to 1873) it was an independent supreme court for criminal and civil cases competent to review the decisions of lower judicial bodies. p. 494

[528] Marx alludes here to the introduction of a 12-pound cannon in the French army on Napoleon III's initiative, the so-called Louis Bonaparte's howitzer; it was planned that this cannon would replace all four calibres of field artillery but the appearance of rifled guns hindered this measure. p. 499

[529] See Note 11. p. 499

[530] See Note 15. p. 499

[531] *"The savior of property"* was the name given to Louis Bonaparte in addresses which municipal councils of various French towns sent him in July 1849. p. 500

532 On Praetorian camps see notes 470 and 471.
On the attempt of January 14 see Note 464. p. 501

533 This title is given according to the entry in Marx's notebook for 1858. p. 504

534 This refers to the first Anglo-Afghan war of 1838-42 (see Note 221). p. 505

535 Marx means the proposals on the budget made on April 18, 1853 by Chancellor of the Exchequer Gladstone and adopted by the House of Commons. p. 511

536 The French surgeon Simon Bernard, residing in England, was accused of being an accomplice of Felice Orsini in the attempt on the life of Napoleon III (making bombs, etc.) and tried in London between April 12 and 17, 1858. By decision of the Central Criminal Court, Bernard was acquitted on April 17. p. 515

537 *Le Moniteur universel* published French colonels' addresses to Napoleon III on the occasion of his surviving after the attempt on his life on January 14, 1858 (see Note 464). These addresses abounded in threats against England. p. 515

538 See Note 463. p. 517

539 Marx presumably used the *Monthly Comparative Return of Paupers relieved in each month in each year* [1857, 1858]. Somewhat later *The Economist*, No. 769, May 22, 1858 carried the article "Pauperism and the State of Trade". Its author analysed the same official reports and gave some statistical data which are also quoted by Marx. p. 523

540 Engels is referring to the oldest form of defences raised by the Burmese around their towns and camps. p. 529

541 The Spanish fortress of *Badajoz* occupied by the garrison under General Phillipon was stormed and taken by English troops commanded by Wellington on April 8, 1812.

The French-held Spanish fortress of *San Sebastian* was stormed on August 31, 1813. Its commandant, General Rey, surrendered on September 8.

The capture of those towns was accompanied by plunder, violence and atrocities against local inhabitants. p. 530

542 On March 3, 1858, Lord Canning, the Governor-General of India, issued a proclamation on the confiscation of land in the province of Oudh in favour of the British Government. The confiscated property included the landed estates of big local feudal lords who had joined the Indian uprising. Canning's point of view was not shared by a number of prominent colonial officials and MPs who favoured a more flexible policy towards the Indian feudal lords and hoped to win them over by promises to leave their domains intact. Marx criticised the proclamation in the articles "The Annexation of Oudh" and "Lord Canning's Proclamation and Land Tenure in India" (see this volume, pp. 533-38 and 546-49). p. 531

543 Engels is referring to the battles fought during the first Anglo-Sikh war of 1845-46. Despite the well-organised army and strong artillery the Sikhs were defeated by the British at Moodka (near Lahore) on December 18, at Ferozeshah (near Ferozepore) on December 21, 1845 and at Aliwal (near the Sutlej) on January 28, 1846 and lost the war. The main cause of their defeat was the treachery on the part of their supreme command. p. 532

544 This title is given according to the entry Marx made in his notebook on May 14, 1858: "India (Politics) (Annexation of Oude)." p. 533

545 See notes 196 and 483. p. 533

546 Marx is referring to the Polish national liberation insurrection of 1830-31. The majority of its participants were revolutionary nobles and most of its leaders came from the aristocracy, whose estates were confiscated. p. 533

547 The *Battle of Novara* between Piedmontese and Austrian troops lasted the whole day of March 22 and ended at dawn on March 23, 1849, in the defeat and withdrawal of the Piedmontese army. p. 533

548 In 1739 Oudh seceded from the Great Mogul Empire and became an independent principality with Lucknow as its capital. Under the treaty of Allahabad (1765) Robert Clive, Governor of Bengal, concluded a subsidiary alliance with Shuja ud-Daulah; the latter had virtually lost power, which passed into the hands of the British Resident. To camouflage this state of affairs the English often referred to the ruler of Oudh as King. p. 534

549 Under the treaty concluded between the East India Company and the Nawab Vizier of Oudh in 1801 Oudh lost a considerable part of its territory between the Ganges and the Jumna, and also Rokhilkhand and Gorakhpur (known as the Ceded Districts) in compensation for failing to repay the Company's subsidies. The Nawab disbanded his troops, and the strength of the Company's troops in Oudh increased. p. 535

550 See Note 368. p. 537

551 Marx informed Engels about the response to his article among the Hungarian émigrés in the USA in his letter of July 2, 1858 (see present edition, Vol. 40, p. 324). p. 539

552 Almost all India was under British rule by the middle of the nineteenth century. Cashmere, Rajputana, part of Hyderabad, Mysore and other smaller principalities were vassals of the East India Company. p. 546

553 On *Zemindars* see Note 402.

Talookdars—big feudal lords in Oudh, the majority of whom came from the ranks of the land-tax collectors who turned the districts taxed by them into their own property.

Sirdars—big Sikh feudal lords. p. 546

554 The reference is to the promulgation of the Permanent Settlement on March 22, 1793 by the Indian Governor-General Charles Cornwallis. It declared almost all lands in Bengal, Bihar and Orissa permanent property of zemindars and the sum of taxes they paid was also established in perpetuity. p. 547

555 See Note 542. p. 548

556 In his dispatch of April 19, 1858 the President of the Board of Control, Lord Ellenborough, severely criticised Lord Canning's proclamation of March 3, 1858 (see Note 542). However, Ellenborough's dispatch was not approved of by the British ruling classes and on May 10, 1858 he had to resign. p. 549

557 In his letter to Engels of May 31, 1858 Marx wrote that during the past week he had prepared two articles for the *New-York Daily Tribune*, presumably this and the preceding one. p. 550

558 See Note 531. p. 550

559 See Note 15. p. 551

560 See Note 470. p. 552

561 See Note 478. p. 552

562 On June 4, 1858, Marx wrote in his notebook: "Army in India", and in the letter to Engels on June 7 he acknowledged the receipt of Engels' article for the *New-York Daily Tribune*: "very amusing one, too" (see present edition, Vol. 40, p. 319). He was probably referring to this article. p. 556

563 An allusion to the fact that Britain's Prime Minister was also First Lord of the Treasury. p. 566

564 The *People's Charter,* which contained the demands of the Chartists, was published in the form of a Parliamentary Bill on May 8, 1838. It contained six points: universal suffrage (for men of 21 and over), annual parliaments, vote by ballot, equal electoral districts, abolition of the property qualification of MPs and payment for MPs. Petitions urging the adoption of the People's Charter were turned down by Parliament in 1839, 1842 and 1848.

The property qualification of MPs was abolished by Parliament in 1858. p. 566

565 The reference is to the policy of the Austrian ruling circles during a big peasant uprising in Galicia in February and March 1846 which coincided with the Cracow national liberation uprising. Taking advantage of class and national contradictions, the Austrian authorities provoked clashes between the insurgent Galician peasants and the Polish lesser nobility (szlachta) who were trying to come to the assistance of Cracow. The peasant uprising began with the disarming of the insurgent szlachta detachments and grew into a mass sacking of landowners' estates. After dealing with the insurgent szlachta, the Austrian Government also suppressed the peasant uprising in Galicia. p. 568

566 See Note 15. p. 569

567 A reference to a Bill tabled in Parliament by the Derby Ministry in March and adopted on August 2, 1858 as the *Act for the Better Government of India.* It placed India under the control of the British Crown, while the East India Company was dissolved, and its shareholders were compensated with £3 million from the Indian budget. The Act also provided for the formation of the Indian Council as a consultative body consisting of 15 military and civil officials in the Anglo-Indian service. The Governor-General of India became the Viceroy, virtually remaining a functionary of the Secretary of State for India in London; the latter kept full control over British colonial administration and the military forces of the former East India Company.

A critical analysis of the Act is given by Marx in his article "The Indian Bill" (see this volume, pp. 585-88). p. 576

568 This title was given in accordance with the entry in Marx's notebook for 1858. p. 580

569 A reference to the colonial war in Algeria, launched by the French Government in 1830. The Algerian people put up a stubborn resistance to the French colonialists; it took them 40 years to turn Algeria into a French colony. p. 583

[570] This title was given in accordance with the entry in Marx's notebook for 1858. p. 585

[571] A reference to the *Act for establishing certain Regulations for the better Management of the Affairs of the East India Company, as well in India as in Europe of 1773.* Its main provisions were as follows: the qualification for a vote in the Court of Proprietors was raised from £500 to £1,000 and was restricted to those who had held their stock for at least twelve months. Measures were taken to prevent the collusive transfer of stock, and the consequent multiplying of votes. The directors were henceforth to be elected for four years, and one-fourth of their number must retire every year, remaining at least one year out of office. There was to be a Governor-General of Bengal assisted by four councillors. They were to have power to superintend the subordinate presidencies in making war or peace. The first governor-general and councillors, Warren Hastings, Clavering, Monson, Barwell and Philip Francis were named in the Act. They were to hold office for five years, and future appointments were to be made by the Company. The Act empowered the Crown to establish by charter a Supreme Court of Justice, consisting of a chief justice and three puisne judges. p. 585

[572] See Note 567. p. 586

[573] See Note 474. p. 587

[574] *Civis Romanus sum* ("I am a Roman Citizen")—an expression used by Foreign Secretary Lord Palmerston in his speech in the House of Commons on June 25, 1850. Palmerston declared that like the formula of Roman citizenship, *Civis Romanus sum,* secured universal respect for the citizens of Ancient Rome, so also a British subject, in whatever land he may be, shall feel confident that the watchful eye and the strong arm of England will protect him against injustice and wrong. p. 588

[575] Marx means the Anglo-Afghan war of 1838-42, in which the British forces were utterly defeated (see Note 221). p. 588

[576] See Note 252. p. 588

[577] A reference to the Second "Opium" War with China, 1856-60. p. 588

[578] About his letter to the *Neue Zeit* Marx wrote to Engels on August 18, 1858 (see present edition, Vol. 40, pp. 340-41). p. 589

[579] This article was written by Engels, on Marx's request, between July 16 and 20, 1858 and sent to New York on July 27. The *New-York Daily Tribune* editors tampered with the text and this is particularly noticeable in the last paragraph. Moreover, the editors changed the title to "How the Indian War Has Been Mismanaged" and published it unsigned. In this volume the title is given in accordance with the entry in Marx's Notebook for 1858. p. 590

[580] The *American War of Independence* (1775-83)—a revolutionary war fought by 13 British colonies in North America. As a result of their victory an independent state was formed, the United States of America. France fought on the side of the Americans. p. 590

[581] See Note 258. p. 597

[582] Marx may have referred to his first article about Lady Bulwer-Lytton written on July 16, 1858, but not published in the *New-York Daily Tribune.* p. 597

583 The *Sikh empire,* a feudal Indian state on the territory of the Punjab, was founded at the end of the eighteenth century and reached its heyday at the beginning of the nineteenth century under Ranjit Singh who brought into subjection all local principalities and some neighbouring regions. Ranjit Singh created strong military organisation and the Sikh army was considered the best in India.

On the subjugation of the Punjab see Note 215. p. 610

584 This became a dictum in the 1840s. It originated with Lord Palmerston who wrote on February 14, 1840 to John Cam Hobhouse, Baron Broughton, President of the Board of Control: "It seems pretty clear that sooner or later the Cossack and the Sepoy, the man from the Baltic and he from the British islands will meet in the centre of Asia." p. 610

585 These notes are to be found in Marx's notebook of excerpts dated November 1854-early 1857. He made them during his work on the articles "Maritime Commerce of Austria" (see this volume, pp. 139-50). p. 615

586 The Genoese obtained privileges under the Nimpha Treaty of 1261 with the Byzantine emperor Mikhail VIII Palaeolog. p. 615

587 On the Treaty of Campo-Formio and of Lunéville see Note 170. p. 616

588 See Note 171. p. 616

589 A reference to the treaty between France and Austria signed in Fontainebleau on October 10, 1807. It specified the boundaries between the Austrian Empire and the Italian Kingdom. p. 616

590 See Note 171. p. 616

591 *Convention money (coin)* was introduced in Austria in 1753. The standard of the 20-gulden, or convention, system was silver. 20 guldens contained 234 grams of pure silver. With the introduction and the growing quantity of paper money in circulation, particularly during the 1848-49 revolution, the rate of exchange of convention money for it constantly increased. p. 616

592 In the summer of 1854 when the fourth bourgeois revolution in Spain (1854-56) broke out, Marx began studying in earnest the history of the nineteenth-century bourgeois revolutions in that country with the aim of ascertaining the specific character of the new revolution, which, he believed, if a success, could give an impact to revolutionary events in other European countries. As can be judged by the notebook in which Marx put down the dates of dispatching the articles to New York and sometimes briefly disclosed their contents, in August-November 1854 he wrote for the *New-York Daily Tribune* nine articles with the general title "Revolutionary Spain". In September-December that year the newspaper published the first six articles dealing with the first (1808-14) and the beginning of the second (1820-23) revolutions and containing a short survey of Spain's preceding history. However, the editors arbitrarily divided the articles, printing them in eight numbers, and thus the printed series of articles "Revolutionary Spain" consisted of eight articles (see present edition, Vol. 13, pp. 389-452). The remaining three articles were not found in the newspaper columns and were regarded as unpublished. Only a small fragment from their draft manuscript has survived dealing with the causes that led to the defeat of the second revolution. It is probably part of the eighth article (Marx's numeration) and may be considered relevant to the entry in the Notebook made on November 21, 1854 (ibid., pp. 654-59).

In 1983, when Volume 14, Section I, of *MEGA* was being prepared for publication, research workers of the Institute of Marxism-Leninism under the Central Committee of the Socialist Unity Party of Germany discovered the seventh (ninth in the newspaper) article of the series. It was published in the morning edition of the *New-York Daily Tribune* for March 23, 1855. This issue is missing in the file of the newspaper available at the library of the Institute of Marxism-Leninism under the CC CPSU. The content of the article corresponds to the entry in the Notebook made on November 14, 1854: "Tuesday, November 14. Spain 1820-July 1822." The article substantially adds to the analysis of the laws governing bourgeois revolutions in general, given by Marx on the example of the nineteenth-century Spanish bourgeois revolutions, and also to the description of certain features of the revolution and counter-revolution in Spain itself determined by its specific historical development.

The article is reproduced here from the photocopy kindly placed at the disposal of the Institute of Marxism-Leninism of the CC CPSU by the Institute of Marxism-Leninism of the CC SUPG. p. 621

593 A reference to the Constitution adopted by the Spanish Cortes in Cadiz on March 19, 1812 (see Note 142). Marx analysed it in one of the articles of this series (see present edition, Vol. 13, pp. 424-33).

For his study of the Constitution Marx used its text in *The Political Constitution of the Spanish Monarchy. Proclaimed in Cadix, 19 March 1812,* London, 1813. p. 621

594 The French Constitution adopted by the Legislative Assembly in 1791 established constitutional monarchy in the country. The king was granted full executive powers and the right of veto. This Constitution was annulled as a result of the popular uprising of August 10, 1792. p. 621

595 An allusion to the description of the absolute monarchy in Spain given by Marx in the first article of this series, namely: "The absolute monarchy in Spain, bearing but a superficial resemblance to the absolute monarchies of Europe in general, is rather to be ranged in a class with the Asiatic forms of government" (see present edition, Vol. 13, p. 396). p. 622

596 Marx is referring to the second bourgeois revolution in Spain (1820-23). p. 622

597 Marx analysed these events in the article "Espartero" (see present edition, Vol. 13, pp. 340-46). p. 622

598 *Ayuntamientos* were organs of local government in Spain, which played a great political role during the Reconquest, or struggle for Spain's liberation from the Arab yoke (eighth-fifteenth centuries), and which were liquidated later. The re-establishment of *ayuntamientos* was one of the democratic demands of the early nineteenth-century bourgeois revolutions. p. 623

599 An allusion to the fact that on the eve of the first bourgeois revolution (1808-14) the power in Spain was actually concentrated in the hands of Manuel Godoy (nicknamed "the sausage-maker"), the favourite of the royal couple, Carlos IV and Maria Luisa. p. 623

600 Ferdinand VII abdicated in May 1808 and lived in Talleyrand's palace in France from 1808 to March 3, 1814. p. 623

601 The reference is to the negotiations between Ferdinand VII and the French Government concerning the terms of Ferdinand's return to Spain terminated in the agreement of December 11, 1813. On December 15, Joseph Bonaparte

abdicated from the Spanish throne in Ferdinand's favour. The Spanish Regency, whom Ferdinand had sent his instructions immediately after December 11, did not fulfil the terms of the agreement. p. 624

602 *Pavillon Marsan*—a building in the Tuileries Palace; during the Restoration it was the residence of the Count of Artois. p. 624

603 This refers to the decree issued by Ferdinand VII on September 30, 1823. p. 624

604 In the course of the national liberation war of the Spanish people against Napoleon I the fortress of Badajoz was many a time the site of fierce battles. p. 624

605 The *Cadiz Cortes*—the constituent assembly in Spain convened on September 24, 1810 and dissolved on September 20, 1813, during the first Spanish revolution (1808-14). The Cortes promulgated a number of laws, and the adoption of the Constitution was of special importance (see notes 142 and 593). p. 624

606 The *Moderados* (see Note 136) were also called *anilleros* (see this volume,p. 629) during the second revolution (1820-23).

The *Exaltados* represented the Left wing in the revolution of 1820-23 and were supported by the democratic section among the officers, urban middle and petty bourgeoisie, artisans and workers. Marx called the Moderados the Liberals of 1812, and the Exaltados the Liberals of 1820. p. 625

607 During the 1820-23 revolution many democratic clubs and secret societies were set up in Spain. The most radical among the secret societies was the Confederation of Spanish Comuneros which numbered 70,000 members. Comuneros favoured resolute struggle against counter-revolution. After the defeat of the revolution the Comuneros were severely persecuted and abandoned their activity. p. 625

608 The *army of the Isla* (of the Island)—an expeditionary corps concentrated in 1819 near Cadiz and on the Isle of Leon to be dispatched to Latin America where the national liberation struggle was waged against the Spanish domination (see Note 615). A plan for an armed revolt against Ferdinand VII's despotism was being hatched in the expeditionary army formed of unreliable elements. The Riego battalion, which mutinied on January 1, 1820, and thus started the second revolution in Spain, was also part of this corps. p. 625

609 Marx is referring here to the detachments formed by the Catholic-absolutist group of Apostolics who called themselves the "army of faith" and staged a revolt against the revolutionary government in 1822 in Catalonia, Navarra and Biscay. In 1823 these detachments joined the French interventionists. p. 625

610 The decree nominating General Carvajal to the post of Captain-General of New Castile was signed by Ferdinand VII on November 16, 1820. Marx drew this information from a book by W. Walton, *The Revolutions of Spain*, 2 volumes, London, 1837. p. 626

611 On October 5-6, 1789, during the French Revolution, the Paris revolutionary masses marched to Versailles and frustrated the counter-revolutionary plot of the Court. The King and the Constituent Assembly were forced to return to Paris. p. 626

612 The Ministry that came to power in 1820 included active participants in the 1808-14 revolution—Evaristo Pérez de Castro, Manuel García Herreros, Augustin de Argüelles and others, who were victims of repressions after its defeat. p. 626

613 In July 1820 bourgeois revolutionaries (Carbonari) started a revolt in the Kingdom of Naples (the Kingdom of the Two Sicilies) and obtained a democratic constitution on the pattern of the Spanish Constitution of 1812. The Congress of the Holy Alliance which opened in Troppau in October 1820 and closed in Laibach in May 1821 took a decision to send Austrian troops to Italy. p. 627

614 The servile party (serviles)—a nickname given to the reactionary clerico-absolutist group which arose during the first bourgeois revolution in Spain (1808-14); later its members formed the Court camarilla of Ferdinand VII. p. 627

615 Marx is referring to the liberation war waged by the Spanish colonies in America (1810-26). General Morillo, who commanded the Spanish army there in 1815-20, was most brutal in suppressing the insurgents. p. 627

616 A reference to the Francisco Martínez de la Rosa Ministry appointed in late February 1822. p. 628

617 A reference to the suppression of the revolt in Naples by the Austrian troops (see Note 613). p. 628

618 *Las Cabezas* (Las Cabezas de San Juan)—a small town north-east of Cadiz, where Riego quartered his battalion at the end of December 1819 and whence he started his revolutionary march (see Note 608). p. 629

619 The *doctrinaire school* included French bourgeois politicians of the Restoration (1815-30), constitutional monarchists who wanted to form in France a bourgeois-aristocratic bloc like that in England. Most prominent among them were the historian François Guizot and the philosopher Pierre Paul Royer-Collard. p. 629

620 Marx is referring to the constitution, the so-called Charter, which was imposed by Louis XVIII in 1814, after Napoleon I's defeat, and established constitutional monarchy in France. p. 629

621 General Elío, who was sentenced to imprisonment in 1820 for having organised a counter-revolutionary coup in 1814, was kept in the citadel of Valencia. p. 630

NAME INDEX

A

uty to the Constituent and Legislative Assemblies during the Second Republic; Bonapartist; member of several cabinets before and after the coup d'état of December 2, 1851.—457

Barrot, Camille Hyacinthe Odilon (1791-1873)—French lawyer and politician, leader of the liberal dynastic opposition until February 1848; headed the monarchist coalition ministry (December 1848-October 1849).—302

Barrot, Théodore Adolphe (1803-1870)—French diplomat; Consul-General in Egypt (1845).—296

Bartrum, R. H.—British army officer in India.—355

Bates, Robert Makin (born c. 1791)—English banker, partner of a firm which went bankrupt in June 1855; was sentenced to penal servitude for financial machinations.—110

Bauer, Bruno (1809-1882)—German philosopher and writer, Young Hegelian.—181-93

Baugh—British lieutenant in India.—298

Bayezid II (1447-1512)—Sultan of Turkey (1481-1512).—80

Beauharnais, Eugénie Hortense de (1783-1837)—Napoleon III's mother, wife of King Louis Bonaparte of Holland.—490

Beautemps-Beaupré, Charles François (1766-1854)—French hydrographer.—148

Bedeau, Marie Alphonse (1804-1863)—French general and moderate republican politician; Vice-President of the Constituent and Legislative Assemblies during the Second Republic; expelled from France after the coup d'état of December 2, 1851; after the amnesty of 1859 returned to France.—476

Bentham, Jeremy (1748-1832)—English sociologist, proponent of utilitarianism.—209

Bentinck, Lord William Cavendish (1774-1839)—British general and statesman; fought in the wars against Napoleonic France; Governor-General of India (1827-35).—536

Bernal Osborne, Ralph (1808-1882)—British liberal politician, M.P., Secretary of the Admiralty (1852-58).—218

Bernard, Simon François (Bernard le Clubiste) (1817-1862)—French republican; emigrated to Britain after the defeat of the 1848 revolution; in 1858 was accused by the French Government of being an accomplice in Orsini's attempt on the life of Napoleon III; acquitted by the British Court.—515, 516

Berryer, Arthur—agent of the French Government in the joint-stock company, Docks Napoléon; son of lawyer Pierre Antoine Berryer; in March 1857 was sentenced to two-year confinement for participating in the financial machinations of the company's governors.—474

Berryer, Pierre Antoine (1790-1868)—French lawyer and politician, deputy to the Constituent and Legislative Assemblies during the Second Republic; Legitimist.—474

Berthier, Louis Alexandre, prince de Neuchâtel, duc de Valengin, prince de Wagram (1753-1815)—Marshal of France, chief-of-staff in Napoleon's army (1799, 1805-07, 1812-14); after the fall of the Napoleonic Empire (1814) sided with the Bourbons.—465

Bertrán de Lys (Lis), Manuel—Spanish statesman, deputy to the Cortes, Minister of Foreign Affairs (1851, 1852) and Minister of the Interior (1851).—630

527, 529-31, 548, 557-59, 580-83, 607

Campbell, Sir George (1824-1892)—British official in India (1843-74 with intervals); Liberal; author of works on India.—579

Canning, Charles John, Earl (from 1859) (1812-1862)—British statesman, Tory, then Peelite; Governor-General of India (1856-62), organised the suppression of the Indian national liberation uprising of 1857-59.—363, 437, 531, 533-34, 547-49, 594

Canning, George (1770-1827)—British statesman and diplomat, Tory, Foreign Secretary (1807-09, 1822-27), Prime Minister (1827).—188, 469

Canrobert, François Certain (1809-1895)—Marshal of France, Bonapartist; an active participant in the coup d'état of December 2, 1851; commander-in-chief of the French army (September 1854-May 1855) during the Crimean war.—466, 483

Cantemir, Demetrius (Demeter), Prince (1673-1723)—Moldavian encyclopaedist and politician; Hospodar of Moldavia (1710-11); in 1711 concluded an agreement with Peter I placing Moldavia under Russian suzerainty.—89

Cardwell, Eduard Cardwell, Viscount (1813-1886)—British statesman, a leader of the Peelites and then a Liberal; President of the Board of Trade (1852-55), Chief Secretary for Ireland (1859-61).—61, 249

Carl Ludvig Eugène (1826-1872)—Crown Prince of Sweden, Regent (1857-59); King of Sweden and Norway under the name of Charles XV (1859-72); son of Oscar I.—334

Carlos Maria Isidro de Borbón (Don Carlos) (1788-1855)—brother of Ferdinand VII; pretender to the Spanish throne under the name of Charles V; head of the feudal clerical party (Carlists) which fomented a civil war in Spain (1833-40).—104, 106

Carmarthen, Marquis of—see *Osborne, Sir Thomas*

Carvajal—Spanish general, nominated by Ferdinand VII Captain-General of New Castile in 1820.—626

Casa-Irujo, Carlos Maria Martinez (1765-1824)—Spanish statesman, ambassador to Paris (1821), Minister of Foreign Affairs (1823).—624

Casimir IV Jagiello (1427-1492)—Grand Duke of Lithuania from 1440; King of Poland (1447-92).—85, 86

Cass, Lewis (1782-1866)—American statesman, general and diplomat, member of the Democratic Party; Secretary of State (1857-60).—570-71

Cassagnac—see *Granier de Cassagnac, Bernard Adolphe*

Castellane, Esprit Victor Elisabeth Boniface, comte de (1788-1862)—Marshal of France, Bonapartist; commanded the garrison of Lyons from 1850.—466, 475

Castello, Mary Anne—English actress, George Canning's mother.—469

Castlereagh, Robert Stewart, Marquis of Londonderry, Viscount (1769-1822)—British statesman, Tory; Secretary for War and for the Colonies (1805-06, 1807-09); Foreign Secretary (1812-22); committed suicide.—114, 222, 471, 491

Catherine I Alexeyevna (1684-1727)—second wife of Peter the Great (from 1712); Empress of Russia (1725-27).—59, 60

Catherine II (1729-1796)—Empress of Russia (1762-96).—28-29, 31-32, 34-37, 39-40, 60, 157, 187, 224

Catiline (Lucius Sergius Catilina) (c. 108-62 B.C.)—Roman politician,

F

I

L

M

ernment of the Roman Republic; in the early 1850s sought for support among the Bonapartists but later opposed them.— 115, 485, 486, 488

Mehemed Bey—see *Bangya, János*

Melbourne, William Lamb, Viscount (1779-1848)—British statesman, Whig, Home Secretary (1830-34), Prime Minister (1834, 1835-41).— 468, 597

Menchikoff (Menshikov), Alexander Sergeyevich, Prince (1787-1869)—Russian general and statesman; ambassador extraordinary in Constantinople (February-May 1853); commander-in-chief of the Russian army and navy in the Crimea (1853-February 1855).— 322, 483

Mengli-Ghirai (Menghi-Ghirei) (d. 1515)—Crimean Khan (1468-1515).— 82, 85, 86

Mercy, de—French army officer; court-martialled and sentenced to death for the sadistic murder of an officer in his regiment in 1858.— 552

Merry, Anthony—British diplomat, envoy to Paris (1802).— 491, 492, 495

Miall, Edward (1809-1881)—English writer and politician, radical, M.P. (1852-57, 1869-74).— 238

Michelet, Jules (1798-1874)—French historian.— 488

Mierosławski, Ludwik (1814-1878)—prominent figure in the Polish national liberation movement; took part in the 1830-31 Polish insurrection and in the 1848-49 revolution in Germany; later headed the moderate wing of the Polish democratic émigrés; sought for support among the Bonapartists in the 1850s.— 62

Mikhail Borisovich (1453-c. 1505)—Grand Duke of Tver (1461-85).— 85

Millaud, Moïse (1813-1871)—French banker, founded a number of newspapers and banks.— 502

Milner Gibson—see *Gibson, Thomas Milner*

Miloš (Milosh) Obrenović I (1780-1860)—Prince of Serbia (1815-39, 1858-60), founder of the Obrenović dynasty.— 62

Mina—see *Espoz y Mina, Francisco*

Minié, Claude Étienne (1804-1879)—French officer, inventor of a new type of rifle.— 450

Minto, Sir Gilbert Elliot, Earl of (1751-1814)—British statesman, Whig, envoy to Vienna (1799-1801), Governor-General of India (1807-13).— 495

Mirès, Jules Isaac (1809-1871)—French banker, owner of a number of newspapers, *Le Constitutionnel* among them.— 467

Moguls—see *Great Moguls*

Mohammed Ali Shah—King of Oudh (1837-42).— 536-38

Mohammed-Amin—Naib in the western part of the North Caucasus (the Abadzekh tribe) (1848-59); led the mountaineers' struggle against Tsarist Russia.— 543

Mohammed Shah (1810-1848)—Shah of Persia (1834-48).— 178-80

Molière (real name *Jean Baptiste Poquelin)* (1622-1673)—French playwright.— 356

Mon, Alejandro (1801-1882)—Spanish politician, liberal; Minister of Finance (1837, 1844-46, 1849), deputy to the Cortes (1836-75).— 286

Moncreiff, James, Baron Moncreiff (from 1874), *Baron of Tullibole* (from 1883) (1811-1895)—British lawyer, M.P., Lord Advocate for Scotland (1851-52, 1852-58, 1859-66, 1868-69).— 216

the Peninsular war (1808-14), in 1842-43 commanded the British troops in India that captured Sind; governor of Sind (1843-47).— 198, 315, 328, 420, 447

Napoleon I Bonaparte (1769-1821)—Emperor of the French (1804-14 and 1815).— 15-16, 75, 98, 139, 141, 146, 149, 167, 169, 171, 356, 365-66, 413, 441, 454, 465-66, 471, 484, 487, 490-98, 616, 623

Napoleon III (Charles Louis Napoleon Bonaparte) (1808-1873)—nephew of Napoleon I, President of the Second Republic (1848-51), Emperor of the French (1852-70).— 5-6, 11, 14-16, 18-21, 24, 98-99, 107, 110, 114-16, 118-19, 122, 124, 131-32, 134, 137, 214, 222-23, 226-27, 230, 250, 270, 273-74, 276, 290-92, 296, 302-03, 320, 323-24, 333, 353, 358, 391, 413-15, 453-59, 464-68, 470-74, 476-80, 483-90, 495, 500-03, 515-19, 531, 533, 550-52, 568-69, 573-74, 595

Napoleon, Prince— see *Bonaparte, Prince Napoléon Joseph Charles Paul*

Narváez, Ramón Maria, duque de Valencia (1800-1868)—Spanish general and statesman, leader of the Moderado Party; head of government (1844-46, 1847-51, 1856-57, 1864-65, 1866-68).— 98-100, 284-88

Nasmyth, James (1808-1890)—British engineer and inventor.— 259

Nasr-ed-Din (1831-1896)—Shah of Persia (1848-96).— 177, 197, 295, 296, 307

Nazar—envoy of the Novgorod Republic in 1477.— 83

Nazir-ed-Din (d. 1837)—King of Oudh (1827-37).— 536

Necker, Jacques (1732-1804)—French banker and politician, several times Director-General of Finance in the 1770s and 1780s; attempted to carry out reforms.— 186

Neill, James George Smith (1810-1857)—British general, fought in the Crimean war; during the national liberation uprising of 1857-59 in India acted with great severity in Cawnpore.— 372

Nemours, Duchess of—see *Marie d'Orléans-Longueville*

Nesselrode, Karl Vasilyevich, Count (1780-1862)—Russian statesman and diplomat, Minister for Foreign Affairs (1816-56), State Chancellor (from 1845).— 193

Newcastle, Henry Pelham Fiennes Pelham Clinton, Duke of (1811-1864)—British statesman, Peelite, Secretary for War and the Colonies (1852-54), Secretary for War (1854-55) and Secretary for the Colonies (1859-64).— 217

Nicholas I (1796-1855)—Emperor of Russia (1825-55).— 178, 187, 264, 466, 533

Nicholson, John (1821-1857)—British general, in 1842 took part in the first Anglo-Afghan war, fought in the second Anglo-Sikh war (1848-49); in 1857, during the national liberation uprising in India, commanded an English unit in the attack on Delhi.— 365, 370, 374

Nocedal, Cándido (1821-1885)—Spanish politician and journalist; member of the Moderado Party; deputy to the Cortes; Minister of the Interior (1856-57).— 284

Nolan, Lewis Edward (c. 1820-1854)—British army officer, served in India, took part in the Crimean war, wrote several books on the cavalry.— 279

Norris, Sir John (c. 1660-1749)—British admiral, in 1709-21 commander of the squadron in the Baltic sent to help Sweden against Russia.— 45, 50, 54, 66, 70, 93

North, Frederick, Earl of Guilford (1732-1792)—British statesman,

Tory; Chancellor of the Exchequer (1767), Prime Minister (1770-82); Home Secretary (1783).—30, 32-35

Northcote, Sir Stafford Henry, Earl Iddesleigh, Viscount St. Cyres (1818-1887)—British statesman, Peelite, later joined the Conservatives, M.P. (1855-57, 1858-85); held a number of ministerial posts.—249

Norton, Caroline Elizabeth Sarah (1808-1877)—English poetess.—597

Norton, George Chapple (c. 1800-1875)—English barrister-at-law, husband of Caroline Norton.—597

O

O'Donnell, Enrique José, conde de la Bisbal (1769-1834)—Spanish general, took part in the war of independence (1808-14); during the period of reaction (1814-20) maintained contacts with the liberals and betrayed revolutionaries to the government.—99

O'Donnell y Jorris, Leopoldo, conde de Lucena y duque de Tetuán (1809-1867)—Spanish general and politician, a leader of the Moderado Party; Captain-General of Cuba (1843-48); in 1854 used the revolutionary crisis in the country to establish military dictatorship; as War Minister directed the suppression of the 1854-56 revolution; head of government (1856, 1858-63, 1865-66); nephew of the above.—97-102, 104-05, 107-08, 284-88, 573

Oleg (d. 912)—Prince of Kievan Rus.—75, 76

Omer Pasha (Michael Lattas) (1806-1871)—Turkish general; Croat by birth; commander-in-chief of the Turkish troops on the Danube (1853-54), in the Crimea (1855) and in the Caucasus (1855-56).—193

Orléans—royal dynasty in France (1830-48).—479, 531, 533, 551

Orleans, Duke of—see *Louis Philippe I*

Orléans, Philip II, duc d' (1674-1723)—Regent of France (1715-23).—24, 359, 488

Orloff (Orlov), Alexei Fyodorovich, Prince (1786-1861)—Russian military figure and statesman, diplomat; headed Russian delegation at the Paris Congress in 1856; President of the State Council and the Committee of Ministers (from 1856); President of the Secret (from 1856) and of the Chief Peasant Question Committee (from 1858); opposed abolition of serfdom.—3

Orsini, Felice (1819-1858)—Italian democrat and republican; a prominent figure in the struggle for Italy's national liberation and unification; executed for his attempt on the life of Napoleon III.—468, 472-75, 477-78, 480

Osborne—see *Bernal Osborne, Ralph*

Osborne, Sir Thomas, Earl of Danby, Marquis of Carmarthen, Duke of Leeds (1631-1712)—British Tory statesman; Prime Minister (1674-79, 1690-95); in 1695 was accused of bribe-taking by Parliament.—187, 585

Oscar I (1799-1859)—King of Sweden and Norway (1844-59).—334

Osten, Adolph Siegfried, Count (1726-1797)—Danish diplomat, ambassador to St. Petersburg (1757-61, 1763-65).—28

Osterman, Andrei Ivanovich, Count (1686-1747)—Russian diplomat and statesman, Vice-Chancellor (1725-41), from 1731 virtually directed Russia's foreign and home policy; exiled after enthronement of Yelizaveta Petrovna in 1741.—27

Osterman, Ivan Andreyevich, Count (1725-1811)—Russian diplomat, ambassador extraordinary to Sweden (1759-74), Vice-Chancellor (1775-96), Chancellor (1796-97); son of the above.—29

Schröder, John Henry (1784-1883)—head of a large banking firm in London; brother of Christian Matthias Schröder.—412

Sébastiani, Horace François Bastien, comte (1772-1851)—Marshal of France, diplomat, Orleanist; Foreign Minister (1830-32), ambassador to London (1835-40).—496

Ségur, Philippe Paul, comte de (1780-1873)—French diplomat, military writer and historian; general, took part in the 1812 campaign.—75, 78, 83, 84, 89, 92

Semyon Ivanovich the Proud (1316-1353)—Grand Duke of Moscow (from 1340) and of Vladimir (from 1341).—79

Sepher Pasha (Sepher Bey) (1795-1859)—Circassian prince in Turkish service; fought in the Russo-Turkish war (1826-28); directed the Circassians' military operations against Russia in 1855-59.—539-44

Serrano y Dominguez, Francisco, conde de San Antonio, duque de la Torre (1810-1885)—Spanish general and statesman, War Minister (1843), took part in the coup d'état of 1856; Foreign Minister (1862-63), head of government (1868-69, 1871, 1874), Regent of the Kingdom (1869-71).—98, 287

Seu (Xu Guangjin) (1785-1858)—Chinese statesman, Governor-General of Kwangtung and Kwangsi.—162

Seymour, Sir Michael (1802-1887)—British admiral, rear admiral of the Baltic fleet (1854-56), commander of the naval forces in the Second Opium War with China (1856-58).—158-62, 218, 222, 234

Shaftesbury, Anthony Ashley Cooper, Earl of (1801-1885)—British politician; in the 1840s headed a group of philanthropic Tories in Parliament; Whig from 1847; Palmerston's stepson-in-law.—219, 599

Shakespeare, William (1564-1616)—English playwright and poet.—211, 219, 269, 457, 492

Shee, Sir William (1804-1868)—Irish lawyer and Liberal politician, M.P.—216

Shelburne—see *Petty, Sir William*

Shore, John, Baron Teignmouth (1751-1834)—British Governor-General of India (1793-98).—535

Shuvalovs (Schuwaloffs)—Russian noble family, close to the Court in the 18th-19th centuries.—31

Sidmouth, Henry Addington, Viscount (1757-1844)—British statesman, Tory; Prime Minister and Chancellor of the Exchequer (1801-04), Home Secretary (1812-21).—222, 494

Sidney—Lord Mayor of London (1857).—231

Sigismund (c. 1361-1437)—German Emperor (1411-37), last of the Luxembourg dynasty.—154-56

Silius Italicus (Titus Catius Silius Italicus) (c. 26-101)—Roman epic poet, author of the poem *De Secundo bello punico*.—65

Simolin, Ivan Matveyevich, Baron (1720-1799)—Russian diplomat, ambassador to Sweden (1774-79), to Britain (1779-85), to France (1785-92).—32, 34

Simonich, Ivan Stepanovich, Count (1792-1855)—Russian general; Serb by birth; envoy to Teheran (1832-39).—179

Simpson, Sir James (1792-1868)—British general, chief of staff (February-June 1855), then commander-in-chief of the British army in the Crimea (June-November 1855).—447

Sindhia, Ali Jah Jaiaji (Bagirat Rao) (born c. 1835)—Mahratta Prince of Gwalior from 1853; sided with the British during the national liberation uprising of 1857-59 in India.—364, 609

Sismondi, Jean Charles Léonard Sismonde de (1773-1842)—Swiss economist, representative of economic romanticism.—147

Sixtus IV (Francesco della Rovere) (1414-1484)—Pope (1471-84).—86

Sleeman, Sir William Henry (1788-1856)—British colonial official, officer, then general, resident at Gwalior (1843-49) and at Lucknow (1849-54).—538

Smith, Sir John Mark Frederick (1790-1874)—British general, military engineer, M.P.—333

Smith, Robert Vernon, Baron Lyveden (1800-1873)—British statesman, Whig, M.P., Secretary at War (1852); President of the Board of Control for India (1855-58).—314, 316, 469

Smythe, John George—British politician, colonel, Peelite, M.P.—249

Solms-Sonnenwalde, Victor Friedrich, Count von (1730-1783)—Prussian diplomat, envoy extraordinary to Sweden (1755-59), envoy to Russia (1762-79).—29

Sophia (Zoë) Palaeologus (c. 1448-1503)—Grand Duchess of Moscow, second wife of Ivan III, niece of the last Byzantine emperor, Constantine XI Palaeologus.—80, 86

Soult, Nicolas Jean de Dieu, duc de Dalmatie (1769-1851)—Marshal of France and statesman, fought in the wars of Napoleonic France, Prime Minister (1832-34, 1839-40, 1840-47).—39, 290

Souwaroff—see *Suvorov, Alexander Vasilyevich*

Stalker, Forster (d. 1857)—British general, commanded British land forces in the Anglo-Persian war of 1856-57; committed suicide.—294

Stanhope, James, Earl (1673-1721)—British military and political figure, diplomat, Whig; participant in the War of the Spanish Succession, envoy to (1706-07, 1708-10) and commander of the British troops in Spain (1708-10); Secretary of State (1714-17), Chancellor of the Exchequer (1717-21); supported Sweden in her war against Russia.—56, 60, 93, 187

Stanley, Edward Henry, Earl of Derby (1826-1893)—British statesman, Tory, Conservative in the 1860s-70s, later Liberal; Colonial Secretary (1858, 1882-85), Secretary of State for India (1858-59), Foreign Secretary (1866-68, 1874-78); son of Edward Derby.—469, 470, 590

Stanley, Edward John, Baron Stanley of Alderley and Baron Eddisbury of Winnington (1802-1869)—British statesman, Whig, M.P.; President of the Board of Trade (1855-58), Postmaster-General (1860-66).—425-26, 428

Stead, Jean—French émigré on Jersey, printer.—496

Stein, Maximilian, Baron (1811-1860)—Austrian army officer; during the revolution of 1848-49 in Hungary was chief of the General Staff of the revolutionary army; then émigré in Turkey under the name of Ferhad Pasha; fought against Russia in the Caucasus (1857-58).—541-43, 545

Stephen III the Great (d. 1504)—Hospodar of Moldavia (1457-1504).—85

Stewart, Sir Donald Martin (1824-1900)—British army officer, later field marshal; took part in suppressing the national liberation uprising of 1857-59 in India, and in the second Anglo-Afghan war (1878-80); commander-in-chief of the British troops in India (1881-85); member of the Council of India (1885-1900).—364

T

revolution in Italy and Germany, émigré in Turkey; fought in the Crimean war on the side of the Allies and in the Caucasian mountaineers' war against Tsarist Russia.—542-43

U

Ummer Singh—see *Amar Singh*

Urquhart, David (1805-1877)—British diplomat, writer and politician; Turkophile; carried out diplomatic missions in Turkey in the 1830s; M.P. (1847-52), Tory; opponent of Palmerston's policy; founder and editor of *The Free Press* (1855-65).—184

Uzbek Khan (c. 1282-1342)—Khan of the Golden Horde (1312-42).—78

V

Vaillant, Jean Baptiste Philibert, comte (1790-1872)—Marshal of France, senator, Bonapartist, Minister of War (1854-59).—465

Vaïsse, Claude Marius (1799-1864)—French statesman, Bonapartist, Minister of the Interior (January-April 1851), prefect of Lyons in the mid-1850s.—466

Valbezen, de—French consul in Calcutta (1854-58).—320

Valdez—Spanish general, participant in the revolution of 1854-56.—100, 101

Valdez (Valdés), Jeronimo (1784-1855)—Spanish general, Governor-General of Cuba (1841-42).—573

Van Cortlandt, Henry Charles (1815-1888)—British general; was in the military service of the Sikhs (1832-39); fought in the first and second Anglo-Sikh wars (1845-46, 1848-49) on the side of the British; participated in suppressing the national liberation uprising of 1857-59 in India.—329, 345, 361, 372

Vaughan, Sir John Luther (1820-1911)—British general, participated in suppressing the national liberation uprising of 1857-59 in India.—307

Velasco y Coello, Manuel (1776-1824)—Spanish general, participant in the first (1808-14) and second (1820-23) revolutions in Spain; Military Governor of Madrid, Captain-General of Extremadura.—626

Veuillot, Louis François (1813-1883)—French journalist, editor-in-chief of clerical newspaper *L'Univers* (1848-60).—483, 488

Victor Emmanuel (Vittorio Emanuele) II (1820-1878)—King of Piedmont (Sardinia) (1849-61), King of Italy (1861-78).—5, 417

Victoria (1819-1901)—Queen of Great Britain and Ireland (1837-1901).—186, 465, 525

Vigodet, Caspar—Governor of Montevideo (1810), Captain-General of New Castile (1820); in 1823 emigrated to France after the defeat of the revolution.—626

Villemain, Abel François (1790-1870)—French politician and writer, Liberal, Minister of Public Education (1839-40, 1840-44).—467, 488

Virgil (Publius Vergilius Maro) (70-19 B.C.)—Roman poet.—43, 188, 486

Vittoria, Duke of—see *Espartero, Baldomero*

Vladimir Svyatoslavich (d. 1015)—Grand Duke of Kiev (980-1015).—75, 76, 86

Vogorides, Alexandros, Prince (Aleko-pasha) (c. 1823-1910)—Turkish statesman and diplomat; Bulgarian by birth; counsellor of the Embassy in London (1856-61), ambassador to Vienna (1876-78), Governor of the Eastern Rumelia (1879-84).—324-25

Whitworth, Charles, Earl (1752-1825)—British diplomat, ambassador to Paris (1802-May 1803), Lord-Lieutenant of Ireland (1813-17).—496-98

William I (1797-1888)—Prince of Prussia, Prince Regent (1858-61), King of Prussia (1861-88), Emperor of Germany (1871-88).—568

William III (1650-1702)—Prince of Orange, Stadtholder of the Netherlands (1672-1702), King of England, Scotland and Ireland (1689-1702).—49, 53, 57, 64-66, 72, 95, 152, 187

William IV (1765-1837)—King of Great Britain and Ireland (1830-37).—536

William "of Kars"—see *Williams, Sir William Fenwick, Baronet "of Kars"*

Williams, Sir William Fenwick, Baronet "of Kars" (1800-1883)—British general; headed the defence of Kars in 1855, during the Crimean war; M.P. (1856-59); commanded the garrison in Woolwich (1856-59).—216, 447-48

Wilson, Sir Archdale (1803-1874)—British general; during the national liberation uprising in India commander of the troops which besieged and stormed Delhi (1857), and of the artillery during the siege of Lucknow (1858).—365, 370, 396, 398, 558

Wilson, George (1808-1870)—British manufacturer and politician, Free Trader, President of the Anti-Corn Law League (1841-46).—241

Wilson, James (1805-1860)—Scottish economist and politician, Free Trader, founder and editor of *The Economist,* M.P. (1847-59), Financial Secretary to the Treasury (1853-58).—206, 517, 518

Wilson, N. (d. 1857)—British colonel, took part in suppressing the national liberation uprising of 1857-59 in India.—451

Windham, Sir Charles Ash (1810-1870)—British general; in 1854-56 fought in the Crimean war; commanded British troops in Lahore (1857-61); took part in suppressing the national liberation uprising of 1857-59 in India.—442, 447-52, 504

Windham, William (1750-1810)—British statesman, Whig, subsequently Tory, M.P., Secretary for War (1794-1801).—491, 495

Winslow, Forbes Benignus (1810-1874)—British physician and journalist, editor of *The Journal of Psychological Medicine and Mental Pathology.*—599

Withworth, M.—British ambassador at the Court of Peter I.—93

Wodehouse, John, Earl of Kimberley (1826-1902)—British statesman, envoy to St. Petersburg (1856-58), Viceroy of Ireland (1864-66), Lord Privy Seal (1868-70), Secretary for Colonies (1870-74, 1880-82).—572

Wood, Sir Charles, Viscount Halifax (1800-1885)—British statesman, Whig; Chancellor of the Exchequer (1846-52), President of the Board of Control for India (1852-55), First Lord of the Admiralty (1855-58), Secretary of State for India (1859-66).—382

Woodburn—British general, in 1857 took part in suppressing the national liberation uprising in India.—316

Woronzoff, Prince—see *Vorontsov, Mikhail Semyonovich, Prince*

Wrangel, Friedrich Heinrich Ernst, Count von (1784-1877)—Prussian general, an active participant in the counter-revolutionary coup d'état in Berlin and in the dispersal of the Prussian National Assembly in November 1848.—107

INDEX OF LITERARY AND MYTHOLOGICAL NAMES

INDEX OF QUOTED AND MENTIONED LITERATURE

WORKS BY KARL MARX AND FREDERICK ENGELS

Marx, Karl

[*The Anglo-Chinese Conflict*] (this volume). In: *New-York Daily Tribune*, No. 4918, January 23, 1857.—355

[*The Bank Act of 1844 and the Monetary Crisis in England*] (this volume). In: *New-York Daily Tribune*, No. 5176, November 21, 1857.—385

British Commerce (this volume). In: *New-York Daily Tribune*, No. 5238, February 3, 1858.—426

The British Revulsion (this volume). In: *New-York Daily Tribune*, No. 5183, November 30, 1857.—401, 411

[*The Causes of the Monetary Crisis in Europe*] (this volume). In: *New-York Daily Tribune*, No. 4843, October 27, 1856.—124

Crédit Mobilier (this volume). In: *New-York Daily Tribune*, Nos. 5027 and 5028, May 30 and June 1, 1857.—303, 357, 358

[*The Financial Crisis in Europe*] (this volume). In: *New-York Daily Tribune*, No. 5202, December 22, 1857.—410

The Formation of a Special Ministry of War in Britain.— The War on the Danube.— The Economic Situation (present edition, Vol. 13). In: *New-York Daily Tribune*, No. 4105, June 14, 1854.—61

The French Crédit Mobilier (this volume). In: *New-York Daily Tribune*, No. 4737, June 24, 1856.—132-33

Indian News (this volume). In: *New-York Daily Tribune*, No. 5091, August 14, 1857.—320

[*Investigation of Tortures in India*] (this volume). In: *New-York Daily Tribune*, No. 5120, September 17, 1857.—353

Lord Palmerston (present edition, Vol. 12). In: *The People's Paper*, Nos. 77, 78, 79, 80, 81, 84, 85 and 86; October 22 and 29, November 5, 12 and 19, December 10, 17 and 24, 1853.—193

WORKS BY DIFFERENT AUTHORS

Aberdeen, G. [Speech in the House of Lords on June 17, 1858.] In: *The Times*, No. 23023, June 18, 1858.—571

Addington, H. [Speech in the House of Commons on December 9, 1802.] In: *Cobbett's Annual Register*. Vol. II. From July to December, 1802. London, 1810.—494

Aesop. *The Fox and The Crow*.—239

[Algarotti, F.] *Lettres du comte Algarotti sur la Russie*. Londres, 1769.—90

Anderson, A. *An Historical and Chronological Deduction of the Origin of Commerce, from the Earliest Accounts. Containing an History of Great Commercial Interests of the British Empire*, Vol. III, London, 1787; Vol. IV, London, 1789.—58-60

Aristoteles. *De Poetica*.—310

Auerbach, B. *Schwarzwälder Dorfgeschichten*.—589

Baillie, H. J. [Speech in the House of Commons on March 16, 1858.] In: *The Times*, No. 22943, March 17, 1858.—536

Bartrum, R. H. *Benares, July 13*. In: *The Times*, No. 22775, September 2, 1857. "The Mutinies in India. Benares."—355

Bauer, B. *De la Dictature occidentale*. Charlottenburg, 1854.—191
— *Die jetzige Stellung Rußlands*. Charlottenburg, 1854.—182-85
— *La Russie et l'Angleterre*. Traduit de l'allemand. Charlottenburg, 1854.—181-93

Beautemps-Beaupré, C. F. *Rapports sur les rades, ports et mouillages de la côte orientale du golfe de Venise, visités en 1806, 1808 et 1809, par ordre de l'empereur*. In: *Annales hydrographiques, recueil d'avis, instructions, documents et mémoires relatifs à l'hydrographie et à la navigation*. T. 2. Année 1849. Paris, Imprimérie administrative de Paul Dupont, 1849.—148

Bedeau, M. A. [Letter to the Editor of *L'Indépendance belge* of March 3, 1858.] In: *L'Indépendance belge*, No. 65, 6 mars 1858.—476

Bible
The Old Testament
Daniel.—296
Isaiah.—95

The New Testament
Luke.—518
Matthew.—115, 191, 216

[Blackstone, W.] *Commentaries on the Laws of England*. In four books, London, 1765-69.—356

Bonaparte, L.-N. *Histoire du canon dans les armées modernes*. Paris, 1848.—482
— *Des idées napoléoniennes*. The first edition appeared in Paris in 1839.—480

Bowring, J. [A letter to Consul Parkes of October 11, 1856.] In: *The Times*, No. 22571, January 7, 1857. "The Bombardment of Canton."—208

Briggs, J. *Average Paid by Each Individual to National Revenue*. In: *The Economist*, No. 772, June 12, 1858. "The Indian Debt and Revenue."—578

Bright, J. [Speech in the House of Commons on June 24, 1858.] In: *The Times*, No. 23029, June 25, 1858.—576, 579

Brougham, H. P. [Speech in the House of Lords on June 17, 1858.] In: *The Times*, No. 23023, June 18, 1858.—572

Bulwer-Lytton, E. G. [Speech in the House of Commons on February 26, 1857.] In: *The Times*, No. 22615, February 27, 1857.—215

Bunyan, J. *The Pilgrim's Progress*.—457

Buràt, J. *Paris, 29 septembre*. In: *Le Constitutionnel*, No. 274, 30 septembre, 1856.—115

Caesar, Gaius Julius. *Commentarii de bello Gallico*.—356

Cairns, H. [Speech in the House of Commons on July 8, 1858.] In: *The Times*, No. 23041, July 9, 1858.—586

Campbell, G. *Modern India: A Sketch of the System of Civil Government*. To which is prefixed, some account of the natives and native institutions. London, 1852.—579

Canning, G. [Speech in the House of Commons on December 12, 1826.] In: *The Speeches of the Right Honorable George Canning with a Memoir of His Life* by R. Therry in six volumes. Vol. VI, London, 1830.—188

Castlereagh, R. St. [Speech in the House of Commons on November 3, 1801.] In: *Cobbett's Annual Register*. Vol. II. From July to December, 1802. London, 1810.—491

Cervantes Saavedra, M. de. *Novelas ejemplares*.—513

Changarnier, N. A. Th. [Letter to the Editor of *L'Indépendance belge* of March 1, 1858.] In: *L'Indépendance belge*, No. 61, 2 mars 1858.—476

Chateaubriand, F. R. (or F. A. de) *Congrès de Vérone. Guerre d'Espagne. Négociations. Colonies espagnoles*. T. I-II, Bruxelles, 1838.—621
— *Les Martyrs ou le Triomphe de la religion chrétienne*.—15

Cicero, Marcus Tullius. *De Natura Deorum*.—282
— *Pro lege Manilia*.—95

Clarendon, G. W. F. [Speech in the House of Lords on June 17, 1858.] In: *The Times*, No. 23023, June 18, 1858.—574

Cobden, R. [Speech in the House of Commons on February 26, 1857.] In: *The Times*, No. 22615, February 27, 1857.—207, 211, 215, 220
— [Speech in the Free-Trade Hall, Manchester, on March 18, 1857.] In: *The Times*, No. 22633, March 20, 1857. "The Representation of Manchester."—228, 230, 239

Cunibert, B.-S. *Essai historique sur les révolutions et l'indépendance de la Serbie depuis 1804 jusqu'à 1850*. Tomes premier et second. Leipzig, 1855.—62

Derby, E. [Speeches in the House of Lords]
— February 24, 1857. In: *The Times*, No. 22613, February 25, 1857.—207, 208, 209, 210
— December 3, 1857. In: *The Times*, No. 22855, December 4, 1857.—425
— March 1, 1858, In: *The Times*, No. 22930, March 2, 1858.—587

Disraeli, B. [Speeches in the House of Commons]
— March 3, 1857. In: *The Times,* No. 22619, March 4, 1857.—215
— July 27, 1857. In: *The Times,* No. 22744, July 28, 1857.—309
— August 11, 1857. In: *The Times,* No. 22757, August 12, 1857.—333
— August 20, 1857. In: *The Times,* No. 22765, August 21, 1857.—333
— April 19, 1858. In: *The Times,* No. 22972, April 20, 1858.—510-12
— May 31, 1858. In: *The Times,* No. 23008, June 1, 1858.—566
[—] *The Young Duke.* "A Moral Tale, though gay." By the author of *Vivian Grey.* In three volumes. London, 1831.—510

Dupont, [E.] *Chronique de l'Intérieur.* In: *La Voix du Proscrit,* No. 8, 15 décembre 1850.—467

Dureau de la Malle, [A.] *Économie politique des Romains.* T. 1-2. Paris, 1840.—486

Edmonstone, G. F. [Telegram.] In: *The Times,* No. 22876, December 29, 1857. "India and China."—423

Ellenborough, [E. L.] [Speeches in the House of Lords]
— July 31, 1857. In: *The Times,* No. 22748, August 1, 1857.—321
— May 7, 1858. In *The Times,* No. 22988, May 8, 1858.—531, 534
— [Speech at the trial of J. G. Peltier on February 21, 1803.] In: *Cobbett's Annual Register.* Supplement to Vol. III. "Important Trials."—497

Elliot, W. [Speech in the House of Commons on November 4, 1801.] In: *Cobbett's Annual Register.* Vol. II. From July to December, 1802. London, 1810.—491

Evans, G. de L. [Speeches in the House of Commons]
— August 11, 1857. In: *The Times,* No. 22757, August 12, 1857.—327
— August 20, 1857. In: *The Times,* No. 22765, August 21, 1857.—331
— February 4, 1858. In: *The Times,* No. 22909, February 5, 1858.—590

Examen critique des révolutions d'Espagne de 1820 à 1823 et de 1836. Tome 1-2, Paris, 1837.—628

Favre, J. [Speech before the Jury on February 26, 1858.] In: *Le Moniteur universel,* No. 58, 27 février 1858.—473, 477

Fourier, Ch. *Théorie des quatre mouvements et des destinées générales.*—21

Fox, Ch. J. *Motion for Papers respecting the State of the French Fleet in Brest.* Feb. 23 [1779]. In: *The Parliamentary History of England, from the earliest period to the year 1803,* Vol. XX, London, 1814.—30
— *Motion for the Removal of the Earl of Sandwich, First Lord of Admiralty.* April 19 [1779]. In: *The Parliamentary History of England, from the earliest period to the year 1803,* Vol. XX, London, 1814.—30
— *Speech in Debates in the Committee of the House of Commons on the Causes of the Want of Success of the British Navy.* Feb. 7 [1782]. In: *The Parliamentary History of England, from the earliest period to the year 1803,* Vol. XXII, London, 1814.—30

Gibbon, E. *The History of the Decline and Fall of the Roman Empire.* Vol. I-IV. The first edition appeared in London in 1776-88.—310

Gladstone, W. E. [Speeches in the House of Commons]
— February 20, 1857. In: *The Times,* No. 22610, February 21, 1857.—205
— June 7, 1858. In: *The Times,* No. 23014, June 8, 1858.—575
— July 6, 1858. In: *The Times,* No. 23039, July 7, 1858.—588

Glyn, G. G. [Speech in the House of Commons on April 19, 1858.] In: *The Times*, No. 22972, April 20, 1858.—512

Graham, J. [Speech in the House of Commons on February 27, 1857.] In: *The Times*, No. 22616, February 28, 1857.—217
— [Speech before the Carlisle constituents on March 16, 1857.] In: *The Times*, No. 22632, March 19, 1857.—228
— [Testimony before the Committee of Roebuck.] In: *The Times*, No. 22054, May 15, 1855.—34

Granier de Cassagnac, A. *La palinodie des honnêtes gens.* In: *Le Constitutionnel*, No. 31, 31 janvier 1858.—467

Granville, G. [Speech in the House of Lords on July 16, 1857.] In: *The Times*, No. 22735, July 17, 1857.—308

Grey, H. G. [Speeches in the House of Lords]
— February 24, 1857. In: *The Times*, No. 22613, February 25, 1857.—211
— June 10, 1858. In: *The Times*, No. 23017, June 11, 1858.—567
— June 17, 1858. In: *The Times*, No. 23023, June 18, 1858.—570, 573

[Gyllenborg, C.] *The Northern Crisis. Or, Impartial Reflections on the Policies of the Czar.* Occasioned by Mynheer Von Stocken's Reasons for delaying the Descent upon Schonen. A True Copy of which is prefix'd, verbally Translated, after the Tenour of that in the German Secretary's Office in Copenhagen, October 10, 1716. 2nd ed., London, 1716.—41, 43-55, 92
— *Letters Which passed between Count Gyllenborg, the Barons Gortz, Sparre, and others; Relating to the Design of Raising a Rebellion in His Majesty's Dominions, To be Supported by a Force from Sweden.* London, 1717.—43, 61

Hauff, W. *Die Bettlerin vom Pont des Arts.*—589

Hawkesbury, R. [Letter to L.-G. Otto, dated July 28, 1802.] In: *Cobbett's Annual Register.* Vol. III. From January to June, 1803. London [s. a.].—493

Heine, H. *Lyrisches Intermezzo.* In: *Buch der Lieder.*—101

Herbert, S. [Speech before the electors of the Southern Division of Wiltshire on April 1, 1857.] In: *The Times*, No. 22644, April 2, 1857. "The Elections."—249

Hesiodus. *Operae et dies.*—209

Hughes, T. S. *The History of England from the Accession of George III., 1760, to the Accession of Queen Victoria, 1837.* Third edition. In seven volumes. Vols I-III. London, 1846.—30, 32-34, 36

Hugo, V. *Napoléon le petit.* Londres, 1852.—490

James, E. [Speech at the court hearing of S. Bernard's case on April 16, 1858.] In: *The Times*, No. 22970, April 17, 1858.—516

[Koch, C. G.] *Tableau des révolutions de l'Europe, depuis le bouleversement de l'empire Romain en occident jusqu'à nos jours par feu M. Koch, correspondant de l'Institut, et recteur honoraire de l'Académie royale de Strasbourg.* Nouvelle édition. Tome second. Paris, 1823.—29

Labouchere, H. [Speech before the Taunton constituents on March 11, 1857.] In: *The Times*, No. 22627, March 13, 1857.—221

[La Guéronnière, A.] *L'Empereur Napoléon III et l'Angleterre.* Paris, 1858.—472

10, 1858.] In: *The Economist*, No. 756, February 20, 1858. "Foreign correspondence"; *Allgemeine Zeitung*, No. 45, 14. Februar 1858 (Beilage).—502

Molière, J. B. *Le bourgeois gentilhomme.*—230

Montalembert, Ch. [Speech at the meeting of the Corps législatif on May 31, 1856.] In: *The Times*, No. 22386, June 5, 1856. "Count Montalembert and the Press in France."—19

[Montesquieu, Ch.-L. de.] *Considérations sur les causes de la grandeur des Romains et de leur décadence.* The first edition was published anonymously in Amsterdam in 1734.—310, 486

Montluc. *La Comédie des Proverbes.* The first edition appeared in Paris in 1618.—326

Mulgrave, G. [Speech before the Scarborough constituents in March 1857.] In: *The Times*, No. 22627, March 13, 1857.—221

Nolan, L. E. *Cavalry, Its History and Tactics.* Sec. ed. London, 1854.—279

Orsini, F. *À Napoléon III, Empereur des Français, 11 février 1858.* In: *Le Moniteur universel*, No. 58, 27 février 1858.—473

— [Testimony at the court session on February 25, 1858.] In: *Le Moniteur universel*, No. 57, 26 février 1858.—473

Otto, L.-G. [Letter to R. Hawkesbury, dated July 25, 1802.] In: *Cobbett's Annual Register.* Vol. III. From January to June, 1803. London [s.a.].—493

Overstone, S. J. L. [Speech in the House of Lords on December 3, 1857.] In: *The Times*, No. 22855, December 4, 1857.—407

Owen, W. D. [Evidence given at a meeting of shareholders of the Royal British Bank at the London Tavern, September 20, 1856.] In: *The Times*, No. 22479, September 22, 1856. "The Royal British Bank."—112

Palmerston, H. J. T. [Speech before the electors of Tiverton on June 28, 1841.] In: *The Times*, No. 1773, July 3, 1841.—483

— [Speech at the Ministerial banquet at the Mansion House on March 20, 1857.] In: *The Times*, No. 22634, March 21, 1857.—232

— [Speech before the electors at the meeting in Tiverton on March 27, 1857.] In: *The Morning Post*, No. 25972, March 28, 1857. "Tiverton. Return of Lord Palmerston and Mr. Heathcoat. From our own reporter."—240

— [Speeches in the House of Commons]

— May 18, 1857. In: *The Times*, No. 22684, May 19, 1857.—293

— August 11, 1857. In: *The Times*, No. 22757, August 12, 1857.—330, 332

— August 20, 1857. In: *The Times*, No. 22765, August 21, 1857.—331, 332

Péreire, I. [The communication, regarding the failure of M. Charles Thurneyssen.] *Paris, May 25.* In *The Times*, No. 22692, May 28, 1857. "Money-Market and City Intelligence."—359

Pindar. *The First Olympian Ode.*—219

Pitt, W. [Speech in the House of Commons on November 3, 1801.] In: *Cobbett's Annual Register.* Vol. II. From July to December, 1802. London, 1810.—491

Price, R. *An Appeal to the Public on the Subject of the National Debt.* 2 ed. London, 1772.—513

— *Observations on Reversionary Payments; on Schemes for providing Annuities for Widows, and for Persons in Old Age; on the Method of Calculating the Values of Assurances on Lives; and on the National Debt.* 2 ed. London, 1772.—513

Puffendorf, S. de. *De Rebus Gestis Friderici Wilhelmi Magni, Electoris Brandenburgici, commentariorum Libri novendecim.* Berolini, Anno MDCLXXXXV (1695).—61

Rawlinson, H. C. [Speech at a meeting of the Royal Geographical Society, held on May 11, 1857.] In: *The Times,* No. 22679, May 13, 1857. "Persia."—294

Reasons for the present conduct of Sweden in relation to the trade in the Baltic set forth in a letter from a gentleman at Dantzick, to his friend at Amsterdam. Translated from the French original, published in Holland: and now submitted to the Consideration of all just and impartial Britons. London, 1715.—64

Régnault, E. *Histoire politique et sociale des Principautés Danubiennes.* Paris, 1855.—62

Renée, Am. *L'acquittement de Bernard a causé...* In: *Le Constitutionnel,* No. 111, 21 avril 1858.—515, 516

Revolution d'Espagne. Examen critique. 1820-1836. Paris, 1836.—627, 628

Ricardo, D. *On the Principles of Political Economy, and Taxation.* London, 1817.—8

Russell, J. [Speech in the House of Commons on February 26, 1857.] In: *The Times,* No. 22615, February 27, 1857.—215
— [Speech before the electors assembled at the London Tavern on March 19, 1857.] In: *The Times,* No. 22633, March 20, 1857.—228
— [Speech before the electors of the City of London on March 27, 1857.] In: *The Times,* No. 22640, March 28, 1857. "The Elections."—249
— [Speech in the House of Commons on April 12, 1858.] In: *The Times,* No. 22966, April 13, 1858.—588

[Russell, W. H.] *The Fall of Lucknow.* In: *The Times,* No. 22986, May 6, 1858.—527-29, 531-32
— *Lucknow, April 5.* In: *The Times,* No. 23007, May 31, 1858. "The British Army in India".—556-57

Rutland, Ch. C. J. [Speech in the House of Lords on June 10, 1858.] In: *The Times,* No. 23017, June 11, 1858.—567

Schiller, J. Chr. Fr. von. *Don Karlos, Infant von Spanien.*—589
— *Die Räuber.* Ein Schauspiel.—586

Segur, Ph. *History of Russia and of Peter the Great.* London, 1829.—75, 78, 83, 84, 89, 92

Shakespeare, W. *King Henry IV.*—457
— *King John.*—219
— *King Richard III.*—219
— *Measure for Measure.*—211
— *The Merchant of Venice.*—492
— *Romeo and Juliet.*—469
— *Timon of Athens.*—269

Silius Halicus. *De secundo bello punico,* Liber II.—65

Smith, [J. M.] F. [Speech in the House of Commons on August 20, 1857.] In: *The Times,* No. 22765, August 21, 1857.—333

Smith, V. [Speeches in the House of Commons].
— June 29, 1857. In: *The Times,* No. 22720, June 30, 1857.—314
— July 27, 1857. In: *The Times,* No. 22744, July 28, 1857.—316

Sophocles. *Antigone.*—453

Spada, A. *Ephémérides russes politiques, littéraires, historiques, et necrologiques.*— Présentant, dans l'ordre des jours de l'année, un tableau des évenements remarquables, qui datent de chacun de ces jours dans l'histoire de la Russie, jusqu'en 1816. Tomes 1-3, St. Pétersbourgs, 1816. (See this volume, Note 222.)—181

Strabo. *Strabonis rerum geographicarum libri 17.* Ad optimorum, librorum fidem accurate editi. T. 1. Lipsiae, 1829.—146

Suetonius G. Tranquillus, *Vitae XII Caesarum.*—164

Talleyrand, Ch. M. [Conversation with Lord Whitworth.] In: *Cobbett's Annual Register.* Vol. III. From January to June, 1803. London [s.a.].—498
— [Conversation with A. Merry, dated June 3, 1802.] In: *Cobbett's Annual Register.* Vol. III. From January to June, 1803. London [s.a.].—491, 492

Tasso, Torquato. *Gerusalemme liberata.*—477

Tausend und Eine Nacht. Arabische Erzählungen. Bd. 2. Pforzheim, 1839.—248

Terence (Publius Terentius Afer). *Andria.*—55
— *Phormio.*—544

Terentianus Maurus. *De litteris, syllabis et metris.* (*Carmen heroicum.*)—15

Theyls, W. *Mémoires pour servir à l'histoire de Charles XII, roi de Suède.* Contenant ce qui s'est passé pendant le sejour de ce Prince dans l'Empire ottoman, et un recit fidèle des troubles survenus de temps en temps entre sa Maj. et la Porte etc. Leyde, 1722.—65

Tite, W. [Speech in the House of Commons on July 22, 1858.] In: *The Times,* No. 23053, July 23, 1858.—600-01

Tooke, Th. *A History of Prices, and of the State of the Circulation, from 1793 to 1837;* Preceded by a Brief Sketch of the State of the Corn Trade in the Last Two Centuries. In two volumes. London, 1838.—402
— *A History of Prices, and of the State of the Circulation, in 1838 and 1839,* with Remarks on the Corn Laws, and on Some of the Alterations Proposed in our Banking System. Being a Continuation of *The History of Prices, from 1793 to 1837.* London, 1840.—402
— *A History of Prices, and of the State of the Circulation, from 1839 to 1847 Inclusive: with a General Review of the Currency Question, and Remarks on the Operation oj the Act 7 & 8 Vict. c. 32.* Being a Continuation of *The History of Prices from 1793 to 1839.* London, 1848.—382, 402
— and W. Newmarch. *A History of Prices, and of the State of the Circulation, during the Nine Years 1848-1856.* In two Volumes; Forming the Fifth and Sixth Volumes of *The History of Prices from 1792 to the Present Time.* Vol. V-VI. London, 1857.—402

Virgil (Publius Virgilius Maro). *Aeneid.*—43, 189, 486

Voltaire. *L'enfant prodigue.* Préface.—309

Walpole, S. H. [Speech in the House of Commons on July 22, 1858.] In: *The Times,* No. 23053, July 23, 1858.—601

Walton, W. *The Revolutions of Spain, from 1808 to the end of 1836.* 2 vols. London, 1837.—626

Winslow, F. *To Edwin James, Esq., Q. C.* In: *The Times,* No. 23049, July 19, 1858. "Lady Bulwer Lytton."—599

Wodehouse, J. [Speech in the House of Lords on June 17, 1858.] In: *The Times,* No. 23023, June 18, 1858.—572

DOCUMENTS

An Account of the Declared Value of British and Irish Produce and Manufactures Exported from the United Kingdom to each Foreign Country and British Possession in the Half-year ended June 30, 1857. In: *The Economist,* No. 732, September 5, 1857.—383

An Account of the Declared Value of British and Irish Produce and Manufactures Exported from the United Kingdom to each Foreign Country and British Possession in the Three Months ended 31st March, 1858, compared with the corresponding period of the Year 1857. In: *The Economist,* No. 770 (supplement), May 29, 1858. "Exports of British and Irish Produce and Manufactures."—560-64

An Account of the Number and Tonnage of Vessels, distinguishing the Countries to which they belonged. Entered Inwards with Cargoes (including their repeated Voyages) in the Four Months ended 30th April, 1858, compared with the corresponding Period of the Years 1856 and 1857. In: *The Economist,* No. 770 (supplement), May 29, 1858. "Vessels employed in the foreign and coasting trade of the United Kingdom."—560, 565

Accounts Relating to Trade and Navigation. For the Four Months ended April, 1857. III.—Exports of the Principal and other Articles of British and Irish Produce and Manufactures in the Four Months ending April, 1857, compared with the corresponding Period of the Year 1856. In: *The Economist,* No. 718, May 30, 1857.—403

Accounts Relating to Trade and Navigation. For the Five Months ended May, 1857. III.—Exports of the Principal and other Articles of British and Irish Produce and Manufactures in the Five Months ending May, 1857, compared with the corresponding Period of the Year 1856. In: *The Economist,* No. 722, June 27, 1857.—403

Accounts Relating to Trade and Navigation. For the Six Months ended June, 1857. III.—Exports of the Principal and other Articles of British and Irish Produce and Manufactures in the Six Months ending June, 1857, compared with the corresponding Months of the Year 1856. In: *The Economist,* No. 727, August 1, 1857.—403

Accounts Relating to Trade and Navigation. For the Seven Months ended July, 1857. III.—Exports of the Principal and other Articles of British and Irish Produce and Manufactures in the Seven Months ending July, 1857, compared with the corresponding Months of the Year 1856. In: *The Economist,* No. 731, August 29, 1857.—403

Accounts Relating to Trade and Navigation. For the Eight Months ended August, 1857. III.—Exports of the Principal and other Articles of British and Irish Produce and Manufactures in the Eight Months ending August, 1857, compared with the corresponding Months of the Year 1856. In: *The Economist*, No. 736, October 3, 1857.—403

Accounts Relating to Trade and Navigation. For the Nine Months ended September, 1857. III.—Exports of the Principal and other Articles of British and Irish Produce and Manufactures in the Nine Months ending September, 1857, compared with the corresponding Months of the Year 1856. In: *The Economist*, No. 740, October 31, 1857.—403

Accounts Relating to Trade and Navigation. For the Ten Months ended October, 1857. III.—Exports of the Principal and other Articles of British and Irish Produce and Manufactures in the Ten Months ended October, 1857, compared with the corresponding Months of the Year 1856. In: *The Economist*, No. 744, November 28, 1857.—403

Accounts Relating to Trade and Navigation for the Three Months ended March 31, 1858. III.—Exports of the Principal and other Articles of British and Irish Produce and Manufactures in the Three Months ended 31st March, 1858, compared with the corresponding Months of the Year 1857. In: *The Economist*, No. 765 (supplement), April 24, 1858.—521-23

Accounts Relating to Trade and Navigation for the Four Months ended April 30. In: *The Economist*, No. 770 (supplement), May 29, 1858.—560

An Act for continuing in the East India Company, for a further Term, the Possession of the British Territories in India, together with certain exclusive Privileges; for establishing further Regulations for the Government of the said Territories, and the better Administration of Justice within the same; and for regulating the Trade to and from the Places within the Limits of the said Company's Charter. [21st July 1813.] In: *The Statutes of the United Kingdom of Great Britain and Ireland. 53 & 54 George III. (1814).* London, 1814.—586

An Act for effecting an Arrangement with the East India Company, and for the better Government of His Majesty's Indian Territories, till the Thirtieth Day of April One thousand eight hundred and fifty-four [28th August 1833.] In: *The Statutes of the United Kingdom of Great Britain and Ireland. 3 & 4 Will. IV.* London, 1835.—444, 586

An Act for the better Government of India. [2nd August 1858.] In: *The Statutes of the United Kingdom of Great Britain and Ireland. 21 & 22 Victoria (1857-58).* London, 1860.—575, 585-86

An Act for the better regulation and management of the affairs of the East India Company, and of the British possessions in India; and for establishing a Court of Judicature for the more speedy and effectual trial of persons accused of offences committed in the East Indies. [August, 1784.]—586

An Act for the Further Amendment of the Laws relating to Labour in Factories.—251

An Act to provide for the Government of India. [20th August 1853.] In: *The Statutes of the United Kingdom of Great Britain and Ireland. 16 & 17 Victoria (1853).* London, 1853.—586

An Act to Regulate the Issue of Bank Notes, and for Giving to the Governor and Company of the Bank of England Certain Privileges for a Limited Period. [19th July 1844.] In: *The Statutes of the United Kingdom of Great Britain and Ireland. 7 & 8 Victoria, 1844.* London, 1844.—379, 382, 383, 385, 389

An Act to Regulate the Labour of Children, Young Persons, and Women in Printworks. In: *The Statutes of the United Kingdom of Great Britain and Ireland, 8 & 9 Victoria, 1845.* London, 1845.—525

[The Address of the President and Council of the Liverpool Financial Reform Association to the Middle, Commercial, Manufacturing and Industrial Classes of the United Kingdom.] In: *The Times,* No. 22561, December 26, 1856. "Liverpool Revision of Taxation."—203

Adresses présentées à l'Empereur. In: *Le Moniteur universel,* No. 17, 17 janvier 1858.—455

[Addresses of the French army men.] In: *Le Moniteur universel,* Nos. 26, 27; 26, 27 janvier 1858.—475

Andréossi (Andréossy), A. Fr. [Note to Lord Hawkesbury, dated 29 March 1803]. In: *Cobbett's Annual Register.* Vol. III. From January to June, 1803. London [s.a.].—496

Annex (B.) To the Treaty between Great Britain, Austria, France, Prussia, and Russia for the Suppression of the African Slave Trade, signed at London, the Twentieth Day of December in the Year One thousand eight hundred and forty-one. Instructions to Cruisers.—571

Articles convenus entre la Grande-Bretagne et la Perse relatifs à l'indépendance de la Ville de Hérat; signés à Téhéran, le 25 janvier 1853.—295

Barnard, H. [W.] [Bulletin of June 8 on the occupation of the hights of Delhi.] In: *The Times,* No. 22748, August 1, 1857. "The Indian Mutinies."—319, 320

[The bill submitted to the Turin Chamber of Deputies on February 17, 1858.] In: *Le Moniteur universel,* No. 54, 23 février 1858. "Partie non officielle. Nouvelles étrangères. Italie."—480

Billault, A. *Rapport à l'Empereur.* In: *Le Moniteur universel,* No. 346, 12 décembre 1857. "Partie officielle."—414

The Board of Trade Returns. In: *The Economist,* No. 765, April 24, 1858.—521, 523

Bourse du mardi 30 septembre 1856. In: *Le Moniteur universel,* No. 275, 1 octobre 1856.—130, 131

Bourse du vendredi 31 octobre 1856. In: *Le Moniteur universel,* No. 306, 1 novembre 1856.—130, 131

Bourse du vendredi 23 octobre 1857. In: *Le Moniteur universel,* No. 297, 24 octobre 1857.—417

Bourse du mardi 22 décembre 1857. In: *Le Moniteur universel,* No. 357, 23 décembre 1857.—417

Calatrava, J. M. [Answer on behalf of the Cortes to Ferdinand VII's message of November 25, 1821.] In: *Revolution d'Espagne. Examen critique. 1820-1836.* Paris, 1836. Marx quotes from his excerpts.—628

Campbell, C. *From his Excellency the Commander-in-Chief to the Right Hon. the Governor-General.* In: *The Times,* No. 22889, January 13, 1858. "The Relief and Evacuation of Lucknow."—435, 436

Canning, Ch. J. *Proclamation.* In: *The Times,* No. 22986, May 6, 1858. "The Fall of Lucknow."—533, 534, 546, 548, 549

Carolus. *Espece de Manifeste du Roi de Suede contre le Roi Auguste.* In: Lamberty de. *Mémoires pour servir à l'histoire du XVIII siècle, contenant les négociations, traités, résolutions et autres documents authentiques concernant les affaires d'état.* Tome sixième. La Haye, 1728.—41

The Case of the Merchants Trading to Russia. [s.l. s.a.]—61

Cavour C. *Note adressée au comte Walewski et à lord Clarendon le 16 avril 1856.*—6

Charles V. *Constitutio criminalis Carolina.*—356

Constitution. 1848. [Paris, 1848.]—465

[Constitution of Spain. March 19, 1812] In: *The Political Constitution of the Spanish Monarchy. Proclaimed in Cadix, 19 March. 1812.* London, 1813.—106

Correspondence, respecting Insults in China. Presented to the House of Commons by Command of Her Majesty, 1857. [London,] 1857.—221

Debate in the Commons on the State of the Navy. 11 Nov. [*1778*]. In: *The Parliamentary History of England, from the earliest period to the year 1803.* Vol. XIX, London, 1814.—30

Debate on the Earl of Effingham's Motion relative to the State of the Navy. March 31 [*1778*]. In: *The Parliamentary history of England, from the earliest period to the year 1803.* Vol. XIX, London, 1814.—30

Décret portant autorisation de la société anonyme formée à Paris sous la denomination de Société générale de Crédit Mobilier. 18 novembre-11 décembre 1852. In: *Collection complète des lois, décrets, réglements et avis du conseil d'Etat.* T. 52, Paris, 1852.—11, 12, 21

The Defensive Treaty concluded in the year 1770, betwixt His Late Majesty King William of ever Glorious Memory, and His Present Swedish Majesty King Charles the XII. Published at the earnest desire of several members of both Houses of Parliament [s.l. s.a.].—41, 56, 57, 63, 65-73, 92

Definitive treaty of Friendship and Alliance between Great Britain and Persia.—Signed at Teheran, 25th November 1814. In: *British and Foreign State Papers.* 1812-1814. Vol. I. Part I. London, 1841.—179

Direction générale des douanes et des contributions indirectes. Tableau comparatif des principales marchandises importées pendant le mois de septembre des années 1856, 1855 et 1854. In: *Le Moniteur universel.* No. 302, 28 octobre 1856.—133

Direction générale des douanes et des contributions indirectes. In: *Le Moniteur universel,* No. 80, 21 mars 1858.—501

East India (Torture), London, 1855-57.—336

Eighth Annual Report of the Commissioners in Lunacy to the Lord Chancellor. 1854.—602

Eleventh Annual Report of the Commissioners in Lunacy to the Lord Chancellor. 1857.—602

[Ellenborough, E. L.] *The Secret Committee of the Court of Directors of the East India Company to the Governor-General of India in Council. April 19, 1858.* In: *The Times,* No. 22989, May 10, 1858. "The Revolt of Oude." An abridged version of this document was published in *The Times,* No. 22988, May 8, 1858.—549, 588

[Espinasse, Ch. M. E.] *La circulaire au sujet des biens immeubles appartenant aux hôpitaux, hospices et bureaux de bienfaisance, et des avantages de la conversion de ces biens en rentes sur l'Etat.* In: *Le Moniteur universel,* No. 142, 22 mai 1858. "Partie non officielle."—550

Extraits de lettres confidentielles adressées au caïmacam de Moldavie par différents personnages politiques. In: *L'Etoile du Danube,* No. 50, 8 août 1857.—324-26

Fanshawe, J. G. [To J. Johnson, Esq.] In: *The Free Press,* No. 26, December 23, 1857. "Excess of Imports over Exports."—425

Ferdinand VII [Speech at the opening of the first session of the Cortes on July 9, 1820.] In: Davis, H. *The War of Ormuzd and Ahriman in the Nineteenth Century.* Baltimore, 1852.—623

— [Speech at the opening of the second session of the Cortes on March 1, 1821.] In: Marliani, M. de. *Historia política de la España moderna.* Barcelona, 1849.—627

— [Message to the Cortes dated November 25, 1821.] Quoted from *Revolution d'Espagne. Examen critique. 1820-1836.* Paris, 1836.—628

— [Decree of September 30, 1823.]—624

Half-yearly Joint Report of the Inspectors of Factories. In: *Reports of the Inspectors of Factories to Her Majesty's Principal Secretary of State for the Home Department for the half year ending 31st October 1856.* London, 1857.—255, 256, 257, 259, 260, 261

Hausmann, G.-E. [Report to the Municipal Council of the Seine.] In: *The Economist,* No. 763, April 10, 1858. "Foreign Intelligence."—502-03

Hawkesbury, R. [Dispatch to A. Merry, dated June 10, 1802.] In: *Cobbett's Annual Register.* Vol. III. From January to June, 1803. London [s.a.].—491-92

— [Dispatch to A. Merry, dated August 28, 1802.] In: *Cobbett's Annual Register.* Vol. III. From January to June, 1803. London [s.a.].—495

Hendriks. [Report before the British Statistical Society on the Finances of India. 1858.] In: *The Economist,* No. 772, June 12, 1858. "The Indian Debt and Revenue."—577

[Horner, L.] "Report of Leonard Horner, Esq., Inspector of Factories, for the half year ended the 31st of October 1856." In: *Reports of the Inspectors of Factories to Her Majesty's Principal Secretary of State for the Home Department for the half year ending 31st October 1856.* London, 1857.—253

[Inglis, J. E. W.] *From Brigadier Inglis, Commanding Garrison of Lucknow, to the Secretary to Government, Military Department, Calcutta.* In: *The Times,* No. 22889, January 13, 1858. "The Siege of Lucknow."—437-41

Johnson, J. [To Lord Stanley of Alderley.] In: *The Free Press,* No. 26, December 23, 1857. "Excess of Imports over Exports."—425

Lettre adressée le 18 mai 1841, par le département des affaires étrangères, aux lords de l'amirauté, au sujet de la poursuite des bâtimens américains soupçonnés de se livrer à la traite.—572

[Lieven.] Copy of a Despatch from Prince Lieven, and Count Matuszevicz, addressed to Count Nesselrode, dated London, 1st (13th) June 1829. In: *The Portfolio. Diplomatic review* (New Series). London, 1843.—192

Otto, L.-G. [Note to R. Hawkesbury, dated August 17, 1802.] In: *Cobbett's Annual Register.* Vol. III. From January to June, 1803. London [s.a.].—495

Palmerston, H. J. T. [Dispatch to the British plenipotentiary at Hong-Kong, August 18, 1849.] In: *The Times,* No. 22616, February 28, 1857. Quoted from J. Graham's speech in the House of Commons, February 27, 1857.—217

— [Correspondence with McNeill in May-July 1838.] In: *Correspondence Relating to Persia and Afghanistan.* London [1839].—179

Parker, H. [Letter to Yeh, Governor-General of the two Kwangs Provinces, October 21, 1856.] In: *The Times,* No. 22571, January 7, 1857. "The Bombardment of Canton."—159

Péreire, I. *Rapport présenté au nom du Conseil d'administration [29 avril 1858.]* In: *Le Moniteur universel,* No. 120, 30 avril 1858.—551

— *Rapport présenté par le conseil d'administration dans l'assemblée générale ordinaire et extraordinaire des actionnaires du 29 avril 1854.* In: *Le Moniteur universel,* No. 121, 1 mai 1854.—16, 357, 360

— *Rapport présenté par le conseil d'administration dans l'assemblée générale ordinaire des actionnaires du 23 avril 1856.* In: *Le Moniteur universel,* No. 117, 26 avril 1856.—9, 22, 23

— *Rapport présenté par le conseil d'administration [de la Société générale du Crédit mobilier] dans l'assemblée générale ordinaire des actionnaires du 28 avril 1857.* In: *Le Moniteur universel,* No. 120, 30 avril 1857.—270, 272, 275

Persigny, F. *Rapport à l'Empereur.* In: *Le Moniteur universel,* No. 172, 21 juin 1854.—18

[*Petition from the Parish St. Mary in Jamaica.*] In: *The Times,* No. 23023, June 18, 1858. "Parliamentary Intelligence."—570

The Political Constitution of the Spanish Monarchy. Proclaimed in Cadix, 19 March 1812. London, 1813.—621

Projet de loi sur les sociétés en commandite par actions. In: *Le Moniteur universel,* No. 153, 1 juin 1856.—15

Protocole de Londres, du 24 mai 1852. In: *Mémoire du Conseil fédéral sur la question de Neuchâtel.* Berne-Neuchâtel, Davoine, 1856.—151

Redgrave, A. *Report of Alexander Redgrave, Esq., Inspector of Factories, for the Half Year ended the 31st October 1857.* In: *Reports of the Inspectors of Factories ... for the Half Year ending 31st October* 1857. London, 1857.—525

— *Le régiment de zouaves de la garde impériale.* In: *Le Moniteur universel,* No. 26, 26 janvier 1858. "Partie non officielle."—457, 475

Report of the Commission for the Investigation of Alleged Cases of Torture at Madras. London, 1855.—336-37

Reports of the Inspectors of Factories to Her Majesty's Principal Secretary of State for the Home Department for the Half Year ending 30th April 1856. London, 1857.—255

Reports of the Inspectors of Factories to Her Majesty's Principal Secretary of State for the Home Department for the Half Year ending 31st October 1856. London, 1857.—251, 252, 255

Reports of the Inspectors of Factories to Her Majesty's Principal Secretary of State for the Home Department, for the Half Year ending 31st October 1857. London, 1857.—521

Return of Lunatic Asylums in England and Wales...; number of patients, etc. London, 1857-58.—604

Russell, J., Wood, Ch. [A letter addressed to the Governor and Deputy Governor of the Bank of England. 25th Oct. 1847.] In: Tooke Th. *A History of Prices, and of the State of the Circulation, from 1839 to 1847 Inclusive: with a General Review of the Currency Question, and Remarks on the Operation of the Act 7 & 8 Vict. c. 32.* Being a continuation of *The History of Prices from 1793 to 1839.* London, 1848.—382

Sebastiani, H. *Rapport fait an Premier Consul.* In: *Gazette nationale, ou Le Moniteur universel,* No. 130, 10 pluviôse an 11 de la République (30 janvier 1803). "Interieur."—496

Several Grievances of the English Merchants in their trade into the Dominions of the King of Sweden, whereby it doth appear how dangerous it may be for the English Nation to depend (as now they do) on Sweden only, for the Supply of the Naval Stores; where they are subjected to so many and great grievances: when they might be amply furnished with the like stores, from the Dominions of the Emperor of Russia, if the English Trade thither was enlarged [s.l. s.a.].—61

Seymour M. [A letter to Yeh, Governor-General of two Kwangs Provinces, October 30, 1856]. In: *The Times,* No. 22567, January 2, 1857. "The Bombardment of Canton."—161

— [A letter to Yeh, Governor-General of the two Kwangs Provinces, November 2, 1856]. *The Times,* No. 22567, January 2, 1857. "The Bombardment of Canton."—159, 161, 162

Situation de la Banque de France et de ses succursales au jeudi 11 septembre 1856. In: *Le Moniteur universel,* No. 256, 12 septembre 1856.—119

Situation de la Banque de France et de ses succursales au jeudi 9 octobre 1856. In: *Le Moniteur universel,* No. 284, 10 octobre 1856.—119, 123

Situation de la Banque de France et de ses succursales au jeudi 13 novembre 1856. In: *Le Moniteur universel,* No. 319, 14 novembre 1856.—137

Situation de la Banque de France et de ses succursales. In: *Le Moniteur universel,* Nos. 282, 317, 345, 9 octobre, 13 novembre, 11 décembre 1857.—415, 417

Situation de la Banque de France et de ses succursales. In: *Le Moniteur universel,* No. 15, 15 janvier 1858.—459

Situation de la Banque de France et de ses succursales. In: *Le Moniteur universel,* No. 43, 12 février 1858.—459

Sixth Annual Report of the Commissioners in Lunacy to the Lord Chancellor. 1852.—602

Traité conclu entre l'Angleterre et l'Espagne relativement à la traité des nègres, signé à Madrid le 23 Sept. 1817.—572

Traité de garantie entre l'Autriche, la France et la Grande-Bretagne, signé à Paris, le 15 avril 1856.—5

Traité de paix, signé à Paris, entre la France et chacune des puissances alliées, le 30 mai 1814; suivi d'articles additionnels distincts et speciaux avec l'Autriche, la Russie, la Grande-Bretagne et la Prusse, et d'articles secrets.—3

Traité signé à Londres, le 8 mai 1852, entre le Danemark d'une part, et l'Autriche, la France, la Grande-Bretagne, la Russie et la Suède de l'autre part, relatif à l'ordre de succession dans la monarchie danoise.—335

Traité supplémentaire entre S. M. la reine du Royaume-Uni de la Grande-Bretagne et d'Irlande et l'empereur de Chine, signé à Houmon-Schai, le 8 octobre 1843.—158

Treaty between His Majesty and the Queen Regent of Spain, during the Minority of her Daughter, Donna Isabella the Second, Queen of Spain, for the Abolition of the Slave Trade.—Signed at Madrid, June 28, 1835.—572

Treaty between the Honorable East India Company and His Excellency the Nabob Vizier-ul-Momalik, Yemeen-Oo-Dowla, Nazim-ul-Moolk, Saadet Ali Khan Behauder, Mobauriz Jung, for ceding to the Company, in perpetual sovereignty, certain portions of His Excellency's territorial possessions, in commutation of the subsidy now payable to the Company by the Vizier,—10th November 1801.—535

Trealy between the Honorable East India Company and His Majesty Abdool Futteh Moeen-ood-Deen Nowshere-Wani-Audil Sultani Zaman Mahammud Alli Shah, King of Oude,—11th September 1837.—536

Treaty of friendship and alliance between His Britannic Majesty and His Catholic Majesty Ferdinand VII, Signed at Madrid the 5th day of July 1814. In the name of the most Holy Trinity.—572.

Treaty of Peace between Her Majesty the Queen of the United Kingdom of Great Britain and Ireland and His Majesty the Shah of Persia, signed, in the English and Persian languages, at Paris, March 4, 1857, and of which the ratifications were exchanged at Bagdad, May 2, 1857. In: *The Times,* No. 22704, June 11, 1857. "The Peace with Persia."—293-96

Treaty with the Nabob Vizier Saadet Ali Khan Behauder,—21st February 1798.—535

Walewski, A. [Despatch to the French Ambassador in London of January 20, 1858.] In: *Le Constitutionnel,* No. 41, 10 février 1858.—470

[Wilson, A.] *Despatch from General Wilson.* In: *The Times,* No. 22839, November 16, 1857. "India."—394

[Windham, C. A.] *Major-General C. A. Windham to the Commander-in-Chief.* In: *The Times,* No. 22904, January 30, 1858. "The Second Relief of Cawnpore."—449

Yeh. [A letter to the Naval Commander-in-Chief M. Seymour of October 31, 1856.] In: *The Times,* No. 22567, January 2, 1857. "The Bombardment of Canton."—160, 162

— [A letter to the Naval Commander-in-Chief M. Seymour of November 3, 1856.] In: *The Times,* No. 22571, January 7, 1857. "The Bombardment of Canton."—160, 162

ANONYMOUS ARTICLES AND REPORTS PUBLISHED IN PERIODIC EDITIONS

Cobbett's Annual Register. Vol. II. From July to December, 1802. London, 1810: *Summary of Politics.*—494

— Vol. III. From January to June, 1803. London [s.a.]. No. 8, February 26, 1803: *Trial of Mr. Peltier.*—497; No. 9, March 5, 1803: *Summary of Politics.*—496

— No. 71, 12 mars 1858: *La Patrie donne les détails suivants sur la tentative...*—475
— No. 86, 27 mars 1858: *Le journal la Patrie publie...* "Nouvelles de France."—483

Journal des Débats politiques et littéraires, 22 juillet 1856. "France."—99

The Leader, No. 333, August 9, 1856. "Continental Notes. Spain."—103

Le Moniteur universel, No. 69, 9 mars 1856. ("Paris, le 8 mars".)—272
— No. 203, 21 juillet 1856. "Partie non officielle."—97
— No. 206, 24 juillet 1856. "Partie non officielle."—97
— No. 280, 6 octobre 1856. "Banque de France."—118
— No. 15, 15 janvier 1858: *Paris, le 14 janvier.* "Partie non officielle."—454, 455
— No. 57, 26 février 1858: *Cour d'assises de la Seine. Audience du 25 février 1858. Attentat du 14 janvier. Acte d'accusation.*—473
— No. 68, 9 mars 1858: *À Chalon-sur-Saône, dans la soirée...*—475, 478
— No. 71, 12 mars 1858: *Paris, le 11 mars.* "Partie non officielle."—500
— No. 86, 27 mars 1858: *Voici en quels termes les principaux organes...* "Nouvelles étrangères. Angleterre".—483
— No. 95-96, 5-6 avril 1858: *Paris, le 5 avril.* "Partie non officielle".—503
— No. 101, 11 avril 1858: *Paris, le 10 avril.* "Partie non officielle".—499

The Morning Advertiser, No. 20686, October 5, 1857: *Our present position in India.*—372

The Morning Post, No. 25971, March 27, 1857: *The circumstances which have marked the canvass of candidates throughout the country...*—238
— No. 26090, August 13, 1857: *The incoming Indian mail...*—328
— No. 26168, November 12, 1857: *The market for the English funds has fluctuated...* "Money Market and City News."—388
— No. 26369, July 5, 1858.—596

New-York Daily Tribune, No. 5343, June 5, 1858: *The Oude Proclamation. The Correspondence between the Governor-General and the Commissioner of Oude.*—546

Punch, or the London Charivari, March 13, 1858: *A Bad Look Out.*—472

The Times, No. 21021, January 26, 1852: *If Louis Napoleon had proceeded to exercise with judgment...*—534
— No. 22381, May 30, 1856: *We have had lately no lack of comparisons between England and France.*—8
— No. 22567, January 2, 1857: *We are now in possession of the full accounts from China...*—163
— No. 22615, February 27, 1857: *The Chinese controversy now raging in both Houses...*—211
— No. 22616, February 28, 1857: [Speeches in the House of Commons, February 27, 1857.]—215
— No. 22620, March 5, 1857: *Had it been possible to make an immediate appeal...*—217
— No. 22648, April 7, 1857: *On what has the General Election turned?...*—247
— No. 22668, April 30, 1857: *In Re Royal British Bank.*—268
— No. 22681, May 15, 1857: *It has been remarked that in war a victory is...*—294
— No. 22719, June 29, 1857: *The details of the Indian mutiny, as given by our correspondent...*—298

— No. 22871, December 23, 1857: *Turin, Dec. 19.* "Italy."—416
— No. 22876, December 29, 1857: *The Relief of Lucknow.* "India."—423-24
— No. 22883, January 6, 1858: *The quotation of gold at Paris is about 1$^{1}/_{2}$ per mille discount...* "Money-Market and City Intelligence."—445
— No. 22889, January 13, 1858: *England has already been informed of how Lucknow was relieved...*—437
— No. 22896, January 21, 1858: [Resolution proposed to a special general court of the East India Company. January 20.] "East India-House."—586
— No. 22902, January 28, 1858: *Cawnpore, Dec. 7; Calcutta, Dec. 24.* "India."—450
— No. 22906, February 2, 1858: *Vienna, Jan. 29.* "Austria."—456
— No. 22954, March 30, 1858: [Telegram from the India-House.] "India".—505-09
— No. 22959, April 5, 1858: *Camp, Cawnpore, Feb. 27, 8 a.m.* "The War in India".—505-09
— No. 22963, April 9, 1858: [Telegram received at the India-House from Malta.] "India."—505-09
— No. 22966, April 13, 1858: *The Siege of Lucknow.* "India and China."—509
— No. 22971, April 19, 1858: *Trial and acquittal of Simon Bernard. Sixth day. Central Criminal Court, April 17.*—515
— No. 22973, April 21, 1858: *Paris, Monday, April 19, 6 p.m.* "France."—515
— No. 22975, April 23, 1858: *Paris, Wednesday, April 21, 6 p.m.* "France."—516
— No. 22988, May 8, 1858: *On Monday it will be exactly a twelvemonth since...*—531
— No. 23000, May 22, 1858: *The Correspondence between the Governor-General and the Commissioner of Oude.*—548, *The late duel at Paris.*—552
— No. 23008, June 1, 1858: [Telegram from our Malta Correspondent.] "India."—554
— No. 23014, June 8, 1858: *Paris, Sunday, June 6, 6 p.m.* "Foreign Intelligence."—569
— No. 23015, June 9, 1858: *Paris, Monday, June 7, 6 p.m.* "Foreign Intelligence."—568
— No. 23016, June 10, 1858: *In those sad days of Ireland's history...*—567
— No. 23017, June 11, 1858: *There was a time within the memory...*—567
— No. 23023, June 18, 1858: [Speech of Bishop of Oxford in the House of Lords on June 17, 1858.] "Parliamentary Intelligence."—570
— No. 23032, June 29, 1858: *Alexandria, June 23; From the India-House.* "India".—581
— No. 23036, July 3, 1858: *Government of India* (No. 3) *Bill.* "Parliamentary Intelligence."—585
— No. 23037, July 5, 1858: *Bombay, June 4.* "India."—582
— No. 23038, July 6, 1858: [Reprint from *The Morning Post.*]—596

INDEX OF PERIODICALS

SUBJECT INDEX

A

J

K

L

M

N

O

P

R

GLOSSARY OF GEOGRAPHICAL NAMES[a]

Amoy	Szeming
Anatolia	Asia Minor
Araxes (river)	Aras
Astrabad	Gurgan
Aurungabad	Aurangabad
Austerlitz	Slavkov
Bahia	Salvador
Barrios	Los Barrios
Bassora	Basra
Boulogne	Boulogne-sur-Mer
Braila	Brăila
British Guiana	Guyana
Bundelcund	Bundelkhand
Cabool, Caboul	Kabul
Canton	Kwangchow
Canton River	Chu-Kiang (Pearl River)
Cattaro	Kotor
Cattaro, Bocche di	Kotor, Gulf of
Ceylon	Sri Lanka
Ching-Kiang-Foo	Chinkiang
Christiania	Oslo
Cilli	Celje
Citate	Chetatea
Coleroon	Cauvery
Constantinople	Istanbul
Cracow	Kraków
Dantzic	Gdańsk
Erivan	Yerevan
Erzeroum	Erzerum or Erzurum
Fiumè	Rijeka
Friuli	Udine
Galatz	Galaţi
Grisons	Graubünden
Gujerat	Gujarat
Hong Kong	Hsiang-Kiang
Illosfalva	Illésfalva
Inkermann	Inkerman
Ivangorod	Dęblin
Jassv	Işşi
Jaxartes	Syr Darya
Jericho	Er Ríha
Kabardinsk	Kabardinka
Kamtchatka	Kamchatka
Karrachee	Karachi
Lambessa	Lambèse
Libau	Liepaja
Luy-chow-foo	Luichow
Macao	Aomen
Malghera	Marghera

[a] This glossary includes geographical names occurring in Marx's and Engels' articles in the form customary in the press of the time but differing from the national names or from those given on modern maps. The left column gives geographical names as used in the original; the right column gives corresponding names as used on modern maps and in modern literature.

Memel	Klaipeda
Mohammerah	Khorramshahr
Montenegro	Crna Gora
Morea	Peloponnesus
Nankin	Nanking
Nepául	Nepal
Neuenburg	Neuchâtel
Newcastle	Newcastle-upon-Tyne
Nizhni Novgorod	Gorky
Nusserabad	Nasirabad
Oltenitza	Oltenița
Oude	Oudh
Oxus	Amu Darya
Palangen	Palanga
Pekin	Peking
Pera	Beyoğlu
Pernambuco	Recife
Pernau	Pärnu
Persia	Iran
Peterhoff	Petrodvorets
Pirano	Piran
Plombières	Plombières-les-Bains
Pola	Pula
Pomerania	Pomorze
Posen	Poznań
Pressburg	Bratislava
Pultawa	Poltava
Punjaub	Punjab
Ragusa	Dubrovnik
Rajpootana	Rajasthan
Revel	Tallinn
Rohilcund	Rohilkhand
Rovigno	Rovinj
St. Petersburg	Leningrad
Salonica	Thessaloniki
San Domingo	Dominican Republic
Schonen	Skåne
Scutari	Üsküdar
Sebenico	Šibenik
Shehustan	Kohistan
Shuster	Shushtar
Silesia	Śląsk
Smyrna	Izmir
Spalato	Split
Stettin	Szczecin
Subbalpore	Jubbulpore
S(o)und	Øresund
Tabreez	Tabriz
Tarnau	Tarnów
Theiss	Tisza
Thorn	Toruń
Tiflis	Tbilisi
Todhpore	Jodhpur
Tornea	Tornio
Transoxiana	Bukhara
Trebizond	Trabzon
Tsang-Ming	Tsungming
Tuabs	Tuapse
Tunis	Tunisia
Turan	Turkestan
Tver	Kalinin
Valengin	Valangin
Wendish Sea	Baltic Sea
Whampoa	Huang-pu
Zara	Zadar